1987

MARKETING PLANNING & STRATEGY

Subhash C. Jain

Assistant Dean and Director
Center for Research and
 Management Development
University of Connecticut

 Published by

S12 **SOUTH-WESTERN PUBLISHING CO.**

CINCINNATI   WEST CHICAGO, ILL.   DALLAS   PELHAM MANOR, N.Y.   PALO ALTO, CALIF.

Printed in the United States of America

To my parents
(for being there)

and

to my teachers and mentor
(for being here)

Preface

Marketing management in a strategic context is the subject of this book. Increasing emphasis on strategic planning by corporations necessitates a repositioning of marketing within the firm. It has become evident that no business can hope to survive, much less grow, on the basis of seat-of-the-pants management. The tactics of conventional wisdom and quantitative approaches, which may be useful in carrying out day-to-day business operations, cannot provide the means for the development of truly imaginative ways to effect business growth in unstable environments. Instead of traditional methods, new perspectives must be made available in order to generate a varied range of innovative strategic options from which to choose a program for action. Management has the responsibility of discovering those realities which are often hidden behind the smokescreen of wishful thinking and short-term perspective. Clearly, then, intuitive decision making based on traditional patterns of behavior now has to yield to strategy formulation based on logical and rational procedures. This book marks one step in this direction.

In recent years a variety of techniques, approaches, frameworks, and methodologies have been worked out, principally by consultants, in the area of strategy formulation. When confronted with this proliferation of methodologies and frameworks (some reliable and useful, others questionable or even spurious; some reasoned speculations, others unreasoned), I am reminded of the ancient legend of the blind men and the elephant:

> It was six men of Indostan,
>   To learning much inclined,
> Who went to see the Elephant
>   (Though all of them were blind),
> That each by observation
>   Might satisfy his mind.
>
> The first approached the Elephant,
>   And, happening to fall
> Against his broad and sturdy side,
>   At once began to bawl,
> "God bless me but the Elephant
>   Is very like a wall" . . .

It may be recalled that each in turn felt a different part of the elephant. The second man, feeling the tusk, thought it was a spear; the third, feeling the trunk, thought it was a snake; the fourth felt the knee and thought it to be a tree; the fifth felt the ear and thought it to be a fan; and the last felt the tail and thought it to be a rope. They argued for a long time, each assuming that his personal experience afforded him a true understanding of the nature of the beast. Mindful of the profound significance of that simple legend and aware that I represent merely a blind man from another age, I present in this book some summary views on the articulation, formulation, and implementation of marketing strategy.

Strategy is usually considered at two different levels: corporate strategy and business strategy. The role of functional areas vis-a-vis strategic planning at either level is still developing. Many scholars argue that strategic planning has forced marketing to assume an insignificant place in business circles. Others disagree and are quick to point out that since marketing inputs are a prerequisite to developing strategy, marketing occupies a crucial position. This latter viewpoint underlies the development of this book. As a matter of fact, the emphasis on strategic planning has broadened the scope of marketing so that instead of being simply a functional area, marketing has gained a corporate orientation.

Because strategic planning goes beyond the traditional marketing concept, such planning gives the company a major focus on marketing. If we pursue an optimistic line of thought, the marketing function has a new opportunity and a new purpose in extending its perspective further from marketing management to marketing strategy. Instruction only in marketing management cannot sufficiently prepare future marketers to occupy strategy-related positions in the business world. The current books on marketing management fail in this regard. New materials and texts with a focus on marketing strategy vis-a-vis business and corporate strategy are needed. This book fills that gap between traditional marketing built upon the marketing concept and the contemporary business trend which emphasizes strategic planning. An attempt is made to discuss marketing's strategic role and to explain the perspectives of the marketing mix from a strategic angle.

The specific areas covered in this book are:

1. The strategic position of marketing in a corporate-wide perspective
2. The place of marketing vis-a-vis other functional areas of business
3. The impact of both macro and product/market environments on marketing-related strategic decisions
4. The state of the environmental scanning art
5. Strategy design from both corporate and product/market viewpoints
6. Establishment of the strategic business unit as an integrating force between the corporation and product/market areas
7. The analysis and means necessary for measuring corporate competencies and for defining objectives and goals

8. Major market, product, price, distribution, and promotion strategies and their relevance in different situations
9. Different approaches to product portfolio development and the assumptions underlying these approaches
10. The theoretical bases and applications in practice of the experience curve concept and the PIMS study
11. The introduction of selected tools, techniques, and models which may be used as aids in strategy formulation, such as cross-impact analysis, the Delphi method, a growth model, and marketing simulation
12. The impact of strategic planning on the structure of marketing organization
13. Examination of the strategic business unit structure at General Electric Co. and the OST system at Texas Instruments Inc. as alternative organizational designs for operationalizing strategic planning

Assumptions about the audience significantly affect the style and content of a book. Primarily, this book is meant for advanced undergraduates and graduate students. Thus, the material is discussed in a lucid fashion developed from a classroom-tested conceptual framework. Many of the conceptual schemes included in the book have been presented at both academic and professional conferences and have been reshaped and modified, based on the feedback provided by many distinguished marketers. The book includes ideas, wherever appropriate, generated by such esteemed strategy development consultants as The Boston Consulting Group, McKinsey & Co., and Arthur D. Little, Inc. The experiences of a large number of companies have been drawn upon and are cited throughout the book as illustrations.

This book concentrates on areas of strategic importance only, especially those which have significant implications and particular relevance for the making of policy decisions in competitive situations. Discussion of routine, day-to-day decisions is intentionally avoided to keep the focus intact. The overall approach of this book is analytic rather than normative. This is necessary because strategy development is, currently at least, more an art than a science. In addition, strategy formulation is a highly complex process for which neat models and econometric equations, no matter how diligently worked out, will not suffice.

This book is far more a record of the work of others than an original document of my own. It is based on ideas and viewpoints of a large number of practitioners and academic colleagues, to whom I express my sincere thanks.

My colleagues at the University of Connecticut have contributed to this task in a variety of ways, and I am indebted to them, especially Donald J. Hempel, Fred W. Kniffin, Peter J. LaPlaca, and Charles Saunders. Further, Chapter 3 is essentially based on work which I did with Donald J. Hempel, and I thank him for this opportunity. I also acknowledge the valuable feedback provided by my undergraduate and graduate students at the University of Connecticut who read early drafts of the text as a part of their assignments during 1978–1980.

A special mention of appreciation must go to Mrs. Yasmin Azad, who edited portions of the manuscript, and to Miss Donna DePellegrini for typing the manuscript.

While it is not feasible to list them all, I must single out the following sources of help whose work, ideas, and writings provided deep insight into strategy formulation: The Boston Consulting Group, General Electric Company, Arthur D. Little, Inc., McKinsey & Co., Planning Executives Institute, S.R.I. International, Strategic Planning Institute, and Texas Instruments Inc. Thanks are also due to a large number of business executives and their corporations for sharing their strategic planning perspectives.

I am also indebted to many writers and publishers, particularly those who have granted me permission to include excerpts from their works. I wish to express gratitude to Derek Abell of the Harvard Business School, Edwin A. Murray of Boston University, C.P. Rao of the University of Arkansas, Gerald Crawford of the University of North Alabama, and Isabelle Schmid of Stanford University for their permission to include cases written by them or under their supervision. Thanks are also due to Iqbal Mathur of Southern Illinois University at Carbondale for the material in Chapter 4, which is based on a joint project. I also would like to take this opportunity to thank Professor Harper W. Boyd, Jr. of the University of Arkansas, who first introduced me to marketing at Stanford University, and Jagdish N. Sheth, Walter H. Stellner Distinguished Professor of Marketing at the University of Illinois, for initiating me into the art of writing a book.

I owe a word of gratitude to my teachers and mentor who taught me all I know and provided the timely advice and counsel to take up projects such as this book. I owe my sincere thanks and appreciation to Professor Dool Singh at Krukshetra University in India, who was instrumental in molding my early college education, and to Professor Stuart U. Rich at the University of Oregon, who taught me what I know about marketing strategy. Dean Ronald J. Patten at the University of Connecticut encouraged me to undertake this project and inspired me to complete it. I owe these individuals my greatest debt of appreciation.

In the final analysis, the book belongs more to my wife and our children than to me. They cheerfully accepted and encouraged a seven-day work week, which meant giving up many weekend social activities and vacations. My son, Amit, deserves special mention for his timely interruptions which forced fresh thinking and generated new ideas.

Storrs, CT   S.C.J.
September 1, 1980

Contents

PART ONE – Introduction

1 Marketing and the Concept of Planning and Strategy   3

Concept of Planning, 4
Concept of Strategy, 11
Process of Marketing Planning and Strategy
    Formulation, 12
Corporate Planning, 18
Relationship Between Marketing Planning and
    Corporate-wide Planning, 27
Marketing Planning and Planning in Other Functional
    Areas, 28
Plan of the Book, 32
Summary, 34

2 Internal Appraisal   39

Meaning of Corporate Appraisal, 40
Factors of Appraisal: Corporate Publics, 41
Factors of Appraisal: Value Orientation of Top
    Management, 47
Factors of Appraisal: Resources of the Firm, 54
Appraising Marketing, 60
Summary, 61

3 Scanning the Environment   67

Importance of Environmental Scanning, 68
The Concept of Environment, 69

State of the Art, 69
Types of Environment, 74
Environmental Scanning and Marketing Strategy, 84
Environmental Scanning—An Example, 88
Organizational Arrangements and Problems, 95
Scanning Techniques, 98
Scanning Approaches, 100
Summary, 100

4   Scanning the Product/Market Environment   102

Social and Cultural Effects, 103
Political Influence, 106
Legal Requirements, 108
Ethical Considerations, 111
Competition, 113
Economic Climate, 114
Technological Changes, 116
Institutional Dynamics, 117
Consumerism, 118
Limits of Growth, 123
Population, 124
Location of Consumers, 126
Income, 128
Expenditure Patterns, 132
Education, 136
Summary, 137

5   Measuring Strengths and Weaknesses   139

Meaning of Strengths and Weaknesses, 140
Studying Strengths and Weaknesses: State of the Art,
    140
Systematic Approach for Measuring Strengths and
    Weaknesses, 142
Present Strategic Posture, 143
Past Performance, 146
Product/Market Thrust, 152
Strengths and Weaknesses, 161
Concept of Synergy, 164
Summary, 164

6   **Developing Marketing Objectives and Goals**   **167**

    Framework for Defining Objectives, 168
    Corporate Objectives, 169
    Strategic Business Unit Objectives, 177
    Product/Market Objectives, 184
    Process of Setting Objectives, 189
    Summary, 194

PART TWO – Product/Market Planning

7   **Framework for Product/Market Planning**   **199**

    Conceptual Scheme, 200
    Measuring the Momentum, 202
    Gap Analysis, 204
    Filling the Gap, 204
    Integration at the SBU Level, 215
    Integration at the Corporate Level, 224
    Strategy Evaluation, 224
    Summary, 226
    Appendix: Business Strategy Concepts, 228

8   **Market Strategies**   **231**

    Dimensions of Market Strategies, 231
    Market-scope Strategy, 232
    Market-geography Strategy, 239
    Market-entry Strategy, 245
    Market-commitment Strategy, 249
    Market-dilution Strategy, 252
    Summary, 254

9   **Product Strategies**   **256**

    Dimensions of Product Strategies, 256
    Product-positioning Strategy, 257
    Product-repositioning Strategy, 262

Product-overlap Strategy, 265
Product-scope Strategy, 269
Product-design Strategy, 273
Product-elimination Strategy, 275
New-product Strategy, 282
Diversification Strategy, 289
Summary, 293

10 Pricing Strategies   **295**

Review of Pricing Factors, 295
Pricing Strategies for New Products, 303
Pricing Strategies for Established Products,
   306
Price-flexibility Strategy, 313
Product-line-pricing Strategy, 315
Leasing Strategy, 318
Bundling-pricing Strategy, 321
Price-leadership Strategy, 322
Pricing Strategy to Build Market Share, 324
Summary, 325

11 Distribution Strategies   **327**

Channel-structure Strategy, 328
Distribution-scope Strategy, 339
Multiple-channel Strategy, 343
Channel-modification Strategy, 348
Channel-control Strategy, 354
Channel-conflict-management Strategy, 358
Summary, 361

12 Promotional Strategies   **363**

Promotion Strategies, 363
Advertising Strategies, 378
Personal Selling Strategies, 390
Summary, 402

PART THREE – Product Portfolio Management

13 Developing a Product Portfolio 407

Product Life Cycle (PLC), 408
Portfolio Matrix, 413
Multifactor Portfolio Matrix, 426
Summary, 433

PART FOUR – Organization and Control

14 Strategy-related Tools and Techniques 437

Experience Curve Concept, 437
Delphi Technique, 446
Scenario Building, 456
Evaluation of Investment Proposals, 457
Summary, 464
Appendix: Experience Curve Construction, 465

15 Strategy-related Models 471

Profit Impact of Market Strategy (PIMS), 472
Growth Potential, 479
Marketing Simulation, 482
Trend-impact Analysis, 487
Cross-impact Analysis, 490
Special-purpose Models, 494
Summary, 507

16 Organizational Structure 508

Strategy and Structure, 509
Integration at the Top, 523
Role of the Chief Executive, 525
Role of the Strategic Planner, 526

Effect of Strategic Planning on Marketing Organization,
528
Summary, 536

Case A   Wilmington Corporation   **538**

Case B   Colonial Manor Hospital   **573**

Case C   Johnston, Inc.   **592**

Case D   Sigtronics, Inc.   **610**

Case E   International Engineering, Inc.   **622**

Index   **643**

Part One
Introduction

CHAPTER 1 – Marketing and the Concept of Planning and Strategy

CHAPTER 2 – Internal Appraisal

CHAPTER 3 – Scanning the Environment

CHAPTER 4 – Scanning the Product/Market Environment

CHAPTER 5 – Measuring Strengths and Weaknesses

CHAPTER 6 – Developing Marketing Objectives and Goals

Chapter 1
Marketing and the Concept of Planning and Strategy

> We must plan for the future, because people who stay in the present will remain in the past.
>
> *Abraham Lincoln*

During the past decade marketers have been presented with a series of approaches to marketing decision making. The first and most widely touted approach is the marketing concept approach, which directs us to develop our product offering, and indeed our entire marketing program, to meet the needs of our customer base. Key elements of the marketing concept approach revolve around the need for an information flow from the market to the decision maker. In recent years this has been expanded to the "societal marketing concept" as have many nontraditional marketing areas. Another paradigm can be found in the systems approach, which originated in other areas of business and scientific endeavors. This approach instructs us to view our product as but a single aspect of the customers' total need-satisfaction system, an aspect that may be significantly different when viewed as a part of the system rather than as an individual entity. The third and most recently discussed approach is the environmental approach, which portrays the marketing decision maker as the focal point of numerous environments within which the firm operates and which affect the success of the firm's marketing program. These environments frequently bear such labels as legal-political, economic, competitive, consumer, market structure, social, technological, and international.

Indeed, these and other approaches to marketing decision making are but descriptive frameworks which stress certain aspects of the firm's role vis-a-vis the strategic planning process. No matter what approach a firm follows, it needs a reference point for its decision which is provided by the strategy and the planning process involved in designing the strategy. Thus the strategic planning process is the guiding force behind decision making, whichever framework one adopts for it. This relationship between the strategic planning process and approaches to marketing decision making is depicted in Exhibit 1-1.

3

EXHIBIT 1-1   Relationship Between Strategic Planning Process and Approaches to Marketing Decision Making

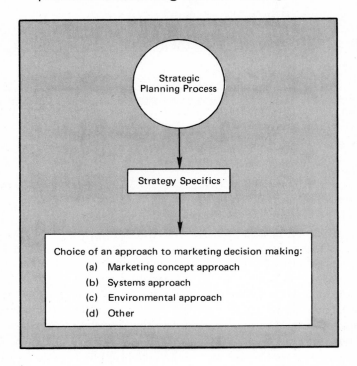

CONCEPT OF PLANNING

Throughout human history, people have been engaged in achieving specific purposes, and in this effort some sort of planning has always found place. In modern times the Soviet Union was the first nation to come up with an economic plan for growth and development. After World War II national economic planning became a popular activity, particularly among the developing countries, with the goal of systematic and organized action designed to achieve stated objectives within a given period. Among the market economies France has gone farthest in planning its economic affairs.

In the business world, Henri Fayol, the French industrialist, is credited with the first successful attempts at formal planning. Today planning has come to be widely recognized as an important activity among business organizations. As Steiner claims:

> No self-respecting growth company today can afford to be without planning capability. It is not surprising that the majority of security analysts and institutional investors passing through companies insist on spending

time with the planner and often emphasize his capabilities in their evaluation reports.[1]

Exhibit 1-2 summarizes what planning can accomplish for a firm.

EXHIBIT 1-2   Accomplishments Attributed to Planning

1. It leads to a better position or standing for the organization.
2. It helps the organization progress in the ways that its management considers most suitable.
3. It helps every manager think, decide, and act more effectively for progress in the desired direction.
4. It helps keep the organization flexible.
5. It stimulates a cooperative, integrated, enthusiastic approach to organizational problems.
6. It indicates to management how to evaluate and check up on progress toward the planned objectives.
7. It leads to socially and economically useful results.

Source: Seven headings from pp. 9–14 in *The Practice of Planning* by David W. Ewing, copyright © 1968 by David W. Ewing. Reprinted by permission of Harper & Row, Publishers, Inc.

In the United States growth is an accepted expectation of a firm; however, it does not happen by itself. Growth must be carefully planned: questions such as how much, when, in which areas, and where to grow, and who will be responsible for different tasks, must be answered. Unplanned growth will be haphazard and may fail to provide the desired levels of profit. Therefore, in order for a company to realize orderly growth, to maintain a high level of operating efficiency, and to achieve its goals fully, it must plan for the future in a systematic manner. Products, markets, facilities, personnel, and financial resources must be evaluated and selected wisely.

Today's business is more complex than ever. In addition to the keen competition that firms face both from domestic and overseas companies, a variety of other concerns such as environmental protection, employees' welfare, consumerism, and antitrust action impinge on business moves. Thus, it is desirable for a firm to be cautious in undertaking risks. This again calls for a planned effort.

Many firms pursue growth internally through the R & D effort. This route to growth not only is time consuming, but also requires a heavy commitment of resources with a high degree of risk. In such a context, planning is needed to choose the right type of risks.

---

[1]George Steiner, *Top Management Planning* (New York: Macmillan Co. Publishers, 1969), p. 14.

Since World War II, technology has had a major impact on markets and marketers. Presumably, the trend of technological changes will continue to rise in the future. The impact of technological innovations may be felt in any industry or in any firm. Therefore, such changes need to be anticipated as far in advance as possible in order for a firm to take advantage of new opportunities and to avoid the harmful consequences of major new developments. Here again planning achieves significance.

Finally, planning is required in making a choice among the many equally attractive alternative investment opportunities a firm may have. No firm can afford to invest in each and every "good" opportunity. Thus, planning becomes essential in making the selection.

Not stressed until the early 1960s, planning activity came up fast during that decade. In 1962, for instance, only about 25 companies in the U.S. had formalized long-range planning in practice.[2] A *Business Week* survey of 1964, however, revealed that 71 percent of the companies in a sample of 139 had formalized corporate planning activity. A similar study by the Conference Board in 1966 reported the percentage to be even higher, i.e., 85 percent among 420 responding companies.[3] Another indication of the popularity of long-range planning is found in a National Planning Association study which showed that 65 percent of the 280 chief executives considered long-range planning to be their most important task, on which they spent 44 percent of their time.[4]

Planning done for future action has been called by different names such as long-range planning, corporate planning, comprehensive planning, and formal planning. Whatever the name used for it, the reference is obviously to the future.

Definition of Planning

Planning has as many definitions as there are writers on the subject. However, there is a common thread underlying planning theory and practice. This is shown in the statement by Warren which defines planning as:

> . . . essentially a process directed toward making today's decisions with tomorrow in mind and a means of preparing for future decisions so that they may be made rapidly, economically, and with as little disruption to the business as possible.[5]

---

[2]Hal R. Mason, "Organizing for Corporate Planning," in *Proceedings of the Long Range Planning Service Client Conference,* February 7–9, 1962 (Menlo Park, Calif.: Stanford Research Institute, 1962), p. 4.

[3]James Brown, Saul S. Sands, and G. Clark Thompson, "The Status of Long Range Planning," *The Conference Board Record* (September, 1966), p. 11.

[4]National Planning Association. "The Use of Economic Projections in Long Range Business Planning: Results of a Questionnaire Study," Report No. 66-J-5 (Washington, D.C.: December, 1966).

[5]Kirby E. Warren, *Long Range Planning: The Executive Viewpoint* (Englewood Cliffs, N.J.: Prentice-Hall, 1966), p. 5.

In practice, however, different meanings are attached to planning. Often a distinction is made between a budget—a yearly program of operations—and a long-range plan. Some people consider planning as something done by staff specialists, while budgeting falls within the purview of line managers.

It is necessary for a company to be sufficiently clear about the nature and scope of planning that it intends to adopt. A definition of planning should then be based on what planning is supposed to be in an organization. It is not necessary for every company to engage in comprehensive planning of the same style. The basis of all planning should be to design courses of action to be pursued for achieving stated objectives in the future such that opportunities are marshalled and threats are guarded against, but the exact planning posture must be custom-made, based on the decision-making needs of the organization.

Operational management, which emphasizes the current programs of an organization, and planning, which essentially deals with the future, are two intimately related activities. Operational management or budgeted programs should emerge as the result of planning. For instance, while the first year of a five-year plan is budgeted and accompanied by detailed operational programs, years two through five are described in more general terms.

A distinction should also be made between planning and forecasting. Forecasting provides an informational input for the planning process by providing an assessment of future changes in areas of importance to a company and interpreting these changes as to their impact on company operations. Planning takes over from there to set objectives and goals and develop strategy.

Significance of Planning

Planning, organizing, directing, staffing, and controlling have been traditionally held as the five functions of a business enterprise. Thus, no business, however small or poorly managed, can do without planning. While planning per se may be nothing new for an organization, the current emphasis on it is indeed different. No longer considered to be just one of the important functions of the organization, in its new role corporate planning demands linkage of various parts of an organization into an integrated system. The emphasis has shifted from planning as an aspect of the organization to planning as a basis of all its efforts and decisions, building the entire organization towards the achievement of designated objectives. As a matter of fact, it can be considered as a new business orientation. Whereas the 1960s required each firm to have a marketing orientation as a condition for growth and survival, the firm of the 1970s reached a point where only long-term direction could underwrite success. The 1980s would demand even greater emphasis on planning. Thus, a planning orientation now supersedes a marketing orientation. This view of business orientation, however, can be questioned. One may claim that the most desirable and only relevant purpose of a business organization is to earn a profit, and as such, a profit orientation is the only valid mission which should guide the workings of a business. This can be argued against since profit, although important, is more a result of good business practice.

A variety of reasons can be ascribed to the recent increase in the emphasis placed on planning. Dynamic technological developments, new dimensions of sociological changes in the environment, increasing involvement of all levels of government, and fierce competition at home and abroad have introduced far-reaching complexities into today's business. To survive in these environments, a firm must look sufficiently far ahead to provide against the uncertainties of a dynamic world. The economic slowdown during the early 1970s led many people to wonder whether they should do something right away to ensure growth in the future or merely accept growth as something built into the system. In the past, corporations were able to adjust themselves to changes in technology, competition, and markets through intuitive leadership. But changes in today's environment are too many and too complex to be marshalled through seat-of-the-pants methods. Further, when a firm becomes large and the new generation of managers emerges, its environment changes substantially. Under these circumstances it becomes essential to use a systematic approach to change. This calls for a planned posture.

There is little doubt about the importance of planning, but to be useful, planning should be done properly. In fact, planning just for the sake of it can be injurious; half-hearted planning can cause more problems than it solves. In practice, however, many business executives simply pay lip service to planning, partly because they find it difficult to incorporate planning into their decision process and partly because they are uncertain how to adapt it.

Requisites for Successful Planning

If planning is to succeed, proper arrangements must be made to put it into operation. The Boston Consulting Group suggests the following concerns for effective planning:

> There is the matter of outlook, which can affect the degree to which functional and professional viewpoints, versus corporate needs, will dominate the work of planning.
>
> There is the question of the extent of involvement for members of the management. Who should participate and to what extent?
>
> There is the problem of determining what part of the work of planning should be accomplished through joint effort, and of how to achieve effective collaboration among the participants in the planning process.
>
> There is the matter of incentives of making planning an appropriately emphasized and rewarded kind of managerial work.
>
> There is the question of how to provide staff coordination for planning, and this raises the issues of how a planning unit should be used in the organization.
>
> And there is the role of the chief executive in the planning process . . . What should it be?[6]

---

[6]*Perspectives on Corporate Planning* (Boston: Boston Consulting Group, 1968), p. 48.

Conceptually, planning is rather simple. However, its implementation is far from being easy. Successful planning requires a blend of many forces in different areas, not the least of which are behavioral, intellectual, structural, philosophical, and managerial. Achieving the proper blend of these forces requires making difficult decisions, as indicated in the above quotation. While planning is complex, indeed, successful planning systems do have common fundamental characteristics despite differing operational details. First, wholehearted support of the chief executive officer is essential. Second, planning must be kept simple, in agreement with the managerial style, unencumbered by detailed numbers and fancy equations. Third, planning is a shared responsibility, and it would be wrong to assume that the president or vice-president of planning, staff specialists, or line managers could do it single-handedly. Fourth, the managerial incentive system should give due recognition to the fact that decisions made with long-term implications may not appear good in the short run. Fifth, the goals of planning should be achievable without excessive frustrations and work load and with a widespread understanding and acceptance of the process. Sixth, overall flexibility should be encouraged in order to accommodate changing conditions.

Initiating Planning Activities

There is no one best time for initiating planning activities in an organization; however, before developing a formal planning system, the organization should be prepared to establish a strong planning foundation. The chief executive should stand behind it wholeheartedly and be willing to perform the necessary functions of the job. A planning framework should be developed to match the company's perspective and should be generally accepted by the executives. A planning manual giving the work flow, information links, format of various documents, and the time schedule for completing various activities must be prepared by the planner. Once these foundations are completed, the company can initiate the planning process anytime.

Planning should not be put off until bad times prevail; it is not a cure for poor performance. While planning is probably the best prevention for keeping away from bad times, planning efforts which are begun when operational performance is at its ebb (e.g., low or no profitability) will only add fuel to the fire since initially these efforts tend to create an upheaval by challenging the traditional patterns of decision making. The company facing the question of survival should concentrate more on alleviating the current crisis.

Planning should evolve gradually over a period of time. It is wishful thinking to expect full-scale planning to be instituted in a few weeks or months. As a matter of fact, initial planning may be formalized in one or more functional areas. As experience is gained, a company-wide planning system may be designed. IBM, a pioneer in formalized planning, followed this pattern for instituting planning. First, financial planning and product planning were attempted in the post-World War II period. Gradual changes toward increased formality occurred over the years. "Since 1966 increased attention has been given to planning contents, and a compatible network of planning data systems was initiated."[7]

Philosophies of Planning

Ackoff defines three different types of planning philosophies which he labels as: satisfying, optimizing, and adaptivizing.[8] The philosophy of *satisfying* planning refers to aiming at easily conceivable achievements and molding the planning efforts accordingly. This type of planning requires setting objectives and goals that are "high enough" and not as "high as possible." Therefore, the satisfying planner devises only one feasible and acceptable way of achieving these goals, which may not necessarily be the best possible way. Under a satisfying philosophy confrontations, which may be caused by conflicts in programs, are avoided through politicking, underplaying change, and accepting a fall in performance as unavoidable.

The philosophy of *optimizing* planning has its foundation in operations research. The optimizing planner seeks to model various aspects of the organization and define them as objective functions. Then efforts are directed so that an objective function is maximized (or minimized), subject to the constraints imposed by the management or forced by the environment. For example, an objective may be to obtain the highest feasible market share; planning will then amount to making a search for different variables that affect market share, such as price elasticity, plant capacity, competitive behavior, the product's stage in the life cycle, and so on. The effect of each variable will be reduced to constraints on the market share. Then an analysis will be undertaken to find out the optimum market share to shoot for.

Unlike the satisfying planner, the optimizer endeavors with the use of mathematical models to find the best available course to realize the objectives and goals. The success of an optimizing planner will depend on how completely and accurately the model framework depicts the underlying situation and how well the planner can figure out solutions from the model once it has been built.

The philosophy of *adaptivizing* planning has been considered by Ackoff as an innovative approach which is yet to be popular in practice. To understand the nature of this type of planning, let us compare it to optimizing planning. In optimization the significant variables and their effects are taken for granted. Given these, an effort is made to achieve the optimal result. On the other hand, with an adaptivizing approach, planning may be undertaken to produce changes in the underlying relationships themselves to create a desired future. The

[7]Harold W. Henry, "Formal Long Range Planning and Corporate Performance," in Subhash C. Jain and Surendra Singhvi, *Essentials of Corporate Planning* (Oxford, Ohio: Planning Executives Institute, 1973), pp. 22–33.

[8]Russell L. Ackoff, *A Concept of Corporate Planning* (New York: John Wiley & Sons, 1970), p. 13.

underlying relationships refer to an organization's internal and external environment and the dynamics of the values of the actors in the environments, i.e., the way values relate to needs and their satisfaction, how changes in needs produce changes in values, and what produces changes in needs.

CONCEPT OF STRATEGY

An explicit statement of strategy is the key to success in the context of a dynamic environment. Where there is no clear concept of strategy, decisions rest on either subjective or intuitive assessments and are made without regard to other decisions. Such decisions become increasingly unreliable as the pace of change accelerates or decelerates rapidly. Strategy is concerned with the development of potential for results and the development of a reaction capability to adapt to environmental changes. Quite naturally, we find that strategy can be formulated at various levels within the firm. Financial strategy, marketing strategy, and other strategies must, of necessity, flow from and be consistent with the overall corporate strategy.

In a great many firms the marketing function represents the greatest degree of contact with the external environment, the environment least controllable by the firm. Marketing strategy consists of establishing a match between the firm and its environment to seek solutions to the problems of deciding (a) what business the firm is in and what kinds of business it may enter in the future, and (b) how the chosen field(s) of endeavor may be successfully run in a competitive environment by pursuing product, price, promotion, and distribution perspectives to serve target markets. Marketing strategy has two dimensions: present and future. The present dimension deals with the *existing* relationships of the firm to its environments. The future dimension encompasses *intended* future relationships—in the form of a set of strategic marketing objectives—and the action programs necessary to reach those objectives. An example of the relationship between corporate strategy and marketing strategy will demonstrate these features.

McDonald's, the hamburger chain, has among its corporate objectives the goal of increasing the productivity of its operating units. Given the high proportion of costs in fixed facilities, it was decided to increase facility utilization during off-peak hours, particularly during the morning hours. The program developed to accomplish these goals was the Egg McMuffin followed by a breakfast menu consistent with the limited product line strategy of McDonald's regular fare. In this example, the corporate strategy of increased productivity of assets led to the marketing strategy of the breakfast fare (intended relationship) built upon realization of variation of store utilization throughout the day (existing relationship) and favorable customer attitudes toward the chain (another existing relationship).

Generally, organizations have indentifiable existing strategic perspectives; however, not many organizations have explicit marketing strategy for the intended future. This is frequently the result of a lack of the top management involvement and commitment required for the development of proper perspectives of the future within the scope of current corporate activities.

The marketing strategy is the core element for future relationships between the firm and its environment. It specifies marketing goals and objectives vis-a-vis the goals of corporate strategy and presents the plans which will be used to achieve those ends.

PROCESS OF MARKETING PLANNING AND STRATEGY FORMULATION

Exhibit 1-3 presents a synopsis of the marketing planning process. Usually companies which undertake formalized planning have well-established planning procedures and time schedules for completion of different planning chores. Following these procedures and time schedules, the chief executive officer triggers the process of marketing planning and strategy formulation by defining corporate objectives and goals.

Corporate objectives, perspectives of planning in other functional areas, corporate resources, and environmental assumptions serve as inputs to the development of overall marketing objectives. These objectives are communicated to the product/market managers for detailed planning in their area of concern.

The product/market planning begins with a review of the following information with reference to a particular product/market: overall marketing and product/market environments, past performance, and current strategic perspectives. Information in these three areas is used to designate the product/market strengths and weaknesses which, along with overall marketing objectives and the information on the momentum of the product/market, serve as basic inputs for undertaking strategic marketing planning for a product/market. This consists of the delineation of specific objectives, action programs, and budget requirements.

The strategic marketing plan for a product/market is submitted to the senior marketing management for a review and an evaluation of consistency with overall marketing objectives and resources. Where necessary, product/market managers may be asked for a revision of their plans. The revised plans are again reviewed and approved. Resources are then committed to different product/market plans for the duration of the planning period. Senior marketing management is responsible for the integration of all the product/market plans into a final product portfolio, which is then approved by corporate management as a part of the corporate planning process.

Regardless of company organization, the perspectives of marketing planning do not change in substance. If a company is organized functionally, the director of product planning reporting to the vice-president of marketing will develop the product/market plans; the development of a product portfolio will be the task of the vice-president. On the other hand, if a company is structured on the product management concept, product or brand managers will be responsible for

EXHIBIT 1-3   Process of Marketing Planning and Strategy Formulation

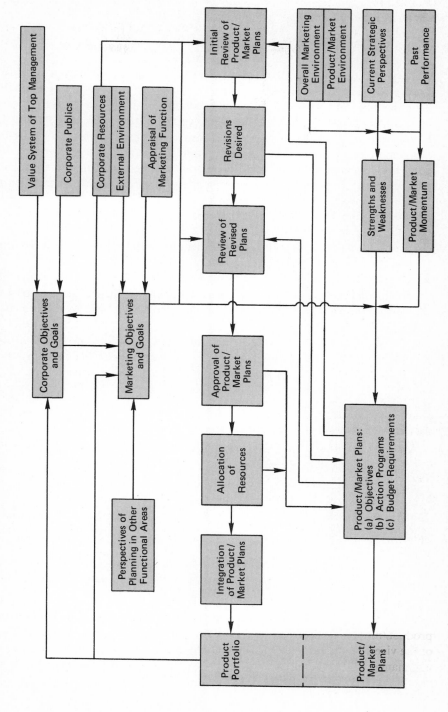

product/market plans. These product/market plans may be integrated at different levels (for example, at the level of group product manager and product marketing manager) before reaching the vice-president of marketing, who is responsible for finalizing the product portfolio.

Large multiproduct, multimarket corporations are usually organized in divisions, groups, units, and even sub-units. Even here the process of marketing planning may not vary much. Initial product/market plans are the domain of the marketing people in the hierarchy at the lowest operating level, say sub-unit. The product portfolio development is undertaken at the corporate level. The sub-unit product/market plans are integrated into unit plans, unit plans into group plans, and group plans into divisional plans before reaching top management. Finally, the corporate vice-president of marketing analyzes the divisional product/market plans to finalize the product portfolio.

In companies where there is no corporate marketing vice-president, the task of developing the product portfolio may become the responsibility of another corporate executive, such as the vice-president for corporate or strategic planning. In many large organizations the product portfolio development is undertaken by the office of the president. Usually in such cases, the office of the president might consist of different executives who share different responsibilities for the chief executive. For example, at Mead Corporation, the office of the president consists of the chairperson of the board, vice-chairperson, and president. The vice-chairperson is responsible for strategic planning and, therefore, product portfolio development. The president is responsible for operations of the company. Both report to the chairperson of the board, who is the chief executive officer. Under such arrangements it may erroneously appear that product portfolio development is not a marketing task.

An Example

The process of marketing planning and strategy discussed above may be illustrated with reference to the Tyrex Company, Incorporated.* The Tyrex Company manufactured various types of equipment used in chemical processing plants, such as pumps, valves, pipes, and fittings. In 1979 the company employed about 1,400 persons. It had 5 operating divisions, 3 wholly-owned subsidiaries, and 22 district sales offices. On the next page is a summary of Tyrex's divisions and their products and sales.

The planning effort at Tyrex began in March, 1979. After a careful evaluation of its corporate publics, corporate resources, and the value system of top management, the following corporate objectives were arrived at:

1. To achieve an average yearly growth in sales and earnings of at least 10 percent
2. To initiate improvements within the industry

---

*Disguised name.

3. To make a 12.8 percent return on total capital invested
4. To develop new products which have innovations or improvements beyond those already on the market, thus permitting engineering ingenuity
5. To enter only growth markets with long-term potentials
6. To be a leader in any field the company enters
7. To consider purchasing other firms which have products, facilities, or skills useful to Tyrex
8. To prefer products utilizing our own unique resources
9. To make regular dividend payments amounting to approximately 40 percent of earnings

Division and Its Location	Nature of Products	1979 Sales (in $1,000s)
Charles Division Cincinnati, Ohio	Pumps	6,314
	Pump parts	6,112
	Valves and parts	11,568
	Sanitary	5,183
	Custom and miscellaneous	2,835
	Jobbing castings	1,050
Miami Valley Plastics Division Cincinnati, Ohio	Laboratory equipment (laboratory sinks, table tops and related laboratory equipment)	2,328
Metzger Division Syracuse, New York	Chemical filters Brewery equipment (filters, coolers, stainless steel tanks)	2,016
Plastics Application Division Cincinnati, Ohio	Custom molding of plastics for engineered applications (all Teflon work)	2,415
Industrial Products Division Morristown, Pennsylvania	Pumps, compressors, reactors and gauges (for high pressure applications)	1,918
	TOTAL	$41,739

Please note that one of the stated objectives of the company was to pay a substantial amount of dividends. This decision was based on the fact that a large majority of the company's stockholders were older persons living on their dividend incomes. This made it necessary for the company to pay regular dividends even at the cost of borrowing from outside for its own capital needs for growth.

An appraisal of the company's marketing function showed:

1. The company has a strong reputation in the market for its quality product.
2. The company's after-sales service is considered best in the industry.
3. The company's sales force is highly qualified and productive.
4. The company has a well-developed system enabling it to make a quick response to customers' requirements concerning product design, delivery, etc.
5. The company's new product development effort has been lacking.
6. The company's prices have been rather high.

Using the corporate perspectives and the appraisal of its marketing function, the company defined its marketing objectives. Before getting to marketing objectives, however, the perspectives of planning in other functional areas of business were also considered. An example is the description of financial objectives below.

Financial Objectives. Financial objectives were defined as goals and limitations. Any downward revision in the goals would not be expected, but any upward revision was an objective in itself. Averages for each of the financial goals are shown in parentheses.

A. Financial Goals
    1. Annual growth rate of 10 percent on sales, profits, and earnings per share (9.9**, not available, 11.8**).
    2. Return on equity of 16 percent (18.7*).
    3. Return on total capital employed of 12.8 percent (14.9*).
    4. Pretax profit on sales of at least 15 percent (16.5*).

B. Financial Limitations
    1. Investment in net working capital of less than 35 percent of annual sales. Investment in net fixed assets of less than 25 percent of annual sales (35%*, 23.5%*).
    2. Dividend payments of approximately 40 percent of earnings (41.6%**).
    3. No significant dilution of shareholders' ownership.

---

*1979 only.
**Average for last 10 years.

Marketing Objectives and Goals.

A. Objectives

   1. To develop new products ahead of competition based on (a) new materials and (b) new design
   2. To aggressively promote company's products as unique and high quality
   3. To monitor customers' requirements on a continuous basis

B. Goals

   1. To develop and introduce at least one new product every year in each division
   2. To hire a new advertising agency to work with the company's promotion department to develop a new promotional strategy
   3. To install a marketing information system
   4. To use product quality and after-sales services as the selling points
   5. To match delivery schedules with customer requirements
   6. To limit marketing efforts to large manufacturers with recurring needs

Using the above information, the Charles Division of the company undertook the following analysis of its environment, current strategy and past performance.

Past Performance.

   1. Sales are up about five percent annually for the past ten years.
   2. Customers desire more sophisticated features in the product but ultimately buy it because of established relationships.
   3. Service expenses are growing at the rate of 10 percent annually.
   4. Customers already resent high prices. There are no easy prospects for increasing prices in the future.

Product/Market Environment.

   1. Technology is fast changing and the company is lagging behind.
   2. Most products are in the maturity stage of the product life cycle.
   3. Competition is emerging from new sources such as European and Japanese manufacturers.
   4. Pollution control requirements which the Charles Division's machinery must satisfy are fairly restrictive and complicated.

Current Strategy.

   The sales made are based on cordial customer relationships established over a long period of time.

The above information was used to determine the following strengths and weaknesses of the Charles Division.

Strengths.
   1. A capable and willing sales force
   2. Good rapport with customers
   3. The customers' appreciation of after-sales services
   4. A network of distributors which foreign competitors lack

Weaknesses.
   1. Products lacking in sophistication
   2. Higher prices
   3. Matured products
   4. No established program to meet the pollution control requirements
       in the products

From here, using product/market forecasts, the Charles Division's objectives and program could be worked out.

CORPORATE PLANNING

As shown in Exhibit 1-4, the overall corporate planning process may be split into three parts: strategic planning, development planning, and functional planning. Each of these will now be explored in detail.

Strategic Planning

Strategic planning is the responsibility of the chief executive. Usually the executive vice-president and selected senior executives are also involved in strategic planning. Underlying factors in strategic planning are: the corporate publics (1)* to whom the business is responsible, such as stockholders, creditors, government, community, customers, and employees; management culture (2), e.g., risk proneness, growth orientation, and the like; and resource potential (3). The last factor needs elaboration. To take an inventory of resources, the model starts with the information available inside the company on competition (4), the posture of current strategy (5), and past performance (6). These three variables are considered individually and in combination in identifying the company's strengths and weaknesses (7).

The description of present strategic posture (say, low price) and evaluation of past performance (comfortable profits) should be examined with reference to competition (very high price) to identify the major advantages (stronghold in the price-conscious segment) or threats (ease of entry into the business, thus potentially new competition) which the company's products/markets may have in the future. The strengths and weaknesses are appraised in relation to technological and socio-economic-political environmental influences (8) and industry dynamics (9), resulting in resource potential.

------

*This number in parentheses and others that follow refer to corresponding boxes in Exhibit 1-4.

EXHIBIT 1-4   Corporate Planning Process

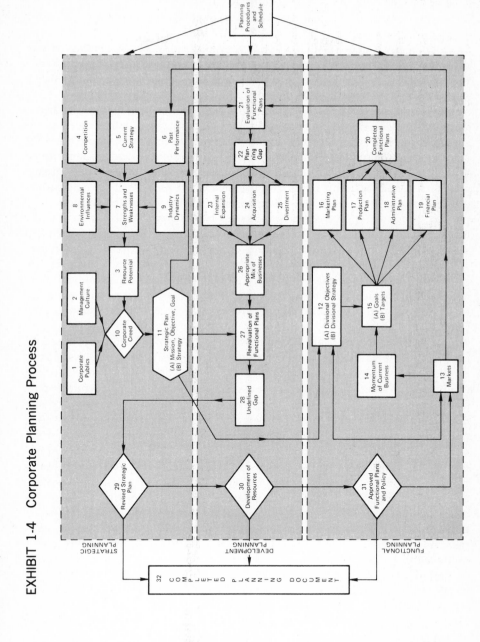

Based on the value orientation of top management, the corporate responsibility to various interests as designated by the management, and the resource potential, a general statement or corporate creed giving the overall philosophy or position of the company is developed (10). The corporate creed, while deeply meaningful, is too general in nature to indicate any specific outlook of the company. Sometimes loosely called policy, the corporate creed is widely made available to the public as a public relations document.

Next is the strategic plan (11). The word strategy has been defined in various ways by scholars. For the purposes of this book, strategy may be defined as the specification of an organization's objectives and goals, and policies and plans for achieving the objectives, including allocation of resources and organizational structure. Briefly, strategy deals with two broad questions: (a) what the company wants to be, and (b) how it hopes to get there, i.e., the purpose of the corporation and the course that should be taken to achieve the designated purpose. The purpose is broken into three parts: mission, objectives and goals. *Mission* is the chief executive's conception of the organization's raison d'etre, what it should work toward in light of the long-range opportunity. *Objective* is a qualitative statement about the direction the company intends to pursue in a given field in order to increase market share and obtain a reasonable return on investment. *Goal* is the specific achievement desired, usually in quantitative terms, with reference to stated time. An example of a goal is to seek 20 percent market share during the next two years.

The scope of the strategic plan differs from company to company, based on its size and the nature of various products or services it handles. Broadly, two levels of strategy should be differentiated: (a) for the corporation as a whole, and (b) for each product/market. In a large corporation, in developing a strategic plan at the corporate level, the major thrust is on corporate strategy. The product/ market strategy is either not considered at all or touched upon briefly. On the other hand, in a smaller company the reverse is true since in such a situation the corporate strategy itself revolves around its products. Thus, strategy for various products/markets is likely to be considered in detail. For example, in a large multi-product company, serving varying markets, the top management cannot concern itself with details. In such a company, therefore, at the corporate level, the emphasis in strategy formulation is likely to be on generalities that apply to all products/markets. In lower echelons of management, of course, a detailed network of strategy formulation will take place for each product/market, making due references to generalities specified at the corporate level.

Objectives and goals can be of three types: measurement, growth/survival, and constraint. Whereas measurement and constraint objectives have more relevance for defining total corporate aims, growth/survival objectives are generally defined in terms of products and markets. Of course, there may be growth objectives for the corporation at large, just as there may be measurement and constraint objectives for each product line.

Measurement objectives are stated largely in financial terms and are intended to serve as control tools for appraising the company's achievements in a given period. One popularly used measurement objective is return on investment. Other measurement objectives are market share, change in market share, sales, return on sales, and return on assets.

Constraint objectives specify the limit imposed by the top management in carrying out company operations. These constraints emerge out of management's own culture, environment, and traditions, and are dictated by the current status of the company. For example, a constraint goal may be to reinvest 50 percent of net income each year. Other constraint objectives may be a minimum (or maximum) amount to spend on R&D, a fixed ratio of promotional expenditures to sales, a given budget for quality control, or a prespecified sales territorial configuration (for example, only New England).

Growth/survival objectives deal with the product/market scope of each product line. A growth objective for a product may be to expand its distribution overseas or to develop and introduce a deluxe model for the higher-income segment of the market.

The last part of the strategic plan deals with the adoption of courses of action. The planner should select a specific course of action from among many feasible alternatives, but a mere decision on a course of action is not enough. The consequences of following the designated course must be determined and evaluated to enable the planner to know in advance what to expect from it and how much it would contribute toward the achievement of the objectives. Every course of action requires certain rules that must be followed, and these rules must be stated explicitly. These rules may be called operational policy. Finally, resource-support and control mechanisms for carrying out the chosen strategy must be established.

In brief, the process of choosing the course of action may be split in four parts:

1. Designation of different courses of action and choice of the most suitable one
2. Evaluation of the chosen action
3. Operational policy to implement the chosen action
4. Financing and administration of the chosen action

The first two aspects of choosing the course of action are dealt with as a part of strategic planning. Operational policy, financing, and administration are considered to be part of development planning.

The chosen course of action should be evaluated in terms of its contribution to the defined objectives, which may be profitability, technological leadership, societal obligation, national security, industry leadership, optimum use of company resources, and the like. The operational policy consists of assigning responsibility to an executive to carry out the chosen course, fixing a time horizon for the action, and considering the geography of the action if it is relevant in a particular case. Resources needed to implement the strategy and the sources which would be tapped to raise the funds are the financing variables. Authority-responsibility relationships and control networks to successfully operate the course of action must be clearly delineated under the proper administrative components.

The strategic plan is reduced to writing, reviewed, and finalized. It is useful to prepare two versions of a strategic plan: (a) a detailed plan, and (b) summary-highlights. The circulation of the former is limited to a few selected executives. The summary-highlights may be distributed comparatively widely but still controlled. On the other hand, the executive responsible for implementing the strategy may be given a copy of the complete plan and asked to communicate only as much information below the line as is considered necessary to implement the specifics of the plan. In either case, the relevant portions of the strategic plan should be communicated to the lower echelons of management. This is essential in order to provide a starting point for functional planning. The objectives and goals of a product/market should either be defined at the corporate level or in the division itself. In the former case, the objectives must be communicated to facilitate the development of functional plans which must be consistent with these objectives. In the second case, the division must be exposed to overall corporate thinking so that its objectives and strategy can be determined. Alternatively, a compromise may be reached between the two approaches. With the help of the divisional head, the objectives for the division may be considered and finalized by corporate management. In other words, the strategic issues concerning the product/market emerge at the top, but the divisional head plays a dominant role.

Functional Planning

Functional planning refers to the detailed network of activities that the company undertakes. This type of planning starts with a definition of the objectives of the function regardless of whether they are defined at the functional or at the corporate level (12). Functional planning is done by the managers who actually implement the programs described in the final edition of the approved corporate plan.

The corporate plan may or may not affect functional planning. In order to encourage creative efforts, the managers may be given a free hand in drawing their plans, virtually to the extent of being free-lancers. For example, a company may state the corporate objective simply as achieving a specific rate of growth, and from thereon the functional managers are free to do their job as they deem fit. Of course, corporate guidelines are provided for following a common format and time schedule such that different functional plans can be integrated without difficulty. On the other hand, functional planning may need to be done strictly according to the instructions detailed in the corporate plan.

With the overall objectives of the function determined, the functional plans begin with the study of markets (13). This is done through information gained from marketing research projects; field-force feedback; ad hoc surveys; the manager's perception of the market situation based on rumors, personal contacts, experience, and intuition; and so on. The market analysis reveals the momentum of current business (14), forces tending to threaten the existing business, and the new opportunities that appear promising. By means of the above analysis, goals and targets are set for each product/market (15). While goals are considered specific aims in the long run, time-phased targets are used to serve as various milestones toward the attainment of goals. For example, the goal may be to achieve 40 percent market share for a given product during the next three years. Targets will specify the movement toward the goal on a periodic basis, such as every six months. The overall objectives of the function serve as check points for determining the suitability of product/market goals and targets. The marketing plan (16) specifies what will be achieved with the existing products, what changes will be made in the products' programs to marshall new opportunities, and what action will be taken to combat threats.

Using the marketing plan as the basis, production planning (17) concentrates on how best to meet the commitments shown in the marketing plan. The present capacity, improvements in plant facilities, training of labor, and availability and prices of raw materials and components represent areas that figure prominently in production planning. Administrative planning is the next step. The administrative plan (18) deals with the potential human resources of the enterprise and components such as organizational structure and development, personnel planning, and the like. Finally, the financial plan (19) is drawn up, specifying different financial needs and their timings. The various functional plans are finally integrated and submitted to the top management (20).

Different functional plans are worked out simultaneously. During this process part of the information is channeled to each functional area through the formal structure. At the same time, informal interdepartmental interactions play an important role. Thus, even before marketing plans are formally completed, the people in the finance department, because of their own knowledge of the company at large and partly through informal communications, know the level of operations being planned by marketing.

The functional plans are handled in one of two ways, depending upon the organization of the company. If the company follows the project management concept, the project team will probably consist of the representatives from manufacturing, engineering, finance, and so on. Thus, after the marketing requirements have been reduced to goals and targets based on the company's capabilities, the financial analysis of the plan can be developed right within the team. In a functional organization, the functional planning will start with marketing; then the production group will develop the scope of its activities; next, the administrative plan would be worked out; and finally, these functional plans will be integrated through a financial plan.

Development Planning

Development planning falls between strategic and functional planning. Development planning is done by a few selected high-ranking executives, including the president. If not directly involved in the planning, the president must approve the completed development plan before it is finalized. Its purpose is to fill, or rather narrow, the gap between strategic and functional plans. Thus, a review of functional plans against the strategic plan constitutes the first step in development planning (21). The review starts with a comparison of corporate objectives, and goals against the projected movement of current operations indicated in functional plans. This designates the total planning gap (22) that needs to be filled.

There are three ways to fill the gap: (a) internal expansion, (b) acquisition, and (c) divestment. Proposals for internal expansion (23) would be included in the functional plans since the functional planners know the progress of internal efforts and the market feasibility of developing a product/service. The internal expansion program, however, must be approved before being pursued. To optimize the overall corporate performance, various expansion proposals as well as other avenues for filling the gap must be considered simultaneously. This is why development planning becomes important. In regard to acquisition (24) as an alternative for expansion, generally a top-ranking individual in the company or a committee of top management is designated to look at various acquisition opportunities. After being screened, evaluated, and analyzed, the acquisition opportunities are developed into definite proposals and made available to development planners. Divestment proposals (25) may be generated either by an ad hoc assignment to an individual or a committee or by the functional heads as a part of functional planning.

The various alternatives under internal expansion, acquisition, and divestment are simultaneously considered to fill the gap and to optimize corporate objectives and goals in the long run. Out of this effort emerge the scope and nature of various businesses to be pursued by the company (26). Now once more the functional plans, along with the approved internal expansion, acquisition, and divestment programs, are compared against the objectives outlined in the strategic plan (27). If the total planning gap discovered under prior evaluation has been filled, the plan is complete. But more often than not, particularly in an ambitious company with high growth objectives, there will still be some remaining gap despite the developmental programs which were accepted in the first round (28). Thus, if the gap still remains, the strategic plan will be reviewed and its objectives and goals modified in order to make the planning effort a realistic one (29). Once action to close the gap between the strategic plan and operational momentum is defined, the necessary resources are deployed (30). Approval on some projects is given, subject to a few constraints spelled out in the form of an operational policy (31). Operational policies will also fix the administrative responsibility for carrying out a project. The three types of plans (e.g., the strategic plan, the functional plan, and the development plan) are now put together as a complete planning document (32).

It should be cautioned that acquisition and divestment opportunities can emerge at any time. Thus, a part of the gap may be left unfilled in the hope that new proposals will be generated to fill the undefined gap later on.

Approaches to Planning

Planning can be approached in one of two ways: the outside-in or the inside-out approach.[9] The outside-in approach can be considered analogous to a marketing orientation in the sense that everything is based on the market and its environment. For example, a manufacturer of water systems might discover that direct selling through company-owned stores is becoming exceedingly popular and will in future years count as an important competitive strategy. As a result of this finding, the company will give serious consideration to opening company-owned stores in various parts of the nation in order to strengthen its position. If the company happens to be small, specializing in a few types of water systems, its limited product lines will not permit it to support direct distribution, and it may be forced to devise alternative strategies. In short, under the outside-in approach to planning, opportunities and threats are picked up in the environment, and decisions are based on the company's resource potential and earlier commitments.

The inside-out approach begins with a self-appraisal which delineates the company's strengths and weaknesses. Then, with the company's strengths in mind, the planners look outside the company for feasible exploitation opportunities. For example, one obvious strength of the Procter & Gamble Company is its distribution network. To make the most of this strength, the company seriously considers only products with a great potential which is realizable through strong distribution.

Each of the two approaches has its advantages and shortcomings. The outside-in approach may be considered more appropriate for fast growth and diversification, but even here it is a mixed blessing. The glamour of opportunities in an area may lead a company to make a myopic evaluation of its capabilities and involve itself in a business which it can not handle. The inside-out approach could be labeled as conservative, which may hamper growth. The shortcoming here is not in the approach, but in management's inability to make a proper evaluation of potential opportunity following the inside-out approach. On the positive side, the inside-out approach prevents undertaking unrealistic ventures.

In practice, a company cannot opt to follow one of these approaches in pure form. In all types of planning, e.g., strategic, development, and functional planning, both inside and outside approaches have to be judiciously blended for simultaneous use. However, one can say that strategic planning, by and large, will be biased in favor of the inside-out approach since financial groups traditionally dominate companies at the top. This approach ensures greater possibilities of acceptable return on investment and of undertaking manageable risks. However, there are exceptions to the rule: Growth through a high debt-equity ratio, acquisition of a variety of unrelated businesses to emerge as a conglomerate, and similar

---

[9]David W. Ewing, *The Practice of Planning* (New York: Harper & Row, Publishers, 1968), pp. 32–45.   *125, 773*

strategies which emphasize the significance of the outside-in approach became quite fashionable during the 1960s. The economic slowdown in the early 1970s, however, brought down the popularity of the outside-in approach at the strategic level. In functional planning, a marketing orientation and hence an outside-in approach is highly desirable in a competitive business environment. Inasmuch as checks and controls exist in the process before a product/market plan becomes final, most of the shortcomings of this approach are held in check. In development planning both approaches are equally important. For example, an acquisition route may seem desirable to fill the planning gap, but the search for acquisition opportunities cannot be made on an ad hoc basis. Thus, following an outside-in approach, acquisition alternatives may be available to fill the gap when it opens up.

Contingency Planning

The marketing plan, as well as other functional plans, should be drawn up in two parts: regular plans and contingency plans. The contingency plans are those that are followed in case environmental conditions evolve in a pattern which differs from that upon which the regular plan was based. As these changes materialize, the efforts of the company can be shifted along contingency plans without ignoring original objectives. Contingency plans are usually drawn up assuming the worst outcomes will occur—e.g., all the underlying assumptions such as sources of finance, appearance of a new competitor, emergence of a new technology tending to take over the company's product completely, sudden announcement of new controls by the government, and occurrence of a natural calamity can go against the company. As an example, the announcement of new economic policy by President Nixon in August, 1971, imposed new demands on the American Express Company overseas. The dollar became unacceptable to overseas hotels and other businesses, creating unimaginable problems for the American tourists in Europe. The American Express Company remained the tourists' only source for conversion of the dollar at the official rate. The company well met its obligation by shifting its gears to contingency plans which, as claimed, had been drawn up way ahead of time. The process of contingency planning is similar to that of regular planning except that parameter-assumptions are taken at their worst values.

Staff and Planning

Planning is necessarily a line function. Staff, however, plays a critical role in the planning function. Staff help can be useful in a variety of ways for different types of planning. The most common functions that staff performs in the realm of planning are: (a) to establish procedures, systems, and time schedules for planning activities; (b) to collect, control, and analyze information on operations within the company; and (c) to collect, control, and analyze information from environments outside the company.

Depending upon the scope of a business, the three tasks listed above can either be performed by an individual or by teams of planners. The staff members also work under various functional/divisional heads. The divisional staff people have administrative responsibility to the divisional head but functional responsibility to the corporate staff.

Planning Processes

In planning literature one comes across two different processes of planning: (a) bottom-up and (b) top-down. The bottom-up process begins at the lower end of the organizational hierarchy, proceeding to the top through several echelons of management. In top-down planning the process is reversed. The top management prescribes the planning course to follow and passes it down the line. Both processes have advantages and limitations. In the bottom-up process, evidently an effort is made to involve many levels of management in the planning activity. But this limits the role of top management to merely approving what has come down the line without an opportunity to reflect its experience and intimate knowledge in the plans. The top-down process, on the other hand, could present the final plans as an authoritative order from the top without the willing involvement and acceptance of the people in the lower ranks. In practice, therefore, no process is pursued in pure form. But major emphasis may be given to one process, depending on the type of planning. We believe that while strategic planning should follow the top-down process, functional planning should be based on the bottom-up process. Development planning may combine both the processes.

Planning Schedule

Planning is a continuing activity which must be done each year in accordance with environmental changes. However, during the course of a year, it is better to design a time schedule showing how the planning cycle would work in the organization. Since opportunities and threats cannot be timed, strategy developments are difficult to schedule. Thus, it would appear naive to fix a time schedule for strategy formulation. Putting this activity in a time slot indicates the point in time up to which strategy may be updated and communicated down the line to trigger action elsewhere in the organization. Of course a change in strategy requires revision of other plans. Such a change, however, can be incorporated without much difficulty unless the strategy is drastically changed.

RELATIONSHIP BETWEEN MARKETING PLANNING AND CORPORATE-WIDE PLANNING

Marketing is one of the functional areas of a business and, as described above, marketing planning is undertaken as a part of functional planning (i.e., along with financial planning, production planning, and administrative planning). In addition, a corporation undertakes strategic planning and development planning. It is important to recognize, however, that all planning has a direct impact on marketing programs. As has been said: ". . . the marketing function is an extension of corporate policy to the extent that the total enterprise exists and is organized as a system of business activities to satisfy market requirements at a profit."[10] Thus, marketing becomes a key concept in any planning activity. For example, corporate strategy defines what business the company is in or will be in and what kind of company it is or will be. Thus, corporate strategy gives shape to the firm's product/market options. Likewise, a firm's product/market posture forces the adoption of corporate strategy, obviously, showing that thought and action at the corporate level must be compatible with the marketing position. Thus, the close relationship between the overall direction of the firm and its marketing emphasis, at least in the long run, is obvious. In brief, effective corporate planning is normally heavily influenced by marketing considerations.

The crucial importance of marketing perspectives in business planning requires that marketing planning and strategy be recognized as a contributor to the corporate-wide planning effort while being guided by corporate planning. In Exhibit 1-4, for example, current strategy, past performance, and a review of the competition considered at the corporate level provide marketing inputs for corporate planning. On the other hand, corporate objectives will trigger the development of marketing planning and strategy.

MARKETING PLANNING AND PLANNING IN OTHER FUNCTIONAL AREAS

Functional planning refers to a detailed network of activities that a company undertakes. It is done by managers who are responsible for implementing the programs laid out in the approved plans. Although different companies follow varied functional planning procedures, there are similar characteristics in successful planning processes.

To be useful, planning should be systematic. This requires proper integration of strategic, development, and functional plans. To ensure such an integration, the genesis of these plans as well as the key assumptions underlying them should be the same. The key assumptions refer to broad socio-economic, political, and technological trends having relevance for the entire corporation. They should be worked out at the corporate level at the beginning of the planning exercise.

To provide a common genesis in a multimarket, multiproduct firm, objectives of a function such as marketing should emerge from corporate objectives and strategies. Generally two different processes are followed to designate functional objectives. They may be worked out at the corporate level with an active involvement of the functional head. Thereafter, the functional head may redefine them in the functional terminology with the help of one or more subordinates. Alternatively, the functional area may be provided with statements of corporate objectives and strategies, then left on its own to define its objectives. Relevant portions

---

[10]Norton Paley, "Corporate Objective and Marketing Aim: What is the Relationship?" *California Management Review,* Vol. II, No. 2 (1968), p. 60.

of the functional objectives may then be communicated down the line to trigger planning activity at the product/market level. In some corporations, however, the product/market heads are given wide latitude without the inhibitions of broad functional objectives. In one large corporation, for example, the product/market managers are simply given the growth rate that the company should achieve, and from then on they are free to do their job as they deem fit. Of course, guidelines are provided for following a common format and a time schedule such that product/market plans can be integrated easily.

As mentioned earlier, there are four principal functional planning areas: marketing, production or manufacturing, finance, and administration. Each department develops its own functional plans. Hierarchically, in functional planning, marketing sits at the top and triggers action elsewhere. This does not mean, however, that planning in other areas must wait until marketing plans are completed. Based on past experience and formal and informal inter-division communications, various functional plans are drawn up simultaneously. Of course, final completion is deferred until the marketing plan is executed.

Functional planning starts with two basic inputs: historical market information and sales forecasts. The market study for each product should be undertaken separately. The word "market" is used here in a comprehensive sense so as to include historical information pertaining to sales, ingredients of the marketing mix, field environment, channel reaction, and so on (see Exhibit 1-3 on page 13). Some of this information should be available in company records; however, ad hoc efforts might be needed to collect other essential information. A good marketing information system and a well-organized marketing research department would be helpful in acquiring adequate information.

After information on markets is obtained, forecasts are developed for the planning period (see product/market momentum in Exhibit 1-3, p. 13). These forecasts assume that no new actions other than normal changes in the marketing mix will be forthcoming as far as the company is concerned. The plan, however, might include a second forecast on a product/market showing how things could improve if a new program were followed. For example, introduction of a new model in a company might require approval of top management. If the manager responsible for making the forecasts infers that introduction of the new model would improve performance substantially, a new forecast including the new model might be made and compared with the old forecast.

These inputs essentially deal with the market and are therefore a responsibility of the marketing management. They may be labelled basic inputs rather than marketing inputs since they are equally important for developing perspectives of other functional plans. These inputs as well as the marketing plan itself serve as points of germination for other functional plans. Sales forecasts generate production schedules, cash flows, manpower needs, and other planning requirements. Media schedules, sales programs, and other aspects of marketing programs also form the basis for a wide variety of functional plans.

Marketing Planning

Marketing planning deals with the development of alternative programs within the scope of the firm's product/market mix. It recommends the most feasible product portfolio in the light of overall corporate goals and strategy, product/market objectives, and marketing environment. Briefly, marketing planning provides two types of information: 1) a product portfolio and 2) the perspectives of different products/markets (via objectives, action programs, and budget requirements) included in the portfolio.

Production Planning

As in other functional plans, production planning is concerned with issues which lie in the realm of top-management activity. This top-management perspective is essential since, tempted by the objectivity of production-related variables, one can become inundated with unnecessary details of the production process. The scope of production planning is determined by corporate strategy and other relevant information such as:

1. Sales forecasts and anticipated inventory requirements
2. New processes, materials, and techniques that have been developed and are available for use
3. Strategy concerning whether to make or buy various parts, etc.
4. Strategy on environmental issues such as waste disposal and the hiring and training of minorities

In addition, many other types of information may be important for production planning, such as buying from more than one source, interdepartmental transfer of parts, and keeping inventory of semi-finished materials. Similarly, quality control can become a strategic issue for a company. To increase productivity or to avoid labor problems, the company might opt for gradually converting the entire labor force to salary. This would, then, be a strategic issue. Similarly, a strategic decision may be made to forbid overtime, or to buy inputs in truckloads in order to cut down on transportation costs. All this information could be significant for production planning.

The next step in formulating a production plan is to take an inventory of departmental resources. These resources can be categorized as:

1. Availability of inputs
2. Status of plant, equipment, and other production-related facilities
3. Productivity
4. Optimum use of resources
5. Quality of output
6. Labor relations
7. Know-how

By using the above information and by making a comparison with major competitors, the dimensions encompassing the planning horizons for each resource may be derived. New developments in the field such as a new process or material should be duly considered. Equipped with all this information, the production head can develop a strategy, which may be broken down into two parts: objectives and action programs.

Given the action programs and the extent of work required in each program, the critical areas where greater effort is needed to enhance efficiency or to avert threat would be defined. In each of these areas, studies should be undertaken and the alternatives available to the company defined. Recommendations should then be made in each area for the approval of top management as a part of development planning. The evaluation of alternatives in the production area should consist of the following:

1. Feasibility analyses: technical, financial, productivity, quality, etc.
2. Cost implications
3. Environmental implications
4. Time implications
5. Investment implications

Finally, the chosen courses of action for different product lines are consolidated to present a complete picture to top management for approval. For example, in deciding plant and facility needs for different lines, the planners could determine the most effective use of existing capacity and what new facilities would be needed and when. Alternatives for facilities, techniques, etc., that are likely to become obsolete in the future would be indicated. In a similar manner, training requirements, pollution control efforts, and so on would be consolidated and presented along with cost-benefit relationships.

Financial Planning

Typically, the financial plan is the last one prepared, but that does not undermine its importance. It is last because of the necessity of incorporating the financial consequences of other functional plans into the financial plan. Financial planning includes both the treasury functions of procurement and management of funds and the controllership functions of budgetary planning and control. The major decision areas in financial planning can be grouped as follows:

A. Financial perspective of operations
1. Sources and uses of funds
2. Cash requirements
3. Impact of operations on profitability

B. Capital projects—evaluation and funding
1. Choosing investment projects
2. Feasible sources for raising funds

The entire spectrum of financial decisions is split between functional planning and development planning. The major emphasis in functional planning is on the first three areas listed above. The last two are in the purview of development planning. In practice development planning is undertaken simultaneously with functional planning, although theoretically it would appear as if the former starts only after the functions have planned the operations. The financial perspective of operations may be called profit planning rather than financial planning. In a decentralized corporation, for example, the financial manager responsible for a specific product/market would deal with the financial perspective of those operations. Corporate financial management would be mainly concerned with capital projects from the standpoint of the entire corporation, which necessitates consolidation of various financial work done in the divisions.

In brief, there are two distinct aspects of financial planning, as mentioned above. In a smaller company the same people may be involved in both the tasks, especially if the corporation is functionally organized. In a corporation with autonomous divisions, entirely different people would perform these two tasks.

Administrative Planning

Administrative planning refers to planning for the human resources of the organization, which would include organizational structure and development and human resource planning. The administrative planning may be done either by people in the personnel department or by those responsible for the company's organizational development. Administrative planning begins with a review of current human resources in the company, which are grouped in different categories such as skilled labor, clerical staff, supervisory people, middle management, managerial personnel, and top management. Next, attempts should be made to forecast organizational needs during the planning period. Here inputs from different areas in the company and the marketing and production plan would be helpful. Studies may also be performed to measure the company's present organizational development status and human productivity.

PLAN OF THE BOOK

Today's business and marketing managers are faced with a continuous stream of decisions, each with its own degrees of risk, uncertainty, and payoff. Ansoff has characterized three broad classes of business decisions:

1. Operating
2. Administrative
3. Strategic[11]

Operating decisions are those dealing with the current operations of the business. The typical objective of these decisions in a business firm is profit

---

[11]H. Igor Ansoff, *Corporate Strategy* (New York: McGraw-Hill Book Co., 1965), pp. 3–10.

maximization. During times of business stagnation or recession as experienced in the past several years, these efforts at increasing efficiency have typically encompassed a cost minimization perspective. Under these conditions managers are pressured into shorter and shorter time horizons. All too frequently decisions are made regarding pricing, discounts, promotional expenditures, collection of marketing research information, inventory levels, delivery schedules, and a host of other areas with far too little regard for the longer-term impact of the decision. As would be expected, the decision which may be optimal for one time period is not so in the long run.

A second type of decision is the administrative one. These decisions pertain to the collection, organization, and development of the firm's resources. These include capital, personnel, and technological resources which must be organized in a manner which provides the greatest potential for the attainment of long-term objectives and goals. Typical decisions in the administrative area involve staffing and organizational structure, degree of decentralization, lines of communication, and information flows. These decisions collectively provide the parameters within which the operational decisions must be made. Indeed, whereas administrative decisions present the firm's potential, operational decisions determine the degree to which that potential is realized.

The third category of decision making deals with the determination of strategy: the selection of the proper markets and the products which best suit the needs of those markets. While strategic decisions may represent a very small fraction of the total plethora of management decisions, they are truly the most important as they provide the definition of the business and the general relationship between the firm and its environment. Despite their importance, the need to make strategic decisions is not always as apparent as is the need (sometimes urgency) for successfully completing operations or administrative decisions.

The strategic decisions are characterized by the following distinctions:

1. They are likely to effect *a significant departure from the established product-market mix.* (This might involve branching out technologically or innovating in other ways.)
2. They are likely to hold provisions for undertaking programs with an unusually *high degree of risk relative to previous experience* (e.g., using untried resources or entering uncertain markets and competitive situations where predictability of success is noticeably limited).
3. They are likely *to include a wide range of available alternatives* to cope with a major competitive problem, the scope of these alternatives providing for significant differences in both the results and resources required.
4. They are likely *to involve important timing options,* both for starting development work and for deciding when to make the actual market commitment.
5. They are likely *to call for major changes in the competitive "equilibrium, "* creating a new operating and customer acceptance pattern.

6. They are likely *to resolve the choice of either leading or following certain market or competitive advances,* based on a trade-off between the costs and risks of innovating and the timing vulnerability of letting others pioneer (in the expectation of catching up and moving ahead at a later date on the strength of a superior marketing force).[12]

This book essentially deals with strategic decisions in the area of marketing. Specifically, Exhibit 1-5 gives an overview of strategic, administrative, and operating decisions in marketing arranged within different decision areas of marketing. The focus of this book will be on the decisions listed as strategic within the areas of market targeting, product, price, promotion, and distribution. The operating and administrative decisions are mainly covered in a typical marketing management course.

SUMMARY

This chapter focuses on the concept of planning and strategy. Planning is the ongoing management process of choosing the objectives to be achieved during a certain period, setting up a plan of action, and maintaining continuous surveillance of results so as to make regular evaluations and, if necessary, to modify the objectives and plan of action. Also described are requisites for successful planning and a time frame for initiating planning activities and philosophies of planning (i.e., satisfying, optimizing and adaptivizing). Strategy is the course of action selected from alternatives as the optimum way to attain objectives, consistent with current policies and in the light of anticipated competitive actions.

Next, the process of marketing planning and strategy formulation is described. Marketing planning begins at the level of a product/market. The product/market plans are reviewed and approved, and resources are allocated. Finally, a product portfolio is developed from the viewpoint of the entire organization. A variety of corporate level inputs such as objectives, resources, and environmental assumptions is required to develop product/market plans. To establish proper perspectives for these inputs, the relationship of marketing planning to corporate planning as well as to planning in other functional areas is examined.

Further, a variety of related concepts is covered. These are approaches to planning, i.e., outside-in and inside-out; contingency plans; line and staff roles in planning; types of planning processes, i.e., bottom-up and top-down; and planning schedule. Finally, the plan to be followed in this book is articulated. Of the three types of business decisions, i.e., operating, administrative, and strategic, this book aims at strategic decision making with reference to marketing. The nature of market-, product-, price-, promotion-, and distribution-related strategic decisions is reviewed vis-a-vis the other two types of decisions in Exhibit 1-5.

---

[12]J. Thomas Cannon, *Business Strategy and Policy* (New York: Harcourt, Brace & World, 1968), p. 20.

EXHIBIT 1-5   Paradigm of Marketing Decisions

Decision Area	Types of Decisions		
	Strategic	Administrative	Operating
(a) Market Targeting: Organizational Customer Markets	1) Scope of market by industry—across-the-board vs. selective industries 2) Scope of market by size—key accounts vs. large customer base 3) Scope of market by application, i.e., market development of new uses for established applications through product substitution	1) Market opportunity analysis 2) Structure for organizational customer buying 3) Building customer feedback system	1) Selection of specific target markets 2) Criteria for establishing contact in chosen markets
(b) Household Consumer Markets	1) Scope of market by geography 2) Choice of markets based on consumer characteristics 3) Limiting the market	1) Evaluating the worth of different segments 2) Organization for household consumer markets	1) Selection of specific target markets 2) Criteria for establishing contact in chosen markets

EXHIBIT 1-5 (cont'd.)

Decision Area	Strategic	Administrative	Operating
	scope, e.g., by distribution-channel selectivity	3) Building customer feedback system	3) Differentiated vs. undifferentiated marketing
(c) Product	1) Product positioning 2) Primary vs. selective demand emphasis 3) Scope of product line 4) Product-system concepts 5) Product customization	1) Analysis of basic technological and marketing strengths and weaknesses 2) Organizational arrangements for product management 3) New product process 4) Product audits	1) Brand decisions 2) Width and depth of product line
(d) Pricing	1) Pricing objectives 2) Sell vs. lease 3) Warranties and guarantees 4) Price bundling 5) "Iceberg" pricing 6) Price changes	1) Price-setting process 2) Gathering information for pricing decision	1) List price 2) Discounts 3) Allowances 4) Trade margins 5) Credits 6) Computation of prices 7) Product line pricing 8) Transfer pricing

EXHIBIT 1-5 (contd.)

Decision Area	Strategic	Administrative	Operating
(e) Promotions	1) Reliance on promotion 2) Promotion mix	1) Internal advertising department vs. outside advertising agency 2) Sales management organization 3) Advertising research 4) Sales communication	1) Objectives for different forms of promotion 2) Media budgets and allocations 3) Message content and format 4) Selling programs 5) Sales promotion programs
(f) Distribution	1) Geographic expansion 2) Location of resources 3) Organizational-Customer channels of distribution 4) Household-Consumer channels of distribution 5) Selectivity of distribution 6) Franchised vs. uncontrolled channels	1) Management of distribution resources 2) Channel communications	1) Selection of channel members 2) Number of channels 3) Channel tactics

DISCUSSION QUESTIONS

1. Is the concept of planning relevant to profit-making organizations alone? Can nonprofit organizations or the national government also embrace planning? Discuss.
2. Traditionally, planning has always been considered an important function of management. How is strategic planning different from traditional planning?
3. Differentiate among operating, administrative, and strategic decisions. Suggest three examples of each type of decision from the viewpoint of a food processor.
4. How might financial planning have an impact on marketing planning? Explain.
5. Adapt the process of marketing planning and strategy formulation presented in Exhibit 1-3 to a small business.
6. Specify the corporate inputs which are needed to undertake marketing planning.
7. Explain the meaning of contingency planning. Do all businesses need such planning? If yes, why?
8. Explain bottom-up and top-down planning processes. Which process is most appropriate for marketing planning?

Chapter 2
Internal Appraisal

We that acquaint ourselves with every zone
And pass both tropics and behold the poles
When we come home are to ourselves unknown
and unacquainted still with our souls.

John Davies

One important reason for undertaking marketing planning is to prepare the company to interact with the changing environment in which it operates. Implicit in this is the significance of predicting what shape the environment is likely to take during the planning period. Then with a perspective of the company's present position the task ahead can be determined. Study of the environment is reserved for the following chapter. This chapter is devoted to self-appraisal.

An analogy to corporate self-appraisal is provided by a career counselor's job. Just as it is relatively easy to make a list of the jobs available to a young person, it is simple to produce a superficial list of investment opportunities open to a company. With the career counselor the real skill comes in taking stock of each applicant, examining the applicant's qualifications, personality, and temperament, defining the areas in which some sort of further development may be required, such as training, and matching these characteristics and the applicant's aspirations against the various options which are open. Well-established techniques exist that can be used to find out most of the necessary information about an individual. Digging deep into the psyche of a company is a more complex operation, but no less important. Failure by the company in the area of self-appraisal can be as stunting to future development in the corporate sense as can be the misplacement of a young graduate in the personal sense.

How should the planner approach the task of appraising corporate perspectives? What needs to be discovered? These and other similar questions are explored in this chapter.

MEANING OF CORPORATE APPRAISAL

Broadly, corporate appraisal refers to an examination of the entire organization from different angles. It is a measurement of the readiness of the internal culture of the corporation to interact with the external environment. Marketing strategists are concerned with those aspects of the corporation which have a direct bearing on corporate-wide objectives and goals because they must be referred to in defining marketing strategy. As shown in Exhibit 2-1, the value systems of top management, corporate publics, corporate resources, and the external environment are all variables which affect the setting of corporate objectives and goals. Of these, the first three variables are discussed in this chapter. An appraisal of the marketing side of a business is also included in this chapter.

Two important characteristics of strategic marketing planning are its concern with issues having far-reaching effects on the entire organization and change as an essential ingredient in its implementation. These two characteristics make the entire process of marketing planning and strategy a difficult job and demand creativity and adaptability on the part of the organization. Creativity, however, is not everybody's forte. By the same token, adaptation to changing conditions

EXHIBIT 2-1   Scope of Internal Appraisal

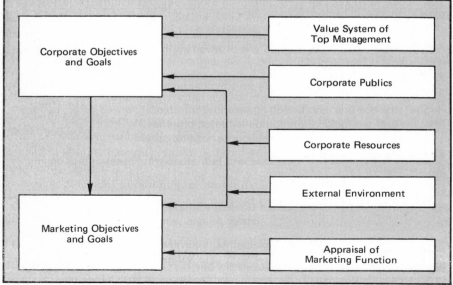

may come to be considered as a threat to existing style, norms of behavior, and relationships. As has been said:

> Success in the past always becomes enshrined in the present by the over-valuation of the policies and attitudes which accompanied that success . . . with time these attitudes become embedded in a system of beliefs, traditions, taboos, habits, customs, and inhibitions which constitute the distinctive culture of that firm. Such cultures are as distinctive as the cultural differences between nationalities or the personality differences between individuals. They do not adapt to change very easily.[1]

Human history is full of instances where communities and cultures were wiped out over time, the apparent reason for downfall being a failure to change to keep up with the times. In the context of business, why is it that organizations like Xerox, R.J. Reynolds, Litton, I.B.M., and Playboy, comparative newcomers among the large organizations, are considered blue-chip companies? Why should NCR, United States Rubber, and American Tobacco lag behind? Why are General Motors, DuPont, and 3M continually ranked as the "successful" companies? The outstanding common denominator found in the successful companies is the element of change. When the perspective of an organization undergoes a change as demanded by time, success is the outcome.

Obviously, the marketing strategist must take a closer look at the perspectives of the organization before formulating future strategy. Strategies must bear a close relationship to the internal culture of the corporation if they are to be successfully implemented.

FACTORS OF APPRAISAL: CORPORATE PUBLICS

Business exists for people. Thus, the first consideration in the strategic process is to recognize the individuals and groups who have an interest in the fate of the corporation and the extent and nature of their expectations.

Meaning of Corporate Publics

The following groups generally constitute the interest-holders in business organizations:

1. Owners
2. Employees
3. Customers
4. Suppliers
5. Banking community and other lenders
6. Government

---

[1] *Perspectives on Corporate Strategy* (Boston, Mass.: Boston Consulting Group, 1968), p. 93.

   7. Community in which the company does business
   8. Society-at-large

For the healthy growth of the organization, all eight groups must be served adequately. Traditionally the concern for community and society was not held important; today, however, service to community and society is widely acclaimed. The community may force a company to refrain from activities which are detrimental to the environment. For example, the Boise Cascade Company was denounced in 1971 as harsh, stingy, socially insensitive, and considerably short of the highest ethical standards for unplanned land development. Ultimately, the community interest prevailed, forcing the company either to give up its land development activities or make proper arrangements for sewage, etc., to keep the environment clean.[2] Similarly, social concern may prevent a company from becoming involved in certain types of business. A publishing company may refuse to publish pornographic material. Student demonstrations against Dow Chemical in the early 1970s for manufacturing napalm provides another example of how societal constraints bear heavily on the operations of a business corporation. Likewise, Gulf Oil's involvement in Angola was resented by various social groups. In brief, the requirements and expectations of today's society must serve as basic ingredients in the development of strategy. As the Committee for Economic Development in its statement on the subject has mentioned:

> The great growth of corporations in size, market power, and impact on society has naturally brought with it a commensurate growth in responsibilities; in a democratic society, power sooner or later begets equivalent responsibility.[3]

Limits of Corporate Response to Different Publics

Historically, a business organization considered its sole purpose to be economic gain, concerning itself with other spheres of society only when required to by law or motivated by philanthropy, charity, etc. The latter was merely a celebration of a corporation's good fortunes which it desired to share with the "outsiders" or a display of pity for the unfortunate. Indirectly, of course, even this meant a good name for the company and thus served the public relations function of the corporation. In slack times, the company reduced its activities in all areas, which meant both inside cost-cutting measures and lowering of commitments to all publics other than stockholders. This system worked well until recently. With economic prosperity almost assured, different stakeholders began to demand a more equitable deal from the corporation. For example, during the 1960s concern over environmental pollution by corporations became a major

---

[2]"Boise Cascade Shifts Toward Tighter Control," *Business Week* (May 15, 1971), p. 90.
[3]*Social Responsibilities of Business Corporations: A Statement on National Policy* (New York: Committee for Economic Development, 1971), p. 21.

issue in both the public and the private sector. Similarly, customers expected the products to be wholesome; employees wanted opportunities for advancement and self-improvement; the community hoped that the local corporation would assume some of its concerns, such as unemployment among blacks. Society thinks that business corporations can help in resolving problems of cities, minorities, etc. In brief, the role of the business corporation has shifted from that of an economic institution solely responsible to stockholders to one of a multifaceted force owing its existence to different stakeholders to whom it must be responsible.

As the most progressive institution in the society, the business corporation is expected to provide balanced prosperity in all fields. This new outlook extends the mission of the business beyond the primary obligation to owners.

Much has been said and written on the desirability and feasibility of enlarging the role of the corporation. *Business Week* states:

> Two generations ago, the idea that business is party to a contract with the society in which it operates would have provoked an indignant snort from most businessmen. Even 10 years ago it was more likely to be material for a corporate president's speech to the stockholders than a basis for policy. It is a measure of how much the middle-of-the-road group of businessmen can set it up as the basic assumption for their statement on the social responsibilities of the business.[4]

In today's environment, corporate strategy must be developed not simply to enhance financial performance, but to maximize performance across-the-board, delivering highest gains to all the stakeholders or corporate publics.

Corporate Publics—Analysis of Expectations

While the expectations of different groups vary, in our society growth and improvement are the common expectations of any institution. But this broad definition does not take into account the stakes of different groups within the business. For planning purposes, a clearer definition of each group's anticipations is needed.

Exhibit 2-2 summarizes the factors against which the expectations of different groups can be measured. The broad categories shown here should be broken down into subcategories as far as possible. For example, in a community where juvenile delinquency is rampant, youth programs become an important area of corporate concern. One must be careful, however, not to make unrealistic or typical assumptions about the expectations of different groups. Take owners, for example. According to the Boston Consulting Group, 50 percent of earnings after taxes must be invested to sustain the normal growth of a business.[5] But the payout desired by the owners may render it difficult to finance growth. Thus, a balance must be

---

4"The New 'Social Contract'," *Business Week* (July 3, 1971), p. 72.
5*The Stockholder* (Boston, Mass.: Boston Consulting Group, 1971).

EXHIBIT 2-2 Corporate Publics and Their Expectations

Publics	Area of Concern	Expectations
Owners	Payout Equity Stock prices Nonmonetary desires	
Customers	Business reliability Product reliability Product improvement Product price Product service Continuity Marketing efficiency	
Employees of All Ranks	Monetary reward Reward of recognition Reward of pride Environment Challenge Continuity Advancement	
Suppliers	Price Stability Continuity Growth	
Banking Community and Other Lenders	Sound risk Interest payment Repayment of principal	
Government (Federal, State, and Local)	Taxes Security and law enforcement Management expertise Democratic government Capitalistic system Implementation of programs	
Immediate Community	Economic growth and efficiency Education Employment and training	
Society-at-Large	Civil rights and equal opportunities Urban renewal and development Pollution abatement Conservation and recreation Culture and arts Medical care	

struck between payment of dividends and plowing back of earnings. A vice-president of finance for a chemical company with yearly sales over $100 million has said:

> While we do recognize the significance of retaining more money, we must consider the desires of our stockholders. They happen to be people who actually live on dividend payments. Thus, a part of long-term growth must be given up in order to maintain their short-term needs of regular dividend payments.

Apparently, this company would not be correct in assuming that growth alone is the objective of stockholders. Thus it behooves the marketing strategists to gain clear insights into the demands of different corporate publics.

Who in the company should undertake the study of stakeholders' expectations? This task constitutes a project in itself and should be assigned either to someone inside the company (such as a corporate planner, an assistant to the president, a director of public affairs and/or a marketing researcher) or to a consultant who may be hired for this purpose. The first time around it will be fairly difficult to specify stakeholders, designate their areas of concern, and make their expectations explicit. Later on, updating from year to year should become fairly routine.

The groups which constitute the stakeholders of a business organization are usually the same from one business to another. Mainly, they are the owners, employees, customers, suppliers, the banking community and other lenders, government, community, and society. The areas of concern of each group and their expectations, however, require surveying. As any other survey project, this amounts to seeking information from an appropriate sample within each group. A structured questionnaire is preferable for obtaining objective answers. Before surveying the sample, however, it is desirable to give in-depth interviews to a few members of each group. The information provided by these interviews is helpful in developing the questionnaire. While overall areas of concern may not vary from one time period to another, expectations certainly do. For example, during a recession stockholders may desire higher payout in dividends than at other times. Besides, in a given time period, the public may not articulate expectations in all of its areas of concern. During inflationary periods, for example, customers may only emphasize stable prices, while product improvement and marketing efficiency may figure prominently in times of prosperity.

Corporate Publics, Objectives, and Goals

The expectations of different publics provide the corporation with a focus for working out its objectives and goals. However, a company may not be able to satisfy the expectations of all stakeholders for two reasons: limited resources and conflicting expectations among stakeholders. For example, customers may want low prices and simultaneously ask for product improvements. Likewise, to meet exactly the expectations of the community the company may be obliged to reduce dividends paid out to the stockholders. Thus, a balance must be struck between the expectations of different stakeholders and the company's ability to honor them.

The corporate response to stakeholders' expectations emerges in the form of its objectives and goals. While objectives and goals are planned to be discussed in Chapter 5, a sample of corporate objectives with reference to customers is given below.

Assume the following customers' expectations for a food processing company:

1. The company should provide wholesome products.
2. The company should clearly state the ingredients of different products in words which are easily comprehensible to an ordinary consumer.
3. The company should make all efforts to keep the prices down.

The company, based on the aforementioned expectations, may set the following goals.

Wholesome Products

1. Create a new position—vice-president, product quality—effective January 1, 19—. No new products will be introduced into the market until they are approved for wholesomeness by this vice-president. The vice-president's decision will be upheld no matter how bright a picture of consumer acceptance of a product is painted by marketing research and marketing planning.
2. Create a panel of nutrient testers to analyze and judge different products for their wholesomeness.
3. Communicate with the consumers about the wholesomeness of the company's products, suggesting that they deal directly with the vice-president of product quality should there be any questions. (Incidentally, a position similar to vice president of product quality was created at Gillette a few years ago. This executive's decisions overruled the market introduction of products despite numerous other reasons for early introduction).

Information on Ingredients

1. Create a new position: director, consumer information. The person in this position will decide what information should be stated on each product so as to provide the consumers with as much information as is feasible on the product ingredients, nutritive value, etc.
2. Seek feedback every other year from a sample of consumers concerning the effectiveness of the information provided.
3. Encourage customers through various forms of promotions to communicate with the director of consumer information on a toll-free phone number to clarify any part of the information which may be unclear.
4. Revise information contents based on numbers 1 and 2.

Keeping Prices Low

1. Communicate with the customers as to what leads the company to raise different prices (i.e., cost of labor is up, cost of ingredients is up, etc.).
2. Design ways to reduce the price pressure on consumers in various ways. For example, develop family packs.
3. Encourage customers to buy family packs, clearly indicating how much they can save by buying family packs. Also assure them that quality of the product will remain intact for a specified period.
4. Work on new ways to reduce costs. For example, a substitute may be found for a product ingredient whose cost has gone up tremendously.

By using the illustration given above, the expectations of each group of stakeholders can be translated into specific goals.

FACTORS OF APPRAISAL: VALUE ORIENTATION OF TOP MANAGEMENT

Values refer to the ideas and desires, ideals and motivations, and outlook and assumptions which an individual cherishes and prizes highly. Management's value orientation bears heavily on efficiency, scrupulous honesty, readiness for change, integrity, self-reliance, energetic enterprise, willingness to take the long view, etc. These in turn have an impact on strategy development. Stated differently, the ideologies and philosophies of the top management as a team and the chief executive as the leader of the team have a profound effect on the managerial policy and the strategic process. As Steiner has said:

> His aspirations about his personal life, the life of his company as an institution, and the lives of those involved in his business are major determinants of choice of strategy. His mores, habits, and ways of doing things determine how he behaves and decides. His sense of obligation to his company will decide his devotion and choice of subject matter to think about.[6]

Presumably, creative men at the top are likely to be more responsive to innovative ideas. Creative leaders foster creativity throughout the organization, giving new perspective to its environment.[7] This creativity may encourage greater R&D effort and smoother adjustment to change.

---

[6]George A. Steiner, *Top Management Planning* (New York: Macmillan Co. Publishers, 1969), p. 241.
[7]Gary A. Steiner (ed.), *The Creative Organization* (Chicago: University of Chicago Press, 1965).

Importance of Value Orientation in the Corporate Environment

It would be wrong to assume that every firm wants to grow. There are companies which probably could grow faster than their current rate indicates. But where top management is averse to expansion, sluggishness prevails throughout the organization, inhibiting growth. A large number of companies started small with the family managing the organization. Some entrepreneurs at the helm of affairs in such companies are quite satisfied with what they have been able to achieve. They would rather not grow than give up their complete control of the organization. Obviously if managerial values promote stability rather than growth, the strategy will be formed accordingly. Of course, if the owners find that their expectations are in conflict with the value system of the top management, they may seek to replace them with a more philosophically compatible team. As an example, a flamboyant CEO may emphasize growth and introduce changes in the organization to the extent of creating suspicion among owners, board members, and colleagues. This may lead to the CEO's exit from the organization. An unconventionally high debt-equity ratio exhibited in the balance sheet can be sufficient cause for a chief executive to be dismissed. Similarly, a CEO's style of management may create upheavals in the organization. As Jennings narrates:

> Under the leadership of William C. Stolk, American Can acquired Marathon Paper Company, and its president, Roy J. Sund, was made head of the parent company. Sund was plainly ticketed to become the chief executive officer when Stolk reached the mandatory retirement age of sixty-five. Now Sund believed in a highly decentralized structure in opposition to the highly centralized organization that Stolk was building. Roy Sund resigned because he did not want to take over a company that did not have his style. Sund went over to Champion Paper and took George Walker with him.[8]

In brief, the value systems of the individual members of the top management serve as important inputs in strategy development. If people at the top hold conflicting values, the chosen strategy will lack the willing cooperation and commitment of all the executives. Generally, differing values are reflected in conflicts over policies, objectives, strategies, and structure.

Measurement of Values

In emphasizing the significance of the value system in strategic planning, several questions become pertinent. Should the corporation attempt to formally establish values for important members of the management? If so, who should

---

[8]Eugene E. Jennings, *Routes to the Executive Suite* (New York: Alfred A. Knopf, 1971), p. 219.

do it? What measures or techniques should be used? If values of the senior executives are in conflict, what should be done? Can values be changed?

It is generally agreed that the values of top management in a company should be measured. If nothing else, it will familiarize the CEO with the orientation of the top executives and will help the CEO to better appreciate their viewpoints. Opinions differ, however, as to who should do the measuring. Various possibilities are: corporate planner, chief executive officer, manpower planner, and outside consultant. While a good case can be made for any one of these alternatives, an outside consultant would probably be the most useful in gaining objective perspective of management values. If a consultant's findings appear to create conflict in the organization, they can be scrapped. Once the initial effort is made with help from the consultant, the human resource planner in the company, working closely with the corporate planner, can design a system for measurement of values.

There are various ways in which values can be measured. A popular technique is the self-evaluating scale developed by Allport et al.[9] This scale divides the values into six classes: religious, political, theoretical, economic, aesthetic, and social. Difficulties with using this scale lie in relating the executives' values to their jobs and in figuring out the impact of these values on corporate strategy. A manual is available that lists the average scores of different groups. Executives can complete the test in about 30 minutes and determine the structure of their values individually.

A more specific way is to pinpoint those aspects of human values which are likely to affect strategy development and measure one's score on these values on a simple five- or seven-point scale. For example, we can measure executives' orientation on factors such as leadership image, performance standards and evaluation, decision-making techniques, use of authority, attitude on change, and nature of involvement. Exhibit 2-3 shows a sample scale for measuring values which ranges from a highly negative to a highly positive attitude.

As a matter of fact, a formal value-orientation profile of executives may not be entirely necessary. By raising questions like the following about each top executive, one can gather insights into value orientations:

Does the executive:
    seem efficiency-minded?
    like repetition?
    like to be first in a new field instead of second?
    revel in detail work?
    seem willing to pay the price of keeping in personal touch with the customer, etc.?

[9]Gordon W. Allport, Philip E. Vernon, and Gardner Lindzey, *Study of Values and the Manual of Study of Values* (New York: Houghton Mifflin Co., 1960).

EXHIBIT 2-3   Measuring Value Orientation

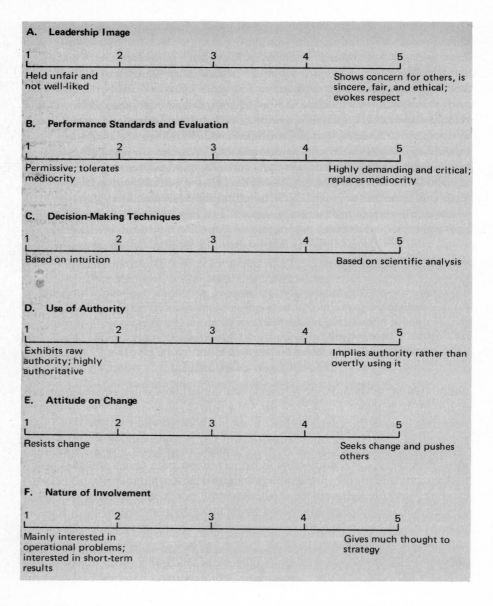

A.   Leadership Image

1	2	3	4	5

Held unfair and
not well-liked

Shows concern for others, is
sincere, fair, and ethical;
evokes respect

B.   Performance Standards and Evaluation

1	2	3	4	5

Permissive; tolerates
mediocrity

Highly demanding and critical;
replaces mediocrity

C.   Decision-Making Techniques

1	2	3	4	5

Based on intuition

Based on scientific analysis

D.   Use of Authority

1	2	3	4	5

Exhibits raw
authority; highly
authoritative

Implies authority rather than
overtly using it

E.   Attitude on Change

1	2	3	4	5

Resists change

Seeks change and pushes
others

F.   Nature of Involvement

1	2	3	4	5

Mainly interested in
operational problems;
interested in short-term
results

Gives much thought to
strategy

   Can the value system of an individual be changed? Traditionally, it has been
held that a person's behavior is determined mainly by the inner self reacting
within a given environment. In line with this thinking, major shifts in values
should be difficult to achieve. In recent years a new school of behaviorists has

begun to emerge who assign a more significant role to the environment. They challenge the concept of "self" as the underlying force in determining behavior.[10] If this "environmental" thesis is accepted, it should be possible to bring about a change in individual values so that the senior executives become more unified. However, the science of human behavior has yet to provide tools that can be used in causing changes in values. Thus it would be appropriate to say that minor changes in pesonal values can be produced through manipulation of the environment. But where the values of an individual executive differ significantly from those of the executive's colleagues, an attempt to alter the former would be difficult.

Differing values caused a key executive, John W. Hanley, to leave the top management of Procter & Gamble for the chief executive officer position at Monsanto. He was passed over for the P&G presidency because other members of the management team found him to be aggressive, eager to experiment and change practices, and constantly challenging his superior. Since he could not be brought around to the conservative style of the other executives, he was passed over for the presidency and eventually left the company.[11]

Value Orientation, Objectives, and Strategy

The influence of the value orientation of top management on the perspectives of their business has already been emphasized. This section examines how a particular type of value orientation may lead to certain objectives and strategy perspectives. Two examples are presented in Exhibit 2-4. In the first example the president is rated high on social and aesthetic values, which seems to indicate a greater emphasis on the quality of a single product than on growth per se. In the second example, again, the theoretical and social orientations of the top management appear to stress "truth and honesty" rather than strictly growth. If the strategic plans of these two companies were to emphasize growth as the major goal, they would undoubtedly fail. Planned perspectives may not be implemented if they are constrained by the top management's value system.

Further evidence on the subject is provided by a study undertaken to find out which approaches, among those that chief executive officers use in their jobs, contribute most to superior performance of companies over time. The study is based on a survey in which 211 CEOs of *Fortune's* 1000 corporations participated. The highlights of the findings are presented in Exhibit 2-5. It is noted in Exhibit 2-5 that an activist exhibits very high involvement in organization and motivation of personnel but low involvement in strategic planning for growth, and very low involvement in anything related to acquisitions. On the other hand,

---

[10]B.F. Skinner, *Beyond Freedom and Dignity* (New York: Alfred A. Knopf, 1971).
[11]Aimee L. Horner, "Jack Hanley Got There by Selling Harder," *Fortune* (November, 1976), p. 162.

EXHIBIT 2-4   Influence of Personal Values on Objectives and
               Strategies

Example A

Values
   The president of a small manufacturer of office duplicating equipment
ranked relatively high on social values, giving particular attention to the
security, welfare, and happiness of the employees. Second in order of
importance to the president were aesthetic values.

Objectives and Strategies
1.   Slow-to-moderate company growth
2.   Emphasis on a single product
3.   An independent-agent form of sales organization
4.   Very high-quality products with aesthetic appeal
5.   Refusal to compete on a price basis

Example B

Values
   The top-management team members of a high-fidelity loudspeaker systems manufacturer placed greater emphasis on theoretical and social
values than on other values.

Objectives and Strategies
1.   Scientific truth and integrity in advertising
2.   Lower margins to dealers than competitors were paying
3.   Maintenance of "truth and honesty" in relationships with suppliers,
dealers, and employees

Source: Reprinted by permission of the *Harvard Business Review*. Excerpts from "Personal
           Values and Corporate Strategies" by William D. Guth and Renato Tagiuri (Septem-
           ber-October, 1965), pp. 137–138. Copyright © 1965 by the President and Fel-
           lows of Harvard College. All rights reserved.

an aloof strategist shows medium involvement in organization and motivation of
personnel and low involvement in product modifications and creation of new-
product ideas. Here again, the message is clear. Strategy formulation should be
based on the orientation of the top management. If not, top management will not
become involved in the activities outlined by the strategic plans, and the strategy
will become meaningless. For example, an executive with activist orientation will
not be very keen on strategic planning. Thus, the strategic planning effort in a
company with an activist CEO should be rather simple.

   In summary, an organization in the process of strategy formulation must study
the values of its important executives. While exact measurement of values may
not be easy to achieve, even preliminary knowledge of the values held by top
management will be helpful to planners in communicating with them. In all
events, attempts are made not to threaten or alienate the executives by challenging

EXHIBIT 2-5   Expressed Degree of Personal Involvement in Important Activities for Different Role Patterns

Nature of involvement	CEO Role Pattern							
	Activist	Growth Entrepreneur	Remote Controller	Product Manager	Aloof Strategist	Acquirer	R&D Planner	Growth Director
New-product development								
Growth source								
Sales, existing products	H	VH	L	H	M	H	M	H
Product modifications	M	M	L	H	L	M	L	H
New products in present markets	H	H	L	H	M	M	M	M
New products in new markets	L	H	VL	M	M	M	M	L
Activities								
Strategic planning for growth	L	M	L	H	H	M	H	M
Direction of growth activities	H	H	L	H	L	M	L	L
Specifying areas for development	H	VH	M	VH	H	L	H	H
Creation of new-product ideas	H	H	VL	M	L	VL	L	L
Specifying development budget	M	VH	M	H	H	L	VH	H
Allocating budget among activities	M	VH	VL	M	M	VL	M	M
Selection of personnel	H	VH	L	M	M	L	H	H
"Go-no go" decisions on products	H	VH	L	H	M	L	H	M
Organization and motivation of personnel	VH	H	L	M	M	M	L	L
Review of progress versus plans	M	M	M	L	VH	L	M	VH
Acquisitions								
Growth source								
Acquisitions in present markets	VL	M	VL	L	H	H	VL	H
Acquisitions in new markets	VL	M	M	L	VH	M	M	M
Activities								
Strategic planning	VL	M	M	VL	H	H	M	L
Identification of candidates and negotiation	VL	H	H	M	VH	VH	H	H
Analysis of candidates	VL	H	M	L	L	H	L	M
Integration and organization of acquired companies	VL	L	L	L	H	M	M	L

Key: VH=Very high involvement   H=High involvement   M=Medium involvement   L=Low involvement   VL=Very low involvement

Source: Reprinted by permission of the *Harvard Business Review.* Exhibit from "CEO's Role in Corporate Growth" by Joseph O. Eastlack, Jr. and Philip R. McDonald (May-June, 1970), p. 156. Copyright © 1970 by the President and Fellows of Harvard College. All rights reserved.

their beliefs, traits, outlooks, etc. Finally, the strategy should be duly formulated considering the value package of the management team even if it means making a compromise with growth and profitability. Where no such compromise is feasible, it is better to transfer or change the assignment of the dissenting executive.

FACTORS OF APPRAISAL: RESOURCES OF THE FIRM

The resources of a firm are its distinctive capabilities and strengths. The resources are relative in nature and must always be measured with reference to competition. The resources can be categorized as: financial strength, human resources, raw material reserve, engineering and production, overall management, and marketing strength. The marketing strategist needs to consider not only marketing resources, but also resources of the company across the board. For example, price setting is a part of marketing strategy, yet it must be considered in the context of the financial strength of the company if the firm is to grow as rapidly as it should. It is obvious that profit margins on sales, combined with dividend policy, determine the amount of funds a firm can generate internally. It is less well understood, but equally true, that if a firm uses more debt than its competitors or pays less dividends, it can generate more funds for growth by decreasing profit margins. Thus it is important in strategy development that all of the firm's resources are fully utilized in a truly integrated way. The firm that will not use its resources fully is a target for the firm that will—even if the latter has fewer resources. Full and skillful utilization of resources can give a distinct competitive edge to a firm.

Resources and Marketing Strategy

Consider the following resources of a company:

1. Has ample cash on hand (financial strength).
2. Average age of key management personnel is 42 years (human resources).
3. Has a superior raw material ingredient in reserve (raw material reserve).
4. Manufactures parts and components that go into the final product using the company's own facilities (plant and equipment).
5. The products of the company, if properly installed and serviced regularly, never stop while being used (technical competence).
6. Has a knowledge of, close relationship with, and expertise in doing business with, the grocery chains (marketing strength).

How do these resources affect marketing strategy? The cash-rich company, unlike the cash-tight company, will be in a position to provide liberal credit accommodation to customers. General Electric Company, for example, helped its dealers and ultimate customers to obtain credit by establishing the General Electric Credit Corporation. In the case of a manufacturer of durable products, which are usually bought on credit, availability of easy credit accommodation to the customers can itself make a difference between success and failure for the company.

If a company has a new raw material reserve, it will not have to depend on outside suppliers when shortages occur. From 1972–74 there was a shortage of high-grade paper. A magazine publisher with its own forests and paper manufacturing facilities did not have to depend on paper companies to acquire paper. Thus, even when there was a shortage which forced the competitors to reduce the sizes of their magazines, the company not dependent on outsiders was still able to provide the same product to the customers.

In the initial stages of the development of color television, RCA was the only company that manufactured color picture tubes. In addition to using these tubes in its own television sets, RCA also sold them to other manufacturers/competitors such as General Electric Company. When the market for color television began to grow, RCA was in a strong position to obtain a larger share of the growth partly because of its easy access to picture tubes. General Electric, on the other hand, was weaker in this respect.[12]

IBM's technical capabilities, among other things, helped it to be an innovator in developing data processing equipment and introducing it to the market. IBM's excellent after-sale service facilities in themselves serve as a promotion for the company's products. The servicing provides a promotional tool in the hands of salespeople to promote the company's products.

Procter & Gamble is noted for its superior strength in dealing with grocery channels. The fact that this strength has served Procter & Gamble well hardly needs to be mentioned. More than anything else, marketing strength has helped Procter & Gamble to supersede established companies like Kimberly Clark and Scott Paper Company in the paper product market.[13]

In brief, the resources of a company help it to establish and maintain itself in the marketplace. It is, of course, necessary for resources to be appraised objectively.

Measurement of Resources

A firm is a conglomerate of different entities, each having a variety of variables which affect its performance. How far should a strategist probe into these variables to designate the resources of the firm? Presumably, only a few of these

---

[12]"General Electric Radio and Television Division," a case copyrighted by the President and Fellows of Harvard College, 1967.
[13]"Marketing Classic: How Firms Put the Big Squeeze on Scott Paper Co., Latter Napped, Diversified, While P&G and Mr. Whipple Invaded Its Paper Business," *The Wall Street Journal* (October 20, 1971), p. 1.

strategic variables must be evaluated. A strategic factor refers to an action, element, or condition which may be of critical importance for a business' success or failure. Exhibit 2-6 lists 85 strategic factors in different areas of a business.

EXHIBIT 2-6   Strategic Factors in Business

A. General Managerial
  1. Ability to attract and maintain high-quality top management
  2. Developing future managers for overseas operations
  3. Developing future managers for domestic operations
  4. Developing a better organizational structure
  5. Developing a better long-range planning program
  6. Achieving better overall control of company operations
  7. Using more new quantitative tools and techniques in decision making at:
      a. Top management levels
      b. Lower management levels
  8. Assuring better judgment, creativity and imagination in decision making at:
      a. Top management levels
      b. Lower management levels
  9. Ability to use computers for problem solving and planning
 10. Ability to use computers for information handling and financial control
 11. Ability to divest nonprofitable enterprises
 12. Ability to perceive new needs and opportunities for products
 13. Ability to motivate sufficient managerial drive for profits

B. Financial
  1. Ability to raise long-term capital at low cost:
      a. Debt
      b. Equity
  2. Ability to raise short-term capital
  3. Ability to maximize value of stockholder investment
  4. Ability to provide a competitive return to stockholders
  5. Willingness to take risks with commensurate returns in what appear to be excellent new business opportunities in order to achieve growth objectives
  6. Ability to apply ROI criteria to R&D investments
  7. Ability to finance diversification by means of:
      a. Acquisitions
      b. In-house research and development

C. Marketing
  1. Ability to accumulate better knowledge about markets
  2. Establishing a wide customer base
  3. Establishing a selective consumer base
  4. Establishing an efficient product distribution system
  5. Ability to get good business contracts (government and others)
  6. Assuring imaginative advertising and sales promotion campaigns

7. Using pricing more effectively (including discounts, customer credit, product service, guarantees, delivery, etc.)
8. Better relationships between marketing and new product engineering and production
9. Producing vigor in sales organization

D. Engineering and Production
  1. Developing effective machinery and equipment replacement policies
  2. Providing more efficient plant layout
  3. Developing sufficient capacity for expansion
  4. Developing better materials and inventory control
  5. Improving product quality control
  6. Improving in-house product engineering
  7. Improving in-house basic product research capabilities
  8. Developing more effective profit improvement (cost-reduction) programs
  9. Developing better ability to mass-produce at low per-unit cost
  10. Relocating present production facilities
  11. Automating production facilities
  12. Better management of, and better results from, research and development expenditures
  13. Establishing foreign production facilities
  14. Developing more flexibility in using facilities for different products
  15. Being in the forefront of technology and being extremely scientifically creative

E. Products
  1. Improving present products
  2. Developing more efficient and effective product-line selection
  3. Developing new products to replace old ones
  4. Developing new products in new markets
  5. Developing sales for present products in new markets
  6. Diversifying products by acquisition
  7. More subcontracting
  8. Getting bigger share of product market

F. Personnel
  1. Attracting scientists and highly technically qualified employees
  2. Establishing better relationships with employees
  3. Ability to get along with labor unions
  4. Better utilizing the skills of employees
  5. Motivating more employees to remain abreast of developments in their fields
  6. Ability to level peaks and valleys of employment requirements
  7. Ability to stimulate creativity in employees
  8. Ability to optimize employee turnover (not too much and not too little)

G. Materials
  1. Getting geographically closer to raw material sources
  2. Assuring continuity of raw material supplies

3. Finding new sources of raw materials
4. Owning and controlling sources of raw materials
5. Bringing "in-house" presently purchased materials and components
6. Reducing raw material costs

Source: George Steiner, *Strategic Factors in Business Success* (New York: Financial Executives Research Foundation, 1969), pp. 4–5.

Not all of these factors will be important for every business. Therefore, the first step in designating resources is to have executives in different areas of the business go through the listing shown in Exhibit 2-6 and choose those variables which they deem strategic. Then each strategic factor may be evaluated either qualitatively or quantitatively. One way of conducting the evaluation is to frame relevant question(s) around each strategic factor, which may be rated on either a dichotomous or a continued scale. As an example, the following questions were found relevant by a man's sportswear manufacturer in different areas of its concern.

Top Management. Which executives form the top management? Which one of them can be held responsible for the firm's performance during the past few years? Is each one of them capable of undertaking future challenges as well as in the past? Is something needed to boost the morale of top management? What are the distinguishing characteristics of each top executive? Are there any conflicts, such as personality conflicts, among them? If so, between whom, and for what reasons? What has been done and is being done for organizational development? What are the reasons for the company's performance during the past few years? Are the old ways of managing obsolete? What more can be done to enhance the company's capabilities?

Marketing. What are the major products/services of the company? Determine the basic facts about each product—e.g., market share, profitability, position in the life cycle, major competitors and their strengths and weaknesses, etc. In which field can the firm be considered a leader? Why? What can be said about the firm's pricing policies (i.e., price compared with value and with prices of competitors)? What is the nature of new product development efforts of the company, such as coordination with R&D and manufacturing? How does the market look in the future for the planning period? What steps are being taken or proposed to meet future challenges? What can be said about the company's channel arrangements, physical distribution, and promotional efforts? What is the behavior of marketing costs? What new products are expected to be launched, when, and with what expectations? What has been done towards consumer satisfaction?

Production. Are people capable of working on new machines, new processes, designs, etc., that may be developed in the future? What new plant, equipment, and facilities are needed? Determine the basic facts about each product—e.g., cost structure, quality control, work stoppages, etc. What is the nature of labor relations? Are any problems anticipated? What steps have been proposed and/or taken to avert strikes, work stoppages, etc.? Does production perform its part effectively in the process of manufacturing new products? How flexible are the operations? Can they be made suitable for future competition and new products well on the way to being produced and marketed commercially? What steps have been proposed and/or taken to cut down pollution? What are the important raw materials being used or that are likely to be used? What are the important sources for each raw material? How reliable are these sources?

Finance. What is the financial standing of the company as a whole and of its different products/divisions in terms of earnings, sales, tangible net worth, working capital, earnings per share, liquidity, inventory, cash flow position, capital structure, etc.? What is the cost of capital? Can money be used in a more productive fashion? What is the reputation of the company in the financial community? How does our performance compare with competitors and other corporations of our size? What steps have been proposed and/or taken to line up new sources of raising capital, to increase return on investment through more productive use of sources, to lower break-even points, etc.? Has the company managed tax matters aggressively? What contingency steps are proposed to avert threats of capital shortage, takeover, etc.?

R & D. What is the R&D reputation of the company? What percentage of sales and profits in the past can be directly attributed to R&D efforts? Are there any conflicts or personality clashes in the department? If so, what has been proposed and what is being done? What is the status of current major projects? When are they expected to be completed? In what way will they help the company's performance? What kind of relationships do the R&D people have with those in marketing and manufacturing? What steps have been proposed and are being taken to cut down overhead and improve quality? Are all scientists/ researchers adequately used? If not, why not? Can we expect any breakthroughs from R&D? Are there any resentments? If so, what are they, and for what reason?

Miscellaneous. What has been proposed and/or done to serve minorities, the community, the cause of education, etc.? What is the nature of productivity gains for the company as a whole and for each part of the company? How do we stand in comparison to industry trend and national goal? How well do we compete in the world market? Which countries/companies constitute tough competitors? What are their strengths and weaknesses? What is the nature and scope of our public relations function? Is it adequate? How does it compare with competitors and other companies of our size and character? Which government agencies— federal, state, or local—do we deal with most often? Are our relationships with them satisfactory? Who are our stockholders? Do a few individuals/institutions hold majority stock? What are their corporate expectations? Do they prefer capital gains or dividend income?

The ratings on the above questions may be added up to compute the total resource score in each area. It must be understood that not all questions can be evaluated using the same scale. In many cases quantitative measurement may be difficult and subjective evaluation will have to be accepted. Further, measurement of resources should be done for current effectiveness and for future perspectives. Exhibit 2-7 shows two nine-point scales: one for current effectiveness and one for future perspectives. These scales can be simplified and/or altered to meet specific needs.

EXHIBIT 2-7   Scales for Measuring Resources

Current Effectiveness	Future Perspectives
(9) Completely effective	(9) Completely sound
(8) Almost completely effective	(8) Almost completely sound
(7) Quite effective	(7) Quite sound
(6) Moderately effective	(6) Moderately sound
(5) As effective as ineffective	(5) As sound as unsound
(4) Moderately ineffective	(4) Moderately unsound
(3) Quite ineffective	(3) Quite unsound
(2) Almost completely ineffective	(2) Almost completely unsound
(1) Completely ineffective	(1) Completely unsound

Source: Adapted from: Robert R. Blake and Jane Srygley Mouton, *How to Assess the Strengths and Weaknesses of Corporate Leadership* (Austin, TX: Scientific Methods, 1972).

APPRAISING MARKETING

As mentioned in Chapter 1, of all the functional areas of a business, marketing plays a unique role in that its inputs intimately affect corporate strategy as much as corporate strategy affects marketing. Thus, to appreciate the true perspectives of marketing planning and strategy and to do it well, it is desirable to have a clear conception of the corporation. For this reason, the discussion so far has been from the viewpoint of the corporation. In this section, an appraisal of the marketing side of business will be made. Marketing is concerned with the activities required to facilitate the exchange process toward managing demand. The perspectives of these activities are founded on marketing strategy. To develop the strategy a company needs a philosophical orientation. Two orientations are relevant here: production orientation and marketing orientation. Briefly, production orientation emphasizes a physical product or service and assumes that the customer will be pleased with the product or service if it has been well conceived and developed. Marketing orientation should first designate the customer group which the firm wishes to serve with its product or service. Then the requirements of a target customer group or segment should be carefully examined. These requirements should become the basis of product or service conception and development.

Marketing has been a buzzword among businessmen for over 30 years. Yet it is one of the most misunderstood functions of a business. According to Kotler only a few corporations, such as Procter & Gamble, Eastman Kodak, Avon, McDonald's, IBM, Xerox, General Electric, and Caterpillar, really understand and practice true marketing.[14] Inasmuch as marketing orientation is a prerequisite to developing successful marketing strategy, it behooves a company to thoroughly examine its marketing orientation.

While much has been said about the virtues of marketing orientation, marketing literature does not go far in providing any objective tool or instrument for measuring it. Fortunately a recent article on the subject does provide an approach for measuring marketing effectiveness. Exhibit 2-8 presents a questionnaire which may be completed to measure the marketing effectiveness of a company. The effectiveness score may be used as a surrogate for marketing orientation. The five effectiveness measures used are: customer philosophy, integrated marketing organization, adequate marketing information, strategic orientation, and operational efficiency. If the questionnaire shown in Exhibit 2-8 is diligently completed, it will reveal the marketing weaknesses of the company. The management may take appropriate action, such as management training, reorganization, or installation of measures designed to seek improvements with or without the help of consultants. If the weaknesses cannot be addressed, the company must live with them, and the marketing strategist should take note of them in the process of outlining the company's future plans.

SUMMARY

Self-appraisal constitutes an important ingredient in the strategy development process since it lays the foundation for the company to interact with the future environment. Corporate publics, value orientation of top management, and corporate resources are the three principal factors of appraisal which were discussed in this chapter.

Corporate publics are all those groups having a stake in the organization, i.e., owners, employees, customers, suppliers, the banking community and other lenders, government, the community in which the company does business, and the society-at-large. Expectations of all stakeholders should be considered in formulating corporate objectives and goals. These goals are also deeply influenced by the value orientation of the corporation's top management. Thus, values of top management should be studied and duly figured in setting objectives. Finally, the company's resources in different areas should be carefully evaluated. They serve as a major criterion for the company to accept certain future perspectives.

This chapter also delved into appraisal of the marketing function and discussed an instrument which can be used to measure a company's marketing effectiveness.

---

[14]Philip Kotler, "From Sales Obsession to Marketing Effectiveness," *Harvard Business Review* (November-December, 1977), p. 68.

EXHIBIT 2-8   Outline for Measuring Marketing Effectiveness

		Customer Philosophy
		A. Does management recognize the importance of designing the company to serve the needs and wants of chosen markets?

Score

0	☐	Management primarily thinks in terms of selling current and new products to whoever will buy them.
1	☐	Management thinks in terms of serving a wide range of markets and needs with equal effectiveness.
2	☐	Management thinks in terms of serving the needs and wants of well-defined markets chosen for their long-run growth and profit potential for the company.

		B. Does management develop different offerings and marketing plans for different segments of the market?
0	☐	No.
1	☐	Somewhat.
2	☐	To a good extent.

		C. Does management take a whole marketing system view (suppliers, channels, competitors, customers, environment) in planning its business?
0	☐	No. Management concentrates on selling and servicing its immediate customers.
1	☐	Somewhat. Management takes a long view of its channels although the bulk of its effort goes to selling and servicing the immediate customers.
2	☐	Yes. Management takes a whole marketing systems view recognizing the threats and opportunities created for the company by changes in any part of the system.

		Integrated Marketing Organization
		D. Is there high-level marketing integration and control of the major marketing functions?
0	☐	No. Sales and other marketing functions are not integrated at the top and there is some unproductive conflict.
1	☐	Somewhat. There is formal integration and control of the major marketing functions but less than satisfactory coordination and cooperation.
2	☐	Yes. The major marketing functions are effectively integrated.

E. Does marketing management work well with management in research, manufacturing, purchasing, physical distribution, and finance?

0 ☐ No. There are complaints that marketing is unreasonable in the demands and costs it places on other departments.

1 ☐ Somewhat. The relations are amicable although each department pretty much acts to serve its own power interests.

2 ☐ Yes. The departments cooperate effectively and resolve issues in the best interest of the company as a whole.

F. How well-organized is the new product development process?

0 ☐ The system is ill-defined and poorly handled.

1 ☐ The system formally exists but lacks sophistication.

2 ☐ The system is well-structured and professionally staffed.

Adequate Marketing Information

G. When were the latest marketing research studies of customers, buying influences, channels, and competitors conducted?

0 ☐ Several years ago.

1 ☐ A few years ago.

2 ☐ Recently.

H. How well does management know the sales potential and profitability of different market segments, customers, territories, products, channels, and order sizes?

0 ☐ Not at all.

1 ☐ Somewhat.

2 ☐ Very well.

I. What effort is expended to measure the cost-effectiveness of different marketing expenditures?

0 ☐ Little or no effort.

1 ☐ Some effort.

2 ☐ Substantial effort.

Strategic Orientation

J. What is the extent of formal marketing planning?

0 ☐ Management does little or no formal marketing planning.

1 ☐ Management develops an annual marketing plan.

2 ☐ Management develops a detailed annual marketing plan and a careful long-range plan that is updated annually.

K. What is the quality of the current marketing strategy?

0	☐	The current strategy is not clear.
1	☐	The current strategy is clear and represents a continuation of traditional strategy.
2	☐	The current strategy is clear, innovative, data-based, and well-reasoned.

L. What is the extent of contingency thinking and planning?

0	☐	Management does little or no contingency thinking.
1	☐	Management does some contingency thinking although little formal contingency planning.
2	☐	Management formally identifies the most important contingencies and develops contingency plans.

Operational Efficiency

M. How well is the marketing thinking at the top communicated and implemented down the line?

0	☐	Poorly.
1	☐	Fairly.
2	☐	Successfully.

N. Is management doing an effective job with the marketing resources?

0	☐	No. The marketing resources are inadequate for the job to be done.
1	☐	Somewhat. The marketing resources are adequate but they are not employed optimally.
2	☐	Yes. The marketing resources are adequate and are deployed efficiently.

O. Does management show a good capacity to react quickly and effectively to on-the-spot developments?

0	☐	No. Sales and market information is not very current and management reaction time is slow.
1	☐	Somewhat. Management receives fairly up-to-date sales and market information; management reaction time varies.
2	☐	Yes. Management has installed systems yielding highly current information and fast reaction time.

Total Score

Rating Marketing Effectiveness

The auditing outline can be used in this way. The auditor collects information as it bears on the 15 questions. The appropriate answer is checked for each question. The scores are added—the total will be somewhere between 0 and 30. The following scale shows the equivalent in marketing effectiveness:

0–5	None
6–10	Poor
11–15	Fair
16–20	Good
21–25	Very good
26–30	Superior

To illustrate, 15 senior managers in a large building materials company were recently invited to rate their company using the auditing instrument in this exhibit. The resulting overall marketing effectiveness scores ranged from a low of 6 to a high of 15. The median score was 11, with three fourths of the scores between 9 and 13. Therefore, most of the managers thought their company was at best "fair" at marketing.

Several divisions were also rated. Their median scores ranged from a low of 3 to a high of 19. The higher scoring divisions tended to have higher profitability. However, some of the lower scoring divisions were also profitable. An examination of the latter showed that these divisions were in industries where their competition also operated at a low level of marketing effectiveness. The managers feared that these divisions would be vulnerable as soon as competition began to learn to market more successfully.

An interesting question to speculate on is the distribution of median marketing effectiveness scores for *Fortune* "500" companies. My suspicion is that very few companies in that roster would score above 20 ("very good" or "superior") in marketing effectiveness. Although marketing theory and practice have received their fullest expression in the United States, the great majority of U.S. companies probably fail to meet the highest standards.

DISCUSSION QUESTIONS

1. How often should a company undertake self-appraisal? What are the arguments for and against yearly self-appraisal?
2. Discuss the pros and cons of a consultant conducting the self-appraisal.

3. Identify five companies which in your opinion have failed to change with time and have either pulled out or continue as laggards. Justify your selection of companies.
4. Identify five companies which in your opinion have kept pace with time as evidenced by their performance.
5. What expectations does a community have of (a) a bank, (b) a medical group, and (c) a manufacturer of cyclical goods?
6. What type of top-management values are most likely to lead to growth orientation?
7. Is growth orientation necessarily good? Discuss.
8. In your opinion what marketing resources are the most critical for success in the cosmetics industry?
9. How should a company go about identifying the critical factors for success in its business?
10. Develop a scheme for measuring the marketing orientation of a firm.

Chapter 3
Scanning the Environment

One does not plan and then try to make circumstances fit these plans. One tries to make plans fit the circumstances.

George Patton

An organization is a creature of its environment. Its very survival and all of its perspectives/resources, problems, and opportunities are generated and conditioned by the environment. Thus, it is important for an organization to monitor the relevant changes taking place in the environment surrounding the organization and plan to adapt to these changes.

In other words, in order for an organization to survive and prosper in the future, the planner must master the challenges of the profoundly changing political, economic, technological, and social environment. In order to achieve this broad perspective, the planner needs to develop and implement a systematic approach to environmental scanning. As the rate and magnitude of change increases, this scanning activity must be intensified and directed by more explicit definitions of purpose, scope, and focus. The efforts of planners to cope with these problems is contributing to the development of systems for exploring alternatives with greater sensitivity to long-run implications. This emerging science has the promise of providing a better framework for maximizing opportunities and allocating resources in anticipation of environmental changes.

This chapter reviews the state of the environmental scanning art and suggests a general approach for environmental scanning which may be used by a marketing planner. Specifically, the chapter discusses the criteria which may be used to determine the scope and focus of scanning, the procedure for examining the relevance of environmental trends, techniques which may be used to determine the impact of an environmental trend on a particular product/market, sources of environmental information in terms of credibility, accuracy, weighting, etc., and linkage of environmental trends and other "early warning signals" to strategic planning processes.

This chapter is mainly based on a study that the author did with Dr. Donald J. Hempel, whose help is gratefully acknowledged.

IMPORTANCE OF ENVIRONMENTAL SCANNING

Without taking into account the relevant environmental influences, a company cannot expect to develop its strategy. It is the environmental influences emerging out of the energy crisis which are responsible for the high popularity of smaller, more fuel-efficient automobiles and which brought the demise of the less-efficient rotary engines. Similar influences resulting from the severe winter of 1976–77 and the uncertainty of fossil fuels have renewed and expanded the interest in solar energy and wind energy and in more energy-conservative homes and buildings. It was the environmental influence of a coffee bean shortage and geometric price increases that spawned the "coffee-saver" modification for Mr. Coffee automatic drip coffee makers, hastened the development of a ground tea for automatic coffee machines, and even produced a coffee substitute, Bravo, made of a common weed. Shopper and merchant complaints of an earlier era contributed to the virtual elimination of deposit bottles; recent pressures from environmental groups have forced their return and have prompted Monsanto to develop a low-cost recyclable plastic bottle, the Easy Goer, for the Coca-Cola Company. Electronic technology has become a threat to many established industries because of new electronically powered products. Established watch companies such as Timex and Bulova now find Texas Instruments, an electronics firm, as a strong new competitor. Likewise, the traditional supremacy of the NCR Corporation in cash registers has been strongly challenged by the new electronic point-of-sale terminals which are tied directly to a store's inventory and accounting computers.

In brief, business derives its existence from the environment. Thus, it should monitor its environment constructively. To do so the business should scan the environment and incorporate the impact of environmental trends on the organization by reviewing the corporate strategy on a continual basis. Glover said the following:

> Perceiving in the environment needs and opportunities for adaptation—even before they actually materialize—and designing and seeing through a continuous procession of actions to carry out adaptive innovation, these are the essence of business *strategy*. More—these are the distinguishing functions of the top management. It is the job of corporate top management to direct and to manage the *transformation* of every aspect of the corporation in response to developments of the dynamic environment. A corporation gets left behind whose management lacks these capacities—The environment represents an everchanging sum total of the "facts of life" with which the corporation has come to terms. Willy-nilly the environment is the unyielding, unforgiving frame of reference for everything top management does as it guides the corporation.[1]

---

[1] J.D. Glover, *Rise and Fall of Corporations: Challenge and Response,* an unpublished note prepared at Harvard Business School, number: 9-367-017, 1967, p. 4.

THE CONCEPT OF ENVIRONMENT

Philosophically, the environment of a corporation includes all those realities whose existence may affect the corporation directly or indirectly in any perceptible way. These realities may be sorted out in the following four categories:

> (1) The *"community"* that is made up of all the human beings that inhabit it and all their social organizations of all kinds; (2) the *"culture"* that is made up of all the constructs of the human mind that affect the behavior of all these individuals and organizations; (3) the *"habitat"* that includes all the physical features of this environment; and (4) the *"product"* that includes all things made and services rendered by man.[2]

Applying the prevailing *culture* and using and consuming natural features of the *habitat* and the *product* of past periods, the entities of the *community* have an existence and generate goods and services.

Operationally, however, there are two main types of environment: corporate environment and product/market environment. Exhibit 3-1 shows these two types of environment and their relationship to strategic planning. The corporate environment is classified in three parts: external, operating, and internal. The external environment comprises political, social, technological, and economic forces at work surrounding the organization. The operating environment refers to interaction with and between those entities having a stake in the organization. The internal environment constitutes forces at work within the organization. The operating environment is significant for day-to-day decisions and is, therefore, excluded from further discussion here. The remaining two environments are appropriate for strategic planning. The internal environment, however, was discussed in the section on internal appraisal. Thus, the emphasis in this chapter will be on the external environment. Constituents of the product/market environment for both day-to-day decisions and strategic decisions are the same and will be discussed in the next chapter.

STATE OF THE ART

Scanning refers to an early warning system for the environmental forces which may impact a company's products and markets in the future. Environmental scanning is a new development. Traditionally corporations evaluated themselves mainly on the basis of financial performance. Generally the environment was studied only for the purpose of making economic forecasts. Other factors of the environment were brought in haphazardly, if at all, and in an intuitive fashion. In recent years a few corporations, such as General Electric, Xerox, and Coca-Cola, have started doing systematic work in this area. For example, the General

---

[2]J.D. Glover, *Environment: "Community", "Culture", "Habitat", and "Product",* an unpublished note prepared at Harvard Business School, number: 9-367-018, 1966, p. 1.

EXHIBIT 3-1 · Constituents of the Environment

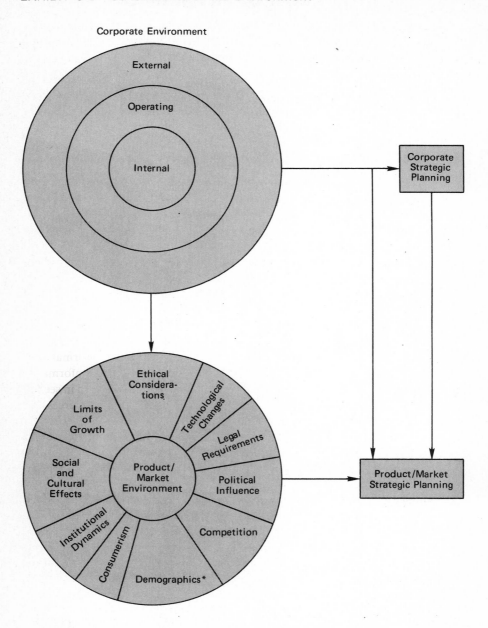

*Population, geographic location, income, expenditure patterns, and education.

Electric Company has taken a hard look at the environment to relate it to its business. Back in 1967, G.E. prepared a 65-page report entitled *Our Future Business Environment: Developing Trends and Institutions* which has been updated since then.[3] The new report indicated 18 different areas where significant value shift has occurred. The slow progress made in relating the environment to one's business can be explained by the difficulty involved in undertaking such an analysis. It is only during the past four or five years that management science has concerned itself with environmental analysis. The work done at or sponsored by institutions like the Hudson Institute, New York; the Rand Corporation, Santa Monica, California; the Stanford Research Institute (via its Business Intelligence Program); the Club of Rome*, Geneva, Switzerland; and the World Future Society, Washington, D.C. has made it easier for business corporations to undertake scientific analysis of the environment.

A pioneering study on environmental scanning has been done by Francis Aguilar. In his investigation of selected chemical companies in the United States and Europe, he found a lack of a systematic approach to environmental scanning. The author consolidated Aguilar's sixteen types of information (see Exhibit 3-2) about the environment that the companies found interesting into five groupings: *market tidings, acquisition leads, technical tidings, broad issues,* and *other tidings.* Among those, market tidings was found to be the dominant category and was of most interest to managers across the board. Aguilar suggests four patterns for viewing information: *undirected viewing* (exposure without a specific purpose), *conditioned viewing* (directed exposure but without undertaking an active search), *informal search* (collection of purpose-oriented information in an informal manner), and *formal search* (a structured process for collection of specific information for a designated purpose). Both internal and external sources were used in seeking the above information. The external was comprised of both personal sources (i.e., customers, suppliers, bankers, consultants, and other knowledgeable individuals) and impersonal sources (publications of sorts, conferences, trade shows, exhibitions, and so on). The internal personal sources included peers, superiors, and subordinates. The internal impersonal sources included regular and general reports and scheduled meetings. Aguilar's study concluded that while the process is not simple, a company can systematize its environmental scanning activity for strategy development.[4]

---

[3]Business Environment Section, *Our Future Business Environment: A Re-evaluation* (New York: The General Electric Co., 1967). See also: Ian H. Wilson, "Changing Values and Institutional Goals," (paper delivered at World Future Society General Assembly session on "Goals and Values for Mankind," May 13, 1971).

*Supported by the Volkswagon Foundation in Germany, the Club of Rome was formed in 1969 by a small group of men from Europe and the United States to analyze global problems in the context of changing environment.

[4]Francis Joseph Aguilar, *Scanning the Business Environment* (New York: Macmillan Co., Publishers, 1967), p. 40.

EXHIBIT 3-2   What External Information Do Managers Obtain?

CATEGORY	GENERAL CONCEPT
Market potential	Supply and demand consideration for market areas of current or potential interest: e.g., capacity, consumption, imports, exports.
Structural change	Mergers, acquisitions, and joint ventures involving competitors, new entries into the industry.
Competitors and industry	General information about a competitor, industry policy, concerted actions in the industry, and so forth.
Pricing	Effective and proposed prices for products of current and potential interest.
Sales negotiations	Information relating to a specific current or potential sale or contract for the firm.
Customers	General information about current or near-potential customers, their markets, their problems.
Leads for mergers, joint ventures, or acquisitions	Information concerning possibilities for the manager's own company.
New products, processes, and technology	Technical information relatively new and unknown to the company.
Product problems	Problems involving existing products.
Costs	Costs for processing, operations, and so forth for current and potential competitors, suppliers, and customers, and for proposed company activities.
Licensing and patents	Products and processes.
General conditions	Events of a general nature: political, demographic, national, and so forth.
Government actions and policies	Governmental decisions affecting the industry.

CATEGORY	**GENERAL CONCEPT**
Suppliers and raw materials	Purchasing considerations for products of current or potential interest.
Resources available	Persons, land, and other resources possibly available for the company.
Miscellaneous	Items not elsewhere classified.

Note: The author grouped the first six categories under *market tidings,* the next one under *acquisition leads,* the next four under *technical tidings,* the next two under *broad issues,* and the last three under *other tidings.*

Source: Francis Joseph Aguilar, *Scanning the Business Environment* (New York: Macmillan Co., 1967), p. 40. Copyright © 1967 by the Trustees of Columbia University in the City of New York. Reprinted by permission.

Aguilar's framework may be illustrated with reference to the Coca-Cola Company. The company looks at its environment through a series of analyses. At the corporate level considerable information is gathered on the economic, social, and political aspects and on competition both in the U.S. and overseas. The corporate office also becomes involved in special studies when it feels that some aspect of the environment requires special attention. For example, to address itself to a top-management concern about the possible market saturation of soft drinks, the company undertook a study to understand "what was going on in the minds of their consumers and what they were looking for. How was the consumption of Coca-Cola related to their life style, to their set of values, to their needs?" Back in the early 1970s the corporate office also made a study of the impact of anti-pollution trends in the government on regulations on packaging. It was noted that at the corporate level environment was scanned rather broadly. Mostly, *market tidings, technical tidings,* and *broad issues* were dealt with. Whenever necessary, in-depth studies were done on a particular area of concern. The corporate information was made available to different divisions of the company.

In addition, at the division level (Coca-Cola, USA) considerable attention is given to the market situation, acquisition leads, and new business ventures. The division also studies general economic conditions (trends in GNP, consumption, income); government regulation (especially antitrust actions); social factors; and even the political situation. Part of this scanning duplicates the efforts of the corporate office. Such redundancy resulted because the divisional planning staff felt that it was in a position to do a better job for its own purpose than could the corporate office, which had to serve the needs of the other divisions as well. The division also undertakes special studies. For example, a few years ago they wondered whether a diet drink should be introduced, and if so, when.

The information received from the corporate office and that which the division had collected itself was analyzed to study events and happenings which could affect the company's current and potential business. Analysis was done mostly through meetings and discussions rather than through the use of any statistical model. It has been said that "the environmental analysis activity is a sort of forum. In the Coca-Cola Company, there is relatively little cohesion among managers. The meetings, therefore, respond to a need for exchange of information between people."[5]

TYPES OF ENVIRONMENT

Traditionally the interaction between operating and internal environments and the impact of the former on the latter have figured into the formulation of corporate strategy. It is the constituents of the external environment and their impacts on operating and internal environments which are often a missing link in the strategic planning effort. These external environments may be categorized as follows: political environment, social environment, economic environment, regulatory environment, and technological environment. The discussion on the following pages deals with these environments.

To do a good job at scanning the environment, one needs to engage in forecasting the shape of things to come. Various methods which are especially relevant for forecasting long-range trends and projection are discussed in a later section of this chapter. Suffice it to say here that environmental scanning necessarily implies a forecasting perspective.

Technological Environment

Technological developments come out of the research effort. Two types of research can be distinguished: basic and applied. A company may engage in applied research only or may undertake both basic and applied research. In either case, a start will have to be made at the basic level, and from there the specific effect on a company's product or process will have to be derived. A company may choose not to undertake any research on its own, accepting a secondary role as an imitator. The research efforts of such a company will be limited mainly to the adaptation of a particular technological change to its business.

Exhibit 3-3 shows three different aspects of technology: type of technology, its process, and the impetus for its development. Five general areas of technology are recognized: energy, materials, transportation, communications and information, and genetic (including agronomic and biomedical developments). The original impetus for technological breakthroughs can come from any or all of three sources: meeting defense needs, seeking the welfare of the masses, and making a mark commercially. The three stages in the process of technological development

---

[5]"The Coca-Cola Company (E), A Case Study," copyrighted by the President and Fellows of Harvard College, 1970.

EXHIBIT 3-3   A Framework for Assessing Technological Conditions at the
National Level

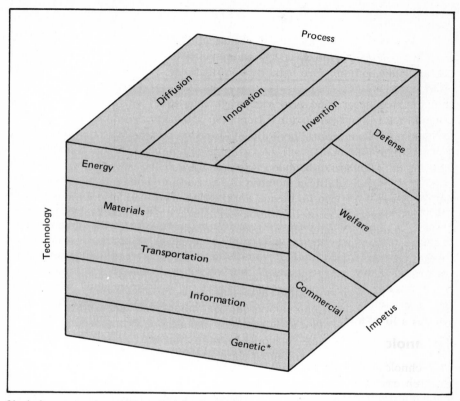

*Includes agronomic and biomedical developments.

Source: Philip S. Thomas, "Environmental Analysis for Corporate Planning," *Business Horizons,*
Vol. XVII (October, 1974), p. 36. Copyright 1974 by the Foundation for the School of
Business at Indiana University. Reprinted by permission.

are: invention (the creation of a new product or process); innovation (the introduction of that product or process into use); and diffusion (the spread of the
product or process beyond first use).[6]

All three aspects of technology mentioned above are important. The area of
technology which a company prefers will indicate where the company's interests
lie. The impetus will point to the market for technological development, and the

---

[6]Philip S. Thomas, "Environmental Analysis for Corporate Planning," *Business Horizons*
(October, 1977), pp. 27–38. See also: George R. White and Margaret B.W. Graham, "How
to Spot a Technological Winner," *Harvard Business Review* (March-April, 1978), pp. 146–
152.

process of development will show the state of technological development and whether the company is in a position to interface with the technology in any state. For example, the invention and innovation stages may call for basic research which is beyond the resources of a company. Diffusion, however, will require adaptation which may not be as difficult as the other two stages.

To illustrate the point, let us take the area of minicomputers. In the 1960s as computers made inroads in the business world, a number of data processing bureaus were born to service small companies which could not afford the computer. Over the years, the bureaus have rendered a very useful service to these companies by processing such information as payroll, accounts receivable, and accounts payable. Developments in the field of computer technology made it feasible in the late 1970s to build and market a small computer (usually called a minicomputer) at a price which is conveniently within the reach of the small business person. While a typical computer in the 1960s sold for over $100,000, in 1979 one could get a small computer for as little as $5,000. The small computer has become a threat to the data processing bureaus because the small customer can now choose between buying a small computer and using the services of the bureau. To protect their business, many bureaus decided to offer minicomputers to the customers themselves. Several small bureaus were acquired by large data processing firms since the minicomputer limited the scope of their business and they could not continue to operate profitably.

Let us also consider technology's impact on the consumer goods industry. Before the 1980s are out, technology will enable a music fan to pull out a small sheet of plastic about as big as a slice of toast and put this "record" containing millions of bits of computer data on a playing machine that reads the computer code with a low-power laser beam. Such computerized or digital records will be capable of playing uninterruptedly for two and a half hours, long enough to encompass a full-length opera on one side alone.

Prototypes of this futuristic gear already exist, and more than 20 manufacturers in Japan, the U.S., and Europe are racing to bring the new technology to a stage suitable for the consumer market by the mid-1980s. This technological development for the record industry has been likened to such breakthroughs as the introduction of electrically made commercial records in 1925 and the switch from 78 RPM shellac records to vinyl LP disks in the 1950s. Needless to say, this new technological leap will pose a great threat to the $3.4 billion-a-year record and tape industry. Many members of the industry may join the race to embrace the new development and themselves offer computerized records. Others may be obliged to leave the industry. A changeover to the new technology cannot be done overnight. A newcomer to the industry, Minnesota Mining & Manufacturing Co., has been working on a variety of digital recording projects since 1971. Thus, those record companies which have scanned their technological environment and followed the trend will be able to make a positive response. Those who have not kept up with the changing technology will have a hard time coping with the technological breakthrough. As a matter of fact, a number of recording companies are already in the front to make a timely response to the development. The 3M

Company, for example, has delivered its first batch of $150,000 studio machines to four recording companies, including two of the nation's biggest, A&M Records and Warner Brothers.[7]

Political Environment

In stable governments the political trends may not be as important as in countries where governments are weak. Yet even in stable countries political trends may have a significant impact on business. For example, in the United States when Democrats are in power in the White House, one can expect greater emphasis on social programs and an increase in government spending. Companies, therefore, in the business of providing social services may expect greater opportunities.

More important, however, are the political trends overseas because the U.S. economy is intimately connected with the global economy. And, therefore, what goes on in the political spheres of other countries (both free world and state-controlled economies) may be significant for U.S. corporations, particularly the multinational corporations. Thus, the marketing planner needs to study both domestic and foreign political happenings. Theoretically a political scientist should be on board to study the impact of political trends on the company's international business operations. But the limited scope of a company's business may not require such detailed analysis. Besides, normally there is sufficient published information analyzing the political trends and their impact on business.

Marketing planners, then, should review selected published information to keep in touch with political trends and interpret the information as it relates to their companies. Exhibit 3-4 shows the type of information which a multinational corporation may find useful to gather and review with reference to the political environment. First, the underlying causes of political risk are analyzed. Then the group channels which may raise political issues out of the causes of risk are recognized. Finally, the impact on business operations is determined.

Economic Environment

Traditionally economic trends formed the basis of future planning. Abundance of information from both government and private sources is available which may be helpful in developing strategic plans. Exhibit 3-5 shows a sample of economic information available from a private source. Many large companies, such as RCA and Chase Manhattan Bank, make their own economic forecasts.

It is not unrealistic to say that all companies, small or large, engaged in strategic planning examine the economic environment. Relevant published information is usually gathered, analyzed, and interpreted for use in planning. In some corporations the entire process of dealing with economic information may be

[7]Bernard Wysocki, Jr., "Computerized System May Free Recordings of Distortion Problems," *The Wall Street Journal* (February 27, 1979), p. 1.

EXHIBIT 3-4   Political Risk: A Conceptual Framework

Sources of Political Risk	Groups Through Which Political Risk Can Be Generated	Effects on International Business Operations
Competing political philosophies (nationalism, socialism, communism)	Government in power and its operating agencies	Confiscation: loss of assets without compensation
Social unrest and disorder	Parliamentary opposition groups	Expropriation with compensation: loss of freedom to operate
Vested interests of local business groups	Nonparliamentary opposition groups (Algerian "FLN," guerrilla movements working within or outside country)	Operational restrictions: market shares, product characteristics, employment policies, locally shared ownership, and so on
Recent and impending political independence	Nonorganized common interest groups: students, workers, peasants, minorities, and so on	Loss of transfer freedom: financial (dividends, interest payments, goods, personnel, or ownership rights, for example)
Armed conflicts and internal rebellions for political power	Foreign governments or intergovernmental agencies such as the EEC	Breaches or unilateral revisions in contracts and agreements
New international alliances	Foreign governments willing to enter into armed conflict or to support internal rebellion	Discrimination such as taxes or compulsory subcontracting
		Damage to property or personnel from riots, insurrections, revolutions, and wars

Source: Stefan H. Robock, "Political Risk: Identification and Assessment," *Columbia Journal of World Business* (July-August, 1971), p. 7.

EXHIBIT 3-5   View of the Economy in 1988

1. GNP
   Real GNP to grow at 3.2% per year to the year 1988.
   GNP in constant 1973 dollars to go up to $2.08 trillion.
   GNP in current dollars to go up to $4.3 trillion.

2. Population
   U.S. population to be 239 million in 1988.

3. Unemployment Rate
   Unemployment rate will decline to around 4.75% in 1988.

4. Employment
   Number of employed people in 1988 will hit 103 million, compared to 84.4 million in 1973.
   Hours of work will decline to 35 in 1988.
   By 1988, output per worker-hour measured in 1973 dollars will top $11, compared to less than $8 in 1973.

5. Business Investment in Plants and Equipment
   By 1988 the capital expenditures in constant 1973 dollars will be $183.17 billion, compared to $100 billion in 1973.

6. Residential Construction
   The net increase in the number of households will average about 1.4 million per year in the years 1974–1988.

Source: *The American Economy: Prospects for Growth to 1988* (New York: McGraw-Hill Int. Bk. Co., 1975).

manual and intuitive. The large ones, however, not only buy more specific and detailed economic information from private sources, over and above what may be available from government sources, but they analyze the information for meaningful conclusions by constructing econometric models. For example, one large corporation with 9 divisions has developed 26 econometric models of its different businesses. The data used for these models is stored in a data bank and is regularly updated. It is available on-line to all the divisions for further analysis anytime. In addition, there are companies which may occasionally buy information from outside and selectively undertake modeling.

Regulatory Environment

Even in a capitalistic society like the United States the government influence on business appears to be increasing. It is said that businesses spend twice as much time on the average fulfilling government requirements today as they did ten years ago. Exhibit 3-6 lists the federal laws that have been passed in the area of consumerism alone during the last ten years.

EXHIBIT 3-6   Selected Federal Laws Concerned with Consumerism

National Traffic and Safety Act (1966)
Fair Packaging and Labeling Act (1967)
Federal Cigarette Labeling and Advertising Act (1967)
Consumer Credit Protection Act (1968)
Toy Safety Act (1969)
Fair Credit Reporting Act (1970)
Environmental Protection Act (1970)
Public Health Cigarette Smoking Act (1971)
Consumer Product Safety Act (1972)
Consumer Goods Pricing Act (1975)

To study the impact of the regulatory environment, i.e., of laws already on the books and pending legislation, legal assistance is required. Usually a company has a legal expert on its staff to relate the regulatory environment to its business. Smaller firms may seek legal assistance on an ad hoc basis. As a matter of fact, the large firms may maintain offices in Washington staffed by people with legal backgrounds and well versed with company business. They know the important government agencies from the point of view of their companies and maintain a close liaison with them. They pass on the relevant information to planners in different departments of the companies. For example, a company which did a substantial amount of business in less-developed countries had a person in Washington who closely followed the developments in the Agency for International Development (AID). As soon as foreign aid to a country was approved, this legal expert signalled the company headquarters, which in turn alerted its office in that country to begin seeking business.

Social Environment

The ultimate test of a business is its social relevance. This is particularly so in a post-industrial society where survival needs are already met. It, therefore, behooves the strategic planner to be familiar with emerging social trends and concerns. The relevance of the social environment will, of course, vary, depending on the nature of one's business. For a technologically oriented business, the scanning of the social environment will be limited to aspects of pollution control and environmental safety. For a consumer products company, however, the impact of the social environment will go much further.

Information on social trends may be derived from published sources. The impact of social trends on the business can either be studied in-house or consultants can be hired to help. A number of consulting firms specialize in providing this type of information. Exhibit 3-7 shows 31 social trends which, according to Yankelovich, Inc., will have a tremendous effect on business in the coming years.

EXHIBIT 3-7   Social Trends Having Marketing Significance

PSYCHOLOGY OF AFFLUENCE TRENDS, reflecting the increasing assumption that the essentials of economic survival are assured, leading to a focus on having more or doing more to improve the quality of living.

Trend
1 Personalization
2 Physical Self-Enhancement
3 Physical Fitness and Well-Being
4 Social/Cultural Self-Expression
5 Personal Creativity
6 Anti-Materialism
7 Meaningful Work

ANTI-FUNCTIONALISM TRENDS, reflecting reaction to the emphasis on the functional and "scientific," seen as leading to drabness and boredom in everyday life.

Trend
8 Mysticism
9 Sensuousness
10 New Romanticism
11 Introspection
12 Novelty and Change
13 Beauty in the Home

REACTION AGAINST COMPLEXITY TRENDS, reflecting the belief that life has become excessively complicated, that the individual has lost control of his destiny, and that there is much to be gained by returning to a more natural and more simple style of life.

Trend
14 Return to Nature
15 Simplification
16 Anti-Bigness
17 Scientism and Technology
18 Ethnic Orientation
19 Local Community Involvement

TRENDS RELATED TO THE WEAKENING OF THE "PROTESTANT ETHIC," reflecting questioning of a value system, termed the "Protestant Ethic" by sociologists, which, put very simply, is based on the belief that ambition, striving, hard work, self-sufficiency, self-denial and other familiar virtues will lead to a successful life.

Trend
20 Living for Today
21 Hedonism
22 Away From Self-Improvement
23 Noninstitutional Religion
24 Liberal Sex Attitudes
25 Blurring of the Sexes
26 Acceptance of Drugs

TRENDS REFLECTING PERMISSIVENESS IN CHILD REARING, deriving from the psychological guidelines which have been widely used in the upbringing of our

current youth population. These guidelines were based largely on concern about
the negative aftereffects of a rigid, demanding, punishment-oriented childhood.

Trend   27   Anti-Hypocrisy
         28   Rejection of Authority
         29   Tolerance for Chaos and Disorder
         30   Female Careerism
         31   Familism

Source: These trends have been extracted from:
          Marketing News, Mid-March, 1971, p. 8; First-of-April, 1971, p. 8; Mid-April, 1971,
          pp. 7–8; First-of-May, 1971, p. 8; Mid-May, 1971, p. 7; and First-of-June, 1971,
          p. 8.

Some large companies do their own research; G.E. stands out in this regard.
Exhibit 3-8 shows the social trends which scanners at G.E. have singled out as
significant for their business.

EXHIBIT 3-8   Basic Trends in "Our Future Business Environment"

The future international scene is expected to be characterized by:
1. Maintenance of the basic international power structure
2. Continued economic growth, despite a conflict between population
   growth and economic development in the emerging nations
3. The emergence of Japan as the third major power
4. Polarization of main world tension on a North-South ("haves" vs.
   "have-nots") axis rather than on an East-West (communist vs. capital-
   ist) axis

The future domestic scene can be interpreted as the interaction of eight basic
trends:
1. Increasing affluence
2. Economic stabilization
3. Rising tide of education
4. Changing attitudes toward work and leisure
5. Growing interdependence of institutions
6. Emergence of the "post-industrial" society
7. Strengthening of pluralism and individualism
8. The black/urban problem

Source: *Our Future Business Environment* (New York: General Electric Co., 1964).

The relevance of a social trend, such as female careerism (see trend #30 in
Exhibit 3-7), to a business can be discussed with reference to the retail industry.
The Bureau of Labor Statistics figures show that the number of working wives
nearly doubled between 1950 and 1975 and that about half of the married women
in this country now hold jobs. Furthermore, the greatest additional growth in job
holders and earnings in the future is most likely to occur among working wives.

In other words, by the middle of the 1980s 60 percent of women as opposed to 80 percent of men will be working. This structural social change leads retailers to ask such questions as: Where does the working wife like to do most of her shopping? What type of store does she prefer? How fashion-conscious is she? What sources of information does she use before she makes a purchase? What kind of services does she expect retailers to provide? A propriety study on the subject (conducted for a major department store) with which the author was associated brought out interesting findings. Working wives are more educated, are more experienced metropolitans, and possess more sophisticated tastes. Their shopping behavior is considerably different from that of the traditional woman shopper. The working-wife market cannot be served by a store which is "all things to all customers." It is predicted that a new store is on the horizon which may emerge either within a department store or as a separate institution to cater to the working-wife market. The working wife prefers suburban stores over the downtown store even though she may be working downtown. The working wife likes to keep more up to date on all fashions and likes her clothes to be functional so that she can wear them at work without losing comfort and efficiency. The above findings bear heavily on retailers' strategies in such areas as merchandising, the role of the suburban store, store positioning, fashion orientation, promotion, and store services.

Let us take two additional trends, personal creativity and anti-materialism (see trends #5 and #6 in Exhibit 3-7), and examine their impact on marketing strategy.

Personal Creativity. Products and services designed to reinforce the idea that creativity is possible for all should represent potential business opportunities. The boom in home sewing that started in the early 1970s gives weight to the marketing significance of this trend. Traditionally wearing a homemade dress was considered a sign of poverty. Not anymore. It has been reported that one important reason for the popularity of home sewing is due to the growing need some women feel for creative outlets.[8]

Anti-Materialism. It has been suggested that the current hierarchy of status symbols, i.e., the possessions and activities that are believed to convey an aura of material success, is undergoing a change. A large car, for example, is not a status symbol anymore. It is getting to the point where people don't want a big car anymore; there is no more status to it. Comfort is not very important either; people just want transportation. According to one source, "where people once viewed cars as fun and something special to own, they are currently frustrated or bored with their cars. The novelty and status of car ownership are long gone.

---

[8]"A $3-Billion Boom in Home Sewing," *Business Week* (October 3, 1970), p. 56.

So they look at their autos as an appliance to get them from place to place economically and to be replaced when it wears out.''[9]

ENVIRONMENTAL SCANNING AND MARKETING STRATEGY

Exhibit 3-9 relates the environment to marketing strategy. Listed below are the procedural steps which explain this relationship.

1. Keep a tab on broad trends appearing in the environment. Once the scope of environmental scanning is determined, broad trends in the chosen areas may be reviewed from time to time. For example, in the area of technology, trends in mastery of energy, material science, transportation capability, mechanization and automation, communications and information processing, and control over natural life may be studied.

2. Determine the relevance of an environmental trend. Everything happening in the environment may not be relevant for a company. Therefore attempts must be made to select those trends in the environment which have significance for the company. There cannot be any hard-and-fast rules for making a distinction between relevant and irrelevant. Consider, for example, the case of the steam locomotive industry. Perhaps its constituents would have been more receptive to changes had these come from within the industry itself. Cooper has said:

> I would hypothesize that if the new threat is very similar to a firm's traditional way of meeting consumer needs, such as the turbine-powered automobile being similar to the internal combustion-powered automobile, then management often would perceive the new development threatening. However, if it meets consumer needs in very different ways, it is less likely to be recognized at an early point. For instance, I suspect that one of the major threats to the future growth of commercial airlines is originating not with transportation companies, but rather with communication firms. I'm thinking in particular of American Telephone and Telegraph's development of the "television phone". As that product is perfected and as the costs of using it are lowered, it may eliminate completely the need for many business flights, with consequent substantial impact upon the future growth of airlines.[10]

---

[9]Walter Mossberg and Laurence G. O'Donnell, "U.S. Love for Auto Wanes as More Demand Cheap Transportation," *The Wall Street Journal,* (March 30, 1977), p. 1.
[10]Arnold C. Cooper, "Identifying, Appraising, and Reacting to Major Technological Change," in *Proceedings,* Winter Conference (Chicago: American Marketing Association, 1967), p. 56.

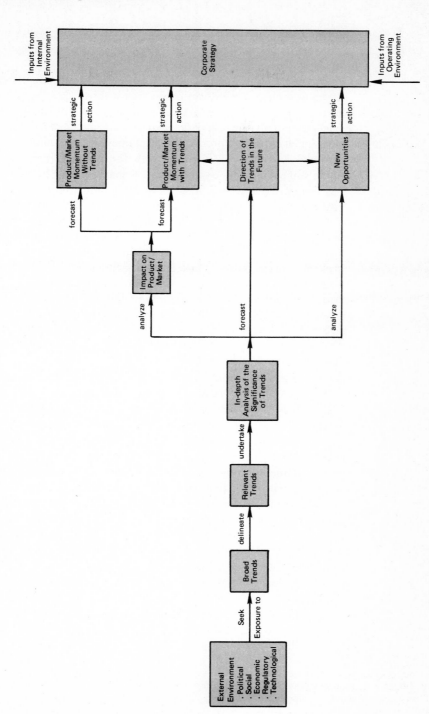

EXHIBIT 3-9 Linking Environmental Scanning to Corporate Strategy

Management's creativity and farsightedness would play an important role in a company's ability to pinpoint the relevant areas of concern.

3. Study the impact of an environmental trend on a product/market. An environmental trend can pose either a threat or an opportunity for a company's product/market; which one it will turn out to be must be studied. The task of determining the impact of a change may be assigned either to a product/market manager or to another executive who is supposedly familiar with the product/market. If the whole subject appears controversial, it may be safer to have an ad hoc committee look into it, or even consultants, either internal or external, may be approached. There is a good chance that a manager who has been involved with a product or service for a good many years would look at any change as a threat to himself. He may, therefore, avoid the issue of a noted impact by declaring it to be irrelevant at the outset. Thus, if such sabotage is feared, perhaps it would be better to rely on the committee or a consultant.

4. Forecast the direction of an environmental trend into the future. If an environmental trend does appear to have significance for a product/market, it is desirable to determine the course that the trend is likely to adopt in the future. In other words, attempts must be made at environmental forecasting.[11]

5. Analyze the momentum of the product/market business in the face of the environmental trend. Assuming the company takes no action, what will be the shape of the product/market performance in the midst of the environmental trend and its direction into the future? The impact of an environmental trend is mostly gradual. While it is helpful to be "first" to recognize and take action when perceiving an environmental trend, not all is lost even if a company waits to see which way the trend proceeds. But how long one can wait depends on the diffusion process of the adoption of change necessitated by the trend. People did not jump to replace black and white television overnight. Such examples abound. There are a variety of reasons which would prohibit an overnight shift in markets due to an environmental trend which may deliver a new product or process. High prices, religious taboos, legal restrictions, and unfamiliarity with the product or service would restrict changeover. In brief, the diffusion process should be predicted before arriving at a conclusion.

6. Study the new opportunities that an environmental trend appears to provide. An environmental trend may not be relevant for a

---

[11]William R. King and David I. Cleland, "Environmental Information Systems for Strategic Marketing Planning," *Journal of Marketing,* Vol. 38 (October, 1974), pp. 35–40.

company's current product/market. But it may indicate promising new business opportunities for a company. For example, the energy crisis provided an easy entry point for Honda cars in the United States. Such opportunities should be duly pinpointed and analyzed for action.

7. Relate the outcome of an environmental trend to corporate strategy. Based on environmental trends and their impacts, the company needs to review its strategy on two counts: changes which may be introduced in the current products/markets, and feasible opportunities which the company may embrace for action. Even if an environmental trend poses a threat for a company's product/market, it is not necessary for the company to come out with a new product to replace the existing one. Neither is it necessary for every competitor to embrace the "change." Even without developing a new product, a company may find a niche in the market which it could cater to despite introduction of a new product by the competitor. The electric razor did not make the use of safety razor blades obsolete. Use of automatic transmission in automobiles did not throw the standard shift out of vogue. New markets and new uses can be found which give the existing product an advantage despite the overall popularity of the new product.

While there are procedural steps listed above for scanning the environment, scanning is nevertheless an art in which creativity plays an important role. Thus, to adequately study the changing environment and relate it to corporate strategy, companies should inculcate a habit of creative thinking on the part of the managers. The following steps adopted by the Coca-Cola Company in this regard are noteworthy:

> Managers concerned with products and new business would ultimately be withdrawn from the line organization and would serve as staff people at the corporate level. There they would be granted considerable freedom of action. A serious effort would have to be undertaken to "open up" line managers to new ideas and to encourage innovation in their plans.[12]

Besides encouraging creative thinking, organizational arrangements should also be made to process new ideas smoothly.

The impact of environmental changes on marketing strategy may be illustrated by means of the following examples. The microwave oven has created new growth opportunities for food processors. Thus, Pillsbury has introduced one-minute pancakes and three-minute popcorn and is working on a number of other products with the goal of a whole line of foods for microwave ovens. Other food

---

[12]"The Coca-Cola Company (E), A Case Study," copyrighted by the President and Fellows of Harvard College, 1970, p. 15.

processors (General Foods, ITT Continental Baking, Standard Brands, and Stouffer's Frozen Foods) are also planning new product lines for microwave ovens.[13] This shows how a technological innovation leads to new perspectives in product strategy. It also shows that the technological advances in one industry can create problems and opportunities in another industry. In the area of economic environment, the decline in the value of the U.S. dollar against major European currencies has opened new markets for U.S. automobiles in Europe. A G.M. executive notes: "The dollar and G.M.'s new smaller cars, closer to European tastes, are working together to create a natural demand that we are trying to exploit from the U.S."[14]

The unisex revolution led Gillette to merge its Personal Care Division (mostly female) with its Toiletries Division (mostly male). Since men and women are not different in what they want in a hair-care product, having two different divisions did not make sense. Thus, the unisex revolution, a sociological change, required a change in product strategy and structural arrangements.[15]

The application of antitrust laws to current-day contexts shows how regulatory and political environments may have an impact on marketing strategy. Our antitrust laws are built on nineteenth century models. These models consider all competition other than price competition to be irrational. Thus, the antitrust laws ignore the realities of doing business in the present era, such as economies of scale, ecological concerns, and consumerism. Additionally, courts are now using antitrust laws to institute social change. Such an application of antitrust laws deeply affects marketing strategy in a variety of ways. For example, ITT Continental Baking Company was ordered by the court to devote one fourth of its media allocations to correct the claim that Profile bread was effective in reducing weight simply because it was sliced more thinly.[16]

ENVIRONMENTAL SCANNING—AN EXAMPLE

Following the steps in Exhibit 3-10, an attempt is made here to illustrate how specific trends in the environment may be systematically scanned.

EXHIBIT 3-10   Systematic Approach to Environmental Scanning

1. Pick up events in different environments (via literature search).
2. Delineate events of interest to the organization in one or more of the following areas: production, labor, markets (household, business, government, foreign), finance, R&D. This could be achieved via trend-impact analysis of the events.

[13]"Microwave Oven Sales Lose Some Speed," *Business Week* (July 31, 1978), p. 100.
[14]"Europe: GM's Big Push to Sell U.S.-Built Cars," *Business Week* (July 31, 1978), p. 45.
[15]"Gillette: A New Shampoo Aims for More of the Unisex Market," *Business Week* (April 3, 1978), p. 96.
[16]G. David Hughes, "Antitrust Caveats for the Marketing Planner," *Harvard Business Review* (March-April, 1978), p. 40.

3. Undertake cross-impact analysis of the events of interest.
4. Relate the trends of the noted events to current corporate strategies in differ-
    ent areas.
5. Select the trends which either appear to provide new opportunities or pose
    threats.
6. Undertake trends' forecasts
    —wild card prediction
    —most probable occurrence
    —conservative estimate
7. Develop three scenarios for each trend based on three types of forecasts.
8. Pass on the information to product/market planners.
9. Product/market planners may repeat steps 4 to 7 and develop more specific
    scenarios vis-a-vis their products/markets. These scenarios will then be incor-
    porated in corporate strategy.

A *literature search* in the area of politics shows that the following new federal
laws may be passed:

1. Eliminating inside directors
2. Requiring companies to meet the cost of "unfriendly" proxy con-
    tests
3. Barring nominee ownership of stock
4. Reducing a company's right to fire workers at will
5. Guarding worker privacy
6. Mandating due process procedures for grievances
7. Disclosing lobbying efforts in detail
8. Requiring that all ad claims be substantiated
9. Publishing corporate actions that endanger workers or the environ-
    ment[17]

The marketing planner of a consumer goods company may want to determine
if these trends have any relevance for the company. To do so the marketing
planner will undertake *trend-impact analysis.* This will require the formation
of a delphi panel to determine the desirability (0-1), technical feasibility
(0-1), probability of occurrence (0-1), and probable time of occurrence (1985,
1990, 1995, beyond 1995) of each event listed above. The panel may also
be asked to suggest the area(s) which may be affected by each event; i.e., production, labor, markets (household, business, government, foreign), finance,
or R&D.

The above information about an event may be studied by managers in areas
which, according to the delphi panel, are likely to be affected by the event. If the
consensus of their opinion is that the event is indeed important, the scanning may
continue (see Exhibit 3-11).

---

[17]*Business Week* (November 21, 1977), p. 64.

EXHIBIT 3-11   Trend-impact Analysis: An Example

Event	Requiring that all ad claims be substantiated	Reducing a company's right to fire workers at will
Desirability	.8	.5
Feasibility	.6	.3
Probability of occurrence	.5	.1
Probable time of occurrence	1985	Beyond 1990
Area(s) impacted	Household markets Business markets Government markets Finance R & D Production	Labor Finance
Decision	Carry on scanning	Drop from further consideration

Note: Two to three rounds of delphi would be needed to arrive at the above probabilities.

Next, *cross-impact analysis* may be undertaken. This type of analysis is planned to study the impact of an event on other events.[18] Where events are mutually exclusive, such analysis may not be necessary. But where an event seems to reinforce or inhibit other events, the cross-impact analysis is highly desirable for uncovering the true strength of an event.

The cross-impact analysis amounts to studying the impact of an event (given its probability of occurrence) upon other events. The impact may be delineated either in qualitative terms (such as critical, major, significant, slight, or none) or in quantitative terms in the form of probabilities.

Exhibit 3-12 shows how cross-impact analysis may be undertaken. The cross-impact ratings or probabilities can best be determined with the help of another

---

[18]James B. Smith and Pamela G. Kruzic, *Analyzing Future Business Environments* (Menlo Park, Calif.: Stanford Research Institute, 1976).

delphi panel. To further sharpen the analysis, it may also be determined whether the impact of an event on other events will be felt immediately or after a certain number of years.

The cross-impact analysis provides the "time" probability of occurrence of an event and indicates other key events which may be monitored to keep track of the first event. Cross-impact analysis is more useful for project-level scanning than for general scanning.

To relate the environmental trends to strategy, consider the following assumed environmental trends and strategies of a cigarette manufacturer.

Trends:

T_1: Requiring that all ad claims be substantiated

T_2: Publishing corporate actions that endanger workers or the environment

T_3: Disclosing lobbying efforts in detail

T_4: Reducing a company's right to fire workers at will

T_5: Eliminating inside directors

Strategies:

S_1: Heavy emphasis on advertising, using emotional appeals

S_2: Seasonal adjustments in labor force for agricultural operations of the company

S_3: Regular lobbying effort in Washington against further legislation imposing restrictions on the cigarette industry

S_4: Minimum number of outside directors on the board[19]

The analysis in Exhibit 3-13 shows that strategy one, heavy emphasis on advertising, is most susceptible and requires immediate management action. Among the trends, trend five, eliminating inside directors, will have the most positive overall impact. Trends one and two—requiring that all ad claims be substantiated and publishing corporate actions that endanger workers or the environment will have a devastating impact. This type of analysis indicates where management concern and action should be directed.

Thus, it will be desirable to undertake forecasts of trends one and two. The forecasts may predict when the legislation will be passed, what will be the major provisions of the legislation, etc. Three different forecasts may be obtained:

1. Extremely unfavorable legislation
2. Most probable legislation
3. Most favorable legislation

---

[19] F. Friedrich Neubauer and Norman B. Solomon, "A Managerial Approach to Environmental Assessment," *Long Range Planning*, Vol. 10, (April, 1977), pp. 13–20.

EXHIBIT 3-12   Cross-impact Analysis: An Example

Event	Probability of Occurrence	Impact								
		a	b	c	d	e	f	g	h	i
a. Eliminating inside directors	.6		.3[b]							
b. Requiring companies to meet the costly 'unfriendly' contests	.3									
c. Barring nominee ownership of stock	.5									
d. Reducing a company's right to fire workers at will	.1									

e. Guarding worker privacy	.4	
f. Mandating due-process procedures for grievances	.3	
g. Disclosing lobbying efforts in detail	.4	
h. Requiring that all ad claims be substantiated	.5	
i. Publishing corporate actions that endanger workers or the environment	.4	0.7[a]

a– This means that if publishing corporate actions that endanger workers or the environment occurs (probability .4), the probability of requiring that all ad claims be substantiated increases from .5 to .7.

b– This means that elimination of inside directors has no effect on the probability of event b.

EXHIBIT 3-13   Use of Matrix to Determine the Impact of Selected Trends on Different Corporate Strategies

Trends	S_1	S_2	S_3	S_4	Impact (I_1) +	Impact (I_1) −
T_1	−8	0	+2	−2		8
T_2	−4	−2	−6	0		12
T_3	0	+4	−4	+2	2	
T_4	0	−4	0	+6	2	
T_5	−2	+6	+4	+2	10	
Impact (I_2) +	−	4	−	8		
Impact (I_2) −	14	−	4	−		

Scale

+8 ⎫ Enhance the implementation of strategy	Critical
+6	Major
+4	Significant
+2 ⎭	Slight
0	No effect
−2 ⎫ Inhibit the implementation of strategy	Slight
−4	Significant
−6	Major
−8 ⎭	Critical

Three different scenarios (using three types of forecasts) may be developed indicating the impact of each trend. This information may then be passed on to product/market managers for action. Product/market managers may repeat steps four through seven (see Exhibit 3-10) to study the selected trend(s) in depth.

ORGANIZATIONAL ARRANGEMENTS AND PROBLEMS

Structuring Responsibility for Scanning

There are three different ways in which corporations organize scanning activity: 1) line managers undertake environmental scanning in addition to their other work, 2) scanning is made a part of the planner's job, and 3) scanning responsibility is instituted in a new office of environmental scanning. Most companies use a combination of the first two types of arrangements. The corporate planner may scan the corporate-wide environment while line managers concentrate on product/market environment. In some companies, notably General Electric Company, a new office of environmental scanning has been established with a responsibility for all types of scanning. G.E.'s environmental scanning office undertakes scanning both regularly and on ad hoc basis (i.e., on a request from one of the groups of the company). Information which is scanned on a regular basis is passed on to all those in the organization for whom it may have relevance. For example, G.E. is organized into sectors, groups, and strategic business units (SBUs).[20] The SBU is the level at which product/market planning takes place. Thus, the scanned information is channeled to those SBUs, groups, and sectors for which it has relevance.

The ad hoc scanning may be undertaken at the request of one or more SBUs. These SBUs then share the cost of scanning and are the principal recipients of the information.

The environmental scanner serves to split the work of the planner. If the planner already has many responsibilities and if the environment of a corporation is complex, it is desirable to have a person specifically responsible for scanning. Further, it is desirable that both planners (and/or scanners) and line managers undertake scanning. This is because managers usually limit their scanning perceptions to their own industry; i.e., they may limit their scanning to the environment with which they are most familiar. At the corporate level, scanning should go beyond the industry. Morrison H. Beach, Chairman of the Board and Chief Executive Officer, Travelers Insurance Companies, advises:

> Traditional planning seeks to identify the environment in which we will be operating and then lays out the alternative strategies for accomplishing our objectives within that environment. It generally assumes that a vast number of organizational regulatory and economic factors are

---

[20]"GE's New Billion-Dollar Small Businesses," *Business Week* (December 19, 1977), pp. 78–79.

beyond our control. I encourage you to challenge such traditional assumptions. In fact, some of these factors may be at least partially within our ability to control, and modifying our environment may be part of the answer to accomplishing our objectives.[21]

Time Horizon of Scanning

Scanning may be for a short term or a long term. Short-term scanning is useful for programming various operations and the term may last up to 2 years. Long-term scanning is needed for strategic planning, and the term may vary from 3 years to 25 years. Rarely does the term of scanning go beyond 25 years. The actual time horizon would be determined by the nature of the product. Forest products may require a longer time horizon since the company must make a decision almost 25 years ahead on tree planting for lumber. The fashion designer, however, may not extend scanning beyond four years. As a rule of thumb, the appropriate time horizon for environmental scanning for a company would be twice as long as the duration of its strategic plan. For example, if a company's strategic plan is extended eight years into the future, the environmental scanning time horizon for this company should be 16 years. Likewise, a company with a five-year planning horizon should scan the environment for ten years into the future. Presumably, then, a multiproduct, multimarket company should have different time horizons for environmental scanning. Working on the above rule of thumb, a company can be sure not only of discovering relevant trends and their impact on its products/markets, but also of implementing necessary changes in its strategy to marshall opportunities provided by the environment or to avert environmental threats.

Problems Faced

Discussed below are the major problems which companies face in the context of environmental scanning. Many of these problems are, in fact, dilemmas which may be attributed to lack of theoretical frameworks on the subject.

1. The environment per se is too broad to be tracked by an organization. Thus, it is necessary to separate the relevant from the irrelevant environment. But this may not be easy since in terms of perceptible realities, the environment of all large corporations is as broad as the world itself. For example, the steam locomotive industry, presumably, would have been more receptive to changes had they emerged within the industry itself rather than outside (via General Motors). A company needs to determine, therefore, what criteria to develop to select information on a practical basis.

---

[21]Morrison H. Beach, "Corporate Planning" (Remarks at Regional Invitational Meeting, American Management Association, November 19, 1976).

2. Another problem is concerned with determining the impact of an environmental trend, i.e., its meaning for business. For example, what does peace on campuses (i.e., no sit-downs, no strikes, etc.) mean for a company's sales and new business opportunities?

3. Even if the relevance of a trend and its impact are determined, making forecasts of the trend poses another problem. For example, how quiet will the students be ten years from now?

4. A variety of organizational problems hinder environmental scanning. Presumably managers are the company's ears and eyes and therefore could be a good source to perceive, study, and channel pertinent information within the organization. But managers are usually so tied up mentally and physically within their little world of specific roles that they simply ignore happenings in the environment.[22] The structuring of organizations by specialized functions can be blamed for this problem to a certain extent. In addition, organizations lack a formal system for receiving, analyzing, and finally disseminating environmental information to the decision points.

5. Environmental scanning requires "blue sky" thinking and "ivory tower" working patterns to encourage creativity. But such work perspectives are often not justifiable in the midst of corporate culture.[23]

6. Frequently the top management, because of their own values, consider dabbling into the future to be a waste of resources; therefore, they adopt an unkindly attitude towards such projects.

7. Many companies as a matter of corporate strategy like to wait and see; therefore, they let the industry leaders act on their behalf, the ones who want to be first in the field.

8. Lack of normative approaches on environmental scanning is another problem.

9. Often the change is too out of the way. It may be perceived, but its relationship to the company is not conceivable.

10. It is also problematic to decide what department of the organization should be responsible for environmental scanning. Also: Should marketing research undertake environmental scanning? How about the corporate planning office? Who else should participate? Is it possible to divide the work? For example, the divisions may concentrate on their products, product lines, markets, and

---

[22]T.P. Merritt, "Forecasting the Future Business Environment," *Long Range Planning,* Vol. 7 (June, 1974), pp. 54–62.
[23]Eli Seger, "How to Use Environmental Analysis in Strategy Making," *Management Review* (March, 1977), pp. 4–13.

industry. The corporate level may deal with the rest of the information.

11. Often information is gathered which is overlapping, leading to a
    waste of resources. Frequently there are informational gaps which
    require duplication of effort.

SCANNING TECHNIQUES

In its early stages environmental scanning has been implemented mainly with
the use of conventional methodologies such as marketing research, economic
indicators, demand forecasting, and industry studies. But the use of such conventional techniques for environmental scanning has not been without pitfalls, for
two major reasons. One, these techniques have failed to provide reliable insights
into the future. As Ewing has said, "the most careful and sophisticated forecasts
of market demand have gone awry, and there is no technical improvement in sight
that promises to change matters."[24] Two, these techniques, in any event, provide
a narrow view of the environment:

> Direct competition . . . is only one of the basic dimensions of the com-
> pany's total strategic environment—The competitive audit must be
> augmented by assessment of the broader governmental, social, economic,
> idealogical and other forces which will influence the company's charac-
> ter, purpose and strategies over the longer term.[25]

Discussed below are a variety of new techniques which have recently been
adapted to scan the environment.

Extrapolation Procedures

These procedures require the use of information from the past to explore
the future. Obviously their use assumes that the future is some function of the
past. There are a variety of extrapolation procedures which range from
a simple estimate of the future (based on past information) to regression
analysis.

Historical Analogy

Where past data cannot be used to scan an environmental phenomenon, the
phenomenon may be studied by establishing historical parallels with other
phenomena. Assumed here is the availability of sufficient information on the other

---

[24]David Ewing, "Corporate Planning at Crossroads," *Harvard Business Review,* Vol. 45, July–
August, 1967, p. 84.
[25]J. Thomas Cannon, "Auditing the Competitive Environment," in John W. Bonge and Bruce
P. Coleman (eds.), *Concepts of Corporate Strategy* (New York: Macmillan Publishing Co.,
1972), pp. 263–264.

phenomena. The turning points in the progression of these phenomena become the guideposts for predicting the behavior of the phenomenon under study.[26]

Intuitive Reasoning

This technique bases the future on the "rational feel" of the scanner. Intuitive reasoning requires free thinking unconstrained by past experience and personal biases. This technique, therefore, may provide better results when used by free-lance think tanks than when used by managers on the job.

Scenario Building

This technique calls for developing a time-ordered sequence of events bearing a logical cause-effect relationship to one another. The ultimate forecast is based on multiple contingencies each with its respective probability of occurring.

Cross-Impact Matrices

When two different trends in the environment point toward conflicting futures, this technique may be used to study these trends simultaneously for their effect. As the name implies, this technique uses a two-dimensional matrix, arraying one trend along the rows and the other along the columns.

Morphological Analysis

This technique requires identification of all possible ways to achieve an objective. For example, the technique can be employed to anticipate innovations and to develop the optimum configurations for a particular mission or task.

Network Methods

There are two types of network methods: contingency trees and relevance trees. A contingency tree is simply a graphical display of logical relationships among environmental trends that focuses on branch-points where several alternative outcomes are possible. A relevance tree is a logical network similar to a contingency tree, but drawn with a view to assign degrees of importance to various environmental trends with reference to an outcome.

Missing Link Approach

The missing link approach combines the morphological analysis and the network method. Many developments and innovations that appear promising and marketable may be held back because something is missing. Under such

---

[26]David T. Kollat, "Environmental Forecasting and Strategic Planning: Perspectives on the Methodology of Futurology," in Fred C. Allvine, *Combined Proceedings,* Spring and Fall Conference (Chicago: American Marketing Association, 1971), pp. 210–213.

circumstances this technique may be used to scan new trends to see if they provide impending answers to the missing links.

Model Building

This technique emphasizes construction of models following deductive or inductive procedures. Two types of models may be constructed: phenomenological models and analytic models. The phenomenological models relate trends into a system for prediction but do not purport to explain the underlying causes. The analytic models seek to identify the underlying causes of change so that future developments may be forecast on the basis of a knowledge of their causes.

Delphi Technique

The delphi technique is the systematic solicitation of expert opinion. Based on reiteration and feedback, this technique is used to seek opinions of a panel of experts on happenings in the environment.[27]

SCANNING APPROACHES

A company can follow an inductive or a deductive approach in studying the impact of an environmental change. The deductive approach, which is predictive in nature, studies the broader changes and analyzes the impact of each change on the company's existing lines, at the same time generating new areas in which it seems feasible for the company to expand. Under the inductive approach the future of each product line can be simulated by exposing its current environment to various changes foreseen in the future. Through the process of elimination changes which bear relevance to one's business can be studied more thoroughly for possible action. Either approach has merits and limitations. The deductive approach, however, is much more demanding since it calls for proceeding from unknowns to specifics. At different levels in the organization both approaches have some contribution to make. At the strategic level the deductive approach is likely to be more useful. In functional planning, however, the inductive approach may be more relevant.

SUMMARY

Because of its growing complexity, the business environment must be constantly monitored. The environment may be conceived as twofold: the corporate environment and the product/market environment. This chapter mainly discusses the corporate environment. Its constituents are: technological environment, political environment, economic environment, regulatory environment, and social environment. The relationship of the environment to marketing

---

[27]Subhash C. Jain, "Predicting Impact of Change Using Delphi Technique," *Managerial Planning,* Vol. 23 (September–October, 1974), pp. 20–28.

strategy is delineated. A systematic approach to environmental scanning using such techniques as trend impact analysis and cross-impact analysis is illustrated. Finally, a variety of techniques which may be useful for scanning the environment are summarized.

DISCUSSION QUESTIONS

1. Explain the meaning of environmental scanning. Which constituents of the environment, from the viewpoint of a business corporation, require scanning?
2. Why did the state of the scanning art not keep pace with the popularity of strategic planning?
3. Illustrate with the help of examples the relevance of technological, political, regulatory, economic, and social environments in the context of marketing strategy.
4. Who in the organization should be responsible for scanning the environment? What role may consultants play to help corporations in their environmental scanning activity?
5. Explain the use of trend impact analysis and cross-impact analysis with reference to environmental scanning.
6. How may the delphi technique be useful in the context of environmental scanning? Give an example.

Chapter 4
Scanning the Product/Market Environment

He who can see three days ahead will be rich for three thousand years.

Japanese Proverb

Chapter 3 was devoted to scanning the environment at the macro level. This chapter looks at the environment from the product/market perspective. Environmental scanning at the macro level is a job of the staff person who may be positioned at the corporate, division, group, or business unit level. The person concerned may go by any of these titles: corporate planner, environmental analyst, environmental scanner, strategy planner, or marketing researcher.

Monitoring of the environment from the viewpoint of products/markets is a line function which should be carried out by those who are involved in making marketing decisions. This is so since the product/market managers, being in close touch with various marketing aspects of the product/market, are in a better position to read between the lines and make more meaningful interpretations of the environment than are the staff people. The constituents of the product/market environment are shown in Exhibit 4-1. Briefly, these constituents are: social and cultural effects, political influences, ethical considerations, legal requirements, competition, economic climate, technological changes, institutional dynamics, consumerism, limits of growth, population, location of consumers, income, expenditure patterns, and education. Not all aspects of the environment will be relevant for every product/market. The scanner, therefore, should first choose which parts of the environment influence the product/market before attempting to monitor them.

This chapter examines the nature of various types of environmental influences which affect product/market strategies. An attempt is made, with the help of examples from the literature, to describe how a particular aspect of the environment may infringe on the formulation of marketing strategies.

EXHIBIT 4-1   Constituents of the Product/Market Environment

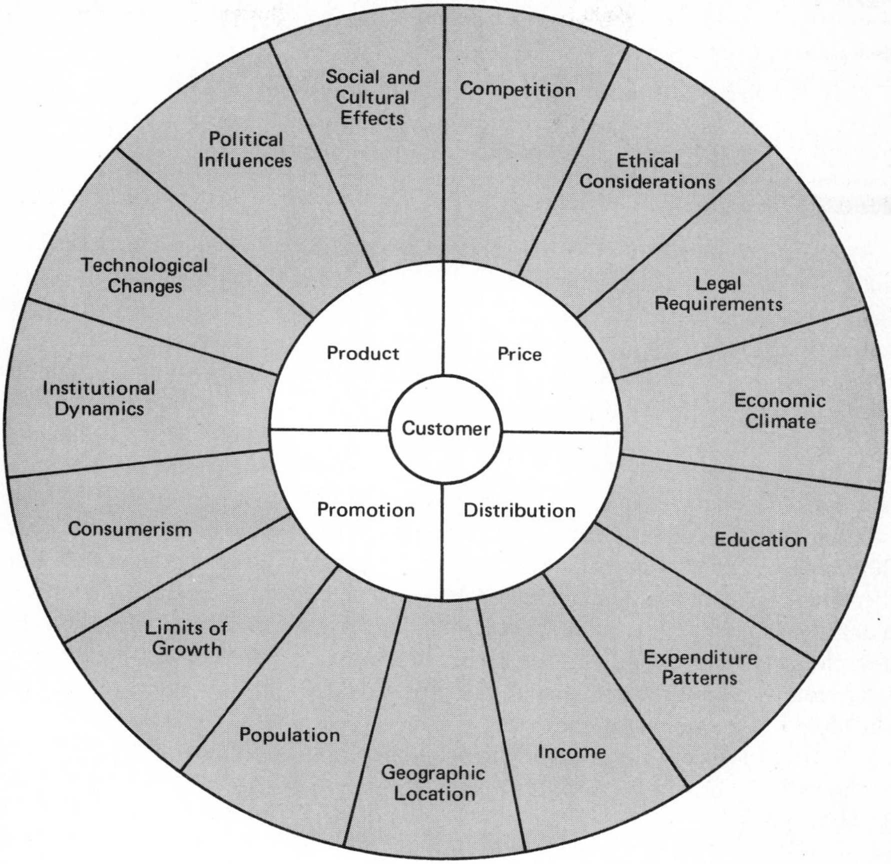

Wheel diagram with concentric rings. Center: Customer. Inner ring: Product, Price, Promotion, Distribution. Outer ring (clockwise from top): Competition, Ethical Considerations, Legal Requirements, Economic Climate, Education, Expenditure Patterns, Income, Geographic Location, Population, Limits of Growth, Consumerism, Institutional Dynamics, Technological Changes, Political Influences, Social and Cultural Effects.

SOCIAL AND CULTURAL EFFECTS

Social and cultural life in the U.S. has changed dramatically in the past 25 years, and the change is continuing at an accelerated rate. A change in social and cultural milieu affects every sector of the marketing front. Thus, out of today's up-heavals, a new type of American consumer is emerging. This development may be a threat or an opportunity, depending on the alertness and plans of the marketer.

Among the social cultural changes that are taking place, changes in the following four areas have direct implications for marketing:

1.   Redefinition of the relationship between institutions (government, industry, education, religion) and the individual

2. Changes in the interpersonal world of the individual
3. Changes in the level of effective functioning of the adult human being
4. New patterns of achievement.[1]

The changing role of woman in the society and the weakening of the Protestant ethic are two changes which we frequently hear about. Let us consider what significance, if any, these changes have on marketing decisions.

Role of Woman

Higher education and affluence, and an intense desire to gain a social status equal to men, are the factors that in combination are molding the life-style of to-day's women. Educated, economically independent young women signify the rapid waning of the era in which the husband made the final buying decisions and brand choices.[2] We can expect a number of new market segments—women in high positions, divorced women—becoming important and requiring different market-ing action. The decline in the traditional role of housewife and mother as women's ultimate destiny should offer new opportunities for providing women with a sense of pride and achievement. The independent working women are becoming a new force behind the youth cult because they look young and act young. In brief, the changing role of women does not merely affect marketing decisions here and there; rather, it tends to require completely new marketing programs with entire-ly different offering, distribution, promotion, and price decisions. For example, in households with working women frozen foods would have greater significance than in households where women are homemakers. By the same token, the changing role of women becomes more pronounced as they begin to make their own buying decisions, thus achieving economic independence and leaving their traditional roles.

Protestant Ethic

Out of the weakening of the Protestant ethic (hard work, self-reliance, and self-denial), new attitudes have emerged such as:

1. Revolution in sex mores (substantiated by the recent trend in movies and legitimate theatre)
2. Immediate rather than deferred gratification (banks advertise—why wait?)
3. General questioning of authority (modes of dress)
4. Search for meaning and purpose in life (Peace Corps service)[3]

---

[1]J.L. Aitken, "Implications for Marketing in Current U.S. Social Trends," *The Conference Board Record,* Vol. 7 (December, 1970), pp. 37–40.
[2]E.B. Weiss, "New Life Styles of 1975–1980 Will Throw Switch on Admen," *Advertising Age,* Vol. 43 (September 18, 1972), pp. 61–67.
[3]"Americans Change," *Business Week,* (February 20, 1978), p. 64.

Currently Americans seem to be embracing a set of values so different from the past that they add up to a whole new outlook on life, work and society. These new values profoundly alter consumer demand. For example, a common style of dress for both men and women is becoming established. Many products such as hair spray, which were traditionally meant for women are being used increasingly by men.

Why the Changes?

We are living in a different world today. The challenges that turned people on yesterday are not challenges anymore. For example, for a vast majority, a house in the suburbs is now a fact of life and not a dream. As has been noted, "In no other comparable period of time in the nation's history did we experience a change of such magnitude. Inevitably, such rapid escalation of affluence, or near affluence, has made extensive changes in our values and in the way we live."[4] Thus, taking industrial efficiency, progress, and productivity for granted, today's youth is seeking new values.

Some students of the future call the new era we are entering the post-industrial society.[5] It is a state of social and economic progress where a vast majority of American people have made social, economic, and cultural achievements which elsewhere in the world are still made by only a small minority. The concept of the post-industrial society has no precedent since in the whole history of humanity no other nation or society has made as much progress in such a short time as the U.S. The post-industrial society is something so new and uncertain that ordinarily very few people like to talk about it. It questions the status quo and established traditions, beliefs, faiths, taboos, and rituals. Marketers have to recognize this and give proper weight to the emerging values if they are to lead a successful operation.

A number of companies are conscious of the new state of social and cultural affairs in American society. They are engaged in studying what changes are, in fact, relevant to their business and how best they can incorporate them in their strategic decisions. The General Electric Company, as was mentioned in Chapter 3, has done a great deal of work studying how our values are changing and what this means for the company's various businesses.

Social Change and Marketing Strategy

The significance of social change for marketing strategy will be explained with reference to the wine industry. Traditionally wine was distributed through liquor stores. However, in recent years women have assumed an important role in making wine-buying decisions. Recognizing this social change, wine companies began distributing wines through grocery stores to make them more readily

---

[4]Fabian Linden, "The Society of the Affluent," *Across the Board* (February, 1978), p. 2.
[5]Herman Kahn, *World Economic Development: 1979 and Beyond* (Boulder, CO: Westview Press, 1979).

available in places where women frequently shop. Simultaneously, wine producers have put great emphasis on wine displays.[6] Another illustration is provided
by food processors. Emphasis on the quality of life among consumers has led
many companies to introduce natural foods into the market with reasonable
success. Likewise, a variety of other ecologically oriented products have been
introduced into the market, such as nonphosphate laundry detergent, to cater to
emerging needs.[7]

POLITICAL INFLUENCE

Even in a free country government exerts significant influence on the
conduct of business. A former chairman of the board of IBM Corporation
remarked:

> In our kind of society, there are times when government has to step
> in and help people with some of their more difficult problems . . .
> If the businessmen insist that free enterprise permits us to be
> indifferent to those things on which people put high value, then the
> people will quite naturally assume that free enterprise has too much
> freedom.[8]

Government intervention in business is usually dictated by political considerations. The government may be local, state, or federal. Specifically, as far as
marketing is concerned, politics come in wherever there is a conflict between
various interests, between two businesses, between business and consumers, or
between business and society-at-large. For example, the U.S. government, in spite
of becoming liberal on trade with China, still bans sales to China of goods deemed
"strategic." However, what is meant by "strategic" is not clearly defined. It
becomes a matter of interpretation for three government agencies: the Commerce
Department, the State Department, and the Defense Department. Two companies interested in trading with China may find a different meaning being assigned
to the word strategic. Political influence may favor one company through a
"right" interpretation of this word.

The political/governmental sector, in attempting to secure the common good,
tries to maintain an orderly balance of competition in the marketplace. In doing
this, the government is sensitive to competitive activity, which may be placed in
three categories: horizontal competition, intertype competition, and vertical competition.[9]

---

[6]"Wine: Selling the New Mass Market," *Business Week* (February 23, 1974), p. 64.
[7]Lewis R. Tucker, Jr., Paul Busch, and Ronald F. Bush, "Multidimensional Marketing: Toward
the Convergence of Instrinsic Value and Profit," in *Proceedings* of the Sixth Annual Meeting
of the Southeast AID's, Atlanta, February, 1976, pp. 60–62.
[8]Thomas J. Watson, Jr., *A Business and Its Beliefs* (New York: McGraw-Hill Bk. Co., 1963),
pp. 88–90.
[9]Joseph C. Palamountain, Jr., *The Politics of Distribution* (Cambridge, MA.: Harvard Univ.
Press, 1955), pp. 24–56.

Horizontal Competition

Competition between two marketing institutions at the same level (such as competition between two types of grocery stores or gasoline stations) is called *horizontal competition.* Horizontal competition is more individualistic in nature since the two interests belong to the same industry group. This type of competition usually takes the form of either monopolistic or oligopolistic competition. Competitive activity gives one institution an edge over another which in turn would like to fight back.

For example, in the 1970s general concern over body weight and the side effects of food additives created a new market for natural foods. To meet the growing demand, initially a number of "health-food" stores, mostly small operations, opened up throughout the country. As the demand for natural foods continued to grow, the sellers were no longer confined to isolated mom-and-pop stores. Many chains came on the scene to promote health foods. General Nutrition Corporation in 1979 owned 700 stores spread all over the country; in fact it was expanding so fast that it opened two additional stores every week. The large companies in the health-food business relied on the same merchandising techniques used by big supermarket chains: heavy advertising, fancy packaging, and selective discounting.

As large chains began to expand, a backlash built against them. The small health-food store owners complained that large competitors were unfairly driving them out of business. They questioned the pricing and promotional techniques of the large competitors and the nutritional value of some of their products. The federal government in 1979 started investigations to examine allegations that the health-food industry had fallen into price fixing and deceptive labeling.[10] The investigations may lead the government to enact laws concerning setting of prices, standards of weights and measures, false advertising, truth in packaging, etc., for the health-food industry.

Intertype Competition

Competition between two institutions of the same type but with different levels of operations may be termed as *intertype competition.* An example is competition between a national grocery chain and a street corner operation. The former can develop into a virtual monopoly with which the smaller operations may not be able to compete. In order to meet the threat of the monopolist, others would probably attempt to compete by means of prices. But in the long run a price war would be more injurious to the smaller merchants. Again, the conflict may have to be resolved at the government level. Political solution to this type of conflict generally takes the form of establishing an authority (such as a commission) which will look out for the interests of the aggrieved.

---

[10]Terri Minsky, "Health-food Chains, In a Rapid Expansion, Cause Some Heartburn," *The Wall Street Journal,* September 28, 1979, p. 1.

Vertical Competition

Conflict between two organizations in the same business venture system, such as conflict between auto manufacturers and dealers over prices or margins, is called *vertical competition*. The dominant feature of this type of competition is the emergence of a power conflict between the two groups. At the governmental level each pleads a case. The auto industry's advertising program, whereby each dealer was required to contribute to a company-operated advertising fund on every purchase made, provides a good example of this type of competition. Unlike the horizontal and intertype struggles, this conflict was between two groups, both of which were strong and had far-reaching governmental contacts.

Political influence can also be exerted through direct action by the government itself in the greater national interest. In 1961, for example, U.S. Steel Corporation raised prices on different types of steel, an action which the federal government considered highly unwarranted for the nation's economy. Through political pressure the Kennedy Administration finally forced U.S. Steel to withdraw the price increase.

Politics and Marketing Strategy

Few studies have been done on the impact of politics on marketing decisions. Therefore, it is difficult to explain. But to illustrate the point, let us take IBM's example. IBM commands a very high share (estimated to be between 60 and 65%) of the computer market. The company could perhaps further increase its market share by employing aggressive marketing strategies. However, other members of the computer industry are already charging IBM with monopolization of the computer field. It is not in the best interests of IBM to implement a strategy for increasing its market share since such activity could make the company susceptible to political action. IBM, therefore, seeks to maintain its current market share. A study done by Greyser showed that politics affects business as much as business affects politics. Comparing his findings of the current study to an earlier study on the subject, Greyser found an increase in the influence of business on politics in general as well as in business' influence on elected officials. The survey noted a substantial executive consensus that business should be more actively involved in politics.[11]

LEGAL REQUIREMENTS

The days of unrestricted competition—when all things were fair in the quest for sales—are over. Previous business philosophies, such as "The public be damned," "The business of the nation is business," and "What's good for us is good for the country," are no longer applicable. Today, the marketing manager's decisions in the areas of product, pricing, promotion, and distribution must be

---

[11]Stephen A. Gryser, "Business and Politics," *Harvard Business Review,* Vol. 46 (November-December, 1968), p. 4.

made in light of legislation enacted at all levels of government: federal, state, and local. Ignorance of the law is no defense when confronted by possible litigation, not to mention the effect of possible litigation on company goodwill. For this reason, it is imperative that the marketing manager have a working knowledge of what can or cannot be done legally.

On an average, 25,000 new regulations, in addition to literally trillions of rules already in existence, are promulgated every year. The new regulations are reported in the *Federal Register* in over 60,000 pages each year. A recent Dow Chemical Company study showed the total costs of compliance with regulatory actions to be $147 million in 1975, including only domestic operations. The benefits of specific regulations vis-a-vis their costs is becoming a matter of concern. In a survey of chief executive officers and top government-liaison staff officers, which was sponsored by the federal government, 86 percent of the respondents felt that government regulations added more to product and service costs than their supposed benefits were worth. Despite such responses, it is safe to predict that regulation of business will not end soon.[12]

Basically, business laws have been enacted with a dual purpose: to maintain and encourage competition and to guarantee fair treatment for the customer. The laws themselves can be grouped into two categories: 1) laws governing monopoly and restraint of trade (Sherman Act, Clayton Act, Federal Trade Commission Act, Robinson-Patman Act, and Antimerger Act); and 2) laws in the area of deceptive practices (Food, Drug and Cosmetic Act, Wheeler-Lea Act, and Federal Trade Commission Act).

The Sherman Antitrust Act (1890)

The Sherman Act is a broadly defined law prohibiting the monopolization or restraint of trade and business within a state, nationally or internationally. Specifically, it is concerned with matters such as price fixing (businesses deciding in consultation with each other to charge the same price and thus harm present competition) and mergers and acquisitions (becoming a monopoly by eliminating competitors).

The Clayton Act (1914)

The Clayton Act is a more specific supplement to the Sherman Act. It prohibits price discrimination (such as a manufacturer charging two customers different prices), exclusive dealing (such as a manufacturer forbidding customers from dealing with anyone else in the manufacturer's line of business), and tying contracts (such as a manufacturer making it obligatory for a customer to buy other products along with the desired product, even if the others can be obtained at lower prices elsewhere).

---

[12]John F. Steiner, "Government Regulation of Business: An Overview," *Los Angeles Business & Economics Journal* (Fall, 1977), pp. 5–8.

The Federal Trade Commission Act (1914)

The Federal Trade Commission Act created the Federal Trade Commission as the enforcing agency of the federal government in antitrust matters. Further, it authorized the enforcement of certain specific prohibitions in the Clayton Act.

The Robinson-Patman Act (1936)

The Robinson-Patman Act amended the Clayton Act, further strengthening the law to maintain competition. Specifically, the Robinson-Patman Act was aimed at price discrimination and price cutting. Nevertheless, its impacts have been felt at all levels of marketing. While the Clayton Act was directed at manufacturers, this act affects both relatively simple individual situations at manufacturers level and the entire structure of marketing relationships—manufacturing, wholesale, retail—of multiproduct and multifunction sellers at all levels.

The Antimerger Act (1950)

The Antimerger Act amended Section 7 of the Clayton Act. It was enacted to broaden the powers of the FTC to regulate those mergers which might substantially lessen competition.

The Food, Drug and Cosmetic Act (1938)

The Food, Drug and Cosmetic Act prohibits adulterated or mislabeled foods, drugs, therapeutic devices, or cosmetics from being manufactured, sold, or transported in interstate commerce, and gives the Food and Drug Administration power to prohibit these abuses.

The Wheeler-Lea Act (1938)

The Wheeler-Lea Act prohibits the use of deceptive advertising in the promotion of foods, drugs, cosmetics, and therapeutic devices.

Legal Requirements and Marketing Strategy

In making decisions the marketing strategist ought to consider the legal implications involved. While a decision might appear logical and sound, the manager may be obliged to accept a different alternative in order to comply with the legal requirements. At Celanese Corporation the question arose whether a distributor should be dropped because he was pushing a product outside his assigned geographic area. Legally the company could not take any action against the distributor since forbidding him to sell in certain areas was in violation of the Robinson-Patman Act. However, the company could drop the distributor if his efforts outside his territory meant he was not meeting sales goals in the market for which he was primarily responsible.[13] Since the legality of a decision may be

---

[13]"How to Avoid Antitrust," *Business Week* (January 27, 1975), p. 84.

difficult to determine, it is safer for a marketing strategist to seek expert help whenever it seems likely that there could be legal aspects to a decision.

A good way to handle the legal aspects is to develop checklists for management personnel which would help them to examine whether a decision may have legal repercussions. For example, in the 1970s the federal government adopted a tough posture in antitrust cases. Shown below are the types of guidelines which companies issued to their employees to keep them in compliance with antitrust laws.

1. Don't discuss with customers the price your company will charge others.
2. Don't attend meetings with competitors (including trade association gatherings) at which pricing is discussed. If you find yourself in such a session, walk out.
3. Don't give favored treatment to your own subsidiaries and affiliates.
4. Don't enter into agreements or gentlemen's understandings on discounts, terms or conditions of sale, profits or profit margins, shares of the market, bids or the intent to bid, rejection or termination of customers, sales territories, or markets.
5. Don't use one product as bait for selling another.
6. Don't require a customer to buy a product only from you.
7. Don't forget to consider state antitrust laws as well as the federal statutes.
8. Don't disparage a competitor's product unless you have specific proof that your statements are true. This is an unfair method of competition.
9. Don't make either sales or purchases conditional on the other party making reciprocal purchases from or sales to your company.
10. Don't hesitate to consult with a company lawyer if you have any doubt about the legality of a practice. Antitrust laws are wide ranging, complex, and subject to changing interpretations.[14]

ETHICAL CONSIDERATIONS

No matter how many laws are enacted to protect the public interest, the corporation is left on its own to act in the best public interest in a variety of matters. Besides, even when there are laws, one can always find loopholes to pursue selfish interests. On such occasions the question of ethics becomes important. The modern corporation, it is believed, has evolved into a social as well as an economic institution. It has concerns, ideals, and responsibilities which go far beyond the profit motive.

The question of the ethics involved in marketing decisions can arise in a number of ways. Consider, for example, the case of a cigarette manufacturer.

---

[14]*Ibid.*

Research has shown that adolescence is a critical time for the establishment of smoking habits in general and perhaps specific brand preference.[15] Given this finding, the cigarette manufacturer faces an ethical dilemma. On the one hand, a promotional campaign directed towards the youth segment of the market would be highly desirable. On the other hand, it may not be good citizenship to induce young people to smoke through advertising techniques. An ethical question may also be raised in connection with companies trying to encourage young children to prefer specific brands of products such as cereal and toys by creating excitement via advertising.

The marketing of prescription drugs poses an interesting ethical problem as well. It is concerned with pricing. Here is a unique situation where not only is the price inelastic, but also the doctor making the buying decision may do so without regard to price. The drug industry has long been criticized for high prices on drugs with brand names. The criticism is based on the following: a comparison with prices in foreign markets, a comparison with similar products sold in the United States, a knowledge of manufacturing and promotion costs, and the industry's high profits.[16] Branded drugs make up a major portion of the pharmaceuticals sold in this country. An ethical question may, therefore, be raised as to why prices of branded drugs are so high. Is it because a firm prices branded products to cover research costs and possibly future research, or is it because the firm has a monopoly on the brand name?

Another major aspect of drug pricing is the large differential between the prices of branded and nonbranded prescriptions. A study of prescription prices of brand name products and their comparative nonbrand competition shows substantial cost differences which may not be justifiable on the basis of quality.[17] The market price level as established by the brand name leader holds a firm umbrella over others entering the market. Yet the nonbranded products have made little progress in spite of the large price advantage since the branded products, backed by heavy promotion, gain a differential advantage over the nonbranded ones. In 1966 it was estimated that $800 million were spent on drug promotion, which comes to about $3,000 per doctor.[18] When doctors prescribe drugs by brand names instead of generic names, this helps the drug business. Having given physicians the habit of prescribing by brand, the pharmaceutical industry as a whole finds it profitable to combine two or more existing drugs to come up with a new product with a different brand name. Since branding becomes an operational mode of the

---

[15]"Kingston Cigarettes: Learning of a Social Practice," in Roger D. Blackwell, James E. Engel, and David T. Kollat, *Cases in Consumer Behavior* (New York: Holt, Rinehart & Winston, 1969), p. 47.

[16]Donald C. King, *Marketing Prescription Drugs* (Ann Arbor: Univ. of Mich. Press, 1968), p. 60.

[17]Morton Mintz, "Drugs: Deceptive Advertising," *The New Republic,* Vol. 159 (July, 1968), pp. 19–21.

[18]F. Marion Fletcher, *Market Restraints in Retail Drug Industry* (Philadelphia: Univ. of Pa. Press, 1967).

drug business, a drug company is put into a situation which it could use to its advantage through large price differentials, a situation which may call for an ethical decision.

The above illustrations underline the importance of ethics in arriving at marketing decisions. Profit is not only desirable, but it also constitutes an essential ingredient in a capitalistic economy. But profits must be earned with due regard to the standards of ethics operating in a social setting. Even if short-term profits have to be given up, standards of ethics must be followed. In this way a business can ensure its long-term growth without being constrained in its role in the society. In the drug example, while there is nothing wrong in creating brand preference through advertising, the drugs must be made recognizable by generic names. Doctors should also be encouraged to use only generic names. Additionally, complete information should be provided on the label so that the consumer can choose between a branded and a nonbranded product.

COMPETITION

One hardly needs to emphasize the significance of studying and evaluating competition before making marketing decisions in a competitive economy. There are several things a firm would not do if it were not for competition. Competition sets the upper limit of a manager's price discretion. "Follow competition" is popular advice on how much a company should be spending on advertising.

In a free market economy each competitor likes to surpass the other in performance. If we draw an analogy from a war situation, a competitor is like an enemy. To outperform its competitors, a company must know how it stands against each one of them with regard to "arms and ammunitions," skill in maneuvering opportunities, preparedness in reacting to threats, and so on. To gain adequate knowledge about competitors, the company will need an excellent intelligence network. The word intelligence signifies that information on competitors must be gathered on a continual basis.

Organizationally, competitive activities can be studied by product managers, market managers, or a staff person (a marketing researcher) attached to a marketing executive. Typically, whenever one talks in terms of competition, the emphasis is placed on price, quality of product, delivery time, and other marketing variables. But this is not enough. One must go much beyond these marketing tactics employed by a competitor. Simply knowing that a competitor has been cutting down prices is not sufficient. What must be known is the flexibility the competitor has in reducing the price further. Implicit here is the significance of gaining knowledge of the competitor's cost structure.

Since competitive factors differ from industry to industry and from company to company in an industry, a separate review should be made of each major competitor. Then a comparative study should be done to determine the company's status vis-a-vis competitors. It must be recognized that competition, not limited to the indsutry only, can come from other industries as well. The history of American business is full of examples where an entire industry has gone out of existence due to competitive inroads. Baldwin Locomotive Works, for example, faced major competition not from other companies in the steam locomotive industry, but from an entirely new industry, the makers of diesel-electric locomotives. Thus, in evaluating competitive activity, it is useful to look beyond one's own industry.

The force of competition may affect the perspective of all four marketing areas. For example, to meet competition a new product may have to be introduced, the price may have to be continually adjusted, distribution may have to be intensified, and the scope of promotion may have to be broadened. To prevent Miller from making inroads into their market shares through Lite beer, other brewers quickly came out with their own versions of light beer. Nestle introduced its brand of decaffeinated coffee to compete against General Foods' Sanka coffee. In Minneapolis, when one bank started giving away gifts to those who opened new accounts, other banks in the city responded with a similar promotional campaign. An auto dealer will frequently slash his price for a car if a customer convinces him that the car can be bought at a lower price at another dealer. Competition in the cosmetics industry led Revlon to broaden its distribution from high-class department stores to discount and drug stores as well.

Competition also affects the timing for implementing various marketing decisions. In 1964 General Foods Corporation had to decide if it should introduce its freeze-dried coffee (branded as Maxim) in the market right away or wait until further marketing research information was gathered. A convincing argument for instant introduction was to gain sufficient time to establish brand loyalty among consumers before Nestle brought out its own freeze-dried coffee.

ECONOMIC CLIMATE

The overall economic climate of the country sets the limit of activity in different sectors of the economy. Thus, when the economy is booming, there will be plenty of jobs, consumers will be optimistic, and the cash registers will ring more often. Under a booming economy a firm will have more opportunity as far as the marketplace is concerned. But opportunities in an industry may attract new competition. When the economy is down, unemployment may rise, interest rates may go up, sales may be difficult to make, and so on. In brief, marketing strategy takes a different shape in a booming economy than in a stagnant or slowly rising economy.

The health of the economy affects consumer confidence, which is then reflected in consumer buying plans. A favorable economic climate generates a spirit of optimism among consumers which makes them more willing to go out and spend money. The reverse is true when economic conditions are unfavorable. Exhibit 4-2 shows how consumer confidence during different time periods is related to different consumer buying plans. During 1969 when consumer confidence was maintained at high levels, consumer buying plans also remained high. However, in 1974–75 a decline in consumer confidence foreshadowed a decline in consumer buying plans as well.

While economic climate affects all businesses, some businesses are affected more deeply than others. The marketing manager has to figure out to what extent

EXHIBIT 4-2   Consumer Confidence and Plans to Buy
(Seasonally Adjusted Index Numbers; 1969–1970=100)

Time	Consumer Confidence	Consumer Buying Plans
1969 January-February	123.4	104.8
1969 March-April	121.6	112.8
1969 May-June	122.9	114.1
1969 July-August	117.3	108.2
1969 September-October	112.6	101.3
1969 November-December	112.0	99.2
1974 January-February	56.0	89.2
1974 March-April	85.9	87.6
1974 May-June	83.3	97.5
1974 July-August	69.1	81.1
1974 September-October	48.9	93.6
1974 November-December	39.9	76.8
1975 January-February	50.9	80.0
1975 March-April	62.5	88.0
1975 May-June	68.0	100.3
1975 July-August	77.3	104.6
1975 September-October	72.1	105.8
1975 November-December	86.8	108.7
1976 January-February	93.3	126.3
1976 March-April	82.2	96.7
1976 May-June	86.7	105.9
1976 July-August	86.8	106.0
1976 September-October	80.2	100.0
1976 November-December	91.5	124.4
1977 January-February	90.3	113.8
1977 March-April	85.2	110.2
1977 May-June	89.6	121.8

Source: Helen Axel, ed., *A Guide to Consumer Markets, 1977/1978* (New York: Conference Bd., 1977), p. 180.

his business is susceptible to economic conditions. For example, in a depressed economic climate consumers tend to postpone buying durables. This means that durable goods manufacturers have to induce consumers to buy by providing new promotional incentives. During 1974–75, automobile companies gave substantial rebates to consumers on new cars. Similar rebates were offered by appliance manufacturers.

Further, it has been found that during times of depressed economic conditions, consumers prefer private brands since they are generally cheaper.[19] For example,

---

[19]Philip Kotler, *Marketing Management* (Englewood Cliffs, NJ: Prentice-Hall, 1976), p. 38.

consumers would prefer canned vegetables sold under the Kroger or A&P brand to those sold under the Del Monte name. This indicates that the marketing manager has to develop a strategy to meet the consumers' growing desire for frugality when the economic climate is not optimistic.

Another area where economic conditions affect prevailing practices is the availability of consumer credit. If the economic climate is depressed, consumer credit becomes scarce. In our economy, however, availability of credit is a prerequisite for buying many products, particularly durables and houses. During depressed economic conditions it is up to the marketing manager to consider how the company can help the consumer obtain adequate financing for buying the product.

TECHNOLOGICAL CHANGES

Advances in the field of technology concerned with mastery of energy; material science (better utilization of existing materials and designing of new materials); transportation capability; mechanization and automation; communication and information processing; and control over natural life (selective breeding, development of hybrids, and elimination of undesirable life) affect marketing in different ways.

A technological development poses either a threat or an opportunity for a company. The company should analyze the impact of technology and take corrective action, which may mean developing a new product or changing the perspective of the existing one to make it more practical for the customer, and by the same token reworking of other marketing decisions.

To identify and develop viable market segments is an important part of the marketing manager's job. Development of computer technology has provided new ways for segmenting the market. For example, computers have been used by retailers to build individual buying profiles. If a store has 500,000 charge customers, the computer can easily come up with 75,000 names of women who have bought higher-priced dresses, shoes, or other special items. These customers can then become a direct-mail target when a new shipment of high-priced dresses or shoes is received. The computer has also been used through a linkage with the cash register to gain up-to-the-minute information about customer reactions on fashion items. This helps in better inventory control and shortens retail inventory replenishment time.

Perhaps technology's main thrust on marketing falls in the area of product decisions. Technological breakthroughs make new products feasible, causing existing products to become obsolete and cutting down their life spans. The steam locomotive became a victim of the diesel locomotive. In the early 1970s the Wankel and the "compound vartex controlled combustion" engines were being considered as efficient, cleaner alternatives to the internal combustion engine in the automobile industry.[20] As American Telephone and Telegraph's picturephone

---

[20]"Detroit's Frantic Hunt for a Cleaner Engine," *Business Week* (December 9, 1972), p. 60; and "Sign of the Times," *Forbes* (March 15, 1974), pp. 26–27.

is perfected and as the costs of using it are lowered, it may eliminate completely the need for many business flights and have subsequent substantial impact upon the future growth of the airlines. Here marketing executives working for the airlines need to study the impact of this technological development on the industry and on their firms and formulate related new marketing strategies.

Technology leads to a variety of efficiencies in operations which can be shared with customers through a reduction in price. The American Telephone and Telegraph Company would never have been able to provide its millions of customers with fast and efficient service if it were not for the development of automatic telephone exchanges.

Technological developments in the field of communications and information processing are tending to revolutionize retailing. Technology is already available to enable consumers to shop through a visual communications system. Orders can be automatically taken by telephone and processed in a central warehouse at any time of the day or night, with speedy delivery the following day. A retailing firm has to evaluate the significance of such changes for itself and the extent to which it should commit itself to new technology.

In the service area, for example, technological change has important implications for the dry cleaning industry. Advances in clothing material have allowed an increasingly large number of items to be cleaned and permanently pressed without dry cleaning. If no steps are taken to meet this change, dry cleaners may find their profits diminishing year after year as a result of new technology. Marketing managers of the dry cleaning industry might try to provide different services for customers such as washing clothes that cannot be dry cleaned as well as dry cleaning clothes. This might offer better service to needs of customers.

Dental researchers are possibly developing a substance that would forever eliminate the development of cavities in most people. In order to effectively cope with this technological advancement the marketing decision makers at Procter & Gamble Company, the makers of Crest, an anti-cavity toothpaste, should know the progress of the research, the probability that it will become widely accepted, and when the new substance will be available.

A final example of technological change having significant implications for marketing decision makers arises from advancements in medical technology. Technological change in this area has induced many social changes. Thanks to advancements in medical technology, people live longer. The older generation is becoming a significant segment of the population. They have needs and wants that provide opportunities for marketing managers. Nursing care, architectural design, transportation, entertainment, etc., all provide new areas in which marketing decision makers can plan for this social change induced by technological change in the field of medicine.

INSTITUTIONAL DYNAMICS

Marketing is essentially an exchange phenomenon. In the performance of the exchange function, a number of institutions besides the manufacturer play a role.

These are wholesaling institutions, retailing institutions, bankers, insurance companies, transportation agencies, and so on. Interaction among these institutions is essential if exchange is to be completed.

An institution functions in an environment that is dynamic in nature and, therefore, subject to change. A firm should make its marketing decisions with due regard to the changes in the interacting institutional settings (such as interaction between wholesaler and retailer).

In the retailing area, as an example, catalog stores (such as E.F. MacDonald, Best, and Service Merchandise) are the latest development. The impact of this development should be evaluated before a firm finalizes its marketing decisions. The catalog store is not a department store in the traditional sense; however, it is not a discount store, either. A number of manufacturers have traditionally avoided placing their established brands with the discounters. But the catalog stores carry well-known brands. This challenges the hold of the regular department stores on quality merchandise. A firm approached by a catalog store wishing to carry its merchandise will need to evaluate its position vis-a-vis the established channels before deciding on the request of the catalog store.

It is not possible to list all the numerous changes that are taking place in different marketing institutions. However, some of these changes expected in the distributive structure in the future are listed below:

1. Rapid growth of vertical marketing systems
2. Intensification of intertype competition
3. Increasing polarity of retail trade
4. Acceleration of institutional life cycles
5. Emergence of the "free-form" corporation as a major competitive reality in distribution
6. Expansion of nonstore retailing.[21]

The trend in these changes is already evident. Their impact on marketing decisions will be far-reaching and challenging. Marketers must study their impact before finalizing their distribution perspective.

CONSUMERISM

Consumerism is a new force in today's marketing environment. It can be defined as ". . . a social movement seeking to augment the rights and power of buyers in relation to sellers."[22] In 1962, President John F. Kennedy proclaimed the consumers' four-pronged Magna Charta: the right to safety, the right to be informed, the right to choose, and the right to be heard. These "rights" in a way

---

[21]William R. Davidson, "Changes in Distributive Institutions," *Journal of Marketing,* Vol. 34 (January, 1970), p. 7.
[22]Philip Kotler, "What Consumerism Means for Marketers," *Harvard Business Review,* Vol. 56 (May-June, 1972), pp. 48–57.

form the core of consumerism. Thus, the movement of consumerism, in its present form, started in the early Sixties.

In pursuing marketing activities which claim the consumer as the focus, in some instances the desire for quick profits has overridden consideration for the consumer. Consequently, in some circles the feeling has grown that the market-place lacks integrity. Others find nothing wrong with the marketing concept, claiming that it has served business well. However, these people suggest that marketing requires a new dimension in the post-industrial era that its current perspective cannot provide. Thus a new and broader philosophy of marketing is needed, which some corporations appear to have acquired already.[23]

Exhibit 4-3 lists the factors that have been claimed as the forerunners of the consumerism movement. In the relatively short history of consumerism, its proponents have made quite an impact in mobilizing public interest in the movement. Studies have been made that have lent support to the movement. For example, it has been found in one study that only 5.8% of the ads that were noticed were perceived as being particularly informative, i.e., helpful in one way or another because of the consumer information they provided.[24] Generally speaking, the consumerism movement stands for the following:

1. Protection against clear-cut abuses (product design, safety)
2. Provision of adequate information
3. Protection of consumers against themselves and other consumers (protection of the inexperienced and underprivileged)[25]

Aaker and Day have discovered an increasing recognition of consumerism in business corporations. Whirlpool, for example, overhauled its aftersales service organization, Safeway stores began unit pricing in their supermarkets, and Feder-ated Department Stores attached tags on small appliances (called tel-tags) to improve the quality of point-of-sale information.[26] In packaging, Reynolds Metals and American Can have developed programs to educate groups and individuals in disposing of packages in nonpolluting ways; 90% of Coca-Cola-owned bottling plants claim to recycle both glass and paper waste material.[27]

Another study, however, showed somewhat different results. In a survey of 157 companies, it was found that business was not responsive to consumerism. The

[23]E.B. Weiss, "Marketers Fiddle While Consumers Burn," *Harvard Business Review,* Vol. 46 (July-August, 1968), pp. 48–57.
[24]Raymond A. Bauer and Stephen A. Greyser, *Advertising in America: The Consumer View* (Cambridge, MA: Harvard Univ. Press, 1968), p. 183.
[25]George S. Day and David Aaker, "A Guide to Consumerism," *Journal of Marketing,* Vol. 34 (July, 1970), p. 13.
[26]David A. Aaker and George S. Day, "Corporate Responses to Consumerism Pressures," *Harvard Business Review,* Vol. 50 (November-December, 1973), pp. 114–124.
[27]William N. Gunn, "Packagers and the Environmental Challenge," *Harvard Business Review,* Vol. 50 (July-August, 1972), pp. 103–111.

EXHIBIT 4-3   Factors Contributing to the Rise of Consumerism in the
             1960s

1. Structural Conduciveness
       Advancing incomes and education
       Advancing complexity of technology and marketing
       Advancing exploitation of the environment

2. Structural Strains
       Economic discontent (inflation)
       Social discontent (war and race)
       Ecological discontent (pollution)
       Marketing system discontent (shoddy products, gimmickry, dishonesty)
       Political discontent (unresponsive politicians and institutions)

3. Growth of Generalized Belief
       Social critic writings (Galbraith, Packard, Carson)
       Consumer-oriented legislators (Kefauver, Douglas)
       Presidential messages
       Consumer organizations

5. Precipitating Factors
       Mass media coverage
       Vote-seeking politicians
       New consumer-interest groups and organizations

6. Social Control
       Business resistance or indifference
       Legislative resistance or indifference

Source: Reprinted by permission of the *Harvard Business Review*. Exhibit from "What
          Consumerism Means for Marketers" by Philip Kotler (May-June, 1972), p. 51.
          Copyright © 1972 by the President and Fellows of Harvard College. All rights
          reserved.

reason for this nonresponsiveness was singled out not as economics or inability
to respond, but as management's attitude that the company had always been
doing a fine job as far as the customer was concerned.[28]

The movement of consumerism is here to stay. The changing circumstances
require that the customer be treated differently than before. This would be possible only when consumerism becomes an ingredient in the decision-making process. Thus, products below minimum acceptable levels of quality should not be
sold, or at least sold only when the customers are informed about it. Similarly,
right and sufficient information should be duly incorporated into promotion
decisions. Consumerism should be embraced on ethical grounds, and in the long
run only an ethically run business can hope to be profitable. If the business fails

---

[28]Frederick E. Webster, Jr., "Does Business Misunderstand Consumerism?" *Harvard Business Review,* Vol. 51 (September-October, 1973), pp. 89–97.

to adopt consumerism, government may be forced to protect consumers' interests legally. The following criteria might be employed by a firm to judge for itself if it has fulfilled the consumerism constraint:

1. The overriding objective of all company responses should be to ensure a satisfied customer in a manner consistent with the public welfare.

2. The essential ingredients in consumer satisfaction are a product that works and an informed customer.

3. There are five mutually supporting ways of ensuring that a product works. These include (a) anticipating customer mistakes and designing them out; (b) informing the consumer about proper product use and care through advertising, packaging, labelling, and other educational programs; (c) establishing warranty and guarantee provisions that are clear, complete, and honest; and (d) maintaining a completely effective service organization.

4. An informed consumer has both good product information and expectations that are realistic.

5. Consumers are more concerned about products and their performance than about companies per se.

6. The essence of effective response to consumerism is an integrated program of product quality, service, and customer information, supported by top management with high-level responsibility for consumer affairs.[29]

The logical course for a firm interested in responding to consumerism is to voluntarily take action on issues where there is a general acceptance of needs and the cost of implementing solutions is not too great. These issues would include product information, health and safety standards, repair and servicing warranties, and product quality. Actions taken by companies on these issues could be very beneficial in terms of long-run company goals.

Overall, businesses should act so as not to expose consumers to abuses in the marketplace. Voluntary action by corporations is slowly gaining momentum. Gillette has established an office of vice president for product integrity to overlook the safety and quality of all 850 Gillette products. This office has been accorded so much power that in 1973 it instigated the $1.5 million recall of two new Gillette antiperspirants because of questions about the long-term effects of inhaling the zirconium in them. The recall was undertaken despite the fact that it publicly embarrassed Gillette and irritated Procter & Gamble Company and Carter-Wallace Inc., both of which sell zirconium antiperspirants of their own and say they are safe.[30]

---

[29]*Ibid.*
[30]Richard Martin, "Gillette's Giovacchini Rules on the Quality, Safety of 850 Products," *The Wall Street Journal,* December 12, 1975, p. 1.

In 1976 Sears, Roebuck & Co. gave a new perspective to its catalog. Instead of using such statements as, "This versatile casual shoe puts you right in step with fall," the text of the new ad listed only such information as construction, size, and color.[31]

If businesses do not respond, government forces will undoubtedly act. Already the government has enacted many laws, as shown in Exhibit 4-4, to promote fair play in the marketplace. To illustrate the nature of laws passed in response to consumerism, selective laws are discussed below. The Automobile Information Disclosure Act (1958) requires all new automobiles to display on their windows a pre-ticket by the manufacturer listing the basic price, federal tax, factory installed accessories, and retailer's service and delivery charges. The Consumer Credit Protection Act (1968), known as the "Truth-in-Lending Law," aims to increase consumer protection in the consumer credit and collection field by requiring lenders to state the true interest rate and other costs of a credit transaction. The Public Health Cigarette Smoking Act, among other things, declared that starting November 1, 1970, cigarette packages must have this notice printed on them: "Warning: The Surgeon General Has Determined That Cigarette Smoking Is Dangerous to Your Health," This act also banned advertising of cigarettes on electronic communications media after January 1, 1971. The Consumer Product Safety Act (1972) has been held as the most far-reaching consumer-oriented law regulating marketing practice since the Federal Trade Commission Act of 1914. This act created an independent Consumer Product Safety Commission which has powers to prescribe mandatory safety standards for virtually all consumer products except those for which specific safety legislation already exists. The Commission is authorized to inspect manufacturing operations, subpoena records, and require compliance tests. It can ban the sale of products, require manufacturers to perform safety tests and keep accident records, and require sellers to repair or recall unsafe products and to rebate the purchase price.

EXHIBIT 4-4   Legal Implications of Consumerism:
Selected Listing of Acts Designed in Consumers' Interest

1. Automobile Information Disclosure Act (1958)
2. National Traffic and Safety Act (1966)
3. Fair Packaging and Labeling Act (1966)
4. Federal Cigarette Labeling and Advertising Act (1967)
5. Consumer Credit Protection Act (1968)
6. Toy Safety Act (1969)
7. National Environmental Policy Act (1969)
8. Public Health Cigarette Smoking Act (1970)
9. Consumer Product Safety Act (1972)

---

[31]"Sears to Pull Puffery from New Catalog, May Do It in Ads," *The Wall Street Journal,* November 18, 1975, p. 5.

The essential legacy of consumerism promises to be beneficial in the long run. It forces business to reexamine its social role. Here are some of the implications of consumerism:

1. Consumerism may increase the amount of product information publicly available, which should help consumers to buy more efficiently.
2. Consumerism may lead to legislation limiting promotional expenditures. Proponents claim that this should help reduce prices for the ultimate consumer.
3. Consumerism may improve the information flow in the form of product performance characteristics, simple language warranty specifications, and safety standards, making it possible for consumers to do shopping more prudently than now.
4. Consumerism may help in reducing the number of unsafe or unhealthy products.[32]

LIMITS OF GROWTH

The world is experiencing a surge of economic growth unprecedented in human history. Simultaneously, however, population is doubling every 30 years. The rates of pollution generation, mineral resource depletion, power production, and destruction of natural areas are accelerating even faster than the population rate. Thus, we are faced with an inevitable transition from worldwide growth to global ecological equilibrium. The shift from growth to dynamic balance may be initiated by some catastrophe such as a global epidemic, war, or starvation. Alternatively, transition could result from an enlightened, concerted, international effort to adopt new values and define new goals.[33] These are the conclusions of a study on world situation undertaken by a team of experts at M.I.T. The study was sponsored by an international elite under the auspices of the Club of Rome (a meeting in Rome led to decision on the study, and gave the group its name). The recent energy crisis attests to the conclusions of the Club of Rome study.

The above study suggests that growth should not be understood as a linear function, something built into the American economic system; growth should be considered in the context of the entire system. It would, therefore, be wrong to assume that sales will continue to rise year after year and that there are no limitations to growth except in the number of customers that can be served at one time. If we accept the findings of the Club of Rome study, the factors of production can no longer be considered in abundance; therefore, different marketing strategies may have to be followed in the future. For example, the firm may have to devote efforts towards demarketing—the reverse of marketing. What the Club

---

[32]Philip Kotler, "What Consumerism Means for Marketers," *Harvard Business Review,* Vol. 56 (May-June, 1972), p. 57.
[33]Donella H. Meadows *et al., The Limits of Growth* (New York: Universe Bks., 1973).

of Rome study has found may not come to pass within one generation or two and thus may not be very relevant to current marketing decisions. In any event, at least philosophically, the thesis mentioned above would be useful in making marketing decisions more socially relevant.

POPULATION

The Department of Commerce statistics show that in the year 1995 the U.S. population will be 252.8 million people, compared to 215.01 million in 1976 (Exhibit 4-5). Historically the annual growth rate of the U.S. population has fluctuated between approximately 1.5 and 1.75 percent. However, toward the middle of the 1970s a downward trend started when the rate dropped to .75 percent; the growth rate is expected to remain below 1 percent up to 1995.

Exhibit 4-5 indicates that about 15 years from now there will be approximately 30 million more Americans. However, the age group 40 and over will grow three times as much as the group 39 and under. More specifically, the group between the ages of 40 and 64 will grow faster than all the other age groups in the population.

Using the above figures as a base, we can state that while during the next decade total population will grow by about 10 percent, there will be proportionately fewer teenagers, more young adults, far more middle-aged adults, and more older adults. Families will tend to be smaller, and a higher proportion of the total population will be working.

Generally business people view slowing down of the population growth rate with some concern since most of them associate more people with more customers, more customers with more sales, and more sales with more profit. In many situations these associations do in fact exist. For example, the total number of cars sold may depend on the total population. But there is no necessary association among population, customers, sales and profit. A lower population growth rate might mean that income per U.S. resident is considerably higher. Thus, with a slower growth rate business people might have approximately the same number of customers as previously, but these customers would have increasingly more purchasing power, and it is purchasing power that counts. What this means is that the total number of cars sold may decrease when population growth rate declines, yet customers may buy higher-priced cars; consequently, total expenditure on cars may actually increase.

To operate within the context of declining population growth and changing age-mix, business will require a new strategic perspective in all areas of marketing —offering, distribution, promotion, and price. Thus a magazine like *Playboy* may reposition itself from serving the post-adolescent group (now its prime target) to serving the adult population. This may be done by emphasizing more sophisticated copy with less fantasy and more useful advice on vacations, investments, and clothes. As the teenage population subsides, a soft-drink company like Coca-Cola may concentrate on diet drinks and citrus-flavored drinks used as mixers.

EXHIBIT 4-5   Population by Broad Age Groups
(Millions of Persons)

		Age Group				
Year	**Total Population**	**Under 5**	**5–17**	**18–39**	**40–64**	**65 and Over**
1920	106.5	11.6	28.0	38.3	23.7	4.9
1925	115.8	12.3	30.2	40.9	26.6	5.8
1930	123.1	11.4	31.6	43.7	29.6	6.7
1935	127.3	10.2	31.4	45.2	32.7	7.8
1940	132.1	10.6	29.8	47.7	35.1	9.0
1945	139.9	13.0	28.6	49.8	38.1	10.5
1950	152.3	16.4	30.9	51.5	41.1	12.4
1955	165.9	18.6	37.2	51.1	44.6	14.5
1960	180.7	20.3	44.2	51.6	47.9	16.7
1965	194.3	19.8	49.9	54.8	51.3	18.5
1970	204.9	17.1	52.5	61.1	54.0	20.1
1975	213.5	15.9	50.4	70.1	54.7	22.4
1976	215.1	15.3	49.9	72.1	54.9	22.9
Projections:						
1980	222.2	16.0	46.0	79.7	55.6	24.9
1985	232.9	18.8	43.5	85.0	58.3	27.3
1990	243.5	19.4	45.3	85.5	63.4	29.8
1995	252.8	18.8	49.6	82.2	70.7	31.4

Source: Helen Axel, ed., *A Guide to Consumer Markets, 1977/1978* (New York: Conference
Bd., 1977), p. 180.

Impact of population change on distribution is well described by a Federated Department Stores executive who asserts that people in their 30s in 1985 will be much more self-confident, discriminating, and less likely to follow the masses. For this reason the Federated stores expect to go into greater specialization within each store, by adding new departments concentrating more on the fashion business and on utilitarian goods, and de-emphasizing hardware and major appliances.[34] The number of women holding jobs in industry may increase because, among other reasons, women will be having fewer children. Via this route population change will affect promotion by companies like Procter & Gamble that now

[34]"How the Changing Age Mix Changes Markets," *Business Week* (January 12, 1976), p. 74.

reach the customers by advertising grooming and cleaning products on daytime television. If more women are spending their days at the office or factory, they will have to be reached in an alternative manner. Pricing decisions will also be affected by population mix. A family with fewer members will be better able to improve the quality of its life and, therefore, will purchase wholesome products and services, irrespective of the price tags. Thus it is not the price, but the adequacy of the product, that will dominate. For example, the Institute of Life Insurance has suggested that insurance companies offer policies that would stay in force during periods of up to two years without premium payments for those who want to take occasional breaks from work. Similarly, Citibank of New York, in response to demographic changes, consolidated all of its consumer financial services together into one group at slightly higher prices. The expectation is that when a consumer takes out a mortgage or opens a credit card account, that contract can be used to sell other programs.[35]

LOCATION OF CONSUMERS

Ours is a land of urban dwellers. In 1960 about two thirds of the U.S. population could be said to be urbanized; in 1970 the proportion was close to three quarters. Large-scale urban growth is leading to the formation of megalopolises, sprawling population belts in which urban areas, once clearly defined, tend to blend into each other. The process of megalopolis formation has been going on for decades. But it is now in such an advanced stage that the top 50 metropolitan areas, which make up the megalopoles, account for about half the U.S. population.

The largest megalopolis runs from Boston to Washington, D.C., a 10-state, 450-mile-long corridor which constitutes 38 million people, or one sixth of the nation. Other megalopoles are: San Francisco to San Diego; Buffalo, New York to Green Bay, Wisconsin; and the Florida peninsula extending down both coasts.

Another interesting geographic development taking place is the varying rate of population growth in different states. Exhibit 4-6 projected that during the period 1970–1980, population growth in only five states (Arizona, California, Nevada, Florida, and Maryland) would exceed 20 percent.

Alaska, Colorado, Connecticut, Delaware, New Hampshire, New Jersey, Oregon, Utah, and Washington were expected to grow between 15 to 20 percent during the years 1970–1980. North Dakota and West Virginia were likely to register a decline. Shifts in the geographic distribution of population will have a bearing on life-styles as a result of geographic conditions such as climate and regional social norms and customs.

For marketers the geographic location of consumers is highly meaningful. Most of the action in our trillion-dollar economy will take place in the urban

---

[35]*Ibid.*

EXHIBIT 4-6 Projected Population Growth by States
Percent Change, 1970 to 1980

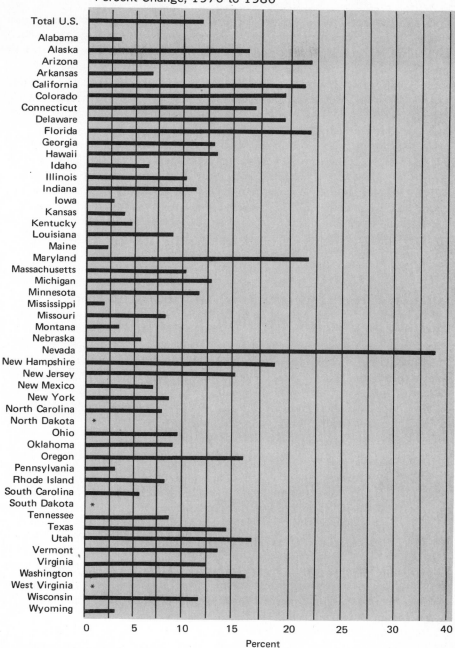

*Projected declines: North Dakota—2.9%, South Dakota—1.2%, and West Virginia—6.3%.

Source: Helen Axel, ed., *A Guide to Consumer Markets, 1977/1978* (New York: Conference Bd., 1977), p. 72.

areas. The urban areas, it is expected, will account for at least 80 percent of all residential construction in the 1980s and will be responsible for the bulk of expenditures for transportation facilities. Further, urban residents are more adventurous as consumers. The consumers in major metropolitan areas, on a per capita basis, are considerably more likely than those in rural areas to buy a long list of goods and services such as automobile rentals, air transportation, liquor, eye makeup, hair coloring, high-priced dresses, stockings, shoes, women's underwear, butter, canned Chinese goods, packaged cookies, frozen cakes, instant breakfast and tea.[36] However, the distinction between rural and urban areas is fast changing; new combined urban areas are emerging. For example, Cleveland and Akron are considered one urban area. So are Miami and Fort Lauderdale.[37] Marketers, therefore, have to determine how the demand for different products changes as urbanization spreads and also how to organize distribution such that newly emerging urban areas may be served adequately. For example, a new store location decision achieves a strategic significance in the midst of changing geographic patterns.

State-by-state growth patterns may also have far-reaching effects on marketing strategy. In terms of product decisions, the growth of sunny states—Florida, California, Arizona—augurs well for products such as suntan lotion, swimsuits, tennis rackets, swimming pools, bicycles, boats, and so on. By the same token, statewide distribution of population has direct relevance to channels of distribution decision since the channels must be developed to provide coverage to the customer, either through the firm's sales branches or through the middlemen's efforts. Formerly, Arizona and Nevada, for example, could probably be served by a warehouse in California. But changing population patterns in these and neighboring states may indicate the desirability of establishing a distribution center in either of these two states.

INCOME

Income is a determinant of ability to buy; thus, it achieves significance. Before discussing income distribution in the United States, it will be useful to gain insights into the different types of incomes which one usually reads about in business and economic writings. The four types of incomes which should be understood are: national income, personal income, disposable income, and discretionary income. *National income* is a macro-economic concept meaning total income of a nation from all sources. Thus, the national income of the United States will constitute all types of income earned by individuals, including employee compensation and corporate profits. *Personal income* is the income that accrues to an individual from all sources. *Disposable income* is the income available to an individual after payment of taxes and other deductions (something in

---

[36]"The Evolution of a Super-Urban Nation," *Business Week* (October 17, 1976), p. 76.
[37]"How the Changing Age Mix Changes Markets," *op. cit.*

the nature of take-home pay). *Discretionary income* is the portion of disposable income left to an individual after paying for essential items such as food, clothing, housing, and transportation.

In the U.S. more than any other nation in the world, a greater proportion of the population has a larger portion of its total income as discretionary income. It is the discretionary dollar that consumers use to buy a vacation, a vacation home, new gadgets, and similar other products and services.

There is no doubt that America is an affluent country and that the future years will see a continuation of the postwar trends towards higher per capita income and hence a steadily rising standard of living. As shown in Exhibit 4-7, by the year 1985 over 30 percent of the families in the country will fall into the income group $25,000 and over, compared to only 14 percent of the families in 1975. Stated differently, in 1985 over half of all incomes will be in the category $25,000

EXHIBIT 4-7   Projections of Families and Income by Income Class
(Percent Distribution, Based on 1975 Dollars)

Income Class	1975	1980	1985
Families (Millions)	56.2	61.2	66.3
Families (Percent)	100.0	100.0	100.0
Under $5,000	12.1	8.5	6.9
$5,000–10,000	21.2	16.2	14.7
10,000–15,000	22.3	18.9	16.3
15,000–20,000	18.7	18.0	17.0
20,000–25,000	11.6	14.4	15.1
25,000–35,000	9.0	15.0	18.2
35,000–50,000	3.6	6.2	8.0
50,000 and over	1.4	2.8	3.9
Income (Percent)	100.0	100.0	100.0
Under $5,000	2.4	1.3	1.0
$5,000–10,000	10.2	6.4	5.2
10,000–15,000	17.8	12.3	9.6
15,000–20,000	20.8	16.4	14.0
20,000–25,000	16.5	16.9	16.0
25,000–35,000	16.4	22.7	25.8
35,000–50,000	9.6	13.1	15.3
50,000 and over	6.3	10.9	13.2

Source: Helen Axel, ed., *A Guide to Consumer Markets, 1977/1978* (New York: Conference Bd., 1977), p. 134.

and over, compared to less than one third in 1975. All these calculations are in
1975 dollars with no inflation built in.

It is not only total income that is going up. There is a simultaneous rise in
supernumerary income, the income over the spending of which the consumer
exercises a choice, as opposed to necessary expenditures on food, shelter, and
other basic necessities. In 1955, as shown in Exhibit 4-8, about 4 percent of the
total family income was supernumerary income, which reached 16 percent in
1980 (in 1974 dollars). In 1955, 5 percent of families were considered to have
supernumerary income, while in 1980 almost one third of all the families had such
income (not shown in the exhibit).

EXHIBIT 4-8   Supernumerary Income
After-tax Figures in 1974 Dollars

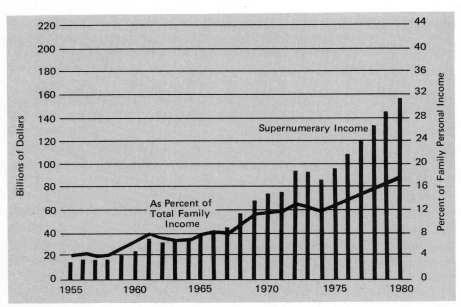

Note: Data are preliminary. The term *supernumerary income,* as used here, refers to that share
of consumer income which is not needed for the essentials and is available for optional
spending. Specifically, it consists of all income in excess of $20,000 a year flowing to each
family unit. The supernumerary income series represents a general measure of rising consumer
affluence. Projections are based on a 4 percent annual growth in real personal income.

Source: Helen Axel, ed., *A Guide to Consumer Markets, 1977/1978* (New York: Conference
Bd., 1977), p. 146.

As a matter of fact, today an individual uses discretion not only in deciding
how to spend income, but also in determining whether more income is wanted:

. . . income has become discretionary in a radically new sense: increasingly, the *size* of a family's income—and not just the way it is allocated

—is a matter of discretion. Instead of spending being a function of income, as John Maynard Keynes argued, income is becoming a function of spending, or, more precisely, of the consumption pattern or life-style that people want to achieve or maintain. In order to live and consume in the desired manner, families may elect to raise their income: wives go to work; husbands moonlight or work overtime; and either may enroll in courses or training programs that enable them to move up the income ladder.[38]

A retailer notes that the number of purchases of furs more than triple as income moves from $10,000 to $15,000, and they increase by a factor of five when income passes $15,000. Spending on boats triples when income is above $10,000 and doubles again after $15,000. The $15,000-and-over consumers also spend three times the amount that $10,000 householders spend on movies, concerts, and plays and five times as much on travel.[39] While the figures used here come from an older source, they do communicate the importance of rising incomes for marketers. In brief, with rising incomes people buy more things that they do not really need, but that please them and complement their life-styles. How does income affect a marketer? The existence of income means that the marketing function of exchange will take place. In other words, income represents the potential for exchange.

The largest segment of the population is called the middle class. As the number of middle-class families increases, intensive distribution of many products becomes feasible. With rising incomes (as more families join the middle-class ranks), for example, a locale may be able to support a large department store. As the mass market develops as a result of rising incomes, a manufacturer may find advertising on a national level more feasible. By the same token, a manufacturer may find itself expanding enough so that taking on the wholesalers' job becomes financially reasonable.

Product planning takes on new dimensions as consumer income changes. As income rises, more is spent on goods, up to a point. Thereafter, services achieve significance. For example, rising incomes have given a boost to the airline industry. Also, rising incomes bring to a larger population goods and services which were hitherto limited to a few people. As more goods and services are demanded, marketing managers must offer a greater variety; thus more research, both on what consumers want and on how to develop products that satisfy these demands, becomes important.

Income levels have an intimate tie to prices since they serve as an important input in what the consumer will buy. People in high income groups buy the products that provide a psychological satisfaction that reflect their social standing. Thus, a bottle of liquor directed toward the high income group must have

---

[38]Charles E. Silberman, " 'Identity Crisis' in the Consumer Markets," *Fortune,* Vol. LXXVII (March, 1971), p. 94.
[39]"What Makes the New Consumer Buy," *Business Week* (April 24, 1971), p. 55.

a high price. A newer view of the relationship between pricing and income may be seen in nonprofit organizations. Their products are often "priced" at what they can convince the public (the individual consumer) those products or services are worth, just as are the goods offered by the retailer. The value of donations, however, directly relates to income and often to cash on hand. The greater the total income, the greater the discretionary income, and the easier it probably is to convince the customer that $5.00 for the Girl Scouts is more valuable than $5.00 for a movie. Promotional efforts would also be dictated by the level of income of the market segment that is being aimed at. Saks Fifth Avenue's "seasonal reductions" might in fact be the same promotion as Penney's "EOM sale", but the income levels of their customers, and supposedly their preferences in vocabulary, do vary.

A further example of the relationship between income and marketing is that marketing has been concerned with creating demands or at least with raising expectations of what is available. To the extent that this affects the consumer's expenditures, perhaps by encouraging use of credit cards, charge accounts, etc., marketing has increased available income. Too much encouragement, however, could lead to overextension, which in turn could lead to the bankruptcy of the consumer, and this in turn may affect the business' income.

EXPENDITURE PATTERNS

Measured in real terms, consumer spending for goods and services will be up about 60 percent between 1973 and 1988. The biggest gain in percentage terms is expected in services, up 65 percent; followed by durable goods, up 60 percent; and nondurable goods, up 56 percent.[40]

The components of consumer expenditures are shown in Exhibit 4-9. Between 1950 and 1976, expenditures in the areas of furniture and equipment and gasoline and oil more than tripled; housing expenditures almost quadrupled during the same period.

The last two columns of Exhibit 4-10 show the income elasticity ratios, i.e., percentage change in personal expenditures for each one percent rise in real disposable personal income. Income elasticity ratios have always been highest for radios, TV, records, and instruments.

Consider Exhibit 4-11(a), which provides statistical data pertaining to dishwashers. With this data the marketing manager could begin to segment the market using as a base historical expenditure patterns in relationship to income distribution and age.

Average expenditures per household, in dollars, indicate that families with incomes of $5,000-$10,000 spent $3 in 1974 toward the purchase of dishwashers and those with incomes of $15,000–$20,000 spent $18, while the average household spent only $10 (data taken from another source). Exhibit 4-11(b) indicates

---

[40] *The American Economy: Prospects for Growth to 1988* (New York: McGraw-Hill Int. Bk. Co., 1975).

EXHIBIT 4-9   Components of Consumer Expenditures

Year	TOTAL	Food, Beverages	Clothing, Shoes	Housing	Household Operation	Furniture, Equipment	Motor Vehicles, Parts	Gasoline, Oil
				Billions of Dollars				
1960	324.9	81.1	26.7	48.1	20.1	17.7	19.7	12.0
1965	430.2	98.9	33.5	65.5	26.3	24.7	29.8	14.7
1966	464.8	106.6	36.6	69.5	28.0	27.7	30.1	16.0
1967	490.4	109.6	38.2	74.1	30.6	29.5	29.7	17.0
1968	535.9	118.3	41.8	79.9	32.7	32.6	35.8	18.4
1969	579.7	126.1	45.1	86.8	35.5	35.0	37.7	20.4
1970	618.8	136.3	46.6	94.0	38.3	36.7	34.9	22.0
1971	668.2	140.6	50.5	102.7	41.6	39.4	43.8	23.4
1972	733.0	150.4	55.1	112.3	45.9	44.8	50.6	24.9
1973	809.9	168.1	61.3	123.2	50.2	50.7	55.2	27.8
1974	887.5	189.9	65.1	136.4	56.1	54.7	47.9	36.3
1975	973.2	209.5	70.0	150.2	63.9	57.6	53.2	38.9
1976	1,079.7	224.4	75.4	165.8	72.1	63.0	70.7	41.5
				Billions of 1976 Dollars				
1950	448.7	129.6	36.2	47.0	25.0	20.5	27.8	13.3
1955	524.3	148.3	39.6	62.1	31.0	23.0	34.6	18.5
1960	601.1	163.9	43.2	79.0	38.0	23.8	32.8	23.3
1965	740.6	185.6	52.2	100.7	46.6	33.6	45.8	27.6
1970	887.6	208.9	58.1	126.0	59.0	45.5	47.7	36.9
1975	1,022.2	213.4	72.3	158.7	68.9	59.8	57.5	40.7
1976	1,079.7	224.4	75.4	165.8	72.1	63.0	70.7	41.5

Source: Helen Axel, ed., *A Guide to Consumer Markets, 1977/1978* (New York: Conference Bd., 1977), p. 160.

that 42.9 percent of those with incomes between $15,000 and $20,000 own or have the availability of a dishwasher. An appliance manufacturer could initially segment the dishwasher market, considering those households with incomes of $15,000 plus per year to be the most likely customers. Then by looking at the age distribution the market could be narrowed further. The age groups 25–34 and 35–44 spent an average of $15 each on dishwasher purchases; those in the 55–64 age group spent $7; in comparison, the national average was $6. In percentages, 31.8 percent of those 25–34 owned a dishwasher; 41.4 percent of

EXHIBIT 4-10   The Pattern of Growth in Consumer Spending, 1960–1975

Average Annual Growth Rates and Income Elasticity Ratios, Selected Items, Based on Constant Dollars

Item	Average Annual Growth Rates 1960– 1975	1967– 1975	Income Elasticity Ratios[1] 1960– 1975	1967– 1975
DISPOSABLE PERSONAL INCOME	4.0	3.3	1.00	1.00
PERSONAL CONSUMPTION EXPENDITURES	3.8	3.2	.95	.97
Durable Goods[2]	5.9	4.8	1.46	1.44
Automobile Purchase	4.0	2.1	.99	.65
Tires, Tubes, Accessories, Parts	4.9	6.6	1.22	2.00
Furniture, Bedding	3.8	3.1	.94	.95
Kitchen, Other Household Appliances	6.0	5.9	1.48	1.78
China, Glassware, Other Durable Hsfgs	6.7	5.8	1.66	1.76
Radios, TV, Records, Instruments	12.2	8.9	3.01	2.69
Wheel Goods, Durable Toys, Sport Equip.	9.6	7.3	2.38	2.20
Nondurable Goods[2]	2.9	2.2	.71	.65
Food, Beverages at Home	2.0	.7	.50	.20
Purchased Meals, Beverages	2.1	2.2	.52	.67
Food Only (excl. Alcoholic Beverages)	1.9	.8	.47	.24
Alcoholic Beverages	2.6	2.4	.63	.73
Tobacco	1.0	1.5	.24	.46
Shoes, Other Footwear	2.6	2.3	.64	.70
Women's, Children's Clothing	3.6	4.0	.90	1.22
Men's, Boys' Clothing (incl. Military)	3.5	3.2	.88	.96
Gasoline, Oil	4.5	3.9	1.11	1.19
Toilet Articles, Preparations	5.8	3.0	1.43	.92
Semidurable Housefurnishings	5.9	5.2	1.45	1.58
Household Supplies, Preparations	5.1	2.3	1.27	.69
Drug Preparations, Sundries	5.4	5.2	1.33	1.56
Services[2]	4.2	3.7	1.03	1.12
Housing: Owner-Occupied (Nonfarm)	5.0	5.1	1.23	1.53
Housing: Renter-Occupied (Nonfarm)	4.6	4.4	1.14	1.31
Household Operation Services, Total	4.2	3.5	1.03	1.04
Electricity	5.9	5.7	1.46	1.72
Gas	3.1	1.4	.76	.43
Telephone	7.8	7.1	1.92	2.13
Auto Transportation Services	4.9	4.8	1.21	1.44
Purchased Local Transportation	−2.8	−2.8	−.68	−.84
Purchased Intercity Transportation	5.6	2.5	1.39	.74
Medical Care Services	5.4	5.6	1.33	1.69
Personal Care Services	−.5	−3.7	−.12	−1.11
Admissions to Spectator Amusements	1.3	2.5	.33	.75
Higher Education	4.6	2.3	1.13	.71
Foreign Travel, U.S. Residents	5.3	2.5	1.30	.77

Note: Growth rates are based on exponential trend growth.
[1] Percentage change in personal consumption expenditures for each 1% rise in real disposable personal income.
[2] Includes items not separately listed.
Source: Helen Axel, ed., *A Guide to Consumer Markets, 1977/1978* (New York: Conference Bd., 1977), p. 170.

EXHIBIT 4-11(a)   Household Expenditures for Selected Durable Goods,
1974
Average Expenditures per Household, for New Purchases,
in Dollars

	Income Class					
Item	**Under $5,000**	**$5,000– 10,000**	**$10,000– 15,000**	**$15,000– 20,000**	**$20,000– 25,000**	**Over $25,000**
TOTAL EXPENDITURES	76	131	184	212	231	255
Washing Machine	10	19	26	29	33	32
Clothes Dryer	5	9	16	18	22	22
Dishwasher	2	3	10	18	19	24

	Age of Head					
	Under 25	**25–34**	**35–44**	**45–54**	**55–64**	**65 and Over**
TOTAL EXPENDITURES	171	209	202	174	141	87
Washing Machine	27	29	28	23	20	10
Clothes Dryer	18	19	17	14	9	5
Dishwasher	3	15	15	13	7	3

Source: Helen Axel, ed., *A Guide to Consumer Markets, 1977/1978* (New York: Conference
Bd., 1977), pp. 191–192.

those 35–44 owned the appliance; 38.1 percent of those 45–54 owned one. The national average was 21.3 percent. On the basis of this limited information alone, the marketing manager could begin to tailor his marketing plan toward those potential customers between the ages of 25 and 54 with incomes greater than $15,000. The marketing mix may then be developed to serve this segment.

The travel service business can also use and interpret statistical data to benefit from customer expenditure patterns. Government data reveals that families with incomes of $15,000 and over, whose heads are professionals or craft workers, live in metropolitan areas, are between the ages of 25–54, and are at least high school graduates, are a travel bureau's most likely customers for both domestic and foreign travel.[41] If nothing else, this information may be helpful in the development of initial marketing strategy.

Perhaps more than any other type of business, the retail firm can benefit from careful analysis of the readily available spending pattern data. Information on virtually every aspect of the retail market, from size and location of markets, to

[41]Helen Axel (ed.), *A Guide to Consumer Markets, 1977/1978* (New York: Conference Bd., 1977), pp. 191–192.

EXHIBIT 4-11(b)   Household Availability of Durables by Selected
                   Characteristics, 1974
                   Percent of Households in Each Group Having Indicated
                   Items Available

	Income Class					
Item	Under $5,000	$5,000– 10,000	$10,000– 15,000	$15,000– 20,000	$20,000– 25,000	Over $25,000
TOTAL HOUSEHOLDS (Mil.)	15.4	17.2	15.9	9.7	5.2	7.1
Percent Having:						
Washing Machine	53.0	65.4	77.2	85.3	86.0	89.2
Clothes Dryer	23.6	40.6	60.9	72.1	76.3	82.2
Dishwasher	7.7	14.9	27.6	42.9	52.8	69.8

	Age of Head					
	Under 25	25–34	35–44	45–54	55–64	65 and Over
TOTAL HOUSEHOLDS (Mil.)	6.1	14.4	12.3	12.6	11.6	13.7
Percent Having:						
Washing Machine	44.1	69.0	83.3	81.7	77.1	63.8
Clothes Dryer	39.1	57.0	67.5	64.3	53.5	32.3
Dishwasher	14.1	31.8	41.4	38.1	25.5	12.8

Source: Helen Axel, ed., *A Guide to Consumer Markets, 1977/1978* (New York: Conference
        Bd., 1977), pp. 191–192.

income distribution, to sales by categories of product and retail establishment,
should provide guidance in planning and decision making. Looking at department
store sales data (1976) by merchandise lines, one finds that clothing accounted
for 41.7 percent of sales, major appliances for 8.1 percent, and draperies/dry
goods for 7.4 percent.[42] Matching this with the customer profile should help
indicate what items stores in various locations may stock, to whom they should
sell, and how they should promote the merchandise.

EDUCATION

Another interesting thing happening in our society is the emphasis on education. As shown in Exhibit 4-12, in 1960 more than one third of the persons
25 years and over had only elementary or less schooling. In 1985, however,
this number is expected to decline to less than 20 percent. On the other
hand, the number of college graduates will increase three times in the period
1960–1985.

---

[42]*Ibid.,* pp. 200–202.

EXHIBIT 4-12   Educational Attainment
                       Persons 25 Years and Over

Year	Total	Years of School Completed				
		Elementary or Less	Some High School	High School Graduate	Some College	College Graduate
Millions of Persons						
1940	74.8	45.2	11.4	10.7	4.1	3.4
1950	86.0	41.8	14.9	17.7	6.3	5.3
1955	91.3	38.0	16.3	23.3	6.9	6.8
1960	97.3	36.3	17.6	27.0	8.3	8.2
1965	103.2	34.0	18.6	31.7	9.1	9.7
1970	109.3	30.3	18.7	37.1	11.2	12.1
1975	116.9	25.5	18.2	42.4	14.5	16.2
1976	118.8	24.5	18.2	43.2	15.5	17.5
Projections:						
1980	128.5	23.5	20.9	48.7	16.1	19.3
1985	139.9	20.1	21.6	54.4	19.2	24.5
Percent Distribution						
1940	100.0	60.4	15.2	14.3	5.5	4.6
1950	100.0	48.6	17.3	20.6	7.3	6.2
1960	100.0	37.3	18.1	27.7	8.5	8.4
1970	100.0	27.8	17.0	34.0	10.3	11.1
1975	100.0	21.9	15.6	36.2	12.4	13.9
1976	100.0	20.6	15.3	36.3	13.0	14.7
Projections:						
1980	100.0	18.3	16.3	37.9	12.5	15.0
1985	100.0	14.4	15.4	38.9	13.7	17.5

Note: Series I (high series) projections.
Source: Department of Commerce.

The educated consumer will offer new opportunities and new challenges to marketers. Presumably, an educated person will be more selective in his choice of products and services than the one who does not have as much education. Thus, education, in addition to creating needs for products such as books, art, travel, and other cultural activities, may lead to consumers demanding quality products without frills. In addition, more education suggests that product promotion may have to be upgraded in both factual content and taste. Distribution may also be affected by education. For example, educated people may not mind buying store brands if the ingredients of a product are clearly stated on the package and if they find them to be in accordance with accepted health norms.

SUMMARY

The concept of marketing regards customers as the focal point of all decisions. The marketing strategies (i.e., product, distribution, promotion, and price) should be formulated to maximize customer satisfaction. The business, however, operates in an environment which limits the manager's decision making. Thus it will be more appropriate to say that a marketing manager should develop product, distribution, promotion, and price strategies within the limits imposed by the environment to provide maximum satisfaction to the customer. The environment refers to: social and cultural effects, political influences, ethical considerations, legal requirements, competition, economic climate, technological changes, institutional dynamics, consumerism, limits of growth, population, location of customers, income, expenditure patterns, and education.

Not all environmental variables are important in every decision situation. Besides, various strategic decisions will be affected differently by environmental variables. For example, politics may become an important factor in a decision to raise prices. On the other hand, the decision about bringing out a new model of an existing product may depend on the influence of technology.

DISCUSSION QUESTIONS

1. Discuss the relevance of environmental variables in developing product/market strategies.
2. Explain the significance of ethical considerations for a cigarette manufacturer.
3. Which social and cultural effects should a department store be aware of in order to serve its clientele?
4. What is consumerism? How does it become a constraint in formulating strategy?
5. In what ways does politics affect marketing strategy? Discuss with reference to a product.
6. Why should a firm be concerned with competition? Indicate how competition may influence strategy in each of these areas: product, price, distribution, and promotion. Give examples involving durable goods.
7. Should a company interested in introducing a new brand of fruit cereal concern itself with the effects of its advertising campaign on children? Why?
8. Choose three external environmental variables which in your opinion would be most relevant for a drug company to consider in developing strategy for a new headache pill.
9. Discuss how changes in consumer incomes may affect a frozen food product.
10. What relevance does the projection that the populations of states like Arizona and Nevada may grow faster in the future have for a brand of beer?

Chapter 5
Measuring Strengths and Weaknesses

To measure is the first step to improve.

Sir William Petty

A business does not perform well by accident. Good performances occur because the people directing its affairs interact well with the environment, capitalizing on the strengths and eliminating underlying weaknesses. In other words, to operate successfully in a changing environment, the business should plan its future objectives around its strengths and downplay moves which bear on its weaknesses. Thus, assessment of strengths and weaknesses becomes an essential task in the strategic process.

In this chapter a framework will be presented for identifying and describing a business' strengths and weaknesses. This framework provides a systematic scheme for an objective appraisal of the performance and strategic moves of the marketing side of business. It can also be used for identifying those perspectives which can be considered as strengths, and those which constitute weaknesses, for meeting the future.

Traditionally the appraisal of the marketing function has been pursued in the form of a marketing audit which stresses the review of current problems. From the strategic point of view, the review should go further to include the future as well. The importance of the measurement of strengths and weaknesses in the context of marketing strategy is well described by Alderson:

> The marketing executive may be visualized as operating on the basis of a sort of map. There are boundaries or limits marking off the class of customers he is trying to reach or the trade channels through which he is willing to sell. There are routes over which he can move in attaining his objectives which experience or investigation has indicated are better than other routes. This map may have to be brought up to date by a validation or a revision of operating assumptions . . .[1]

---

[1]Wroe Alderson, *Marketing Behavior and Executive Action* (Homewood, IL: Richard D. Irwin, 1957), p. 419.

Strengths and weaknesses in the context of marketing are a relative phenomenon. Strengths today may become weaknesses tomorrow and vice versa. This is why a penetrating look at the different aspects of a business' marketing program is essential. This chapter is directed toward this end (i.e., searching for opportunities and the means for exploiting them, as well as identifying weaknesses and the ways in which they may be eliminated).

MEANING OF STRENGTHS AND WEAKNESSES

Strengths refer to the competitive advantages and other distinctive competencies which the company can exert in the marketplace. Andrews notes:

> The distinctive competence of an organization is more than what it can do; it is what it can do particularly well. Thus, the hapless manufacturer of chocolate candy who finally lost his chain of candy stores was not really a surpassingly efficient retailer of candy. He just thought he was. His real skill lay in production, in his ability to design special machinery to permit quality production at low cost. The proper application of his real strengths would probably have confined him to manufacturing for wholesalers and supermarket chains.[2]

Weaknesses are constraints which hinder movements in certain directions. For example, a business short of cash cannot afford to undertake a large-scale promotional offensive. In developing marketing strategy, the business should, among other things, dig deeply into its skills and competencies and chart its future in accordance with these competencies.

STUDYING STRENGTHS AND WEAKNESSES: STATE OF THE ART

A systematic scheme for analyzing strengths and weaknesses is still in embryonic form. One hardly finds any scholarly work on the subject of strengths and weaknesses. The only formal study with which the author is familiar was done by Stevenson, who studied six companies. He was interested in the process of defining strengths and weaknesses in the context of strategic planning. He was concerned with the company attributes examined, the organizational scope of the strengths and weaknesses identified, the measurement employed in the process of definition, the criteria used for distinguishing a strength from a weakness, and the sources of information utilized. Stevenson found a general lack of agreement on suitable definitions, criteria, and information used to measure strengths and weaknesses.[3] Despite the primitive state of the art, however, the author's inter-

---

[2]Kenneth R. Andrews, *The Concept of Corporate Strategy* (Homewood, IL: Dow Jones-Irwin, 1971), pp. 97–98.
[3]Howard H. Stevenson, "Defining Corporate Strengths and Weaknesses: An Exploratory Study," an unpublished doctoral dissertation, Harvard Business School, 1969.

views with strategic planners indicate that many more companies review their strengths and weaknesses today than did ten years ago.

The strengths and weaknesses may be found in the functional areas of the business, or they may result from some unusual interaction of functions. According to Conrad, the strengths of a company may be varied and may include such factors as dealing with tough unions, living with unstable prices, exploiting new product ideas, being sensitive to customer needs, administering franchises, negotiating in secret, doing it oneself, making intuitive decisions, manipulating technical services, and having an investment know-how in distribution.[4]

The following example illustrates how a study of strengths and weaknesses may discover opportunities which otherwise may not have even been conceived of. A national distiller and marketer of whiskeys may possess such strengths as:

> . . . sophistication in natural commodity trading associated with its grain purchasing procedures; knowledge of complex warehousing procedures and inventory control; ability and connections associated with dealing in state political structures—i.e., state liquor stores, licensing agencies, and so on; marketing experience associated with diverse wholesale and retail outlets; advertising experience in creating brand images.[5]

If these strengths are properly analyzed with a view to seeking diversification opportunities for the whiskey distiller, it will appear that the distiller has unique abilities for successfully entering the business of selling building products, e.g., wood flooring or siding, composition board, and the like. This is because experience in commodity trading can be transferred to trading in lumber; experience in dealing with political groups can be used to gain building code acceptances; and experience in marketing can apply to wholesalers (e.g., hardware stores and do-it-yourself centers) of building products.

The Apeco Corporation case illustrates how a company can get into trouble if it does not carefully consider its strengths and weaknesses. Apeco is a Des Plaines, Illinois company. It has a penchant for diversifying into businesses that are in vogue in the stock market. It has been, or still is, in the following businesses: office copying machines, mobile homes, recreational vehicles, speed boats and cabin cruisers, computers, video recording systems, and small buses. Despite entry into some glamorous fields, Apeco did not share the growth and profits that other companies in some of these fields achieved. This is because Apeco entered new and diverse businesses without relating its moves to its basic skills and competencies. For example, despite the fact that it was the first company to develop a photocopy process, even before Xerox, its total market share for all types of copier machines and supplies is now well under 5%. Apeco could not

---

[4]Gordon R. Conrad, "Unexplored Assets for Diversification," *Harvard Business Review* (September-October, 1963), pp. 69–70.
[5]*Ibid.,* p. 71.

keep pace with the technological improvements and service on installed machines, essential in the copier business. In addition, it overextended itself so much that managerial controls were rendered inadequate.[6]

SYSTEMATIC APPROACH FOR MEASURING STRENGTHS AND WEAKNESSES

The strengths and weaknesses of a business can be measured at different levels in the organization. The scheme planned to be utilized in this book is shown in Exhibit 5-1. A major portion of the discussion will be devoted to the measurement of the marketing strengths and weaknesses of a product/market. The strengths and weaknesses of the strategic business unit (SBU) will be a composite of the strengths and weaknesses of different products. A *strategic business unit* is a part of a larger organization with a clear market focus and a manager who has complete responsibility for integrating all functions into a strategy. An SBU may be a division, a product department, or even a product line or major market. It is designated as a business unit because it is a self-contained business for which a strategic plan can be developed, balancing short- and long-term considerations; it also has an identifiable external competitor.

EXHIBIT 5-1   Levels for Measuring Marketing Strengths and Weaknesses

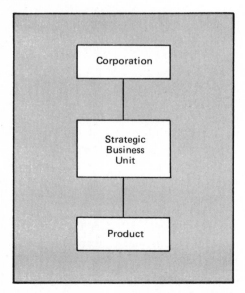

[6]"Apeco Puts Its Money on a Small Bus," *Business Week* (February 2, 1974), pp. 40–41.

In modern complex corporations, traditional structuring into groups and divisions has been found to be less than conducive to strategic planning. This is because different products or groups of products within a division may have different focuses, objectives, and potential. For this reason as strategic planning made inroads into corporations, many of them found it useful to break the organization into SBUs.

The strengths of different SBUs will culminate in corporate strengths (or weaknesses). Of course, at the corporate level there may be additional strengths of a general nature, such as those which were discussed in Chapter 3.

Exhibit 5-2 illustrates the factors which require examination in order to delineate the strengths and weaknesses of a product/market environment. These factors, along with the overall marketing effectiveness of the company, describe the strengths and weaknesses of the product.

EXHIBIT 5-2   Measurement of Product Strengths and Weaknesses

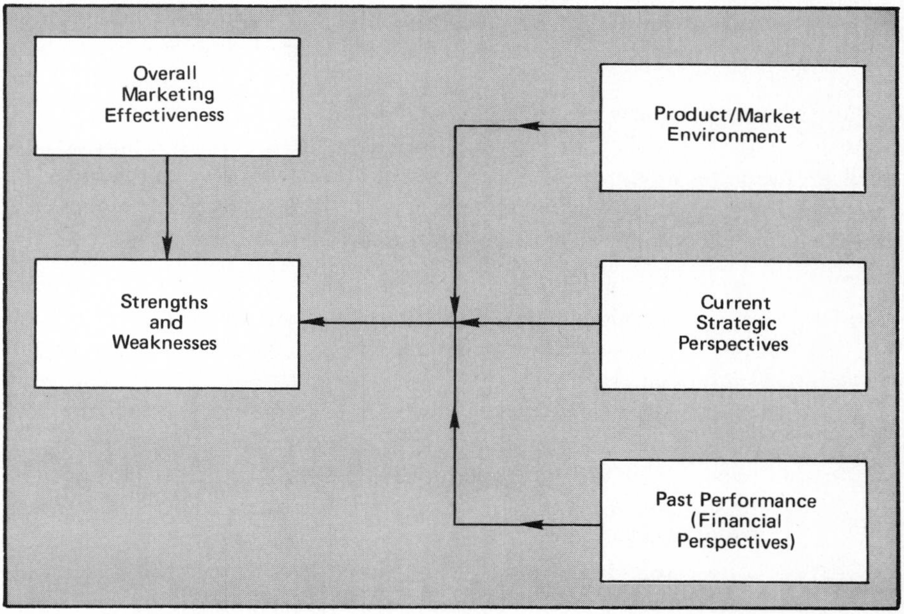

PRESENT STRATEGIC POSTURE

The present strategic posture constitutes a very important variable in developing future strategy. While it is difficult and painful to try to understand current strategy if formal planning has not been done in the past, it is worth the effort for a good beginning in strategic planning.

The emphasis here is on the study of the current strategy of a product/market. Before examining the present strategy of a product/market, however, it is desirable to gain company-wide perspectives by raising such questions as:

1. What underlies our company's success, given competitor's patterns of doing business?
2. Are there any characteristics and traits which have been followed regularly?
3. To what strategic posture do these characteristics and traits lead?
4. What are the critical factors which could make a difference in the success of the strategy?
5. To what extent are critical factors likely to undergo a change? What may be the direction of change?[7]

These questions cannot be answered entirely objectively; therefore, they call for creative responses. Often managers will have disagreements on various issues. For example, the vice-president of marketing of a company which had recently made a heavy investment in sales training considered this investment to be a critical factor in success. He thought well-trained salespeople would be more productive in listing new customers. On the other hand, the vice-president of finance claimed that the investment in training had increased overheads. Despite such problems, however, a review of current strategy is very important. The following operational scheme for studying current strategy from the point of view of the entire corporation has been found useful:

1. Begin with an identification of the actual current scope of the company's activities. The delineation of customer/product/market emphasis and concentration would give an indication of what kind of a company it is currently.
2. This analysis should be followed by identification of the pattern of actual past and existing resource deployments. This description would show which functions and activities have received the greatest management emphasis and where the greatest sources of strength currently lie.
3. Given the identification of scope and deployment patterns, an attempt should be made to deduce the actual basis on which the company has been competing. Such competitive advantages or distinctive competences represent the central core of present performance and future opportunities.
4. Next, on the basis of observation of key management personnel, the actual performance criteria (specifications), emphasis, and priorities

[7]*Perspectives on Corporate Strategy* (Boston: Boston Consulting Group, 1968), p. 42.

which have governed strategic choices in the past should be determined.[8]

Inasmuch as strategy by itself has no relevance, it must be tied to a purpose, division, or function. Thus, one needs a classification scheme for strategy. One can employ countless schemes for this purpose such as classification by major product lines, by divisions, by customers, or by functions. The discussion in this chapter is planned around classification by product/market.

Present Strategy of a Product/Market

As far as marketing is concerned, the strategy for a product is formulated around one or more marketing mix variables. In examining present strategy our purpose is to pinpoint those perspectives of the marketing mix which currently dominate strategy. The current strategy of a product may be examined by seeking answers to the following two questions:

1.   What markets do we have?
2.   How is each market served?

What Markets Do We Have?

1.   Recognize different market segments in which the product is sold.
2.   Build a demographic profile of each segment.
3.   Identify important customers in each segment.
4.   Identify also those customers who, while important, also do business with competitors.
5.   Reasons which each important customer may have in buying the product from us (i.e., customer's objectives in buying from us). These reasons may be economic (i.e., lower prices); functional (e.g., product features not available in competing products); and psychological (e.g., "this perfume matches my individual chemistry").
6.   Strategic perspective of each important customer as it concerns the product's purchase. This aspect will primarily be relevant for business customers. For example, an aluminum company should attempt to study the strategy which a can manufacturer may have as far as its aluminum can business is concerned. Suppose prices of aluminum are consistently rising, and more and more can manufacturers are replacing aluminum cans with cans of a new alloy of plastic and paper. Such strategic perspectives of the important customer, the can manufacturer in this case, should be examined.
7.   Anticipated changes in each customer's perspectives which may

---

[8]Robert L. Katz, *Cases and Concepts in Corporate Strategy* (Englewood Cliffs, NJ: Prentice-Hall, 1970), p. 210.

occur in the next few years. These changes may become necessary because of shifts in the customer's environment (both internal and external), abilities and resources.

The above information should, if properly analyzed, provide a good knowledge of customers: why they buy our products, and their likelihood of doing business with us in the future. For example, a paper manufacturer discovered that most customers did business with him because, in their opinion, his delivery schedules were most flexible. The quality of paper might have been superior too, but this was not strategically important for the customers.

How Is Each Market Served? The means which the company employs to serve its different customers may be studied by analyzing the information contained in Exhibit 5-3.

A careful examination of this information will reveal the current strategy which the company utilizes to serve its main markets. For example, analysis of the information in Exhibit 5-3 may reveal the following facts pertaining to a breakfast cereal:

> Of the seven different segments in the market, the product is extremely popular in two segments. Customers buy the product mainly for health reasons or because of their desire to be "natural." This desire is strong enough for them to pay a premium price for the product. Further, customers are willing to make a trip to another store (other than their regular grocery store) to buy this product. Different promotional devices keep the customers conscious of the "natural" ingredients of the product.

This may point toward the following strategy for the product:

1. Concentrate on limited segments.
2. Emphasize the naturalness of the product as its unique attribute.
3. Keep the prices high.
4. Pull the product through with heavy doses of consumer advertising.

Where strategy in the past has not been systematically formulated, recognition of current strategy will be more difficult. In such situations, strategy must be inferred from the perspectives of different marketing decisions.

The discussion above on present strategy of a product has been approached from two angles: which strategic aspects of the product are indeed valued by the customer, and what constitutes marketing strategy in the eyes of the company.

PAST PERFORMANCE

Evaluation of past performances is invaluable in measuring strengths and weaknesses since it provides historical insights into a company's marketing strategy and its success. Historical examination should not be limited to simply noting the directions the company adopted and the results it achieved, but should also

EXHIBIT 5-3   Information for Recognizing Present Marketing Strategy

1. Basis for segmenting the market
2. Definition of the markets for the product
3. Profile of customers in each segment: age, income level, occupation, geographical location, etc.
4. Scope and dimensions of each market: size, profitability, etc.
5. Expected rate of growth of each segment
6. Requirements for success in each market
7. Market standing with established customers in each segment: market share, pattern of repeat business, expansion of customer's product use
8. Benefits which customers in different segments derive from the product: economics, better performance, displaceable cost, etc.
9. Reasons for buying the product in different segments: product features, awareness, price, advertising, promotion, packaging, display, sales assistance, other
10. Customer attitudes in different segments: brand awareness, brand image (mapping), etc.
11. Overall reputation of the product in each segment
12. Purchase or use habits which contribute to these attitudes
13. Reasons which reinforce customer's faith in the company and product
14. Reasons which force customers to turn elsewhere for help in using the product
15. Life cycle status of the product
16. Story of the product line: quality development, delivery, service
17. Product research and improvements planned
18. Market share—overall and in different segments
19. Deficiencies in servicing or assisting customers in using the product
20. Possibility of reducing services in areas where customers are becoming more self-sufficient
21. Resource base: nature of emerging and developing resources—technical, marketing, financial—which could expand or open new markets for the product
22. Geographic coverage of the product market
23. Identification of principal channels (dealer or class of trade)
24. Buying habits and attitudes of these channels
25. Sales history through each type of channel
26. Industry sales by type of outlet (i.e., retail, wholesale, institutional, and further by major types of outlets within each area, i.e., department store, chain store, specialty store, etc.)
27. Overall price structure for the product
28. Trade discount policy
29. Variations in price in different segments
30. Frequency of price changes
31. Promotional deals offered for the product
32. Emphasis on different advertising media
33. Major thrust of advertising copy
34. Sales tips or promotional devices used by salespeople

include a search for reasons which may be behind the occurrence of these results. Exhibit 5-4 shows the type of information which is helpful in measuring past performance. In our discussion in this section we do not plan to deal with all the different types of information listed therein; market share and competitive analysis will be taken up in the next section. However, this exhibit recapitulates the type of past information which a company uses in its marketing planning efforts.

As far as marketing is concerned, the following three types of analysis should be undertaken to measure past performance: product performance profile, market performance profile, and financial performance profile.

Information utilized for developing a product performance profile is shown in Exhibit 5-5. A product may contribute to company performance in six different ways: through profitability, image of product leadership, furnishing a base for further technological growth, support of total product line, utilization of company resources (i.e., utilization of excess plant capacity), and provision of customer benefits (vis-a-vis the price paid). An example of this last type of contribution is a product which is a small but indispensable part of another product or process with low cost relative to the value of the whole finished product. Tektronics, Inc., manufacturer of oscilloscopes, is an example. When a computer is installed, an oscilloscope is sold along with it and is used to help set up the computer to test it, and to monitor its performance. The cost of the oscilloscope is small when one considers the essential role it plays in the use of the much more expensive computer.

The market performance profile is illustrated in Exhibit 5-6. In analyzing how well a company is doing in the segments it serves, a good place to begin is the marginal profit contribution of each customer or customer group. Other measures used here are market share, growth end-user markets, size of customer base, distribution strength, and degree of customer loyalty. Of all these, only distribution strength requires some explanation. Distribution and dealer networks can greatly influence a company's performance. This is because it takes an enormous effort to cultivate dealers' loyalty and get repeated business from them. Distribution strength, therefore, can make a significant difference in overall performance.

The real value of a strategy must be reflected in financial gains and market achievements. To measure financial performance, four types of standards may be employed for comparison. These are: 1) the company's performance, 2) competitors' performance, 3) management expectations, and 4) performance in terms of resources committed. With these standards, for the purposes of marketing planning and strategy, financial performance can be measured with respect to the following variables:

1. Growth rate (percentage)
2. Profitability (percentage), i.e., rate of return on investment
3. Market share (percentage as compared with principal competitors)
4. Cash flow

EXHIBIT 5-4   General Foods: Post Division
Historical and Supporting Data for Marketing Plans

A. The Consumer

Identify if possible the current "light," "moderate," and "heavy" user of the product in terms of:
   1. Recent trends in % of brand's volume accounted for by each group.
   2. The characteristics of each group as to sex, age, income, occupation, income group, geographical location.
   3. Attitudes towards the product and category and copy appeals most persuasive to each group.

B. The Product

Identify the current consumer preference of the brand versus primary competition (and secondary competition if available), according to:
   1. Light, moderate, heavy usage (if available).
   2. The characteristics of each group as to sex, age, income, occupation, income group, geographical location, size of family, etc.

C. Shipment History

Identify the recent shipment trends on the brand by total units and units/M population (brand development) according to districts, regions, and nationally.

D. Spending History

Identify the recent spending trends on the brand by total dollars, dollar/M population, per unit sold for advertising, for promotion, and for total A & P by districts, regions, and nationally.

E. Profitability History

Identify the recent trends of list price, average retail price (by sales areas), gross profit margins, and PBT *in addition* to trends in:
   1. Gross profit as % of net sales.
   2. Total marketing as % of gross profit and per unit sold.
   3. PBT as % of net sales and per unit sold.
   4. ROFE (Return of Funds Employed) for each recent fiscal year.

F. Share of Market History

Identify recent trends of:
   1. The brands of share-of-market nationally, regionally, district-wide.
   2. Consumption by total units and % gain/loss versus year ago nationally, regionally, district-wide.
   3. Distribution by pack size nationally, regionally, district-wide.

Where applicable, trends in all of the above data should also be identified by store classification, chain versus independent (large, medium and small).

G. Total Market History

Identify recent trends of the total market in terms of units and % gain/loss versus year ago nationally, regionally, district-wide, per M population, store type, county size, type of user (exclusive versus partial user), retail price trends, by user characteristics (age, income, etc.).

H. Competitive History (major brands), where available

Identify significant competitive trends in share, consumption levels by sales areas, store types; media and promotion expenditures; types of media, promotion; retail price differentials, etc.

Source: E. Raymond Corey and Steven H. Star, *Organization Strategy: A Marketing Approach* (Boston: Division of Research, Harvard Business School, 1971), p. 224. Reprinted by permission of Harvard University Press.

EXHIBIT 5-5   Product Performance Profile
Contribution to Company Performance

Product Line	Profit- ability	Product Leader- ship	Techno- logical Growth	Support of Total Product Line	Utiliza- tion of Company Resources	Provision of Customer Benefits
_ _ _ _ _						
_ _ _ _ _						
_ _ _ _ _						
_ _ _ _ _						

Source: Stuart U. Rich, "Planning the Future Strategy of Your Business," *Oregon Business Review* (April, 1964), p. 3.

EXHIBIT 5-6   Market Performance Profile
Contribution to Company Performance

Market Segments	Profit- ability	Market Share	Growth End-user Markets	Size of Customer Base	Distribu- tion Strength	Degree of Customer Loyalty
_ _ _ _ _ _						
_ _ _ _ _ _						
_ _ _ _ _ _						
_ _ _ _ _ _						

Source: Stuart U. Rich, "Planning the Future Strategy of Your Business," *Oregon Business Review* (April, 1964), p. 4.

It is desirable to analyze financial performance for a number of years to determine the historical trend of performance. To show how financial performance analysis may figure in formulating marketing strategy, the following excerpt from a recent study on the subject may be used:

> A maker of confectionery that offers more than one hundred brands, flavors and packagings, prunes its lines—regularly and routinely—of those items having the lowest profit contribution, sales volume, and vitality for future growth.
>
> Since the early 1970s each individual product has been ranked on these three factors, and an "index of gross profitability" has been prepared for each in conjunction with annual marketing plans. These plans take into account longer-term objectives for the business, trends in consumer wants and expectations, competitive factors in the marketplace and, lastly, a deliberately ordered "prioritization" of the company's resources. Sales and profit performance are then checked against projected targets at regular intervals through the year, and the indexes of gross profitability are adjusted when necessary.
>
> The firm's chief executive emphasizes that even individual items whose indexes of profitability are ranked at the very bottom are nonetheless profitable and paying their way by any customary standard of return on sales and investment. But the very lowest-ranking items are regularly reviewed; and, on a judgmental basis, some are marked for pruning at the next convenient opportunity. This opportunity is most likely to arrive when stocks of special ingredients and packaging labels for the items have been exhausted.
>
> In a recent year, the company dropped 16 items that were judged to be too low on its index of gross profitability. Calculated and selective pruning is regarded within the company as a healthy means of working toward the best possible mix of products at all times. It has the reported advantages of increasing efficiencies in manufacturing as a result of cutting the "down time" between small runs, reducing inventories, and freeing resources for the expansion of the most promising items— or the development of new ones—without having to expand productive capacity. Another important benefit is that the sales force concentrates on a smaller line containing only the most profitable products with the largest volumes. On the negative side, however, it is acknowledged that pruning, as the company practices it, may result in near-term loss of sales for a line until growth of the rest of the items can compensate.[9]

---

[9]David S. Hopkins, *Business Strategies for Problem Products* (New York: Conference Bd., 1977), p. 29.

PRODUCT/MARKET THRUST

Product/market thrust refers to all activities concerned with customers and prospects—present, potential and shifting—and all the direct competitors for that demand. In Chapter 4 the perspectives of the product/market environment were discussed. Here environment will be examined to study the driving forces which determine the future direction of the product/market concerned. In addition to competition, many other influencing factors must be considered for this. For example, the sociological, political, legal, economic, technological, and ethical trends of the product/market environment can profoundly influence changes in the industry in the long run. In order to make an effective, strategically oriented evaluation of the product/market thrust, the discussion will be planned under the following headings: competition, industry dynamics, and demand.

Competition

In a free market economy, each competitor likes to exceed the other in performance. A competitor is like an enemy. To outperform its competitors a company must know how it stands against each one of them with regard to 'arms and ammunitions'—skills in maneuvering opportunities, preparedness in reacting to threats, and so on. To get adequate knowledge about the competition it faces, the company needs an excellent intelligence network.

Organizationally, competitive activities can be monitored by product managers, market managers, or a staff person, such as a marketing researcher. Typically, whenever one talks in terms of competition, emphasis is placed on price, quality of product, delivery time, and other marketing variables. For the purposes of strategy development, however, one needs to go much beyond these marketing tactics employed by a competitor. Simply knowing that a competitor has been lowering prices is not sufficient. Over and above that, we must know how much flexibility the competitor has in reducing the price further. Implicit here is the need for getting information about the competitor's cost structure.

The following procedure may be adopted to review competition:

1. Recognize key competitors in market segments in which the company is active. Presumably, a product will be positioned to serve one or more market segments. In each segment there may be different competitors to reckon with; an attempt should be made to recognize all important competitors in each segment. If the number of competitors is excessive, it is sufficient to limit the consideration to the first three competitors. Each competitor may be briefly profiled to indicate total corporate proportion.

2. Analyze track record of each competitor in terms of sales, profits, growth, and share. Performance of a competitor can be measured with reference to a number of criteria. As far as marketing is concerned, sales growth, market share, and profitability are the impor-

tant measures of success. Thus, a review of each competitor's sales growth, market share, and profitability for the past several years will be desirable. In addition, any ad hoc reasons which bear upon a competitor's performance should be noted. For example, a competitor may have lined up some business, in the nature of a windfall from Saudi Arabia, without making any strategic moves to secure the business. Such events should be duly pointed out. Occasionally a competitor may intentionally pad up the result to reflect good performance at year end. Such tactics should be noted too. Rothschild advises the following:

> To make it really useful, you must probe how each participant keeps its books and records its profits. Some companies stress earnings; others report their condition in such a way as to delay the payment of taxes; still others bookkeep to increase cash availability.
>
> These measurements are important because they may affect the company's ability to procure financing and attract people as well as influence stockholders' and investors' satisfaction with current management.[10]

3. Study how satisfied each competitor appears to be with his performance. To study this question reference will have to be made to the objective(s) which each competitor has for the product. If the results are in concert with the expectations of the firm's management and stakeholders, the competitor will be satisfied. A satisfied competitor is most likely to follow the current successful strategy. On the other hand, if the results as exhibited by the track record are at odds with management expectations, the competitor is most likely to come out with a new strategy.

4. Probe each competitor's marketing strategy. The strategy of each competitor can be inferred from the game plans (i.e., different moves in the area of product, price, promotion, and distribution) which are pursued to achieve the objective. Information on the game plans will be available partly from published stories on the competitor and partly from the company salespeople in contact with the competitor's customers and salespeople.

    To clarify the point, consider a competitor in the small appliances business who spends heavily for consumer advertising and sells products mainly through discount stores. The prices that consumers pay to this firm are lower than those they pay to established firms. From this brief description it will be safe to conclude that as a matter

---

[10]William E. Rothschild, *Putting It All Together: A Guide to Strategic Thinking* (New York: AMACOM, 1976), p. 85.

of strategy, the competitor desires to establish the brand in the mass market through the discounters. In other words, the competitor is trying to reach customers who would like to buy a reputed brand at discount prices and hopes to make money by creating a large sales base.

5. Analyze current and future resources and competencies of each competitor. In order to study a competitor's resources and competencies, the first step is to designate the broader areas of concern; these may be facilities and equipment, personnel skills, organizational capabilities, and management capabilities. Each area may then be examined generally with reference to different functional areas (i.e., general management and finance, research and development, operation, and especially marketing). In the area of finance, availability of a large credit line will be a strength under "management capabilities." Owning a warehouse and refrigerated trucks could be a strength under "Facilities and Equipment," as far as marketing is concerned. Exhibit 5-7 provides a checklist which may be used for designating each competitor's strengths and competencies. With the use of the checklist in Exhibit 5-7, an attempt should be made to specifically pinpoint those strengths which one's competitor can utilize to pursue goals against one's firm and other firms in the market. Simultaneously, those areas where the competitor looks particularly vulnerable should also be noted. The purpose here is not to get involved in a ritualistic, detailed account of each competitor, but to demarcate those aspects which may account for substantial difference in performance.

6. Prediction concerning future marketing strategy of each competitor. The above competitive analysis provides enough information to make predictions concerning the future strategic directions which each competitor may pursue. The prediction, however, must be made qualitatively, using management consensus. The use of management consensus as the basic means for developing forecasts is based on the presumption that, by virtue of their experience in gauging market trends, executives should be able to make some credible predictions about each competitor's behavior in the future. A senior member of the marketing research staff may be assigned the task of soliciting executive opinions and consolidating the information into specific predictions on the moves competitors are likely to make in the future. Management consensus may, however, be systematized to a certain extent by using the delphi method. The delphi method will be described in Chapter 14. Briefly, the executive in charge of the product may develop perspectives on the future strategy of each competitor. Then the marketing researcher may present these predictions to a selective group of marketing executives who

EXHIBIT 5-7   Checklist for Competitive Strengths and Competencies

	Facilities and Equipment	Personnel Skills	Organizational Capabilities	Management Capabilities
General Management & Finance				
R&D				
Operations				
Marketing	Warehousing Retail outlets Sales offices Service offices Transportation equipment Training facilities for sales staff Data processing equipment	Door-to-door selling Retail selling Wholesale selling Direct industry selling Department of Defense selling Cross-industry selling Applications engineering Advertising Sales promotion Servicing Contract administration Sales analysis Data analysis Forecasting Computer modeling Product planning Backround of people Corporate culture	Direct sales Distributor chain Retail chain Consumer service organization Industrial service organization Department of Defense product support Inventory distribution and control Ability to make quick reponse to customer requirements Ability to adapt to sociopolitical upheavals in the marketplace Loyal set of customers Cordial relations with media and channels Flexibility in all phases of corporate life Consumer financing Discount policy Teamwork Product quality	Industrial marketing Consumer merchandising Department of Defense marketing State and municipality marketing Well-informed and receptive management Large customer base Decentralized control Favorable public image Future orientation Ethical standards

Source: Adapted from: H. Igor Ansoff, *Corporate Strategy* (New York: McGraw-Hill Bk. Co., 1965), pp. 98–99.

would presumably be familiar with the industry-wide marketing of the product. Their opinions can then be used to refine the predictions made by the product executive.

7.   Impact of competitive strategy on the company's product/market. The delphi panel discussed above can also be used to specify the impact of competitive strategy. Here again, the product executive must first analyze the impact using as a basis competitive information and his or her experiences on the job. Thereafter, the consensus of a larger group of executives can be obtained on the impact analysis performed by the product executive.

Needless to say, an analysis of impact using the delphi method, besides being expensive, will be time-consuming. Thus, the amount of effort that can be devoted to analyze such matters will depend on the strategic importance of the product.

Industry Dynamics

Every industry has a few peculiar characteristics of its own. These characteristics are bound by time and thus subject to change. We will call them the dynamics of the industry. No matter how hard a company tries, if it fails to fit into the dynamics of the industry, ultimate success may be difficult to achieve. Consider the aluminum industry. Integration—both forward and backward—is a prerequisite to operating successfully in this industry. Canada's Alcan Aluminum, Ltd., which did not recognize the peculiar dynamics of its industry, lagged behind. For this reason, it has not yet been able to regain its earlier position. As *Business Week* reports:

> The big U.S. aluminum producers learned one basic lesson years ago: if you get into the aluminum business, you have to go all the way. Turning out aluminum ingots is not enough because the real potential for profit lies in integrating production as far up and down the line as possible. It was a lesson that came late to Nathaniel V. Davis, President of Alcan Aluminum, Ltd., the giant Canadian producer. Not until the early 1960s did Alcan start moving into the fabrication business in a big way. But when Davis finally made the change, he pulled out all the stops. Ever since, his company has been playing the costly and problem-plagued game of catch-up.[11]

Still another example of the perspectives of an entire industry and how they may change over time is provided by the cosmetics industry. The cosmetics business has traditionally been run according to a seat-of-the-pants method with ultimate dependence on the marketing genius of the inventors. In the 1970s a

---

[11]"Why Alcan Spends So Much," *Business Week* (July 10, 1971), p. 78.

variety of pressures began to engulf the industry. The regulatory climate became tougher. Consumers became more demanding and unpredictable. Inflationary economic conditions and rising costs made profits smaller. Many leading companies were acquired by large corporations. For example, Eli Lilly bought Elizabeth Arden, Squibb acquired Lanvin-Charles of the Ritz, Pfizer got Coty, Norton Simon added Max Factor, Colgate-Palmolive bought Helena Rubinstein, and British-American Tobacco scooped up Germaine Monteil. These changes have made competition in the industry fierce. Capital investment in the industry is small, but inventory and distribution costs are extremely high, partly because of the number of shades and textures in each product line. For example, nail polish and lipstick have to be available in over 50 different shades. Briefly, in comparison with the Fifties and Sixties, the cosmetics industry has gone through a tremendous change. Now mass distribution has become a prerequisite for the successful operation of a cosmetics business. Basic inventory and financial controls, budgeting, and planning are utilized to the fullest extent to cut costs and waste. This type of shift in direction and style in the industry may have important ramifications for marketing strategy.[12]

Back in the 1950s and 1960s, to succeed in the cosmetics business one needed a glamorous product. As has been said, Revlon manufactured lipstick in its factories, but sold what satisfied the desire to have lovely lips. In the 1970s, however, the main strength was in securing distribution to achieve specific objectives in sales, profit, and market share.

Exhibit 5-8 provides a checklist of items which may be examined to get an understanding of the dynamics of industry. Basically considered here are:

1. Scope of competitors' business (i.e., location and number of industries)
2. New entrants in the industry
3. Other current and potential offerings which appear to serve similar functions or satisfy the same need
4. Industry's ability to raise capital, attract people, avoid government probing, and compete effectively for the consumers' dollars
5. Industry's current practices (i.e., price setting, warranties, distribution structure, after-sales service, etc.)
6. Trends in volume, costs, prices, and return on investment, compared with other industries
7. Industry profit economics: key factors determining profits, such as volume, materials, labor, capital investment, market penetration, and dealer strength
8. Ease of entry into the industry, including capital investment

---

[12]"Management Realists in the Glamour World of Cosmetics," *Business Week* (November 29, 1976), p. 42.

9. Relationship between current and future demand and manufacturing capacity, and its probable effects on prices and profits
10. Effect of integration, both forward and backward
11. Effect of cyclical swings in the relationship between supply and demand

For planning purposes the company should determine the relevance of each of the above factors in its industry and the position it occupies compared to competitors with regard to these factors. An attempt should be made to highlight the dynamics of the company in the industry environment. It should be emphasized here that the study of dynamics does not mean sheer projections of the industry growth rates and the company's likelihood to match the industry's growth pattern, since the fortunes of a particular company may not necessarily be related to the overall growth of its industry.

Demand

An analysis of demand may also help in recognizing strengths. There are three types of demand: existing demand, latent demand, and incipient demand. *Existing demand* exists when a product has been bought to satisfy a particular need. *Latent demand* refers to a situation where a particular need has been recognized, but no products have been offered to satisfy the need. *Incipient demand* is the demand in which certain trends project the emergence of a need although the customer is not aware of one.[13]

To analyze demand for strategy development three product categories may be considered: breakthrough products, competitive products, and improved products. A breakthrough product is a unique innovation which is mainly technical in nature, such as a digital watch, a color television, a jet plane, etc. A competitive product is one of the many brands currently available in the market which has no special advantage over the competing products. An improved product is one which, while it is not unique, is generally superior to many existing brands.[14]

The three types of demand may be analyzed with reference to these three types of products to ascertain which type of demand the company is strategically most competent to pursue.

A few observations are in order here. The most risky proposition is the pursuit of incipient demand with a competitive or improved product. The most attractive alternative is to serve latent demand with a competitive offering. In the economically healthy years of 1960s, for example, K-Mart recognized the price-conscious segment which was ignored by both Sears and Penney. As inflation became rampant in the 1970s this demand became all the more pro-

---

[13]H. Igor Ansoff, *Corporate Strategy* (New York: McGraw-Hill Bk. Co., 1965), pp. 190–191.
[14]*Ibid.*

EXHIBIT 5-8   Industry Dynamics Checklist

Classification of Competitors

1. List all of your current major competitors and then classify them in terms of the following categories: United States, foreign, international, multinational; single industry or multi-industry.
2. Anticipate changes which you think may take place over the next five to ten years.
3. What are the positive (opportunities) and negative (threats) implications of these changes?

New Entries

Draw a diagram depicting:
1. Competitors in other geographic regions or other segments who do not currently, but may decide to, compete in your markets or segments.
2. Customers served by your industry. Note those who may want to move backwards, and consider the reasons why such a move may make sense.
3. Suppliers to your industry; note movement and reasons.
4. Companies on the periphery—those who serve the same customers with different but related products. This might include other pieces of equipment related to yours or equipment that would be included in a broader definition of the market. It is impossible to list all related items, but those of closest proximity should be included.
5. Any other companies that might be enticed to serve your customers or markets. This should include conglomerates or diversified companies that might be attracted by the growth, size, or profitability of your markets. Choose the most likely new entries and quiz yourself about what you know about them and their strategies.

Substitutions and Innovations

1. List other products or services that provide the same or a similar function. Record the percentage of total market sales for each substitute product.
2. Anticipate product innovations which can replace or reduce the sales of your products. When do you think these products will be commercially feasible? (Note: Information about potentially competitive products can be found by searching the U.S. Patent Office or foreign patent offices.)

Other Forms of Competition

1. Think about your industry's and product's ability to compete effectively for the consumers' dollar and how this may be modified in the future.
2. Identify the type of financial resources required, and evaluate the ability of the industry to obtain capital and at what cost.
3. Record the image your industry has and how this can impact on its ability to attract the quantity and quality of people it requires now and in the planning period. There is also a cost dimension to this aspect of competition, since people can be bought.

Other Industry Characteristics

1. Who are the trend setters?
2. Will a new practice be introduced which will force you to follow? What is it and what is the likely cost of this change?
3. Describe the current type of distribution prevalent in the industry. What changes do you anticipate? What about the mix of dealers? Will this mix change?
4. How about the pre- and postsales service requirements: Is service bundled (that is, included in the purchase price) or unbundled?
5. Are there any changes in the types of warranties or guarantees?
6. Describe the level of capacity utilization now and in the next five years. Does the industry anticipate demand and add capacity in advance of demand, or does it react and cause an oversupply situation?
7. What type of people lead the industry? Do the behavior and values vary from segment to segment?
8. List key suppliers, including type, size, and location. Are suppliers increasing or decreasing in number, or are they holding? What is the financial condition of key suppliers?

Source: Reprinted, by permission of the publisher, from *Putting It All Together: A Guide to Strategic Thinking,* by William E. Rothschild, © 1976 by AMACOM, a division of American Management Associations, pp. 80–81. All rights reserved.

nounced, and K-Mart found itself fully equipped to capitalize on it, to the extent that in 1977 K-Mart became the second largest retailer in the country, next to Sears.

It is not necessary, however, for a company to always search for latent demand. Sometimes the existing demand may provide a more lucrative opportunity than latent demand. In the late 1970s when all major tire companies were spending more on diversification, Goodyear opted for new commitment to the tire industry despite a seemingly unfavorable environment for the industry which is described below:

> The long-lasting and popular radial tire has cut off growth in unit volume at the same time that U.S. population growth has stabilized. Moreover, the auto makers are downsizing cars and thus are buying smaller tires. Both developments have adversely affected the tire-makers' profitability. In addition, the auto makers are laying plans to remove the spare tire altogether.[15]

According to industry observers, Goodyear's technological breakthrough in designing highly automated machinery which would vastly improve productivity, and its marketing talent which enabled it to sell its tire innovations when others failed, put the company in a unique position to serve the existing demand for radial tires.

---

[15]"Goodyear's Solo Strategy," *Business Week* (August 28, 1978), p. 67.

STRENGTHS AND WEAKNESSES

The study of product/market thrust, current strategic perspectives, and past performance provides insights into information necessary for designating strengths and weaknesses. Exhibit 5-9 provides a rundown of areas of strength as far as marketing is concerned. Where feasible, strengths should be stated in objective terms. Exhibit 5-9 does not provide an all-inclusive listing, but it is indicative of the kind of strength which a company may have over its competitors. It will be noted that most areas of strength are related to the excellence of outstanding personnel or are resource based. Not all factors will have the same significance for every product. Therefore, it will be desirable to first recognize the critical factors which could directly or indirectly bear on a product's perform-ance. For example, the development of an improved product may be strategic for drug companies. On the other hand, in the case of cosmetic products, where image building is usually important, advertising may be a critical factor. After-sales service may have significance for products such as copying machines, com-puters, and elevators. The critical factors may be chosen with reference to Exhibit 2-6 (p. 56). From among the critical factors, an attempt should be made to sort out strengths. It will be desirable to rate different strengths for a more objective analysis.

EXHIBIT 5-9   Areas of Strength

1. Excellence in product design and/or performance (engineering ingenuity)
2. Low-cost, high-efficiency operating skill in manufacturing and/or in distribu-tion
3. Leadership in product innovation
4. Efficiency in customer service
5. Personal relationships with customers
6. Efficiency in transportation and logistics
7. Effectiveness in sales promotion
8. Merchandising efficiency—high turnover of inventories and/or of capital
9. Skillful trading in volatile price movement commodities
10. Ability to influence legislation
11. Highly efficient, low-cost facilities
12. Ownership or control of low-cost or scarce raw materials
13. Control of intermediate distribution or processing units
14. Massive availability of capital
15. Widespread customer acceptance of company brand name (reputation)
16. Product availability, convenience
17. Customer loyalty
18. Dominant market share position
19. Effectiveness of advertising
20. Quality sales force

Source: Points 1 through 16 are taken from: Robert L. Katz, *Cases and Concepts in Corpo-rate Strategy,* © 1970, p. 215. Reprinted by permission of Prentice-Hall, Engle-wood Cliffs, NJ.

The strengths should be further examined to undertake what may be called opportunity analysis (i.e., matching strengths or competencies to opportunity). The opportunity analysis will serve as an input in establishing a company's economic mission. The opportunity analysis is useful in developing both an individual product's objectives and the corporate-wide mission. In Exhibit 5-10 the objectives for a food product are shown as they emerged from a study of its strengths. These objectives are a premium product, an unscored segment, and a new channel outlet. In other words, at the level of a product the opportunity analysis seeks to answer such questions as: What opportunity does the company have for overcoming the weaknesses of competition? modify or improve the product line or add new products? serve the needs of more customers in existing markets, or develop new markets? improve the efficiency of current marketing operations?

As far as the corporate-wide mission is concerned, consider the case of a ball-point pen manufacturer. One of the strengths of a successful manufacturer is the ability to handle extensive advertising and massive distribution. This strength is transferable and could be used for running a successful razor-blade business as well. This is what has happened, of course, at BIC Pen Corporation. In other words, the opportunity analysis can direct a company toward the course it should pursue.

An interesting observation with regard to opportunity analysis, made by Andrews, deserves mention here:

> The match is designed to minimize organizational weakness and to maximize strength. In any case, risk attends it. And when opportunity seems to outrun present distinctive competence, the willingness to gamble that the latter can be built up to the required level is almost indispensable to a strategy that challenges the organization and the people in it. It appears to be true, in any case, that the potential capability of a company tends to be underestimated. Organizations, like individuals, rise to occasions, particularly when the latter provide attractive reward for the effort required.[16]

In the process of analyzing strengths, certain weaknesses will also be noted. Exhibit 5-11 shows a sample of weaknesses of a paper manufacturer. Basically, appropriate action must be taken to correct the weaknesses. However, some weaknesses may have corporate-wide bearing, while others may be weaknesses of a specific product. The corporate-wide weaknesses must be examined, and necessary corrective action must be incorporated into the overall marketing strategy. For example, weaknesses #3, 5, and 6 could have corporate-wide ramifications. These must be addressed by the chief marketing strategist. The remaining three

---

[16]Kenneth R. Andrews, *The Concept of Corporate Strategy* (Homewood, IL: Dow Jones-Irwin, 1971), p. 100.

EXHIBIT 5-10   Matching Strengths with Opportunities

Strength	Likely Impact	Opportunity (Furnished by the Environment)	Objectives and Goals
Customer loyalty	Incremental product volume increases Price increases for premium quality/service New product introductions	A trend of changing taste An identified geographic shift of part of the market A market segment neglected by the industry A product-related subconscious need not solicited by competition A product weakness of competition A distribution weakness of competition Technical feasibility for improving existing package design A discovered new use for the product or container	Develop a premium product Introduce the existing product in the segment hitherto not served Develop a new channel outlet for the product, etc.
Cordial relationships with channels	New product introductions Point-of-purchase advertising Reduction of delivered costs through distribution innovations Tied-in products Merchandising differentiation		

EXHIBIT 5-11   Marketing Weaknesses as Related to a Paper Product

1. Inadequate definition of customer for product/market development
2. Ambiguous service policies
3. Too many levels of reporting in the organizational setup
4. Overlapping channels
5. Lack of top-management involvement in new product development
6. Lack of quantitative goals

weaknesses can be corrected by the person in charge of the product with which these weaknesses are associated.

CONCEPT OF SYNERGY

Before concluding the discussion on strengths and weaknesses, it will be desirable to briefly introduce the concept of synergy. Synergy refers to the combined effect of certain parts which is greater in total effect than the sum of their individual effects. For example, individually, Product 1 contributes X, while Product 2 contributes Y. If they are produced together, they may contribute X + Y + Z. Then, Z is the synergistic effect of X and Y being brought together, and Z represents positive synergy. There can be negative synergy as well. Study of synergy helps in analyzing new growth opportunities. A new product, for instance, may have such a high synergistic effect on a company's existing product(s) that it may be an extremely desirable addition.

Quantitative analysis of synergy is far from easy. Ansoff, however, has provided a framework for evaluation of synergy which will be discussed here with reference to a new product-market entry. A new product-market entry contribution could take place at three levels: contribution to the parent company (from the entry), contribution to the new entry (from the parent), and joint opportunities (i.e., benefits which will accrue to both as a result of consolidation). As far as it is feasible, entries in Exhibit 5-12 should be assigned a numerical value, such as increase in unit sales by 20 percent, time saving by 2 months, reduction in investment requirements by 10 percent, and so on. Finally, various numerical values may be given a common value in the form of return on investment or cash flow.[17]

SUMMARY

This chapter provided a scheme for an objective measurement of strengths and weaknesses of a product/market. Strengths and weaknesses are tangible and intangible resources which may be utilized for seeking growth for the product. Three major factors which need to be studied in order to designate strengths and weaknesses are: product/market thrust, current strategic perspectives, and past

---

[17]H. Igor Ansoff, *Corporate Strategy* (New York: McGraw-Hill Bk. Co., 1965), pp. 88–90.

EXHIBIT 5-12   Measurement of Synergy of a New Product-market Entry

Synergistic Contribution to:	Synergy Measures							
	Startup Economies			Operating Economies		Expansion of Present Sales	New Product and Market Areas	Overall Synergy
	Investment	Operating	Timing	Investment	Operating			
Parent								
New entry								
Joint opportunities								

Source: Adapted from: H. Igor Ansoff, *Corporate Strategy* (New York: McGraw-Hill Bk. Co., 1965), p. 189.

performance. An additional influential factor is overall marketing effectiveness, which was dealt with in Chapter 2. Present strategy was examined in this chapter with reference to the markets being served and the means utilized to serve these markets. Past performance was considered in the form of financial analysis which ranges from simple measurements such as market share and profitability to developing product and market performance profiles.

Competition, industry dynamics, and demand constitute the aspects of the product/market thrust. Operational frameworks were suggested to analyze these aspects. Finally, the analysis under current strategy, past performance, and product/market thrust was brought together to delineate strengths and weaknesses. Also discussed here was the concept of synergy, which refers to a combined return on the resources of two products vis-a-vis their individual returns. The analysis of strengths and weaknesses sets the stage for defining objectives and goals.

DISCUSSION QUESTIONS

1. Why is it necessary for a corporation to measure its strengths and weaknesses?
2. Is it feasible to make an objective appraisal of strengths and weaknesses since people may naturally indulge in self-praise and thus may see everything they do as "right," and hence a strength?
3. Evaluate the current strategy of (a) Westinghouse, (b) IBM, and (c) Chrysler in view of their declining performance in the later part of the 1970s.
4. Develop a conceptual scheme to evaluate the current strategy of a bank and a department store.
5. Evaluate the past performance of United Airlines in the light of its comeback since 1978.
6. Examine the dynamics of the cigarette industry in the light of continuing controversy on the effects of smoking. What are the essential ingredients needed to keep making profits in the industry?
7. Develop a framework for an auto manufacturer to measure the foreign competition.
8. From McDonald's point of view, what sort of demand appears most promising for growth?
9. Explain the meaning of synergy. Examine what sort of synergy Procter & Gamble achieved by going into the potato chip business.

Chapter 6
Developing Marketing Objectives and Goals

"Would you tell me, please, which way I ought to go from here?" said Alice. "That depends a good deal on where you want to get to," said the Cheshire cat.

Lewis Carroll
Alice in Wonderland

An organization must have an objective to guide its destiny. While the objective does not in itself guarantee the success of a business, its presence will certainly mean more economical and financially less wasteful management of operations.

Objectives form a specific expression of purpose, thus helping to remove any uncertainty about the company's policy or about the intended purpose of any effort. To be effective, objectives must provide a startling challenge to jolt managers away from traditional in-a-rut thinking. If properly designed, objectives permit measurement of progress. Without some form of progress measurement, it may not be possible to know whether adequate resources are being applied or whether these resources are being managed effectively. Finally, objectives facilitate the relationships between units, especially in a diversified corporation where the separate goals of different units may not be consistent with some higher corporate purpose.

Despite their overriding importance, defining objectives is far from easy. "There is no mechanical or expert instant answer method. Rather, defining goals as the future becomes the present is a long, time-consuming, and continuous process."[1] In practice, many businesses are run either without any commonly accepted objectives and goals or with conflicting objectives and goals. In some cases objectives may be understood in different ways by different executives. At times the objectives may be defined in "mundane" terms so that their significance for the job is not understood. For example, one product manager of a large company said, "Our objective is to satisfy the customer and increase sales." After

---

[1]Myles L. Mace, "The President and Corporate Planning," *Harvard Business Review* (January–February, 1965), p. 56.

cross-checking with the vice-president of sales, however, it was found that the company had a goal of making a minimum of six percent after-tax profit even if it meant losing market share. "Our objective, or whatever you choose to call it, is to grow," the vice-president of sales said. "This is a profit-oriented company, and thus, we must earn a minimum profit of ten percent on everything we do. You may call this our objective." These are examples of how different departments in a company define their objectives. In brief, setting a company's direction is a difficult task. It is the task of the chief executive to set the company's objectives and goals and obtain for them the support of his or her senior colleagues, thus paving the way for other parts of the organization to do the same.

The purpose of this chapter is to provide a framework for goal setting in a large, complex organization. Usually a first step in planning is to state your objectives so that, knowing where you are trying to go, you can figure out how to get there. However, objectives cannot be stated in isolation without the perspectives of the company's current business, past performance, resources, and environment. Thus, the subject matter discussed in chapters 2, 3, 4, and 5 becomes the background material for defining objectives and goals.

FRAMEWORK FOR DEFINING OBJECTIVES

Objectives and goals will be discussed at three different levels: the corporate level, the strategic business unit (SBU) level, and the product/market level. For example, consider General Electric, whose large appliances business constitutes an SBU. Thus, G.E. may have overall corporate objectives, objectives of the large appliances business, and, finally, objectives of a different type of product/market, such as household refrigerators. In a small company which manufactures a limited line of related products, corporate and SBU objectives may be common. Likewise, in a company with a few unrelated products, an SBU's objectives may be no different from those of the product/market.

It will be desirable to define a few terms which one often confronts in the context of goal setting. These are mission, policy, objective, and goal. A *mission* is the chief executive officer's conception of the organization's raison d'etre, or what it should work toward, in the light of long-range opportunity. A *policy* is a written definition of general intent or company position designed to guide and regulate certain actions and decisions, especially those of major significance or of a recurring nature. An *objective* is a long-range purpose or aim which is not quantified or limited to a time period, such as increasing the return on the stockholders' equity. A *goal* is a measurable objective of the business, judged by management to be attainable at some specific future date through planned actions. An example of a goal is to achieve ten percent growth in sales within the next two years.

In the following sections objective and goal will be further examined for their significance at different levels. Although we recognize the distinction between an objective and a goal, we will consider these terms simultaneously in order to give the discussion more depth.

The following are the qualities that objectives and goals should have: credibility, communicability, practicality, competitive advantage, and normality (i.e., common business wisdom expressed in common business language). On the other hand, the following are the frequently cited types of frustrations, disappointments, or troubling uncertainties which should be avoided when dealing with goals:

1. Lack of credibility, motivation, and/or practicality
2. Poor information inputs
3. Defining objectives without considering different options
4. Lack of consensus regarding corporate values
5. Disappointing committee effort to define objectives
6. Sterility (lack of uniqueness and competitive advantage).[2]

Briefly, if objectives and goals are to serve their purpose well, they should represent a careful weighing of the balance between the performance desired and the probability of its being accomplished:

> Strategic objectives which are too ambitious result in the dissipation of assets and the destruction of morale, and create the risk of losing past gains as well as future opportunities. Strategic objectives which are not ambitious enough represent lost opportunity and open the door to complacency.[3]

CORPORATE OBJECTIVES

Corporate objectives are defined in a variety of ways. In some corporations they take the form of a corporate creed or code of conduct which defines the perspectives from the viewpoint of different stakeholders. At other corporations objectives are presented as corporate policy, providing guidelines for implementing strategy. Either way, corporate objectives consist of broad statements which represent a company's position on various matters and serve as inputs in defining objectives and formulating strategy at lower echelons in the organization.

Exhibit 6-1 illustrates the corporate policies of Armco Steel Corporation. Notice that very broad statements are made to illustrate where the company stands on various matters of corporate life. Exhibit 6-2 lists the objectives of another company, Barnes Group Inc. Here objectives have been defined in greater detail although the tone is still very general in nature. Another interesting point to note is that while Armco did not specify any rate of return or growth figures, the Barnes Group did. This may be because in the steel industry making such information public may have negative repercussions vis-a-vis labor negotiations, setting of import quotas, and adherence to EPA requirements.

---

[2]Robert F. Stewart, "Setting Corporate Aims," a report of the Long Range Planning Service of the Stanford Research Institute, 1971, p. 5.
[3]*Perspectives on Corporate Strategy* (Boston: Boston Consulting Group, 1970), p. 44.

EXHIBIT 6-1   Armco Policies

Ethics:

To do business guided and governed by the highest standards of conduct so the end result of action taken makes a good reputation an invaluable and permanent asset.

Square Deal:

To insist on a square deal always. To make sure people are listened to and treated fairly, so that men and women really do right for right's sake and not just to achieve a desired result. For everyone to go beyond narrowness, littleness, selfishness in order to get the job done.

Organization:

To develop and maintain an efficient, loyal, aggressive organization of people who believe in their company, to whom work is a challenge and to whom extraordinary accomplishment is a personal goal.

Working Conditions:

To create and maintain good working conditions . . . to provide the best possible equipment and facilities . . . and plants and offices that are clean, orderly and safe.

Quality and Service:

To adopt "Quality and Service" is an everyday practice. Quality will be the highest attainable in products, organization, plant, property and equipment. Service will be the best possible to customers, to shareholders, to city, state and nation.

Opportunity:

To employ people without regard to race, sex, religion or national origin. To encourage employees to improve their skills by participating in available educational or training programs. To provide every possible opportunity for advancement so that each individual may reach his or her highest potential.

Compensation:

To provide not only fair remuneration, but the best compensation for service rendered that is possible to pay under the changing economic, commercial and other competitive conditions that exist from time to time. It's Armco's ambition to develop an organization of spirit, loyalty and efficiency that can and will secure results which will make it possible for individual members to earn and receive better compensation than would be possible if performing a similar service in other fields of effort.

Incentive:

To provide realistic and practical incentive as a means of encouraging the highest standard of individual performance and to assure increased quantity and quality of performance.

Cooperation:

To recognize cooperation as the medium through which great accomplishments are attained. Success depends more on a spirit of helpful cooperation than on any other one factor.

Objectivity:

To always consider what is right and best for the business as a whole, rather than what may be expedient in dealing with a single, separate situation.

Conflict of Interest:

To prohibit employees from becoming financially interested in any company with which Armco does business, if such financial interest might possibly influence decisions employees must make in their areas of responsibility.

The above policy does not apply to ownership in publicly-owned companies. This is not considered a conflict of interest but, rather, is encouraged as part of the free enterprise system.

Citizenship:

To create and maintain a working partnership between industry and community in this country and throughout the world. To support constructive agencies in communities where Armco people live and work in an effort to create civic conditions that respond to the highest needs of the citizens.

Source: "Armco Policies," a brochure published by Armco Steel, 1969.

EXHIBIT 6-2   Barnes Group Inc.: Corporate Objectives

CORPORATE CONCEPT

To continually improve and expand Barnes Group as a worldwide company conducting its business on a multi-operations basis, consisting of one or more profit centers, with emphasis on critical component parts manufactured for the durable goods segment of industrial markets and on distribution markets for consumable maintenance, repair and service parts.

INTERNAL GROWTH

The continuation of internal growth has the highest priority in the overall corporate plans. Internal growth is the profitable expansion of the business of the presently existing groups in the Corporation.

It is expected that internal growth will be built upon the following factors:

1. Increased demand from present markets
2. Increased penetration of present markets
3. Growth in the gross national product both inflationary and real
4. Development of new markets
5. Introduction of new products and services
6. Development of manufacturing and marketing specializations

7. Organizational development
8. Additions to present operations

To provide capability beyond that presently existing for a product, manufacturing or market area closely related to an operation's present activity, "add-on" acquisitions will be considered when they offer an advantage over the internal generation of the additional capability. "Add-on" acquisitions will be sufficiently small in size to fit into an existing operation and will have annual sales normally not to exceed about $10 million.

Proposals for "add-on" acquisitions will originate and be stimulated from within the individual operation, as a natural adjunct to its planning activity. Final approval and the actual acquisition process will, however, remain the responsibility of the corporate function.

The Corporation recognizes that business cycles, economic trends, technological change, and political or social environment will have an effect on the achievement of growth. In continuing its basic reliance on internal growth, the Corporation counts on the innovative ingenuity of its employees and their ability to anticipate, plan for, and adapt to changing conditions to minimize negative factors and maximize new opportunities. It is corporate policy to encourage and support employees in the taking of reasonable business risks for the purpose of achieving profitable growth.

Overall business conditions, together with recognition of the different markets served by the operating groups and the different relative penetration and maturities of those markets, cause each of the groups to produce different rates of sales growth by internal means. It is anticipated that each of the groups shall continue with annual sales growth rates in excess of their historic levels, which have been 6% for Associated Spring North America, 12% for Associated Spring International, and 13% for Bowman Distribution. These historic sales growth rates have included inflation and currency fluctuations but without "add-on" acquisitions. Recognition of inflationary rates and currency fluctuations substantially different from the historical norm will be taken for purposes of determining the acceptability of annual and five-year performance plans.

EXTERNAL GROWTH

In addition to the primary objective of internal growth, Barnes Group will achieve external growth to accelerate total corporate growth and to add further stability and balance to the Corporation. This program for external growth includes the following:

Additional Operations

To provide significant increments of growth, additional operations will be added to Barnes Group. Such additions shall be a matter totally reserved for corporate initiation, action and decision. In considering acquisitions, the Corporation shall seek candidates that will provide diversification and balance to the Corporation's present operations and whose products and services will enhance the Corporation's image for growth and competence as an industrial supplier. Candidates shall preferably have annual sales in the range in $30,000,000–$75,000,000, and shall have forecast profit levels which will, over the longer term, contribute to rather than dilute the overall earnings of the Corporation.

Opportunities here will be measured on growth potential as well as their ability to provide enhanced profit margins. As they will be diversification steps, they will occupy a substantial share of their present market and bring experienced operating management in their field. In the period through 1980, Barnes Group shall seek to add one new operation to the Corporation.

International

To expand Barnes Group further as an international corporation throughout the industrialized world is a prime corporate objective. It is the Corporation's intention to limit international activity to business fields where competence has already been established.

It is the Corporation's desire to maintain 100% ownership of international operations, but consideration will be given to shared ownership with local nationals when this is a necessary or preferable alternative in Barnes Group's long-term interest.

In the past ten years during which Barnes Group carried out its determination to proceed in multinational markets, the emphasis on international activity, of necessity, was a corporate function. In the process of further international development during the time to 1980, it is intended to shift increasing responsibility to the operation as the ability of each to handle competently this expansion is demonstrated. This expansion shall be by acquisition or establishment of new businesses; however, all acquisitions in final decision and process shall remain the responsibility of the corporate function.

Specific goals and priorities, in order of importance, for international expansion are:

First, in each of the operations to consolidate and expand the interaction of the profit centers presently within each, to maximize the benefits for the commitments that have already been undertaken.

Second, to emphasize further expansion in the Associated Spring operations into the heartland of European markets with special emphasis on establishing substantial manufacturing operations in Germany; and to achieve a goal of $80,000,000 Associated Spring sales by 1980 divided between its European and Latin American operations. In the Bowman Distribution operation, targets in the next five years shall include a minimum of $30,000,000 sales in Europe and establishment of $10,000,000 sales in Latin America including its present operations in Mexico.

Third, additional areas of emphasis for Associated Spring shall include operations covering the Middle East and establishment of an Associated Spring manufacturing location within the Pacific shore area in the Far East with a potential for supplying that broad geographic area, as well as exploration of opportunities in European Communist Bloc countries.

SALES GOAL

The goal for total corporate sales shall be U.S. $500,000,000 in the year 1980. This goal shall consist of total corporate sales of U.S. $400,000,000 from internal growth which will be achieved by having an annual increase in sales of at least 12% and by the addition of U.S. $100,000,000 from all acquisitions and new operations established.

FINANCIAL

The Corporation's measure of profit performance is the return on capital employed. Capital employed is the sum of all assets plus the accumulated reserves for depreciation.

It is recognized that all operations are not directly comparable, and targets for individual profit centers and operations will be set, taking into account the nature of the operation, its performance plans and its record of achievement against them.

Target profit performance shall consist of:

1. A competitive return on capital employed with a basic minimum pretax return of 15 per cent which shall be inflation-adjusted from time to time, and
2. An annual growth rate of pretax profits of at least 12 per cent.
3. New projects and further capital commitments shall be subject to a minimum hurdle rate of 25 per cent return on capital unless deemed otherwise necessary or desirable by the Corporation in view of legal requirements or in the corporate best long-term interest.

Emphasis on asset management at all levels will include annual targets for cash generation, capital expenditures and balance sheet items, including inventory and receivables management.

Particular attention is drawn to the differences between actual cash-generating capacity and book results. Each group and profit center is expected to develop not only net cash-generating capacity for its own requirements, but also sufficient funds for the corporation to meet its high-priority investment commitments and opportunities.

In the Corporation's international businesses the special problems of shifting funds across international borders, differing tax treatments and currency-exchange matters make cash self-sufficiency even more important.

It is intended to repatriate surplus funds for redeployment by the Corporation as required. As a guideline the Corporation intends each of its non-U.S. dollar organizations to remit as dividends or otherwise an amount of its annual aftertax earnings equal to the same percentage that the Corporation is currently paying from its consolidated aftertax income to its stockholders. Deviations from this policy may be expected when international restrictions exist or when it is in the Corporation's best long-term interest.

Recognition of the basic differences in the businesses of the Corporation extends to the enhanced profitability and income-statement contributions from the distribution operations as balanced by the enhanced financial solidarity of fixed-asset stability by those in the metal parts manufacturing operations. The anticipated pretax return on sales for each operation shall continue to be expected to maintain or exceed their historic range of 15% for Bowman Distribution and 8% for Associated Spring North America and 8% for Associated Spring International.

PLANNING FOR GROWTH AND PERFORMANCE

To meet its overall objectives, the Corporation considers that annual planning on a 5-year basis is essential. The Corporation considers that the critical elements of planning for growth and performance by the individual profit centers in the groups are:

1. The establishment of specific attainable market, manufacturing and management objectives,
2. The preparation of definite plans and programs to meet these objectives, and
3. The quantification of these plans and their presentation in the established financial planning format.

When these have been determined by the operations to be acceptable in terms of overall operation objectives, they become, in aggregate, the operation performance plan. The consolidation of the operation plans with any other overall corporate plans forms the corporate performance plan for the period.

MANAGEMENT AND PERSONNEL

The Corporation has earned a reputation as a respected, professionally-managed company and intends to maintain and enhance this reputation. Recognition of the importance of each individual shall continue to be a basic primary concern for the success of the Corporation.

Barnes Group will continue to develop a management environment that will encourage and welcome change, new ideas, and the assumption by managers of reasonable business risks as means for assuring profitable growth of the Corporation.

The Corporation will seek to attract, develop and hold personnel of the highest caliber throughout the organization, and will provide compensation and incentives commensurate with performance.

As well as continuing its policy of promotion from within, the Corporation intends to continue a steady infusion of talented new personnel at all levels to assure both the broadest possible balance and an accelerated rate of innovation.

Specifically, Barnes Group commits to a policy of upward mobility in its key management personnel and will give full consideration to implementing this concept by seeking new or changed responsibilities and duties for key management personnel when they have continually occupied the same responsibilities over a period of approximately ten years. It will seek to constantly provide sufficient challenge and growth for all personnel in the Corporation by the growth of the

Corporation and its ability to stimulate and move along key management personnel into positions of enhanced responsibility.

CORPORATE CITIZENSHIP

Barnes Group intends to conduct its business so as to merit the respect of employees, local communities, owners and governments at all locations. The Corporation commits itself to make a status report from time to time with regard to its activities of Corporate Citizenship.

The Corporation aspires to a position of leadership in the following fields:

1. Affirmative action programs at all levels for equal opportunity to minority and disadvantaged persons and groups, including women.
2. Aggressive action to reduce or eliminate throughout its operations any sources or causes of environmental pollution or destruction.
3. In the international field, a positive and responsible attitude as a foreign owner to the national policies and interests of the host country. It is intended that the Corporation will continue its policy of seeking and holding local resident nationals for key positions in all of its international organizations.
4. The encouragement of employees to participate and assert personal leadership in activities directed toward the solution of social and human problems.
5. At all levels of the company, the maintenance of the highest standards of business and professional ethics. The delivery of high-quality products and services and to fulfill this economic role with a minimum of resource waste.

STOCKHOLDERS AND FINANCIAL COMMUNITY

The Corporation recognizes the need to continue to enhance and develop its image for continuity of growth from an investor's point of view:

1. By continuing, and improving where possible, contact with and information flow to the financial community and stockholders.
2. By continuing to provide an adequate return through dividends and appreciation of stock value to the stockholders—the owners of the business. The Corporation will strive to continue its policy of the last 14 years of frequent increases in dividends to shareholders. Within the framework of this objective the maximum amount possible will be reinvested in the business to sustain its planned growth.

Barnes Group commits itself in principle to a course of independent growth and development and believes the shareholders' interest is best served by the expansion of the Corporation as an independent entity.

Through this image of growth and successful performance, the Corporation will strive to continue to merit the confidence of the financial community and the stockholders who supply the funds required by the Corporation to meet its objectives.

Source: *Corporate Objectives: 1975-1980* (Bristol, CT: Barnes Group, 1976).

Corporations define objectives in various ways. Some companies make only brief statements while others elaborate on each policy in detail. Lockheed Corporation, for example, breaks down each statement into the following four parts: introduction, basic policy, assignment or responsibilities, and interpretation. The Green Giant Company defines its objectives, which it calls policies, separately for each functional area in a 38-page report. In other words, corporations vary enormously in the way they state their objectives.

The statements on objective at the corporate level serve two purposes. First, these statements convey corporate perspectives to the community in the form of a public relations document. Second, they spell out the boundaries within which the SBU's objectives and strategy may be formulated. Exhibit 6-3 illustrates how corporate objectives and goals may be organized.

Objectives and goals are split into three categories: measurement, growth/survival, and constraint. Measurement objectives are usually financial in nature. Growth/survival objectives have a reference to the marketing side of the business. Constraint objectives indicate certain external and internal limitations and impositions which must be adhered to. For example, the objective of giving a square deal to all people may prohibit a company from seeking a course which would hurt the interest of a special group. Also, the objective of equal opportunity has led many corporations to encourage employment of women executives.

STRATEGIC BUSINESS UNIT OBJECTIVES

A strategic business unit (SBU) was defined as a unit comprised of one or more products having a common market base whose manager has complete responsibility for integrating all functions into a strategy against an identifiable external customer. The term SBU was defined in Chapter 5. Even at the cost of repetition, it will be desirable to examine the development and meaning of strategic business units here again. This will indicate why objectives must be defined at this level. Abell's explanation is as follows:

> The development of marketing planning has paralleled the growing complexity of business organizations themselves. The first change to take place was the shift from functionally organized companies with relatively narrow product lines and served-market focus to large diversified firms serving multiple markets with multiple product lines. Such firms are usually divided into product or market divisions, divisions may be divided into departments, and these in turn are often further divided into product lines or market segments. As this change gradually took place over the last two decades, "sales planning" was gradually replaced by "marketing planning" in most of these organizations. Each product manager or market manager drew up a marketing plan for his product line or market segment. These were aggregated together into an overall divisional "marketing plan." Divisional plans in turn were aggregated into the overall corporate plan.

EXHIBIT 6-3 Classifying Corporate Objectives and Goals

Measurement		Growth/Survival		Constraint	
Objectives	Goals	Objectives	Goals	Objectives	Goals
1. Make satisfactory profit.	a. 10 percent return on investment. b. $2 per share earnings.	1. Become leader in the industry.	Achieve 55 percent market share in the traditional business.	1. Do not dilute stockholder equity.	Growth should be achieved without equity financing. A small amount of dilution of shareholders' equity will be tolerated as a result of present stock option and incentive compensation plans.
2. Control water pollution in the area.	Reduce the fluoride concentration in the waste discharge of a plant from 3.8 milligrams per liter to the government-prescribed limit of 1.0 mg.	2. Be among *Fortune's* first 500 corporations.	Add another $100 million to sales by 1983-1984.		
3. Fight back acquisition efforts by other corporations.	a. Seek recapitalization by borrowing to repurchase 10 percent common shares. b. Trim marketable current assets to raise enough funds to double dividend payouts.	3. Achieve a stronger position in the Eastern European markets.	a. Undertake a study of market potential, country by country. b. Choose a country for initial entry and for opening an office.	2. Do not do business with countries that pursue apartheid policy. 3. Depend less on government business. 4. New venture must provide satisfactory return on investment.	Attempts to develop business with South Africa may be called off. Government business should not constitute more than 50 percent of sales. Aim at 12 to 15 percent return on investment.

But a further important change is now taking place. There has been over the last decade a growing acceptance of the fact that individual units or subunits within a corporation, e.g., divisions, product departments, or even product lines or market segments, may play different *roles* in achieving overall corporate objectives. Not all units and subunits need to produce the same level of profitability; not all units and subunits have to contribute equally to cash flow objectives.

This concept of the organization as a "portfolio" of units and subunits having different objectives is at the very root of contemporary approaches to strategic marketing planning. It is commonplace today to hear businesses defined as "cash cows," "stars," "question marks," "dogs," etc.* It is in sharp contrast to practice in the 1960s and earlier which emphasized primarily sales and earnings (or return on investment) as a major measure of performance. Although different divisions or departments were intuitively believed to have different capabilities to meet sales and earning goals, these differences were seldom made explicit. Instead, each unit was expected to "pull its weight" in the overall quest for growth and profits.

With the recognition that organizational entities may differ in their objectives and roles, a new organizational concept has also emerged. This is the concept of a "business unit." A business unit may be a division, a product department, or even a product line or major market, depending on the circumstances. It is, however, usually regarded by corporate management as a reasonably autonomous profit center. Usually it has its own "general manager" (even though he may not have that title, he has general managerial responsibilities). Often it has its own manufacturing, sales, research and development, and procurement functions although in some cases some of these may be shared with other businesses (e.g., pooled sales). A business unit usually has a clear market focus. In particular it usually has an identifiable strategy and an identifiable set of competitors. In some organizations (the General Electric Company, for example), business units are clearly identified and defined. In other organizations, divisions or product departments are treated as relatively autonomous business units although they are not explicitly defined as such.

A business unit will usually comprise several "program" units. These may be product lines, geographic market segments, end-user industries to which the company sells, or units defined on the basis of any other relevant segmentation dimension. Program units may also sometimes differ in their objectives. In such cases, the concept of a portfolio exists both in terms of business units within a corporate structure (or substruc-

*These terms are defined in Chapter 13.

ture, such as a group) or in terms of programs within a business unit. Usually, however, the business unit is a major focus of strategic attention, and strategic market plans are of prime importance at this level.[4]

As the above quotation notes, in a large, complex organization there may be a number of SBUs, each playing its unique role for the organization. Obviously, then, at the corporate level, objectives can be defined only in generalities. It is only at each SBU level that more specific statements of objectives can be made. Actually it is the SBU mission and its objectives and goals that product/market managers will need to consider in their strategic plans.

Business Mission

Mission is a broad term that refers to the total perspectives or purpose of an organization. Examples are: "General Motors is people" and Du Pont's "Better things for better living through chemistry." Traditionally the mission of a business corporation was framed around its product line and expressed in mottoes such as: "Our business is textiles," "We manufacture cameras," and so on. With the advent of marketing orientation and technological innovations, the traditional method of defining the business mission has been decried. It has been held that building the perspectives of a business around its product limits the scope of management to enter new fields and thus make use of growth opportunities. Levitt has said:

> The railroads did not stop growing because the need for passengers and freight transportation declined. That grew. The railroads are in trouble today not because the need was filled by others (cars, trucks, airplanes, even telephones), but because it was not filled by the railroads themselves. They let others take customers away from them because they assumed themselves to be in the railroad business rather than in the transportation business. The reason they defined their industry wrong was because they were railroad-oriented instead of transportation-oriented; they were product-oriented instead of customer-oriented.[5]

According to Levitt's thesis, the mission of a business should be defined broadly so that an airline could perhaps consider itself in the vacation business, a publisher in the learning industry, an appliance manufacturer in the business of preparation of nourishments, and so on. Recently Levitt's proposition has been criticized and the question asked whether the simple extension of the scope of a business leads far enough. For example, the railroads could not protect themselves by defining their business as transportation. The Boston Consulting Group says:

---

[4]Derek F. Abell, "Metamorphosis in Marketing Planning," in Subhash C. Jain, (ed.), *Research Frontiers in Marketing: Dialogues and Directions* (Chicago: American Marketing Association, 1978), p. 257.
[5]Theodore Levitt, "Marketing Myopia," *Harvard Business Review* (July–August, 1960), p. 46.

Unfortunately, there is a prevalent notion that if one merely defines one's business in increasingly general terms—such as transportation rather than railroading—the road to successful competitive strategy will be clear. Actually, that is hardly ever the case. More often, the opposite is true. For example, in the case of the railroads, passengers and freight represent very different problems, and short haul vs. longer haul are completely different strategic issues. Indeed, as the unit train demonstrates, just coal handling is a meaningful strategic issue.[6]

The problem with Levitt's thesis is that it is too broad and does not provide what those involved in finance call a *common thread:* a relationship between a firm's past and future which indicates where the firm is bound and helps management to institute directional perspectives. The common thread may be found in the area of marketing, production technology, finance, or management. ITT ventured into such diverse businesses as hotels and bakeries, taking advantage of its managerial abilities in order to manage and operate far-fetched businesses. Armco Inc. found a common thread via finance in entering the airplane leasing business. BIC Pen Company used its marketing strength to involve itself in the razor blade business. The Singer Company considered common technology as the basis for entering the business machines industry. Thus, the mission cannot be defined by making abstract statements which one hopes will pave the way for the business to enter new fields.

It would appear that the mission of a business is neither a statement of current business nor a random extension of current involvements. It signifies the scope and nature of business, not as it is today, but as it could be in the future. The mission plays an important role in designating opportunities for diversification either through R & D or acquisitions. To be meaningful, the mission should be based on a comprehensive analysis of the business' technology and customer mission. Examples of companies with technology-based definitions are computer companies and aerospace companies. Customer mission refers to the fulfillment of a particular type of customer need, such as the basic nutritional need, the maintenance of household need, or the entertainment need.

Whether the company has a written business mission statement or not is immaterial. What is important, however, is that due consideration has been given to technological and marketing factors (as related to particular segments and their needs) in defining the mission. Ideally, business definitions should be based on a combination of technology and market mission variables, but some companies venture into new fields just depending on a one-way definition. For example, Texas Instruments entered the digital watch market on the basis of its integrated circuits technology lead. Procter & Gamble added Folger's coffee to its business out of its experience in fulfilling the customer's daily requirements.

Cited below, as an illustration, are mission statements of Swissair.

---

[6]*Perspectives on Corporate Strategy* (Boston: Boston Consulting Group, 1970), p. 42.

1. to provide worldwide service for the Swiss industry and the Swiss
    people, and to develop the service as these needs develop.
2. to maximize long-run profits, earning at least a minimum amount
    of dividend each year.[7]

To sum up, the mission deals with the questions: What type of business do we
want to be in at some future time? What do we want to become? At any given
point in time, most of the resources of a business are frozen or locked into their
current uses, and the outputs in services and/or products are for the most part
defined by current operations. Over an interval of a few years, however, environmental changes place demands on the business for new types of resources. Further, because of personnel attrition and depreciation of capital resources, management has the option of choosing the environment in which the company will
operate and acquiring commensurate new resources rather than replacing the old
ones in kind. This explains the importance of defining the business' mission. The
mission should be so defined that it has a bearing on the business' strengths and
weaknesses.

The relevance here of a discussion on the definition of the business mission can
be questioned. This topic could as well be included under corporate objectives.
However, in a large diversified company where one part of the business may have
little in common with another, a statement of business mission may be difficult
to make. It is assumed that as a matter of strategy the SBU of a company may
consider new roles for itself. For such actions a statement of business mission will
be useful. It is possible, however, that once an SBU expands its role, the expanded
role may be assigned by top management to another SBU.

Objectives and Goals

Objectives and goals may be stated in terms of activities (manufacturing a
specific product, selling in a particular market); financial indicators (achieving
targeted return on investment); desired positions (market share, quality leadership); and combinations of these factors. Generally an SBU has a series of objectives to cater to the interests of different stakeholders. One way of organizing
objectives is to split them into the following classes: measurement objectives,
growth/survival objectives, and constraint objectives. It must be emphasized that
objectives and goals should not be based just on facts, but also on values and
feelings. What facts should one look at? How should they be weighed and related
to one another? It is in seeking answers to such questions that value judgments
become crucial.

The perspectives of an SBU will determine how far the objective can be broken
down into minute details. If the objective applies to a number of products, only
broad statements of objectives specifying the role of each product/market from

---

[7]"Swissair (c)," a case copyrighted by IMEDE, Lausanne, Switzerland, 1960, p. 406.

the vantage point of the SBU will be feasible. On the other hand, when an SBU has been created around one or two products, objectives may be stated in detail.

Exhibit 6-4 illustrates how SBU objectives and goals can be identified and split into three groups: measurement, growth/survival, and constraint. Measurement objectives and goals define an SBU's aims from the point of view of the stockholders. Traditionally the word *profit* would have sufficed instead of measurement. But, as is widely recognized today, a modern corporation has several corporate publics besides the stockholders. Therefore it is erroneous to use the word *profit*. On the other hand, the company's very existence and ability to serve different stakeholders depend on financial viability. Thus, profit constitutes an important measurement objective. To emphasize the real significance of profit, it is more appropriate to label it as a measurement tool.

It will be useful here to draw a distinction between corporate objectives and measurement objectives and goals at the level of an SBU. Corporate objectives define the company's outlook for various stakeholders as a general concept. But the SBU's objectives and goals are specific statements. For example, keeping the environment clean may be one of the corporate objectives. Using this as a basis,

EXHIBIT 6-4   Illustration of an SBU's Objectives

I.   SBU

Major Appliances

II.   Mission

To be the leading company (in terms of sales and innovations) in the power-consuming apparatus/appliances.

III.   Objectives (General statements in the following areas):

A. Measurement
  1. Profitability
  2. Cash flow
B. Growth/Survival
  1. Market standing
  2. Productivity
  3. Innovation
C. Constraint
  1. Capitalize on our research in certain technologies
  2. Avoid style businesses with seasonal obsolescence
  3. Avoid antitrust problems
  4. Assume responsibility to public

IV. Goals

Specific targets and time frame for achievement of each objective listed above.

in a particular time frame an SBU may define prevention of water pollution as one of its objectives. In other words, it is not necessary to repeat the company's obligation to various stakeholders in defining an SBU's objectives since this is already covered in the corporate objectives. In summary, objectives and goals should underline the areas that need to be covered during the time horizon of planning.

Growth objectives and goals have a reference to getting ahead. "Leap ahead" is accepted as sound advice in a capitalistic society. Shunning growth is equivalent to being against motherhood. Thus, companies often aim at growth. While measurements are usually stated in financial terms, growth is prescribed with reference to the market. Depending on its internal environment and how it wishes to interact with the outside world, a company may avoid doing a few things in certain ways. This imposes definite constraints on carrying out operations. Such constraints, which are self-imposed, may be stated as constraint objectives and goals.

An orderly description of objectives may not always work out. Overlapping may occur among the three types of objectives and goals. It is important, however, that the final draft of objectives is based on investigation, analysis, and contemplation. The SBU's objectives and goals as outlined in Exhibit 6-4 comprise all functional areas of a business; the objectives mainly concerned with marketing are the growth/survival objectives. However, as far as planning is concerned, at the SBU level, the functional breakdown of a business is outdated.

PRODUCT/MARKET OBJECTIVES

Product/market objectives may be defined in terms such as profitability, market share, and growth. Most companies state their product/market purpose in a combination of these terms. Some companies, especially the very small ones, may use just one of these terms to communicate their product/market objectives.

Profitability

Profits in one form or another constitute a desirable goal to pursue for a product/market venture. As objectives they may either be expressed in absolute monetary terms or as a percentage of capital employed or total assets.

At the corporate level emphasis on profit to state objectives is sometimes avoided since it seems to convey only limited perspectives of the corporate purpose. Besides, many economic theorists find it to be a non-operational concept. But at the product/market level an objective in terms of profitability provides a measurable criterion with which the management can evaluate performance. Since product/market objectives are an internal matter, the corporation is not constrained by any ethical questions in its emphasis on profits. Of course, attainment of objectives should always be subject to good across-the-board conduct and be within the ethical standards laid down by the corporate management.

Burroughs Corporation, a computer manufacturer, is an ardent user of the profitability objective. The company aims at achieving a pretax margin of 20 percent and increasing pretax return on invested capital to 20 percent. Burroughs' emphasis on profits is something unusual in the computer industry. The orthodox view has been that before the computer business could be expected to pay off, many years of unprofitable investment were required. But Burroughs' chief executive officer, Ray Macdonald, insisted on the profit goal in his company, and the outcome has been quite satisfactory. Burroughs' overall performance has been twice as good as that of any other competitor in the industry except IBM.[8]

How can the profitability goal be realized in practice? First, the corporate management determines the desired profitability, i.e., rate of return on investment. There may be a single goal set for the entire corporation, or it may vary for different businesses. Using the given rate of return, the SBU may compute the percent of markup on cost for its product(s). To do so, the normal rate of production, averaged over the business cycle, is computed. The total cost of the normal production then becomes the standard cost. Next, the ratio of invested capital (in the SBU) to a year's standard cost (i.e., capital turnover), is figured out. The capital turnover multipled by the rate of return gives the markup percentage to be applied to standard cost. This markup is an average figure which may be adjusted both among products and through time.

Market Share

In many industries, the cigarette industry for example, gain of a few percentage points in the market share has a positive effect on profits. Thus, market share has traditionally been considered as a desirable goal to pursue. In recent years extensive research on the subject has discovered new evidence on the positive impact of market share on profitability. This has added new dimensions to market share as a viable goal to pursue.

While market share was traditionally considered in absolute terms, current thinking on it requires that it be defined in relative terms (i.e., in relation to the share of the leader). It is held that absolute share is only meaningful to the extent that it is an indicator of market stability and competitive maturity.

The importance of market share is explainable by the fact that it is related to cost. Cost is a function of scale or experience. Thus the market leader has a lower cost than the competitors because superior market share permits the accumulation of more experience. Prices, however, are determined by the cost structure of the least effective competitor. The high cost competitor must generate enough cash to hold the market share and meet finances. If this is not accomplished, the high-cost competitor drops out and is replaced as the marginal competitor by a more effective, lower-cost competitor. The profitability of the market leader is

---

[8]Bro Uttal, "How Ray Macdonald's Growth Theory Created IBM's Toughest Competitor," *Fortune* (January, 1977), p. 94.

ascertained by the same price level that determines the profit of even the least effective competitor. Thus, higher market share gives a competitive edge to a firm. As a matter of fact, effect of market share goes much further. Henderson states:

> Ability to have a basic cost differential in a market sector provides the opportunity to gain a differential growth rate and a differential market share in that sector. This leads to an even greater differential advantage in cost. This advantage can be compounded until it becomes an advantage of such proportions that quite adequate profits can be earned even though competitors can barely finance the maintenance of their own shares.[9]

One strong proponent of market share goal is Texas Instruments. The company takes a long-term view and commits itself to obtaining a big share of the growth market. It keeps building new plants even though its first plant for a product has yet to run at full capacity. It does so hoping large-scale operations will provide a cost advantage which it can utilize in the form of lower prices to customers. The latter in turn leads to a higher market share.[10]

While market share is a viable goal to pursue, tremendous foresight and effort is needed to achieve and maintain the market share position. A company aspiring to aim at a large share of the market should carefully consider two aspects: 1) its ability to finance the market share, and 2) its ability to effectively defend itself against the antitrust action which may be instigated by large increases in market share.[11] For example, both G.E. and RCA found that to meet their corporate profitability objectives they needed to achieve specific market share positions in the computer business. To realize the targeted market share positions required huge investment. The question, then, was whether they should gamble in an industry which was dominated by one large competitor (IBM) or invest their monies in other fields where there was the probability of earning a return equal to or higher than in the computer field. Both G.E. and RCA decided to get out of the computer field.[12] Fear of antitrust suits also prohibits the seeking of higher market shares. A number of corporations—Kodak, Gillette, Xerox, and IBM, for example—have been the target of such action.

The above reasons have led Bloom and Kotler to suggest that while market share should be pursued as a desirable goal, companies should opt not for share maximization, but for an optimal market share. They suggest the following procedure for figuring out the optimal point:

---

[9]Bruce D. Henderson, "Market Share," an informal statement by the Boston Consulting Group, 1978.
[10]"The Strategy that Took T.I. to the Top," *Business Week* (September 18, 1978), p. 67.
[11]William E. Fraham, Jr., "Pyrrhic Victories in Fights for Market Share," *Harvard Business Review* (September–October, 1972), p. 100.
[12]Allan T. Demaree, "G.E.'s Costly Ventures into Futures," *Fortune* (October, 1970), p. 158.

1. Estimate the relationship between market share and profitability.
2. Estimate the amount of risk associated with each share level.
3. Determine the point at which an increase in market share can no longer be expected to bring enough profit to compensate for the added risks to which the company would expose itself.[13]

Virtues of higher market share do not mean that a company with lower share may not have a chance in the industry. There are companies which earn a respectable return on their equity despite low market shares. Examples of such corporations are Burroughs, Crown Cork & Seal, Union Camp, and Inland Steel. The following characteristics explain the success of low-share companies: They compete only in those market segments where their strengths have the greatest impact, they make efficient use of their modest R & D budgets, they shun growth for growth's sake, and they have innovative leaders.[14]

In brief, market share goal should not be taken too lightly. Rather a firm should aim at a market share after careful examination.

Growth

Growth is an accepted phenomenon of American life. All institutions should progress and grow. Those which do not grow invite extinction. The static corporations are often subject to a proxy fight.

There are a variety of reasons which make growth a viable objective to pursue. These are growth expectations of the stockholders, growth orientation of top management, employees' enthusiasm, growth opportunities furnished by the environment, corporate need to compete effectively in the marketplace, and corporate strengths and competencies which make it easy to grow. Exhibit 6-5 elaborates these under customer reasons; competitive reasons; company reasons; and distributer, dealer, and agent reasons.

An example of growth encouraged by corporate strength is provided by Time Inc. Around 1978 the company was in an extremely strong cash position. This helped it to acquire Book-of-the-Month Club, Inc., American Television & Communications Corp., and the *Washington Star* newspaper.[15] Also, H.S. Geneen's passion for growth led ITT into different industries (bakeries, car-rental agencies, hotels, insurance firms, parking lots) in addition to its traditional communications business. Any field that promised growth was acceptable to him. Thus, the chief executive officer's growth orientation is the most valuable prerequisite for growth.

---

[13]Paul N. Bloom and Philip Kotler, "Strategies for High Market Share Companies," *Harvard Business Review* (November–December, 1975), p. 63.
[14]R.G. Hamermesh, M.J. Anderson, Jr., and J.E. Harris, "Strategies for Low Market Share Businesses," *Harvard Business Review* (May–June, 1978), p. 95.
[15]"Time Inc.: A Bold Bid for Growth in all Four Lines of Business," *Business Week* (March 20, 1978), p. 130.

EXHIBIT 6-5   Reasons for Growth

Customer Reasons

The product line or sizes too limited for customer convenience.
Related products needed to serve a specific market.
Purchasing economies: one source, one order, one bill.
Service economies: one receiving and processing, one source of parts, service, other assistance.
Ability to give more and better services.
Production capacity not enough to fill needs of important customers who may themselves be growing.

Competitive Reasons

To maintain or better industry position, growth is necessary in any but a declining industry.
To counter or better chief competitors on new offerings.
To maintain or better position in specific product or market areas where competition is making strong moves.
To permit more competitive pricing ability by greater volume.
To possess greater survival strength in price wars, product competition and economic slumps by greater size.

Company Reason

To fulfill the growth expectations of stockholders, directors, executives and employees.
To utilize available management, selling, distribution, research or production capacity.
To supplement existing products and services that are not growth markets or are on downgrade of the profit cycle.
To stabilize seasonal or cyclical fluctuations.
To add flexibility by broadening the market and product base of opportunities.
To attain greater borrowing and financial influence with size.
To be able to attract and pay for better management personnel.
To attain the stability of size and move to management-by-planning.

Distributor, Dealer and Agent Reasons

To add products, sizes, and ranges necessary to attract interest of better distributors, dealers and agents.
To make additions necessary to obtain needed attention and selling effort from existing distributors, dealers and agents.

Source: John M. Brion, *Corporate Marketing Planning,* copyright © 1967 by John Wiley & Sons, Inc., pp. 70–71. Reprinted by permission of John Wiley & Sons, Inc.

Other Objectives

In addition to the commonly held objectives of profitability, market share, and growth, which were discussed above, a company may sometimes pursue a unique objective. Such unique objectives may be: technological leadership, social contribution, strengthening of national security, and international economic development.[16]

Technological Leadership. A company may consider technological leadership as a worthwhile goal to achieve. In order to accomplish this, it may develop new products or processes or adopt innovations ahead of competition, even when economics may not justify doing so. The underlying purpose of seeking this objective is to keep the name of the company in the forefront as a technological leader among security analysts, customers, distributors, and other stakeholders. Pan Am, for example, was the first airline to fly a Boeing 747 jumbo jet. This conveyed the image of a modern airline which uses up-to-date equipment.

Social Contribution. A company may pursue as an objective something which will make a social contribution. Ultimately that something may lead to higher profitability, but initially it is intended to provide a solution to a social problem. A beverage company, for example, may set the objective of not using throw-away bottles, or some other company may decide to hire an excessive number of minority youths during the summer to keep the streets calm.

Strengthening of National Security. In the interest of strengthening national defense, a company may undertake activities which may not be justifiable otherwise. For example, national concern may lead a company to deploy resources to develop a new fighter plane. The company may do so despite little encouragement from the Air Force, if only because the company sincerely feels that the country will need the plane in the coming years to match the Russian stockpile.

International Economic Development. Improvement of human welfare, the economic progress of less-developed countries, perpetration of a worldwide free enterprise system, etc., may also serve as objectives. For example, a company may undertake the development of a foolproof method of birth control which can be easily afforded and conveniently used by poor and illiterate masses in the less-developed countries of the world.

PROCESS OF SETTING OBJECTIVES

At the very beginning, in order to define objectives, an attempt should be made to take an inventory of objectives as they are understood now. For example, the

---

[16]J. Thomas Cannon, *Business Strategy and Policy* (New York: Harcourt, Brace & World, 1968), pp. 41–42.

SBU's head and senior executives may state what the current objectives of the SBU are and what type of SBU they want it to be in the future. Various executives will perceive current objectives differently; of course they will have varying ambitions for the SBU's future. It will take several top level meetings and a good deal of effort on the part of the head to settle on the final objectives.

Each executive may be asked to make a presentation on the objectives and goals he or she would like the corporation, SBU, or product/market to adopt for accomplishment in the future. The executives should be asked to justify the significance of each objective in terms of measuring performance, satisfying environmental conditions, and achieving growth. Foreseeably, the executives will have different objectives, but there will emerge, on analysis, a desire for a common destiny for the corporation, SBU, or product/market. In other words, people could have the same thing in mind, but put it across in such a way that it appears different. Sometimes inharmony of objectives may be based on diverse perceptions of a business' resource potential and corporate creed. Thus, before embarking on setting objectives, it is helpful if information on the resource potential and corporate creed is circulated among the executives.

Before finalizing the objectives, it is necessary that the executive team show a consensus; i.e., each one of them should believe in the viability of the set objectives and willingly agree to work toward their achievement. A way must be found to convince a dissenting executive to cooperate. For example, if a very ambitious executive works with stability-oriented people, in the absence of an opportunity to be creative the executive may fail to perform adequately even on routine matters, thus becoming a liability to the organization. In such a situation, it may be better to encourage the executive to look around for another job. This is useful for the organization as well as for the dissenting executive. This type of situation occurs when most of the executives have risen through the ranks and an "outsider" joins them. The dynamism of the latter is perceived as a threat, which may result in conflict. The author is familiar with a $100 million company where the vice-president of finance, an "outsider," in his insistence on long-range planning came to be recognized as such a danger by the old-timers that they made it necessary for him to quit.

To sum up, objectives should be set through a series of executive meetings. The organizational head plays the role of mediator in the process in screening varying viewpoints and perceptions and developing consensus from them.

Once broad objectives have been worked out, they should be translated into specific goals. This is an equally challenging task. Should the goals be set so high that only an outstanding manager can achieve them, or should they be set so that they are attainable by the average manager? At what level does frustration inhibit a manager's best efforts? Does an attainable budget lead to complacency? Presumably a company should start with three levels of goals: 1) easily attainable, 2) most desirable, and 3) optimistic. Thereafter, the company may choose a position somewhere between the most desirable and optimistic goals, depending on the organization's resources and the value orientation of the management. In no case, however, should the performance fall below the easily attainable level, even if everything goes the wrong way. Attempts should be made to make the goals realistic and achievable. Overly elusive goals can cause discouragement and affect motivation.

There are no acceptable standards, procedures, or measures for defining objectives. Thus, each organization must work out its own definitions of objectives and goals—what constitutes growth, what measures to adopt for their evaluation, etc. For example, consider the concept of return on investment. Almost for decades this has been considered to be a good measure of corporate performance. There are a large number of corporations which consider a specified return on investment as the most sacrosanct of goals to achieve. But ponder over its limitations. In a large, complex organization, ROI tends to optimize divisional performance at the cost of total corporate performance. Further, its orientation is a short-term one. Investment refers to assets. Different projects require a varying amount of assets before beginning to yield results, and the return may be slow or fast, depending on the nature of the project. Thus the value of assets may lose significance as an element in performance measurement. As the president of a large company remarked, "Profits are often the result of expenses incurred several years previously." The president also suggested that the current amount of net cash flow in dollars serves as a better measure of performance than the potential amount of net cash flow: "The net cash contribution budget is a precise measure of expectations with given resources."

Authors have suggested different procedures for developing objectives and goals. According to Boyd and Levy, the following six sources may be used to generate objectives and goals:

1. Focus on material resources (e.g., oil, minerals, forest).
2. Concern with fabricated objects (e.g., paper, nylon).
3. Major interest in events and activities requiring certain products or services, such as golfing and handling emergencies (Emery Air Freight).
4. Emphasis on the kind of person whose needs are to be met: "Babies Are Our Business" (Gerber).
5. Catering to specific parts of the body; i.e., eyes (Maybelline), teeth (Dr. West), feet (Florsheim), skin (Noxzema), hair (Clairol), beard (Gillette), and legs (Hanes).
6. Examination of wants and needs and seeking to adapt to them; i.e., generic use to be satisfied (nutrition, comfort, energy, self-expression, development, conformity, etc.) and consumption systems (for satisfying nutritional needs, for example).[17]

---

[17]Harper W. Boyd, Jr. and Sidney J. Levy, "What Kind of Corporate Objectives?" *Journal of Marketing* (October, 1966), pp. 53–58.

The above categories are especially useful for defining growth/survival objectives, particularly at the SBU or product/market level.

A different scheme for defining objectives has been proposed by SRI International. As shown in Exhibit 6-6, three approaches for working out objectives are: the "rational" approach, the "experimental" approach, and the "creative" approach. Each approach follows a different cause, means, and outcome sequence to arrive at objectives.[18] The SRI scheme appears to be more suited to defining corporate objectives than SBU and product/market objectives.

Whichever approach is utilized for finally coming out with a set of objectives and goals, the following serve as basic inputs in the process. At the corporate level objectives are influenced by corporate publics, the value system of top management, corporate resources, and external environment. The setting of an SBU's objectives and goals will be affected by its resources, strengths, and weaknesses and by the overall environment. Finally, product/market objectives are impacted by its strengths and weaknesses and its momentum. The strengths and weaknesses are based on the SBU's objectives, its current strategic perspectives, its past performance, and the product/market thrust. The momentum refers to future trends by extrapolation of past performance with the assumption that no major changes occur either in the product/market environment or in its marketing mix.

Identified above are the conceptual frameworks and underlying information useful in defining objectives at different levels. Unfortunately there is no computer model which would neatly relate all the available information to give a set of

EXHIBIT 6-6 Approaches to Objective Selling

	Cause	Means	Outcome
"Rational" Approach	Recognize Need	Formulate Options	Rate and Choose
"Experimental" Approach	Determine Priority	Explore Options	Evaluate Merit
"Creative" Approach	Determine Priority	Test Feasibility	Conceptualize Outputs

Source: Robert F. Stewart, *Setting Corporate Aims* (Menlo Park, CA: Stanford Research Institute, 1971), p. 5.

---

[18]Robert F. Stewart, "Setting Corporate Aims," a report of the Long Range Planning Service of the Stanford Research Institute, 1971, p. 8.

acceptable objectives. Thus, whichever conceptual scheme is followed and no matter how much information is available, in the final analysis objective setting remains a creative exercise. A creativity test which SRI International recommends to executives for determining their creativity vis-a-vis objective setting is shown in Exhibit 6-7.

EXHIBIT 6-7   Creativity Test

A group whose members would like to test how far out in the spectrum of creative methodology it can go can do so by a rather simple experiment. To illustrate:

Question: What are the end products of our business?

Conventional answer: We make light, off-the-road vehicles and ancillary mowing, raking, and baling equipment.

Generic answer: We are in the motorized agricultural equipment business.

Analog answer: Our products are to sickle and rake as seining nets are to the fishing pole.

Metaphor answer: We are obstetricians to Mother Earth.

Let us assume that Mr. A. offered the analog that mentioned the fishing pole. Mr. B asks derisively, "What the hell have fish got to do with making tractors?" Mr. C interrupts before A can answer with, "Say! Speaking of fish—have we ever looked into either the threats or opportunities of hydroponics?" Mr. D: "I thought of worms. Has anybody ever tried mechanically stocking a field with fertile earthworm eggs like they stock streams with trout?" The power of unconventional ways of looking at familiar things is illustrated without Mr. A's having to rationalize his analogy.

Or, let us also assume that the group agrees that the metaphoric allusion to obstetricians is interesting but too abstract to be useful. The fact that the group acknowledges interest—especially if accompanied by any evidence of humor or elation—may be the kind of signal that W.J.J. Gordon refers to in his research at Synetics. If the moderator deems it to be such, a short exercise called "force fit" may be tried. This consists of asking the group to imagine some line of thought by which the metaphor and the existing business might be connected. For example, one individual trying to force the Mother Earth metaphor and power mowers might muse: "It seems to me that obstetricians, like ourselves, only get into the life stream on 'labor day' when the sweat and tears and pressure are greatest." (Grins break out around the table.) "All right, you guys are ahead of me. What should our role be at planting time?"

If the above experiment indicates that the planning committee finds the latter two levels of abstraction more stimulating than frustrating, it is probably worthwhile to take advantage of this stimulation by seeking professional counsel in group creativity.

Source: Robert F. Stewart, *Setting Corporate Aims* (Menlo Park, CA: Stanford Research Institute, 1971), p. 5.

Once an objective has been set, it may be tested for validity using the following criteria:

1.   Is it, generally speaking, a guide to action? Does it facilitate decision making by helping management select the most desirable alternative courses of action?

2.   Is it explicit enough to suggest certain types of action? In this sense, "to make profits" does not represent a particularly meaningful guide to action, but "to carry on a profitable business in electrical goods" does.

3.   Is it suggestive of tools to measure and control effectiveness? "To be a leader in the insurance business" and "to be an innovator in child-care services" are suggestive of measuring tools in a helpful way; but statements of desires merely to participate in the insurance field or child-care field are not.

4.   Is it ambitious enough to be challenging? The action called for should in most cases be something in addition to resting on one's laurels. Unless the enterprise sets objectives which involve reaching, there is the threat that the end of the road may be at hand. It might be perfectly appropriate for some enterprises which have accomplished their objectives to quietly disband. However, for an undertaking to have continuity, it needs the vitality of challenging objectives.

5.   Does it suggest cognizance of external and internal constraints? Most enterprises operate within a framework of external constraints (e.g., legal and competitive restrictions) and internal contraints (e.g., limitations in financial resources). For instance, if objectives are to be a guide to action, it appears that American Motors, because of its particular set of constraints, should have somewhat different objectives than General Motors.

6.   Can it be related to both the broader and the more specific objectives at higher and lower levels in the organization? For example, are the SBU's objectives relatable to the corporate objectives, and in turn do they also relate to the objectives of one of its products/markets?[19]

SUMMARY

This chapter discusses the setting of objectives and goals. Objectives may be defined as general statements on the purpose and directions that the corporation wants to pursue. Goals are specific targets that the corporation would like to

---

[19]Reprinted by permission of the *Harvard Business Review*. Excerpt from "The Hierarchy of Objectives" by Charles H. Granger (May-June, 1964), p. 65. Copyright © 1964 by the President and Fellows of Harvard College. All rights reserved.

achieve within a given time frame. For example, the intent to increase market share is an objective. To aim at increasing the market share to, say, 20 percent within a period of two years is a goal.

Three levels of objectives and goals are examined: the corporate level, the strategic business unit (SBU) level, and the product/market level. At the corporate level, objectives emphasize overall perspectives.

At the SBU level, the business mission is first considered. Then the SBU's objectives and goals are defined, either in terms of financial indicators or desired positions, or in combinations of these factors. The product/market objectives are defined in terms of profitability, market share, growth, and several miscellaneous aspects.

DISCUSSION QUESTIONS

1. What informational inputs does a company need to define its objectives and goals?
2. Define the terms policy, objective, and goal.
3. Why is it necessary for a corporation to have a hierarchy of objectives (i.e., at the corporate level, the SBU level, and the product/market level)? Why can't a common set of objectives and goals be pursued at all these levels?
4. Develop a scheme for developing the corporate objectives of an insurance company, a fast-food chain, and a television manufacturer.
5. What is meant by the term *business mission?* Why is it necessary to define the mission?
6. How may an airline define its business mission?
7. How may a department store and a camera manufacturer define their product/market objectives? (Make your own choice of a product/market.)
8. Give two examples of product/market objectives in terms of technological leadership, social contribution, and strengthening of national security.

Part Two
Product/Market Planning

CHAPTER 7 – Framework for Product/Market Planning

CHAPTER 8 – Market Strategies

CHAPTER 9 – Product Strategies

CHAPTER 10 – Pricing Strategies

CHAPTER 11 – Distribution Strategies

CHAPTER 12 – Promotional Strategies

Chapter 7
Framework for Product/Market Planning

Induce your competitors not to invest in those products, markets, and services where you expect to invest the most. That is the most fundamental rule of strategy.

Bruce D. Henderson

Two things were achieved in the earlier chapters. First, the internal and external information required for undertaking marketing planning and strategy formulation was identified, and methods for analyzing such information were examined. Second, using the available information, the formulation of objectives was covered. The discussion on objectives, it will be recalled, was treated at three different levels: the product/market, strategic business unit, and corporate levels. This chapter takes us to the next step toward strategy formulation by establishing a framework for it.

Essentially, the strategy framework emphasizes starting at the product/market level, then seeking integration at the SBU level and the corporate level. This framework has two unique characteristics. Firstly, it emphasizes strategy consideration at the product/market level. Traditionally planning at that level was concerned primarily with operational rather than strategic matters. It focused on one-year budgets, and longer-term plans, though based on corporate strategies, contributed little toward selecting these strategies themselves. In stressing strategy formulation right at the product/market level, the proposed framework influences overall corporate strategy as a stepping-stone toward a superstructure. Secondly, the strategy framework introduces the strategic business unit as an integrating force between products/markets and the corporation. In strategy formulation all the factors of technology, finance, marketing, and competitive economics must be simultaneously considered. Optimizing all these factors at the corporate level in complex organizations is far from easy. Many companies have tried to solve this difficulty by adopting the profit center concept. Unfortunately, the profit center concept emphasizes short-term consequences, which are often transient, rather than shifts in environment, which take place over a period of time. Even worse, it is dysfunctional when it optimizes the profit center instead of the corporation as a whole. Additionally, a profit center may easily gain so much autonomy that the chief executive officer and the corporate executives become spectators rather than shapers of major strategic decisions. The division of the corporation into strategic business units (SBUs), however, overcomes the difficulties posed by the profit center concept. A typical SBU is composed of product lines with identifiable independence from other products or product lines in terms of competition, prices, substitutability of product, style/quality, and impact of product withdrawal. It becomes the satellite center for managing various products/markets.

Briefly, the framework suggests that strategic decisions might best be made at three different levels in a diversified company: by the product/market managers and the SBU manager jointly when questions of implementation are involved, by the chief executive officer and the SBU manager jointly when the formulation of strategy is the concern, and by the chief executive officer when the mission of the business is at issue.

CONCEPTUAL SCHEME

Exhibit 7-1 depicts the framework for developing product/market strategy. Product/market planning consists mainly of the following steps:

1. Start with the present business. Predict what the momentum of the business will be over the planning period if no significant change

EXHIBIT 7-1   Framework for Product/Market Planning

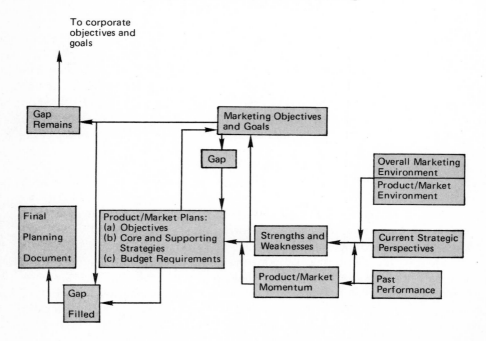

in the policies or methods of operation are made. The prediction will be based on historical performance.

2. Forecast what will happen to the environment over the planning period. This will include overall marketing environment and product/market environment.

3. Modify the prediction in step 1 in the light of shifts in the environment in step 2.

4. Stop if the predicted performance is fully satisfactory (vis-a-vis objectives) since nothing more is needed to be done. Continue if the prediction is not fully satisfying.

5. Appraise the significant strengths and weaknesses that exist in comparison with more important competitors. This appraisal should include any factors which may become important both in marketing (market, product, price, promotion, and distribution) and in other functional areas (finance, R&D, costs, organization, morale, reputation, management depth, etc.).

6. Evaluate the differences between your marketing strategies and those of your major competitors.

7. Undertake an analysis to discover some variation in marketing strategy which would produce a more favorable relationship in your competitive posture in the future.

8. Evaluate the proposed alternate strategy in terms of possible risks, competitive response, and potential payout.

9. Stop if the alternate strategy appears satisfactory (i.e., in terms of objectives).

10. Broaden the definition of the present business and repeat steps 7, 8, and 9 if there is still a gap between the objective and the alternative strategy. Here, re-defining the business means looking at other products that can be supplied to a market which is known and understood. Sometimes this means supplying existing products to a different market. It may also mean applying technical or financial abilities to new products and new markets simultaneously.

11. The process of broadening the definition of the business to provide a wider horizon can be continued until one of the following occurs:
    a. The knowledge of the new area becomes so thin that a choice of the sector to be studied is determined by intuition or obviously inadequate judgment.
    b. The cost of studying the new area becomes prohibitively expensive because of lack of related experience.
    c. It becomes clear that the prospects of finding a competitive opportunity have become remote.

12. Lower the objectives if the existing business is not satisfactory and if broadening of the business offers unsatisfactory prospects.

There are three tasks involved in the strategy procedure described above: information analysis, strategy formulation, and implementation. At the product/ market level these tasks are performed by either the product/market manager or an SBU executive. In practice, analysis and implementation are usually handled entirely by the product/market manager, while strategy formulation is done jointly by the product/market manager and the SBU executive.

Essentially, all firms have some kind of strategy and plans to carry on their operations. In the past, both the plans and the strategy were made intuitively. However, the increasing pace of change is forcing businesses to make their strategies explicit and often to change them. Strategy per se is getting more and more attention.

Any approach to strategy formulation leads to a conflict between objectives and capabilities. Attempting the impossible is not a good strategy; it is just a waste of resources. On the other hand, setting inadequate objectives is obviously self-defeating. Setting the proper objectives depends upon prejudgment of the potential success of the strategy; however, you cannot determine the strategy until you know the objectives. Strategy development is a reiterative process requiring art as well as science. The above dilemma may explain why many strategies are intuitively made rather than logically and tightly reasoned. But there are concepts which can be usefully applied in approximating the opportunities and speeding up the process of strategy development. Take market segmentation, for example. A market can be viewed in many different ways; a product can be used in many different ways. Each time the product/market pairing is varied, the relative competitive strength is varied, too. Thus, a key element in strategy is choosing the competitor whom you wish to challenge, as well as choosing the market segment and product characteristics with which you will compete. The above procedure is designed not only to systematically analyze information, but also to formulate or change strategy in an explicit fashion and implement it.

MEASURING THE MOMENTUM

Planning is undertaken to achieve a desired future which, while the probability is low, may come about without any changes in strategy being made. The first phase in developing product/market plans is to determine the state of affairs in the future, assuming that the environment and the strategy remain the same. This future state of affairs is what we call momentum. If the momentum projects a desirable future, little planning is needed. More often, however, the future implied by the momentum may not be the desired future.

The momentum may be measured using modeling, forecasting, and simulation techniques. Let us describe how these techniques were applied to a bank. This bank grew by opening two to three new branches per year in the trading area defined by state law. The measurement of momentum consisted of projecting income statement and balance sheet figures for new branches and merging them with the projected income statement and balance sheet of the original bank. A model was constructed to project the bank's future performance. The first step in the model construction was the prediction of B_{ijt}, i.e., balances for an account of type i in area j and in time period t. Account types included checking, savings, and certificates of deposit, and areas were chosen to coincide with counties in the state. County areas were desirable since most state data were available by county and the current branching areas were defined by counties. Balances were projected using multiple linear regression. County per capita income and rate of population growth were found to be important variables for predicting total checking account balances, and these variables, along with the last period's savings balance, were shown to be important in describing savings account balances.

The next step in the model construction was to predict M_{jt} (i.e., the market share of the bank being considered in area j and time period t). This was done using a combination of data of past performances and managerial judgment. The total expected deposit level for the branch being considered, D_{it}, was then calculated as:

$$D_{it} = \sum_{jb} (\ B_{ijt} \ M_{jt})$$

For the existing operations of the bank, the past data was utilized to produce a ten-year set of deposit balances. These deposit projections were added to those of new branches. Turning to other figures, certain line items on the income statement could be attributed directly to checking accounts, others to savings accounts. The remaining figures were related to the total of account balances.

For this model, ratios of income and expense items to appropriate deposit balances were predicted by a least-squares regression on historical data. This was not considered the most satisfactory method since some changing patterns of incurring income and expenses were not taken into account. However, more sophisticated forecasting techniques, such as exponential smoothing and Box-Jenkins, were rejected due to the potential amounts of management misunderstanding they could generate. As Ackoff points out, managers will rarely use results of a model they do not understand.[1]

Once the ratio matrix was developed, the income statements could be generated by simply multiplying the ratios by the proper account balance projection to arrive at the ten-year projection for the income statement line items. These income statements, in conjunction with the bank's policy on dividends and capitalization, were then used to generate a ten-year balance-sheet projection. The net results were presented to the bank's senior executive committee to be reviewed and modified. After incorporating executive judgment, final ten-year income statements and balance sheets were obtained, indicating the bank's momentum into the future.[2]

---

[1]Russell L. Ackoff, *A Concept of Corporate Strategy* (New York: John Wiley & Sons, 1970).
[2]Robert J. Graham, "Some Useful Techniques for Implementing a Planning Process," in Justin D. Stolen and James J. Conway (eds.), *Ninth Annual Conference Proceedings* (Atlanta: American Institute for Decision Sciences, 1977), pp. 525–527.

GAP ANALYSIS

In the preceding example, momentum was extrapolated from the historical data. Little attention was given to either internal or external environmental considerations in developing the momentum. However, for a realistic projection of future outcomes, careful analysis of the overall marketing environment as well as the product/market environment is necessary.

As a part of gap analysis, therefore, the momentum should be examined and adjusted with reference to environmental assumptions. Analysis of the industry, the market, and the competitive environment should be performed to identify important threats and opportunities. This should be combined with a careful evaluation of the product/market competitive strengths and weaknesses. On the basis of this, the momentum should be evaluated and refined.

In the midst of continued inflation toward the end of 1979, the new chairman of the Federal Reserve System, Paul Volcker, decided to restrict the money supply. Consequently, the prime and short-term rates of interest increased quite a bit. For example, the rate of interest on a six-month money market certificate went up to 12.651 percent annually. This led many depositors to withdraw their money (even at the cost of substantial penalty for early withdrawal) from the six-year certificates of deposit which earned 7.75 percent annual interest. In the illustration discussed in the previous section, the impact of such an increase in interest rate was not considered in arriving at the momentum (i.e., in making forecasts of deposit balances). But as a part of gap analysis, this shift in the environment should be duly taken into account by making adequate adjustments in the momentum.

The 'new' momentum should then be measured against the objectives to see if there will be a gap between expectation and potential realization. More often than not, there will be a gap between what objectives are desired and what momentum, as revised with reference to environmental assumptions, can deliver. How this gap may be filled will be discussed in the next section.

FILLING THE GAP

The gap must be filled in order to bring the planned results as close to goals as possible. Essentially, gap filling amounts to reformulating the product/market strategy. Exhibit 7-2 describes a six-step procedure which may be used for examining the current strategy and coming up with a new one which can fill the gap.

While basically using a procedure similar to the one depicted in Exhibit 7-2, the discussion here is planned under the following headings: issue assessment, identification of key variables, and strategy selection. The experience of companies with which the author is familiar suggests that the gap-filling exercise should be assigned to a multi-functional team. Non-marketing people often provide outside inputs into the process; their objectivity and healthy skepticism are generally of great help in sharpening the focus and in maintaining business-wide

EXHIBIT 7-2   Procedure for Filling the Gap

1. Record current strategy:
   a. What is the current strategy?
   b. What kind of business does management want to operate (considering such management values as desired return on investment, growth rate, share of market, stability, flexibility, character of the business, and climate)?
   c. What kind of business does management feel it ought to operate (considering management's concepts of social responsibility and obligations to stockholders, employees, community, competitors, customers, suppliers, government, and the like)?
2. Identify problems with the current strategy:
   a. Are trends discernible in the environment that may become threats and/or missed opportunities if the current strategy is continued?
   b. Is the company having difficulty implementing the current strategy?
   c. Is the attempt to carry out the current strategy disclosing significant weaknesses and/or unutilized strengths in the company?
   d. Are there other concerns with respect to the validity of the current strategy?
   e. Is the current strategy no longer valid?
3. Discover the core of the strategy problem:
   a. Does the current strategy require greater competence and/or resources than the company possesses?
   b. Does it fail to exploit adequately the company's distinctive competence?
   c. Does it lack sufficient competitive advantage?
   d. Will it fail to exploit opportunities and/or meet threats in the environment, now or in the future?
   e. Are the various elements of the strategy internally inconsistent?
   f. Are there other considerations with respect to the core of the strategy problem?
   g. What, then, is the real core of the strategy problem?
4. Formulate alternative new strategies:
   a. What possible alternatives exist for solving the strategy problem?
   b. To what extent do the company's competence and resources limit the number of alternatives that should be considered?
   c. To what extent do management's preferences limit the alternatives?
   d. To what extent does management's sense of social responsibility limit the alternatives?
   e. What strategic alternatives are acceptable?
5. Evaluate alternative new strategies:
   a. Which alternative best solves the strategy problem?
   b. Which alternative offers the best match with the company's competence and resources?
   c. Which alternative offers the greatest competitive advantage?
   d. Which alternative best satisfies management's preferences?
   e. Which alternative best meets management's sense of social responsibility?

f. Which alternative minimizes the creation of new problems?
6. Choose a new strategy:
    a. What is the relative significance of each of the preceding considerations?
    b. What should the new strategy be?

perspectives. The process the team follows should be carefully structured and the
analytical work punctuated with regular review meetings to synthesize findings,
check progress, and refocus work when such is considered desirable. The SBU
staff should be deeply involved in the evaluation and approval of the strategies.

Issue Assessment

The primary purpose of this step is to raise issues about the status quo to
evaluate the business' competitive standing in view of present and expected
market conditions. Typically, a beginning should be made by working through
a series of questions in order to identify those few issues that will most crucially
affect the future of the business. The following questions might be included:
How mature is the product/market segment under review? What new avenues
of market growth are conceivable? Is the industry becoming more cyclical?
Are competitive factors changing (for example, is product-line elaboration declining and cost control gaining in importance)? Is our industry as a whole
likely to be hurt by continuing inflation? Are new regulatory restrictions pending?

As the company moves toward its own competitive position, the following
questions may be raised: How mature is our product line? How do our products
perform compared with those of leading competitors? How does our marketing
capability compare? What about our cost position? What are our customers' most
common criticisms? Where are we most vulnerable to competitors? How strong
are we in our distribution channels? How productive is our technology? How
good is our record in new-product introduction?

Some critical issues are immediately apparent in many companies. For example, a company in a highly concentrated industry may find it difficult to hold on
to its market share if a stronger, larger competitor were to launch a new low-
priced product with intensive promotional support. Also, in a capital-intensive
industry the cyclical pattern and possible pressures on pricing are usually critical.
If a product's transport costs are high, preemptive investments in regional manufacturing facilities may be desirable. Other important issues may be concerned
with threats of backward integration by customers or forward integration by
suppliers, technological upset, new regulatory action, or the entry of foreign
competition into the home market. Most strategy teams supplement this brain-
storming exercise with certain basic analyses that often lead to fresh insights and

a more-focused list of critical business issues. Three such issues which may be mentioned here are: profit economics analysis, market segmentation analysis, and competitor profiling.

Profit economics analysis will indicate how product costs are physically generated and where the economic leverage lies. The contribution of the product to fixed costs and profits may be calculated by classifying the elements of cost as fixed, variable, or semi-variable and by subtracting variable cost from product price to yield contribution-per-item-sold. It is then possible to test the sensitivity of profits to possible variations in volume, price, and cost elements. Similar computations may be made for manufacturing facilities, distribution channels, and customers.

Segmenting the market will show alternate methods of segmentation and whether there are any segments not being properly cultivated. Once the appropriate segment is determined, efforts should be made to project the determinants of demand (including cyclical factors and any constraints on market size or growth rate) and to explain pricing patterns, relative market shares, and other determinants of profitability.

Profiling competitors may involve examining their sales literature, talking with experts or representatives of industry association, and interviewing shared customers and any known former employees of competitors. If more information is needed, the team may acquire and analyze competing products and perhaps even arrange to have competitors interviewed by a third party. With these data competitors may be compared in terms of product features and performance, pricing, likely product costs and profitability, marketing and service efforts, manufacturing facilities and efficiency, and technology and product development capabilities. Finally, each competitor's basic strategy may be inferred from these comparisons.[3]

Identification of Key Variables

The above information on issues should be analyzed to isolate the critical factors on which success in the industry depends. In any business there are usually about five to ten factors which have a decisive effect on performance. However, these factors may vary from industry to industry. Even within a single company they may vary according to shifts in industry position, product superiority, distribution methods, economic conditions, availability of raw materials, and the like. Therefore, suggested here is a set of questions which may be raised to identify the key success factors in any given situation:

1. What things have to be done exceptionally well to win in this industry? In particular, what must we do well today to lead the industry in profit results and competitive vitality in the years ahead?

---

[3]Carter F. Bales, "Strategic Control: The President's Paradox," *The McKinsey Quarterly* (Autumn, 1977), pp. 9–16.

2. What factors have caused or could cause companies in this industry to fail?
3. What are the unique strengths of our principal competitors?
4. What are the risks of product or process obsolescence? How likely are they to occur and how critical could they be?
5. What things have to be done to increase sales volume? How does a company in this industry go about increasing its share of the market? How could each of these ways of growing affect profits?
6. What are our major elements of cost? In what ways might each of them be reduced?
7. What are the big profit leverage points in this industry—i.e., what would be the comparative impact on profits of equal management efforts expended on each of a whole series of possible improvement opportunities?
8. What key recurring decisions have to be made in each major functional segment of the business? What impact on profits could a good or bad decision in each of these categories have?
9. How, if at all, could the performance of this function give the company a competitive advantage?[4]

Once these key factors have been identified, they should be examined with reference to the current status of the product/market to define alternative strategies which may be pursued to gain competitive advantage over the long term. Each alternative strategy should be evaluated for profit payoff, investment costs, feasibility, and risk.

It is important that strategy alternatives be described as specifically as possible. Simply stating "maintain product quality," "provide high-quality service," and "expand market overseas" is not enough. Precise and concrete descriptions, such as "extend the warranty period from one year to two years," "enter English, French, and German markets by appointing agents in these countries," and "provide a $25 cash rebate to every buyer to be handed over by the company directly," are essential before alternatives can be adequately evaluated.

Initially the strategy group may generate a long list of alternatives, but informal discussion with management can soon pare these down to a handful. Each surviving alternative should be weighed in terms of projected financial consequences (sales, fixed and variable costs, profitability, investment, and cash flow) and relevant nonfinancial measures (market shares, product quality and reliability indices, channel efficiency, and so on) over the planning period.

At this time due attention should be paid to examining any contingencies and making appropriate responses to them. For example, if market share increases only by half of what was planned, what pricing and promotional actions might

---

[4]Richard F. Nenschel, "Improving Management Information Systems," *The McKinsey Quarterly* (Winter, 1976), pp. 51–52.

be undertaken? If customer demand instantly shoots up, how can orders be filled? What ought to be done if the Consumer Product Safety Commission should promulgate new product usage controls? Additionally, if the business is in a cyclical industry, each alternative should also be tested against several market-size scenarios, simultaneously incorporating varying assumptions about competitive-pricing pressures. In industries dominated by a few competitors, an evaluation should be made of the ability of the business to adapt each strategy to competitive actions such as pricing moves, shifts in advertising strategy, or attempts to dominate a distribution channel.[5]

Strategy Selection

The above discussion culminates in providing information on trade-offs between alternate strategies. At this stage, then, a preferred strategy will be chosen for recommendation to management. Usually the chosen strategy will have a focus on one of the areas of the marketing mix (i.e., product, price, promotion, or distribution). For example, the preferred strategy may be to "reduce prices to maintain market share." Here the emphasis of the strategy is on pricing. Thus, pricing may be labeled as the *core strategy,* i.e., area of primary concern. However, in order to make an integrated marketing decision, appropriate changes may have to be made in product, promotion, and distribution areas. The strategic perspectives in these areas may be called *supporting strategies.* Thus, once strategy selection has been undertaken, the core and supporting strategy areas should be delineated.

Occasionally more than one decision area may constitute core strategy. For example, in holding prices and introducing a new improved version of the product, both product and price are core strategies, while promotion and distribution are supporting ones. Exhibit 7-3 shows core and supporting strategies for an industrial product and a consumer product. Notice that in the case of the microcomputer, product constitutes the only core strategy. For the movie camera, however, both price and promotion are core strategies.

Let us examine the concept of core and supporting strategies with reference to a furniture store in New Jersey. For a long time this store stocked furniture of the Early American style. With the change in consumers' tastes, the Early American style was going out of fashion, and the future of the business looked bleak. The store, therefore, needed a new strategy. On further analysis, it was found that the store catered to 20-35-year-old professionals struggling to establish careers and households. To continue to serve this segment adequately, the store decided that the product and price areas would constitute the core strategy while promotion and distribution strategies would be supporting ones. To implement the core strategy, the store needed a line of furniture which would be appropriate for those with "a high level of taste and a not-so-high level of income." It finally

[5]Carter F. Bales, *op. cit.*

EXHIBIT 7-3   Illustrations of Core and Supporting Strategies

Product/Market	Core Strategy	Supporting Strategy
1. Microcomputer for Small Business People	*Product:* Develop new stand-alone product within 3 years for companies with annual sales of less than $5 million.	*Price:* Keep the price low to compete aggressively. *Promotion:* Hire and train a new sales force to call on the customers; provide excellent after-sales service. *Distribution:* Seek intensive distribution through office equipment wholesalers.
2. Movie Camera for Upper-Middle Class Families	*Promotion:* Promote heavily by mail among families with annual income over $25,000. Follow through with telephone calls. *Price:* Keep prices down. Make up for reduced prices by selling a package deal for film and processing.	*Product:* Develop instructions in a very lucid fashion (i.e., a step-by-step procedure in easy-to-comprehend language). Develop appropriate packaging for mail delivery. *Distribution:* Arrange with a mail delivery organization such as UPS for fast and dependable delivery.

decided on contemporary furniture to be sold unassembled and packed in cartons. This type of furniture, known as K-D (for "knock-down") in the trade, was developed in Europe about 30 years ago with the intention of having it shipped to the U.S. K-D had a low profile in this country until recently. Either high-price retailers imported the furniture in K-D form and assembled it in their workrooms, or cheap K-D shelving made of plastic or pressboard was sold at budget houseware prices. Now retailers are finding a growing demand for K-D since it satisfies the desire for contemporary furniture at moderate prices. The following supporting strategies were required: 1) promoting the new line in appropriate media, 2) emphasing K-D as tasteful furniture at a reasonable price which required only that the customer assemble it, and 3) stocking the right mix of furniture so that the product was available without delay.[6]

Exhibit 7-4 describes the major elements of marketing strategy, which obviously revolve around the product, price, promotion, and distribution decisions. For each of these four marketing decisions, the exhibit lists the "effort" and "activities" involved. The marketing strategy is formulated around the "effort"; the implementation of the strategy is achieved through the "activities." In other words, when a change in marketing strategy is called for, look under "effort" to develop strategy alternatives in each area.

EXHIBIT 7-4   Major Elements of Marketing Strategy and Component Activities

A. **PRODUCT EFFORT.** Includes product planning, product research and development, product testing, and the service accompanying the product.
   Activities:
   1. Market research relating to product planning, development, and product testing.
   2. Technical research, development, and laboratory testing of new products and improvements of existing products.
   3. Product research relating to the development of product styling and fashions.
   4. Presale service such as product application engineering.
   5. Postsale service such as product installation, maintenance, and guarantee service.

B. **SALES EFFORT.** Includes such areas as sales management, personal selling, advertising, promotional programs, and all other forms of marketing communications.
   Activities:
   1. Product branding and promotional packaging.
   2. Printed media advertising in newspapers, magazines, and brochures.
   3. Broadcast media advertising on radio and television.
   4. Sales management and personal selling including all sales management

---

[6]"The Upswing in Knock-down Furniture," *Business Week* (September 18, 1978), p. 61.

activities (e.g., training supervision) and the sales efforts of company management personnel.

5. Special promotional activities such as promotional warranties, trade shows, dealer aids, and product displays.

C. **DISTRIBUTION.** Includes the selection, coordination, and evaluation of channels, transportation, warehousing, and inventory control.
Activities:
1. Transportation.
2. Warehousing and inventory control.
3. Determination of the basic channels of distribution to be utilized.
4. Selection of individual establishments within the basic channels.
5. Manufacturer's efforts to develop and assist the channel of distribution.

D. **PRICING EFFORT.** Includes price determination, pricing policies, and specific pricing strategies over which some degree of control is exercised.
Activities:
1. Cost plus desired profit or standard cost pricing.
2. Pricing according to competitive levels, pricing at the prevailing competitive price.
3. Pricing at a certain percent above or below competitors' prices.
4. Pricing according to what the market will bear based on estimated value of the product to the consumer.
5. Pricing based on governmental rules and regulations.

Source: Clyde E. Harris, Jr., Richard R. Still, and Melvin R. Crask, "Stability or Change in Marketing Methods?" *Business Horizons* (October, 1978), p. 33. Copyright 1978 by the Foundation for the School of Business at Indiana University. Reprinted by permission.

Once strategy alternatives in each area (i.e., product, price, promotion, and distribution) have been generated and before an alternative is selected, a decision must be made on core strategy. What this is, is a very difficult question to answer. Conceptually, all major facets of marketing strategy are essential in a situation. But which particular area is the most critical is something which depends on a variety of factors. While this question has not been examined deeply in the literature, an original study on the relative importance of the elements of marketing strategy was reported by Udell in the 1960s.[7] A team of professors updated this study in the 1970s and found that sales effort remained the most important facet of marketing strategy, followed by product effort, pricing effort, and distribution effort. While the emphasis on different areas as such did not vary in the two studies, the activities comprising these areas did reveal changes, especially when respondents were classified according to the type of product produced.

---

[7] Jon G. Udell, "The Perceived Importance of the Elements of Strategy," *Journal of Marketing* (January, 1968), pp. 34–40.

Mid-1970 industrial goods manufacturers assigned less importance to presale service, technical research and development, warehousing and inventory control, pricing at the competitive level, and pricing according to government rules and regulations. Conversely, these manufacturers gave less weight to style research and development, branding and promotional packaging, cost-plus pricing, and pricing according to what the market will bear.

Mid-1970 consumer durable goods manufacturers de-emphasized the importance of pre-sale service, technical research and development, selection of establishments in the channel, assisting channel members, and pricing at the competitive level. Upgraded in importance were style research and development, marketing research, transportation, determination of channels used, and cost-plus pricing.

Finally, mid-1970 producers of consumer nondurable goods placed less emphasis on presale service, postsale service, technical research and development, print advertising, assistance to channel members, and pricing according to a percentage above or below competition. The producers gave more weight to style research and development, and branding and promotional packaging.[8]

While the above findings are helpful, the fact remains that determination of core strategy will vary from case to case. What may be said, however, is that the core strategy is formulated around the critical variable(s) which, for the same product, may differ from one segment to another. This is well supported by the following quote taken from a case study of the petroloids business, which deals with manufactured substances based on the synthesis of organic hydrocarbons into a family of such unique materials as oils, petro-rubbers, foams, adhesives, and sealants.

Major producers competed with one another on a variety of dimensions. Among the most important were price, technical assistance, advertising and promotion, and product availability. Price was used as a competitive weapon primarily in those segments of the market where products and applications had become standardized. However, where products had been developed for highly specialized purposes and represented only a small fraction of a customer's total material cost, the market was often less price sensitive. Here customers were chiefly concerned with the physical properties of the product and operating performance.

Technical assistance was an important means of obtaining business. A sizeable percentage of total petroloid sales were accounted for by

---

[8]Clyde E. Harris, Jr., Richard R. Still, and Melvin R. Crask, "Stability or Change in Marketing Methods?" *Business Horizons* (October, 1978), p. 40.

products developed to meet the unique needs of particular customers. Products for the aerospace industry were a primary example. Research engineers of petroloid producers were expected to work closely with customers to define performance requirements and to insure the development of acceptable products.

Advertising and promotional activities were important marketing tools in those segments which utilized distribution channels and/or which reached end users as opposed to OEM's. This was particularly true of foams, adhesives and sealants which were sold both to industrial and consumer markets. A variety of packaged consumer products were sold to hardware, supermarkets, and "do-it-yourself" outlets by our company as well as other competitors. Advertising increased awareness and stimulated interest among the general public while promotional activities improved the effectiveness of distribution networks. Since specialty petroloid products accounted for only a small percentage of a distributor's total sales, product promotion insured that specific products received adequate attention.

Product availability was a fourth dimension on which producers competed. With manufacturing cycles from 2–16 weeks in length and thousands of different products, no supplier could afford to keep all his items in stock. In periods of heavy demand, many products were often in short supply. Those competitors with adequate supplies and quick deliveries could readily attract new business.[9]

Apparently, strategy development is difficult since different emphasis may be needed in different product/market situations. This emphasis is built around the critical variables, which may be difficult to identify. Luck plays a part in making the right move; occasionally sheer intuition suffices. Despite all this, a careful review of past performance, current perspectives, and environmental changes should go a long way in choosing the right areas to concentrate on. The appendix at the end of this chapter gives a framework of business strategy concepts and provides an interesting review for strategic direction. This framework is not meant to introduce a new scheme for strategy development. Rather, it provides an opportunity for philosophically reflecting on the business strategy formulation, which helps in articulating a system for one's own use.

Reformulation of current strategy may range from making slight modifications in the existing perspectives to coming out with an entirely different strategy. For example, in the area of pricing, one alternative for an automobile manufacturer may be to keep the prices from year to year stable (i.e., no yearly price increases). A different alternative may be to lease cars, instead of selling them, directly to

[9]"Tex-Fiber Industries—Petroloid Products Division (A)," a case developed by John Craig under the supervision of Derek F. Abell, copyrighted by the President and Fellows of Harvard College, 1970, p. 7.

consumers. The decision on the first alternative may be made by the strategic business unit executive. But the second alternative, being far reaching in nature, may require the review and approval of top management. In other words, how much examination and review a product/market strategy will require depends on the nature of the strategy (in terms of the change it seeks from existing perspectives) and the resource commitment required.

INTEGRATION AT THE SBU LEVEL

Product/market plans must be reviewed at the strategic business unit (SBU) level. This is done to ensure that product/market strategies are those best suited to take the SBU where it wants to go. Alternatively, it is necessary to examine and integrate different product/market strategies toward the optimum realization of SBU goals. Before describing the integration process, it will be desirable here to digress for a moment and discuss the process for constituting SBUs.

Identification of Strategic Business Units (SBUs)

Since formal strategic planning began to make inroads in corporations in the 1970s, a variety of new concepts have been developed for approximating the opportunities of a corporation and speeding up the process of strategy development. These newer concepts create problems of internal organization. In a dynamic economy all functions of a corporation (i.e., R&D, finance, and marketing) are interrelated. Optimizing some functions instead of the whole company is far from adequate for exhibiting superior corporate performance. Such an organizational perspective leaves only the chief executive officer in a position to think in terms of the corporation as a whole. Large corporations have attempted many structural designs to broaden the scope of the chief executive in dealing with complexities. One such design is the profit center concept. Unfortunately, the profit center concept emphasizes short-term consequences; also, its emphasis is on optimizing the profit center instead of the corporation as a whole.

The strategic business unit concept has been developed to overcome the difficulties posed by the profit center type of organization. Thus, the first step in integrating the product/market strategies is to identify the SBUs or "strategy centers." This amounts to identifying natural businesses in which the corporation is involved. SBUs are not necessarily synonymous with existing divisions or profit centers. An SBU is composed of a product or product lines having identifiable independence from other products or product lines in terms of competition, prices, substitutability of product, style/quality, and impact of product withdrawal. It is around this configuration of products that a business strategy should be designed. In today's organizations this strategy may encompass products found in more than one division. By the same token, some managers may find themselves managing two or more natural businesses. This does not necessarily mean that divisional boundaries need to be redefined; often a strategic business unit can overlap divisions, and a division can include more than one unit.

Strategic business units may be created by applying a set of criteria consisting of price, competitors, customer groups, and shared experience. To the extent that price changes in a product entail a review of the pricing policy of other products, these products may have a natural alliance. If various products/markets of a company share the same group of competitors, they may be amalgamated into an SBU for the purpose of strategic planning. Likewise, products/markets sharing a common set of customers belong together. Finally, products/markets in different parts of the company having common R&D, manufacturing, and marketing components may be included in the same SBU. For illustration purposes, consider the case of a large diversified company, one division of which manufactures car radios. The following possibilities exist: the car radio division, as it stands, may represent a viable SBU; alternatively, luxury car radios with automatic tuning may constitute a different SBU from the SBU for standard models; or it may be that other areas of the company, such as the TV division, are combined with all or parts of the car radio division for the creation of an SBU.[10]

A conceptual question becomes relevant in identifying SBUs: How much aggregation is desirable? Higher levels of aggregation give a relatively smaller and more manageable number of SBUs. Besides, the existing management information system may not have to be modified since a higher level of aggregation yields SBUs of the size and scope of present divisions or product groups. However, higher levels of aggregation permit at the SBU level only general notions of strategy, which may lack relevance for promoting action at the operating level. On the other hand, lower levels of aggregation make SBUs identical to product/market segments which may lack "strategic autonomy."[11] For example, two SBUs may compete with one another, thereby shifting the strategic issue to which SBU should formulate what strategy to higher levels of management. The answer to the above debate is that the aggregation should be at neither a higher nor a lower level, but should be maintained at optimum. The optimum can be determined by applying the set of criteria exemplified above, then further refining it by using managerial judgment. Exhibit 7-5 points out factors which may be considered in the process.

Situation Analysis of the SBU

Once SBUs have been created, the next step is to classify them in a way that will be useful for the purpose of strategy formulation. The experience of different companies shows that this can be achieved by placing SBUs in a two-by-two matrix with industry maturity or attractiveness as one dimension and competitive position as the other. Industry attractiveness may be studied with reference to the life-cycle stage of the industry (i.e., embryonic, growth, mature, or aging). Such

---

[10]Peter Patel and Michael Younger, "A Frame of Reference for Strategy Development," *Long Range Planning* (April, 1978), pp. 7–8.
[11]*Ibid.*

EXHIBIT 7-5   Factors to Consider when Identifying/Creating SBUs

1. All SBUs must have:
   a. A distinct mission
   b. Identifiable external competitors
   c. Control over all functional activities
2. Overall, one should consider:
   a. The total # of SBUs that will be created
   b. The size of each individual SBU
   c. The degree to which it is meaningfully possible to separate or combine markets, distribution systems, production technologies, and R & D technologies
   d. The degree of SBU overlap
   e. Competitor SBU selection
3. Remember:
   The choice of how an organization will be broken down into SBUs is really the choice of the number, the level, and the nature of the points at which competitive resource allocation decisions will occur in the organization.

Source: "Conceptual Constructs for Formulating Corporate and Business Strategies" (a case prepared by Charles W. Hofer, Stanford University, 1977), p. 5. Reprinted from *Stanford Business Cases 1977* with permission of the publishers, Stanford University Graduate School of Business, © 1977 by the Board of Trustees of the Leland Stanford Junior University.

factors as growth rate, growth potential, distribution and stability of markets, breadth of product line, number of competitors, customer stability, ease of entry, and technological stability may be rated for determining an industry's stage in the life cycle. The experience of different industries shows that the above factors behave in a certain manner in each stage of the life cycle.

An industry adopts a different perspective in embryonic, growth, mature and aging stages with reference to such factors as growth rate, number of competitors, customer stability, etc. The maturity of an industry has implications for business strategy selection. For example, the number of competitors tends to reach a peak during the growth stage and decline during the mature stage as marginal firms leave the industry.

Industries generally start in an embryonic stage, pass through growth and maturity, and can eventually be classified as aging. This process can take decades or a few years. The different stages are generally of unequal duration. To cite a few examples, home computers and solar energy devices are in the embryonic category. Home smoke alarms and sporting goods in general fall into the growth category. Golf equipment and steel represent mature industries. Finally, men's hats and rail cars are included in the aging category. It is important to remember that industries can experience reversals in their aging processes. For example, roller skates have experienced a tremendous resurgence (i.e., moving from the aging stage back to the growth stage) due to the addition of polyurethane skateboard wheels. It should also be emphasized that there is no "good" or "bad" life cycle position. A particular stage of maturity becomes "bad" only if the expectations or strategies adopted by an industry participant are inappropriate for a given stage of maturity.

The four different stages in the life cycle are characterized as follows:

Embryonic industries usually experience rapid sales growth, frequent changes in technology, and fragmented, shifting market shares. The cash deployment to these businesses is often high relative to sales as investment is made in market development, facilities, and technology. These businesses are generally not profitable, but investment is usually warranted in anticipation of gaining position in a developing market.

The growth stage of maturity is generally characterized by a rapid expansion of sales as the market develops. Customers, shares, and technology are better known than in the embryonic stage, and entry into the industry can be more difficult. Growth businesses are usually capital borrowers from the corporation, producing low to good earnings.

In mature industries the competitors, technology, and customers are all known and there is little volatility in market shares. The growth rate of these industries is usually about equal to the GNP. Businesses in these industries tend to provide cash for the corporation through high earnings.

The aging stage of maturity is characterized by:

1. Falling demand for the product and limited growth potential.
2. A shrinking number of competitors. Survivors gain market share through attrition.
3. Little product line variety.
4. Little, if any, investment in research and development or plant and equipment even though the business generates extremely high earnings.[12]

The competitive position of an SBU should depend not only on market share, but also on such factors as capacity utilization, current profitability, degree of integration (forward or backward), distinctive product advantages (such as patent protection), and management strength (such as willingness to take risk). The above factors may be studied for classifying a given SBU as one of the following competitive positions: dominant, strong, favorable, tenable, or weak.

The industry maturity and competitive position analysis may also be used in further refining the SBU itself. In other words, after an SBU has been created and it is analyzed for industry maturity and competitive position, it may be found that it has not been properly constituted. This would require redefining the SBU and undertaking the analysis again. Using the car radio example, considerable differences with reference to industry maturity may become apparent between the car

---

[12]*A Management System for the 1980s* (Cambridge, MA: Arthur D. Little, Inc., no date), pp. 18-20.

radios with built-in cassette players and traditional car radios. Differences in industry maturity and/or competitive position may also exist with regard to regional markets, consumer groups, and distribution channels. For example, the market for cheap car radios sold by discount stores to end users doing their own installation may be growing faster than the market served by specialty retail stores providing installation services. Such revelations may require further refinement in formulating SBUs. This may continue until the SBUs represent the highest possible level of aggregation which is consistent with the requirement to derive clear-cut analyses of industry maturity and competitive position.[13]

Strategy Review of the SBU

Once the position of an SBU is determined in the matrix of product life cycle stage and competitive position, a compendium of strategies, as shown in Exhibit 7-6, may be used to determine the relevant strategy the SBU should pursue. Actually the strategies shown in Exhibit 7-6 provide strategic guidelines rather than strategies per se. They show the normal strategic path a business unit may adopt, given its position in product life cycle stage and its competitive position.

To bridge the gap between broad guidelines and specific strategies for implementation, further analysis is required. A three-stage process is suggested here. First, using the broad guidelines, the SBU management may be asked to state the strategies pursued during the previous years. Second, these strategies may be reviewed by using selected performance ratios to analyze the extent to which the strategies were successfully implemented. Similarly, current strategies may be identified and their link to past strategies established. Third, having identified and analyzed past and current strategy with the help of strategic guidelines, the management, using the same guidelines, selects the strategy it proposes to pursue in the future. The future perspective may call for the continuation of current strategies and/or the development of new ones. Before accepting the future strategic course, however, it is desirable to measure its *cash consequences* or *internal deployment* (i.e., percentage of funds generated which are reinvested). Exhibit 7-7 illustrates an SBU earning 22 percent on assets with an internal deployment of 80 percent. Such an SBU would normally be considered to be in the mature stage. However, if the previous analysis showed that the SBU was in fact operating in a growth industry, the corporation would need to rethink its investment policy for this SBU. The entire quantitative information pertaining to an SBU may be summarized on one sheet, as shown in Exhibit 7-8. In this way all past accounting information is readily available.

Review of Product/Market Strategies

Different product/market plans are reviewed at the SBU level. The underlying criterion for evaluation is a balanced achievement of SBU goals which may be

---

[13]Patel and Younger, *op cit.,* p. 8.

EXHIBIT 7-6 Compendium of Strategies for an SBU

	Embryonic	Growth	Mature	Aging
Dominant	All-Out Push for Share Hold Position	Hold Position Hold Share	Hold Position Grow With Industry	Hold Position
Strong	Attempt to Improve Position All-Out Push for Share	Attempt to Improve Position Push For Share	Hold Position Grow With Industry	Hold Position or Harvest
Favorable	Selective or All-Out Push for Share Selectively Attempt to Improve Position	Attempt to Improve Position Selective Push for Share	Custodial or Maintenance Find Niche and Attempt to Protect	Harvest or Phased Withdrawal
Tenable	Selectively Push for Position	Find Niche and Protect It	Find Niche and Hang on or Phased Withdrawal	Phased Withdrawal or Abandon
Weak	Up or Out	Turnaround or Abandon	Turnaround or Phased Withdrawal	Abandon

Source: Arthur D. Little, Inc.

EXHIBIT 7-7 Profitability and Cash Position of a Business

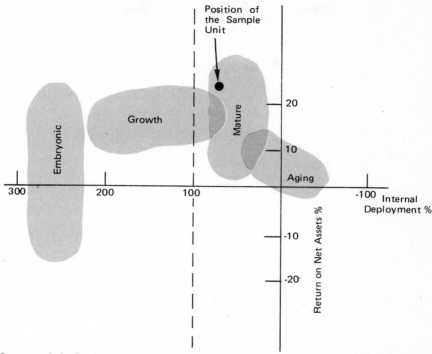

Source: Peter Patel and Michael Younger, "A Frame of Reference for Strategy Development," *Long Range Planning* (April, 1978), p. 78.

specified in terms of profitability and cash consequences. If there is a conflict of interest between two product/market groups in the way the strategy is either articulated or implemented, the conflict should be resolved so that SBU goals are maximized. Assume that both product/market groups seek additional investments during the next two years. Of these, the first product/market will start delivering positive cash flow in the third year. The second one, however, is not likely to generate positive cash flow until the fourth year, but it will provide a higher overall return on capital. If the SBU's need for cash is urgent and if it desires additional cash for its goals during the third year, the first product/market group will appear more attractive. Thus, despite higher profit expectations out of product/market group two, the SBU may approve investment in product/market group one with a view to maximizing the realization of its own goals.

At times the SBU may require a product/market group to make additional changes in its strategic perspective before giving its final approval. On the other hand, a product/market plan may be totally rejected and required to pursue its current perspective.

EXHIBIT 7-8   Financial Record of an SBU

PERFORMANCE

| | INDICES OF: | | | | RETURN | | | | | |
| | | | | | Investment (per $ sales) | | | | | |
Year	Industry Capacity (A)	Business Unit's Product Capacity (B)	Business Unit's Sales (C)	Profits After Taxes (D)	Net Assets (E)	Receivables (F)	Inventories (G)	Net Current Liabilities (H)	Working Capital (I)	Other Assets (J)	Total Net Assets (K)

INVESTMENT

| | RETURN (continued) | | | | | | | RONA | FUNDS GENERATION AND DEPLOYMENT | | | |
| | Cost and Earnings (per $ sales) | | | | | | | | (per $ sales) | | | (%) |
Year	Cost of Goods Sold (L)	Research and Development (M)	Sales and Marketing (N)	General and Administrative (O)	Other Income and Expenses (P)	Profit Before Taxes (Q)	Profit After Taxes (R)	Return on Net Assets (S)	Operating Funds Flow (T)	Change in Assets (U)	Net Cash Flow to Corporation (V)	Internal Deployment $(U \div T)$ (W)

Source: Arthur D. Little, Inc.

INTEGRATION AT THE CORPORATE LEVEL

Integration at the corporate level is reflected in the form of corporate strategy. Corporate strategy, it should be noted, differs from business strategy in a fundamental way. The primary focus of business strategy is on gaining competitive advantage. Corporate strategy, however, deals mainly with developing business unit configurations, their organization and management systems, and their financial transactions in a manner conducive to the achievement of the desired corporate growth, profitability, and risk levels. One way of achieving integration at the corporate level is by developing a balanced portfolio of different businesses for the corporation. This will be discussed in Chapter 13.

STRATEGY EVALUATION

"The time required to develop resources is so extended, and the time-scale of opportunities is so brief and fleeting, that a company which has not carefully delineated and appraised its strategy is adrift in white water." This quotation from an article by Seymour Tilles underlines the importance of strategy evaluation. He suggests the following six criteria for evaluating the adequacy of a strategy:

1. Internal consistency
2. Consistency with the environment
3. Appropriateness in the light of available resources
4. Satisfactory degree of risk
5. Appropriate time horizon
6. Workability[14]

An attempt is made in this section to evaluate product/market strategy using these criteria.

Internal Consistency

The strategy should be in tune with the different policies of the corporation, the SBU, and the product/market area. For example, if the corporation has decided to limit the government business of any unit to 40 percent of total sales, a product/market strategy emphasizing greater than 40 percent reliance on the government market will be internally inconsistent.

Consistency with the Environment

The strategy should be consistent with the external product/market environment. After the fall of the Shah of Iran in 1979, gas prices shot up very high and

---

[14]Seymour Tilles, "How to Evaluate Corporate Strategy," *Harvard Business Review* (July–August, 1963), pp. 111–121.

a nationwide gas shortage for the coming years became imminent. In such an environment as this, an automobile company which introduces to its middle-of-the-line car new features which will substantially increase gas consumption may not be doing the right thing. At a time when more and more women are seeking jobs, a strategy assuming traditional roles for women (i.e., raising children and staying home) is inconsistent with the environment.

Appropriateness in the Light of Available Resources

Money, competence, and physical facilities are the critical resources which a manager should be aware of in finalizing strategy. A resource may be examined in two different ways: 1) as a constraint limiting the achievement of goals, and 2) as that which the company will exploit as the basis for its strategy. It is desirable for a strategist to make correct estimates of the resources available without being excessively optimistic about them. This implies that even if the resources are there in the corporation, a particular product/market group may not be able to lay claim to them. Alternatively, the resources currently available to a product/market group may be transferred to another group if the SBU strategy deems it necessary.

Satisfactory Degree of Risk

The degree of risk may be determined, based on the perspectives of the strategy and the available resources. A pertinent question here is: Will the resources be continually available as planned in appropriate quantities and for as long as it is necessary to implement the strategy? The overall proportion of resources committed to a venture becomes a factor to be reckoned with here since the greater these quantities, the greater the degree of risk that is involved.

Appropriate Time Horizon

A viable strategy will have attached to it a time frame for its realization. It is desirable for the time horizon of the strategy to be appropriate enough to allow its implementation without either creating havoc in the organization or missing market availability. For example, in introducing a new product to the market, enough time should be allotted for market testing, salespeople's training, etc. But the time should not be so long that a competitor can enter the market first and skim the cream off the top.

Workability

The workability of a strategy should be realistically evaluated with reference to quantitative data. Sometimes, however, it may be difficult to undertake such objective analysis. In such a case, other indications may be used to assess the contributions of a strategy. One such indication could be the degree of consensus among key executives about the viability of the strategy. The feasibility of identifying ahead of time alternate strategies for achieving the goal is another indication of the workability of the strategy. Finally, the discovery of resource requirements in advance, which eliminates the necessity of instituting crash programs of cost reduction or seeking reduction in planned programs, also substantiates the workability of the strategy.

In addition to reviewing the strategy with reference to the above criteria, a quick evaluation for judging the viability of specific strategies (i.e., product, price, promotion, and distribution strategies) can be made by referring to a compendium of strategies. The matrix in Exhibit 7-9 illustrates such a compendium. It lists marketing decision areas on one side and objectives on the other side. Relevant strategies for a particular decision area/objective are stated therein. It is desirable that such a compendium be custom developed for a company, either internally or with the help of a consultant.

SUMMARY

This chapter introduced a framework for developing product/market strategy. Essentially, the framework requires predicting the momentum of current operations into the future (assuming constant conditions), modifying the momentum in the light of environmental changes, and reviewing the adjusted momentum against goals. If there is no gap between the set goal and the prediction, the present strategy may well be continued. Usually, however, there is a gap between the goal and expectations from current operations. Thus, the gap must be filled.

The following three-step process has been suggested for filling the gap: 1) issue assessment (i.e., raising issues with the status quo vis-a-vis the future); 2) identification of key variables (i.e., isolating the key variables on which success in the industry depends) and developing alternative strategies; and 3) strategy selection (i.e., choosing the preferred strategy). The thrust of the preferred strategy is on one or more of the four variables of the marketing mix (i.e., product, price, promotion, and distribution). The major emphasis of marketing strategy, the core strategy, is on this chosen variable. Strategies for the remaining variables are supporting strategies.

The product/market strategies are reviewed for approval by the strategic business unit (SBU) management. A detailed procedure has been outlined for constituting the SBUs and for formulating SBU strategies. The outcomes of both the SBU strategy and the product/market strategy are then reduced to a common denominator (for example, cash flow or return on assets). At this time, the SBU examines the product/market strategies in order to maximize its performance. The SBU strategies are then integrated at the corporate level in the form of a product portfolio (which will be discussed in a later chapter).

The chapter concludes with a procedure for evaluating product/market strategies. This consists of examining the following aspects of the strategy: internal consistency, consistency with the environment, appropriateness in the light of available resources, satisfactory degree of risk, appropriateness of time horizon, and workability.

EXHIBIT 7-9 Impact of Multibusiness Strategic Planning on Marketing

Marketing Decision Area	Strategy Adopted for Division or Product Line		
	Invest for Future Growth	Manage for Earnings	Manage for Immediate Cash
Market share	Aggressively build across all segments	Target efforts to high-return/high-growth segments. Protect current franchises	Forego share development for improved profits
Pricing	Lower to build share	Stabilize for maximum profit contribution	Raise, even at expense of volume
Promotion	Invest heavily to build share	Invest as market dictates	Avoid
Existing product line	Expand volume. Add line extensions to fill out product categories	Shift mix to higher-profit product categories	Eliminate low-contribution products/varieties
New products	Expand product line by acquisition, self-manufacture or joint venture	Add products selectively and in controlled stages of commitment	Add only sure winners

Source: Louis V. Gerstner, "Can Strategic Planning Pay Off?" *Business Horizons* (December, 1972), p. 15. Copyright 1972 by the Foundation for the School of Business at Indiana University. Reprinted by permission.

DISCUSSION QUESTIONS

1. Describe how a manufacturer of television sets may measure the momentum of his or her business for the next five years.
2. Discuss how the increasing impact of Japanese competition may be taken into account by the television manufacturer to adjust momentum.
3. List five issues which Sears may raise to review its large-appliances strategy.
4. List five key variables on which success in the home-construction industry depends.
5. Give examples of core strategies in product, price, promotion, and distribution areas. Specify the industry where a particular core strategy will be relevant.
6. How does a strategic business unit differ from a profit center?
7. Discuss how the strategy evaluation criteria may be employed to review the strategy of an industrial goods manufacturer (assume a particular type of company).
8. Apply the product/market strategy framework outlined in this chapter to a service business such as a bank, an airline, etc.

APPENDIX: BUSINESS STRATEGY CONCEPTS

Spectacular business successes are usually new ways of doing business in familiar markets with familiar products. These are the true strategic victories, won by using corporate resources to substantially outperform a competitor with superior strength.

The concept of superior performance without superior resources is usually identified with trying harder. Yet most companies seem to work very hard to produce only minor differentials in performance.

The underlying principle of a good strategy is simple: "Concentrate your strength against your competitor's relative weakness." This principle has a major corollary in a dynamic competitive environment—concentration of effort will inevitably produce a counter-concentration by competition; therefore, timing and sequence are critical. A major attack should never be launched against a competent well-entrenched competitor without first eliminating his ability or willingness to respond in kind.

There are many prerequisites to a successful strategy:

1. The characteristics of the competition must be known in detail, including their characteristic attitude and behavior.
2. The environment in which competition will take place must be equally well understood.
3. Your own relative strengths must be accurately and objectively appraised.
4. The strategic concept must not be based on the obvious exercise of known strengths. If it is, you don't need a strategy, just a plan.
5. It must be possible to achieve stability if the strategy succeeds.

6. Your own organization must not be misled by your efforts to outmaneuver competition. Strategic goals must be very explicit.

Once the strategic framework has been designed, the tactics of attack must be selected. Concentration of resources can be achieved in several ways:

1. Choose the most vulnerable market segment.
2. Choose products or markets that require response rates beyond a competitor's ability.
3. Choose products or markets which require capital that a competitor is unwilling to commit.
4. Recognize the commercial potentials of new technology early.
5. Exploit managerial differences in style, method, or system such as overhead rate, distribution channels, market image, or flexibility.

The value of the initiative depends on when and how the competition responds. Therefore, an effective strategy must choose the best initiative and also dissuade competition from responding. This is a fundamental strategic concept that is often neglected. Most strategic success depends upon the competition's decision not to compete. Therefore, strategic success almost always depends upon the ability to influence competitors' decisions. It is necessary to win in the mind of the competition.

Diversion and dissuasion fall into classic categories:

1. Appear to be unworthy of attention. Quickly cut off a part of the market which is too small to justify a major response. Repeat, and repeat, etc.
2. Appear to be unbeatable. Convince competition that if they follow your lead and practices, they will gain nothing since you will equal or better any market actions they take.
3. Avoid attention. Be secretive. Do not let competition know about new products, new policies or capabilities until it is too late to respond effectively.
4. Redirect attention. Focus competitive attention on the major volume areas of company sales, not the high potential areas.
5. Attract attention but discredit significance. Overstate and overpublicize the potentials of new products or policies.
6. Be apparently irrational. Take actions which seem emotional or impulsive but which make competitive investment unattractive.

These and other patterns have exact counterparts in military behavior. In business as in war, the lessons of experience teach the same thing.

> . . . We can at least crystallize the lessons into two simple maxims—one negative, the other positive. The first is that, in the face of the overwhelming evidence of history, no general is justified in launching his

troops in a direct attack upon an enemy firmly in position. The second, that instead of seeking to upset the enemy's equilibrium by one's attack, it must be upset before a real attack is, or can be, successfully launched.

(Liddell Hart, *Strategy,* Praeger)

Source: Bruce D. Henderson, "Business Strategy Concepts" (Boston: The Boston Consulting Group, Inc., 1969). Perspectives No. 61.

Chapter 8
Market Strategies

Three women and a goose make a marketplace.

Italian Proverb

In the final analysis, all business strategies must be justified by the availability of a viable market. When a viable market is lacking, even the best strategy will flop. Additionally, the development of marketing strategies for each product/market business should be realistically tied to the target market. Since market should be the focus for successful marketing, strategies aligned to market(s) point the way for each present business, serve as underpinnings for overall corporate long-range planning, and provide direction for programming key activities and projects in all functional areas.

When corporate resources are scarce and corporate strengths are limited, it is fatal to spread them across too many markets. Rather, these critical resources should be concentrated on those key markets (key in terms of type of market, geographic location, time of entry, and commitment) that are decisive for a business' success. Merely allocating resources in the same way as other firms do will yield no competitive differential. If, however, it can be discovered which markets really hold potential, the business will be able to lever itself into a position of relative competitive superiority.

This chapter will identify different aspects of market strategies which companies commonly pursue and analyze their impact on performance vis-a-vis product/market objectives. The use of these strategies will be illustrated with examples from the marketing literature.

DIMENSIONS OF MARKET STRATEGIES

Market strategies deal with the perspectives of markets to be served. These perspectives can be determined in different ways. For example, a company may serve the entire market or dissect it into key segments on which to concentrate its major effort. Thus, market scope is one aspect of market strategy. The geographic dimensions of the market constitute another aspect: a company may focus on a local, regional, national, or international market. Another strategic variable is the time of entry into a market. A company may be the first, among the first few, or among the last to enter the market. Commitment to a market is still another aspect of market strategy. This commitment can be to achieve market domination, to become a major factor in the market, or merely to play a meager role in it. Finally, a company may intentionally decide to dilute a part of its market as a matter of strategy. Exhibit 8-1 summarizes these market strategies. There are different alternatives which a company may choose to follow under each strategy. These alternatives will be explored in the next five sections.

EXHIBIT 8-1   Market Strategies

Market-scope Strategy
Market-geography Strategy
Market-entry Strategy
Market-commitment Strategy
Market-dilution Strategy

MARKET-SCOPE STRATEGY

The United States represents the largest market in the world for most products. But it is not a homogeneous market. This large market has a variety of sub-markets or segments which vary substantially from one another. One of the crucial elements of market strategy is to choose the segment or segments that are to be served. This, however, is easier said than done. There can be different methods for dissecting the market. Choosing which method to select for segmentation may pose a problem.

Virtually all strategists segment their markets. Typically, they use SIC code, annual purchase volume, age, and income as differentiating variables. Categories based on these variables, however, may not suffice as far as the development of strategy is concerned.

RCA, for example, initially classified potential customers for color televisions according to age, income, and social class. The company soon realized that these segments were not crucial ones for continued growth since buyers were not confined to those groups. Later analysis discovered that there were "innovators" and "followers" in each of the above groups. This finding led the company to tailor its marketing strategy to various segments according to their "innovativeness." Mass acceptance of color television might have been delayed substantially if RCA had followed a more traditional approach.[1]

An American food processor achieved rapid success in the French market after discovering that "modern" French women like processed foods while "traditional" French housewives look upon them as a threat. A leading industrial manufacturer discovered that its critical variable was the amount of annual usage

---

[1]"Strategy and Market Segment Research," an informal statement on marketing issued by the Boston Consulting Group, 1968.

per item, not per order or per any other conventional variable. This proved to be critical since heavy users can be expected to be more sensitive to price and may be more aware of and responsive to promotional perspective.

The above illustrations underscore not only the significance of dissecting the market, but also the importance of carefully choosing the dissecting variable. The market-scope strategy deals with these issues. Specifically, it amounts to: 1) identification of the bases for forming market segments or establishing criteria for segmentation, and 2) choosing to serve a single market, several distinct markets, or the entire market.

Segmentation Criteria

One may use simple demographic and socioeconomic variables, personality and life-style variables, or situation-specific events (such as use intensity, brand loyalty, attitudes, etc.) as the bases for segmentation. For example, a Japanese shipbuilding company dissects its tanker market into large, medium, and small markets; similarly, its cargo ship market is classified into high-, medium-, and low-grade markets. A forklift truck manufacturer divides its market on the basis of product-performance requirements. Many consumer goods companies, General Foods, Procter & Gamble, and Heublein among them, base their segments on life-style analysis. Exhibit 8-2 provides an inventory of different bases for market segmentation. Most of these bases are self-explanatory. For a detailed account, however, reference may be made to an advanced book on the subject, such as the Frank, Massy, and Wind book.[2]

EXHIBIT 8-2   Bases for Segmentation

1. Demographic Factors (Age, income, sex, etc.)
2. Socioeconomic Factors (Social class, stage in the family life cycle)
3. Geographic Factors
4. Psychological Factors (Life-style, personality traits)
5. Consumption Patterns (Heavy, moderate, and light users)
6. Perceptual Factors (Benefit segmentation, perceptual mapping)
7. Brand-loyalty Patterns

Data for forming market segments may be analyzed with the use of simple statistical techniques (e.g., averages) or multivariate methods. Caution is necessary to avoid the impression that a good job in forming segments necessarily calls for the use of multivariate techniques or other high-level statistical analysis. As a Lever Brothers executive has said:

> Clearly, all this exotic segmentation research—multivariate, life-style, benefits, nonparametric, factor analytic—is an expensive toy for hypothesis generation. It is an over-intellectualized exercise of powerful statisti-

[2]Ronald E. Frank, William F. Massy, and Yoram Wind, *Market Segmentation* (Englewood Cliffs, NJ: Prentice-Hall, 1972).

cal methods which, unfortunately, too often are hooked up to inadequate marketing theory. If hypothesis generation is the goal, there are other ways (and talking to your spouse is a respectable substitute for all that statistical manipulation).[3]

Conceptually, the following procedure may be adopted to choose a criterion for segmentation:

1. Identify potential customers and the nature of their needs.
2. Segment all customers into groups having:
   a. Common requirements
   b. The same value system with respect to the importance of these requirements.
3. Determine the theoretically most efficient means of serving each market segment, making sure that the distribution system selected will keep each segment separate from all others with respect to cost and price.
4. Adjust this ideal system to the constraints of the real world: existing commitments, legal restrictions, practicality, and so forth.

Besides products and customers, a market can also be segmented by level of customer service, stage of production, price-performance characteristics, credit arrangements with customers, location of plants, characteristics of manufacturing equipment, channels of distribution, and financial policies.

The key is to choose a variable or variables which so divide the market that customers in a segment have similar responsiveness to some aspect of the marketer's strategy. The variable should be measurable; i.e., it should represent an objective value such as income, rate of consumption, frequency of buying, etc., not simply a qualitative viewpoint such as the degree of customer happiness. Also, the variable should create segments which may be accessible through promotion. Even if it is feasible to measure happiness, segments based on the happiness variable cannot be reached by a specific media. Thus, happiness may not serve as an appropriate criterion as far as accessibility is concerned.

Once segments have been formed, the next strategic issue is deciding which segment should be selected. The selected segment should comply with the following conditions:

1. It should be one in which the maximum differential in competitive strategy can be developed.
2. It must be capable of being isolated so that the competitive advantage can be preserved.
3. It must be valid, even though imitated.

---

[3]William T. Moran, "Segments Are Made, Not Born," in Earl L. Bailey (ed.), *Marketing Strategies* (New York: Conference Bd., 1974), pp. 15–16.

The success of Volkswagen in the U.S. can be attributed to its fit into a market segment which had two unique characteristics. First, the segment served by VW could not be adequately served by a modification of conventional U.S. cars. And second, the manufacturing economies of scale could not be brought to bear by U.S. manufacturers to the disadvantage of VW. In contrast, American Motors was equally successful in identifying a special segment to serve with its compact car, i.e., the Rambler. The critical difference was that American Motors could not protect that segment from the superior scale of manufacturing volume of the other three automobile manufacturers.

The choice of strategically critical segments is not a straightforward task. It requires a careful evaluation of corporate strength as compared with the competition. It also requires analytical marketing research to uncover market segments in which these differences can be significant.

Single-market Strategy

A variety of reasons may lead a company to concentrate its efforts on a single segment. For example, a small company, in order to avoid confrontation with large competitors, may find a unique niche in the market and devote its energies to serving this market. Design and Manufacturing Corporation presents an illustration of a successful single-market strategy. In the late 1950s, Samuel Regenstrief studied the dishwasher market and found: 1) a high growth potential, 2) market domination by G.E., and 3) absence of a manufacturer to supply large retailers like Sears with their own private brand. These conclusions led him to enter the dishwasher market, concentrating his efforts on the single segment of national retailers. Today the company is the largest producer of dishwashers in the world with over 25 percent of the U.S. market. A D & M executive states his company's strategy in the following words: "Sam knew precisely what segment of the market he was going after; he hit it at exactly the right time; and he has set up a tightly run organization to take full advantage of these opportunities."[4]

The story of the Tampax product illustrates the success of the single-market strategy. The product had a minimal share of the market dominated by Kimberly-Clark's Kotex and Personal Products' Modess sanitary pads. Tampax could not afford to compete head-on with these major brands to sell its different concept of sanitary protection. But the company found that newer, younger users are more open-minded in this matter and these customers are very loyal to a brand. Starting from a premise of greatest appeal to the young user—that internal protection offers greater freedom of action—Tampax concentrated on reaching young girls. The single-market strategy has proved to be highly beneficial to the company. The sales have grown to more than 35 percent of the total sanitary

---

[4]"Design and Manufacturing Corporation" a case copyrighted in 1972 by the President and Fellows of Harvard College, p. 4.

protection market. Even today the company's advertising is scarcely distinguishable from the firm's first efforts.[5]

There is no magic formula in choosing a segment. A business should analyze the market carefully to find a segment which is currently being ignored or served inadequately. Then it should concentrate on the chosen segment wholeheartedly despite initial difficulties and in a manner which avoids competition from the established firms. VW's long-standing position in the small car market in the U.S., discussed above, succinctly explains how a single-market strategy can be implemented in the midst of keen competition.

Often new segments emerge in the market as a result of changes in the environment. For example, the women's liberation movement motivated the General Broadcasting Corp. of New Haven, Connecticut, to orient its radio station to strictly working women. The station (rated among the "top 40 AM stations") features the Ladies Professional Golf Association before reporting on the Red Sox. It employs women on a two to one ratio and carefully screens advertising to avoid ads which may put down women in any way.[6]

The single-market strategy consists of seeking out a market segment which larger competitors may consider too small, too risky, or just plain unappealing. The strategy will not work in areas such as the extractive and process industries, where big-company market power becomes important in realizing economies of scale. Companies concentrating on a single market have the advantage of making a quick response to market opportunities and threats via appropriate changes in policies. For example, the Rival Manufacturing Co. strengthened its position in the sale of slow-cooking crock pots by gaining control over the sole source of earthenware liners, a backward integration step that ensured its domination of this highly attractive, growing market segment.[7]

So far, the discussion on single-market strategy has seemingly implied that a single segment is necessarily a small segment. There can be cases, however, where a single segment constitutes a large market. For example, up until recently IBM pursued only a single segment, although a very large one, with any vigor. Similarly, Coca-Cola Company served only the large segment of coke drinkers. In the long run, however, competitors move in to break the large segment into several smaller segments. For instance, the computer market has been divided into such different segments as the markets for computers for scientific uses, computers for military purposes, and computers for financial institutions.

As far as the impact of the single-market strategy is concerned, it affects profitability in a positive manner. Due to concentrated effort in a market, particularly when competition is meagre, it is feasible to keep costs down while prices

---

[5]George W. Schiele, "How to Reach the Young Consumer," *Harvard Business Review* (March–April, 1974), p. 83.

[6]"A Radio Station with a Feminist Air," *Business Week* (October 2, 1978), p. 32.

[7]Donald K. Clifford, Jr., "Thriving in Recession," *Harvard Business Review* (July–August, 1977), p. 63.

are kept high, and thus earn substantially higher profits. Although the growth objective may not be achieved when this strategy is followed, a company may be able to increase its market share if the chosen segment is large enough vis-a-vis the overall market.

Multimarket Strategy

Instead of limiting business to one segment and thus laying all its eggs in one basket, a company may opt to serve several distinct segments. To successfully implement the multimarket strategy, it is necessary to choose those segments with which the company feels most comfortable and in which the company is able to avoid confronting companies serving the entire market. The point can be illustrated with reference to Crown Cork & Seal Company. The company is a major producer of metal cans, crowns (bottle caps), closures (screw caps and bottle lids), and filling machinery for beer and soft drink cans. The two dominant companies in this industry are American Can and Continental Can. The industry is characterized by a really dynamic environment: technological breakthroughs, new concepts of packaging, new materials, and the threat of self-manufacture by large users. Crown Cork & Seal, as a matter of strategy, decided to concentrate on two segments: 1) cans for such "hard-to-hold" products as beer and soft drinks, and 2) aerosol containers. The new strategy paid off. The company outperformed its two larger competitors both in sales growth and in return on sales in the 1964-1975 period. As it should with any strategic choice, the company fully committed itself to its strategy despite the lure of serving other segments. For example, in spite of its 50-percent share in the motor-oil-can business, Crown Cork decided not to continue to compete aggressively in this market.[8]

The multimarket strategy can be executed in one of two ways: either by selling different products in different segments, or by distributing the same product in a number of segments. Texas Instruments, Inc., for example, introduced in 1978 the first all-electronic analog watch, showing the traditional hands on the face of a liquid-crystal display. The watch was directed toward that segment of people who like to stick to tradition whatever it costs (i.e., they are used to reading time by the hands and do not want to read time as numbers). With Swiss-made stainless steel and gold-plated cases, the four models of this watch ranged in price from $275 to $325. TI developed a new market by introducing a new product.[9] On the other hand, the Green Giant Company (now a division of Pillsbury) expanded itself into another segment by distributing its existing product—i.e., supplying its frozen corn on the cob to all Church's Fried Chicken and some Kentucky Fried Chicken fast-food outlets.[10]

---

[8]E. Raymond Corey, "Key Options in Market Selection and Product Planning," *Harvard Business Review* (September–October, 1975), p. 119.

[9]"This Electronic Watch Has 'Hands'," *Business Week* (July 31, 1978), p. 37.

[10]"Green Giant: The New Course That Makes It Attractive to Pillsbury," *Business Week* (October 2, 1978), p. 66.

Total-market Strategy

A company using the total-market strategy serves the entire spectrum of the market by selling different products directed toward different segments in the market. The strategy evolves over a great number of years of operations. Initially a company may start with a single product to serve the market. As the market grows and gets into different segments, leading competitors may attempt to compete in all the segments. This may be done by employing different combinations of product, price, promotion, and distribution strategies. These dominant companies may also attempt to enter new segments as they emerge. As a matter of fact, the leading companies may themselves create new segments and try to control them at the outset.

A number of companies in different industries follow this strategy. General Motors, for one, has traditionally directed its effort to securing the entire market: "A car for every pocket and taste." With its five auto divisions (Chevrolet, Pontiac, Oldsmobile, Buick, and Cadillac) and with a number of car lines manufactured by each of these divisions, the company attempts to compete in all conceivable segments.

IBM also follows an across-the-board strategy. It has a system for meeting the requirements of all types of customers. In the middle 1970s as the minicomputer segment emerged, IBM was somewhat delayed, but finally developed a minicomputer to market in the new segment. Similarly, in the consumer products areas, Coca-Cola has the following soft drinks to satisfy different drinking tastes: Coca-Cola, Tab, Sprite, Fresca, and Fanta. The company even has a brand of orange juice, Minute Maid, to serve those who like to drink orange juice and nothing else (to the extent that orange juice competes with soft drinks).

The total-market strategy is highly risky. For this reason only a very small number of companies in an industry may follow this strategy. It requires a top-management commitment to embracing the entire market. Additionally, a company needs an ample amount of resources to implement this strategy. Finally, only companies in a strong financial position may find this strategy attractive. As a matter of fact, a deteriorating financial position may force a company to move backward from across-the-board market strategy. Chrysler Corporation's financial woes led it to reduce the scope of its markets overseas at a time when experts were looking to the emergence of a single global market. As a Chrysler official remarked: "This company has only a limited amount of management talent and money to go around. It can't go after every part of the U.S. market, let alone around the world."[11]

The total-market strategy can be highly rewarding in terms of achieving growth and market share. It may or may not lead to increased profitability.

---

[11]"Chrysler Corp.: Bullish on the Future, BUT . . . ," *Business Week* (November 20, 1978), p. 115.

Seeking Changes in Market Scope

Companies may not necessarily get tied to a particular market strategy permanently. Environmental shifts may necessitate a new perspective from one time period to another. Consider the Household Finance Corporation (HFC). It gave such short shrift to its traditional business in the 1960s that the company appeared to be a prime candidate for a name change; in 1977 only 46% of its $139 million in net income came from consumer lending, compared with 78% in 1965. At the time, the big banks were beginning to promote their new national credit cards aggressively, mass merchandisers were touting their own credit cards more actively, and credit unions were capitalizing on their tax-exempt status to attract more borrowers with low-interest loans. In response to these trends the company had to take it easy in the household finance business as a defensive measure. Thus, HFC reduced the scope of its market as far as household finance was concerned. In 1978, as new opportunities emerged for expanding its financial services, the company decided to revitalize its position in the household finance market.[12]

The J.C. Penney Company, after 75 years of being identified as a retailer of private label soft goods to price-conscious customers, decided around 1978 to change the scope of its market. The company transformed itself so that it occupied a position between a traditional department store and a discount store (something along the lines of a moderately priced department store chain with emphasis on higher-priced fashion) in hardgoods, housewares, and especially apparel.[13]

Disney's emphasis on the 5 to 13-year-old age market has been a phenomenon in itself. During the 1960s this segment continued to grow, providing the company with opportunity for growth and expansion. In the 1970s, however, this segment shrank; it was headed for a further decline in population in the 1980s. This led the company to change its strategic perspectives to begin serving the over-25 age group of customers by making changes in its current offerings and undertaking new projects. For example, the company is lining up sponsors (such as Exxon) to build a massive adult-oriented addition to Walt Disney World.[14]

Briefly, then, market is a moving target, and a company's strategic perspectives must undergo a change accordingly.

MARKET-GEOGRAPHY STRATEGY

Geography has long been used as a strategic variable in shaping market strategy. Business history provides many examples of how businesses started locally and gradually expanded nationally or even internationally. Products like the

---

[12]"Household Finance: Revitalizing the Business That Got It Started," *Business Week* (September 25, 1978), p. 124.
[13]"J. C. Penney's Fashion Gamble," *Business Week* (January 16, 1978), p. 66.
[14]"Can Disney Still Grow on Its Founder's Dreams?" *Business Week* (July 31, 1978), p. 59.

automobile, telephone, television, and jet aircraft have brought all parts of the country together so that the distance factor ceases to be important. Thus, geographic expansion becomes an attractive choice when seeking growth.

Take the case of Ponderosa System, Inc., a fast-food chain of steak houses. The company started in 1969 with four restaurants in Indiana. By 1970 it had added ten more restaurants in Indiana and Southern Ohio. At the end of 1975 there were almost 400 Ponderosa Steak Houses, from St. Louis to New York. The company continues to expand geographically; by the early 1980s it may be nationwide. The Ponderosa story provides an interesting illustration of the pattern of geographic growth: initially a business limits its operations to a small community, from there it moves on to two or three neighboring states, then to about 7–10 states, then to 15–20 states, and finally it becomes national or even international.

There are a variety of reasons for seeking geographic expansion: to achieve growth, reduce dependence on a small geographic base, use national advertising media, realize experience (i.e., economies of scale), utilize excess capacity, and guard against competitive inroads by moving into more distant sectional markets.

This section examines various alternatives included in the market-geography strategy. The purpose here is to highlight strategic issues which may dictate the choice of a geographic dimension in the context of market strategy.

Local-market Strategy

In modern days the relevance of the local-market strategy may be limited to: 1) retailers and 2) service organizations such as airlines, banks, doctors, etc. In many cases, geographic dimensions of doing business are decided by law. For example, until recently, an airline needed permission from the Civil Aeronautics Board (CAB) concerning the areas it could fly between. By the same token, banks, by state law, may only operate locally.

As far as retailers are concerned, there are 1.5 million retailers which make less than $100,000 annually. Presumably, these are all local operations. Even manufacturers may initially limit the distribution of their new products to a local market.

While the number of businesses operating only locally is large, their share of the total business is meagre. The strategy to operate only in local markets may be fine initially, but in the long run a business must expand outside its immediate vicinity in order to prosper.

Regional-market Strategy

The regional scope of a business may vary from operations in two or three states to those spread over a part of the country such as New England, the Southwest, the Midwest, the West, etc. Regional expansion provides a good compromise between doing business locally and going national.

Regional expansion ensures that if business in one part of the region is depressed, favorable conditions may operate in other parts so that overall business will be satisfactory. Further, it is culturally easier to handle a region than the entire country. Logistics of handling a business are much simpler regionally than nationally. As a matter of fact, many companies may prefer to limit their business to a region as a matter of strategy in order to avoid competition and keep control centralized.

Many businesses continue to operate successfully regionally. Large grocery chains such as the following, for example, are regional in character: Safeway in the West, Kroger's in the Midwest, and Stop & Shop in the East. Regional expansion of a business helps in achieving growth and, to an extent, in gaining market share. Simply expanding a business regionally, however, may or may not affect its profitability.

Geographic expansion of a business to a region may become necessary either to achieve growth, or to keep up with a competitor. For example, a small pizza chain with about 30 restaurants in the Dayton, Ohio, metropolitan area had to expand its territory to survive when Pizza Hut started to compete aggressively with it.

At times a regional strategy is much more desirable than going national. For example, a company operating nationally may do a major portion of its business in a region, with the remainder spread over the rest of the country. It may find it much more profitable to concentrate its effort on the region where it is most successful and divest itself of its business elsewhere. Coors Beer, for example, is distributed in only 20 percent of the U.S. market—a 12-state area where it has a 40-percent market share. If it expands its market nationally, it may lose some of the mystique attached to this brand.[15]

National-market Strategy

Presumably, going from a regional to a national market further opens up opportunities for growth. This may be illustrated with reference to Acton Corp. Traditionally a cable television and telephone interconnect business, it went into the consumer-product arena in 1977 by buying up a dozen regional snack-food companies. It became the nation's second largest potato- and corn-chip maker, doing business in 18 states including most of the Mid-Atlantic, Midwest, and Southwest. The company plans to go national in order to achieve further growth, thus providing stiffer competition for PepsiCo's Frito-Lay division.[16]

It is the prospect of growth that influenced the Radisson Hotel Corp. of Minneapolis to go national and become a major factor in the hotel business. The company operated 19 hotels in 1978. But to double its hotels to 37 by 1982, it

---

[15]"Miller's Fast Growth Upsets the Beer Industry," *Business Week* (November 8, 1976), p. 62.
[16]"Acton: A Switch to Snack Foods Has Turned It Profitable," *Business Week* (September 25, 1978), p. 126.

decided to move into prime "gateway" markets such as New York, Los Angeles, Boston, Chicago, and San Francisco where it could compete against such giants as Marriott Corp. and Hyatt Corp.[17]

Going national, however, is far from easy. Each year a number of brands enter the markets, hoping eventually to become national brands. Ultimately, however, only a small percentage of them hit the national market, and a still smaller percentage succeeds.

A national market strategy requires a top-management commitment since a large investment is needed initially for promotion and distribution. This makes it easier for large companies to introduce new brands nationally, partly because they have the resources and are in a position to take the risk, and partly because a new brand can be sheltered under the umbrella of a successful brand. For example, a new product introduced under GE's name has a better chance of succeeding than if it is introduced by an unknown company.

To successfully implement the national-market strategy, a company needs to institute proper controls to make sure things are satisfactory in different regions. Where controls are lacking, competitors, especially regional ones, may find it easy to break in. If such a situation comes about, the company may find itself losing business in one region after the other. The national-market strategy, if implemented properly, can go a long way in providing growth, market share, and profitability.

International-market Strategy

A number of corporations have adopted international-market posture. The Singer Company, for example, has for a long time been operating overseas. The international-market strategy, however, became a popular method of growth for large corporations in the post-World War II period.

In attempts to reconstruct war-torn economies, the U.S. government provided financial assistance to European countries through the Marshall Plan. Since the postwar American economy emerged as the strongest in the world, its economic assistance programs in the absence of competition stimulated extensive corporate development of international strategies. As Sanford Rose remarked:

> . . . in those halcyon years, nothing seemed more seductive to U.S. business than a foreign climate. American manufacturing companies of all types trekked abroad in prodigious numbers, and wherever they migrated, their banks, advertising agencies, and accounting firms went with them. The book value of U.S. foreign direct investment swelled from about $12 billion in 1950 to more than $50 billion in 1966. It is now estimated at between $140 billion and $150 billion.[18]

[17]"Radisson Hotel Corp.: A Budding Chain Challenges the Big Operators," *Business Week* (December 4, 1978), p. 113.
[18]Sanford Rose, "Why the Multinational Tide Is Ebbing," *Fortune* (August, 1977), p. 112.

Exhibit 8-3 provides not only an appreciation of the extensiveness of U.S. direct investments overseas, but also an indication of where American business has concentrated its efforts. It can be observed that 60 percent of U.S. investments overseas have been in Western Europe and Canada. However, as many under-developed countries (LDCs) gained political freedom after the war, the national governments of these countries also sought U.S. aid to modernize their economies and improve living standards. Thus, LDCs provided additional opportunities for U.S. corporations, especially those in more politically stable countries where the U.S. foreign aid programs were in progress. It is apparent, though, that for a variety of reasons (cultural, political, and economic), U.S. corporations found more viable opportunities in Western Europe, Canada, and, to a lesser extent, Japan.

In recent years, overseas business has become a matter of necessity from the viewpoint of both U.S. corporations and the U.S. government. The increased

EXHIBIT 8-3   U.S. Cumulative Direct Investment Abroad
(In Billions of U.S. Dollars)

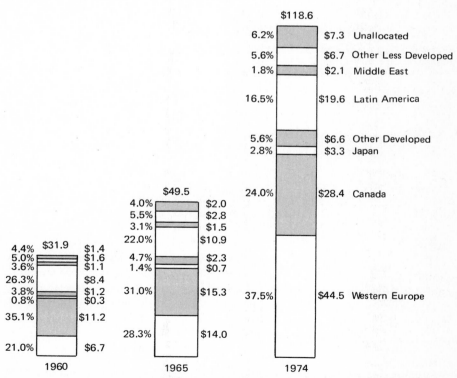

Source: *International Economic Report of the President* (Washington: U.S. Printing Office, 1976), p. 66.

competition facing many industries, resulting from the saturation of markets and competitive threats from overseas corporations doing business domestically, has forced U.S. corporations to look to overseas markets. At the same time, the unfavorable balance of trade, partly due to increasing energy imports, has made the need to expand exports a matter of vital national interest. Thus, while in the Fifties and Sixties international business was considered to be a means of capitalizing on new opportunity, in today's changing economic environment it has become a matter of survival.

Generally speaking, international markets provide additional opportunities over and above domestic business. In some cases, however, a company may find the international market segment as an alternative to the domestic market. Massey-Ferguson decided long ago to concentrate on sales outside of North America rather than compete with the powerful U.S. farm equipment producers. Massey's entire organization, including engineering, research, and production, is geared to market changes overseas. It has learned to live with the instability of foreign markets and to put millions of dollars into building its worldwide manufacturing and marketing networks. The payoff for the company from its emphasis on the international market has been encouraging. In 1975, with 70 percent of its sales abroad, Massey's earnings jumped 38 percent, compared to declines for both Deere & Co. and International Harvester Co.[19]

Other Dimensions of Market-geography Strategy

A company may be regional or national in character, yet it may not be covering its entire trading area. These gaps in the market provide another opportunity for growth. For example, the 7-Eleven stores have traditionally avoided downtown areas. Southland Corporation has about 6,500 of these stores in suburban areas which provide it with over $2 billion in sales. In 1978 the company opened a store at 34th and Lexington in New York and thus signaled the beginning of a major drive into the last of the U.S. markets that 7-Eleven had not yet tapped.[20] Similarly, Hilton Hotels Corporation has hotels in all major cities, but not in medium-sized cities. The company may decide to seek expansion by opening hotels in smaller cities as well. Bloom and Kotler label such strategic posture as "market fortification." The advantage of this strategy is to prevent the competition from moving in.[21]

The gaps in the market were left either because certain markets did not initially promise sufficient potential or because local competition appeared too strong to confront. However, a corporation may find later on that these markets are easy to tap if it consolidates its position in other markets or if changes in the environment develop favorable conditions.

---

[19]"Massey-Ferguson's Success Story," *Business Week* (February, 1976), p. 40.
[20]"Southland: Moving Downtown with Its 7-Eleven Food Stores," *Business Week* (October 30, 1978), p. 180.
[21]Paul N. Bloom and Philip Kotler, "Strategies for High Market-Share Companies," *Harvard Business Review* (November–December, 1975), p. 63.

MARKET-ENTRY STRATEGY

The market-entry strategy refers here to the timing of entering the market. Basically, there are three options from which a company can choose: 1) be first in the market, 2) be among the early entrants, or 3) be a laggard. The importance of the time of entry may be shown with reference to computers. Experience has shown that if new product lines are acceptable to the user and if their impact is properly controlled through pricing and contractual arrangements, this can stimulate sales of an older line. Customers are more content to upgrade within the current product line if they know that a more advanced machine is available whenever they need it. A successful introduction, therefore, requires that the right product be announced at the right time. If it is announced too early, the manufacturer will make the product obsolete unnecessarily. If too late, the manufacturer will suffer a drop in revenues and a loss of customers to the competition.

Be-first-in-the-market Strategy

To be the first in the market with a product provides definite advantages. The company can create a lead for itself which others will find difficult to match. Following the experience curves concept, if the first entrant gains a respectable share of the market, across-the-board costs should go down by a fixed percentage every time experience doubles. This cost advantage can be transferred to customers in the form of lower prices. Thus, competitors will find it difficult to challenge the first entrant in the market since in the absence of experience their costs, and hence prices, for a similar product will be higher. If the new introduction is protected by a patent, of course, the first entrant has an additional advantage since for a specific number of years, a virtual monopoly will exist.

This strategy, however, is not without risks. The first entrant must stay ahead of technology in the field, failing which, competitors may dethrone him. Here Docutel Corp. provides an interesting case. This Dallas-based company was the first to introduce the automated teller machine (ATM) for banks in the late 1960s. These machines made it feasible for the customers to withdraw cash from and make deposits to their savings or checking accounts at any time by pushing a few buttons. It had virtually no competition until 1975, and as recently as 1976 the company had a 60-percent share of the market for ATMs. Then the downfall began. The market share fell to 20 percent in 1977 and 8 percent in 1978. Docutel's fortunes changed because the company failed to maintain its technological lead. Its second-generation ATM failed miserably and thus made way for the competitors. The Diebold corporation was the major beneficiary arising from Docutel's troubles: Its share of the market jumped to 70 percent in 1978 from barely 15 percent in 1976.[22]

---

[22]"Docutel: Trying for a Comeback by Dovetailing the New with the Old," *Business Week* (October 30, 1978), p. 179.

As a matter of fact, if the company plans to be the first in the market, it must stay ahead no matter what happens since the cost of yielding the first position to someone else later can be very heavy. The first entrant must create a primary demand for the product when none exists through heavy investment in promotion. The competitors, however, will find it convenient to piggyback since by the time they enter the market, the primary demand is already there. This shows that even if a company has been able to develop a new product for an entirely new need, it should carefully evaluate its strengths in order to command the market for a long time through technological and marketing innovations. The competitors will make every effort to break in, and if the first company is unsure of itself, it should wait. The strategy to be first, however, if properly implemented, can be highly rewarding in terms of growth, market share, and profitability.

Early-entry Strategy

Several firms may be working on the same track to develop a new product, one of which will introduce the product first. Then the remaining ones are forced into early-entry strategy either because the leader merely beat them in the race, or because they waited in order to let someone else take the lead first. If the early entry takes place just on the heels of the first entrant, it usually causes a dogfight between the firms involved. By and large, the fight is between two firms: the leader and a strong follower (even though there may be several other followers). The reason for the fight is that both firms work hard on the new product and aspire to be the first in the market. Both of them make a strong commitment to this product in terms of resources. In the final phases of their new-product development, if one of the firms introduces the product first, the other one must rush to the market right away to prevent the first one from creating a stronghold in the market. Ultimately, the competitor with an overall superior marketing strategy in terms of positioning, product, price, promotion, and distribution comes out ahead.

After the two firms find their natural positions in the market and the market launches itself on the growth course, there may be other entrants into it. These firms exist on the growth wave of the market and exit as the market matures.

Back in the 1960s, the General Foods Corporation was working on the development of a new type of coffee produced by a freeze-drying process. The company already had a strong position in the regular and instant coffee markets. As General Foods was finalizing various aspects of the marketing strategy of its new coffee, later to be called Maxim, Nestle introduced its own brand (Taster's Choice) of freeze-dried coffee. General Foods immediately followed suit, and the two firms aggressively fought for the market share. Nestle, however, carried the ball since General Foods rushed to the market when it was not quite ready.[23]

---

[23]John C. Maxwell, "Coffee Intake Rose in 1972, After Sliding for Five Years," *Advertising Age* (July 23, 1973), p. 68.

Early entry on the heels of the leader is desirable if a company exhibits across-the-board superior marketing strategy and has the resources to fight the leader. As a matter of fact, the later entrant may get an additional advantage out of the groundwork (in the form of creation of primary demand) done by the leader. A weak early entrant, however, will be conveniently swallowed by the leader. The Docutel Corp. case discussed above illustrates the point. This company was the leader in the ATM market. However, being a weak leader, it paved the way for a later entrant, i.e., Diebold, to take over the market which Docutel had developed.

As the market reaches the growth phase, a number of other firms may enter it. Depending on the length of the growth phase and the point at which firms enter the market, some of them could be labeled as early entrants. Most of these early entrants prefer to operate in specific niches in the market rather than compete against the major firms. For example, a firm may concentrate on doing private branding for a major retailer. Many of these firms, particularly the marginal operations, may be forced out of the market as growth slows down.

Early entry, therefore, can be a rewarding experience if the entry is made with a really strong thrust directed against the leader's market or if it is carefully planned to serve an untapped market. The early entry can contribute significantly to profitability and growth. For the firm that takes on the leader, the early entry may also help in gaining market share.

Laggard-market-entry Strategy

The laggard-market-entry strategy refers to entering the market toward the tail end of the growth phase of the market or in the maturity phase of the market. There are two principal alternatives to choose from in making an entry in the market as a laggard: to enter as imitator or as initiator. An imitator will enter the market as a "me too" competitor, i.e., by developing a product which, for all intents and purposes, is similar to the one already on the market. An initiator, on the other hand, questions the status quo and, after doing some innovative thinking, enters the market with unconventional strategies. Between these two extremes there are companies which enter stagnant markets with modified products.

The entry into the market as an imitator is short-lived. Initially the company may be able to tap a portion of the market by capitalizing on the customer base of the major competitor(s). In the long run, as the leader discards the product in favor of a new or improved one, the imitator is left with nowhere to go. In the early 1970s Honeywell Inc. was faced with the decision about which type of advanced computer system it should develop: an imitation of the IBM 360, or its own new version? As is evident from the following, the company favored the second alternative:

But while the copy might make it easier to tap IBM's huge customer base, it was rejected on several counts. First, it relegated Honeywell to the status of a "me too" company. Secondly, even if a high performance/low cost system were developed, there was no assurance that customers would want an imitation. "After all, if you are looking for a Ford, you go to a Ford dealer." It was agreed that the Task Force would develop its own state-of-the-art system.[24]

The initiator starts by seeking ways to dislodge the established competitor(s) in some way. Consider the following examples:

> The blankets produced by an electrical appliance manufacturer carried the warning: "Do not fold or lie on this blanket." One of the company's engineers wondered why no one had designed a blanket that was safe to sleep on while in operation. His questioning resulted in the production of an electric underblanket that was not only safe to sleep on while in operation, but was much more efficient: being insulated by the other bed clothes, it wasted far less energy than conventional electric blankets, which dissipate most of their heat directly into the air.
>
> A camera manufacturer wondered why a camera couldn't have a built-in flash that would spare users the trouble of finding and fixing an attachment. To ask the question was to answer it. The company proceeded to design a 35 mm camera with built-in flash, which has met with enormous success and swept the Japanese medium-priced single-lens market.[25]

The above two examples illustrate how through creativity and initiative a latecomer may be able to make a mark in the market.

The Wilmington Corporation adopted the middle course to enter the pressed glass-ceramic cookware market in 1977. Until that time, Corning Glass Works was the sole producer of this product; Corning held a patent on it which expired in January, 1977. The Wilmington Corporation opted against entering the market with a "me too" product to compete with Corning Glass. It sought entry into the market with a modified product line, i.e., products with round shape and solid colors, unlike Corning's product, which has a square shape, white color, and a cornflower emblem. The company felt that these changes should enlarge the market since consumers would be able to use glass-ceramic products in a variety of new ways.[26]

Whatever course a company may pursue to enter the market, as a laggard it cannot expect much in terms of profitability, growth, or market share. The

---

[24]"Honeywell Inc.—E.D.P. Division," a case copyrighted in 1975 by the President and Fellows of Harvard College, p. 10.

[25]Kenichi Ohamae, "Effective Strategies for Competitive Success," *The McKinsey Quarterly* (Winter, 1978), p. 55.

[26]"Wilmington Corporation," a case copyrighted in 1976 by the President and Fellows of Harvard College.

market is already saturated, and only established firms can operate profitably. As a matter of fact, their built-in experience affords an even greater advantage to the established competitors. The imitator, however, may be able to make a profitable entry, at least until the established firm obsoletes the imitator's innovation by adding it to its own line.

MARKET-COMMITMENT STRATEGY

The market-commitment strategy refers to the degree of involvement that a company seeks in a particular market. It is widely held that not all customers are equally important to a company. Often, statements such as "17 percent of the customers account for 60 percent of the sales; 56 percent of the customers provide 11 percent of the sales, and so on," are made, which indicate that a company should make varying commitments to different customer segments. The commitment can be in the form of financial or managerial resources or both. Presumably, results from any venture will be commensurate with the commitment made, which explains the importance of the commitment strategy.

The commitment to a market may be categorized as strong, average, or light. Whatever may be the nature of the commitment, it must be duly honored. If a company fails to regard its commitment, it could get into trouble. Back in 1946 the Liggett & Meyers Tobacco Co. had a 22-percent share of the U.S. cigarette market. In 1978 its share of the market was down to less than 3.5 percent. A variety of reasons are ascribed to the company's declining fortunes, amounting to a lack of commitment to the market which at one time it commanded with an imposing market share. These reasons are: responding too slowly to changing market conditions, using poor judgment in positioning brands, and failing to attract new and younger customers. The company lagged behind when filters were introduced. It also missed industry moves to both king size and extra-long cigarettes. It missed the market move toward low-tar cigarettes. Its major entry in the category, Decade, wasn't introduced until 1977, well after competitors had established similar brands.[27] The Liggett & Meyers example illustrates that a company can lose a comfortable position in the market if it fails to serve the market to which it is committed.

Strong-commitment Strategy

The strong-commitment strategy requires that the company plan to operate in the market optimally by realizing economies of scale in promotion, distribution, manufacturing, etc. If a competitor challenges the company's position in the market, the latter must fight back aggressively by employing different forms of product, price, promotion, and distribution strategies. In other words, since the

---

[27]John Koten, "Liggett's Cigarette Unit Lags, and Some Believe It May Be Snuffed Out," *The Wall Street Journal,* November 27, 1978, p. 1.

company has a high stake in the market, it should do all it can to defend its position.

A company with a strong commitment to the market should refuse to be content with the way things are. It should foresee its own obsolescence by developing new products, customer services, channels of distribution, and cost-cutting processes. The point may be illustrated with reference to the Polaroid Corporation. The company continues to do research and development to stay ahead in the field. The original Land camera, introduced in 1948, produced brown-and-white pictures. Thereafter, the company developed film which took truly black-and-white pictures with different ASA speeds. Also, the time involved in the development of film was reduced from the original 60 seconds down to 10 seconds. In 1963, the company introduced a color print film with a development time of 60 seconds; in the early 1970s, the company introduced the SX-70 camera, which made earlier Polaroid cameras obsolete. Since its introduction, a variety of changes and improvements have been made both in the SX-70 camera and in the film that goes into it. In brief, the Polaroid Corporation had a strong commitment to the instant photography market, and it took all the necessary steps to maintain its position there.

The nature of a company's commitment to a market may, of course, change with time. Until 1971 the Procter & Gamble Co. had a light commitment in the coffee market, especially in the East. Its Folger's coffee was almost an unknown product east of the Mississippi. In the early 1970s the company made a strong commitment to the coffee market in the East, city by city. Thus, in 1971 a small company called Breakfast Cheer Coffee Co. made $12 million a year in sales and had an 18-percent share of the coffee market in Pittsburgh. By 1974, this company's sales had plummetted to $2.3 million and its market share had dwindled to under 1 percent. On the other hand, P&G became a major factor in coffee in the Pittsburgh market.[28]

The strong commitment to a market can be highly rewarding in terms of achieving growth, market share, and profitability. A warning is in order here, however. The commitment made to a market should be based on the company's resources, strengths, and willingness to take risks to live up to this commitment. For example, P&G could afford to implement its commitment to the Pittsburgh market since it had a good rapport with distributors and dealers and the resources to launch an effective promotional campaign. A small company, however, could not have afforded to do all that.

Average-commitment Strategy

When a company has a stable interest in the market, it must stress the maintenance of the status quo. This leads it to make only an average commitment to

---

[28]Bill Henderickson, "Tiny Firms Are Losers in Coffee War Fought by Two Big Marketers," *The Wall Street Journal,* November 3, 1977, p. 1.

the market. The average-commitment strategy may be triggered by the fact that a strong-commitment strategy is not feasible for a variety of reasons: The company may lack the resources to make a strong commitment; strong commitment may be in conflict with top management's value orientation; or the market in question may not constitute a major thrust of the company in, for example, a multiproduct or multimarket company.

In April, 1976, when the Eastman Kodak Company announced its entry into the instant photography field, the company most worried was the Polaroid Corporation. This was because Polaroid had a strong commitment to the instant photography market and did not like Kodak being there just for the sake of competition. As Polaroid's president commented: "This is our very soul that we are involved with. This is our whole life. For them it's just another field . . ."[29] A company with an average commitment to a market can afford to make occasional mistakes since it has other businesses to compensate.

Essentially, this strategy requires keeping customers happy by providing them with what they are accustomed to. This can be done by making appropriate changes in the marketing program as desired by environmental shifts, thus making it difficult for competitors to lure the customers away. Where the commitment is average, however, the company becomes vulnerable to the lead company in the market as well as the underdog. The leader may wipe out the average-commitment company by price cutting, which should be feasible due to the experience effect. The underdog may challenge the average-commitment company by introducing new products, shifting out new segments within the market, trying out new forms of distribution, or launching new types of promotional thrusts. The best defense for the company with an average commitment to the market is to keep the customers satisfied by being vigilant about the developments in the market.

Even an average commitment may be adequate, as far as profitability is concerned, if the market is growing. In a slow-growth market the average commitment is not conducive to achieving either growth or market share.

Light-commitment Strategy

A company may have only a passing interest in a market, by virtue of which it will make only a light commitment to it. The passing interest may be explained by the fact that the market is stagnant, its potential is limited, it is overcrowded with many large companies involved, etc. Additionally, a company may opt for light commitment to a market to avoid antitrust difficulties.

The General Electric Company maintains a light commitment in the color television market because the field is overcrowded, particularly by the Japanese companies. The Procter & Gamble Company, in the early 1970s, adopted the light-commitment strategy in the shampoo market presumably to avoid antitrust

---

[29] *The New York Times,* April 28, 1976, p. 23.

difficulties like those it had encountered with Clorox several years previously; P & G let its share of the shampoo market slip from around 50 percent to a little over 20 percent, delayed reformulating its established brands (Prell and Head and Shoulders), introduced only one new brand in many years, and substantially cut down on its promotional effort on shampoos.[30]

A company with a light commitment to a market operates passively without making any new moves. It is satisfied as long as the business continues to be in the black, and thus seeks very few changes in its marketing perspectives. Overall, this strategy is not of much significance for the company pursuing increasing profitability, greater market share, and/or growth.

MARKET-DILUTION STRATEGY

In many situations a company may find reducing a part of the business strategically more useful than expanding. The dilution strategy works out well when the overall benefit that a company derives from a market, either currently or potentially, is less than it could achieve elsewhere. Besides unsatisfactory profit performance, desire for concentration in fewer markets, lack of top-management knowledge of the market, negative synergy of the market vis-a-vis other markets that the company serves, and lack of resources to fully develop the market are other reasons for diluting market position.

There was a time when dilution of a market was considered to be a confession of failure on the part of management. In the 1970s dilution came to be accepted purely as a matter of strategy. Different ways of diluting the market are: demarketing, pruning of marginal accounts, key account strategy, and harvesting strategy.

Demarketing Strategy

Demarketing, in a nutshell, is the reverse of marketing. This term became popular in the early 1970s when, due to the Arab oil embargo, the supply of a variety of products became short. Demarketing may be defined as: ". . . attempts to discourage customers in general or a certain class of customers in particular on either a temporary or permanent basis."[31]

The demarketing strategy may be implemented in different ways. One way involves keeping close track of time requirements of different customers. Thus, if one customer needs the product in July and another in September, the former's order is filled first even though the latter confirmed the order first. A second way of demarketing is rationing supplies to different customers on an equitable basis. Shell Oil followed this route to institute demarketing strategy toward the end of 1978 when a gasoline shortage occurred. Each customer was sold up to ten

---

[30]Nancy Giges, "Shampoo Rivals Wonder When P & G Will Seek Old Dominance," *Advertising Age* (September 23, 1974), p. 3.
[31]Philip Kotler and Sidney J. Levy, "Demarketing, Yes Demarketing," *Harvard Business Review* (November–December, 1971), p. 74.

gallons of gasoline at each filling. Third, recommending that customers use a substitute product temporarily is a form of demarketing. The fourth demarketing method is to divert a customer with an immediate need for the product to another customer to whom the company has supplied the product recently and who is not likely to use it until later. The company becomes an intermediary between the two customers, providing supplies of the product to the supplying customer whenever they are needed if present supplies are transferred to the customer in need.

The demarketing strategy is directed toward maintaining customer goodwill during times when the customers' demands cannot be adequately met due to reasons beyond the company's control. This is achieved by helping out customers in the different ways discussed above. The company does so hoping that the situation leading to demarketing is temporary in nature and that when conditions are normal again, the customers will be favorably inclined toward the company. In the long run, the demarketing strategy should lead to increased profitability.

Pruning-of-marginal-markets Strategy

A company must undertake a conscious search for those markets which do not provide rates of return comparable to those that could be attained if it were to shift its resources to other markets. These markets potentially become pruning candidates as a result of this search. The pruning of marginal markets may result in a much higher growth rate for the company as a whole. Consider two markets, one providing 10 percent and the other 20 percent on original investments of $1,000,000. After 15 years the first one will show an equity value of $4 million as opposed to $16 million for the second one. Pruning can improve the return on investment and growth rate both by ridding the company of markets which are growing slower than the rest of the markets and by providing cash for investment in faster-growing, higher-return markets. Several years ago A&P, the number two grocery chain in the country, closed over 100 stores in markets where its competitive position was weak. This pruning effort helped the company to fortify its position and concentrate on markets where it felt strong.[32]

Pruning also helps in restoring balance in the business. A company may face an out-of-balance condition when the business has too many diverse and difficult markets to serve. By pruning the company may limit its operations to growth markets only. Since growth markets require heavy doses of investment (in the form of price reductions, promotion, market development, etc.), and since the company may have limited resources, the pruning strategy can be very beneficial. Chrysler Corporation, for example, decided in 1978 to quit the European market to be able to use its limited resources to restore its position in the U.S. market. The pruning strategy is especially helpful in achieving market share and profitability.

---

[32]"A & P Follows N.Y.C.'s Lead with 'Instant Money Game'," *Advertising Age* (January 17, 1977), p. 50.

Key-markets Strategy

In most industries a few customers buy a major portion of the volume. This characteristic may be extended to markets. If the breakdown of markets is properly done, a company may find that a few markets account for a very large share of its revenues. These key markets, as a matter of strategy, may then call for extra emphasis in terms of the selling effort, after-sales service, product availability, etc. As a matter of fact, the company may decide to limit its business to these key markets alone.

The key-markets strategy may be illustrated with reference to Royal Crown Companies, Inc. (RC). For years this company, with a market share of 5.6 percent, pursued the mission to challenge head-on both Coca-Cola Co. and PepsiCo Inc., which had market shares of 35 percent and 21 percent, respectively. It tried to duplicate Coke and Pepsi in both product line and advertising. On his arrival in 1976 the new head of the company, Donald McMahon, decided to pursue the key-markets strategy. He put nearly all of RC's marketing efforts in markets where they were already successful, such as New York and Los Angeles. The key-markets strategy not only raised the company's market share in the soft drink industry slightly, but led to a substantial increase in profitability as well. With growth in the industry settled down to 3.5 percent, the key-markets strategy worked out well for Royal Crown.[33]

Market-harvesting Strategy

The market-harvesting strategy refers to a situation where a company may decide to deliberately let its market share slide down. The harvesting strategy may be pursued for a variety of reasons: to increase badly needed cash flow, to increase short-term earnings, and to avoid antitrust action. Usually only companies with high market share can expect to harvest successfully.

If a product reaches the stage where continued support can no longer be justified, it may be desirable to realize a short-term gain by raising the price or by lowering quality and cutting advertising to turn an active brand into a passive one. In any event, the momentum of the product may continue for years with sales declining but useful revenues still coming in.

SUMMARY

This chapter illustrates various types of market strategies which a company may pursue. Market strategies refer to a company's perspective of the customer. This customer focus is a very important factor in market strategies. By diligently delineating the markets to be served, a company can effectively compete in an industry even with the established firms.

Five different types of market strategies and various alternatives under each strategy which were examined in this chapter are outlined below:

---

[33]"Royal Crown Cola Gets a Lot More Fizz," *Business Week* (March 14, 1977), p. 84.

1. Market-scope Strategy
   a. Single-market strategy
   b. Multimarket strategy
   c. Total-market strategy
2. Market-geography Strategy
   a. Local-market strategy
   b. Regional-market strategy
   c. National-market strategy
   d. International-market strategy
3. Market-entry Strategy
   a. Be-first-in-the-market strategy
   b. Early-entry strategy
   c. Laggard-market-entry strategy
4. Market-commitment Strategy
   a. Strong-commitment strategy
   b. Average-commitment strategy
   c. Light-commitment strategy
5. Market-dilution Strategy
   a. Demarketing strategy
   b. Pruning-of-marginal-markets strategy
   c. Key-markets strategy
   d. Market-harvesting strategy

Application of each strategy was illustrated by citing examples from marketing literature. The impact of each strategy was considered in the form of its effect on marketing objectives (i.e., profitability, growth, and market share).

DISCUSSION QUESTIONS

1. Outline the procedure for a new cosmetic company to use in segmenting the market to gain competitive advantage.
2. How far is it advisable for a company to utilize multivariate analysis to segment the market? Discuss.
3. How may a company choose the criteria for segmenting the market?
4. Under what conditions may a company adopt across-the-board market strategy?
5. Can a company operating only locally go international? Discuss with examples.
6. Examine the pros and cons of being the first in the market.
7. What underlying conditions must be present before a company can make a strong commitment to a market?
8. Define the term demarketing. What circumstances dictate the choice of demarketing strategy?

Chapter 9
Product Strategies

How many things there are here that I do not want.

Socrates

Product strategies specify the market needs which may be served by offering different products. It is the product strategies, duly related to market strategies, which eventually come to dominate both the overall strategy and the spirit of the company, and opportunities and threats are seen accordingly. Product strategies deal with such matters as number and diversity of products, product innovations, product scope, and product design. In this chapter different dimensions of product strategies are examined for their essence, their significance, their limitations, if any, and their contributions to objectives and goals. Each strategy will be exemplified with illustrations from marketing literature.

DIMENSIONS OF PRODUCT STRATEGIES

The implementation of product strategies requires cooperation among different groups, i.e., finance, R & D, corporate staff, and marketing. This makes product strategies a difficult thing to develop and implement, as may be illustrated with reference to Chrysler Corporation. The engineering department in the company had such dominance that all other considerations were subordinated:

> Engineering considerations, for example, dictate what kinds of cars the company makes. In the late fifties, when the auto makers were developing their first compacts, Chrysler's management wanted to build a rear-engined compact to compete with G.M.'s Corvair. "Our engineers were not willing to go into the weight distribution that it would entail. There was no way this management could have even ordered that engineering department to do a rear-engined car." A decade later, as Ford and G.M. were preparing subcompacts, Chrysler's engineers concluded they could not design one that would both be competitive in styling and meet their standards for interior comfort.[1]

---

[1]Peter Vanderwicken, "What's Really Wrong at Chrysler," *Fortune* (May, 1975), p. 176.

According to the above author, too much engineering emphasis in arriving at strategic decisions was one of the major reasons for the Chrysler Corporation's poor showing in the turbulent 1970s.

As a matter of fact, in many companies, to achieve proper coordination among diverse groups the product strategy decisions are made at the top-management level itself. At Gould Inc., for example, the top management decides what kind of a business it is and what type it wants to be. The company pursues products in the areas of electromechanics, electrochemistry, metallurgy, and electronics. The company works to dispose of products which do not fall strictly into its areas of interest.

In some companies, the overall scope of product strategy is laid out at the corporate level while actual design is left to business units. It is contended that this alternative is more desirable since in a diverse company it is difficult for the top management to deal with the details of product strategy. In this chapter eight different dimensions of product strategies are recognized (see Exhibit 9-1). Each strategy is examined from the point of view of a strategic business unit; the use of each strategy is discussed with reference to illustrations from marketing literature.

PRODUCT-POSITIONING STRATEGY

The term "positioning" refers to placing a brand in that part of the market where it will have a favorable reception compared to competing products. Since the market is heterogeneous, one brand cannot make an impact on the entire market. As a matter of strategy, therefore, the product should be matched with that segment of the market where it is most likely to succeed. McGirr advises the following:

> Position your product in the marketplace so that it stands apart from competing brands. You can cover that consumer space as if you had a patent on it. Find a strong product position and sit on it. Positioning tells what you stand for, what you are, how you would like customers to evaluate you. Your position telegraphs the simple truth of your products.[2]

Positioning is achieved by using marketing mix variables, especially design and communication efforts. The desired position for a product may be determined by use of the following procedure:

1. Analyze product attributes which are salient to consumers.
2. Examine the distribution of these attributes among different market segments.
3. Determine the optimal position for the product in regard to each

---

[2]William I. McGirr, "The Taster's Choice Story—Establish a Strong Product Position," *Marketing Times* (November–December, 1973), p. 26.

EXHIBIT 9-1   Dimensions of Product Strategies

Product-positioning Strategy
Product-repositioning Strategy
Product-overlap Strategy
Product-scope Strategy
Product-design Strategy
Product-elimination Strategy
New-product Strategy
Product-diversification Strategy

        attribute, taking into consideration the positions occupied by exist-
        ing brands.

    4. Choose an overall position for the product (based on the overall
        match between product attributes and their distribution in the popu-
        lation and the positions of existing brands).

For example, cosmetics for the career woman may be positioned as "natural"
ones which supposedly make her appear as if she were wearing no makeup at all.
An alternate position could be "fast" cosmetics: smoky mauve eye shadow and
dark red lipstick which give the customer a mysterious aura in the evenings.
There can be still a third position: light cosmetics to be worn for tennis and other
leisure activities.

Another example could be made in the positioning of beer. Two position
decisions for beer are light vs. heavy and bitter vs. mild. The desired position for
a new brand of beer can be determined by discovering its rating in the above
attributes and the size of the beer market, which is divided into segments according to these attributes and the positions of other brands. It may be found that the
heavy and mild beer market is large and that Schlitz and Budweiser compete in
it. In the light and mild beer market, another big segment, only Miller may be
positioned. The management may decide to position the new brand in competition with Miller.

Two types of positioning strategy are discussed here: single-brand strategy and
multiple-brand strategy. A company may have just one brand which it may place
in one or more chosen segments in the market. Alternatively, it may have several
brands positioned in different segments.

Positioning a Single Brand

To maximize its benefits with a single brand, a company must try to associate
itself with a core segment in the market where it can play a dominant role. In
addition, it may attract customers from other segments outside its core as a fringe
benefit. Coors beer, for example, is positioned in a limited geographic segment,
the mountain states, and does very well there.

An alternative single-brand strategy would be to consider the market as undifferentiated and cover it with a single brand. Several years ago, for example, the

Coca-Cola Company followed a strategy whereby Coke supposedly quenched the thirst of the total market. Such a policy, however, can only work in the short run. To seek entry into a market, competitors segment and challenge the dominance of the single brand by positioning themselves in small, viable niches. Even the Coca-Cola Company now has a number of brands to serve different segments: Fanta, Sprite, Tab, Fresca, and even orange juice.

Take the case of beer. Traditionally brewers operated as if there were one homogeneous market for beer that could be served by one product in one package. Miller, in order to seek growth, took the initiative to segment the market and positioned its High Life brand to serve the younger people. Thereafter, it introduced a 7-ounce pony bottle which turned out to be a favorite of women and older people, who thought the standard 12-ounce size was simply too much beer to drink. But Miller's big success came with the introduction of another brand in 1975, low-calorie Lite. Lite now stands to become the most successful new beer introduced in the United States in this century.[3]

Kotler reports that Heublein's Smirnoff brand had a 23-percent share of the Vodka market when its position was challenged by another brand, Wolfschmidt, priced at one dollar less a bottle. Instead of cutting the price of its Smirnoff brand to meet the competition, Heublein raised the price by one dollar and used increased revenues for advertising. At the same time it introduced a new brand, Relska, positioning it against Wolfschmidt, and also marketed Popov, a low-price vodka. This strategy effectively met Wolfschmidt's challenge and gave Smirnoff an even higher status. Thus, Heublein resorted to multiple brands to protect its single brand which was challenged by a competitor.[4]

Whether a single brand should be positioned in direct competition with the dominant brand already on the market or be placed in a secondary position is another strategic issue. The direct head-on route is usually risky, but some variation in this type of strategy is quite common. Avis seemingly accepted a number-two position in the market next to Hertz. Gillette, on the other hand, positioned Earth Born directly against Clairol's Herbal Essence, Johnson's Baby Shampoo, and P & G's Head and Shoulders.[5]

Generally a single-brand strategy is a desirable choice in the short run, particularly where the task of managing multiple brands will be beyond the managerial and financial capability of a company. Supposedly, this strategy is more conducive to achieving higher profitability since a single brand permits better control of operations than do multiple brands.

There are two requisites to successfully managing a single brand in the market: the brand must be so positioned in the market that it can stand competition from

---

[3]"Miller's Fast Growth Upsets the Beer Industry," *Business Week* (November 8, 1976), p. 58.
[4]Philip Kotler, *Marketing Management* (Englewood Cliffs, NJ: Prentice-Hall, 1977), p. 169.
[5]*Advertising Age,* June 17, 1974, p. 1.

the toughest rival, and its unique position should be maintained by creating the aura of a different product. Take the case of Hanes Corporation. Recently it entered the cosmetics field, a crowded and highly competitive industry. But the segment it has picked out—sales in supermarkets and discount drug stores—is one that large business companies such as Revlon, Avon, and Max Factor have not tapped. Hanes's brand of cosmetics, L'erin, formerly L'aura, is sold at a free-standing display (similar to L'eggs) placed near checkout counters.[6] As far as the second requisite is concerned, an example is VW's success in protecting its position in the small car market until Japanese cars entered the market in the 1970s. Additionally, Coors beer continues to protect its position because of the mystique attached to its name. In other words, a single brand must have some advantage to save it from competitive inroads.

Positioning Multiple Brands

Primarily, two reasons lead companies to introduce multiple brands to a market: 1) to seek growth by offering varied products in different segments of the market, and 2) to avoid competitive threats to a single brand. General Motors has a car to sell in all conceivable segments of the market. Coca-Cola has a soft drink to offer for each different taste. IBM sells computers for different customer needs. Procter & Gamble offers a laundry detergent for each laundering need. Briefly, offering multiple brands oriented toward different segments of the same market is an accepted route to growth.

To realize desired growth, multiple brands should be diligently positioned in the market so that they do not compete with each other and create cannibalism. For example, 20–25 percent of sales for Anheuser-Busch's Michelob Light brand come from the existing Michelob brand because of the Light brand's low-calorie appeal among current customers.[7] General Foods took a loss with the Maxwell House brand as a result of Maxim's linkage to it. Ford's introduction of the Falcon as a "new-sized Ford" at a lower price led consumers to substitute Falcons for existing Ford models.[8] Thus, it is necessary to be careful in segmenting the market and to position the product through design and promotion as uniquely suited to a particular segment.

Of course, some sort of cannibalism is unavoidable. But the question is how much cannibalism is acceptable when introducing another brand. It has been said that 70 percent of Mustang sales in the car's introductory year were to buyers who would have purchased another Ford had the Mustang not been introduced; the remaining 30 percent of the sales came from new customers. Cadbury's experience with a recent introduction of a chocolate bar in England indicates that

---

[6]"A Hosiery Giant Jumps from L'eggs to Faces," *Business Week* (August 22, 1977), p. 87.
[7]"Anheuser-Busch, Inc., Has Another Entry in 'Light Beer' Field," *The Wall Street Journal,* February 13, 1978, p. 4.
[8]William Copulsky, "Cannibalism in the Marketplace," *Journal of Marketing* (October, 1976), pp. 103–105.

over 50 percent of its volume came from market expansion, with the remaining volume coming from the company's existing products. Both the Mustang and the chocolate bar were rated successful by the introducing companies. The apparent difference in cannibalism rates shows that cost structure, degree of market maturity, and the competitive appeal of alternative offerings will affect cannibalism sales and their importance to the sales and profitability of a product line and individual items.[9]

An additional factor to consider in figuring out actual cannibalism is the vulnerability of an existing brand to a competitor's entry into the presumably open spot in the market. For example, suppose that a company's new brand derives 50 percent of its sales from customers who would have bought its existing brand. However, if 20 percent of the sales of this existing brand were susceptible to a competitor's entry (assuming a fairly high probability that the competitor would have indeed positioned its new brand in that open spot), the actual cannibalism should be considered as 30 percent. This is because 20 percent of the revenue from sales of the existing brand would have been lost to a competitive brand had there been no new brand.

Multiple brands can be positioned in the market either head-on with the leading brand or with an idea. The relative strengths of the new entry and the established brand will dictate which of the two positioning routes is more desirable. While head-on positioning usually appears risky, some companies have successfully carried it out. IBM's copier was positioned in head-on competition with Xerox. Bristol-Myers' Datril was introduced to compete directly with Tylenol. Positioning with an idea, however, may prove to be a better alternative, especially when the leading brand is well established. Positioning with an idea was attempted by Kraft Inc. to position three brands (Breyers and Sealtest ice cream and Light n' Lively ice milk) as complementary rather than competitive. Vick Chemical positioned Nyquil, a cold remedy, with the idea that Nyquil assured a good night's sleep. Seagram successfully introduced its line of cocktail mixes, Party Tyme, against heavy odds in favor of National Distillers' Holland House line by promoting it with the Snowbird winter drink.[10]

Positioning of multiple brands and their management in a dynamic environment calls for ample managerial and financial resources. When these resources are lacking, the company is better off with a single brand. Additionally, if a company already has a dominant position, its attempt to increase its share of the market by introducing an additional brand may invite antitrust action. Such an eventuality should be guarded against. On the other hand, there is also a defensive or share-maintenance issue to be considered here even if one has the dominant

[9]Roger A. Kerin, Michael G. Harvey, and James T. Rothe, "Cannibalism and New Product Development," *Business Horizons* (October, 1978), p. 31.
[10]John P. Maggard, "Positioning Revisited," *Journal of Marketing* (January, 1976), pp. 63–66.

entry. A product with high market share may not remain in this position forever if competitors are permitted to chip away with unchallenged positions.

As a strategy, the positioning of multiple brands, if properly implemented, can lead to increases in growth, market share, and profitability.

PRODUCT-REPOSITIONING STRATEGY

Often a product may require repositioning. This can happen if 1) a competitive entry has been positioned next to the brand with an adverse effect on its share of the market, 2) consumer preferences have undergone a change, 3) new customer-preference clusters have been discovered with promising opportunities[11], or 4) a mistake has been made in the original positioning.

Citations from marketing literature will illustrate how repositioning becomes desirable under different circumstances. Simmons Company introduced its Hide-A-Bed (convertible sofa) in 1940. Soon after, hundreds of competitors followed suit and affected Simmons' business. At the same time consumer preferences shifted in favor of living room sofas, which plateaued the industry sales. Also, the consumers were becoming more quality conscious. These conditions led Simmons to reposition the product by reversing the emphasis from the bed that converted to a sofa, to the sofa that converted to a bed. The repositioning was implemented by making appropriate changes in product design (i.e., using elegant upholstery and style), and by advertising (i.e., stressing utilitarian demand for living room sofas, quality, and fashion consciousness). Following the repositioning in 1960, Simmons' sales increased rapidly.[12]

Over the years, Coca-Cola's position has been shifted to keep up with the changing mood of the market. In recent years, the theme of Coca-Cola's advertising has evolved from "Things go better with Coke" to "It's the real thing." The current perspective of Coca-Cola's positioning is to seek to reach a generation of young people and those young at heart. Recently Procter & Gamble changed the name of its brand of toothpaste, Gleem II, back to just Gleem to revitalize and reposition it primarily as a whitener with fresh taste, thereby reverting to Gleem's original position. In 1968 with the addition of fluoride to Gleem, P & G had emphasized Gleem's cavity-fighting properties and had changed its name to Gleem II. Continued poor performance of the brand, however, led to thorough research of the problem, which showed that Gleem was still perceived as a whitener despite its cavity-fighting emphasis. This is what led the company to seek again the original position for Gleem.[13]

---

[11]Philip Kotler, op. cit., p. 108.

[12]Carl Spielvogel, "Brand Positioning and Repositioning," in Earl L. Bailey (ed.), Marketing Strategies (New York: Conference Bd., 1974), p. 10.

[13]Nancy Giges, "P & G Busy: Repositioned Gleem; Folger's Addition; Revamped Sure," Advertising Age (January 17, 1977), p. 1.

Basically, there are three ways to reposition a product: among existing users, among new users, and for new uses. The discussion that follows will elaborate these repositioning alternatives.

Repositioning Among Existing Customers

Repositioning among existing customers is sought by the promotion of more varied uses of the product. Du Pont adopted this strategy to revitalize its nylon business by promoting the "fashion smartness" of tinted hose. The effort was directed toward expanding women's collections of hosiery by creating a new fashion image for hosiery: not simply a *"neutral* accessory to a central integration of fashion, but a *suitable* tint and pattern for each outer garment in the lady's wardrobe." The repositioning effort was also expected to reinforce the leg as a mark of sex appeal and thus help hosiery sales.

General Foods Corporation repositioned Jell-O to boost its sales by promoting it as a base for salads. To facilitate this usage, the company introduced a variety of vegetable-flavored Jell-Os. Similar strategy was adopted by 3M on behalf of Scotch tape. 3M introduced a line of colored, patterned, waterproof, invisible, and write-on Scotch tapes for different types of gift wrapping.[14]

The purpose of repositioning among current users is to revitalize the product's life by giving it new character as something which is needed not merely as a staple product, but also in order for one to be unique and fashionable. The repositioning among users should help the brand in its sales growth as well as in its increasing profitability.

Repositioning Among New Users

Repositioning among new users requires that the product be presented with a different twist to the people who have not hitherto been favorably inclined toward it. In so doing, care must be taken to see that in the process of enticing new customers, the current customers of the product are not acerbated. Miller's attempts to win over new customers for the Miller High Life beer are noteworthy. Approximately 15 percent of the population consumes 85 percent of all the beer sold in the U.S. Miller's slogan, "the champagne of bottled beer," tended to have more appeal for light users than heavy users. Also, the image projected too much elegance for a product in the indulgence category. Miller decided to reposition the product slightly to offer greater appeal to a wider range of beer drinkers without weakening the current franchise of the brand. "Put another way, the need was to take Miller High Life out of the champagne bucket, but not to put it in the bathtub." After conducting a variety of studies, Miller came up with a new

---

[14]Examples of Du Pont and General Foods discussed here and in the discussion that follows are from: Theodore Levitt, "Exploit the Product Life Cycle," *Harvard Business Review* (November–December, 1965), pp. 81–94.

promotional campaign built around this slogan: "If you've got the time, we've got the beer." The campaign proved to be highly successful. Through its new slogan the brand communicated three things: it was a quality product worth taking time out for; the idea of an invitation, offered in a friendly low-key manner, suggested the use of the product at leisure; and the idea of a pleasant ambience of relaxation and reward removed the pressures of the work day.[15]

At Du Pont new users of nylon were created by legitimizing among early teenagers and subteenagers the necessity of wearing hosiery. This was achieved by working out a new ad campaign with emphasis on the merchandising of youthful products and styles to tempt the young consumers. Jell-O attempted to develop new users among those who would not perceive Jell-O as a popular dessert or salad product. Thus, during the Metrecal boom, Jell-O was advertised with a new concept—a fashion-oriented, weight-control appeal.

The addition of new users to a product's customer base helps enlarge the overall market and thus puts the product on a growth route. Repositioning among new users also helps increase the profitability since an essentially old product is marketed, but in a revitalized fashion. Except for promotional costs, very few new investments have to be made to seek repositioning among new users.

Repositioning for New Uses

The repositioning for new uses requires searching for latent uses of the product, if any. While all products may not have latent uses, there are products which may be used for purposes not originally intended. The case of Arm & Hammer's baking soda offers a classic example of an unexplored use of a product. Today this product is popular for killing odors. Yet this was not the use originally conceived for the product. While new uses for a product can be discovered in a variety of ways, the best way to discover them is to gain insights into the customer's style of consuming the product. If a large number of customers are using the product for a purpose other than the one originally intended, this other use could be developed into an alternative use with whatever modifications are necessary.

The positioning for new-use strategy may be illustrated with reference to a United States Borax & Chemical Corporation product. Initially it was positioned primarily as a laundry deodorant. The company stressed deodorizing and freshening as the benefits of the product. After nine years in the market, the company found that a large number of women who had a negative feeling about using a bleach considered a modified version of this company's product named Borateem (labeled as Borateem Plus) as a good substitute for bleach. This led the United States Borax & Chemical Corporation to seek a new position for Borateem—that

---

[15]Carl Speilvogel, *op. cit.,* pp. 13–16.

of a bleach substitute. The repositioning provided consecutive month-to-month sales gains for the product.[16]

At Du Pont, new uses for nylon sprang up in the form of varied types of hosiery (such as stretch stockings and stretch socks), tires, bearings, etc. It is the new uses which kept nylon on the growth path: wrap knits in 1945, tire cord in 1948, textured yarns in 1955, carpet yarns in 1959, and so on. Without the new uses nylon would have hit the saturation level as far back as 1962.

As far as Jell-O is concerned, General Foods found that women used powdered gelatin dissolved in liquids as a means of strengthening their fingernails. Working on this clue, General Foods introduced a flavorless Jell-O as a bone-building agent.

The new-use strategy is directed toward revamping the sales of a product whose growth based on its original conceived use has slowed down. This strategy potentially can be followed to increase sales growth, market share, and profitability.

PRODUCT-OVERLAP STRATEGY

The product-overlap strategy refers to a situation where a company decides to compete against its own brand. Many reasons lead companies to adopt such a strategic posture. The A & P stores themselves cannot keep the 42 manufacturing operations working at full capacity. A & P, therefore, decided to distribute many of its products through independent food retailers. A & P's Eight O'clock coffee, for example, is sold through the 7-Eleven stores.[17] Procter & Gamble has different brands of detergents virtually competing in the same market. Each brand has its own organization for marketing research, product development, merchandising, and promotion. Although sharing the same sales force, each brand behaves aggressively to outdo the other in the marketplace. Sears, Roebuck and Co.'s large appliances bearing its brand name are actually manufactured by the Whirlpool Corporation. Thus, Whirlpool's appliances compete against those it sold to Sears.

These are alternative ways in which the product-overlap strategy may be operationalized. Principal among them are: having competing lines, doing private labeling, and dealing with original-equipment manufacturers. These are discussed in the ensuing pages.

Competing Brands

In order to gain a larger share of the total market, many companies introduce competing products to the market. When a market is not neatly delineated, a single brand of the product may not be able to make an adequate impact on the

---

[16]*Ibid.,* pp. 11–12.
[17]Robert E. Weigand, "Fit Products and Channels to Your Markets," *Harvard Business Review* (January–February, 1977), p. 97.

market. If the second brand is placed to compete with the first one, while there will still be some cannibalism, overall sales of the two brands should increase substantially. In other words, the two competing brands provide a more aggressive front against the competitors.

Often the competing-brands strategy works out to be a short-term phenomenon. When a new version of the product is introduced, the previous version is allowed to continue until the new one has fully established itself. In this way competition is prevented from stealing sales during the time that the new product is coming into its own.

In 1977 Gillette introduced the Atra razor, which was a revolutionary new product. It has a pivoting head mechanism that permits a closer shave. At the same time, its previous twin-blade razor, Trac II, introduced in 1971, continued to be promoted as before. It is claimed that the two brands put together have been very effective in the market. It is estimated that 46 percent of Atra users have converted from Trac II; this figure would have been 60 percent if Trac II had not been promoted. Besides, Atra, the new razor, would have become more vulnerable to the Schick Super II and other rigid Trac II lookalikes.[18]

To expand its overall coffee market, Procter & Gamble introduced in 1977 a more economical form of ground coffee under the Folger's label branded as Folger's Flaked coffee. A more efficient milling process which refines the coffee into flakes allows hot water used in brewing to come into contact with more of each coffee particle. This can result in savings of up to 15 percent per cup. The new product is packaged in 13-, 26-, and 32-ounce cans yielding the same number of cups of coffee as standard 16-, 32-, and 48-ounce jars, respectively. Both the new and the old formulations were allowed to be promoted aggressively, competing with each other and at the same time providing a strong front against brands belonging to other manufacturers.[19]

The competing-brands strategy is useful in the short run only. Ultimately each brand should find its special niche in the market. If that does not happen, they will create confusion among customers and the sales will be hurt. Alternatively, in the long run, one of the brands may be withdrawn, yielding its position to the other brand. This strategy is a useful device for achieving growth and increasing market share.

Private Labels

Private labeling refers to a manufacturer producing a brand under someone else's name. In the areas of goods where middlemen have significant control of

---

[18]"Gillette Renews Its Love for Television Sports," *Business Week* (October 23, 1978), p. 142.
[19]Nancy Giges, "P & G Busy: Repositioned Gleem; Folger's Addition; Revamped Sure," *Advertising Age* (January 17, 1977), p. 1.

the distribution sector, private labeling or branding has become quite common. For large food chains, items bearing their own brand name contribute significantly toward their sales. Sears, J.C. Penney, and other such companies merchandise different types of goods: textile goods, electronic goods, large appliances, sports goods, and others with their own brand names on them.

The private-label strategy may be discussed from two viewpoints: the manufacturer's purpose to offer a private brand, and the middleman's purpose to have a private brand. A manufacturer offers a private brand if this will help increase total revenues. Of course, the manufacturer's first effort will be to push its own brand, but if the choice is between producing a private brand and having no business, it will seriously consider labeling for others. Many companies manufacture solely for others. For example, the Design & Manufacturing Corporation was begun exclusively for manufacturing privately branded dishwashers for large distributors. This, however, can be a risky position since the manufacturer is at the mercy of middlemen who will negotiate a hard bargain. They know the manufacturer is not known in the market and will be forced to come to terms. The situation becomes critical if the manufacturer deals mainly with one customer, such as Sears, for example. There have been many cases where a small manufacturer gave up and sold its business to a distributor with whom it did a major part of its dealings because it just could not operate profitably and still meet the distributor's demand for price reductions.

Many large manufacturers deal in private brands while simultaneously offering their own brands. In such a situation they are competing against themselves. They do so, however, hoping overall revenues will be higher with the offering of the private brand than without it. Coca-Cola, for example, supplies its Minute Maid orange juice to A & P so that in an A & P store both its own brand (supplied by Coca-Cola) and Minute Maid are offered side by side. At one time, many companies equated offering private brands with lowering their brands' images. But the business swings of the 1970s made them change their attitude on this issue. For example, the Frigidaire Division of General Motors at one time did not offer its appliances under a private label. However, in 1975 it started offering them under Montgomery Ward's name.

The middlemen's interest in selling goods under their own brand names is also motivated by economic considerations. They buy goods with their brand name on them at lower costs, then offer them to the customers at a price which is slightly lower than the price of a manufacturer's brand (also referred to as a national brand). The assumption is that the customer motivated by the lower price will buy a private brand, assuming that its quality is on par with the national brand. This assumption is based on the premise that a reputed middleman will not offer something under its name if it is lacking in quality. Needless to say, the predominance of such an assumption among the customers will vary depending on the status of the middleman.

Dealing With an Original Equipment Manufacturer (OEM)

Following the strategy of dealing with an OEM, a company may sell the components used in its product to competitors. This enables the competitors to compete with the company in the market. For example, in the initial stages of color television, RCA was the only company that manufactured the picture tube. It sold these picture tubes to General Electric and other competitors, enabling them to compete with RCA color television sets in the market.

The relevance of this strategy may be discussed from the viewpoint of both the seller and the OEM. The motivation for the seller to engage in this strategy comes from two sources: desire to work at near-capacity level, and desire to share the effort to promote primary demand. Working at full capacity becomes essential in the case of products where the experience effect works. Thus, by selling a component to competitors, a company may reduce the across-the-board costs of the component for itself. This way it will have the price leverage to compete with those to whom it sold the component. Besides, the company will always have the option of refusing to do business with a competitor who becomes a problem.

The second type of motivation is based on the support which competitors can provide in stimulating primary demand for the new product. Many companies may be working on a new-product idea. One of them successfully introduces the product while others are unable to do so since they lack an essential component or technology which the former has. Since the product is new, the innovator may find it tedious to undertake the task of developing primary demand by itself. It may make a strategic decision to share the essential component technology with other competitors, thus encouraging them to enter the market and sharing the burden of stimulating primary demand.

A number of companies follow the OEM strategy. The auto manufacturers sell parts to each other. Texas Instruments sold electronic chips to its competitors during the initial stages of the calculator's development. Back in the 1950s Polaroid bought certain essential ingredients from Kodak to manufacture film. IBM shared a variety of technological components with other computer producers. In many situations, however, the OEM strategy may be forced upon companies by the Justice Department in its efforts to promote competition in an industry. Both Kodak and IBM shared the products of their technology with competitors at the demand of the government. Thus, as a matter of strategy, when government interference may be expected, a company will gain more by sharing its components with others and assuming industry leadership. From the standpoint of results, this strategy is useful in seeking increased profitability. It may not have much effect on market share or growth.

As far as the OEMs are concerned, the strategy of depending upon a competitor for an essential component will only work in the short run. This is because the supplier may at some point in time refuse entirely to sell or it may make it difficult for the buyer by delaying deliveries or periodically making enormous price increases.

PRODUCT-SCOPE STRATEGY

The product-scope strategy deals with the perspectives of the product mix of a company (i.e., the number of product lines and items in each line that the company may offer). The product-scope strategy is determined by making a reference to the overall company mission. Presumably, the mission defines what sort of company it is going to be, which helps in selecting the products and services which are to become a part of the product mix. Standard Brands Inc., for example, was traditionally in the business of food ingredients such as corn sweeteners; it also had such branded consumer products as Planter's nuts and Fleischmann's margarine. The company is interested in adding more branded food and beverage products to its business. It also wants to branch out to nonfood products as well. For example, Standard Brands would like to add to its line a product like Elmer's glue, which belongs to another food company, Borden, Inc. However, before arriving at any decision, the management felt that it should define the mission of its business: "A crucial choice is whether we define our mission as that of a consumer food company or, more broadly, as a consumer product company."[20]

The product-scope strategy must be finalized after a careful review of all facets of the business since it involves a long-term commitment. Additionally, the strategy must be reviewed from time to time to make any changes called for because of shifts in the environment. The point may be elaborated with reference to Eastman Kodak Co.'s decision to enter the instant-photography market. Traditionally Polaroid bought the negatives, worth $50 million, for its films from Kodak. In 1969 Polaroid built its own negative plant. This meant Kodak would lose some $50 million worth of business and be left with idle machinery that had been dedicated to filling Polaroid's needs. Further, by producing its own film, Polaroid could lower its costs; if it then cut prices, instant photography might become more competitive with Kodak's business. Alternatively, if Polaroid held prices high, it would realize high margins, and would soon be very rich indeed. Encouraged by such achievements, Polaroid could even develop a marketing organization rivaling Kodak and threaten it in every sphere. In brief, Kodak was convinced that it would be shut out of the instant photography market forever if it delayed its entry any longer. Subsequently, however, a variety of reasons led Kodak to change its decision to go ahead with the instant-photography project. Its pocket instamatic cameras turned out to be highly successful, and some of the machinery and equipment allocated to instant photography had to be switched over to the pocket instamatics. Capital shortage also occurred, and Kodak, as a matter of financial policy, did not like to borrow to support the instant-photography project.[21] Kodak again revised its position and did enter the field of instant

---

[20]"Standard Brands: A Blueprint for a New Packaged Goods Drive," *Business Week* (February 6, 1978), p. 90.
[21]Bro Uttal, "Eastman Kodak's Orderly Two-Front War," *Fortune* (September, 1976), p. 123.

photography in 1976. In brief, the product-scope strategy required a deep review of a large number of factors both inside and outside the organization.

The three variants of product-scope strategy which will be discussed in this section are: single-product strategy, multiple-products strategy, and system-of-products strategy. It will be recalled that in the previous chapter three alternatives were discussed under market-scope strategy: single-market strategy, multimarket strategy, and total-market strategy. These market strategies may be related to the three variants of product-scope strategy, which provides nine different product/market-scope alternatives.

Single Product

A company may have just one product in its line and try to live on the success of this one product. Concentration on a single product leads to specialization, which helps in scale and productivity gains. Besides, management of operations is much more efficient when a single product is the focus. Further, in today's environment where growth leads most companies to other multiple products, a single-product company may become so specialized in its field that it can stand any competition. Lukens Steel Co. ranks 19th in U.S. steel production. It specializes in plate steel, making more grades and sizes than anybody else in the industry. Even in its chosen field, Lukens has been a specialist in higher margin lines, such as unusually heavy-guage plates, low-sulfur grades, and special shapes such as dome-like caps. This sharp product focus differentiates Lukens from many of its larger competitors which have much broader product lines, and it has given the company much higher earnings than most. In 1977, its profits rose by 10.3% while steel makers as a group barely broke even. In 1978, the industry enjoyed recovery although Lukens was far ahead of them all.[22]

It is the narrow product focus, i.e., cancer insurance, that has given American Family Life Assurance Co. of Columbus, Georgia, a fast track record. Cancer is probably more feared than any other disease in the U.S. today. Although it kills fewer people than heart ailments, its victims' suffering is often lingering and painful. Cashing in on this fear, American Family Life became the nation's first marketer of insurance policies that cover the expenses of treating cancer. Today 60 percent of all cancer policies in force have been written by American Family. The company ranked 69th in 1979 among North American life, accident, and health insurance companies as measured by premiums, while in 1969 its rank was 372. In just five years American Family's premium income increased 294 percent while earnings went up by 18 percent.[23]

---

[22]"Lukens Steel: A Specialist Blankets a High-margin Market," *Business Week* (December 11, 1976), p. 127.
[23]"American Family Life: Expanding Beyond Its Cancer Insurance Market," *Business Week* (January 15, 1979), p. 100.

Despite its obvious advantages, the single-product company has one drawback: It amounts to laying all the eggs in one basket, and if the changes in the environment make the product obsolete, the single-product company can be in deep trouble. American history is full of instances where entire industries got wiped out. The disposable diaper, initially introduced by Procter & Gamble via its brand Pampers, pushed the cloth diaper business out of the market. The Baldwin Locomotive Company's steam locomotives were made obsolete by General Motors' diesel locomotives.

Currently another company, indeed the entire industry, is being challenged by technological inroads. De Luxe Check Printers, Inc., has been a leader in the basic check-printing business for decades. But now the company must decide how to broaden its one-product revenue base because, as the more efficient electronic funds-transfer systems (EFTS) gain increasing acceptance in the 1980s, growth in check printing is sure to decline. A recent study by IBM indicated electronic funds transfer could displace as much as 20 percent of check transactions by 1985. Further slowdown is likely from a saturation of the check market. One reason for the recent high rates of check growth has been the wider use of checks. Two or more checking accounts in families with wives and teens working is not uncommon. But such growth prospects will decline by the early 1980s. In brief, De Luxe needs to do something in the long run to offset the slowdown.[24]

The single-product strategy has an additional drawback. It is not conducive to seeking growth or market share. Its main advantage is profitability. If a company with a single-product focus is not able to earn higher margins, it is better to seek a new posture. Companies interested in growth and/or market share will find the single-product strategy to be of limited value.

Multiple Products

The multiple-product strategy amounts to offering two or more products. As a matter of fact, this strategy covers a wide range of situations from just having a few products to having virtually hundreds of products. A variety of reasons lead companies to choose this strategic posture. A company having a single product has nowhere to go if that product gets into trouble. With multiple products, however, some may be low contributors while others are high contributors. This way overall performance balances out. Besides, to seek growth it becomes essential to have multiple product offerings. Even when growth can also be sought by opening new markets, this itself may not suffice since economies of scale may want to serve different markets with multiple products, not just one.

In 1970, when Philip Morris, Inc., bought the Miller Brewing Co., it was a one-product business ranking seventh in beer sales. Growth prospects led the

---

[24]"De Luxe Check Printers: Facing the Age of Electronic Banking," *Business Week* (August 28, 1978), p. 110.

company to offer a number of other products. Thus, by May 1978 the United States National Beer Competition showed Anheuser-Busch first with 23 percent of the market and Miller second with 15 percent of the market.[25] The Chicago-based Dean Foods Co. is a $347 million (1978 sales) dairy concern. Over the years, diet-conscious and aging consumers have increasingly shunned high-fat dairy products in favor of low-calorie foods, and competition for the business that remains is increasingly fierce. To successfully operate in such an environment, the company decided to add on other refrigerated foods such as party dips and cranberry drink which are faster-growing, higher-margin businesses than the company's traditional dairy business. Dean Foods' moves have been so successful that while many milk processors are looking to sell out, it is concerned that it might be bought.[26]

Multiple products can be either related or unrelated. The unrelated products will be discussed later in the section on diversification. The related products consist of different product lines and items. For example, a food company may have a frozen vegetable line, a yogurt line, a cheese line, and a pizza line. In each line the company may have different items (such as strawberry, pineapple, apricot, peach, plain, and blueberry flavors in the yogurt line). Notice that there is a consistency in different lines of the food company on three counts: 1) They are sold through grocery stores, 2) they must be refrigerated, and 3) they are meant for the same target market. These underpinnings make them related products.

While not all products may be fast-moving items, they must complement each other in a portfolio of products. The subject of product portfolio will be treated in a separate chapter later on. Suffice it to say here that the multiple-products strategy is directed toward achieving growth, market share, and profitability. Not all companies may get rich simply by having multiple products. This is because growth, market share, and profitability are the functions of a large number of variables, only one of which is having multiple products.

System of Products

The word "system" as applied to products is a post-World War II phenomenon. Two related forces have been responsible for the emergence of this phenomenon. These are the popularity of the marketing concept which requires that businesses do not sell products, but customer satisfactions, and the complexities of the product itself which call for the use of complementary products (with the main product) and after-sales services. For example, an airline should not be selling plane tickets but a pleasureful vacation. A cosmetics company does not

---

[25]"Miller's Fast Growth Upsets the Beer Industry," *Business Week* (November 8, 1976), p. 58.
[26]"Dean Foods: Diversifying to Supplement a Low-Growth Business," *Business Week* (December 18, 1978), p. 74.

sell lipstick but the hope of looking pretty. A person taking a vacation needs not only an airline ticket, but also hotel accomodation, ground transportation, and sightseeing. Following the marketing concept, an airline may define itself as selling a vacation package which includes the air transportation, hotel reservations, meals, sightseeing, etc.

IBM offers a single source for all of the customer's data processing requirements which includes hardware, operating systems, packaged software, maintenance, emergency repairs, and consulting services to train customer personnel and assist them in using the system. Thus, IBM offers a system consisting of different products and services to solve data processing problems. Xerox sells a system for duplicating written documents consisting of the copying machine, repair service, and paper which is fed into the machine.

Offering a system of products rather than a single product is a viable strategy in a number of ways. It makes the customer fully dependent on the company which in turn achieves a monopolistic control over the market. Additionally, the system-of-products strategy blocks the way for the competition to move in. With such benefits this strategy is extremely useful for seeking growth, profitability, and market share. If this strategy is stretched beyond its limits, however, a company can get into legal problems. IBM, for instance, was charged by the Justice Department with monopolizing the computer market. In the aftermath of this, IBM has had to make amendments in its strategy.

The successful implementation of this strategy requires a deep understanding of customer requirements (the processes and functions the consumer must perform when using the product). Effective implementation of this strategy broadens both the company's concept of its product and the market opportunities for it, which in turn help meet the marketing objectives of growth, profitability, and market share.

PRODUCT-DESIGN STRATEGY

A company may offer a standard or custom-designed product for each individual customer. The decision about whether to offer a standard or customized product can be simplified by asking these questions, among others: "What are our capabilities?" and "What business are we in?" With respect to the company's capabilities, there is a danger of overidentification of capabilities for a specific product. If capabilities are overidentified, the company might be in trouble when the need for the product declines since it will have difficulty relating the capabilities to other products. It is, therefore, desirable for a company to have a clearer perspective of its capabilities. The second question determines the limits within which customizing may be pursued.

Between the two extremes of standard and customized products, a company may also offer standard products with modifications. These three strategic alternatives, which come under the product-design strategy, are discussed below.

Standard Products

The offering of standard products leads to two benefits. First, standard products are more amenable to the experience effect than are customized products, giving the company a cost benefit. Second, standard products can be merchandised nationally much more efficiently. Ford's Model T is a classic example of a successful standard product. However, the standard product has one major problem. It orients management thinking toward realization of per-unit cost savings to such an extent that even ordinary changes in the product design necessitated by shifts in market requirements may be ignored.

There is considerable evidence to suggest that larger firms derive greater profits from standardization by taking advantage of economies of scale and long production runs to produce at a low price.[27] Small companies, on the other hand, must make use of the major advantage they have over the giants, i.e., flexibility. Hence the standard products strategy is generally more suitable for large companies. Small companies are better off as job shops, doing customized individual work at a higher margin.

A standard product is usually offered in different grades and styles with varying prices. This way, even though it is a standard product, customers will be offered broader choices. Likewise, distribution channels get the product in different price ranges. In terms of results, the standard-product strategy helps in achieving the marketing objectives of growth, market share, and profitability.

Customized Products

Customized products are sold on the basis of the quality of the finished product, i.e., the extent to which the product meets the customer's specifications. Usually, the producer will work closely with the customer, reviewing the progress of the product until completion. Unlike the standard products, for customized products price is not a factor to be reckoned with. A customer expects to pay a premium price for a customized product. As was mentioned above, a customized product is more suitable for small companies to offer. This is a broad statement which should not be interpreted to mean that large companies cannot successfully offer customized products. This will actually depend on the nature of the product. A small men's clothing outlet is in a better position to offer custom suits than a large men's suit manufacturer. On the other hand, G.E. is more suited to manufacture a custom-designed airplane engine for a military craft than a smaller company.

Over and above the price flexibility, dealing in customized products provides the company with useful experience in developing new standard products. A number of companies have been able to develop mass market products out of their

---

[27]Sidney Schoeffler, Robert D. Buzzell, and Donald F. Heany, "Impact of Strategic Planning on Profit Performance," *Harvard Business Review* (March–April, 1974), p. 142.

custom work experience on the NASA projects. The microwave oven, for example, is an offshoot of the experience which companies gained on government contracts. The customized products also provide opportunities for inventing new products to meet other specific needs. In terms of marketing objectives, this strategy is directed more toward realizing higher profitability than are other product-design strategies.

Standard Product with Modifications

The standard-product-with-modifications strategy represents a compromise between the two strategies discussed above. In being offered a standard product, a customer may be given the option to specify a limited number of desired modifications. A popular example of this strategy is provided by the auto industry. A new car buyer can choose among the following modifications: type of shift (standard or automatic), air conditioning, power brakes, power steering, size of engine, type of tires, and color of the car. While some modifications may be free, for the most part the customer will be expected to pay extra. The customer may not have to pay anything extra for the color of the car, but for other options additional charges will be made.

Supposedly, this strategy is directed toward realizing the benefits of both a standard and a customized product. By manufacturing a standard product, the company seeks the economies of scale; at the same time, by offering modifications the product is individualized to meet the specific requirements of the customer. This is borne out by the experience of a small water pump manufacturer which sold its products through distributors nationally. The company manufactured the basic pump in its facilities in Ohio and then had it shipped to its four branches in different parts of the country. At each branch the pumps were finished according to specifications requested by the distributors. Following this strategy, the company saved money in transportation (since the standard pump could be shipped in bulk) even while it provided customized pumps to the distributors.

Among other benefits, this strategy permits the company to keep in close contact with the market needs which may be satisfied through product improvements and modifications. It also enhances the company's reputation for flexibility in meeting customer requirements. It may also encourage new uses of the product. Other things being equal, this strategy can be useful in seeking growth, market share, and profitability.

PRODUCT-ELIMINATION STRATEGY

Marketers have believed for a long time that sick products should be eliminated. It is only in recent years that this belief has achieved strategic dimensions. It is believed that a company's various products represent a portfolio and that each of these products has a unique role to play in making the portfolio viable. If a product's role diminishes or if it does not fit into the portfolio, it ceases to be important.

When a product reaches the stage where continued support can no longer be justified because its performance falls short of expectations, it is desirable to pull the product out. Reasons for poor performance of a product are notorious and evident to everybody. These may be any of the following:

1. Low profitability
2. Stagnant or declining sales volume or market share which would be too costly to build up
3. Risks of technological obsolescence
4. Entry into a mature or declining phase of the product life cycle
5. Poor fit with the company's strengths or declared mission

Products which are not able to limp along must be eliminated. They are a drain on a company's financial and managerial resources, which can be used more profitably elsewhere.

The two alternatives in the product-elimination strategy are line simplification and total-line divestment. These are examined below.

Line Simplification

Line-simplification strategy refers to a situation where a product line is trimmed to a manageable size by pruning the number and variety of products or services being offered. This is a defensive strategy which is adopted to keep the falling line stable. It is hoped that the simplification effort will help in restoring the health of the line. This strategy becomes especially relevant during times of rising costs and resource shortages.

The application of this strategy in practice may be illustrated with the example of General Electric Co.'s housewares business. In the early 1970s, the housewares industry faced soaring costs and stiff competition from Japan. G.E. took a hard look at its housewares business and raised such questions as: "Is this product segment mature? Is it one we should be harvesting? Is it one we should be investing money in and expanding?" Analysis showed that there was a demand out there for housewares, but it was just not attractive enough for G.E. at that time. The company ended production of blenders, fans, heaters, and vacuum cleaners since they were found to be on the down side of the growth curve and did not fit in with G.E.'s strategy for growth.[28]

The following excerpt indicates how and why a confectionery firm simplified its line:

> A maker of confectionery that offers more than one hundred brands, flavors and packagings prunes its lines—regularly and routinely—of those items having the lowest profit contribution, sales volume, and vitality for future growth.

---

[28]"G.E.'s New Strategy for Faster Growth," *Business Week* (July 8, 1972), p. 54.

Since the early 1970's, each individual product has been ranked on these three factors, and an "index of gross profitability" has been prepared for each in conjunction with annual marketing plans. These plans take into account longer-term objectives for the business, trends in consumer wants and expectations, competitive factors in the marketplace and, lastly, a deliberately ordered "prioritization" of the company's resources. Sales and profit performance are then checked against projected targets at regular intervals through the year, and the indexes of gross profitability are adjusted when necessary.

The firm's chief executive emphasized that even individual items whose indexes of profitability are ranked at the very bottom are nonetheless profitable and paying their way by any customary standard or return on sales and investment. But the very lowest ranking items are regularly reviewed; and, on a judgmental basis, some are marked for pruning at the next convenient opportunity. This opportunity is most likely to arrive when stocks of special ingredients and packaging labels for the items have been exhausted.

In a recent year, the company dropped 16 items that were judged to be too low on its index of gross profitability. Calculated and selective pruning is regarded within the company as a healthy means of working toward the best possible mix of products at all times. It has the reported advantages of increasing efficiencies in manufacturing as a result of cutting the "down time" between small runs, reducing inventories, and freeing resources for the expansion of the most promising items—or the development of new ones—without having to expand productive capacity. Another important benefit is that the sales force concentrates on a smaller line containing only the most profitable products with the largest volumes. On the negative side, however, it is acknowledged that pruning, as the company practices it, may result in near-term loss of sales for a line until growth of the rest of the items can compensate.[29]

The implementation of line-simplification strategy can lead to a variety of benefits: potential cost savings from longer production runs; reduced inventories; and a more forceful concentration of marketing, R & D, and other efforts behind a shorter list of products. According to one point of view, a company with an extensive line could trim costs and add to revenues by cutting ten percent of the varieties being offered.[30]

Despite the obvious merits, the simplification efforts may sometimes be sabotaged since people at the helm feel slighted by it. They sincerely feel either that

---

[29]David S. Hopkins, *Business Strategies for Problem Products* (New York: Conference Bd., 1977), p. 29.
[30]David S. Hopkins, "New Emphasis in Marketing Strategies," *The Conference Board Record* (August, 1976), p. 35.

the line as it is will make it when appropriate changes are made in the marketing mix, or that the sales and profits will turn up once the temporary conditions in the marketplace turn around. Thus, careful maneuvering is needed on the part of management to successfully simplify the line unhindered by corporate rivalries and intergroup pressures. As has been said:

> New products have glamour. Their management is fraught with great risks. Their successful introduction promises growth in sales and profits that may be fantastic. But putting products to death—or letting them die —is a drab business, and often engenders much of the sadness of a final parting with old and tried friends . . . Too often management thinks of this as something that should be done but can wait until tomorrow . . . This is why a definite procedure for deletion of products should be set up, and why the authority and responsibility for the various activities involved should be clearly and definitely assigned.[31]

The decision to drop a product from the line is more difficult if it is one of those core products which served as a foundation for the company to start the business. Such a product achieves the status of motherhood, and a company may like to keep it for nostalgic reasons. For example, the decision by General Motors to drop the Cadillac convertible was probably a difficult one to make in light of the prestige attached to the vehicle. On the other hand, the BIC Pen Corporation probably had little difficulty in disposing of the nonprofitable Waterman pen and ink products because the company viewed the decision from purely a business perspective: "Marcel Bic (BIC Pen Corporation's founder) was not the founder of Waterman and supposedly did not have strong feelings about the product."[32] Despite the emotional aspects of a product-deletion decision, the need to be objective in this matter cannot be overemphasized. Companies establish their own criteria to screen different products for elimination.

An industrial company uses the following procedure to eliminate a product line:

> Assuming that a product is beginning to show a decline in terms of profitability, we try to determine the causes. It may simply be volume; and, if so, this would be reflected by the fact that the product has a variable margin which is good but still inadequate to absorb fixed costs. In such cases, we try to determine why the sales are low and whether something can be done to change the situation.
>
> If the variable margin is bad, we try to see if it cannot be changed by product design, better purchasing, or additional automation to reduce labor costs. In those cases where either the variable margin cannot be

---

[31]Ralph S. Alexander, "The Death and Burial of Sick Products," *Journal of Marketing* (April, 1964), pp. 1–7.

[32]"BIC Pen Corporation," a case copyrighted by the President and Fellows of Harvard College, 1974, p. 2.

improved, or volume cannot be increased to absorb fixed costs, we have no alternative but to abandon the product.

All of these continuing efforts are examined annually when we update our three-year plan. All staff members participate in this effort; and it is not difficult to determine whether a problem product has a solution or whether it should be written off.

A specific example of this is our line of a component for electric motors. We began to get information back from the field that our prices were no longer competitive. On the other hand, an examination of costs indicated that if we lowered the price, the line would go from a marginally profitable position to one of significant loss.

We analyzed our manufacturing techniques and compared them with the reasonable knowledge that we had concerning our competition. It became apparent that without an expenditure of approximately $500,000 for new equipment, we would not be able to produce the product for a price that would approach that of our two major competitors.

At the time, we sold about $1 million worth of this product, and we projected that the increased investment in manufacturing would provide a profit of approximately $14,000 before taxes on this volume. We decided that a three-and-one-half-year payout was inadequate and, therefore, phased out the line.

We have benefitted from this decision. First, the capital was invested in other product lines, thus increasing their profitability. In addition, by focusing our strengths on fewer products, we were able to increase market penetration on those remaining products so significantly that our total sales today are probably much higher than they would have been had we continued to manufacture the special component.[33]

In finalizing the decision, due attention must be given to honoring prior commitments. For example, replacement parts must be provided even though an item is dropped. Alexander cautions: "The firm that leaves a trail of uncared-for 'orphan' products cannot expect to engender much goodwill from dealers or users. Provision for the care and maintenance of the orphan is a necessary cost of deletion."[34]

A well-implemented program of product simplification can lead to both growth and profitability. It may, however, be done at the cost of market share.

Total-line Divestment

Divestment is a situation of reverse acquisition. It might also be a dimension of market strategy. But to the extent that the decision is approached from the product's perspective (i.e., to get rid of the product which is not doing well even

---

[33]David S. Hopkins, *Business Strategies for Problem Products* (New York: Conference Bd., 1977), p. 32.
[34]Ralph S. Alexander, *op. cit.*

in a growing market), it is an aspect of product strategy. Traditionally companies resisted divestment for the following reasons, which are principally economical and psychological in nature:

1. Divestment means negative growth in sales and assets, which runs counter to the business ethic of expansion.
2. It suggests defeat.
3. It requires changes in personnel, which can be painful and can result in perceived or real changes in status or have an adverse effect on the entire organization.
4. It may have to be effected at a price below book and thus have an adverse effect on the year's earnings.
5. The candidate for divestment may be carrying overhead, buying from other units of the company, or contributing earnings.

With the advent of strategic planning in the 1960s, divestment became an accepted option for seeking faster growth. More and more companies are now willing to sell a business if the company will be better off strategically. These companies feel that divestment should not be regarded solely as a means of ridding the company of an unprofitable division or plan; rather, there are some persuasive reasons supporting the divestment of even a profitable and growing business which should be considered. For example, selling a part of the business will release assets for use in other parts of the business where opportunities are growing: Divestment can improve the return on investment and growth rate both by ridding the company of units which are growing more slowly than the basic business and by providing cash for investment in faster-growing, higher-return operations.

Divestment also helps restore a balanced portfolio for a business. If the company has too many high-growth businesses, particularly those at an early stage of development, its resources may be inadequate to fund growth. On the other hand, if a company has too many low-growth businesses, it will often generate more cash than is required for investment and will build up redundant equity. For a business to grow evenly over time while showing regular earnings increments, a portfolio of fast- and slow-growth businesses is necessary. Divestment can help achieve this kind of balance. Finally, divestment helps restore a business to a size which will not raise the eyebrows of the Justice Department and lead it to an antitrust action against the company.

The use of this strategy is reflected in G.E.'s decision to divest its computer business. In order to realize a return which G.E. considered adequate, the company needed to make additional heavy investments in its computer business. It figured it could use the money to greater advantage in an area other than computers. Hence, it divested its computer business by selling it to Honeywell.[35]

---

[35]William E. Fruhan, Jr., "Pyrrhic Victories in Fights for Market Share," *Harvard Business Review* (September–October, 1972), pp. 100–107.

Essentially following the same reasoning, Olin Corporation divested its aluminum business on the grounds that maintaining its small four-percent share required big capital expenditures which could be more usefully employed elsewhere in the company.[36] Westinghouse Electric sold its major appliance line because it needed at least an additional three percent beyond the five-percent share it held before it could compete effectively against the industry leaders, G.E. and Whirlpool, which divided about half the total market between them.[37]

Union Carbide Corp. in 1978 sold eight small businesses and its European petrochemical interests, whose sales exceeded $300 million a year. As a matter of fact, in 1978 the company had plans to redeploy some 15 percent of its $7.42 billion in assets in a few months. The company considered these divestments necessary to transform itself into a manageable organization.[38]

It is difficult to prescribe generalized criteria to determine the desirability of divestment of a business. The Boston Consulting Group, however, suggests raising the following questions, the answers to which should provide a starting point for considering divestment:

1.   What is the earnings pattern of the unit? A key question is whether the unit is acting as a drag on corporate growth. If so, then management must determine whether there are any offsetting values. For example, are earnings stable compared to the fluctuation in other parts of the company; and if so, is the low growth unit a substantial contributor to the overall debt capacity of the business? Management should also ask a whole series of "what if" type of questions relating to earnings: the effect of additional funding? new management? a change in location? etc.

2.   Does the business generate any cash? In many situations, a part of a company will be showing a profit but not generating any discretionary cash. That is, every dime of cash flow must be pumped right back into the operation just to keep it going at *existing levels.* Does this type of operation make any real contribution to the company? Will it eventually? What could the unit be sold for? What would be done with cash from this sale?

3.   Is there any tie-in value—financial or operating—with the existing business? Are there any synergies in marketing, production, R & D? Is the business counter-cyclical? Does it represent a platform for growth—internally-based or through acquisitions?

4.   Will selling the unit help or hurt the acquisitions effort? What will be the immediate impact on earnings (write-offs, operating expenses?) What effect, if any, will the sale have on the image in the

---

[36]*Business Week* (August 10, 1974).
[37]*Forbes* (May 15, 1975).
[38]Jeffrey A. Tannenbaum, "Sliding Earnings Spur Union Carbide Corp. to Big Reform Effort," *The Wall Street Journal,* January 3, 1979, p. 1.

stock market? Will the sale have any effect on potential acquisitions
("will I be sold down the river")? Will the divestment be functional
in terms of the new size achieved? Will the smaller size facilitate
acquisitions by broadening the "market" of acceptable candidates,
or, by contrast, will the company become less credible because of the
smaller size?[39]

In conclusion, a company should undertake a continuing in-depth analysis of
the market share, growth prospects, profitability, and cash-generating power of
each business. As a result of such a review, a business may have to be divested
to maintain balance in the company's total business. This, however, is feasible
only when the company develops enough self-discipline to avoid increasing sales
volume beyond a desirable size and instead buys and sells companies with the sole
objective of enhancing overall corporate performance.

NEW-PRODUCT STRATEGY

New-product development is an essential activity for companies seeking
growth. By adopting the new-product strategy as their posture, companies are
better able to sustain competitive pressures on their existing products and make
headway. The implementation of this strategy has become easier due to technological innovations and the willingness of customers to accept new ways of doing
things.

According to *New Product News,* new products in grocery and drug lines were
introduced at the rate of 3.3 per day during 1977, for a total of 1218.[40] This shows
the importance that companies attach to new products. Despite their importance
in strategy determination, implementation of new-product programs is far from
easy. Too many products never make it in the market. Booz, Allen & Hamilton
Inc. studies indicate that of every 58 product ideas only one leads to a successful
product in the marketplace: Forty-six ideas are dropped during the initial screening, another five fail to qualify during the business analysis stage, four go down
during development stages, one is screened out via test marketing, and of the
remaining two only one makes it in the market.[41] In other words, risks and
penalties of product failure require that companies move judiciously in adopting
the new-product strategy.

Top management can affect the implementation of this strategy: first, by
establishing policies and broad strategic directions for the kinds of new products
the company should seek; second, by providing the kind of leadership that will
create the environmental climate needed to stimulate innovative drive in the

---

[39]"Divestment and Growth," an informal statement published by the Boston Consulting
Group, 1969.
[40]*Business Week* (March 6, 1978), p. 82.
[41]*Management of New Products* (New York: Booz, Allen & Hamilton, 1968).

organization; and third, by instituting review and monitoring procedures so that the manager is involved at the right decision points and can know whether or not work schedules are being met in ways that are consistent with the broad policy direction.

The term "new product" sometimes leads to problems of semantics. To avoid any confusion, for our purposes, new-product strategy will be split into three alternatives: 1) product improvement/modification, 2) product imitation, and 3) new-product development.

Product improvement/modification is the introduction of a new version or improved model of the product, such as "new improved Crest." Usually the improvements and modifications are achieved by adding new features or style, changing processing requirements, and altering product ingredients. When a company introduces a product which is already in the market but new to the company, it is following product-imitation strategy. For example, Schick was imitating when it introduced a double-blade razor to compete with Gillette's Trac II. For our purposes, a *new product* will be defined as one which has a completely new approach in fulfilling customer desires (examples: Polaroid camera, television, typewriter, etc.) or one which replaces existing ways of satisfying customer desires (example: replacement of slide rules by pocket calculators).[42]

Product Improvement/Modification

An existing product of a company may reach a stage which requires that something be done to keep it viable. The product may have reached the maturity stage of the product life cycle due to shifts in environment, thus ceasing to provide an adequate return. Alternatively, new-product, pricing, distribution, and promotion strategies employed by competitors reduce the status of the product to a "me-too" category. At that stage management has two options: either to eliminate the product or to revitalize it by making improvements and/or modifications. Improvements and/or modifications are achieved by redesigning, remodeling, or reformulating so that the product satisfies customer needs more fully. This strategy seeks not only to restore the health of the product, but also sometimes to help in distinguishing it from those of competitors. *Fortune's* description of Kodak's strategy is relevant here:

> On the one hand, the longer a particular generation of cameras can be sold, the more profitable it will become. On the other hand, amateur photographers tend to use less film as their cameras age and lose their novelty; hence it is critical that Kodak keep the camera population eternally young by bringing on new generations from time to time. In each successive generation, Kodak tries to increase convenience and reliability in order to encourage even greater film consumption per cam-

---

[42]Ben M. Enis, Raymond La Garce, and Arthur E. Prell, "Extending the Product Life Cycle," *Business Horizons* (June, 1977), pp. 46–56.

era—a high "burn rate," as the company calls it. In general, the idea is to introduce as few major new models as possible while ringing in frequent minor changes powerful enough to stimulate new purchases.

Kodak has become a master of this marketing strategy. Amateur film sales took off with a rush after 1963. That year the company brought out the first cartridge-loading, easy-to-use instamatic, which converted many people to photography and doubled film usage per camera. A succession of new features and variously priced models followed to help stimulate film consumption for a decade. Then Kodak introduced the pocket instamatic, which once again boosted film use—both because of its novelty and because of its convenience. Seven models of that generation have since appeared.[43]

Kodak's strategy as described above points out that it is never enough just to introduce a new product. The real payoff comes if it is managed in such a way that it continues to flourish year after year in a changing and competitive marketplace.

It is said that Procter & Gamble has made 55 significant modifications in Tide since it was introduced in the 1950s.[44] G.M.'s downsizing efforts in its different cars to meet the demands of the marketplace and the federal government for better gas mileage provides another illustration of the effectiveness and usefulness of the product-modification strategy. When the Arab oil embargo was imposed toward the end of 1973, G.M. had the worst average gas mileage, 12 miles per gallon, among U.S. automakers. Following the embargo in 1974, as buyers turned away from gas-guzzlers in panic, G.M.'s share of the U.S. new car market slid to 42 percent, its lowest share since 1952 (excluding the strike year of 1970). Just three years later, in the 1977-model year, the average mileage of G.M. cars, 17.8 miles per gallon, was the best among the three largest automakers. G.M.'s big cars alone average 15 miles per gallon, or 3 miles per gallon better than the entire 1974 fleet. Largely as a result of the downsizing modifications, the company's market share rebounded to about 46 percent.[45]

There is no magic formula for restoring the health of a product. Occasionally it is the ingenuity of the manager that may bring to light the desired cure for the product. Generally, however, a complete review of the product from marketing perspectives will be needed to analyze the underlying causes and come up with the modifications and improvements necessary to restore it to health.

To identify these options it may be necessary to tear down the competing product or products and make a detailed comparative analysis of quality and price. One framework for such an analysis is illustrated in Exhibit 9-2.

---

[43]Bro Uttal, "Eastman Kodak's Orderly Two-Front War," *Fortune* (September, 1976), p. 123.
[44]Nancy Giges, "P & G Busy: Repositioned Gleem; Folger's Addition; Revamped Sure," *Advertising Age* (January 17, 1977), p. 1.
[45]Charles G. Burck, "How G.M. Turned Itself Around," *Fortune* (January 16, 1978).

EXHIBIT 9-2   Product-change Options After Competitive Tear-down

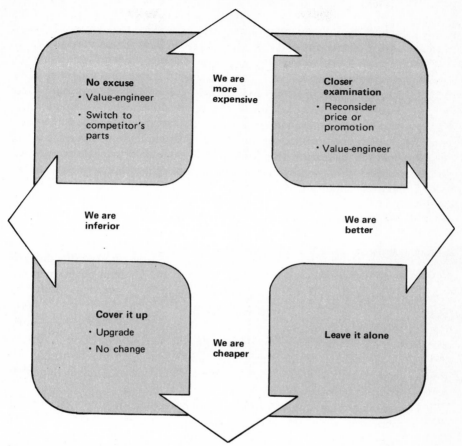

No excuse
- Value-engineer
- Switch to competitor's parts

We are more expensive

Closer examination
- Reconsider price or promotion
- Value-engineer

We are inferior

We are better

Cover it up
- Upgrade
- No change

We are cheaper

Leave it alone

Source: Kenichi Ohmae, "Effective Strategies for Competitive Success," *The McKinsey Quarterly* (Winter, 1978), p. 57.

The basic premise of Exhibit 9-2 is that by comparing its product with that of its competitors, a company will be able to identify unique product strengths on the basis of which to pursue modifications and improvements. The use of the analysis suggested by Exhibit 9-2 may be illustrated with reference to a Japanese manufacturer. Back in 1978, Japan's amateur color film market was dominated by three companies, Kodak, Fuji, and Sakura, the last two being Japanese companies. For the past 15 years Fuji had been gaining market share, while Sakura, the market leader in the early 1950s with over half the market, was losing the market to both its competitors. By 1976 it held only about 16 percent of the market share. Marketing research showed that, more than anything else, Sakura was the victim of an unfortunate word association. Its name in Japanese means "cherry blossom," suggesting a soft, blurry, pinkish image. The name Fuji, however, was associated with the blue skies and white snow of Japan's sacred mountain. Being in no position to change perceptions, the company decided to analyze the market from structured, economic, and customer points of view.

The company found a growing cost-consciousness among film customers: Amateur photographers commonly left one or two frames unexposed in a 36-exposure roll, but they almost invariably tried to squeeze extra exposures onto the 20-exposure rolls. Here Sakura saw an opportunity. It decided to introduce a 24-exposure film. Its marginal costs would be trivial, but its big competitors would face significant penalties in following suit. Sakura was prepared to cut down its prices if the competition lowered the price of their 20-frame rolls. Its aim was twofold. First, it would exploit the growing cost-mindedness of users. Second, and more important, it would be drawing attention to the economic issue, where it had a relative advantage, and away from the image issue, which it could not win. Sakura's strategy paid off. Its market share increased from 16 percent to over 30 percent.[46] Overall, the product-improvement strategy is conducive to achieving growth, market share, and profitability alike.

Product Imitation

Not all companies like to be the first in the market with a new product. They let someone else take the initiative. If the innovation is successful, they ride the bandwagon of the successful innovation by imitating. In the case of innovations protected by patents, imitation must wait until the patent expires. In the absence of a patent, however, the imitating companies work diligently to design and produce a product not very different from the innovator's product and to compete vigorously with the innovator.

The imitation strategy can be justified in that it transfers the risk of introducing the unproven idea/product to someone else. It also saves investments in research and development. This strategy particularly suits companies with limited resources. Many companies, as a matter of fact, develop such talent that they can imitate any product, no matter how complicated. With a little investment in R & D, the imitator may sometimes have a lower cost which gives it a pricing advantage in the market over the leader.

Another important reason for pursuing the imitation strategy may be to gainfully transfer the special talent a company may have for one product to other similar products. For example, the BIC Pen Corp. decided to enter the razor blade business since it thought it could successfully use its aggressive marketing posture there. In the early 1970s Hanes Corp. gained resounding success with L'eggs, an inexpensive pantyhose that sold on free-standing racks in food and

---

[46]Kenichi Ohmae, "Effective Strategies for Competitive Success," *The McKinsey Quarterly* (Winter, 1978), pp. 56–57.

drugstore outlets. A few years later, the company decided to apply the L'eggs marketing talent to cosmetics through its brand named L'aura.

The imitation strategy may also be adopted on defensive gounds. Being sure of its existing product(s), a company may initially ignore new developments in the field. If the new developments, however, become overbearing, they may cut into the ground held by the existing product. In such a situation, a company may be forced into imitating the new development as a matter of survival. Colorado's Adolph Coors Company conveniently ignored the introduction of light beer and dismissed Miller Lite as a fad. Many years later, however, the company was getting bludgeoned by Miller Lite beer. Also, Anheuser-Busch with its light beer began to challenge Coors' supremacy in the California market, where Coors's market share went down from 41 percent to 23 percent. The matter became so serious that Coors decided to abandon its one-product tradition, and in the summer of 1978 it introduced a low-calorie light beer.[47]

Imitation also works well for companies that want to enter new markets without resorting to expensive acquisitions or special new-product development programs. For example, Owens-Illinois, Inc., is adapting heavy-duty laboratory glassware into novelty drinking glasses for home bars.[48]

While imitation does prevent the risks involved in innovation, it is wrong to assume that any imitation of a successful product will succeed. In other words, the market program of an imitation should be as carefully chalked out and implemented as that of an innovation. This point may be illustrated with reference to R.J. Reynolds Tobacco Company's Real cigarette. Real, with 9 mg. of tar, is suffering from the massive shakeout that is occurring in the low-tar segment (15 mg. or less) of the market. In less than three years, that segment came from almost nowhere to 25 percent of unit sales as millions found low-tar cigarettes to be an acceptable alternative which had a lower risk of damage to their health. Low-tar brands such as Reynolds' 11-mg. Vantage and Philip Morris' 9-mg. Merit are selling well because they were available before the low-tar craze took off. Kent Golden Lights did well because they capitalized on smokers' familiarity with parent brands. But the brands that were late entries, such as Real and Liggett & Myers' Decade, are hurting. Real's performance is disappointing because the company spent a huge amount of money in promoting it —almost $40 million in just six months. Among other reasons given, it is said that Real failed to perform well in the market because the company violated its own system by bypassing traditional test marketing.[49] Thus, even a proven imitation may fail unless all elements of the marketing mix are properly scrutinized and implemented.

---

[47]John Huey, "Men at Coors Beer Find the Old Ways Don't Work Anymore," *The Wall Street Journal,* January 19, 1979, p. 1.
[48]*Business Week* (June 1, 1974), p. 67.
[49]"Why Real Missed Its Target," *Business Week* (April 24, 1978), p. 27.

Imitation strategy is most useful for seeking increases in market share and growth.

Product Innovation

Product-innovation strategy includes introducing a new product to replace an existing product in order to satisfy a need in an entirely different way or to provide a new approach to satisfy an existing or latent need. This strategy connotes that the entrant is the first firm to develop and introduce the product. The ballpoint pen is an example of a new product which replaced the fountain pen. The electronic computer was a new approach for handling the information needs of people.

Product innovation is an important characteristic of U.S. industry. Year after year companies spend billions of dollars on research and development to innovate. In 1977, for example, American industry spent more than $18 billion on R & D over and above the R & D supported by the federal government.[50] This shows that industry takes a purposeful attitude toward new-product and new-process development.

Product innovation, however, does not come easily. Besides involving major commitment in terms of dollars, it requires heavy doses of managerial time spent in cutting across organizational lines. And still the innovation may fail to make a mark in the market. For this reason most innovations are produced by large organizations. Initially an individual or a group of individuals may be behind it. But a stage is reached where individual efforts require corporate support to finally develop and launch the product in the market.

Typically the development of a product innovation passes through various stages such as idea, screening, business analysis, development of a prototype, test market, and commercialization. The idea may emerge from different sources such as customers, private researchers, university researchers, employees, research labs, and so on. An idea may be generated in recognizing a consumer need, or just in pursuing a scientific endeavour, hoping it may lead to a viable product. Companies follow different procedures to screen ideas and choose a few for further study. If an idea appears promising, it will be carried to the stage of business analysis, which may consist of investment requirements, revenue and expenditure projections, and financial analysis regarding return on investment, pay-back period, and cash flow. Thereafter, a few prototype products will be produced in order to examine engineering and manufacturing aspects of the product. A few sample products based on the prototype will be produced for market testing. After changes suggested in market testing have been incorporated, the innovation may be commercially launched.

Procter & Gamble's development of Pringle's is a classic case of recognizing a need in a consumer market and then painstakingly working away to meet it.

---

[50]"R & D Spending Patterns for 600 Companies," *Business Week* (July 3, 1978), p. 58.

Americans consume about $1 billion worth of potato chips annually. The manufacturers of potato chips have traditionally faced a variety of problems. The chips are so fragile that they can rarely be shipped for more than 200 miles, and even at that distance a quarter of the chips get broken. They also spoil quickly—their shelf life is hardly two months. These characteristics have kept potato chip making a fragmented industry, and nobody before P & G had applied much technology to the product since it was invented in 1853.

P & G knew these problems since it sold edible oils to the potato-chip industry, and it set out to solve them. Rather than slicing potatoes and frying them in the traditional way, engineers developed a process somewhat akin to papermaking. They dehydrated and mashed the potatoes and pressed them for frying into a precise shape like a hyperbolic paraboloid which looks like a potato chip. P & G found this to be an easy way to manufacture which permits the chips to be stacked neatly on top of one another in a hermetically sealed container that resembles a tennis ball can. Pringle's potato chips stay whole and have a shelf life of at least a year.[51]

After a new product is screened through the lab, the division that will manufacture it takes over and finances all further development and testing. In some companies division managers show little interest in taking on the new products because the costs of introduction are heavy and hold down short-term profits. At P & G, executives ensure that a manager's short-term record is not marred by the cost of a new introduction.

Before a new P & G product is actually introduced in the market, it must prove that it has a demonstrable margin of superiority over its prospective competitors. A development team begins refining the product by trying variations of the basic formula, testing its performance under almost any conceivable condition, and altering its appearance. Eventually a few alternative versions of the product are produced and tested with a large number of P & G employees. If the product passes the tests by the employees, the company presents it to panels of consumers for further testing. P & G feels satisfied if a proposed product is chosen by fifty-five out of a hundred consumers tested.

There is hardly any doubt that if an innovation is successful, it pays off lavishly. However, it is a highly risky strategy requiring heavy commitment and having a low probability of achieving a breakthrough. Thus, the choice of this strategy should be dictated by a company's financial and managerial strengths and risk proneness.

DIVERSIFICATION STRATEGY

Diversification refers to seeking unfamiliar products, markets, or both in pursuing growth. Every company is best at certain products; diversification requires

---

[51]Peter Vanderwicken, "P & G's Secret Ingredient," *Fortune* (July, 1974), p. 75.

substantially different knowledge, thinking, skills, and processes. Thus, diversification is at best a risky strategy and a company should choose this path only when current product/market orientation does not seem to provide further opportunities for growth. A few examples will illustrate the point that diversification does not automatically promise success. CNA Financial Corp. faced catastrophe on expanding the scope of its business from insurance to real estate and mutual funds and ended up being acquired by Loews Corporation. Shrafft's restaurants did little for Pet Incorporated. Pacific Southwest Airlines acquired rental cars and hotels, only to see its stock decline from 49¼ before diversification in 1969 to 4¼ in 1975.[52] The diversification decision is, therefore, a major step which must be taken carefully.

The term "diversification" must be distinguished from integration and merger. *Integration* refers to accumulation of additional business in a field through participation in more of the stages between raw materials and the ultimate market, or through more intensive coverage of a single stage. *Merger* implies a combination of corporate entities which may or may not result in integration. Diversification, of course, is a strategic alternative which implies deriving revenues and profits from different products and markets.

Ansoff states the following reasons which lead companies to seek diversification:

1. Firms diversify when their objectives can no longer be met within the product-market scope defined by expansion.
2. A firm may diversify because the retained cash exceeds the total expansion needs.
3. A firm may diversify when diversification opportunities promise greater profitability than expansion opportunities.
4. Firms may continue to explore diversification when the available information is not reliable enough to permit a conclusive comparison between expansion and diversification.[53]

Essentially, there are three different forms of diversification which a company may pursue: concentric diversification, horizontal diversification, and conglomerate diversification. These will be examined below.

Diversification may be achieved by developing the new product internally or through acquisition. Caterpillar Tractor Co.'s entry into the field of diesel engines is a case of internal diversification. Since 1972 the company has poured over $1 billion into developing new diesel engines ". . . in what must rank as one of the largest internal diversifications by a U.S. corporation." By 1981 as much as 20 percent of Caterpillar's sales will be from diesel engines. Caterpillar's decision is justified by the soaring energy costs. Because a diesel is 45 percent more fuel

---

[52]Paul I. Brown, "Diversifying Successfully," *Business Horizons* (August, 1976), p. 85.
[53]H. Igor Ansoff, *Corporate Strategy* (New York: McGraw-Hill Bk. Co., 1965), pp. 129–130.

efficient than a gasoline engine, Caterpillar is moving into a variety of smaller-road and off-the-road vehicles.[54]

Hershey Foods Corp.'s venture into the restaurant business was achieved by buying the Friendly Ice Cream Corporation. This illustrates diversification by acquisition. Hershey adopted the diversification strategy for growth since its traditional business, chocolate and candy, is stagnant due to the decline in candy consumption with the sharp increases in cocoa prices.[55]

Concentric Diversification

Concentric diversification bears a close synergistic relationship to either the company's marketing or its technology. Thus, new products that are introduced share a common thread with the firm's existing products either through marketing or production. Usually the new products are directed to a new group of customers. Texas Instruments' venture into digital watches illustrates this type of diversification. Using its expertise in the integrated-circuits technology, the company developed a new product which appealed to a new set of customers. On the other hand, Pepsico's venture into the fast-food business through the acquisition of Pizza Huts is a case of concentric diversification in which the new product bears a synergistic relationship to the company's existing experience in the area of marketing.

While a diversification move per se is risky, concentric diversification does not lead a company into an entirely new world since in one of the two major fields (technology or marketing), the company will operate in a known territory. The relationship of the new product to the firm's existing product(s), however, may or may not mean much. All that the realization of synergy does is make the task easier; it does not necessarily make it successful. For example, Gillette entered the market for pocket calculators in 1974 and digital watches in 1976, but abandoned both businesses later. Both pocket calculators and digital watches were sold to mass markets where Gillette had the expertise and experience. Despite the marketing synergy, it failed to successfully sell either calculators or digital watches. Gillette found that these lines of business called for strategies totally different from those it followed in selling its existing products.[56] Two lessons can be drawn from Gillette's experience. One, there may be other strategic reasons for successfully launching a new product in the market besides commonality of markets or technology. Two, the commonality should be analyzed in breadth and depth before drawing conclusions on the transferability of current strengths to the new product.

---

[54]"A Revved-up Market for Diesel Engine Makers," *Business Week* (February 5, 1979), p. 76.
[55]"Hershey: Joining With Friendly to Diversify Away From Chocolate," *Business Week* (January 29, 1979), p. 118.
[56]"Gillette: After the Diversification That Failed," *Business Week* (February 28, 1977), pp. 58–62.

Horizontal Diversification

Horizontal diversification refers to new products which technologically are unrelated to a company's existing products, but can be sold to the same group of customers to whom existing products are sold. A classic case of this form of diversification is Procter & Gamble's entry into different businesses such as potato chips (Pringles), toothpaste (Crest and Gleem), coffee (Folger's), etc. Traditionally a soap-products company, P & G diversified into the above products, which were aimed at the same customer who bought soap.

Note that in the case of concentric diversification, the new product may have certain common ties with the marketing of an existing product of the company, but it is sold to a new set of customers. In horizontal diversification the customers for the new product are drawn from the same ranks as those of the existing product.

Other things being equal, in a competitive environment the horizontal-diversification strategy is more desirable if the present customers are favorably disposed toward the company and if one can expect this loyalty to continue for the new product. Loyalty can help initially in successfully introducing the product; in the long run, however, the new product must stand on its own. Thus, for example, if product quality is lacking, or promotion is not effective, or the price is not right, the new product will flop despite customer loyalty to the company's other products. In other words, horizontal diversification should not be regarded as a route to success in all cases. An important limitation of horizontal diversification is that the new product is introduced to be marketed in the same economic environment as the existing product, which leads to rigidity and instability. Stated differently, horizontal diversification tends to increase the company's dependence on a few market segments.

Conglomerate Diversification

In conglomerate diversification, the new product bears no relationship to either the marketing or technology of the existing product. In other words, through conglomerate diversification a company launches itself into an entirely new product/market arena. International Telephone and Telegraph Corporation's ventures into bakery products (Continental Baking Company), insurance (Hartford Fire Insurance Co.), car rentals (Avis Rent A Car System, Inc.), and the hotel business (Sheraton Corporation) illustrate the implementation of conglomerate diversification in practice. ITT divested some of these businesses a few years ago upon the demand of the Justice Department.

It is necessary to remember here that companies do not flirt with unknown products in unknown markets without having some hidden strengths to handle a conglomerate diversification. For example, the managerial style required for a new product to prosper may be just the same as the one the company already has. Thus, managerial style becomes the basis of synergy between the new product and an existing product. By the same token, another single element may serve as a dominant factor in making a business attractive for diversification. As Conrad has said:

> Such could be the case for a cigarette manufacturer. Its general business acumen might not seem to suggest diversification opportunities, yet its extensive capabilities in advertising might hold an answer. Many companies would be afraid of the massive advertising techniques and budgets wielded in the cosmetics field, but this might be just what a cigarette company is basically suited to handle. Similarly, a cigarette manufacturer might do well in the razor blade business, and a razor blade manufacturer might succeed in the ballpoint pen business.[57]

Inasmuch as conglomerate diversification does not bear an obvious relationship to a company's existing business, there is some question as to why companies adopt it. There are two major advantages of conglomerate diversification. One, it improves the profitability and flexibility of a firm by venturing into businesses which have better economic prospects than the firm's existing business. Two, a conglomerate firm, due to its size, gets a better reception in capital markets.

Overall, this type of diversification, if successful, has the potential of providing increased growth and profitability.

SUMMARY

Product strategies reflect the mission of the company and the business it is in. Following the marketing concept, the choice of product strategy should bear a close relationship to the market strategy of the company. The various product strategies, and the alternatives under each strategy, discussed in this chapter are listed below:

1. Product-positioning Strategy
   a. Positioning a single brand
   b. Positioning multiple brands
2. Product-repositioning Strategy
   a. Repositioning among existing customers
   b. Repositioning among new users
   c. Repositioning for new uses
3. Product-overlap Strategy
   a. Competing brands
   b. Private labels
   c. Dealing with an original equipment manufacturer (OEM)
4. Product-scope Strategy
   a. Single product

---

[57]Gordan R. Conrad, "Unexplored Assets for Diversification," *Harvard Business Review* (September–October, 1963), p. 71.

   b. Multiple products
   c. System of products
  5. Product-design Strategy
   a. Standard products
   b. Customized products
   c. Standard product with modifications
  6. Product-elimination Strategy
   a. Line simplification
   b. Total-line divestment
  7. New-product Strategy
   a. Product improvement/modification
   b. Product imitation
   c. Product innovation
  8. Diversification Strategy
   a. Concentric diversification
   b. Horizontal diversification
   c. Conglomerate diversification

The nature of different strategies was discussed, and their relevance for different types of companies was examined. Adaptations of different strategies in practice were illustrated with citations from published sources.

DISCUSSION QUESTIONS

 1. Discuss how a company may avoid problems of cannibalism among competing brands.
 2. How may a church reposition itself among existing and new "customers" to increase its membership?
 3. Conceptualize how a stale brand (assume a grocery product) may reposition itself for new uses.
 4. What criteria may be employed to determine the viable position for a brand in the market?
 5. What conditions justify a company's dealing in multiple products?
 6. Discuss the pros and cons of offering customized products.
 7. Are there reasons other than profitability for eliminating a product? Discuss.
 8. What factors must be weighed to determine the viability of divesting the entire product line?
 9. Under what circumstances is it desirable to adopt product imitation strategy?
10. Is conglomerate diversification a safe way to grow? Discuss why and why not.
11. What may a company do to encourage successful product innovation?

Chapter 10
Pricing Strategies

The real price of everything is the toil and trouble of acquiring it.

Adam Smith

Pricing has traditionally been considered a "me too" variable in developing marketing strategy. The stable conditions of the 1960s may be particularly responsible for the low status ascribed to the pricing variable. Strategically, the function of pricing was to provide adequate return on investment. Thus, the timeworn cost-plus method of pricing and its sophisticated version, return-on-investment pricing, have historically been the basis of arriving at a price.

In the 1970s, however, a variety of happenings have given a new twist to the task of making pricing decisions. Double-digit inflation, material shortages, the high cost of money, consumerism, and post-price-controls behavior have all contributed in making pricing an important part of marketing strategy.

Despite the importance attached to it, effective pricing is not easy. Even under the most favorable conditions, a large number of internal and external variables must be systematically studied in formulating pricing strategy. For example, the competitor's reactions often figure as an important consideration in developing pricing strategy. Simply knowing that a competitor has a lower price is insufficient; a price strategist must know how much flexibility the competitor has in further lowering the price. This presupposes a knowledge of the competitor's cost structure. In the dynamics of today's environment, however, where rampant inflation can render cost and revenue projections obsolete as readily as they are developed, pricing strategy becomes much more difficult to formulate.

This chapter provides a composite of pricing strategies. Each strategy is examined for its underlying assumptions and relevance in specific situations. The application of different strategies is illustrated with the help of examples from pricing literature.

REVIEW OF PRICING FACTORS

Basically, there are four factors a pricer needs to review to arrive at a price. These are pricing objectives, cost, competition, and demand. This section briefly reviews these factors which underlie every pricing strategy alternative.

Pricing Objectives

Broadly, pricing objectives can be either profit oriented or volume oriented. The profit objective may be defined either in terms of net profit percentage desired or as a target return on investment. Traditionally the latter objective has been more popular among large corporations. The volume objective may be stated as the percentage of market share that the firm would like to achieve. Alternatively, it may simply be stated as the desired sales growth rate. Many firms also consider the maintenance of a stable price as a goal. Particularly in cyclical industries, price stability sustains confidence among customers and thus smoothens operations through thick and thin.

In addition to the above, there is a variety of other ways of defining pricing objectives, as shown in Exhibit 10-1.

EXHIBIT 10-1   Potential Pricing Objectives

1. Maximum long-run profits.
2. Maximum short-run profits.
3. Growth.
4. Stabilize market.
5. Desensitize customers to price.
6. Maintain price-leadership arrangement.
7. Discourage entrants.
8. Speed exit of marginal firms.
9. Avoid government investigation and control.
10. Maintain loyalty of middlemen and get their sales support.
11. Avoid demands for "more" from suppliers—labor in particular.
12. Enhance image of firm and its offerings.
13. Be regarded as "fair" by customers (ultimate).
14. Create interest and excitement about the item.
15. Be considered trustworthy and reliable by rivals.
16. Help in the sale of weak items in the line.
17. Discourage others from cutting prices.
18. Make a product "visible."
19. "Spoil market" to obtain high price for sale of business.
20. Build traffic.

Source: Alfred R. Oxenfeldt, "A Decision-Making Structure for Price Decisions," *Journal of Marketing* (January, 1973), p. 50.

The objectives listed in Exhibit 10-1 show that for many firms there can be pricing objectives other than those of profitability and volume. Each firm should evaluate the different objectives and choose its own priorities from among these objectives in the context of the pricing problems that the firm may be facing. The following are illustrations of pricing problems:

1. Decline in sales
2. Prices higher or lower than those of competitors

3. Excessive pressure on middlemen to generate sales
4. Imbalance in product-line prices
5. Distortion vis-a-vis the offering in the customers' perceptions of the firm's prices
6. Frequent changes in prices without any relationship to environmental realities[1]

These problems suggest that a firm may have more than one pricing objective even though these objectives may not be articulated as such. Essentially, the objectives will deal directly or indirectly with these three areas: profit (setting a high enough price to enable the company to earn an adequate margin for profit and reinvestment), competition (setting a low enough price to discourage competitors from adding capacity), and market share (setting a price below competition to gain market share).

Cost

Fixed and variable costs are the major concerns of a pricer. In addition, the pricer may sometimes have to consider other types of costs, such as out-of-pocket costs, incremental costs, opportunity costs, controllable costs, and replacement costs.

To study the impact of costs on pricing strategy, the following three relationships may be considered: 1) the ratio of fixed costs to variable costs, 2) the economies of scale available to a firm, and 3) the cost structure of a firm vis-a-vis competitors. If the fixed costs of a company in comparison with variable costs form a high proportion of its total costs, adding sales volume will be a great help in increasing earnings. Consider, for example, the case of the airlines, whose fixed costs are as high as 60 to 70 percent of the total costs. Once fixed costs are recovered, the additional tickets sold add greatly to earnings. Such an industry would be called *volume sensitive.* There are some industries, such as the paper industry, where variable costs constitute a higher proportion of total costs. Such industries are *price sensitive* since even a small increase in price adds much to earnings.

If the economies of scale obtainable from a company's operations are substantial, one should plan to expand market share and, in considering long-term prices, take expected declines in costs into account. Alternatively, if the experience is expected to produce a decline in costs, then prices may be lowered in the long run to gain higher market share.

If a manufacturer is a low-cost producer relative to competitors, it will earn additional profits by maintaining prices at competitive levels. The additional profits can be used to promote the product aggressively and increase the overall perspective of the business. If, however, the costs of a manufacturer are high

---

[1]Alfred R. Oxenfeldt, "A Decision-making Structure for Price Decisions," *Journal of Marketing* (January, 1973), pp. 48–53.

compared to those of competitors, the manufacturer is in no position to reduce prices since this may lead to a price war which it is bound to lose.

Different elements of cost must be differently related in setting prices. Exhibit 10-2 shows, for example, how computations of full cost, incremental cost, and conversion cost may vary and how these costs affect product-line prices. Exhibit 10-3 shows the procedure followed for setting target-return pricing.

EXHIBIT 10-2   Effect of Costs on Pricing

COST PRICING

Costs	Product A	Product B
Labor (L)	$20	$30
Material (M)	40	20
Overhead (O)	10	20
Full Cost (L+M+O)	70	70
Incremental Cost (L+M)	60	50
Conversion Cost (L+O)	30	50

PRODUCT-LINE PRICES

	Markup (M′)	Product A	Product B
Full-cost Pricing $P = FC+(M')FC$	20%	$84	$84
Incremental-cost Pricing $P = (L+M)+M'(L+M)$	40%	84	70
Conversion-cost Pricing $P = (L+O)+M'(L+O)$	180%	84	140

Source: Philip Kotler, *Marketing Management,* © 1972, Table 14-2, p. 544. Reprinted by permission of Prentice-Hall, Inc., Englewood Cliffs, NJ.

EXHIBIT 10-3   Computation of Target-return Pricing

Manufacturing Capacity	200,000
Standard Volume (80%)	160,000
Standard Full Cost Before Profit	$100/unit
Target Profit	
Investment	$20,000,000
ROI Target	20%
ROI Target	$4,000,000
Profit Per Unit at Standard ($4,000,000 ÷ 160,000)	$25/unit
Price	$125/unit

Competition

Exhibit 10-4 shows the competitive information needed for pricing strategy. The information may be analyzed with reference to the following competitive characteristics: number of firms in the industry, relative size of different members of the industry, product differentiation, and ease of entry.

EXHIBIT 10-4   Competitive Information Needed for Pricing Strategy

1. Published competitive price lists and advertising
2. Competitive reaction to price moves in the past
3. Timing of competitor's price changes and initiating factors
4. Information on competitor's special campaigns
5. Competitive product-line comparison
6. Assumptions of competitor's pricing/marketing objectives
7. Competitor's reported financial performance
8. Estimates of competitor's costs—fixed and variable
9. Expected pricing retaliation
10. Analysis of the capacity to retaliate and duration
11. Financial viability of engaging in price war
12. Strategy posture
13. Overall competitive aggressiveness

In an industry where there is only one competitor, competitive activity is absent and the firm is free to set any price, subject to constraints imposed by law. Conversely, in an industry comprised of a large number of active firms there is fierce competition, which limits the discretion of a firm in setting its prices. Where there are a few firms manufacturing an undifferentiated product (such as in the steel industry), only the industry leader may have the discretion to change prices. Other industry members will tend to follow the leader in setting their prices.

The firm with a large market share in an industry will be in a position to initiate price changes without worrying about competitors' reactions. Presumably, a competitor with a large market share will have the lowest costs. The firm can, therefore, keep its prices low, thus discouraging other members of the industry from adding capacity and further improving its cost advantage in a growing market.

If a firm operates in an industry where there are opportunities for product differentiation, it can have some control over pricing even if the size of the firm is small and there are many competitors in the industry. This may occur if customers consider one brand to be different from other competing brands; whether the difference is real or imaginary, they will not object to paying a higher price for their preferred brand. To establish product differentiation of their brand in the minds of consumers, companies spend heavily for promotion. Product differentiation, however, offers an opportunity to control prices only within a certain range.

In an industry which is easy to enter, the price setter has less discretion in establishing prices; if barriers to market entry exist, however, the firm already in the industry will have greater control over prices. Barriers to entry may take any of the following forms:

1. Capital investment
2. Technological requirements
3. Nonavailability of essential materials
4. Economies of scale which existing firms are enjoying and which would be difficult for a newcomer to achieve
5. Control over natural resources by existing firms
6. Marketing expertise

In an industry where barriers to entry are relatively easy to surmount, a firm will follow what can be called keep-away pricing. This is necessarily on the lower side of the pricing spectrum.

Demand

Exhibit 10-5 contains the information required for analyzing demand. Demand is based on a variety of considerations, of which price is just one. Some of these considerations are:

1. Ability of customers to buy
2. Willingness of customers to buy
3. Place of the product in the customer's life-style (whether a status symbol or a daily-use product)
4. Prices of substitute products
5. Potential market for the product (if there is an unfulfilled demand in the market or if the market is saturated)
6. Nature of nonprice competition
7. Customer behavior in general
8. Segments in the market

All these factors are interdependent, and it may not be easy to estimate their relationship to each other precisely.

Demand analysis involves predicting the relationship between price level and demand while considering the effects of other variables on demand. The relationship between price and demand is called *elasticity of demand* or *sensitivity of price*. It refers to the number of units of a product that would be demanded at different prices. Price sensitivity should be considered at two different levels: total industry price sensitivity and price sensitivity for a particular firm.

Industry demand for a product is considered to be elastic if, by lowering prices, demand can be substantially increased. If lowering of price has little effect on demand, the demand is considered inelastic. The environmental factors previously mentioned will have a definite influence on demand elasticity. Let us illustrate with a few examples. In today's energy crisis the price of gasoline is going

EXHIBIT 10-5 Customer Information Needed for Pricing Strategy

1. The customers' value analysis of the product: performance, utility, profit-rendering potential, quality, etc.
2. Market acceptance level: the price level of acceptance in each major market, including the influence of substitutes
3. The price the market expects, differences in different markets
4. Price stability
5. The product's S-curve and its present position on it
6. Seasonal and cyclical characteristics of the industry
7. The economic conditions now and during the next few periods
8. The effect of depressions to anticipate; the effect of price change on demand in such a declining market (e.g., very little with luxury items)
9. Customer relations
10. Channel relations, and channel costs to figure in calculations
11. The mark-up at each channel level, company vs. intermediary goals
12. Advertising and promotion requirements and costs
13. Trade-in, replacement parts, service, delivery, installation, maintenance, pre-order and post-order engineering; inventory, obsolescence, and spoilage problems and costs
14. The product differentiation that is necessary
15. Existing industry customs and reaction of the industry
16. Stockholder, government, labor, employee, and community reactions

Source: John M. Brion, *Corporate Marketing Planning.* Copyright © 1967 by John Wiley & Sons, New York, p. 181. Reprinted by permission of John Wiley & Sons, Inc.

up, and the average consumer seeks to conserve. By the same token, if by some miracle gasoline prices go down, people will use gas more freely. They may drive large cars again and take long-distance vacations by car. Thus, demand for gasoline can be considered as somewhat elastic.

A case of inelastic demand is provided by salt. No matter how much the price fluctuates, people are not going to change the amount of salt they consume. Similarly, demand for luxury goods such as yachts is inelastic since yachts fit into the life-style of only a small proportion of the total population.

Sometimes the market for a product is segmented so that demand elasticity in each segment must be studied. Demand for certain types of beverages in the senior citizens' market might be inelastic although it is especially elastic in the younger market. If the price of a product goes up, customers have the option of switching to another product. Thus, availability of substitute products is another factor that needs consideration.

When the total demand of an industry is highly elastic, the industry leader may take the initiative to lower prices. The loss in revenues due to decreased prices will be more than compensated for by the additional demand expected to be generated; therefore the total dollar market expands. Such a strategy is highly attractive in an industry where economies of scale are achievable. Where demand is inelastic and there are no conceivable substitutes, the prices may be increased, at least in the short run. In the long run, however, the government may impose controls, or substitutes may be developed.

The demand for the products of an individual firm will be derived from the total industry demand. An individual firm will be interested in finding out how much market share it can command by changing its own prices. In the case of undifferentiated standardized products, lower prices should help a firm to increase its market share as long as competitors do not retaliate by matching the firm's prices. Similarly, when business is sought through bidding prices, lower prices should be of help. In the case of differentiated products, however, market share can be improved even by maintaining higher prices (within a certain range). The products may be differentiated in various real and imaginary ways.

For example, by providing adequate guarantee and after-sale services, an appliance manufacturer may maintain higher prices and still increase market share. Brand name, an image of sophistication, and the perception of high quality are other factors which may help to differentiate the product and thus create for the firm an opportunity to increase prices and not lose market share. Of course, other elements of the marketing mix should reinforce the image suggested by the price. In brief, a firm's best opportunity lies in differentiating the product and then communicating this fact to the customer. A differentiated product offers more opportunity for increasing earnings through price increases.

The sensitivity of price can be measured by taking into account historical data, consumer surveys, and experimentation. Historical data can either be studied intuitively or manipulated through quantitative techniques such as regression analysis to see how demand goes up or down based on prices. A consumer survey planned for studying sensitivity of prices is no different from another market research study. Experiments can be conducted either in a laboratory situation or in the real world to judge what level of prices will generate what level of demand. For example, a company interested in studying the sensitivity of prices may introduce a newly developed grocery product in a few selected markets for a short period of time at different prices. Information obtained from this experiment should provide insights into elasticity of demand for the product. In a recent study on the subject, the prices of 17 food products were varied in 30 cooperative food stores. It was found that the product sales generally followed the "law of demand": When prices were raised 10 percent, sales decreased about 25 percent; an increase of 5 percent in prices led to a decrease in sales by about 13 percent; a lowering of prices by 5 percent increased sales by 12 percent; and a 10-percent decrease in price improved sales by 26 percent. In another study, a new deodorant priced at 63 cents and at 85 cents in different markets resulted in the same volume of sales. Thus, price elasticity was found to be absent, and the manufacturer set the product price at 85 cents.[2]

---

[2]Mark I. Alpert, *Pricing Decisions* (Glenview, IL: Scott, Foresman and Co., 1971), p. 96.

Laboratory experiments can be conducted in simulated environments to test the effects of various prices on demand. For example, consumers can be invited to an auditorium where they may be exposed to a number of products and asked to state their preferences. This information can then be analyzed to determine how demand behaved at various prices. Laboratory experiments can be performed in a variety of ways. In the studies that have been reported on laboratory experiments, students have generally been used as consumers. The consumers are asked to choose a brand from among several different ones without being shown the actual products, or they may be asked to go on a simulated shopping trip. In any event, if properly planned, the results obtained from laboratory experiments can be reliable.

PRICING STRATEGIES FOR NEW PRODUCTS

Pricing strategy for a new product should be so developed as to make the desired impact on the market while at the same time discouraging competition from emerging. There are two basic strategies that may be used in pricing a new product. The two strategies are referred to as skimming-pricing strategy and penetration-pricing strategy.

Skimming Pricing

Skimming pricing is a strategy of establishing a high initial price for a product with a view to "skimming the cream off the market" at the upper end of the demand curve. It is accompanied by heavy expenditure on promotion. A skimming strategy may be recommended when the nature of demand is uncertain, when a company has expended sums of money in the research and development of a new product, when the competition is expected to develop and market a similar product in the near future, or when the product is so innovative that the market is expected to mature very slowly.

In these circumstances, a skimming strategy has several advantages. At the top of the demand curve, price elasticity is low. Besides, in the absence of any close substitute, cross elasticity is also low. These factors, along with heavy emphasis on promotion, tend to help the product make significant inroads into the market. The high price also helps in segmenting the market. Only nonprice-conscious customers will buy the new product during the initial stage. Later on, the mass market can be tapped by lowering the price.

If there are doubts about the shape of the demand curve, and the initial price is found to be too high, the price may be slashed. But it is very difficult to start low and then raise the price later on. Raising a low price may annoy potential customers, and further anticipated drops in price may retard demand at a particular price. For a financially weak company, a skimming strategy may provide immediate relief. This model depends upon selling enough units at the higher price to cover promotion and development costs. If price elasticity is higher than anticipated, a lower price will be more profitable and "relief giving."

Modern patented drugs provide a good example of skimming pricing. At the time of its introduction in 1942, penicillin was priced as high as $20 for a 100,000 unit vial. By 1944 the price was down to $2, and it had decreased to a few cents in 1949. Many new products are priced following this policy. Color television, long-playing records, frozen foods, and instant coffee were all priced very high at the time of their initial appearance in the market. But different versions of these products are now available at prices ranging from very high to very low.

No conclusive research has been done yet to indicate how high the initial price should be in relation to the cost. The following suggestion provides a guideline:

> A rule of thumb in the relationship between factory door cost and consumer's price is that the final price to the consumer should be at least three or four times the factory door cost. Such markup is frequently used to provide adequate margins for the promotional outlays needed for new-product flotation and for anticipated reductions in the retail price as distributor competition intensifies.[3]

A decision concerning how high a skimming price should be will depend on two factors: 1) chances of competitors entering the market and 2) price elasticity at the upper layer of the demand curve. If competitors are expected to bring out their own brands quickly, it may be safe to price rather high. On the other hand, if competitors are years behind in product development and a low rate of return to the firm would slow the pace of their research, a low-skimmed price would be useful. However, price skimming in the face of impending competition may not be wise if a larger market share might make entry more difficult. If limiting the sale of the new product to a few selected individuals will produce sufficient sales, a very high price may be desirable.

Determining the duration of time for keeping prices high will depend entirely upon the competition's activities. In the absence of patent protection, skimming prices may be forced down as soon as competitors join the race. However, in the case of products such as drugs, which are protected through patents, the first manufacturer slowly brings down the price as the patent period draws near an end, and then, a year or so before the expiration of the patent period, the first manufacturer saturates the market with a very low price. This is done to establish a foothold in the mass market before competitors enter it, thereby frustrating their expectations.

So far, skimmed prices have been discussed as high prices in the initial stage. There are other forms of initial high prices, called *premium* and *umbrella* prices, which remain more or less high.[4] Some products carry *premium* prices (high prices) permanently and build an image of superiority for themselves. Where a

---

[3]Joel Dean, *Managerial Economics* (Englewood Cliffs, NJ: Prentice-Hall, 1951), p. 419.
[4]Robert A. Lynn, *Price Policies and Marketing Management* (Homewood, IL: Richard D. Irwin, 1967), pp. 134–137.

mass market cannot be developed and the upper-end demand seems adequate, manufacturers will not take the risk of distorting the prestigious image by lowering prices and offering the product to everybody. Estee Lauder cosmetics, Olga intimate apparel, Brooks Brothers' clothes and Johnston & Murphy's shoes are some products which fall into this category.

Sometimes higher prices are maintained in order to provide an *umbrella* for the small high-cost competitors. The umbrella pricing policy has been aided by limitation laws passed by state governments, which specify minimum prices for a variety of products, such as milk.

Du Pont provides an interesting example of a skimming-pricing strategy. The company tends to focus on higher-margin specialty products. Initially it prices them high, then it gradually lowers the prices as the market builds and competition grows.[5]

Penetration Pricing

Penetration pricing is the strategy of entering the market with a low initial price so that a greater share of the market can be captured. A penetration strategy is resorted to when an elite market does not exist and demand seems to be elastic over the entire demand curve, even during the early stages of product introduction. High price elasticity of demand is probably the most important reason for adopting a penetration strategy. The penetration strategy is also used to discourage competitors from entering the market. When competitors seem to be encroaching on the market, an attempt is made to lure them away by means of penetration pricing, which requires lower margins. A competitor's costs play a decisive role in this since a cost advantage over the existing manufacturer might persuade a firm to enter the market, however low the margin of the former may be.

One may also turn to penetration strategy with a view to achieving economies of scale. Savings in production costs alone may not be an important factor in setting prices low since in the absence of price elasticity it is difficult to generate sufficient sales. Finally, before adopting penetration pricing, one must make sure that the product will be appropriate and will fit the life-styles of the mass market. For example, while it would not be difficult for people to accept imitation milk, cereals made out of petroleum products would probably have difficulty in becoming popular.

How low the penetration price should be will differ from case to case. There are several different types of prices used in penetration strategy: *restrained prices, elimination prices, promotional prices,* and *keep-out prices.* Restraint is applied so as to maintain prices at a certain point during inflationary periods. Environmental circumstances, therefore, serve as a guide to what the level of price should be. *Elimination prices* are fixed at a point where the survival of a competitor is

---

[5]"Pricing Strategy in an Inflation Economy," *Business Week* (April 6, 1974), p. 43.

threatened. A large multiproduct company can lower prices to a level where a smaller competitor might be wiped out of the market. Pricing of suits at factory outlets illustrates *promotional prices.* Factory outlets constantly promote their prices as low compared to brand names while advertising their product as equally durable. *Keep-out prices* are fixed at a level where the competitor is just kept out. Here the objective is to keep the market to oneself at the highest chargeable price. A low price acts as the sole selling point under penetration strategy, but the market should be broad enough to justify low prices. Thus, price elasticity of demand is probably the most important relationship that determines how low prices can go.

Unlike Du Pont, Dow Chemical Co. stresses a penetration-pricing strategy. It concentrates on lower-margin commodity products and low prices, builds a dominant market share, and holds on for the long pull.[6]

PRICING STRATEGIES FOR ESTABLISHED PRODUCTS

Changes in the product/market environment may require a review of prices of products already on the market. For example, an announcement by a large firm about lowering its prices will make it necessary for other firms in the industry to examine their prices. Back in 1976 Texas Instruments Inc. announced that it would soon sell a digital watch for about $20. The T.I. announcement jolted the entire industry since only 15 months earlier, the lowest priced digital was selling for $125. It forced a change in everyone's strategy and has given some producers real problems.

Fairchild Camera & Instrument Corp. reacted with its own version of a $20 plastic-cased watch. So did National Semiconductor Corp. American Microsystems, Inc., however, decided to get completely out of the finished watch business.[7]

A review of pricing strategy may become necessary due to shifts in demand. In the late 1960s, for example, it seemed that with miniskirts in popularity the pantyhose market would continue to boom. But the fashion emphasis on pants slowed down the growth. Pants hide runs or tears in pantyhose, making it unnecessary to buy as many pairs. The pant fashion has also led to a preference for knee-high hose over pantyhose. The knee-high hose cost less to the customer and mean lower profits for the manufacturers. While the market has been dwindling, two new entrants, Bic Pen Corp. and Playtex Corp., were readying their brands for introduction. This made it necessary for the Big Three—Hanes Corp., Burlington Industries, Inc., and Kayser-Roth Corp.—to review their prices and protect market shares.[8]

---

[6]*Ibid.*

[7]"How T.I. Beat the Clock on Its $20 Digital Watch," *Business Week* (May 31, 1976), pp. 62–63.

[8]"The New Sag in Pantyhose," *Business Week* (December 14, 1974), p. 98.

An examination of existing prices may lead to one of three strategic alternatives: maintaining the price, reducing the price, or increasing the price.

Maintaining the Price

If the market segment from which the company derives a big portion of its sales is not affected by changes in the environment, the company may decide not to initiate any change in its pricing strategy. The gasoline shortage in the aftermath of the fall of the Shah of Iran did not affect the luxury car market. Buyers of Cadillac, Mercedes-Benz, and Rolls Royce were not concerned about higher gas prices. Thus, General Motors did not need to redesign the Cadillac to reduce gas consumption or lower its price so as to make it attractive to the average customer, despite its heavy gas usage.

This strategy will be appropriate in circumstances where a price change may be desirable, but the magnitude of change is indeterminable. This may be because the reaction of customers and competitors to a price change cannot be predicted. Alternatively, the price change may have an impact on the product image or sales of other products in the line, which it is not practical to assess. Back in the early 1970s when Magnavox and Sylvania cut the prices of their colored televisions, Zenith maintained prices at their current level. Zenith could not tell why competitors were adopting such a strategic posture since the industry appeared to be in good shape. Zenith continued to maintain prices for six years until 1977, when it sought multiple cuts in prices during a period of six months.[9] Thus, price may also be maintained when a company is not sure why a price change may be desirable.

Politics may be still another reason for maintaining prices. During 1978–1979 President Carter urged voluntary control of wages and prices. Many companies restrained themselves from seeking a price change in order to align themselves behind government efforts to control inflation.

Still further, prices may be maintained on social grounds. Even when supply is temporarily short of demand, some business people may continue to charge the current prices to adopt a socially responsible posture. For example, taxi drivers in a large city may not hike fares when subway and bus service operators are on strike.

Reducing the Price

Prices may be lowered mainly for three reasons. First, as a defensive strategy, prices may be cut in response to competition. For example, in late 1977 when airlines were permitted to propose promotional fares, United Airlines offered a variety of low-fare packages between major cities. Its major competitors on these routes, American Airlines and Trans World Airlines, followed suit.

---

[9]"Troubled Zenith Battles Stiffer Competition," *Business Week* (October 10, 1977), p. 128.

A second reason for lowering prices is offensive in nature. Following the experience curve concept, costs across the board go down by a fixed percentage every time experience doubles. This means that a company with a greater experience will have lower costs than one whose experience is limited. Lower costs have a favorable impact on profits. Thus, as a matter of strategy in order to gain a cost and, hence, profit advantage, it behooves a company to shoot for higher market share and secure as much experience as is feasible.

Texas Instruments Inc. has followed the experience curve concept in gaining cost reductions of integrated circuits for a long time. This has been duly reflected in its strategy to slowly lower prices of such products as electronic calculators and digital watches. Even in other businesses such a strategy may work out to be viable. Take the case of Metpath Inc., a clinical laboratory. At about the time Metpath was formed in the late 1960s, the industry leader, Damon Corp., was acquiring local labs all around the country; by the early 1970s, large corporations in the business, Revlon, Bristol-Myers, Diamond Shamrock, and W.R. Grace, began doing the same. Metpath, however, adopted a price-cutting strategy. In order to implement this strategy, it took a variety of measures to seek economies of scale, thus reducing costs. Figuring that there were not many economies of scale involved in simply putting together a chain of local labs that continue to operate mostly as separate entities, Metpath focused on centralizing its testing at a super-lab that did have those economies and on creating a nationwide network to collect specimens and distribute test results. Metpath's strategy paid off well. In 1979 it was on the verge of becoming the industry leader with sales of $53.4 million in the $12 billion clinical-lab-testing field. Meanwhile, Damon Corp., with revenues of $76 million in 1978, has been stumbling. Heavy price competition, much of it being attributed to Metpath, led some of the big diversified companies, including W.R. Grace and Diamond Shamrock, to pull out of the business.[10]

The third and final reason for price cutting may be in response to customer need. If low prices are a prerequisite for inducing the market to grow, customer need may then become the pivot of marketing strategy, all other aspects of the marketing mix being developed accordingly. In the late 1970s continued inflation and higher prices made customers sensitive to shopping alternatives. Around this time, a new type of grocery store named Aldi opened its door in the Chicago area. The biggest attraction of this store has been its rock-bottom prices. It carried only 450 food items (as against some 10,000 different food items in a large supermarket), most of them being dry or canned foods; there was no fresh meat, eggs, milk, or anything refrigerated. Aldi provided no carry-out service, and there were no bags (customers brought their own bags), boxes, or check cashing. Needless to say, Aldi is doing well. As a matter of fact, it became a legend for the establishment of similar stores throughout the country. Even some large chains moved in

---

[10]"Metpath: Price Cutting with a Super-Lab Creates New Growth," *Business Week* (February 26, 1979), p. 128.

to adopt a strategic posture similar to Aldi's. The Jewel Companies initiated their generic label product line with more than 100 products and introduced it in many of their Midwest supermarkets and in their Star Market Co. subsidiary in New England. *Generic products* are those sold without brand names and marketed with stenciled labels reading "apple juice," "baking soda," and so on. It is expected that about 10 percent of the total industry sales of about $140 billion in the early 1980s will go to stores like Aldi.[11]

In adopting a low-price strategy for an existing product, a variety of considerations must be taken into account. The long-term impact of a price cut against a major competitor is a factor to be reckoned with. For example, a regional pizza chain can cut prices to prevent Pizza Hut from gaining a foothold in the market only in the short run. Eventually Pizza Hut (a division of Pepsico, Inc.) will prevail upon the local chain through price competition. Pizza Hut may lower prices to such an extent that the local chain may find it difficult even to recover its costs. Thus, competitive strength should be duly evaluated in opting for low-price strategy.

In a highly competitive situation, a product may continue to command a higher price than other brands if it is marketed as a "different" product, such as, for example, one of deluxe quality. If the price of this product is reduced, the likely impact on its position should be looked into. Sony televisions have traditionally been sold at a premium price since they were promoted as a quality product. Sony's strategy paid off: The Sony TV rose to prominence as a quality product capturing over seven percent of the market share between 1970 and 1975. Around that time, growing consumer movement pressures led Sony dealers to reduce prices. This not only hurt Sony's overall prestige, but also made some retailers stop selling Sony since it became just one of the many brands they carried.[12] In other words, the price cut, though partly initiated by its dealers, lost Sony its distinction. Even if its sales might have increased in the short run, in the long run this did not prove to be a viable strategy since the lower price tended to go against the perception which consumers had of Sony's being a distinctive brand of television.[13] Ultimately, consumers may perceive Sony as just another brand, which will affect both sales and profits.

It is desirable to examine the impact of a price cut of one product on other products in the line. Price is often considered to be an indication of product quality. Thus, the same product with a different price tag may be perceived differently. Let us apply this to the whole product line. If the price of a particular item is reduced, it is necessary to thoroughly consider what impact, if any, it will

---

[11]David P. Garino and Paul Ingrassia, " 'No Frills' Food Shops Attract Customers, Unsettle Supermarkets," *The Wall Street Journal*, April 27, 1978, p. 1.
[12]Paul Ingrassia, "In a Color-TV Market Roiled by Price Wars, Sony Takes a Pounding," *The Wall Street Journal*, March 16, 1978, p. 1.
[13]See Zarrel V. Lambert, "Product Perception: An Important Variable in Price Strategy," *Journal of Marketing* (October, 1970), pp. 68–71.

have on other products in the line. Wilson Sports Co., for example, manufactures tennis rackets and golf clubs. If the price of a tennis racket is substantially reduced to gain higher market share (assuming prices of all types of rackets are cut), the question of what impact it will have on golf clubs must be weighed.

The impact of lowering prices is illustrated with reference to the Bulova Watch Company, Inc. In 1972, the company was considering reducing the prices of its tuning-fork Accutron watches for men. Before finalizing the decision, the company had to consider the following effects of reducing the prices:

1. The pricing decision extended beyond Bulova's Accutron watches for men. In 1972 Bulova had, for the first time, started to market Accutron watches for women. This new line could more than double the market for Accutron watches. Also, in 1972 Bulova had started to market Accuquartz watches for men, Bulova's entry into the new market for quartz watches. If the prices for men's Accutron watches were reduced, the prices for the other two lines would have to be adjusted downwards as well.

2. A reduced-price Accutron line might affect Bulova's long-established conventional watch line. In 1972 the sale of "Bulova" brand watches—jeweled-lever watches retailing at prices across the entire mid-price segment of the market—contributed a major piece of Bulova's business. In the past, a price gap separated most Bulova brand watches from those in the more expensive Accutron line. If the gap were closed, the company might find that it was trading sales of its most expensive Bulova brand watches for sales of its least expensive Accutron watches.

3. The price reduction, if approved, could not be limited strictly to Bulova's domestic business. Bulova's watch prices overseas, though not identical with those in the United States, were related to its watch prices at home. Eventually, to maintain some sort of order on a worldwide basis, Bulova's foreign prices would have to ease down, too.

4. Related to point 3, Bulova's operations, particularly its manufacturing activities, were highly international in nature. Most of what the firm sold in the United States came from its overseas plants. But, with recurring monetary crises and currency realignments, the pricing decision had to be made against a backdrop of confused international economic conditions.

5. Finally, Bulova's financial performance in the preceding two years was nothing to cheer about. Declining defense orders since 1970 had, by 1972, cut $26 million out of Bulova's sales, and even though increases in Bulova's consumer business had picked up some of the slack, profits had suffered badly. Bulova's net income for its fiscal year ending March 31, 1972, was $3.9 million, down 40% from its

record 1970 net income of $6.8 million. While fiscal 1973 looked more promising, the company clearly had some distance to go to get back to its previous performance level.[14]

Finally, the impact of a price cut on a product's financial performance must be reviewed before the strategy is implemented. If a company is financially so positioned that a price cut will weaken its profitability, it may decide not to lower the price even if that may be in all other ways the best posture to follow. It has been said that in the late 1960s when BankAmericard and Master Charge were made available to consumers free of charge, the American Express Company had a big dilemma facing it. To stop the growth of BankAmericard and Master Charge, it was strategically considered desirable to offer American Express at a nominal price, i.e., $5 or even less as opposed to the former annual charge of $15. But the American Express Company could ill afford loss of revenues. Since it was not sure if reduction in price would generate enough additional business to provide about the same amount of revenues it originally had, the American Express Company decided to stick to its price.

Increasing the Price

An increase in price may be sought for various reasons. First, in an inflationary economy, prices may have to be adjusted upward in order to maintain profitability. During inflation all types of costs go up, and to maintain profits at an adequate level, increase in price becomes necessary. The desired level of increase in price is a matter of strategy which varies from case to case. Conceptually, however, price should be increased to such a level that the profits before and after inflation are approximately equal. The increase in price should also take into account any decline in revenue caused by shift in demand due to the price increase. Mention must be made that it is not always necessary for a company to increase prices to offset inflationary pressure. A company can take nonprice measures as well to reduce inflationary effect. For example, many fast food chains have increased their menus and seating capacity, thus partially offseting the rise in costs.

Prices may also be increased when a brand has a monopolistic control over the market segments that it serves. In other words, when a brand has a differential advantage over competing brands in the market, it may increase the price so as to maximize its benefits and take advantage of its unique position. The differential advantage may be real or may just exist in the psyche of the consumer. In seeking a price increase in a monopolistic situation, the increase should be such that the customers will absorb it and still remain loyal to the brand. If the price increase is abnormal, the differential advantage may be lost, and the customer will strictly choose a brand based on price. This may be explained with reference to coffee.

[14]"Bulova Watch Company, Inc. (A)," a business case copyrighted by the President and Fellows of Harvard College, 1973, pp. 1–2.

Let us say there is a segment of customers who ardently drink Maxwell House coffee. In their minds Maxwell House has something special. If the price of Maxwell House coffee goes up (assuming prices of other brands of coffee remain unchanged), these coffee drinkers may continue with it because the brand has virtually a monopoly over their coffee-drinking behavior. There is a limit, however, to what these Maxwell House loyalists will pay for their favorite brand of coffee. Thus, if the price of Maxwell House coffee is increased too much, these customers may shift their preference.

This indicates that in monopolistic situations, strategically, the price of a brand may be set high to increase revenues. The extent of the increase will depend on the boundaries of customer loyalty, which must be determined by a market research study.

Sometimes prices must be increased to adhere to the industry situation. Of the few firms in an industry, one of them (usually the largest) emerges as a leader. If the leader firm raises its price, other members of the industry must do so too, if only to maintain balance of strength in the industry. If they refuse to do so, they are liable to be challenged by the leader. Usually no firm likes to fight the industry leader since it has more at stake than the leader.

In the auto industry there are four firms: General Motors, Ford, Chrysler, and American Motors. General Motors is the industry leader. If General Motors increases its prices, all other members of the industry follow suit. Thus, a firm may be compelled to seek a price increase in response to a similar increase by the industry leader. The leader also sets the limit to price increases, and followers frequently set their prices very close to those of the leader. While the increase is forced on a firm in this situation, it is a good strategic move to set a price which, without becoming obviously different, is higher than the leader's price.

Prices may also be increased to segment the market. For example, a soft drink company may come out with a new brand and direct it toward busy executives/professionals. This brand may be differentiated as one that provides stamina and invigoration without adding calories. To substantiate the brand's worth and make it appear different, the price may be set at double the price of existing brands of soft drinks.

Hewlett-Packard Co. operates in the highly competitive pocket calculator industry, where the practice of price cutting is quite common. Nonetheless, Hewlett-Packard thrives by offering high-priced products for a select segment of the market. It seems to appeal to a market segment that is highly inelastic with respect to price, but highly elastic with respect to quality. The company equips its products with special features and then offers its calculators at a price that is much higher than the industry average.

The increase in price should be considered for its effect on long-term profitability, demand elasticity, and competitive moves. While in the short run a higher price may mean higher profits, the long-run effect of a price increase may be disastrous. The increase may encourage new entrants to the industry and competition from substitutes. Thus, before the price-increase strategy is implemented, its long-term effect should be thoroughly examined. Further, an increase in price may lead to shifts in demand which could be detrimental. Likewise, the increase may negatively affect market share if competition decides not to seek similar increases in price. Thus, the competitive posture must be studied and predicted. Additionally, a company should review its own ability to live with higher prices. A price increase may mean decline in revenues, but increase in profits. Whether such a situation will create any problem needs to be looked into. Will laying off people or reassignment of sales territories be problematic? Is a limit to price increases called for as a matter of social responsibility? For example, in 1979 President Carter asked businesses to voluntarily adhere to seven-percent increases in prices and wages. In such a situation, should a company which otherwise finds a ten-percent increase in price strategically sound go ahead with it? Finally, the price increase should be duly reinforced by other factors of the marketing mix. A Chevy cannot be sold at a Cadillac price. A man's suit bearing a K-Mart label cannot be sold on par with one manufactured by Brooks Brothers. An Estee Lauder cosmetic cannot be promoted by an ad in *TV Guide.* Thus, the increased price should be evaluated before being finalized to see whether the posture of other market-mix variables will substantiate such an increase.

PRICE-FLEXIBILITY STRATEGY

Price-flexibility strategy usually consists of two alternatives: a one-price policy and a flexible-pricing policy. Influenced by a variety of changes in the environment such as double-digit inflation, Japanese competition, shortages, and the consumer movement, more and more companies have been adhering in recent years to flexibility in pricing in different forms. The flexibility may consist of setting different prices in different markets based on geographic location, varying prices depending on the time of delivery, or customizing prices based on the complexity of the product desired.

One-price Strategy

A *one-price strategy* means that the same price is given to all customers who purchase goods under essentially the same conditions and in the same quantities. The one-price strategy is fairly typical in situations where mass distribution and mass selling are employed. There are several advantages and disadvantages that may be attributed to a one-price strategy. Some advantages of this type of pricing strategy are that it allows for administrative convenience and that it serves to make the pricing process easier. Also, this strategy contributes to the maintenance of goodwill among customers due to the fact that no one customer is receiving special pricing favors over another customer.

A general disadvantage of a one-price strategy is that the firm usually ends up broadcasting its prices to competitors, who may be capable of undercutting the price. Total inflexibility in pricing may have highly adverse effects on corporate growth and profits in certain situations. It is very important that the company remain responsive to the general trends of its economic, social, legal, and competitive environments. Realistically, then, a pricing strategy should be reviewed to incorporate environmental changes as they become pronounced. Any analysis of this type would have to include a close look at a company's position relative to the actions of other firms operating within the industry. As an example, it is generally believed that one reason for the success of discount houses is that conventional retailers rigidly hold to traditional prices and margins.

Flexible-pricing Strategy

A flexible-pricing strategy refers to situations where the same products and/or quantities are offered to different customers at different prices. A flexible-pricing strategy is more common in industrial markets than in consumer markets. An advantage of a flexible-pricing strategy is the freedom allowed to sales representatives to make adjustments for competitive conditions rather than refuse an order. Also, a firm is able to charge a higher price to customers who are willing to pay it and a lower price to those who are unwilling. However, legal difficulties may be encountered if price discrimination becomes an issue. Besides, other customers may become upset upon learning that they have been charged more than their competitors. In addition, bargaining may tend to increase the cost of selling, and some sales representatives may let price cutting become a habit.

Recently many of the large U.S. companies have added new dimensions of flexibility to their pricing strategy. While companies have always shown some willingness to adjust prices or profit margins on specific products as and when market conditions varied, this kind of flexibility is now being carried to the state of a high art. The concept of price flexibility can be implemented in four different ways: by market, by product, by timing, and by technology.

Price flexibility with reference to the market can be achieved either from one geographic area to another or from one segment to another. Both Ford Motor Co. and General Motors Corp. charged less for their 1978 compacts marketed on the West Coast than for those marketed anywhere else in the country. Different segments make different uses of a product. Many companies, therefore, consider customer usage in setting price. For example, a plastic sold to industry might command only 30¢ a lb., but sold to a dentist it might bring $25 a lb. Here again, the flexible-pricing strategy will call for different prices in the two segments.[15]

Price flexibility via product is implemented by considering the value that a product provides to the customer. Careful analysis may show that some products are underpriced and can stand an upgrading in the marketplace. But others, competitively priced to begin with, cannot stand any additional margin because the match-up between value and cost would be lost.

Costs of all transactions from raw materials to delivery at the customer's door may be analyzed, and if some costs are unnecessary in a particular case, due

---

[15]"Flexible Pricing," *Business Week,* December 12, 1977, p. 78.

adjustments may be made in pricing a product to sell to a particular customer. Such cost optimization is very effective from the customer's point of view since the customer does not pay for those costs for which no value is received.

Price flexibility can also be practiced by adding to the price an escalation clause based on cost fluctuations. This is especially relevant in situations where there is a substantial time gap between confirmation of an order and delivery of the finished product. In the case of products susceptible to technological obsolescence, price is set to recover all sunken costs within a reasonable period of time.

There are two main characteristics of the flexible-pricing strategy: emphasis on profit or margins rather than simply volume and willingness to change price with reference to the existing climate. Caution will be in order here. In many instances building market share may be essential to cut costs and hence increase profits. Thus, where the experience curve concept makes sense, companies may be willing to reduce prices to hold or increase market shares. However, a reduction in price simply as a reactionary measure to win a contract is discounted. Implementation of this strategy requires that the pricing decision be instituted away from the salespeople in the field by someone high up in the organization. In some companies the pricing executive may report directly to the chief executive officer. Additionally, a systematic procedure for price review at quarterly or biannual intervals must be established. A computer may even be used if necessary. Finally, an adequate information system is required to help the pricing executive examine different pricing factors.

PRODUCT-LINE-PRICING STRATEGY

A modern business enterprise manufactures and markets a number of product items in a line with differences in quality, design, size, and style. Products in a line may be complementary to or competitive with each other. This influences the cross elasticities of demand between competing products and the package-deal buying of products complementary to each other. For example, instant coffee prices must bear some relationship to the company's regular coffee since these items are substitutes for one another: therefore, this represents a case of cross elasticity. Similarly, the price of a pesticide must be related to that of a fertilizer if customers are to use both. In other words, a multiproduct company cannot afford to price one product without giving due consideration to the effect on other products in its line.

The pricing strategy of a multiproduct firm should be developed to maximize the profits of the entire organization rather than the profitability of a single product. For products already in the line, the pricing strategy may be formulated by classifying them according to their contribution as follows:

1. Products which contribute more than their pro rata share toward overhead after direct costs are covered
2. Products which just cover their pro rata share
3. Products which contribute more than incremental costs, but do not cover their pro rata share

4. Products which fail to cover the costs savable by their elimination

With such a classification in mind, management is then in a better position to study ways of strengthening the performance of its total product line. Pricing decisions on individual products in the four categories listed above are made in the light of demand and competitive conditions facing each product in the line. This means that some products (new products) may be priced to yield a very high margin of profit while others (highly competitive standard products) may have to show an actual loss. By retaining these marginal products to "keep the machines running" and to help absorb fixed overhead costs, management may be able to maximize the total profits from all of its lines. A few items which make no contribution may have to be kept to round out the line offered.

General Motors' pricing structure provides a good illustration of the above procedure. To offset the lower profit margins on lower-priced small cars, the company raises the prices of its large cars. Additionally, the prices of luxury cars are raised much more than those of standard cars. For example, Cadillac Seville was sold in 1978 for more than $14,000, four times the price of the lowest-priced car. Ten years ago the top of the line was three times as costly as the lowest-priced car. The gap, however, is widening since the growing market for small cars with low markups makes it necessary for the company to generate high profits on luxury cars to meet the profit goal. Thus, it is expected that by 1985 General Motors will be selling a Cadillac for $30,000.[16]

For a new product being considered for addition to the line, strategy development will proceed with an evaluation of the role assigned to it. The following questions could be asked:

1. What would the effect be on the company's competing products at different prices?
2. What would be the best new-product price (or range), considering its impact on the total company offering as a whole? Should other prices be adjusted? What, therefore, would be the incremental gain or loss (volumes and profits of existing lines plus volumes and profits of the new line at different prices)?
3. Is the introductory product necessary for staying ahead of or catching up with competition anyhow?
4. Can it enhance the corporate image, and if so, how much is the enhancement worth?[17]

If the product/market strategy has been adequately worked out, it will be obvious whether the new product can profitably cater to a particular segment. If

---

[16]Brian S. Moskal, "Pricing: New Forces Prompt New Philosophies," *Industry Week,* December 11, 1978, pp. 48–56.
[17]John M. Brion, *Corporate Marketing Planning* (New York: John Wiley & Sons, Inc., 1967), p. 183.

so, pricing will be considerably easier; costs, profit goals, marketing goals, experience, and external competition will be the factors around which price will be determined.

Where there is no specific product/market match, pricing strategy for a new product considered for the line will vary depending on whether the product is complementary or competitive vis-a-vis other products in the line. For the complementary product, an examination of the industry price schedule which will furnish the primary guides for the bottom price, top price, and conventional spread between items may be necessary. There are three particularly significant factors in product-line-pricing strategy. The lowest price in the market is always the most remembered and unquestionably generates the most interest, if not the most traffic; having the top market price implies the ability to manufacture quality products; and a well-planned schedule structure (one that optimizes profit and at the same time is logical to the customers) is usually carefully studied and eventually followed by the competition regardless of who initiated it. In addition, however, there can be a product included in the line with the objective of "pricing to obtain the principal profit from a product's supplies or supplementary components."

If the anticipated product is competitive, a start will have to be made with the following market analysis:

1. Knowledge of the industry's pricing history and characteristics regarding the line
2. Comparison of company vs. competitor items and volumes, showing gaps and areas of popularity
3. Volume and profit potentials of the company line as is
4. Volume and profit potentials with the new internally competitive product
5. Effect on company volume and profit if competition added the proposed product and the company did not
6. Impact of a possible introduction delay or speedup

With the above information on hand, the cost-plus-markup computations should be undertaken. Thereafter, the pricer has three alternatives to set the price: 1) add a uniform or individual markup rate to the total cost of the product, 2) add a markup rate that covers all the constant costs of the line, and 3) add the rate necessary for achieving the goal. The three alternatives have different characteristics. The first one hides the contribution margin opportunities. The second alternative, while revealing the minimum feasible price, tends to spread the constant-cost coverage in such a manner that the product absorbing the most overhead is made the most price attractive. The third alternative assigns the burden on the high-material-cost product which may be competitively necessary. No matter which alternative is pursued, the final price should only be arrived at after it has been duly examined with reference to market and competitive factors.

LEASING STRATEGY

The major emphasis of a pricing strategy is on buying a product outright rather than leasing it. Actually leasing, other than in housing, is more common in the marketing of industrial goods than in that of consumer goods. A large number of people lease apartments or houses rather than buying them. Even leasing of other items in recent years has been found to replace purchasing. For example, some people lease cars. Usually by paying a specified sum of money every month, like a rental on the apartment, one can lease a new car. Again, as in the case of housing, a lease is binding for a minimum period, such as two years. Thus, the consumer can lease a new car every other year. Since repairs in the first two years of a car's life may not amount to much, one is saved the bother of such problems.

While there may be different alternatives for setting the lease price, the lessor usually likes to recover the investment within a few years. Thereafter, a very large portion of the lease price (or rent) will be profit. A lessor may set the monthly rental on a car so that within a few months, say 30, the entire cost can be recovered. For example, the monthly rental on a Chevette, based on the 1978 price (assuming no extras), may be about $100 a month. With the term set at 30 months, the dealer will get all his money back in about 27 months (it should be noted that a dealer gets a car at a wholesale price and not the sticker price, which is the suggested retail price). The important thing is to set the monthly lease rate and the minimum period for which the lease is binding in such proportions that the total amount which the lessee pays for the duration of the lease is less than what he would pay as monthly installments on a new car. As a matter of fact, the lease rate has to be substantially less in order for the buyer to opt to lease.

Furniture renting may be attractive to young adults, people of high mobility (e.g., executives, stewardesses), and certain senior citizens whose children have left home and who need appropriate furnishings only temporarily when their children's families come to visit. In addition, apartment owners may rent furniture to provide furnished units to the tenants. The following excerpts from a case provide the pricing mechanics of furniture renting.

> Custom Furniture Rental Corporation (CFRC) leased home furnishings for one month or longer. On direct-to-tenant business the firm realized a nine-month payback (i.e., 11% per month of the purchase price) but 20 months, 15% on commercial.
>
> CFRC's customers had the option of buying part or all of the rented furniture. The purchase price amounted to 25 times the monthly rental fee. A selection of furniture carrying a monthly rental of $30 would bear, therefore, a total purchase price of $750. The purchase option offered provided that credit toward the total purchase price be given as follows:
> 100% of the first year's rent;
> 75% of the second year's rent;
> 50% of the third year's rent; or

80% of this credit could be applied to the purchase of a similar piece of new furniture

Using the example of a $30-per-month rental and a $750 purchase price, the customer, having paid the first year's rental fees, would be given a credit of $360 and would pay the balance of $390 to complete the purchase. The customer who had completed making rental payments for two years would be given credit of $630 (100% of $360 plus 75% of $360) toward the $750 purchase price, leaving a balance of $120.

Persons opting to buy their rented furniture generally did so after the first year and certainly not beyond the second year. In 1971 there were 1,400 customers who decided to purchase one or more pieces of rented furniture. Gross receipts from those sales were $330,000. However, less than 8% of the total customer base exercised their buying option.

Used furniture was sent out for rental "like new," but the company openly invited all of its customers to return any piece that failed to meet the "like new" test.

A deposit of $35 was required for each account and was returned if the lease was in effect at least 12 months. This fee covered the cost of delivery and installation. Customers could make additions, deletions, or changes of items, but there was a $15 charge for each such order. The rate was in effect a delivery charge and applied to any and all pieces of furniture involved in the service call.

If the lessee moved, there was a $20 charge to shift the furniture. If a customer transferred to another geographical area serviced by CFRC, the lessee could return the furniture and ask for delivery at the new location.[18]

In industrial markets the leasing strategy is employed by essentially all capital goods and equipment manufacturers. Traditionally shoe machinery, postage meters, packaging machinery, textile machinery, and other heavy equipment has been leased. Recent applications of the strategy include the leasing of computers, copiers, cars, and trucks. As a matter of fact, just about any item of capital machinery and equipment can be leased. From the customer's point of view, the leasing strategy makes sense for a variety of reasons. First, it reduces the capital required to enter a business. Second, it protects the customer against technological obsolescence. Third, the entire lease price or rental may be written off as an expense for income tax purposes. This advantage, of course, may or may not be relevant depending on the source of funds the customer would have used for the outright purchase (i.e., his or her own money or borrowed funds). Finally, leasing

---

[18]"Custom Furniture Rental Corporation," a case in Harper W. Boyd, Jr. and Robert T. Davis, *Marketing Management Casebook* (Homewood, IL: Richard D. Irwin, 1976), pp. 11–12.

gives the customer the freedom not to get stuck with a product which may prove later on to be not quite useful.

From the viewpoint of the manufacturer, the leasing strategy is advantageous in many ways. First, income is smoothed out over a period of years, which is very helpful in the case of equipment of high unit value in a cyclical business. Second, market growth can be boosted since more customers can afford to lease the product than can afford to buy. Third, revenues are usually higher when a product is leased than when it is sold.

The following quote from a book on the Xerox Corp. illustrates the manner in which a leasing strategy was adopted for a new product:

> Immediately the plan had opponents. They argued vigorously. "When you sell a machine you instantly get your investment back, or a substantial part of it," they said. "That gives you the necessary capital to build more machines. But when you lease, at what has to be a small fee per month, your costs cannot be recouped for years. How can we afford to sink millions into this venture and get back only a small rental fee? How can we afford to wait a long time for our investment to be amortized before we can begin to show profits? We're too small to think of leasing. We simply haven't that much money to play with. We've got to sell copying equipment to regain our investment as quickly as possible. There's no other way to carry on."
>
> Joe Wilson* listened attentively. Then he said, "If we try to sell a machine that costs upward of four thousand dollars to produce (as the first ones did), we'll have to charge more than eight thousand dollars, maybe more than ten thousand dollars to show any profit, allowing for maintenance, advertising, administration, and other costs. Will people make that big an investment in something so new and unproved? Won't it be easier to offer them the machine at a low rental price so that they don't have to gamble a big sum on reproducing papers?
>
> "Another point to consider is this," Joe went on. "A rented machine will in time amortize its production costs. Thereafter all fees are profit, less an allowance for maintenance. So in the long run, with rental fees continuing, we're bound to show greater profits than an outright sale. IBM found the system works on other types of business equipment. Why shouldn't it work for us?
>
> "IBM has the financial resources for it. We haven't."
>
> "We can borrow the resources," Joe said. "Or we can issue stock."
>
> Then one of the men protested, "Suppose some other company comes out with a better copier that makes ours obsolete. The leased machines will quickly be returned to us. If this happens before rental fees have

---

*President of the Haloid Company that originally developed the xeroxing process.

amortized our costs, we'll never recover our investment. And we'll never pay off our indebtedness. Haloid could be wiped out."

Joe granted, "There's no doubt that leasing means we have to produce a machine that's at all times the best on the market. This will be the responsibility of the research and development staff—always to stay ahead of competition. I'm confident they can do it."

In spite of his assurance, however, Joe Wilson had some grave doubts about one phase of leasing. It concerned the fee Haloid would have to charge if monthly payments were to amortize costs in a reasonable time, cover maintenance, yet yield a profit. They might amount to two hundred or even two hundred fifty dollars a month. Would potential users pay so much?

We all doubted it. A way had to be found, we all agreed, to reduce monthly rentals. Many of us sat at our desks with paper and pencil, trying to calculate the lowest fee we could profitably quote.

We could not ignore the fact that there was a subsidiary form of profit in leasing. This was pointed out by a tax-wise member of our Board. Only the owner of a piece of equipment may claim a depreciation allowance on it. Therefore, if we sold a machine, its new owner would enjoy this tax deduction. But if we leased it, thereby retaining ownership, Haloid itself could claim the depreciation.

"Which," one director declared, "could amount to several million dollars a year if we ever get a hundred thousand or so machines on the market."[19]

BUNDLING-PRICING STRATEGY

This strategy refers to the inclusion of an extra margin (for support services) in the price over and above the price of the product as such. This type of strategy has been most popularly followed by companies which lease rather than sell their products. Thus, the rental price when using a bundling strategy will include an extra charge to cover a variety of support functions and services needed to sell and maintain the product throughout its useful life.

The bundling strategy is a very viable strategy for firms that lease their products. Since the unit profit increases sharply after the product completes the planned amortization life, it is desirable for the company to keep the product in good condition and hence enhance its working life for high resale or re-leasing value. The bundling strategy permits the company to do so since a charge for upkeep or "iceberg" services is included in the price.

IBM had traditionally followed the bundling strategy, whereby it supposedly charged rentals for hardware and provided service, software, and consultancy free

---

[19]John H. Dessauer, *My Years with Xerox* (New York: Doubleday & Co., 1971), pp. 68–70.

to its customers. In 1969, however, the Justice Department charged IBM with monopolizing the computer market. While the case proceedings were still in progress in 1979, the company unbundled its prices in 1970. It started selling computers, software, service, and technical input separately.

Under the bundling strategy not only are costs of hardware and profits covered, but also included are the anticipated expenses for extra technical sales assistance, design and engineering of the system concept for a customer, software and applications to be used on the system, training of the customer's personnel, and maintenance. While the bundling strategy can be criticized for tending to discourage competition, one has to consider the complexities involved in delivering and maintaining a fault-free, sophisticated system. Without the manufacturer taking the lead in adequately keeping the system in working condition, customers would have to deal with a variety of people to make use of such products as computers. At least in the initial stages of a technologically oriented product, a bundling strategy is highly useful from the customer's point of view.

For the company, this strategy 1) covers the anticipated expenses of providing services and maintaining the product, 2) provides revenues for supporting after-sales service personnel, 3) provides contingency funds to meet unanticipated happenings, and 4) ensures the proper care and maintenance of the leased product.[20] The bundling strategy also permits an ongoing relationship with the customer. In this way the company gains firsthand knowledge of the customer's needs which may help to shift the customer to the new generation of the product. Needless to say, the very nature of the bundling strategy makes it most relevant to technologically sophisticated products, particularly those marked by rapid technological obsolescence.

On the negative side, the bundling strategy tends to inflate costs and distort prices and profitability. For this reason, in the inflationary years of the 1970s many businesses that have in the past pursued this strategy began unbundling their services and charging separately for them. Grocery wholesalers, for instance, may pass through a straight invoice cost and then charge for delivery, packaging, etc., separately. A growing number of department stores now charge extra for home delivery, gift wrapping, and shopping bags. Thus, people who don't want a service need not pay for it.

PRICE-LEADERSHIP STRATEGY

The price-leadership strategy prevails in oligopolistic situations. One member of an industry, due to its size or command over the market, emerges as the leader of the entire industry. The leading firm then makes pricing moves which are duly acknowledged by other members of the industry. Thus, this strategy places the

---

[20]J. Thomas Cannon, *Business Strategy and Policy* (New York: Harcourt, Brace & World, 1968), p. 135.

burden of making critical pricing decisions on the leading firm; others simply follow the leader. The leader is expected to be careful in making the decisions. A faulty decision could cost the firm its leadership since other members of the industry would then stop following in its footsteps. For example, if the leader, in increasing prices, is motivated only by self-interest, it will be left alone and will ultimately be forced to withdraw the increase in price.

The leadership strategy is a static concept. In an environment where growth opportunities are adequate, companies would rather maintain stability than fight each other by means of price wars. Thus, the leadership concept works out well in this case. In the auto industry, General Motors is the leader. The other three members of the industry have traditionally adjusted their prices to come very close to any price increase by General Motors.

Usually, the leader is the company with the largest market share, such as U.S. Steel Corporation or International Business Machines Corporation. The leadership strategy is designed to stave off price wars and "predatory" competition which tend to force down prices and hurt all parties. Companies that deviate from this form are chastised through discounting or shaving by the leaders. Price deviation is quickly disciplined.

In an unfavorable business environment it may not be feasible to implement the leadership strategy. This is because firms may be differently placed to interact with the environment. Thus, the leader hesitates to make decisions on behalf of the entire industry since other firms may not always find its decisions to their advantage. For this reason, the price leader-follower pattern may be violated.

In order to survive during unfavorable conditions, even smaller firms take the initiative to undercut the price leader. For example, during 1978, while the list prices of steel displayed similarity, companies freely discounted their prices. Likewise, during the turbulent years of the 1970s, with increasing competition from overseas, the price-leadership strategy did not work in the chemical industry. Thus, companies planned a variety of temporary allowances to generate business. The following quote highlights how the leadership strategy is being eroded in the glass container industry:

> Traditional patterns of price leadership also are breaking down in the glass container industry, with smaller companies moving to the fore in pricing. Last year, for example, Owens-Illinois, Inc.—which is larger than its next five competitors combined—increased its list prices by 4½%. Fearing that the increase would hurt sales to brewing companies that were just beginning to switch to glass bottles, the smaller companies broke ranks and offered huge discounts. The action not only negated O-I's increase but served notice that the smaller companies were after O-I's market share.[21]

---

[21]"Flexible Pricing," *Business Week* (December 12, 1977), p. 81.

An automatic response to a leader's price adjustment assumes that all firms are more or less similarly positioned vis-a-vis different price variables (i.e., cost, competition and demand) and that different firms have common pricing objectives. Such an assumption, however, is far from being justified. The leadership strategy is an artificial way to force similar pricing response throughout the industry. It is a strategic mistake for a company to price in a manner identical to that of its competitors. It should price either above or below the competition to set itself apart.

PRICING STRATEGY TO BUILD MARKET SHARE

Some recent work in the area of marketing strategy has delineated the importance of market share as a key variable in strategy formulation. While market share has been discussed earlier with reference to other matters, this section examines the impact of market share on pricing strategy.

Time and again it has been noted that higher market share or experience leads to lower costs. Thus, the new product should be priced to gain experience and market share. This will provide the company such a cost advantage that it cannot ever profitably be overcome by any competitor of normal performance. Competitors will be prevented from entering the market and will have to learn to live in a subordinate position.

Assuming the market is price sensitive, it is desirable to develop it as early as possible. One way of achieving this is to reduce the price. Unit costs are necessarily very high in the early stages of any product; if price is set to recover all costs, there may be no market for the product at its initial cost in competition with existing alternatives. Following the impact of the market share or experience on prices, it may be worthwhile to set prices at a level which will move the product. During the early stages operations may have to be conducted even at a loss. As the volume is gained, costs go down, and even at the initial low price the company makes money. This implies that the competitive cost differential of the future should be of greater concern than current profitability. Of course, such a strategic posture makes sense only in a competitive situation. In the absence of competition there is every reason to set prices as high as possible, to be lowered only when total revenue would not be effected by such an action.

The lower the initial price set by the first producer, the more rapidly the producer builds up volume and a differential cost advantage over succeeding competitors and the faster the market develops. In a sense this is a purchase of time advantage. However, the lower the initial price, the greater the investment required before the progressive reduction of cost will result in a profit. This in turn means that the comparative investment resources of the competitors involved can become a significant, or even the critical, determinant of competitive survival.

Two types of limitations, however, make the implementation of this type of strategy difficult. First, the resources required to institute this strategy are more than that which a firm normally has available. Second, the price, once set, will not be raised, but maintained until costs fall below price; therefore, the lower the price, the longer the time needed for any return and the larger the investment. When future return is discounted to present value, there is obviously a limit.[22]

It is these difficulties which lead many firms to set initial prices which cover all costs. This is particularly so when there is no clear competitive threat. As volume builds up and costs decline, this produces visible profitability which in turn induces new competitors to enter the field. As the competitors make their moves, the innovating firm has the problem of choosing between current profitability and market share. Strategically, however, pricing of a new product, following the relationship between market share and cost, should be dictated by a product's projected future growth.

SUMMARY

Pricing strategy is of interest to the very highest management levels of a company. Yet there are few management decisions that are more subject to intuition than pricing. There is a reason for this. Pricing decisions are primarily affected by factors which are difficult to articulate and analyze, such as pricing objectives, cost, competition, and demand. For example, assumptions must be made about what a competitor will do under certain hypothetical circumstances. There is no way to know that for certain; hence, the characteristic reliance on intuition.

This chapter reviews the pricing factors mentioned above and examines important strategies which a pricer may pursue. The following strategies are discussed:

1. Pricing strategies for new products
2. Pricing strategies for established products
3. Price-flexibility strategy
4. Product-line-pricing strategy
5. Leasing strategy
6. Bundling-pricing strategy
7. Price-leadership strategy
8. Pricing strategy to build market share

Mainly, there are two new product strategies, skimming and penetration. The former is a high-price strategy while the penetration strategy is one of low price directed toward generating volume. Three strategies for established products are discussed: maintaining the price, reducing the price, and increasing the price. A flexible-pricing strategy provides leverage to the pricer in terms of duration of commitment both from market to market and from product to product. Product-line-pricing strategy is directed toward maintaining a balance between different

---

[22]"New Product Pricing," an informal statement by the Boston Consulting Group, 1973.

products offered by a company. The leasing strategy constitutes an alternative to an outright sale of the product. The bundling strategy is concerned with packaging products and associated services together for the purposes of pricing. Price-leadership strategy is a characteristic of an oligopoly where one firm in an industry emerges as a leader and sets the pricing tone for other members of the industry. Finally, the pricing strategy to build market share emphasizes the strategic significance of setting an initially low price to gain volume and market share and thereby achieve cost reductions.

DISCUSSION QUESTIONS

1. Is the maintenance of a stable price a viable objective? Why?
2. Is there a conflict between profit and volume objectives? Doesn't one lead to the other? Discuss.
3. What are the advantages of using incremental costs instead of full costs for pricing? Are there any negative implications of using incremental costs which a pricing strategist needs to be aware of?
4. What assumptions need to be made about competitive behavior for formulating pricing strategy?
5. "Short-term price increases tend to depress industry profits in the long run by accelerating the introduction of new capacity and depressing market demand." Discuss.
6. Following the experience curves concept, the initial price of a new product should be set rather low; as a matter of fact, it may be below the cost. Taking into account the popularity of this thesis, discuss the relevance of the skimming strategy.
7. "Price policies are in fact a derived product of investment policies. Conversely, it appears that the true consequence of price changes is to affect the investment decisions of competitors." Discuss.
8. What factors are ascribed to the decline in popularity of the price-leadership strategy?

Chapter 11
Distribution Strategies

The art of getting rich consists not in industry, much less in saving, but in a better order, in timeliness, in being at the right spot.

Ralph Waldo Emerson

Distribution strategies are concerned with the channels which a manufacturer may employ to make the goods and services available to customers. The channels are organized structures of buyers and sellers which bridge the gap of time and space between the manufacturer and the customer.

In the beginning of this book, marketing was defined as an exchange process. In relation to distribution, exchange poses two problems. First, goods must be moved to a central location from the warehouses of producers who make heterogeneous goods and who are geographically widespread. Second, the goods that are accumulated from diversified sources should represent a desired assortment from the viewpoint of customers. These two problems can be solved by the process of sorting, which combines *concentration* (i.e., bringing the goods from different sources to a central location) and *dispersion* (i.e., picking an assortment of goods from different points of concentration). There are several strategic questions that need to be answered here. Who should perform the concentration and dispersion tasks—the manufacturer or intermediaries? Which intermediary should the manufacturer select to take the goods close to the customer? These questions are central to distribution strategies.

In addition to the above, there are other strategy-related matters which are discussed in this chapter. The focus of other strategic questions is on the scope of distribution (i.e., how widespread distribution may be), use of multiple channels to serve different segments, modification of channels to accommodate environmental shifts, resolution of conflict among channels, and use of vertical systems to institute control over channels.

Each strategic issue raised above is examined with reference to its relevance to different circumstances. The application of each strategy is illustrated by examples from marketing literature.

CHANNEL-STRUCTURE STRATEGY

The *channel-structure strategy* refers to the number of intermediaries which may be employed in moving goods from manufacturers to customers. A company may undertake to distribute its goods to customers or retailers without involving any intermediary. This comprises the shortest channel and may be labeled as a *direct-distribution strategy.* Alternatively, goods may pass through one or more middlemen, such as wholesalers and/or agents. This is an *indirect distribution strategy.* Exhibit 11-1 shows alternative channel structures for consumer and industrial products.

The decision on channel-structure strategy is based on a variety of factors. To put the discussion in proper perspective, first a conceptual framework is presented. It is built around the principle of postponement-speculation theory. Then two different approaches for choosing channel structure are examined.

An underlying factor here is the use of middlemen in channel structure. The importance of using middlemen may be illustrated with reference to an example cited by Alderson. In a primitive economy five producers produced one type of item each: hats, hoes, knives, baskets, and pots. Since all of them needed the others' products, a total of ten exchanges were required to accomplish trade. However, with a market (or middlemen), once the economy has reached equilibrium (that is, each producer-consumer has visited the market once), only five exchanges need take place to meet everyone's needs. Let n denote the number of producer-consumers. Then the total number of transactions without a market is given by:

$$T_{without} = \frac{n\,(n-1)}{2}$$

and total number of transactions with a market is given by:

$$T_{with} = n$$

The efficiency created in distribution by utilizing a middleman may be viewed as:

$$\text{Efficiency} = \frac{T_{without}}{T_{with}} = \frac{n\,(n-1)}{2} \times \frac{1}{n} = \frac{n-1}{2}$$

For the example with five producer-consumers, the efficiency of having a middleman is 2. The efficiency increases as n increases. Thus, in many cases middlemen may perform the task of distribution more efficiently than the manufacturers would.[1]

---

[1]Wroe Alderson, "Factors Governing the Development of Marketing Channels," in Richard M. Clewett (ed.), *Marketing Channels for Manufactured Products* (Homewood, IL: Richard D. Irwin, 1964), p. 7.

EXHIBIT 11-1   Typical Channel Structures

(a) Consumer Products

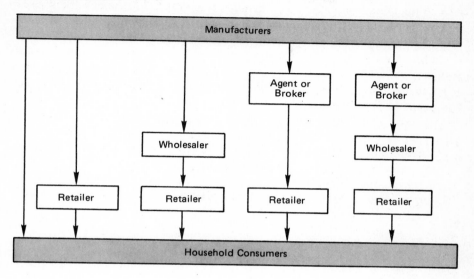

(b) Industrial Products

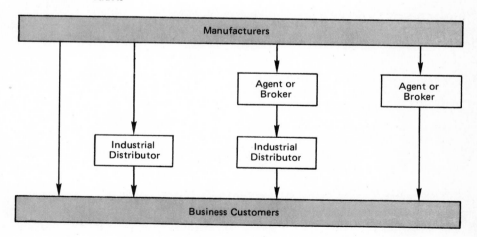

Postponement-speculation Theory[2]

Conceptually, the selection of channel structure may be explained with reference to Bucklin's postponement-speculation framework. The framework is based on risk, uncertainty, and costs involved in facilitating exchanges. Postponement refers to transfer of risk to match with actual customer demand. Presumably, it should produce efficiency in marketing channels. For example, the manufacturer may produce and ship goods only on confirmed orders. Speculation, on the other hand, requires undertaking risk through changes in form and movement of goods within the channels. Speculation leads to economies of scale in manufacturing, reduces costs of frequent ordering, and eliminates opportunity cost.

Exhibit 11-2 shows the behavior of variables involved in the postponement-speculation framework. The vertical axis shows the average cost of undertaking a function for one unit of any given commodity; the horizontal axis refers to the time involved in delivering a confirmed order. Together, the average cost and the delivery time measure the cost of marketing tasks performed in a channel with reference to delivery time. The nature of the following three curves in Exhibit 11-2 should be understood: C (costs to the buyer for holding an inventory), AD' (costs involved in supplying goods directly from manufacturer to buyer), and DB (costs involved in shipping and maintaining speculative inventories, i.e., in anticipation of demand).

Following Bucklin's framework, one determines the channel structure by examining the behavior of the C, AD', and DB curves:

1. The minimal cost of supplying the buyer for every possible delivery time is derived from curves AD' and DB. As may be seen in Exhibit 11-2, especially fast delivery service can be provided only by the indirect channel (i.e., by using a stocking intermediary). However, at some delivery time, I', the cost of serving the consumer directly from the producer will intersect and fall below the cost of indirect shipment. The minimal costs derived from both curves are designated DD'. From the perspective of channel cost, it will be cheaper to service the buyer from a speculative inventory if delivery times shorter than I' are demanded. If the consumer is willing to accept delivery times longer than I', then direct shipment will be the least expensive.

2. The minimal total cost curve for the channel with respect to delivery time is derived by summing the cost of moving goods to the buyer, DD', and the buyer's costs of holding inventory, C. The curve is

[2]Louis P. Bucklin, *A Theory of Distribution Channel Structure* (Berkeley, CA: IBER Special Publications, 1966); and Louis P. Bucklin, "Postponement, Speculation and Structure of Distribution Channels," in Bruce E. Mallen (ed.), *The Marketing Channel: A Conceptual Viewpoint* (New York: John Wiley & Sons, 1967), pp. 67–74. See also: Louis W. Stern and Adel I. El-Ansary, *Marketing Channels* (Englewood Cliffs, NJ: Prentice-Hall, 1977), pp. 231–236.

EXHIBIT 11-2   Using the Postponement-speculation Concept to Determine Channel Structure

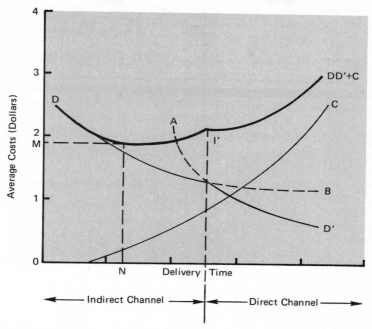

Source: Louis P. Bucklin and Leslie Halpert, "Exploring Channels of Distribution for Cement with the Principle of Postponement-speculation," in Peter D. Bennett (ed.), *Marketing and Economic Development* (Chicago: American Marketing Association, 1965), p.698.

represented in Exhibit 11-2 by DD' + C. Total channel costs initially fall as delivery time lengthens because increased buyer expenses are more than made up for by savings in other parts of the channel. Gradually, however, the savings from these sources diminish and buyer costs begin to rise more rapidly. A minimal cost point is reached, and expenses for the channel rise thereafter. Channel structure is controlled by the location of this minimum point. If, as in the present case, it falls to the left of I', then goods would be expected to flow through the speculative inventory (i.e., an intermediary). If, on the other hand, the savings of the buyer from postponement had not been as great as those depicted, the minimum point would have fallen to the right of I' and shipments would have been made directly from the producer to the consumer.[3]

---

[3]Louis P. Bucklin and Leslie Halpert, "Exploring Channels of Distribution for Cement with the Principle of Postponement-speculation," in Peter D. Bennett (ed.), *Marketing and Economic Development* (Chicago: American Marketing Association, 1965), p. 699.

Goods Approach

The goods approach is advanced by Aspinwall. According to him, the marketing characteristics of a product determine the most appropriate and economical method for distributing it. The product characteristics considered here are:

1. *Replacement rate* (rate at which a product is bought and used by buyers in order to derive the satisfaction one expects from the product)
2. *Gross margin* (difference between sale price and direct costs incurred at different levels in bringing the goods closer to the buyer)
3. *Adjustment* (services that must be provided to ensure requisite satisfaction to the buyer from goods)
4. *Time of consumption* (time frame within which the product must be used to provide the required value)
5. *Searching time* (time that the buyer requires to travel to a retail store and the distance he or she must travel to purchase the product)[4]

Based on these characteristics, products may be differentiated in three color categories as follows:[5]

	Color Classification		
Characteristics	Red Goods	Orange Goods	Yellow Goods
Replacement Rate	High	Medium	Low
Gross Margin	Low	Medium	High
Adjustment	Low	Medium	High
Time of Consumption	Low	Medium	High
Searching Time	Low	Medium	High

The above analysis may now be used to develop a schematic diagram showing how goods of different color classifications require different methods of distribution. Such a diagram is shown in Exhibit 11-3. A simple percentage scale of 0 to 100 is laid out on both coordinates, representing all possible graduations in goods from red through orange to yellow. For example, line AB represents a good with an ordinate value of 63, which indicates that it has 63-percent yellow characteristics and 37-percent red characteristics. Ladies' ready-to-wear is an example of such a good, sold through department stores and small specialty stores. Department stores are directly supplied by the factory, while small specialty stores are

---

[4]Leo V. Aspinwall, "The Characteristics of Goods and Parallel Systems Theories," in Leo V. Aspinwall, *Four Marketing Theories* (Boulder, CO: Bureau of Business Research, Univ. of Colorado, 1961).
[5]*Ibid.*

EXHIBIT 11-3   Schematic Array of a Few Selected Goods
(Plotted in Terms of Yellow Goods)

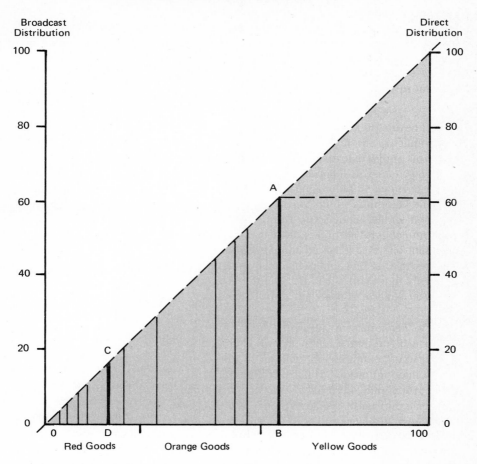

Source: Leo V. Aspinwall, *Four Marketing Theories* (Boulder, CO: Bureau of Business Research, Univ. of Colorado, 1961).

served through specialty wholesalers. On the other hand, line CD represents a good which is characterized as 15-percent yellow and 85-percent red. A good of this type is soap, which is mainly sold through different types of intermediaries.

The 15-percent-yellow characteristics might indicate specialty salespeople's activity involving factory drop shipments (direct distribution). A real-world example of this type of good is illustrated by the Bic pen. Back in 1979, Bic products were sold to retailers and commercial accounts by 120 company salespeople who called on approximately 10,000 accounts. These accounts represented large retailers (such as chains) as well as wholesale distributors. Through these 10,000 accounts Bic achieved distribution for its products in approximately 2,000,000 retail outlets, of which 12,000 were commercial supply stores. In addition, the salespeople called on 20,000 independent retail accounts which were considered important in the marketplace. In the case of these accounts, the Bic salespeople merely filled orders for the distributors. Although Bic did do some direct selling (yellow characteristic), it was limited to chain retailers.[6]

The goods approach suggests that the color characteristic of a product, which is a function of five variables (replacement rate, gross margin, adjustment, time of consumption, and searching time), will determine the appropriate channel structure for the good. Thus, for yellow goods direct distribution is desirable, while red goods should be channeled through middlemen. Orange goods may be distributed partly directly and partly through the middlemen.

Three reservations must be noted here, however. First, the color concept introduced here is dynamic in nature. Thus, many goods during introduction may be characterized as yellow. But as they reach the growth stage in their life cycles, the replacement rate increases and the goods shift toward the red end of the scale. For example, Texas Instruments at first distributed digital watches directly. About five years later, as the product became popular, a large portion of the inventory moved through middlemen. Similarly, Hallmark Cards' many new products which have come out in the market in the past few years (i.e., books, candles, jewelry, pewter, crystal items, etc.) may now be characterized as red. Yet at the time of introduction they were considered to be yellow. Unquestionably, therefore, the company initially planned to sell them exclusively through Hallmark dealers.[7]

Second, one or more of the five product characteristics noted above may be given higher importance for a particular good. This will mean that while four characteristics may qualify a product as the yellow type, one characteristic may be given such a high value that it is placed in the red category. For example, to provide customers with an instant delivery of pre-recorded cassette tapes for use on videotape recorders, the Paramount Pictures Corp. has collaborated with Fotomat Corp. stores for both the sale and rental of its film list. Since immediate delivery is important in a business such as this, the customer can call a toll-free number to order a cassette, which can be picked up after twenty hours at a neighborhood Fotomat store.[8] Apparently, the searching time characteristic had a major influence in Paramount Pictures Corporation's decision to channel the films for household use through Fotomat Corp.

---

[6]"Bic Pen Corporation (A)," a case study copyrighted by the President and Fellows of Harvard College, 1974.

[7]"Hallmark Now Stands for a Lot More Than Cards," *Business Week* (May 29, 1978), p. 57.

[8]"Video Corp. of America: A Big Bet on Software for TV Recorders," *Business Week* (July 9, 1979), p. 76.

The third reservation which must be noted here is that a company may always follow an innovative course to distribute its product. For example, Avon Products, Inc., distributes its products door to door using about a quarter of a million sales girls. This strategy not only suits the informal life style of suburbia, but it also provides the customer with an opportunity to make a decision on an intimate product in the privacy of the home. When following the goods approach, beauty aids do not qualify for direct distribution, but this strategy helped to make Avon the world's largest cosmetics and toiletries company.[9] Similarly, Hanes Corp. decided to distribute L'eggs pantyhose directly to supermarkets and drugstores even though it was a "red" product. The company did so because their marketing research showed that the unique distribution problem faced by pantyhose customers was in not being able to find it in stock. To overcome the out-of-stock problem that hurt other hosiery manufacturers, L'eggs opted for direct store delivery and established a market information system which permitted regular replenishment of sold-out items.[10]

Financial Approach

With the financial approach, a manufacturer's choice of a channel should be determined by its financial resources and need to control the distribution of its product.[11] The term *control* refers to the desire of the manufacturer to determine retail price, distribution outlets, customer service, storage facilities, and advertising. As a matter of fact, the term is used here in a broad fashion to also include other factors involved in the selection of channel structure, such as the nature of the product, the nature of the market, and selectivity of distribution.

The relationship between these two determining factors for channel selection, i.e., financial resources and control, is an inverse one. The following are the four major channel alternatives:

1. Manufacturer to consumer
2. Manufacturer to retailer to consumer
3. Manufacturer to wholesaler to retailer to consumer
4. Manufacturer to agent to wholesaler to retailer to consumer

Alternative 1 provides an organization with a good deal of control, but also requires an enormous amount of resources. Alternative 4, on the other hand, requires the least financial resources, but provides the firm with minimum control on distribution. Alternatives 2 and 3 stand between the two extremes. The above

[9]"Troubled Avon Tries a Face-lifting," *Business Week* (May 11, 1974).
[10]"Our L'eggs Fit Your Legs," *Business Week* (March 25, 1972), pp. 96–100.
[11]Eugene W. Lambert, Jr., "Financial Considerations in Choosing a Marketing Channel," *MSU Business Topics* (Winter, 1966), pp. 17–26.

considerations provide a firm with four choices (A, B, C, and D) in selecting channel structure, as shown below:

Control Desired

		Yes	No
	Yes	A	B
Adequate Financial Resources	No	C	D

In situations A and D, the financial considerations do not play a major part since in the former case, the firm has adequate resources, while in the latter, the need for financial resources is minor. In situations B and C, however, financial consideration becomes a dominating factor. In the case of C, if the firm desires control, adequacy of financial resources becomes a limiting factor. For example, the firm may like to use direct distribution to maintain control; however, excessive financial resources needed to implement such a channel structure would prohibit such a choice. This may lead the firm to opt for indirect distribution through wholesaler (or wholesaler to agent) to retailer to consumer. In situation B the firm can choose among all four; since control is a determining factor here, the choice rests on financial resources alone. Commitment of the firm's financial resources, however, has to be made in the light of the opportunity cost of these resources in the firm elsewhere. In other words, in situation B, channel-structure strategy becomes a capital budgeting problem, and the investment in channels is evaluated vis-a-vis other investment opportunities available to the firm.

The importance of the control factor in choosing channel structure is found in a case study on petrochemicals. A common feature of the petrochemical industry is that its base product can be finished in several different ways to produce several different end products. Therefore, in certain situations (such as sales in foreign countries a long way from a plant), it was found to be profitable to store the base product and finish it to an end product as and when the market dictated. This called for an effective control of channels such that required inventories could be processed in time to provide timely delivery to the customer. Of extreme importance here were the logistics involved in setting up systems such as this. The distance between the end market and the main plant was so great that there was a high probability of stockouts and overstocks occurring because of fluctuating demands. The number of orders and amount of total sales were also major considerations in seeking control.[12] Another instance of the importance of control is provided by the Sherwin-Williams Co. The company found the wholesalers and retailers lacking in the effort to do an effective job. In order to institute necessary controls, therefore, the company established its own retail stores: as many as 2,000 outlets throughout the country.[13]

But even when control may necessitate opting for direct distribution, the financial resources of a company may not permit this. The point may be illustrated with reference to The J.B. Kunz Company, a leading supplier of savings passbooks to the U.S. banking industry. The company relies on distributors to reach its bank customers. J.B. Kunz sells to thousands of different banks spread out through a wide region. The company was able to handle distribution through approximately forty distributors. Besides additional executives, this small family-run company would have had to hire more salespeople, a luxury it could neither afford nor justify, in order to opt for direct distribution.[14]

An intermediary for a financially weak company may provide a cushion even though this may not be realized when choosing a channel structure. Back in 1979, the Chrysler Corporation got into such trouble that it had to go to the federal government for a $1 billion advance against its taxes. At that time, while the government decision was still pending, its dealers offered aid in the form of a surcharge. The dealers' proposal called for imposing a special $50 surcharge on each vehicle delivered to them by the factory in the next three years. The extra $50 was proposed to be a direct investment in the company to help protect jobs and meet the cash-flow problem. The proposal was to generate $120 million in three years.[15] This illustrates how a middleman can come to the aid of a manufacturer in trouble.

Additional Considerations

The framework and the two approaches discussed above for determining channel structure are mainly based on economic considerations. Examined in this section are a variety of environmental influences on channel-structure strategy formulation. These influences may be categorized as technological, social and ethical, governmental, geographical, and cultural. Many aspects of channel structure are affected by technological advances. For example, mass retailing in food has been feasible due to the development of automobiles, highways, refrigerated

---

[12]"Tex-Fiber Industries: Petroloid Products Division (A)," a case study copyrighted by the President and Fellows of Harvard College, 1976.

[13]"A Paintmaker Puts a Fresh Coat on Its Marketing," *Business Week* (February 23, 1976), p. 95.

[14]"J.B. Kunz Company (A)," a case study copyrighted by the President and Fellows of Harvard College, 1977.

[15]"Chrysler Offered Aid by Its Own Dealers in the Form of Surcharge," *The Wall Street Journal,* August 10, 1979, p. 2.

cars, cash registers, packaging improvements, and mass communications (television). In the coming years, television shopping with household computer terminals should have a far-reaching impact on distribution structure. Technological advances permitted BSR Ltd., an English company, to become dominant in the U.S. market for low-priced phonograph record changers. They developed a prepackaged, all-in-one changer which could be sold through mass retailers so that even sales clerks without technical know-how could handle customers.[16]

Social taboos and ethical standards may also affect the channel-structure decision of a product. Mallen describes that *Viva,* a woman's magazine, had achieved a high circulation in supermarkets and drug stores in Canada. In response to readers' insistence and *Playgirl's* competition, *Viva* began to introduce nude male photos. This led most supermarkets to ban this magazine. Since supermarkets accounted for over half of *Viva's* circulation, *Viva* dropped nude photos so that it could continue being sold there.[17] Social and ethical considerations do not permit the distribution of birth control pills through supermarkets. The channel-structure strategy can be influenced by local, state, and federal laws in a variety of ways. For example, door-to-door selling of certain goods may be prohibited by law in some localities.[18] In many states (for example, California and Ohio) wine can be sold through supermarkets, but other states (e.g., Connecticut) do not permit this.

Geographic size, population patterns, and typology also influence the channel-structure strategy. In urban areas direct distribution to large retailers may make sense. The rural areas, however, may be covered only by wholesalers.

Often it may appear that with the inception of large grocery chains, an accepted phenomenon, the independent grocery stores are dying. The truth is, however, that independent grocery stores as recently as 1975 accounted for 49 percent of all grocery sales in the country, i.e., over $70 billion. Thus, a manufacturer can ill afford not to deal with the independents, and to reach them it must go through wholesalers. Wetterau Inc., for example, is a grocery wholesale firm in Hazelwood, Missouri, which did $832 million worth of business in 1978, serving only 700 IGA retail grocery stores and all of the Red & White grocery stores. It does not do any business with chain stores. But because of Wetterau's determination to offer its customers relatively low prices, a wide selection of brands, service programs carefully designed to make the brands more profitable, and a personal interest in their success, its customers are almost fanatically loyal. The company offers its customers,—small, independent retail stores—a variety of services, such as lease arrangements, store design, financing packages, training,

---

[16]"Why BSR Dominates the Record-changer Market," *Business Week* (June 7, 1976), pp. 84–85.
[17]Bruce Mallen, *Principles of Marketing Channel Management* (Lexington, MA: Lexington Bks., 1977), p. 179.
[18]See Marvin A. Jolson, "Direct Selling: Consumer vs. Salesman," *Business Horizons* (October, 1972), pp. 87–95.

and computerized inventory systems. These services tend to enhance customers' competitiveness by reducing their operating costs and simplifying their bookkeeping, which in turn helps Wetterau to earn extra profits.[19] The Wetterau example shows that to reach smaller retailers, particularly in areas far removed from large metropolises, the indirect distribution strategy is appropriate. The wholesaler provides services to small retailers which a large manufacturer can never match on its own.

Finally, cultural traits may require the adoption of a certain channel structure in a setting which otherwise may seem an odd place for one. For example, in many parts of Switzerland, fruits and vegetables are sold in a central marketplace in the morning by small vendors even though there are modern supermarkets all over. This practice continues since it provides consumers with an opportunity to socialize with each other while shopping.

DISTRIBUTION-SCOPE STRATEGY

For an efficient channel network, the manufacturer should clearly define the target customers it intends to reach. Implicit in the definition of target customers is a decision on the scope of distribution the manufacturer wants to pursue. The strategic alternatives here are: exclusive distribution, selective distribution, and intensive distribution.

Exclusive Distribution

Exclusive distribution means that one particular retailer serving a given area is granted sole rights to carry the product. For example, Hart, Schaffner & Marx suits are distributed exclusively through one store in a town. There are several advantages to be gained by the use of exclusive distribution. It brings tremendous dealer loyalty, greater sales support, a higher degree of control over the retail market, better forecasting, and better inventory and merchandising control. The impact of dealer loyalty can be helpful when the manufacturer has seasonal or other kinds of fluctuating sales. An exclusive dealership is more willing to finance inventories and thus bear a higher degree of risk than an otherwise more extensive dealership. A smaller number of dealers gives the manufacturer or wholesaler greater opportunity to provide the dealer with promotional support. And, with fewer outlets it is easier to control such aspects as margin, price, and inventory. Dealers are also more agreeable in providing data which may be used for marketing research and forecasts. Exclusive distribution is especially relevant for products that customers seek out. Examples of such products may include certain brands of appliances (such as G.E. dishwashers); clothing (such as Brooks Brothers suits); watches (such as Seiko); cameras (such as Minolta); and luggage (such as American Tourister briefcases).

---

[19]"Wetterau: A Maverick Grocery Wholesaler," *Business Week* (February 14, 1977), p. 121.

There are several obvious disadvantages to exclusive distribution. First, sales volume may be lost due to exclusive distribution. Second, the manufacturer places its fortunes in a geographic area in the hands of one dealer. Exclusive distribution brings with it the characteristics of high price, high margin, and low volume. If the product is highly price elastic in nature, this combination of characteristics can mean significantly less than optimal performance. Having one sole retailer can mean that if sales are depressed for any particular reason, the retailer is then likely to be in a position to dictate terms to other channel members (i.e., the retailer becomes the channel captain).

For example, assume a company manufacturing traditional toys deals exclusively with J.C. Penney Company, Inc. For a variety of reasons its line of toys may not do well. These reasons may be a continuing decline in the birthrate, an economic depression, the emerging popularity of electronic toys, higher prices of the company's toys compared to competitive brands, Penney's poor promotional effort, etc. J.C. Penney, however, may put the blame on the manufacturer's higher prices since it is the exclusive distributor, and it may demand a reduction in prices from the manufacturer. Inasmuch as the manufacturer has no other reasons to give that could explain the poor performance, it must depend on J.C. Penney's analysis.

The last disadvantage of exclusive distribution is one that is easy to overlook. In certain circumstances exclusive distribution has been found to be in violation of antitrust laws because of its restraint on trade. The fine line of distinction between legal and illegal practices was shown in the *United States* v. *Sealy Inc.* case, as described below:

> Another significant case was concerned with the arrangement under which bedding manufacturers were licensed to manufacture and sell in an exclusive territory under the Sealy brand name. The district court had held that the system of exclusive regional licensees used by Sealy was an effective way to achieve maximum market development and found no evidence that the system was developed for the purpose of protecting the markets of licensees or for eliminating competition among them. When the case reached the Supreme Court, however, the Court decided that the arrangements among regional manufacturers and Sealy were essentially horizontal rather than vertical since Sealy was controlled by the regional franchise holders. Consequently, the effect was one of collusion and restraint of trade in which territorial restrictions were combined with unlawful price fixing and policing.[20]

As Sealy's case indicates, it is difficult to show that any given exclusive distribution channel is not set up to protect the markets of the retailers involved.

---

[20]Edwin H. Lewis, *Marketing Channels: Structure and Strategy* (New York: McGraw-Hill Bk. Co., 1968), p. 77.

Therefore, when one is dealing with exclusive distribution, the legal consideration should be one of the primary concerns.

The legality of an exclusive contract will vary from case to case. As long as an exclusive contract does not undermine competition and create a monopoly, it is acceptable. The courts appear to use the following criteria to determine if indeed an exclusive distribution lessens competition:

1. Whether the volume of the product in question is a substantial part of the total volume for the product type
2. Whether the exclusive dealership excludes competitive products from a substantial share of the market.[21]

Thus, a company considering an exclusive distribution strategy should review its decision in the light of above two ground rules. If we state it differently, based on past Supreme Court decisions, it appears that exclusive distribution should be avoided unless it involves the reasonable use of a trademark or patent or is justifiable by unusual circumstances, such as the economic survival or maintenance of a company.

Intensive Distribution

The inverse of exclusive distribution is intensive distribution. An *intensive distribution* strategy makes a product available at all possible retail outlets. This may mean that the product is carried at a wide variety of different, and also competing, retail institutions in a given area. The distribution of convenience goods is most consistent with this strategy. If the nature of the product is such that a consumer will generally not bother to seek out the product, but will buy it on sight if available, then it is to the seller's advantage to have the product visible in as many places as possible. The Bic Pen Corp. is an example of a firm which uses this type of strategy. Bic makes its products available in a wide variety of retail establishments ranging from drug stores to "the corner grocery store" to large supermarkets. In all, Bic sells through 200,000 retail outlets representing competing as well as noncompeting stores. The advantages to be gained by this strategy are increased sales, wider customer recognition, and impulse buying. All of these qualities are desirable for convenience goods.

There are two main disadvantages associated with intensive distribution. First, the items are characteristically low-priced and low-margin products which require a fast turnover. Second, it is difficult to provide any degree of control over a large number of retailers. The uncontrolled distribution may not become a problem if the intensive distribution leads to increased sales. In the long run, however, it may have a variety of devastating effects. For example, if durable products such as Sony televisions were to be intensively distributed (i.e., through

---

[21]Louis W. Stern and Adel I. El-Ansary, *Marketing Channels* (Englewood Cliffs, NJ: Prentice-Hall, 1977), p. 320.

drug stores, discount stores, variety stores, etc.), Sony's sales would probably increase. But intensive distribution would lead to the problems of price discounting, provision of adequate customer service, and continued cooperation of traditional channels (e.g., department stores). Not only might these problems affect sales revenues in the long run, but the manufacturer might also lose some of its established channels. For example, a department store might decide to drop the Sony line for another brand of television. In addition, the distinctive brand image of Sony televisions could suffer. In other words, the advantages furnished by intensive distribution should be carefully related to the type of product to decide if this form of distribution would suit it. It is because of the problems outlined above that one finds intensive distribution limited to such products as candy, newspapers, cigarettes, aspirin, soft drinks, etc., where turnover is usually high and channel control is usually not as strategic as it would be, say, for television sets.

Selective Distribution

Between exclusive and intensive distribution, there is selective distribution. *Selective distribution* is the strategy in which several, but not all, retail outlets in a given area distribute the product. *Shopping goods* are frequently distributed through a selective distribution strategy; these are goods which consumers seek on the basis of the most attractive price or quality characteristics. Because of this, competition among retailers is far greater for shopping goods than for convenience goods. Naturally they wish to reduce the competition as much as possible. This causes them to pressure the manufacturer to reduce the number of retail outlets in their area in order to reduce competition.

The number of retailers should be limited by criteria which allow the manufacturer to choose only those retailers who will make a contribution to the firm's overall distribution objectives. For example, some firms may choose those retail outlets that can provide acceptable repair and maintenance service to consumers who have purchased their products. In the automotive industry selective criteria are used by the manufacturer in granting dealerships for given areas. These criteria consist of such considerations as showroom space, service facilities, and inventory levels.

Selective distribution is best applied under circumstances in which high sales volume can be generated by a relatively small number of retailers, or in other words, in which the manufacturer would not appreciably increase its coverage by adding additional dealers.

Selective distribution can also be used effectively in situations where a manufacturer requires a high-caliber firm to carry a full product line and provide necessary services. A dealer in this position is likely to require promotional and technical assistance. The technical assistance will be needed not only in conjunction with the sale, but also after the sale in conjunction with repair and maintenance service. Again, by limiting the number of retail outlets to a selective few which are capable of covering the market, the manufacturer can avoid unnecessary costs that may be associated with signing on additional dealers.

Obviously, the greatest danger associated with a strategy of selective distribution is the risk of not adequately covering the market for the product. The consequences of this error are greater than the consequences of initially having one or two extra dealers. Therefore, when in doubt, it is better to have too much coverage than not enough.

In selective distribution it is extremely important for a manufacturer to choose those dealers (retailers) who most closely match the marketing goals and image intended for the product. There can be segments within retail segments; therefore, identifying the right retailers can be the key to penetrating a chosen market.

Thus, every department store cannot be considered the same. Among them there can be price, age, and image segmentation. One does not have to be very accurate in distinguishing between stores of the same type in the case of products that have no special image (i.e., those which lend themselves to unsegmented market strategies and mass distribution). But for products with any degree of fashion or style content or with highly segmented customer groups, a selective distribution strategy requires an adequate choice of outlets.[22]

To appraise what type of product would be suitable for what form of distribution, let us refer to Exhibit 11-4. This exhibit combines the traditional threefold classification of consumer goods, (convenience, shopping, and specialty goods) with a threefold classification of retail stores (convenience, shopping, and specialty stores) to determine the appropriate form of distribution. This initial selection may then be examined in the light of other considerations to make a final decision on the scope of distribution.

MULTIPLE-CHANNEL STRATEGY

The *multiple-channel strategy* refers to a situation in which two or more different channels are employed for distribution of goods and services. The market must be segmented so that each segment is provided the services it needs and pays for them, but it is not charged for services it does not need. Usually, this cannot be done effectively by direct selling alone or by exclusive reliance upon distribution. The Robinson-Patman Act makes the use of price for segmentation almost impossible when selling to the same kind of customer through the same distribution method. Market segmentation, however, may be possible when selling to one class of customer directly and to another only through distributors, thus providing different services, prices, and support. Thus, a multiple-channel strategy permits an optimal access to each individual segment.

---

[22]Arthur I. Cohen and Ana Loud Jones, "Brand Marketing in the New Retail Environment," *Harvard Business Review* (September-October, 1978), pp. 141–148.

EXHIBIT 11-4   Selection of Suitable Distribution Policies Based on the
Relationship Between Type of Product and Type of
Store

Classification	Consumer Behavior	Most Likely Form of Distribution
Convenience store/ convenience good	The consumer prefers to buy the most readily available brand of product at the most accessible store.	Intensive
Convenience store/ shopping good	The consumer selects his purchase from among the assortment carried by the most accessible store.	Intensive
Convenience store/ specialty good	The consumer purchases his favorite brand from the most accessible store carrying the item in stock.	Selective/ exclusive
Shopping store/ convenience good	The consumer is indifferent to the brand of product he buys but shops different stores to secure better retail service and/or retail price.	Intensive
Shopping store/ shopping good	The consumer makes comparisons among both retail-controlled factors and factors associated with the product (brand).	Intensive
Shopping store/ specialty good	The consumer has a strong preference as to product brand but shops a number of stores to secure the best retail service and/or price for this brand.	Selective/ exclusive
Specialty store/ convenience good	The consumer prefers to trade at a specific store but is indifferent to the brand of product purchased.	Selective/ exclusive
Specialty store/ shopping good	The consumer prefers to trade at a certain store but is uncertain as to which product he wishes to buy and examines the store's assortment for the best purchase.	Selective/ exclusive
Specialty store/ specialty good	The consumer has both a preference for a particular store and for a specific brand.	Selective/ exclusive

Source: Louis P. Bucklin, "Retail Strategy and the Classification of Consumer Goods,"
Journal of Marketing (January, 1963), pp. 50–55. The specific exhibit was devel-
oped in Burton Marcus *et al., Modern Marketing,* copyright © 1975 by Random
House, Inc. Reprinted by permission of Random House, Inc.

Basically, there are two types of multiple channels of distribution, the complementary and the competitive.[23] These are discussed below.

Complementary Channels

Complementary channels exist when each channel handles a different noncompeting product or noncompeting market segment. An important reason to pro-

---

[23]Martin L. Bell, *Marketing Concepts and Strategy* (Boston: Houghton Mifflin Co., 1966), p.
402.

mote a complementary channel is to reach market segments which cannot otherwise be served. For example, American Tourister sells to discount stores the same type of luggage it distributes through department stores, with some cosmetic changes in design. In this way the company is able to reach the middle- and low-income segments of consumers who may never shop for luggage in department stores. Similarly, magazines use newsstand distribution as a complementary channel to mailing subscriptions. As a matter of fact, catalog business serves as a complementary channel for such large retailers as Sears and Penney.

The simplest way to create complementary channels is through private branding. This permits entry into markets which would otherwise have been lost. The Coca-Cola Company sells its Minute Maid frozen orange juice to A&P to be sold under the A&P name. At the same time, the Minute Maid brand is available in A&P stores. Presumably, there are customers who perceive the private brand to be no different in quality than the manufacturer's brand. Inasmuch as the private brand is always a little less expensive than a manufacturer's brand, such customers prefer the former. Thus, private branding helps to broaden the market base.

There is also another reason which may lead a manufacturer to choose this strategy. In instances where other firms in the industry have saturated the traditional distribution channels for a product, a new entry may be distributed through a different channel. This new channel may then in turn be different from the traditional channel used for the rest of the manufacturer's product line. Hanes Corp., for example, decided to develop a new channel for L'eggs since the traditional channels were already crowded with competing brands. Likewise, R. Dakin & Co. developed nontraditional complementary channels to distribute its toys. While most toy manufacturers sell their wares through toy shops and department stores, Dakin distributes over 60 percent of its products through a variety of previously ignored outlets such as airports, hospital gift shops, restaurants, amusement parks, stationery stores, and drug stores. This way it avoids direct competition. The success of Dakin's strategy is revealed by the fact that the company's sales went up from $11 million in 1975 to $57 million in 1979.[24] In recent years many companies have developed new channels in the form of mail ordering for such diverse products as men's suits, shoes, insurance, records, newly published books, and jewelry.

Complementary channels may also be necessitated on geographic grounds. Many industrial companies undertake direct distribution of their products in areas such as New York, Chicago, Detroit, Cleveland, etc. Since the market is dense, orders are large, and a salesperson can make over ten calls a day because of the proximity of customers to each other. The same company, however, uses manufacturer's representatives or some other type of middlemen in the hinterlands since the market there is too thin to support full-time salespeople.[25]

---

[24]"R. Dakin: Marketing Old-style Toys Through Offbeat Outlets," *Business Week* (December 24, 1979), p. 94.
[25]Robert E. Weigand, "Fit Products and Channels to Your Markets," *Harvard Business Review* (January-February, 1977), pp. 95–105.

Another reason to promote complementary channels is to seek distribution of noncompeting items. For example, many food processors package for institutional customers cans of fruits and vegetables which have no market among household customers. These products, therefore, are distributed through different channels. Procter & Gamble manufactures toiletries for hotels, motels, hospitals, airplanes, etc., which need to be distributed through different channel arrangements. The volume of business may also require the use of different channels. Many appliance manufacturers sell directly to builders, while distributors and dealers may be used for selling to household consumers.

The basis of employing complementary channels is to enlist customers and segments which cannot be served when limiting distribution to a single channel. Thus, the addition of a complementary channel may be considered in a simple cost-benefit analysis. If by employing an additional channel the overall business can be increased without jeopardizing quality and/or service and without any negative impact on long-term profitability, it may be worthwhile to do so. Care is needed to ensure that the enhancement of the market through multiple channels does not lead the company to be charged by the Justice Department with monopolizing the market.

Competitive Channels

The second type of multiple-channel strategy is termed a *competitive channel.* *Competitive distribution* occurs when the same product is sold via two different and competing channels. This distribution posture may be illustrated with reference to a boat manufacturer, the Luhrs Company. It sold and shipped boats directly to dealers. It used one franchise to sell Ulrichsen wood boats and Alura fiberglass boats and another to sell Luhrs wood and fiberglass/wood boats. The two franchises could have been issued to the same dealer, but they were normally issued to separate dealers. Competition between dealers holding separate franchises was both possible and encouraged.[26] The two dealers competed against each other to the extent that their products satisfied similar consumer needs in the same segment.

The reason for choosing this competitive strategy was the hope that it would provide increased sales. It was thought that if the dealers had to compete against themselves as well as against other manufacturers' dealers, the extra effort would serve to benefit the overall sales of the manufacturer. The effectiveness of this strategy does leave some room for debate. It could be argued that a program utilizing different incentives, such as special discounts for attaining certain given levels of sales, could be just as effective as this competition. It could be even more effective since the company would eliminate the costs associated with developing additional channels.

---

[26]"Bangor Punta Operations Inc.," a case study copyrighted by the President and Fellows of Harvard College, 1969, pp. 28–29.

Sometimes a company may be forced into developing competing channels in response to a changing environment. For example, nonprescription drugs were traditionally sold through drug stores. But as supermarkets' merchandising perspectives underwent a change during the post-World War II period, grocery stores became a viable channel for such products since shoppers expected to find convenience drug products there. This made it necessary for drug companies to deal with grocery wholesalers and retail grocery stores along with drug wholesalers and drugstores.

The argument behind this strategy is that while two brands of the same manufacturer may essentially be the same, they cater to different sets of customers. Thus, General Motors engages different dealers for its Buick, Cadillac, Chevrolet, Oldsmobile, and Pontiac cars. These dealers vigorously compete with each other. A more interesting example of competing multiple channels adopted by automobile manufacturers is provided by their dealings with car rental companies, to whom they sell cars directly. Hertz, for example, buys from an assembly plant and regularly resells some of its slightly used cars in competition with new cars through its over 100 offices across the U.S. Many of these offices are located in close proximity to manufacturers' new-car dealers.[27] Despite such competition, a manufacturer undertakes distribution through multiple channels to come off, on the whole, with increased business.

In adopting multiple competing channels, a company needs to make sure that it does not overextend itself; otherwise it may spread itself too thin and face competition from all sources to such an extent that the ultimate results are disastrous. McCammon cites the case of a wholesaler who adopted multiple channels and thus exposed itself to a grave situation. This holds true for a manufacturer as well. McCammon states:

> Consider, for example, the competitive milieu of Stratton & Terstegge, a large hardware wholesaler in Louisville. At the present time, the company sells to independent retailers, sponsors a voluntary group program, and operates its own stores. In these multiple capacities, it competes against conventional wholesalers (Belknap), cash and carry wholesalers (Atlas), specialty wholesalers (Garcia), corporate chains (Wiches), voluntary groups (Western Auto), cooperative groups (Colter), free-form corporations (Interco), and others. Given the complexity of its competitive environment, it is not surprising to observe that Stratton & Terstegge generates a relatively modest rate of return on net worth.[28]

---

[27]Weigand, *op. cit.*
[28]Bert C. McCammon, Jr., "Future Shock and the Practice of Management," a paper presented at the Fifth Annual Attitude Research Conference of the American Marketing Association, Madrid, Spain, 1973, p. 9.

One of the dangers involved in setting up multiple channels is dealer resentment. This is particularly true when competitive channels are established. When this happens, it obviously means that an otherwise exclusive retailer will now suffer a loss in sales. Such a policy can result in the retailer electing to carry a different manufacturer's product line. This will happen if a comparable product line which is generally feasible is available. For example, if a major department store, the R.H. Macy & Co., Inc., is upset with a manufacturer, the Arrow Shirt Company, for doing business with discounters (i.e., for adopting multiple channels), it can conveniently take its order to another shirt manufacturer.

Multiple channels also create control problems. National Distillers & Chemical Corp. had a wholly owned distributor, Peel Richards in New York, which strictly enforced manufacturer-stipulated retail prices and refused to do business with price cutters. Since R.H. Macy discounted National Distillers' products, Peel Richards stopped selling to them. R.H. Macy retaliated by placing an order with an upstate New York distributor of National Distillers.[29] National Distillers had no legal recourse against either R.H. Macy or the upstate New York distributor, who was an independent business person.

The above problems do not discount the importance of dual distribution. They only suggest the difficulties which may arise with the multiple-channel arrangement and which the management must live with. A manufacturer's failure to use multiple channels gives the competitors an opportunity to segment the market by concentrating on one or the other end of the market spectrum. This is particularly disastrous to a leading manufacturer because the manufacturer must automatically forego access to a large portion of the market potential if it cannot make use of the economies of dual distribution.

CHANNEL-MODIFICATION STRATEGY

The *channel-modification strategy* is the introduction of a change into the existing distribution arrangements based on evaluation and critical review. Channel evaluation should be undertaken on an ongoing basis so that appropriate modification may be made as and when it becomes necessary. A shift in existing channels may become desirable because of any of the following factors:

1. Changes in consumer markets and buying habits
2. Development of new needs in relation to service, parts, or technical help
3. Changes in competitors' perspectives
4. Changes in relative importance of outlet types
5. Changes in manufacturer's financial strength
6. Changes in the sales volume level of existing products
7. Changes in product (addition of new products), price (substantial

---

[29]Weigand, *op. cit.*

reduction in price to gain dominant position), or promotion (greater emphasis on advertising) strategies

Channel Evaluation

Channels of distribution may be evaluated on such primary criteria as cost of distribution, coverage of market (penetration), customer service, communication with the market, and control of distribution networks. Occasionally such secondary factors as support of channels in the successful introduction of a new product and cooperation with the company's promotional effort also become evaluative criteria. To arrive at a distribution channel which will satisfy all these criteria requires simultaneous optimization of every facet of distribution, something which is usually not operationally possible. Consequently, a piecemeal approach which consists in suboptimizing the various aspects may be followed. Also, all the suboptimized choices may be reviewed together and their interactive effect evaluated.

Cost of Distribution. A detailed cost analysis of distribution is the first step in evaluating various channel alternatives on a sales-cost basis. This requires classification of total distribution costs under various heads and subheads. Exhibit 11-5 gives an illustration of such a cost classification which is based on general accounting practices; the information on each item should be conveniently available from the controller's office.

The question of evaluation comes up only when the company has been following a particular channel strategy for a number of years. Presumably, the company will have pertinent information to undertake distribution cost analysis by customer segment and product line. This sort of data allows the analyzer to find out how cost under each head varies with sales volume, e.g., how warehousing expenses vary with sales volume, how packaging and delivery expenses are related to sales, etc. In other words, the purpose here is to establish a relationship between annual sales and different types of cost. These relationships are useful in predicting the future cost behavior for the established dollar-sales objective, assuming present channel arrangements are continued.

To find out the cost of distribution for alternative channels, estimates should be made of all the relevant costs under various sales estimates. The cost information can be obtained from published sources and interviews with selected informants. For example, assume that a company has been selling through wholesalers for a number of years and is now considering distribution through its own branches. To follow the latter course, the company will need to rent a number of offices in important markets. Estimates for the rent or purchase of an office can be made by real estate agents. Similarly, the cost of recruiting the additional help needed to staff the offices should be available at the personnel office. With the relevant information gathered, simple break-even analysis can be used for computing the attractiveness of the alternative channel.

EXHIBIT 11-5   Representative List of Distribution Costs by Function

1. Direct Selling

   Salaries: Admin. & supervisory
   Clerical
   Salespeople
   Commission
   Travel and entertainment
   Training
   Insurance: Real & property
            Liability
            Workmen's comp.
   Taxes: Personal property
          Social security
          Unemployment ins.
   Returned-goods expense
     chargeable to salespeople
   Pension
   Rent
   Utilities
   Repair & maintenance
   Depreciation
   Portage & office supplies

2. Advertising & Sales Promotion

   Salaries: Admin. & supervisory
            Clerical
            Advtg. production
   Publication space
     Trade journals
     Newspaper
   Product promotion
     Advtg. supplier
     Advtg. agency fees
     Direct mail expenses
     Contests
     Catalogs & price list
     Cooperative advtg.
       Dealers
       Retail stores
       Billboards

3. Product & Package Design

   Salaries: Admin. & supervisory
   Wages
   Materials
   Depreciation

4. Sales Discounts and Allowances

   Cash discounts on sales
   Quantity discounts
   Sales allowances

5. Credit Extension

   Salaries: Admin. & supervisory
            Credit representatives
            Clerical
   Bad-debt losses
   Forms and postage
   Credit rating services

Legal fees: Collective efforts
Travel
Financial cost of accounts receivable

6. Market Research

   Salaries: Admin.
            Clerical
   Surveys: Distributors
           Consumers
   Industry trade data
   Travel

7. Warehousing & Handling

   Salaries: Administration
   Wages: Warehouse services
   Depreciation: Furniture
                Fixtures
   Insurance
   Taxes
   Repair & maintenance
   Unsalable merchandise
     Warehouse responsibility
   Supplies
   Utilities

8. Inventory Levels

   Obsolescence markdown
   Financial cost of carrying
     inventories

9. Packing, Shipping, & Delivery

   Salaries: Administration
            Clerical
   Wages: Truck drivers
          Truck maint. men
          Packers
   Shipping clerks
   Truck operators
   Truck repairs
   Depreciation: Furniture & fixtures
                Trucks
   Insurance
   Taxes
   Utilities
   Packing supplies
   Postage & forms
   Freight: Factory to warehouse
            Warehouse to customer
            Factory to customer
   Outside trucking service

10. Order Processing

    Order forms
    Salaries: Administration
    Wages: Order review clerks
           Order processing
           Equipment operators
    Depreciation: order processing
                 equipment

11. Customer Service
Salaries: Administration
Customer service representatives
Clerical
Stationery & supplies

12. Printing and Recording of Accounts Receivable
Sales invoice forms
Salaries: Clerical
Admin.
Accounts receivable clerks

Sales invoicing equipment operators
Depreciation: sales invoicing equipment

13. Returned Merchandise
Freight
Salaries: Administration
Clerical
Returned-goods clerical
Returned-goods processing:
Material labor
Forms & supplies

Assume a company has 20,000 potential customers and, on an average, each one of them must be contacted every 2 weeks. A salesperson making 10 calls a day and working 5 days a week can contact 100 customers every two weeks. Thus, the company will need $20,000 \div 100 = 200$ salespeople. If each salesperson receives $20,000 in salary and $10,000 in expenses, the cost of salespeople will be $6,000,000. Further, assume 10 sales managers will be required for control and supervision, and each one will be paid, say, $35,000 a year. The cost of supervision would then be $350,000. Let $5,650,000 be the cost of other overheads, i.e., office and warehouse expenses, etc. The total cost of direct distribution will then be $6,000,000 + $350,000 + $5,650,000, or $12 million. Assuming that distribution through wholesalers (the arrangement currently being pursued) costs the company 25 percent of sales. Assuming sales to be $x, we can equalize $.25x = \$12$ million, and solve for x, which will be $48 million. This means that the company must generate a sales volume of $48 million before it can break even on costs if it follows direct distribution. Thus, if the sales potential is well above the $48 million mark, direct distribution is worth considering.

One problem with the break-even analysis is that the distribution alternatives which are considered equally effective may not always be so. It is a pervasive belief that the choice of a distribution channel affects the total sales revenue just as the selection of an advertising strategy does. For example, the retailer may receive the same number of calls under each of two channel alternatives: from the company's salesperson and from a wholesaler's salesperson. The question is, however, whether the effect of these calls is the same. The best way to handle this problem is to calculate the differences which would be necessary in order to make the channel alternatives equally effective. To an extent, this can be achieved either intuitively or by using one of the mathematical models reported in marketing literature.[30]

Coverage. An important aspect of predicting future sales responses is the penetration which will eventually be achieved in the market. For example, in the

---

[30]See William R. King, *Quantitative Analysis for Marketing Management* (New York: McGraw-Hill Bk. Co., 1967), pp. 526–528.

case of a drug company, the customers can be divided into three groups: 1) drug stores, 2) doctors, and 3) hospitals.

One measure of the coverage of market (or penetration of market) will be the number of customers in a group contacted or sold, divided by the total number of customers in that group. Another measure may be the penetration in terms of geographical coverage of territory. But these measures are too general. Just the ratio of customers contacted and total number of customers is not a proper indication of coverage because all types of customers are not equally important. For example, all types of druggists (large, medium, and small sized) are not equally important to the company. Therefore, customers may be further classified as follows:

Customer Group	Classification	Basis of Classification
Druggists	Large, Medium, and Small	Annual turnover
Hospitals	Large, Medium, and Small	Number of beds
Doctors	Large, Medium, and Small	Number of patients attended

Then the desired level of penetration for each subgroup should be specified, i.e., 90 percent of the large, 75 percent of the medium, and 50 percent of the small druggists may be penetrated. With the use of simple proportions, these percentages can be used for examining the effectiveness of an alternative channel.

An advanced analysis is possible, however, by building a penetration model. The basis of the model is that increments in penetration for equal time periods are proportionate to the remaining distance to the limiting (objective or target) value of penetration. The increment in penetration in a time period t will be: $t = rp (1 - r)^{t-1}$, where p = targeted or aimed penetration, and r = penetration ratio. This ratio signifies how rapidly the cumulative penetration will approach aimed penetration. For example, if aimed penetration is 80 percent and if r = 0.3, then first-year penetration is $80 \times 0.3 = 24\%$. Next year, the increment in penetration will be $80 \times 0.3 \times 0.7 = 16.8\%$. Hence, cumulative penetration at the end of the second year will be $24 + 16.8 = 40.8$. The value of p for each subgroup is a matter of policy decision on the part of the company. The value of r depends on the time period during which aimed penetration is to be achieved and the sales efforts in terms of the number of medical representative-salespeople and their call pattern for each subgroup.

For the existing channel (selling through the wholesalers), the value of r can be determined from past records. For the alternate channel (direct distribution), the approximate value of r can be computed in one of two ways:

1. The company executives should know how many salespeople would be kept on the roll if alternate channels were used. The executives can also estimate the average number of calls a day a salesperson would make and hence the average number of customers in a subgroup he

or she could contact. With this information, the value of r can be determined as follows:

$$\frac{\text{Number of customers in a subgroup contacted under existing channel}}{\begin{array}{l}\text{Number of customers in a subgroup}\\\text{that would be contacted in alter-}\\\text{nate channel}\end{array}} = \frac{\text{Value of r for existing channel}}{\begin{array}{l}\text{Value of r}\\\text{for alternate channel}\end{array}}$$

2. A second approach may be to find out (or estimate) the penetration that would be possible after one year if an alternate channel were used, then substitute this in the penetration equation to find r when p and t are known values.

From the penetration model it is easier to predict the exact coverage in each subgroup of customers over a planning period (say, 5 years hence). The marketing strategist should determine the ultimate desired penetration p and the time period in which it is to be achieved. Then the model would be able to predict which channel would take the penetration closer to the objective.

Customer Service. The level of customer service will differ from customer to customer for each business. Generally speaking, the sales department, with feedback from the field force, should be able to designate the standards of various services that the company should offer to different customer segments. If this is not feasible, a sample survey may be planned to find out which services the customers expect and which services are currently being offered by competitors. This information can be utilized to develop a viable service package. Then the capability and willingness of each channel alternative may be matched to single out the most desirable channel. This can be done intuitively. Alternatively, a more scientific approach would be to list and assign weights to each type of service, then rate different channels for various services. The accumulated score can be used for the service ranking of channel alternatives.

Communication and Control. *Control* may be defined as the process of taking steps to bring actual results and desired results closer together. *Communication* refers to the information flow between the company and the customers. To evaluate alternate channels on these two criteria, the communication and control objectives should be defined. With reference to communication, for example, information may be desired on the activities of competitors, new products from competitors, the special promotional efforts of competitors, the attitudes of customers toward a company's and competitor's services, and the reasons for success of a particular product line of the company. Each channel alternative may then be evaluated in terms of its willingness, capabilities, and interest in providing the required information. In the case of wholesalers, communications perspectives will also depend on the terms of contract. But the mere fact that they are legally bound by the contract may not motivate them to cooperate willingly. Finally, the information should be judged for accuracy, timeliness, and relevance.

Channel Modification

Environmental shifts, internal or external, may require a company to modify existing channel arrangements. A shift in the trade practice, for instance, may render distribution through a manufacturer's representative obsolete. Similarly, technological changes in the product design may require frequent service calls on customers which wholesalers may not be able to make, thus leading the company to opt for direct distribution.

Generally speaking, a new company in the market starts distribution through middlemen. This becomes necessary because during the initial period, the technical and manufacturing problems are big enough to keep the management busy. Besides, at this time, the company has neither the insight nor the capabilities needed to successfully deal with the vagaries of the market. Therefore, middlemen are used. With their knowledge of the market they play an important role in establishing a demand for the company's product. But once the company establishes a foothold in the market, it may discover that it does not have the type of control on distribution which it must have to make further headway. At this time, modification becomes essential.

Managerial astuteness requires that the company do a thorough study before deciding to change existing channel arrangements. In other words, half-hearted measures could create insurmountable problems resulting in loose control and poor communications. Further, the affected middlemen should be duly taken into confidence about a company's plans and compensated for any breach of terms. Any modification of channels should match the perspectives of the total marketing strategy. This means that the effect of a modified plan on other ingredients of the marketing mix (such as product, price, and promotion) should be considered. The managers of different departments (as well as the customers) should be informed so that the change does not come as a surprise. In other words, care needs to be taken to ensure that a modification in channel arrangements does not cause any distortion in the overall distribution system.

CHANNEL-CONTROL STRATEGY

Traditionally channel arrangements have consisted of loosely aligned manufacturers, wholesalers, and retailers, all of whom trying to serve their own ends regardless of what went on elsewhere in the channel structure. In such arrangements, the channel control was generally missing. Each member of the channel negotiated aggressively with others and performed a conventionally defined set of marketing functions.

Importance of Channel Control

Control, for a variety of reasons, is a necessary ingredient in running a successful system. Having control is likely to have a positive impact on profits since inefficiencies are caught and corrected in time. This is evidenced by the success of voluntary and cooperative chains, corporate chains, franchise alignments, manufacturer's dealer organizations, and sales branches and offices. Control also helps to realize cost effectiveness vis-a-vis experience curves. For example, warehousing, data processing, and other facilities, if centrally organized, will provide scale efficiencies. Through a planned perspective of the total system, effort is directed to achieving common goals in an integrated manner.[31]

Channel Controller

The focus of channel control may be any member of a channel system, such as the manufacturer, wholesaler, or retailer. Unfortunately there is no established theory to indicate whether any one of them makes a better channel controller than the others. When the literature was surveyed, it was found that one appliance retailer in Philadelphia with a 10-percent market share, Silo Incorporated, served as the channel controller. This firm had no special relationship with any manufacturer, but if a supplier's line did not do well, Silo was immediately contacted and asked to do something about it.[32] Sears (in addition to J.C. Penney, Montgomery Ward, and K-Mart) can be expected to be the channel controller for a variety of products it carries. Among manufacturers, Kraft ought to be the channel controller for refrigerated goods in supermarkets. Likewise, Procter & Gamble is a channel controller for detergents and related items. Ethan Allen, Inc., decided to control the distribution channels for its line of Early American furniture by establishing a network of 200 dealer outlets.[33] The Sherwin-Williams Co. decided to take over channel control to guide its own destiny since the traditional channels did not show enough aggressiveness. The company established its own chain of 2000 retail outlets.[34]

The above examples underscore the importance of someone taking over channel leadership in order to establish control. Conventionally, market leadership and the size of a firm determined its suitability for channel control. Strategically, a firm should attempt to control the channel for a good if it can make a commitment to fulfill its leadership obligations and if such a move is likely to be economically beneficial in the long run for the entire channel system.

Vertical Marketing Systems

Vertical marketing systems may be defined as:

> . . . professionally managed and centrally programmed networks (which) are pre-engineered to achieve operating economies and maximum mar-

[31]Bert C. McCammon, Jr. and Robert W. Little, "Marketing Channels: Analytical Systems and Approaches," in George Schwartz, (ed.), *Science in Marketing* (New York: John Wiley & Sons, 1965).

[32]"An Appliance Dealer with a Real Clout," *Business Week* (November 6, 1971), p. 76.

[33]"Ethan Allen Breaks with Tradition," *Business Week* (June 10, 1972), p. 22.

[34]"A Paintmaker Puts a Fresh Coat on Its Marketing," *Business Week* (February 23, 1976), p. 95.

ket impact. Stated alternatively, vertical marketing systems are rationalized and capital-intensive networks designed to achieve technological, managerial, and promotional economies through the integration, coordination, and synchronization of marketing flows from points of production to points of ultimate use.[35]

The vertical marketing system is an emerging trend in the American economy. It seems to be replacing all the conventional marketing channels as the mainstay of distribution. As a matter of fact, according to one estimate, the vertical marketing systems in the consumer-goods sector account for about 64 percent of the available market.[36] In brief, the vertical marketing system (sometimes also referred to as a centrally coordinated system) has emerged as the dominant ingredient in the competitive process and thus plays a strategic role in the formulation of distribution strategy.

Vertical marketing systems may be classified into three types: corporate, administered, and contractual. Under the *corporate vertical marketing system,* successive stages of production and distribution are owned by a single entity. This is achieved through forward and backward integration. As mentioned earlier, Sherwin-Williams, the paint maker, owns and operates 2,000 retail outlets in a corporate vertical marketing system (a case of forward integration).[37] Other examples of such systems are Hart, Schaffner & Marx (operating over 200 stores); Singer; International Harvester; Goodyear; and Sohio.[38] Not only a manufacturer, but also a corporate vertical system, might be owned and operated by a retailer (a case of backward integration). Sears, like many other large retailers, has financial interests in many of its suppliers' businesses. For example, about one third of DeSoto, Inc. (a furniture and home furnishings manufacturer) stock is owned by Sears. Finally, W.W. Grainger, Inc., provides an example of a wholesaler-run vertical marketing system. This firm, an electrical distributor with 1974 sales of $315 million, has seven manufacturing facilities.[39]

In an administered vertical marketing system, a dominant firm within the channel system, such as the manufacturer, wholesaler, or retailer, coordinates the flow of goods by virtue of its market power. For example, the firm may exert influence to achieve economies in transportation, order processing, warehousing, advertising, merchandising, etc. As can be expected, it is the large organizations like Sears, Safeway, Penney, General Motors, Kraft Inc., General Electric, Procter & Gamble, Lever Brothers, Nabisco, and General Foods which emerge

---

[35]Bert C. McCammon, Jr., "Perspectives for Distribution Programming," in Louis P. Bucklin, (ed.), *Vertical Marketing Systems* (Glenview, IL: Scott, Foresman and Co., 1970), p. 43.
[36]Philip Kotler, *Marketing Management* (Englewood Cliffs, NJ: Prentice-Hall, 1972), p. 282.
[37]"A Paintmaker Puts a Fresh Coat on Its Marketing," *op. cit.*
[38]Louis W. Stern and Adel I. El-Ansary, *Marketing Channels* (Englewood Cliffs, NJ: Prentice-Hall, 1977), p. 419.
[39]*Ibid.,* p. 422.

as channel captains to guide their channel networks, while not actually owning them, to achieve economies and efficiencies.

In a *contractual vertical marketing system,* independent firms within the channel structure integrate their programs on a contractual basis to realize economies and market impact. Primarily, there are three types of contractual vertical marketing systems: wholesaler-sponsored voluntary groups, retailer-sponsored cooperative groups, and franchise systems. Independent Grocers Alliance (IGA) is an example of a wholesaler-sponsored voluntary group. At the initiative of the wholesaler, small grocery stores agree to form a chain to achieve economies with which to compete against corporate chains. The joining members mutually agree to adhere to a variety of contractual terms, such as the use of a common name which helps to realize economies in large orders. Except for these terms, each store continues to operate independently. A retailer-sponsored cooperative group is essentially the same as a wholesaler-sponsored voluntary group except that the former is constituted at the initiative of a retailer. Retailers form their own association (cooperative) to compete against the corporate chains by undertaking wholesale functions (possibly even a limited amount of production), i.e., by operating their own wholesale companies which serve the member retailers. This type of contractual vertical marketing system is mostly operative in the food line. Associated Grocers Co-op., Inc., and Certified Grocers are examples of retailer-sponsored cooperative groups.

A *franchise system* refers to an arrangement where a firm licenses others to market a product or service using its trade name in a defined geographic area on specified terms and conditions. Four different types of franchise systems which can be distinguished are defined below:

1. The manufacturer-retailer franchise as exemplified by franchised automobile dealers and franchised service stations.
2. The manufacturer-wholesaler franchise as exemplified by Coca-Cola, Pepsi-Cola, Royal Crown Cola, and Seven-Up, which sell the soft drink syrups they manufacture to franchised wholesalers who, in turn, bottle and distribute soft drinks to retailers.
3. The wholesaler-retailer franchise as exemplified by Rexall Drug Stores and Sentry Drug Centers.
4. The service sponsor-retailer franchise as exemplified by Avis, Hertz, and National in the car rental business; McDonald's, Chicken Delight, Kentucky Fried Chicken, and Taco Tico in the prepared-foods industry; Howard Johnson's and Holiday Inn in the lodging and food industry; Midas and AAMCO in the auto repair business; and Kelly Girl and Manpower in the employment service business.[40]

---

[40]William P. Hall, "Franchising: New Scope for an Old Technique," *Harvard Business Review* (January-February, 1964), pp. 60–72.

The vertical marketing systems help in achieving economies that cannot be realized by conventional marketing channels. In strategic terms, vertical marketing systems provide opportunities for building experience, thus allowing even small firms to derive the benefits of market power. If present trends are any indication, in the 1980s vertical marketing systems should account for over 85 percent of the total retail sales. Considering their growing importance, conventional channels will need to adopt new distribution strategies to compete against the vertical marketing systems. Stern and El-Ansary recommend that conventional channels should take the following steps:

1. Develop programs to strengthen customers' competitive capabilities. This alternative would involve manufacturers and wholesalers in such activities as sponsoring centralized accounting and management reporting services, formulating cooperative promotional programs, and cosigning shopping center leases.
2. Enter new markets. For example, building supply distributors have initiated cash-and-carry outlets. Steel warehouses have added glass and plastic product lines to their traditional product lines. Industrial distributors have initiated stockless buying plans and blanket order contracts so that they may compete effectively for customers who buy on a direct basis.
3. Effect economies of operation by developing management information systems. For example, some middlemen in conventional channels have installed the IBM IMPACT program to improve their control over inventory.
4. Determine, through research, the focus of power in the channel and urge the channel member designated to undertake a reorganization of the marketing flows.[41]

CHANNEL-CONFLICT-MANAGEMENT STRATEGY

It is quite conceivable that independent firms which constitute a channel of distribution (i.e., manufacturer, wholesaler, retailer) may sometimes find themselves in conflict with each other. The underlying causes of conflict are the divergent goals that different firms may pursue. If the goals of one firm are being challenged because of the strategies followed by another channel member, conflict is the natural outcome. Thus, *channel conflict* may be defined as ". . . a situation in which one channel member perceives another channel member(s) to be engaged in behavior that is preventing or impending him from achieving his goals."[42]

Disagreement between channel members may arise due to incompatible desires and needs. Weigand and Wasson cite four examples of this:

---

[41]Stern and El-Ansary, *op. cit.,* pp. 428–429.
[42]*Ibid.,* p. 282.

A manufacturer promises an exclusive territory to a retailer in return for the retailer's "majority effort" to generate business in the area. Sales increase nicely, but the manufacturer believes it is due more to population growth in the area than to the effort of the store owner, who is spending too much time on the golf course.

A fast-food franchisor promises "expert promotional assistance" to his retailers as partial explanation for the franchise fee. One of the retailers believes that the help he is getting is anything but expert and that the benefits do not correspond with what he was promised.

Another franchisor agrees to furnish accounting services and financial analysis as a regular part of his service. The franchisee believes that the accountant is nothing more than a "glorified bookkeeper" and that the financial analysis consists of several pages of ratios that are incomprehensible.

A third franchisor insists that his franchisees should maintain a minimum stock of certain items that are regularly promoted throughout the area. Arguments arise as to whether the franchisor's recommendations constitute a threat, while the franchisee is particularly concerned about protecting his trade name.[43]

To cite an example from the literature, STP Corp. provides an interesting case. When the STP Corporation introduced STP additives to the market, it bypassed parts of the industry's elaborate setup. This alienated many auto supply middlemen, who retaliated by threatening not to stock STP filters either.[44] Also, In the early 1970s, dealers and jobbers of petroleum products were pressing damage suits against oil companies because of their pricing policies in six states. The conflict arose because the oil companies were supposedly selling gasoline to independent dealers at lower prices than to their own affiliates. The oil companies were also charged with threatening to cancel the dealers' leases if they did not follow the companies' marketing practices and operating procedures.[45]

The four strategic alternatives available for resolving the conflict between channel members are: bargaining, boundary, interpenetration, and superorganizational strategies.[46] Under the *bargaining strategy,* one member of the channel takes the lead in activating the bargaining process by being willing to concede something, with the expectation that the other party will reciprocate by adopting flexibility. For example, a manufacturer may agree to provide interest-free loans

---

[43]Robert E. Weigand and Hilda C. Wasson, "Arbitration in the Marketing Channel," *Business Horizons* (October, 1974), p. 40.

[44]Frederick C. Klein, "Andy Granatelli, His STP Additive Labeled Superfluous, Tries to Get Firm Rolling Again," *The Wall Street Journal,* June 13, 1972, p. 32.

[45]"The Oil Giants Fight the Independents," *Business Week* (May 13, 1972), p. 135.

[46]The following discussion is taken from: Louis W. Stern and Adel I. El-Ansary, *Marketing Channels* (Englewood Cliffs, NJ: Prentice-Hall, 1977), pp. 292–309.

for up to 90 days to a distributor if the distributor will carry twice the level of inventory that it previously did and will furnish warehousing for the purpose. Likewise, a retailer may propose to continue to carry the television line of a manufacturer if the manufacturer will supply televisions under the retailer's own name (i.e., the retailer's private brand). The bargaining strategy will work out only if both parties are willing to adopt the attitude of give-and-take and if the bottom-line results for both are favorable enough to induce them to accept the terms of the bargain.

The *boundary strategy* handles the conflict through diplomacy; i.e., by nominating the employee most familiar with the perspectives of the other party to take up the matter with his or her counterpart there. For example, a manufacturer may nominate a veteran salesperson to communicate with the purchasing agent of the customer to see if some grounds can be worked out to resolve the conflict. A department store manager may be upset with a manufacturer for the decision to start supplying the product to a mass retailer, such as Montgomery Ward. To resolve such a conflict, the manufacturer's salesperson may meet with the purchasing agent to talk over business in general, and in between the talks the salesperson may indicate in a subtle way that the company's decision to supply the product to Montgomery Ward for sale through catalogs is motivated by its desire to help the department store: In the long run, the department store will reap the benefits of the brand-name popularity which is triggered by the deal with Montgomery Ward. Besides, the salesperson may propose that his company will agree not to sell the top of the line to Ward, thus ensuring that it would continue to be available only through major department stores. In order for this strategy to succeed, it is necessary that the diplomat (i.e., the salesperson in the above example) is fully briefed on the situation and is provided leverages with which to negotiate.

The *interpenetration strategy* is directed toward resolving conflict through frequent informal interactions with the other party which lead to a proper appreciation of each other's perspectives. One of the easiest ways to develop interaction is for one party to invite the other to join its trade association. For example, television dealers felt that there was inadequate communication between various channel members, with the result that the manufacturers did not understand dealers' problems. To correct the situation, the television manufacturers were invited to become members of the National Appliance and Radio-TV Dealers Association (NARDA). Currently manufacturers take active interest in NARDA conventions and seminars, and, according to industry sources, the channel relationships in the television industry have improved a great deal.[47]

Finally, the focus of *superorganizational strategy* is to employ conciliation, mediation, and arbitration to resolve the conflict. Essentially, a neutral third

---

[47]Henry Assall, "Constructive Role of Interorganizational Conflict," *Administrative Science Quarterly,* Vol. 14 (1969), p. 287.

party is brought into the conflict to resolve the matter. *Conciliation* is an informal attempt by the third party to bring the two conflicting organizations together and make them come to an agreement amicably. For example, an independent wholesaler may serve as a conciliator between a manufacturer and its customers. Under *mediation,* the third party plays a more active role. If the parties in conflict fail to come to an agreement, they may be willing to consider the procedural or substantive recommendations of the mediator.

Arbitration may also be applied to resolve channel conflict. Arbitration may be compulsory or voluntary. Under *compulsory arbitration,* the dispute must by law be submitted to a third party, the decision being final and binding on both the conflicting parties. For example, the courts may arbitrate between two parties in dispute. Years ago, when automobile manufacturers and their dealers had problems relative to distribution policies, the court arbitrated. *Voluntary arbitration* is a process whereby the parties in conflict submit their disputes for resolution to a third party on their own. For example, in 1955 the Federal Trade Commission arbitrated between television set manufacturers, distributors, and dealers by setting up 32 industry rules to protect the consumer and to reduce distributive conflicts. The distributive conflict areas involved were: tie-in sales; price fixing; mass shipments used to clog outlets and foreclose competitors; discriminatory billing; and special rebates, bribes, refunds, and discounts.[48]

Of all the methods of resolving conflict, arbitration is the fastest. Additionally, under arbitration, secrecy is preserved and less expense is incurred. Inasmuch as industry experts serve as arbitrators, one can expect a fairer decision. Thus, as a matter of strategy, arbitration may be more desirable than other methods for managing conflict.[49]

SUMMARY

Distribution strategies are concerned with the flow of goods and services from manufacturers to customers. The discussion in this chapter is conducted from the manufacturer's viewpoint. Six major distribution strategies may be distinguished. These are: channel-structure strategy, distribution-scope strategy, multiple-channel strategy, channel-modification strategy, channel-control strategy, and channel-conflict-management strategy.

The channel-structure strategy determines whether the goods should be distributed directly from manufacturer to customer or indirectly, allowing goods to pass through one or more intermediaries. Formulation of this strategy was discussed with reference to Bucklin's postponement-speculation theory. Additionally, two approaches (goods and financial) were dealt with in this discussion. The distribution-scope strategy specifies whether exclusive, selective, or intensive dis-

[48]Stern and El-Ansary, *op. cit.,* p. 305.
[49]Weigand and Wasson, *op. cit.*

tribution should be pursued. The question of simultaneously employing more than one channel is discussed under multiple-channel strategy. The channel-modification strategy involves evaluating current channels and making necessary changes in distribution perspectives so as to accommodate environmental shifts. The channel-control strategy focuses on vertical marketing systems to institute control. Finally, the resolution of conflict among channel members is examined under the channel-conflict-management strategy.

The merits and demerits of each strategy are discussed. Examples from marketing literature are also given to illustrate the practical applications of different strategies.

DISCUSSION QUESTIONS

1. What factors may a manufacturer consider to determine whether to distribute the products directly to customers? Can automobiles be distributed directly to customers?
2. Is intensive distribution a prerequisite for gaining experience? Discuss.
3. What precautions are necessary to ensure that exclusive distribution is not liable to challenge as a restraint in trade?
4. What strategic reason makes the multiple-channel strategy a necessity for a multiproduct company?
5. What criteria may a food processor adopt to evaluate its channels of distribution?
6. What kinds of environmental shifts require a change in channel arrangements?
7. What reasons may be ascribed to the emergence of vertical marketing systems?
8. What strategies may conventional channels adopt to meet the threat of vertical marketing systems?
9. What are the underlying sources of conflict in distribution channel relations? Give examples.
10. What is the most appropriate strategy for resolving a channel conflict?

Chapter 12
Promotional Strategies

Advertisements contain the only truths to be relied on in a newspaper.

Thomas Jefferson

Promotion strategies are concerned with the planning, implementation, and control of persuasive communication with customers. These strategies may be designed around advertising, personal selling, sales promotion, or any combination of these. The first strategic issue involved here is how much money may be spent on the promotion of a specific product/market. The distribution of the total promotional budget among advertising, personal selling, and sales promotion is another strategic matter. The formulation of strategies dealing with these two issues determines the role that each type of promotion may play in a particular situation.

Clearcut objectives and a sharp focus on target customers are necessary for an effective promotional program. In other words, merely undertaking an advertising campaign or hiring a few salespeople to call on customers may not suffice. Rather, an integrated communication plan consisting of various promotion methods should be designed to ensure that customers in a product/market cluster get the right message and maintain a long-term cordial relationship with the company. Besides, promotional perspectives must also be properly matched with the product, price, and distribution perspectives.

In addition to the strategic issues mentioned above, this chapter discusses strategies in the areas of advertising and personal selling. The advertising strategies examined here are media strategy and copy strategy. Strategic matters explored in the area of personal selling are those concerned with designing a selling program and supervising salespeople. The formulation of each strategy is illustrated with reference to examples from the literature.

PROMOTION STRATEGIES
Promotion-expenditure Strategy

The amount that a company may spend on its total promotional effort, which consists of advertising, personal selling, and sales promotion, is not easy to determine. There are no appropriate standards which indicate how much should be spent on promotion in a given product/market situation. This is so because the decision on promotion expenditure is influenced by a complex set of circumstances.

Promotion expenditure makes up part of the total marketing budget. Thus, the allocation of more or less funds to one department, such as advertising, will affect the level of expenditure elsewhere within the marketing function. For example, it may be debated whether additional expenditures on advertising are more desirable than a new package design. In addition, the perspectives of promotion expenditure must be examined in the context of pricing strategy. A relatively higher price provides more funds for promotion than does a lower price. The amount set aside for promotional expenditure is also affected by the sales response of the product, which is very difficult to estimate accurately. A related matter here is the question of the cumulative effect of promotion. The major emphasis of research in this area, even where the issue is far from being resolved, has been on the duration of advertising effects. While it is generally accepted that advertising effects, and maybe that of other forms of promotion as well, may last over a long period, there is no certainty about the duration of these benefits. According to one source, the cumulative effect depends on the loyalty of customers, frequency of purchase, and competitive efforts, each of which may be influenced in turn by different set of variables.[1]

Promotion expenditures will vary from one product/market situation to another. There is, however, no normative framework which may suggest what form of promotion will be appropriate for a given product-market combination. Consider the case of the H.J. Heinz Company. In early 1977 the company decided to reverse its emphasis on overseas markets and concentrate on the U.S. To successfully compete in the U.S. market, the company significantly boosted its advertising budget from $34 million in 1976 to $63 million in 1977.[2] There is no ready-made formula which may be used to explain whether the $63 million committed to advertising by Heinz was the optimum in the light of a change in market strategy (i.e., a greater dependence on the U.S. market).

Promotion induces competitors to react, and there is no way to accurately anticipate competitive response and thus decide on a budget. For example, from 1975 to 1977, Chesebrough-Pond's Inc. spent about $7.5 million annually to advertise its Ragu brand of spaghetti sauce. In 1977 Hunt-Wesson Foods, Inc., challenged Ragu with its Prima Salsa brand, and Ragu's market share went down from 63.5% in mid-1976 to 57.5% by early 1977. To regain its position, Chesebrough-Pond, among other measures, increased its 1978 advertising budget to $11

[1]Nariman K. Dhalla, "Assessing the Long-term Value of Advertising," *Harvard Business Review* (January–February, 1978), pp. 87–95.
[2]"Heinz Comes Home and Discovers Advertising," *Business Week* (November 14, 1977), p. 224.

million.[3] According to the company sources, this proved helpful since in early 1979 Ragu's market share went up to 64%. Clearly the level of promotion must be adjusted as the competitive situation changes.

Despite the difficulties involved, practitioners have developed rules of thumb for determining promotion expenditures which are strategically sound. These rules of thumb may be distinguished as being of two types: breakdown and buildup methods.[4] Before discussing these methods, however, it will be worthwhile to briefly review the application of marginal analysis to the promotion expenditure decision.

Marginal Approach The *marginal approach* was the earliest organized framework for developing a promotion budget. With this approach, the expenditure of each ingredient of promotion (i.e., communication mix, personal selling, advertising, and sales promotion) should be made so that marginal revenue is equal to marginal cost. For example, the outlay on advertising should be incurred to the point where it just equals the incremental profit earned on the additional business generated by advertising. Similarly, the expenditure on personal selling should be equal to the profit on sales generated by the sales force. For the total communication mix as a whole, the optimum budget should be set where the marginal revenues per dollar of cost from advertising, personal selling, and sales promotion are equal. In other words, the appropriation on each of the three ingredients of promotion should be increased or decreased until the stage is reached in which marginal revenues are equal.

Theoretically the approach appears sound. However, measurement of marginal costs and revenues poses a difficult problem. Even if margins can be estimated, the marginal approach may not be feasible. For example, no firm may like to hire and fire salespeople in an attempt to reach the optimum point where marginal cost is equal to marginal revenue. Besides, what if the margin is reached at three fourths of a salesperson? Likewise, in advertising, either one places an ad in a magazine or one does not advertise at all. A half-page ad in *Time* costs approximately $70,000 (1979 estimate). Either one advertises in *Time* or one does not. Even though a firm may know that its margin is achieved at a level of expenditure which is much less than $70,000, it is not possible to haggle with *Time* over the cost of its advertising space. Measurement of the carry-over effect of advertising or computation of profits may be still another problem.

The question of the carry-over effect of advertising is a complex one, and there is no agreement as to how long advertising affects sales. Traditionally it was held that advertising's effect on sales lasts several years. Recent work in the area, however, suggests that the duration of the cumulative effect of advertising on sales

[3]Stanley H. Slom, "Careful Planning, Aggressive Marketing Help Chesebrough-Pond's Stave Off Foes," *The Wall Street Journal,* March 23, 1979, p. 40.
[4]See G. David Hughes, *Marketing Management: A Planning Approach* (Reading, MA: Addison-Wesley Publishing Co., 1978), p. 368.

is between 3 and 15 months, which renders the carry-over effect of advertising as a short-term phenomenon.[5] Either way, it may not be easy to determine the duration of the cumulative effect of advertising on sales. In brief, then, while the marginal approach for allocating promotional expenditures provides a good theoretical framework, its practical use is limited.

Breakdown Methods. Included in breakdown methods are the percentage-of-dollar sales, spend-as-much-as-can-be-afforded, return-on-investment, and competitive-parity approaches. Under the *percentage-of-sales approach,* promotion expenditure is a specified percentage of the previous year's or predicted future sales. Initially this percentage is arrived at by a hunch. Later on, historical information is used to decide what percentage of sales should be allocated for promotion expenditure. The rationale behind the use of this approach is that expenditure on promotion must be justified by sales. This approach is followed by many companies since it is simple, it is easy to understand, and it leaves managers the flexibility to cut corners during periods of economic slowdown. Among its flaws is the fact that basing promotion appropriation on sales puts the chicken before the egg. Further, the logic of this approach fails to consider the cumulative effect of promotion. In brief, this approach considers promotion a necessary expenditure that must be apportioned from sales revenue without considering the relationship of promotion to competitors' activities or its influence on sales revenues.

Another approach for allocating promotion expenditure is to *spend as much as can be afforded.* In this approach the availability of funds or liquid resources is the main consideration in making the decision on promotion expenditure. In other words, even if a company's sales expectations are high, the level of promotion will be kept low if its cash position is tight. This approach can be questioned on several grounds. It assumes a close relationship between promotion expenditures and the liquid resources of a company, an assumption which may not be accurate. As a matter of fact, even a cash-short company must spend more on promotion if it expects to improve sales. Further, this approach involves an element of risk. At a time when the market is tight and sales are slow, a company may spend more on promotion if it happens to have the resources available. This approach, however, does consider the fact that promotion outlays have long-term value, i.e., the cumulative effect of advertising. Also, under conditions of complete uncertainty, this approach is a cautious one.

According to the *return-on-investment approach,* promotion expenditures are considered as an investment whose benefits will be derived over the years. Thus, as in the case of any other capital investment, the appropriateness of promotion expenditure should be determined by comparing the expected return with the

---

[5]Darral G. Clarke, "Econometric Measurement of the Duration of Advertising Effect on Sales," *Journal of Marketing Research* (November, 1976), pp. 345–357.

desired return. The expected return on promotion may be computed by using present values of future returns. Inasmuch as some promotion is likely to produce immediate results, the total promotion expenditure may be partitioned between current expense and investment. Alternatively, the entire promotion expenditure can be considered as an investment, in which case the immediate effect of promotion can be conceived as a return in period zero. The basic validity and soundness of the return-on-investment approach cannot be disputed. But there are several problems in its application. First, determination over time of the outcomes of different forms of promotion may be difficult. Second, what is the appropriate return which one might expect from an advertising investment? These limitations put severe constraints on the practical use of this approach.

The *competitive-parity approach* assumes that promotion expenditure is directly related to market share. The promotion expenditure of a firm should, therefore, be in proportion to those of competitors in order to maintain its position in the market. Thus, if the leader in the industry allocates two percent of its sales revenue on advertising, other members of the industry should spend about the same percentage of their sales on advertising. Considering the competitive nature of the economy, this seems a reasonable approach for allocating promotion expenditures. This approach, however, has a variety of limitations. Promotion is but one variable which affects market performance. Thus, simply maintaining a promotion parity with the competitors may not be enough for a firm to preserve its market share. Further, this approach requires a knowledge of competitors' perspectives on promotion, and this information may not always be available. Still further, a goal can sometimes be achieved by following one of two approaches. First, greater emphasis can be put either on promotion or on reducing prices. This approach can be misleading if a firm follows competitive leads in advertising without reference to its prices. Second, with judicious selection of media, timely advertising, well-drawn copy, a good sales-supervision program, etc., it is possible for a firm to realize the same results as another firm which has twice as much to spend. Again, it is difficult in this case to ensure market share by simply maintaining a promotional balance with competitors.

Buildup Method. Companies have advertising, sales, and sales promotion (merchandising) managers who report to the marketing manager. Using as a basis the factors discussed for determining the promotional task, the marketing manager specifies the objectives of promotion separately for the advertising, personal selling, and sales promotion of each product line. Ideally the spadework for defining objectives should be done by a committee consisting of executives concerned with product development, pricing, distribution, and promotion. Committee work helps in bringing inputs from different areas; thus, the decision on promotion expenditure is made in the context of the total marketing mix. For example, it may be agreed upon that promotion should be undertaken to expose at least 100,000 household customers to the product, while institutional customers may be sought through reductions in price.

In practice it may not always be easy to pinpoint the roles of advertising, personal selling, and sales promotion objectively. These can be overlapping so that all three methods of promotion compete with each other. Management, therefore, may in some fashion have to blend advertising, personal selling, and sales promotion. Unfortunately, there are no formulas for blending different methods of promotion in all situations. Each company must work out its own rules for a promotion mix. Once the tasks to be performed by each method of promotion have been designated, they may be defined formally as objectives. These objectives, established separately for advertising, sales promotion, and personal selling, are communicated to the respective managers. On the basis of these objectives, each promotion manager will probably redefine his or her own goals in more operational terms. These redefined objectives then become the modus operandi of each department.

Once departmental objectives have been defined, each area works out a network of details for advertising or personal selling. A budget is drawn up by costing each item required to accomplish the objectives of the program. The total budget figure gives the amount required by each department. As each department prepares its own budget, the marketing manager may also prepare individual budgets for all of them. The marketing manager, however, does not work out a detailed program but simply lists the major expenditures in the light of overall marketing strategy. A marketing manager's budget is mainly a controlling device.

When the individual departments have arrived at their estimates of necessary allocation, the marketing manager meets with each of them to approve the budgets. At that time, the marketing manager's own estimates help in making a close examination of the department budgets. Finally, an appropriation is made to each department for advertising, personal selling, and sales promotion. Needless to say, the emphasis on different tasks is revised and the total budget refigured several times before an acceptable program emerges. A committee, instead of just the marketing manager, may approve the final appropriation for each department.

The buildup method forces the managers to analyze scientifically the role they expect promotion to play and the contribution it can make toward achieving marketing objectives. It also helps maintain control over promotion expenditure and avoid the frustrations often faced by promotion managers as a result of cuts in promotion appropriations due to economic slowdown. On the other hand, this approach can become overly scientific. Sometimes profit opportunities which may require incurring additional promotion expenditure may appear unannounced. Involvement with the objective and task exercise to decide how much more should be spent on promotion will take time, perhaps leading to the loss of the unexpected opportunity.

The buildup method may be illustrated with the following example. International Products Company, Inc.,* a large grocery-products company, had success-

---

*Disguised name.

fully introduced its brand of freeze-dried coffee to the market back in the 1960s. In the mid-1970s, the company planned to introduce the freeze-dried coffee to the vending machine market. It followed the build-up method to budget promotional allocations for the purpose. As background on the subject, it was found that vending machines sold $8.8 billion of products in 1974 in the United States. There were approximately 8,300 operating companies which were directly concerned with the business of machine selling, and there were almost 7 million vending machines on over 1 million locations in 1974.

The following objectives were set up in each area of promotion.

Advertising.
1. Make the entire population of vending machine operating companies aware of the International Products Company's freeze-dried coffee program in three years.
2. Make them knowledgeable about International's plan to help them by selling conversion kits for vending machines (i.e., kits which operators may buy to convert a machine usable for freshly brewed coffee so that it is usable for freeze-dried coffee).
3. Make the entire population of vending machine manufacturers aware of the desirability of converting their machines from freshly brewed to freeze-dried coffee in two years.

Personal Selling.
1. Make calls on 2000 selected vending machine operators to present them with International's freeze-dried coffee program in a two-year period.
2. Follow up to finalize deals with at least 500 operators mainly in the East and Midwest.
3. Call upon five leading vending machine manufacturers to buy conversion kits from International.

Sales Promotion.
1. Organize a one-day seminar at International's headquarters in Stamford, Connecticut, to be attended by top-management executives of selected vending machine operating firms. The attendees will be given an overview of International's vending machines program in an elegant setting.
2. Develop promotional material, which salespeople can leave with the vending machine operators, which is designed to restate the sales pitch by characterizing different selling features (i.e., savings, profits, consumer acceptance, purchase or conversion assistance, and free products).

The above objectives were used to arrive at advertising, personal-selling, and sales-promotion expenses. As far as possible, all direct items of cost were included. Due adjustments were made when intracompany transactions were involved. For example, International's sales force currently calling on the vending machine operators was to be utilized to introduce freeze-dried coffee. It was agreed by the top management that an amount equal to five percent of the sales force expenses should be charged to the new undertaking for the next three years.

An attempt was made to conceive each program in detail so that all expenses were included in the budget. For example, the one-day seminar program was detailed as follows:

> Attending executives will receive "red carpet" treatment all the way: personal letters of invitation with round-trip first-class tickets enclosed; special limousines to meet arriving guests at airports; catered lunches, etc.
>
> After a guided tour of the Stamford facilities, the visitors will be introduced to the freeze-dried coffee program by means of a two-step presentation:
> 1. A large flip chart outlining the advantages of freeze-dried coffee over fresh brew, the extra profits and other benefits for the operators, and the cooperation of the machine manufacturers in the program
> 2. A preview of the audiovisual presentation which the International salespeople will make later in the fall to each operator's purchasing department
>
> Following the presentation, the guests will be returned to the appropriate airport for their return flights.

Such a detailed outline of each aspect of promotion is helpful in making sure all items of expenditure have been included in the budget. The budgets are then submitted to marketing management for its approval.

Promotion-mix Strategy

Another strategic decision in the area of promotion concerns the allocation of effort among different methods of promotion (i.e., advertising, personal selling, and sales promotion). *Advertising* refers to nonpersonal communication transmitted through the mass media (radio, TV, print, outdoors, and mail). The communication is identified with a sponsor who compensates the media for the transmission. *Personal selling* refers to face-to-face interaction with the customer. Unlike in advertising, in personal selling communication flows both ways — from the source to the destination and back. All other forms of communication with the customer other than those included in advertising and personal selling constitute *sales promotion*. Thus, coupons, samples, demonstrations, exhibits, premiums, trade allowances, sales and dealer incentives, cents-off packs, rebates, and point-of-purchase material are all sales promotion devices.

In some cases the three types of promotion may be largely interchangeable; however, they should be blended judiciously to complement each other for a balanced promotional perspective. Illustrated below is the manner in which a chemical company mixed advertising with personal selling and sales promotion to achieve optimum promotional performance.

An advertising campaign aimed at customer industries, employees, and plant communities carried the theme, "The little chemical giant." It appeared in *Adhesive Age, American Paint & Coating Journal, Chemical & Engineering News, Chemical Marketing Reporter, Chemical Purchasing, Chemical Week, Modern Plastics,* and *Plastics World.*

Sales promotion and personal selling were supported by publicity. Editorial tours of the company's new plants, programs to develop employee understanding and involvement in the expansion, and briefings for local people in towns and cities where USIC (the company) had facilities provided a catalyst for publicity.

Personal selling was aggressive and provided direct communication about the firm's continued service. USIC reassured producers of ethyl alcohol, vinyl acetate monomer, and polyethylene that "we will not lose personal touch with our customers."[6]

Development of an optimum promotion mix is by no means easy. Companies use haphazard and seat-of-the-pants procedures to determine the respective roles of advertising, personal selling, and sales promotion in a product/market situation. A Marketing Science Institute (MSI) study on the subject revealed the following:

1. Decisions on the promotional mix were often diffused among many decision makers. This inhibited the formation of unified promotion strategy, and indecision and conflict often occurred.
2. Personal selling plans were sometimes divorced from the planning of advertising and sales promotion.
3. Frequently the decision makers were not adequately aware of the objectives and broad strategies of the overall product program which the promotion plan was designed to implement.
4. Sales and market share goals tended to be constant, regardless of decreases or increases in promotional expenditures. Thus they became unrealistic as guides and directives for planning, or as criteria of promotional effectiveness, or even as a fair basis for application of the judgment of the decision makers.
5. The working planner was usually expected to prepare only one allocation plan for a product . . . Alternate marketing or promotion strategies did not receive full consideration . . . Decisions on the

---

[6]"USIC Chem. Ads Start to Support Effort to Double Sales in 5 Years," *Industrial Marketing* (June, 1976), pp.1–4.

funds allocated among alternative promotional methods usually lacked objective measures of effectiveness or reliable sets of guidelines. Lacking alternative strategies, planners were unprepared to meet contingencies and to adapt the program readily to feedback of its effects or environmental changes.

6. Negative planning, to be implemented should expenditures be cut back, was missing . . . Unforeseen cutbacks were perennial in most companies . . . Promotion funds were often the first to be reduced when profits were threatened.

7. In most of the companies there seemed to be a minimum of emphasis on record keeping and a reluctance to worry about what actually happened in the past as opposed to what was intended.

8. Frequently, senior marketing . . . personnel were not clearly informed of assumptions and conditions underlying lower-echelon decisions . . . the programs submitted for management review often lacked necessary details for upstream decision making.

9. Lower-echelon persons in some companies were not given the authority necessary to carry out their assignments. . . . yet they were responsible for results.

10. Top management seldom asked for support from knowledgeable line and staff groups in arriving at their final decisions . . . these communications difficulties were a source of confusion and a demoralizing influence.

11. Expenditure levels for promotion were typically derived by working backward rather arbitrarily from sales revenue forecasts . . . Quantifying the objective, and then referring all contributory factors to systematic and comprehensive promotional planning procedures, was rare. In those cases when this was found, it did not appear well documented or complete . . .

12. The allocation of total budgets among the various tasks and tools of promotion was sometimes determined by: sheer intuition, comparing past patterns of decisions, mechanically working backward from the more fixed items to a residual for flexible items, relying on competent judgment of others, and arbitrary "rules of thumb."

13. In policy committee meetings, marketing management often presented well-rationalized, but not necessarily well-structured, arguments in favor of various promotional mixes. These presentations suffered in comparison with the more logical and rational financial and technical proposals presented by other line and staff people . . . Even less prevalent than systematic planning was the practice of looking at prior years' performances through postaudits or reviews intended to enhance the forward-planning process.

14. The present state of the art in marketing administration is such that cause and effect relationships, and other basic insights, are not

sufficiently understood to permit knowledgeable forecasts of what to expect from alternate courses of action. Even identifying feasible alternatives can prove difficult.[7]

The MSI study clearly underlines the critical need for developing a conceptual framework to make promotion-mix decisions. Apparently, a variety of factors needs to be considered to determine the appropriate promotion mix in a particular product/market situation. These factors may be categorized as product factors, market factors, customer factors, budget factors, and marketing mix factors.[8] The details of these factors are shown in Exhibit 12-1. Discussed below is the significance of each of these categories of factors in determining the promotion mix.

EXHIBIT 12-1 Criteria for Determining Promotion Mix

Product Factors
1. Nature of product
2. Perceived risk
3. Durable versus nondurable
4. Typical purchase amount

Market Factors
1. Position in its life cycle
2. Market share
3. Industry concentration
4. Intensity of competition
5. Demand perspectives

Customer Factors
1. Household versus business customers
2. Number of customers
3. Concentration of customers

Budget Factors
1. Financial resources of the organization
2. Traditional promotional perspectives

Marketing Mix Factors
1. Relative price/relative quality
2. Distribution strategy
3. Brand life cycle
4. Geographic scope of market

---

[7]Patrick J. Robinson and David J. Luck, *Promotional Decision Making: Practice and Theory* (New York: McGraw-Hill Bk. Co., 1964) pp. 21–22.
[8]See Paul W. Farris, "Determinants of Advertising Intensity: A Review of the Marketing Literature," *Working Paper* (Cambridge, MA: Marketing Science Institute, 1977).

Product Factors. Factors in this category are mainly related to the way in which the product is bought, consumed, and perceived by the customer. For industrial goods, especially technical products, personal selling is more significant than advertising since these goods usually need to be inspected and compared before being bought. Salespeople can explain the workings of a product and provide on-the-spot answers to customers' queries. For consumer goods such as cosmetics and processed foods, advertising is of primary importance. In addition, advertising plays a dominant role when used for products which provide an opportunity for differentiation and for those being purchased with emotional motives.

The perceived risk of a purchase decision is another variable here. Generally speaking, the more risk a buyer perceives to be associated with buying a particular product, the higher will be the importance of personal selling over advertising. A buyer generally likes to have more information on the product when the perceived risk is high, and this necessitates an emphasis on personal selling. Durable goods are bought less frequently than nondurables and usually require a heavy commitment of resources. These characteristics make personal selling of greater significance than advertising for durable goods. However, since many durable goods are sold through franchised dealerships, the influence of each type of promotion should be determined in light of the additional push it would provide in moving the product. Finally, products purchased in small quantities are presumably purchased frequently and require routine decision making. For these products advertising should be preferable to personal selling. Often such products are of low value; therefore, a profitable business in these products can only be conducted on volume. This underlines the importance of advertising in this case.

Market Factors. The first market factor is the position of a product in its life cycle. The creation of primary demand, hitherto nonexistent, is the primary task during the introductory stage; therefore, a high level of promotion effort is needed to explain a new product to potential customers. For consumer goods in the introductory stage, the major thrust is on heavy advertising supported by missionary selling to help distributors move the product. Additionally, different measures of sales promotion (e.g., sampling, couponing, free demonstrations, etc.) are employed to entice the customer to try the product. In the case of industrial products, personal selling alone is useful during this period. During the growth phase there is increasing demand, which means enough business for all competitors. In the case of consumer goods, however, the promotional effort shifts to reliance on advertising. Industrial goods, on the other hand, begin to be advertised as the market broadens and continue to require a personal selling effort. In the maturity phase competition becomes intense, and advertising, along with sales promotion measures, is resorted to in order to differentiate the product (a consumer good) from competitive brands and to provide an incentive to the customer to buy the product. Industrial goods during maturity call for intensive personal selling. During the decline phase, the promotional effort does not vary much initially from that during the maturity phase except that the intensity of promotion declines. Later on, as price competition becomes keen and demand continues to decline, overall promotional perspectives are reduced.

For a given product class, if market share is high, both advertising and personal selling are used. If the market share is low, the emphasis is placed on either personal selling or advertising. This is because high market share seems to indicate that the company does business in more than one segment and uses multiple channels of distribution. Thus, both personal selling and advertising are utilized to promote the product. Where market share is low, the perspectives of the business are limited, and either advertising or personal selling will suffice, depending on the nature of the product.

If the industry is concentrated among a few firms, advertising will achieve additional significance for two reasons. One, heavy advertising may help discourage other firms from entering the field. Two, it sustains a desired position for the product in the market. Heavy advertising constitutes an implied warranty of product performance and perhaps decreases the uncertainty consumers associate with new products. In this way new competition is discouraged and existing positions are reinforced.

Intensity of competition tends to impact promotional blending along the same lines as market share. When competition is keen, all three types of promotion are needed to sustain the product's position in the market. This is because promotion is needed to inform, remind, and persuade customers to buy the product. On the other hand, if competitive activity is limited, the major function of promotion is to inform and perhaps remind customers about the product. Thus, either advertising or personal selling is mainly used.

Hypothetically, advertising is more suited for products which have relatively latent demand. This is because advertising investment should open up new opportunities in the long run, and if the carry-over effect is counted, expenditure per sales dollar would be more beneficial. If demand is limited and new demand is not expected to be created, advertising outlay would be uneconomical. Thus, future potential becomes a significant factor in determining the role of advertising.

Customer Factors.   In this section, factors which relate to the type of customers a business serves are dwelled upon. One of the major dimensions used to differentiate businesses is the issue of whether they market products for household consumption or for organizational use. There are several significant differences in the way products are marketed to these two customer groups, and these differences exert considerable influence on the type of promotion that should be used. In the case of household customers, it is relatively easy to identify the decision maker for a particular good; therefore, advertising is more desirable. Also, the self-service nature of many consumer-product sales makes personal selling less important. Finally, household customers do not go through a formal buying process utilizing objective criteria as organizational customers do. This again makes advertising more useful for reaching household customers. Essentially the same reasons make personal selling more relevant in promoting the product among organizational customers.

The number of customers and their geographic concentration also influence promotional blending. For a small customer base, especially if it is geographically concentrated, advertising does not make as much sense as it does in cases where customers are spread all over and represent a significant mass. Caution is needed here because some advertising may always be necessary for consumer goods, no matter what the market perspectives are. Thus, the above analytical statements only provide a conceptual framework and should not be understood as exact yes/no decision criteria.

Budget Factors. Ideally the budget should be based on the promotional tasks to be performed. However, intuitively and traditionally, companies place an upper limit on the amount that they will spend on promotion. Such a limit may influence the type of promotion which may be undertaken. For example, a company with a promotional budget of $50,000 cannot afford insertions in a national magazine even though such a coverage might provide the best results. Budget factors affect the promotional blend in two ways. First, a financially weak company will be constrained in undertaking certain types of promotion. For example, TV advertising necessitates a heavy commitment of resources. Second, in many companies the advertising budget has been traditionally linked to revenues as a percentage. This method of allocation continues to be used so that expected revenues will indicate how much might be spent on advertising in the future. The allocated funds, then, automatically determine the role of advertising. Similarly, personal selling perspectives are determined independently.

Marketing Mix Factors. The promotion decision should be made in the context of other aspects of the marketing mix. This section examines the relevance of other marketing decisions to the promotion mix. The price and quality of a product relative to competition impact the nature of its promotional perspectives. Higher prices must be justified to the consumer by actual or presumed product superiority. Thus, in the case of a product which is priced substantially higher, advertising achieves significance in communicating and establishing the product's superior quality in the minds of the customers.

The promotion mix is also influenced by the distribution structure employed for the product. If the promotion is distributed directly, the sales force will largely be counted on to promote the product. Indirect distribution, on the other hand, requires greater emphasis on advertising since the sales force push is limited. As a matter of fact, the further the manufacturer is removed from the ultimate user, the greater is the need for the advertising effort to stimulate and maintain demand. The influence of the distribution strategy may be illustrated with reference to two cosmetic companies: Revlon and Avon. The two companies deal in similar products. Revlon distributes its products through different types of intermediaries and advertises them heavily. Avon, on the other hand, distributes directly to end users in their homes and spends relatively little on advertising.

Earlier, we examined the effect on the promotion mix of a product's position in its life cycle. The position of a brand in its life cycle also influences promotional perspectives. When an existing brand reaches the maturity phase in its life cycle, the marketer has three options: to employ life-extension strategies, to harvest the brand for profits, and/or to introduce a new brand which may be targeted at a more specific segment of the market. Positioning the new brand during the introduction phase in the desired slot in the market requires higher advertising. As it enters the growth phase, advertising will have to be blended with personal selling. In the growth phase the overall level of promotion will decline in scope. In brief, the new brand will have to be treated like a new product as far as promotion is concerned.

Finally, the geographic scope of the market to be served is another consideration here. Advertising, relatively speaking, is more significant for products marketed nationally than for those marketed locally or regionally. One study showed that even spot television advertising proved to be more expensive vis-a-vis the target-group exposures gained when the market was geographically limited.[9] Thus, since advertising works out to be an expensive proposition, regional marketers should rely less on advertising and more on other forms of promotion, or substitute for television advertising another element of the marketing mix. For example, a regional marketer may manufacture private-label brands.

Conclusion. While the above factors are helpful in establishing roles for different methods of promotion, actual appropriation among them should take into consideration the effect of any changes in the environment. For example, until 1977 soft drink companies frequently used sales promotion (mainly cents off) to vie for customers. In 1978, however, the makers of soft drinks changed their promotion-mix strategy to concentrate more on advertising. This is evidenced by the fact that the five largest soft drink makers spent about $200 million on advertising in 1979, 40% more than they spent in 1977. One reason for this change in promotional perspective has been the realization that price discounting hurt brand loyalties; since Coke and Pepsi had made colas into commodities by means of cents-off promotion, the consumer now shopped for price.[10] Briefly, then, the promotion-mix strategy should be reviewed periodically to incorporate changes necessitated by environmental shifts both inside and outside the company.

In addition, the promotion mix may also be affected by a desire to be innovative, i.e., to do something different and seek uniqueness. For example, Puritan

---

[9]Michael E. Porter, "Interbrand Choice, Media Mix and Market Performance," *American Economic Review* (May 16, 1976), pp. 190–203.
[10]"Soft-Drink Companies Prime Their Weapons in Market-Share Battle," *The Wall Street Journal,* April 26, 1979, p. 1.

Fashions Corporation, an apparel company, traditionally spent little on advertising. In the late 1970s, the company had been continually losing money. Then in 1977, the company introduced a new product, body-hugging jeans, and employed an unconventional promotion strategy. It placed the designer Calvin Klein's label on the jeans, sold them as a prestige trouser priced at $35 (double the price of nonlabeled styles), and advertised them heavily. This provided the company with instant success. Although Puritan had no previous experience in jeans, the company's production soared within one year to 125,000 pairs a week. This meant a 25% share of the $1 billion retail market.[11] While promotional innovation may not last long because competitors may soon copy it, it does provide the innovator with a head start.

Promotional blending requires consideration of a large number of variables, as outlined above. Unfortunately the effect of these variables on promotion is stated only in generalizations. This makes it difficult to assign quantitative values to each influencing factor. The difficulty arises on two counts. First, the state of the art of normative work in this area has not been developed very far. Second, in practice, advertising and personal selling are generally treated differently, which limits the feasibility of case studies on the subject. Thus, the decision on promotion blending must necessarily be made subjectively. The above factors, however, provide a checklist for reviewing the soundness and viability of the subjective decision.

ADVERTISING STRATEGIES

Media-selection Strategy

Media may be defined as those channels through which messages concerning a product or service are transmitted to the targets. The following media are available to advertisers: newspapers, magazines, television, radio, outdoor advertising, transit advertising, and direct mail. Selection of an advertising medium is influenced by such factors as the product or service itself, the target market, the extent and type of distribution, the type of message to be communicated, the budget, and the competitors' advertising strategy. Presumably, information on most of these factors is available inside the company, except for the advertising perspectives employed by the competition. To obtain this information, it may be necessary to undertake a marketing research project to find out what sort of advertising strategy the competitors had in the past and what might be expected of them in the future. In addition, medium selection also depends on the advertising objectives for the product/market concerned. These objectives form the basis for arriving at media objectives. With the above information in place, there are different methods which may be used to select a medium. Before finalizing the

---

[11]"Puritan Fashions: Trying to Protect a Bonanza Built on Designer Jeans," *Business Week* (August 13, 1979), p. 56.

media strategy, however, it is desirable to evaluate it for viability against predeter-mined criteria.

Advertising Objectives. To build a good advertising program, it is necessary first to pinpoint the objectives of the ad campaign. It would be wrong to assume that all advertising leads directly to sales. A sale is a multiphase phenomenon, and advertising can be used for transferring the customer from one phase to the next: "Advertising attempts to move consumers from unawareness of a product or service—to awareness—to comprehension—to conviction—to action."[12] Thus, the advertiser must specify at what stage or stages he or she wants advertising to work. The objectives of advertising may be defined by any one of the following approaches.

Inventory Approach. A number of scholars have worked out an inventory of functions performed by advertising. The objectives of an ad campaign should be defined from an inventory based on a firm's overall marketing perspective. For example, the following inventory may be used to develop a firm's advertising objectives.

A. Increase sales by:
1. Encouraging potential purchasers to visit the company or its dealers
2. Obtaining leads for salesmen or dealers
3. Inducing professional people (i.e., doctors, architects) to recom-mend the product
4. Securing new distributors
5. Prompting immediate purchases through announcements of special sales and contests
B. Create an awareness about a company's product or service by:
1. Informing potential customers about product features
2. Announcing new models
3. Highlighting the unique features of the product
4. Informing customers as to where the product may be bought
5. Announcing price changes
6. Demonstrating the product in use[13]

The inventory approach is helpful in highlighting the fact that there are different objectives which can be emphasized in advertising and that the selection of objectives cannot be made without reference to overall marketing objectives. Thus, this approach helps the advertiser to avoid operating in a vacuum. How-ever, inherent in this approach is the danger that the decision maker may choose

[12]Russell H. Colley (ed.), *Defining Advertising Goals for Measured Advertising Results* (New York: Association of National Advertisers, 1961), pp. 49–60.
[13]Adapted from Harry D. Wolfe *et al., Measuring Advertising Results,* Studies in Business Policy No. 102 (New York: Conference Bd., 1962), pp. 10–11.

nonfeasible and conflicting objectives if everything listed in the inventory seems worth pursuing.

Hierarchy Approach. According to Lucas and Britt, the objectives of advertising should be stated in an action-oriented psychological form. Thus, the objectives of advertising may be defined as: gaining customers' initial attention, perception, continued favorable attention, and interest; or affecting customers' comprehension, feeling, emotion, motivation, belief, intentions, decision, imagery, association, recall, and recognition. The thesis behind this approach is that customers move from one psychological state to another before actually buying the product. Thus, the purpose of advertising should be to move customers from state to state and ultimately towards purchasing the product. While it makes sense to define the purpose of an individual ad in hierarchical terms, it may become difficult to relate the purpose so defined to marketing goals. Besides, the measurement of psychological states which form the basis of this approach will be difficult and subjective compared to the measurement of goals such as market share.[14]

Attitudinal Approach. Boyd *et al.* consider advertising to be instrumental in producing changes in attitudes and therefore suggest defining advertising goals to influence attitudinal structures. According to them, advertising may be undertaken to accomplish any of the following goals:

1. Affect those forces which influence strongly the choice of criteria used for evaluating brands belonging to the product class.
2. Add characteristic(s) to those considered salient for the product class.
3. Increase/decrease the rating for a salient product class characteristic.
4. Change the perception of the company's brand with regard to some particular salient product characteristic.
5. Change the perception of competitive brands with regard to some particular salient product characteristic.[15]

The attitudinal approach is an improvement over the hierarchical approach since it attempts to relate advertising objectives to product/market objectives. This approach indicates not only the functions which advertising will perform, but also the specific results that it will achieve.

Advertising objectives should be defined by a person completely familiar with all the product/market perspectives. A good definition of objectives is an aid in writing an appropriate ad copy and selecting the right media. It should be

---

[14]Darrell B. Lucas and Stuart H. Britt, *Measuring Advertising Effectiveness* (New York: McGraw-Hill Bk. Co., 1962), p. 16.
[15]Harper W. Boyd, Jr., Michael L. Ray, and Edward C. Strong, "An Attitudinal Framework for Advertising Strategy," *Journal of Marketing* (April, 1972), pp. 29–30.

recognized that different ad campaigns for the same product can have varied objectives. But all ad campaigns should be complementary to each other so as to maximize the total advertising impact.

Product/market advertising objectives may be used to derive media objectives. Media objectives should be defined so as to answer such questions as: Are we trying to reach everybody? Are we aiming to be selective? If housewives under 30 with children under 10 are really the target, what media objectives should be developed? Are we national or regional? Do we need to concentrate in selected counties? Do we need reach or frequency or both? Are there creative considerations which should control our thinking? Do we need color or permanence (which might mean magazines and supplements), or personalities and demonstration (which might mean TV), or the best reminder for the least money (which might mean radio or outdoor), or super selectivity (which might mean direct mail), or going all the way up and down in the market (which could mean newspapers)? The following is a sample of media objectives based on the questions raised above:

1. We need a national audience of women.
2. We want them between 18 and 34.
3. Because product is a considered purchase, we need room to explain it thoroughly.
4. We need color to show product to best advantage.
5. We have to keep after these women more than once, so we need frequency.
6. There's no way to demonstrate product except in store.[16]

Media-selection Procedure. Media-selection calls for two decisions: 1) which particular medium to use and 2) within a given medium, which specific vehicles to choose. For example, if magazines are to be used, which particular ones should ads be placed in? The following two approaches can be used in media selection: 1) cost-per-thousand-contacts comparison and 2) matching of audience and medium characteristics.

Cost-per-thousand-contacts Comparison. Traditionally the *cost-per-thousand-contacts* comparison has been the most popular method of media selection. Although simple to apply, the cost-per-thousand method leaves much to be desired. Basing media selection entirely on the number of contacts to be reached ignores the quality of contacts made. For example, an advertisement for a women's dress line appearing in *Vogue* would make more of an impact on those exposed to it than would the same ad appearing in *True Confessions.* Similarly, *Esquire* would perhaps be more appropriate than many less-specialized magazines for introducing men's fashions.

---

[16]The above discussion on media objectives is taken from William J. Colihan, Jr., "How to Read and Judge a Marketing Plan," *Financial Executive* (March, 1975), pp. 26–30.

Further, the cost-per-thousand method can be highly misleading if one considers the way in which advertisers define the term *exposure*. According to the media definition, exposure occurs as soon as an ad is inserted in the magazine. Whether the exposure actually occurs is never considered. This method also fails to consider editorial images and the impact power of different channels of a medium.

Matching of Audience and Media Characteristics. An alternative approach to media selection is to specify the target audience and match their characteristics with those of the medium. The step-by-step procedure for using this method is described below.

1. Build a profile of customers detailing who they are, where they are located, when they can be reached, and what their demographic characteristics are. Media objectives defined earlier will be helpful in building the customer profile.
2. Study media profiles in terms of audience coverage. Implicit in this step is the study of the audience's media habits (i.e., an examination of who constitutes a particular medium's audience).
3. Match the customer profiles to media profiles. The customer characteristics for a product should be matched to the audience characteristics of different media. This should lead to the preliminary selection of a medium, based primarily on the grounds of coverage.
4. The preliminary selection should be examined further in regard to product and cost considerations. For some products, other things being equal, one medium will be superior to another. For example, in the case of beauty aids a demonstration should be helpful; hence, television would be a better choice than radio. Cost is another concern in media selection; information on cost is available from the media themselves. Cost should be balanced against the benefit expected to be derived from the campaign under consideration.
5. Finally, the total budget should be allocated to the different media and the various media vehicles. The final selection of a medium should maximize the achievement of the media objectives. For example, if the objective is to make people aware of a product, then the medium selected should be one which affords optimal awareness.

Basically, two types of information are required for medium selection: customer profile and audience characteristics. The advertiser should build a customer profile for this product/market.

Information on media is usually available from media owners. Practically all media have complete information available to them concerning their audiences (demographics and circulation figures). Each medium, however, presents the information in a fashion that makes the medium look best. It is desirable, therefore, to validate the audience information supplied by the media with reference to the audit bureaus of the various media, which authenticate this information. The Audit Bureau of Circulations, the Traffic Audit Bureau, and the Business Publications Audit of Circulations are examples of such bureaus.

There are many private sources which may also be tapped to collect media-related information. One prominent source is Standard Rate and Data Service, Inc., which supplies monthly directories of rates, mechanical requirements, circulation figures, and other information about the key media. In addition, various types of specific information may be sought from such sources as American Business Press (reports annual investment by business firms in business papers), Broadcast Advertisers Report (reports the costs of all network TV programs and monitors network and local television), Leading National Advertising, Inc. (gives monthly cumulative reports of schedules and expenditures in selected national magazines and supplements), and Media Records (provides monthly cumulative reports of schedules and expenditures in daily and Sunday newspapers). Most advertising agencies subscribe to information provided by the above sources and make it available to their clients. As a matter of fact, companies with large advertising departments may also purchase the information for in-house consumption. Additionally, the ad agencies may collect primary data as well on certain aspects for the benefit of their clients.

Evaluation Criteria. Before dollars are committed to a selected medium, it is desirable to review the medium's viability against a set criteria. Colihan suggests using the following criteria to evaluate the medium decision: Is the decision maker being thorough, progressive (imaginative), measure minded, practical, and optimistic?[17] Thoroughness requires that all aspects of media selection be given full consideration. For maximum impact, the chosen medium should be progressive; i.e., it should have a unique way of doing the job. An example of progressiveness is putting a sample envelope of Sanka coffee in millions of copies of *TV Guide.* Because of postal regulations, this could not be done in a magazine that is mainly purchased through subscriptions. But *TV Guide* is mainly a newsstand magazine. Measure-mindedness refers to more than just the number of exposures. It refers not only to frequency and timing in reaching the target audience, but also to the quality of the audience; i.e., the proportion of heavy to light TV viewers reached, proportion of men to women, working to nonworking women, etc. Practicality requires choosing a medium on factual, not emotional, grounds. For example, it is not desirable to substitute a weak newspaper for a strong one just because the top management of the company does not agree with the editorial policy of the latter. Finally, the overall media plan should be optimistic in that it takes advantage of the lessons to be learned from experience.

---

[17]*Ibid.*

Advertising-copy Strategy

Copy refers to the content of an advertisement. The term is used in a broad sense to include the words, pictures, symbols, colors, layout, and other ingredients of an ad. Copywriting is a creative job, and its quality depends to a large extent on the genius of the creative person in the advertising agency or the company. However, creativity alone may not produce good ad copy. A marketing strategist needs to have his or her own perspectives on the copy (what to say, how to say it, and whom to say it to) and needs to furnish information on ad objectives, product, target customers, competitive activity, and ethical and legal considerations. The creative person will carry on from there. In brief, although copywriting may be the outcome of a flash of inspiration on the part of an advertising genius, it must have a systematic, logical, step-by-step presentation of ideas.

The point may be illustrated with reference to Perrier water, a brand of bottled water that comes from mineral springs in Southern France. In Europe this product is quite popular; in the U.S., however, it used to be a rare product available in gourmet shops only. In 1977, the company introduced the product to the U.S. market as a soft drink by tapping the adult-user market with heavy advertising. Perrier's major product distinction is that its water is naturally carbonated spring water. The product was aimed at the affluent adult population, particularly those concerned with diet and health, as a status symbol and a sign of maturity. Perrier faced competition from two sources: regular soft drink makers and potential makers of a mineral water. The company took care of the soft drink competition by segmenting the market on the basis of price (Perrier was priced 50 percent above the average soft drink) and thus avoiding direct confrontation. In regard to competition from new brands of mineral water, Perrier's association with France and the fact that it was constituted of naturally carbonated spring water were expected to continue as viable strengths. The above information was used to develop ad copy for placement in high-fashion women's magazines and in TV commercials narrated by Orson Welles. The results were astonishing. In just 18 months, at the end of 1978, sales had soared to around $30 million from less than $1 million two years before in 1976.[18]

Essentially, an ad copy constitutes an advertiser's message to the customer. To ensure that the proper message gets across, it is important that no form of noise distorts what is intended to be communicated. *Noise* may emerge from three sources: 1) dearth of facts (e.g., the company is unaware of the unique distinctions of its product); 2) competitors (e.g., competitors make changes in their marketing mix to counter the company's claims or position); and 3) behavior traits of the customers or audience. Often, the last source of noise remains a missing link in developing an ad copy. One is conveniently motivated to use one's own perspec-

---

[18]"Perrier: The Astonishing Success of an Appeal to Affluent Adults," *Business Week* (January 22, 1979), p. 64.

tives of what the customer will like or believe on the assumption that they apply to the audience as well. It is desirable, therefore, to gain, through some sort of marketing research, insights into the behavior patterns of the audience and make this information available to the creative person. For example, based on his research, Schiele provides the following clues for making an effective appeal to young consumers:

1. *Never talk down to a teenager.* While "hip" phraseology and the generally flippant tone observed in the teenager's conversation may be coin of the realm from one youngster to another, it comes across as phony, foolish, and condescending when directed at him or her by an advertiser. Sincerity is infinitely more effective than cuteness. Entertainment and attention-getting approaches by themselves do little to attract a teenager to the merits of a product. In fact, they often dissuade the youngster from making a purchase decision.

2. *Be totally, absolutely, and unswervingly straightforward.* Teenagers may act cocky and confident in front of adults, but most of them are still rather unsure of themselves and are wary of being misled. They are not sure they know enough to avoid being taken advantage of, and they do not like to risk looking foolish by falling for a commercial gimmick. Moreover, teenagers as a group are far more suspicious of things commercial than adults are. Advertising must not only be noticed; it has to be believed.

3. *Give the teenager credit for being motivated by rational values.* When making a buying selection, adults like to think they are doing so on the basis of the benefits the product or service offers. Teenagers instinctively perceive what's "really there" in an offering. Advertising must clearly expose for their consideration the value a product or service claims to represent.

4. *Be as personal as possible.* Derived from the adult world of marketing, this rule has an exaggerated importance with teenagers. In this automated age, with so many complaining of being reduced en masse to anonymity, people are becoming progressively more aware of their own individuality. The desire to be personally known and recognized is particularly strong with young people, who are urgently searching for a clear sense of their own identity.[19]

The following findings from communications research are helpful in further refining the attributes of ad copy which an advertising strategist needs to spell out for the creative person.

---

[19]George W. Schiele, "How to Reach the Young Consumer," *Harvard Business Review* (March–April, 1974), pp. 85–86.

Source Credibility. An ad may show a celebrity recommending the use of a product. It is hoped that the credibility of the celebrity will help give the ad additional credence which will, in turn, be reflected in higher sales.

Research on the subject has shown that an initially credible source, such as Miss America claiming to use a certain brand of hair spray, is more effective in changing the opinion of an audience than if a similar claim is made by a lesser-known source, such as a housewife. However, as time passes, the audience tends to forget the source or to dissociate the source from the message. Some consumers who might have been swayed in favor of a particular brand because it was recommended by Miss America may revert back to their original choices, while those who did not initially accept the housewife's word may later become favorably inclined toward the product she is recommending. The decreasing importance of the source of the message over time has been called the *sleeper effect.* [20]

Several conclusions can be drawn from the *sleeper effect.* In some cases it may be helpful if the advertiser is disassociated completely from the ad, particularly when the audience may perceive that a manufacturer is trying to push something. On the other hand, when source credibility is important, advertisements should be scheduled so that the source may reappear to reinforce the message.

Balance of Argument. When preparing copy, there is the question of whether only the good and distinctive features of a brand should be highlighted, or whether its demerits should be mentioned as well. Traditionally the slogan has been, "Put your best foot forward." In other words, the messages should be designed to emphasize only the favorable aspects of the product. Recent research in the field of communication has questioned the validity of indiscriminately detailing the favorable side. It has been noted that:

1. Presenting both sides of an issue was found to be more effective than giving only one side among individuals who were initially opposed to the point of view presented.
2. Better-educated people are more favorably affected by presentation of both sides; the poorly educated are more favorably affected by communication that gives only supporting arguments.
3. For those already convinced of the point of view presented, the presentation of both sides is less effective than a presentation featuring only those items favoring the general position being advanced.
4. Presentation of both sides is least effective among the poorly educated already convinced of the position advocated.

---

[20]See Carl I. Hoveland, Irving L. Janis, and Harold H. Kelley, *Communication and Persuasion* (New Haven, CT: Yale Univ. Press, 1953), p. 225.

5. Leaving out a relevant argument is more noticeable and detracts more from effectiveness when both sides are presented than when only the side favorable to the proposition is being advanced.[21]

These findings have important implications for developing the copy. If one is trying to reach executive customers through an ad in the *Harvard Business Review,* it probably will be better to present both favorable and unfavorable qualities of a product. On the other hand, for status products and services such as Bulova diamond watches, the Playboy Club, and Chanel No. 5 perfume, emphasis on both pros and cons can distort the image. Thus, when status is already established, a simple message is more desirable.

Message Repetition. Should the same message be repeated time and again? According to the learning theory, reinforcement over time from different directions increases learning. It has been said that a good slogan never dies and that repetition is the surest way of getting the message across. However, some feel that while the central theme should be maintained, the message should be presented with variations.

Communication research questions the value of wholesale repetition. Repetition, it has been found, leads to increased learning up to a certain point. Thereafter learning levels off and may, in fact, change to boredom and loss of attention. Continuous repetition may even counteract the good effect created earlier.[22] Thus, advertisers must keep track of the shape of the learning curve and develop a new product theme when the curve appears to be flattening out.

Rational vs. Emotional Appeals. Results of studies on the effect of rational and emotional appeals presented in advertisements are not conclusive. Some studies show that emotional appeals have definite positive results.[23] However, Cox feels that arousing emotions may not be sufficient unless the ad can rationally convince the subject that the product in question will fulfill the need.[24] It appears that emphasis on one type of appeal—rational or emotional—will not be enough. The advertiser must strike a balance between emotional and rational appeals. For example, Procter & Gamble's Crest toothpaste ad, "Crest has been recommended by the American Dental Association," has a rational content; but its reference to "cavity prevention" also excites emotions. Similarly, Lever Brothers' Close-up

---

[21]Carl I. Hoveland, Arthur A. Lumsdaine, and Fred D. Sheffield, "The Effect of Presenting 'One Side' Versus 'Both Sides' in Changing Opinions on a Controversial Subject," in Wilbur Schramm (ed.), *The Process and Effects of Mass Communication* (Urbana, IL: Univ. of Illinois Press, 1960), p. 274.

[22]Donald F. Cox, "Clues for Advertising Strategists," *Harvard Business Review* (September-October, 1961), p. 170; and "Admen Suffer from Overskill," *Business Week* (October 17, 1970), p. 132.

[23]Hoveland, Janis, and Kelley, *op. cit.,* p. 57.

[24]Cox, *op. cit.,* p. 166.

toothpaste ad is principally emotional in nature: "Put your money where your mouth is." However, it also has an economic aspect: "Use Close-up both as a toothpaste and mouthwash."

An interesting example of how emotional appeal complemented by service can get a market niche for an unknown company is provided by Singapore Airlines. Singapore is a Southeast Asian nation barely larger than Cleveland. Many airlines have tried to sell the notion that they have something unique to offer, but not many have succeeded. Singapore Airlines, however, thrives mainly on the charm of its exotic cabin hostesses, who serve the passengers with warm smiles and copious attention. A gently persuasive advertising campaign glamorizes the cabin hostess as "the Singapore girl." To convey the idea of in-flight pleasure of a lyrical quality, most of the airline's ads are essentially large, soft-focus color photographs of various hostesses. A commercial announces: "Singapore girl, you look so good I want to stay up here with you forever." Of course, its emotional ad appeals are duly supported by excellent services (rational appeals to complement emotional ones). It is claimed that the airline provides gifts, free cocktails, and free French wines and brandy to even economy-class passengers. The airline flies with an average of 74 percent of its passenger seats filled—the highest load factor of any major scheduled international carrier.[25] In brief, emotional appeal can go a long way in the development of an effective ad campaign, but it must have rational underpinnings to support it.

Humor Appeals. Researchers have expressed divergent views on the role of humor in advertising. Some feel that appeals with a humorous touch are persuasive. Others find humor to be a regional, rather than universal, phenomenon which depreciates with repetition. A recent study found humorous messages to be more effective when they did not interfere with comprehension. The study concluded that:

1. Humorous messages attract attention.
2. Humorous messages may detrimentally affect comprehension.
3. Humor may distract the audience, yielding a reduction in counterargumentation and an increase in persuasion.
4. Humorous appeals appear to be persuasive, but the persuasive effect is, at best, no greater than that of serious appeals.
5. Humor tends to enhance source credibility.
6. Audience characteristics may confound the effect of humor.
7. A humorous context may increase liking for the source and create a positive mood. This may increase the persuasive effect of the message.
8. To the extent that a humorous context functions as a positive rein-

---

[25]Louis Kraar, "Flying High with the 'Singapore Girls,' " *Fortune* (June 18, 1979), pp. 132–139.

forcer, a persuasive communication placed in such a context may be more effective.[26]

Presentation of a Model's Eyes in Pictorial Ads. Traditionally it has been known that the size of the eye's pupil reflects mental attitude. The pupil tends to expand with excitement and contract when interest is lacking. One study tried to measure the effect of the size of the pupil and the direction of the model's eyes in an ad. The study found that:

> Enlarged pupil size is indicative of favorable attitude toward others and covertly influences consumers' interests and attitude toward the communicator. Message communication appears to be influenced by the direction of the eyes, and whether their angle is consistent with the appeal of the message and the receiver's attitude toward the message. When eye direction is to the right, rational and objective thoughts are reinforced; eyes directed toward the left reinforce emotional and subjective expressions.[27]

Apparently, if properly treated, eye size and direction in the picture can increase the effectiveness of an ad.

Comparison Advertising. Comparison advertising refers to the comparison of one brand against one or more competitive brands by explicitly naming them on a variety of specific product or service attributes. Such advertising became popular in the early 1970s; today one finds comparison ads for all forms of goods and services. While it is still debatable whether or not comparative ads are more or less effective than individual ads, limited research on the subject does indicate that in some cases such ads are more useful.[28]

Many companies have successfully used comparison advertising. One that stands out is Helene Curtis Industries, Inc. Starting in 1972, the company used comparison ads on TV for its Suave brand of shampoo. The ad said: "We do what theirs does for less than half the price." Competitors were either named or their labels were clearly shown. The message—that Suave was comparable to top-ranking shampoos—was designed to allay public suspicion that low-priced merchandise is somehow shoddy. In 1972 the brand had had less than 1 percent of the $850 million retail market for shampoo. The campaign was so successful, however, that Suave's sales and market share doubled in 1973, the campaign's

[26]Brian Sternthal and C. Samuel Craig, "Humor in Advertising," *Journal of Marketing* (October, 1973), p. 12.

[27]Albert S. King, "Pupil Size, Eye Direction, and Message Appeal: Some Preliminary Findings," *Journal of Marketing* (July, 1972), p. 57.

[28]E.C. Hackleman and S.C. Jain, "An Experimental Analysis of Attitudes Toward Comparison and Non-Comparison Advertising," in William L. Wilkie (ed.), *Advances in Consumer Research,* Proceedings, Association for Consumer Research Conference, Miami, October 26–29, 1978, pp. 90–94.

first full year, and nearly doubled again in 1974. In 1976 Suave surpassed both Procter & Gamble's Head & Shoulders and Johnson & Johnson's Baby Shampoo in volume.[29] Clearly, comparison advertising provides an underdog with the chance to make a comeback.

PERSONAL SELLING STRATEGIES

Selling Strategy

There was a time when the problems of selling were simpler than they are today. For example, in 1971 material shortages and spiraling costs produced a variety of changes in the selling strategies of businesses. The story is told of a drilling rig company in Texas which ordered a huge quantity of steel plate from the Los Angeles-based metal distributor, Ducommun Inc. Ducommun could not possibly fill the order from its regular sources. To help the customer out, the Ducommun salesperson searched around and found a Rumanian factory which could supply steel plates to the drilling company. A Ducommun executive remarked, "Our salesmen have turned consultants on everything from scheduling a customer's future needs to drumming up substitute materials."[30] Apparently the complexities involved in selling in the 1970s required different perspectives than those in the 1960s. The 1980s may call for a still different selling strategy. Discussed below are objectives and strategic matters pertaining to selling strategies.

Objectives. Selling objectives should be derived from overall marketing objectives and properly linked with promotional objectives. For example, if the marketing goal is to raise the current 35-percent market share in a product line to 40 percent, the sales manager may stipulate the objective to increase sales of specific product items by different percentage points in various sales regions under his or her control.

The sales management objectives may be broken down further into objectives for each region and even for each salesperson within a region. Using as a base the total sales management objectives, each sales office may work out its own objectives in terms of sales quotas for its territories and customers. The quotas may be further subdivided for each salesperson, who may set his or her own objectives (i.e., whom to call on and with what frequency, and which strategies to employ to sell to different customers).

Selling objectives are usually defined in terms of sales volume. The objectives, however, may also be defined for: 1) gross margin targets, 2) maximum expendi-

---

[29]Gwen Kinkead, "A 'Me Too' Strategy That Paid Off," *Fortune* (August 27, 1979), pp. 86–89.

[30]"The Salesman's New Job: Drumming Up Suppliers," *Business Week* (October 26, 1974), p. 54.

ture levels, and 3) fulfillment of specific activities, such as converting a stated number of competitors' customers into company customers.

The sales strategist should also specify the role of selling in terms of personal-selling push (vis-a-vis advertising pull). This decision will depend on the consumer decision process, the influence of different communication alternatives, and the cost of these alternatives. Personal selling introduces flexibility and helps to offer tailor-made, customer-to-customer sales presentation. Further, personal selling offers an opportunity to develop a tangible personal rapport with the customer which can go far toward building a long-term relationship. Finally, personal selling is the only method which can secure immediate feedback. This helps in taking timely corrective action and avoiding mistakes. The benefits of personal selling, however, must be considered in relation to its costs. For example, according to the research department of the McGraw-Hill Publications Company, per-call personal selling expenditures for all types of personal selling in 1977 came to $96.79, up by 36 percent from 1975.* Thus, the high impact of personal selling should be considered in light of its high cost.

Strategic Matters. As a part of selling strategy, several strategic matters should be resolved. The decision must be made as to whether greater emphasis should be put on maintaining existing accounts or on converting customers. According to one study, the retention and conversion of customers is related to the time salespeople spend with them.[31] Thus, before salespeople can make the best use of their efforts, they must know how much importance can be attached to each of the two functions of retention and conversion. The decision is influenced by such factors as the growth status of the industry, the company's strengths and weaknesses, the competitors' strengths, and marketing goals. For example, a manufacturer of laundry detergent will think twice before attempting to convert customers from Tide (Procter & Gamble's brand) to its own brand. On the other hand, there may be factors which make a company challenge the leader. For example, Bic Pen Corp. is aggressively promoting its disposable razor among Gillette's customers. The decision to maintain or convert customers cannot be made in isolation, but must be considered in the context of the total marketing strategy.

Another aspect of selling strategy deals with the question of who should be contacted in the customer organization. The buying process may be divided into four phases: consideration, acceptance, selection, and evaluation. Different executives in the customer organization may exert influence on any of the four phases. The sales strategist may work out a plan specifying which salesperson should call

---

*The same source noted that the larger the sales force, the lower the cost. For instance, companies with fewer than 10 salespeople spent $128.69 per call; companies with more than 50 spent $70.06. This underscores the significance of the experience effect.
[31]"Penstock Press," a case study copyrighted by the President and Fellows of Harvard College, 1966.

upon whom in the customer organization and when. On occasion, a person other than the salesperson may be asked to call on the customer. Sometimes as a matter of selling strategy a team of people may visit the customer. For example, Northrop Corp., an aerospace contractor, assigns aircraft designers and technicians—not salesmen—to call on potential customers. When Singapore indicated interest in Northrop's F-5 fighter, Northrop dispatched a team to Singapore that included an engineer, a lawyer, a pricing expert, a test pilot, and a maintenance specialist.[32]

Van Leer cites this example from the literature: A manufacturer of vinyl acetate latex (used as a paint base of latex paint) built its sales volume by having its people call on the "right people" in the customer organization. The manufacturer recognized that its product was used by the customer to produce paint which is sold through its marketing department, not the purchasing agent or manager of research. So the manufacturer planned for its people to meet with the customer's sales and marketing personnel to find out what their problems were, what kept them from selling more latex paint, and what role the manufacturer could play (concerning the supply of vinyl acetate latex) to help the customer. It was only after the marketing personnel had been sold on the product that the purchasing department was contacted.[33] Thus, a good selling strategy requires a careful analysis of the situation, which helps to determine the key people to contact in the customer organization. A simple routine call on the purchasing agent may not suffice.

The selling strategy should also determine the size of the sales force needed to perform an effective job. This decision is usually made intuitively. A company starts with a few salespeople, adding more as it gains experience. Some companies may go a step beyond the intuitive approach to determine how many salespeople should be recruited. For instance, consideration may be given to factors such as the number of customers who must be visited, the amount of market potential in a territory, and so on. But all these factors are weighed subjectively. Discussed below are three different methods which may be employed in making an objective decision about the optimum size of the sales force.

Semlow recommends a step-by-step procedure for deciding how much should be spent on personal selling. He believes additional salespeople should be hired to the point where profit on sales generated by the additional staff is greater than or equal to the cost of these employees. Algebraically, this reads as follows:

$$S(p) - C \text{ is greater than } 0.$$

S refers to the sales volume each additional salesperson is likely to produce, p is the expected profit margin on additional sales volume, and C denotes the total

---

[32]Louis Kraar, "Everyone at Northrop Is in Marketing," *Fortune* (April 10, 1978), pp. 52–55.
[33]R. Karl van Leer, "Industrial Marketing with a Flair," *Harvard Business Review* (November-December, 1976), pp. 117–124.

cost of maintaining the additional staff. In this equation the values of p and C are usually known. A company can devise its own methods for computing the value of S. Semlow has elaborated his procedure with an example. He discusses a simple case of 25 one-person territories. Semlow's method consists of:

1. Computing sales per one percent of potential for each territory by dividing its dollar sales with the percentage of the total potential for the same territory.

2. Smoothing out a trend line of sales volume per one percent of potential for territories of various sizes. This is achieved by plotting the percentage of potential of each territory and sales volume per one percent of potential on a graph.

3. Assigning a number of salespeople to territories based on different average percentage potentials, and computing sales per average salesperson in each case (assuming one salesperson for one percent of total potential). If territory size were taken to be .5 percent, 200 salesmen would be employed. Further, if sales per one percent of potential (with .5-percent-size territory) were $20,000, total sales would be $200,000. Dividing $200,000 by the number of salespeople, the sales per average salesperson comes to $1,000.

This process is repeated with different average territory sizes in percentages such as two percent, three percent, etc. Semlow's analysis shows that sales increased with the number of salespeople in territories rated high, but the increase in sales was less than proportionate to the increase in sales potential.

Semlow's method continues with the following procedures:

4. Estimating operating profit after deducting all costs from sales volume computed in point 3 above.

5. Determining total investment—plant investment and working capital—required at alternative sales volume.

6. Expressing operating profit as a ratio to sales volume and investment.

Semlow found that both these ratios were highest with 65 salespeople (in the case he was considering), which was then considered to be the optimum size of the sales force. With experience, one can derive a curve for various categories of products for ready reference as to the number of people needed for the selling job. Semlow's approach considers territorial sales potential to be the crucial factor in determining the size of the sales force.[34]

Talley proposes a method based on the work load for determining the size of the sales force. He suggests grouping major customers into different categories

[34]Walter J. Semlow, "How Many Salesmen Do You Need?" *Harvard Business Review* (May-June, 1959), pp. 126–132.

according to the desired frequency of calls. From this estimate, the total number of calls that must be made in a year is divided by the average number of calls a salesperson can make in a year. This gives the number of salespeople needed. Talley's method can be stated mathematically:

$$N = \frac{\sum_{i=1}^{n} (C_i \, F_i)}{P}$$

In the above formula:

N = desirable number of salespeople.

C_i = number of customers in class size i.

F_i = required number of annual calls for customers in class i.

P = average number of calls made by a salesperson annually.

n = number of customer classes.

Suppose that a company has 10 customers to be called on 100 times a year, 80 customers to be called on 50 times a year, 140 customers to be contacted 10 times a year, and 500 customers to be called on twice a year. Further, it is expected that a salesperson can make an average of 200 calls a year. Using Talley's approach, this company needs 37 salespeople, as shown below.

$$N = \frac{10 \times 100 + 80 \times 50 + 140 \times 10 + 500 \times 2}{200}$$
$$= 7400/200 = 37$$

The size of the sales force can also be determined by comparing the expected monetary values of various sizes of sales forces of salesmen in relationship to different market potentials. In other words, given the various levels of potential projections in a territory, different profits will accrue depending on the size of the sales force. Profit estimates for each market potential will give the expected values when multiplied by a probability of potential being realized. A summation of expected values for each decision rule (size of the sales force) can be prepared in order to pick the one which is highest. This specifies the desired number of salespeople.[35]

Examined above are the major strategic issues involved in developing selling strategy. In addition, matters of price concessions (within the limits of law) to

---

[35]Walter J. Talley, "How to Design Sales Territories," *Journal of Marketing* (January, 1961), pp. 7–13.

different customers and trial installations of the company's products on selected customers' premises may also occasionally require strategic inputs.

Sales-motivation-and-supervision Strategy

To ensure that salespersons perform to their utmost capacity, they must be adequately motivated and properly supervised. Often it has been found that salespeople fail to do well because the management has failed to carry out its part of the job, especially in the area of motivation and supervision. While motivation and supervision may appear to be mundane day-to-day matters, they have far-reaching implications for marketing strategy. The purpose of this section is to give insights into the strategic aspects of motivation and supervision.

Motivation. Salespeople may be motivated through both financial and nonfinancial means. Financial motivation is provided by monetary compensation. Nonfinancial motivation is usually tied in with evaluation programs.

Compensation. People work to make a living; their motivation to work is deeply affected by the remuneration they receive. A well-designed compensation plan keeps turnover low and helps to increase the salesperson's productivity. A compensation plan should be simple; understandable; flexible (cognizant of the differences between individuals); and economically equitable. It should also provide incentive and build up morale. It should not penalize the salespeople for conditions beyond their control, and it should help in developing new business, provide stable income, and, above all, meet the objectives of the corporation. Some of these requisites may conflict with each other. Thus, there cannot be any perfect plan. All that can be done is to balance each variable properly and design a custom-made plan for each sales force. It is conceivable that within the same company there may be different compensation plans for the two sales forces.

Different methods of compensating salespeople are: the salary plan, commission plan, and combination plan. Exhibit 12-2 shows the relative advantages and disadvantages of each plan.

EXHIBIT 12-2 Advantages and Disadvantages of Various Sales-compensation Alternatives

SALARY PLAN

<u>Advantages</u>
1. Assures a regular income.
2. Develops a high degree of loyalty.
3. Makes it simple to switch territories or quotas or to reassign salesmen.
4. Ensures that nonselling activities will be performed.
5. Facilitates administration.
6. Provides relatively fixed sales costs.

Disadvantages
   1. Fails to give balanced sales mix because salesmen would concentrate on products with greatest customer appeal.
   2. Provides little, if any, financial incentive for the salesman.
   3. Offers few reasons for putting forth extra effort.
   4. Favors salesmen or saleswomen who are the least productive.
   5. Tends to increase direct selling costs over other types of plans.
   6. Creates the possibility of salary compression where new trainees may earn almost as much as experienced salesmen.

COMMISSION PLAN

Advantages
   1. Pay relates directly to performance and results achieved.
   2. System is easy to understand and compute.
   3. Salesmen have the greatest possible incentive.
   4. Unit sales costs are proportional to net sales.
   5. Company's selling investment is reduced.

Disadvantages
   1. Emphasis is more likely to be on volume than on profits.
   2. Little or no loyalty to the company is generated.
   3. Wide variances in income between salesmen may occur.
   4. Salesmen are encouraged to neglect nonselling duties.
   5. Some salesmen may be tempted to "skim" their territories.
   6. Service aspect of selling may be slighted.
   7. Problems arise in cutting territories or shifting men or accounts.
   8. Pay is often excessive in boom times and very low in recession periods.
   9. Salesmen may sell themselves rather than the company and stress short-term rather than long-term relationships.
  10. Highly paid salesmen may be reluctant to move into supervisory or managerial positions.
  11. Excessive turnover of sales personnel occurs when business turns bad.

COMBINATION PLAN

Advantages
   1. Offers participants the advantages of both salary and commission.
   2. Provides greater range of earnings possibilities.
   3. Gives salesmen greater security because of steady base income.
   4. Makes possible a favorable ratio of selling expense to sales.
   5. Compensates salesmen for all activities.
   6. Allows a greater latitude of motivation possibilities so that goals and objectives can be achieved on schedule.

Disadvantages
   1. Is often complex and difficult to understand.
   2. Can, where low salary and high bonus or commission exist, develop a bonus

that is too high a percentage of earnings; when sales fall, salary is too low to retain salesmen.

3. Is sometimes costly to administer.

4. Can, unless a decreasing commission rate for increasing sales volume exists, result in a "windfall" of new accounts and a runaway of earnings.

5. Has a tendency to offer too many objectives at one time so that really important one can be neglected, forgotten, or overlooked.

Source: Reprinted by permission of the *Harvard Business Review.* Excerpts from "How to Pay Your Sales Force" by John P. Steinbrink (July–August, 1978), pp. 111–122. Copyright © 1978 by the President and Fellows of Harvard College. All rights reserved.

The greatest virtue of the straight-salary method is the guaranteed income and security that it provides. However, it fails to provide any incentive to the ambitious salesperson and therefore may adversely affect productivity. Most companies work on a combination plan, which means that salespeople receive a percentage of sales as commission for exceeding the periodic quotas set for them. Conceptually, the first step in designing a compensation plan is to define the objective (such as rewarding extraordinary performance, providing security, and so on). Every company would probably prefer to grant some security to its people and, at the same time, distinguish the top employees through incentive schemes. In designing such a plan, the company may determine the going salary rate for the type of sales staff which it is interested in hiring. The company should match the market rate and retain people of caliber. The total wage should be fixed somewhere near the market rate after making adjustments for the company's overall wage policy, environment, and fringe benefits.

A study of the income spending habits of those in the salary range of salespeople should be made. Based on this study, the percentage of nondiscretionary spending may be linked to an incentive income scheme whereby extra income could be paid as commission on sales or as a bonus, or both. Care must be taken in constructing a compensation plan. In addition to being equitable, the plan should be simple enough to be comprehensible by the salespeople. Webster recommends the following procedure for constructing a compensation plan:

1. Establish clear and consistent compensation objectives, such as guaranteed income, stimulation, individual sales incentives, group incentives, and flexibility for local modification.

2. Determine the level of income for each salesperson.

3. Establish the proportions of fixed and incentive income.

4. Select measurement criteria for each component. For example, the size of the fixed component may be determined by the amount of servicing, follow-up work, and prospecting required. The incentive component may be determined by some measure of sales volume, such as total sales in dollars, in units, or the gross formula.

5.   Establish the compensation formula.

6.   Pretest the formula.[36]

Once compensation has been established for an individual, it is difficult to reduce it. It is desirable, therefore, for management to consider all the pros and cons of fixed compensation for a salesperson before finalizing a salary agreement. While it is always possible to revise wages upwards, people are seldom penalized downwards. This raises an important ethical and managerial problem. Doesn't the equality concept demand periodic adjustments—both upward and downward —to the compensation? Some blue-collar workers are paid a piece rate and can be penalized for a bad showing. However, in white-collar jobs such as that of a salesperson, no such penalties are planned. Thus, initial salary fixation achieves importance.

Evaluation. Evaluation is the measurement of a salesperson's contribution to corporate goals. For any evaluation, one needs standards. Establishment of standards, however, is a difficult task, particularly when salespeople are asked to perform different types of jobs. In pure selling jobs, quotas can be set for minimal performance, and salespeople achieving these quotas can be considered as doing satisfactory work. Achievement of quotas can be classified as follows: those exceeding quotas between 1 to 15 percent may be designated as average salespeople; those between 16 to 30 percent, well-performing; and, finally, those over 30 percent can be considered extraordinary salespeople. Sales contests and awards, both financial and nonfinancial, may be instituted to give recognition to salespeople in various categories. For example, NCR Corporation awards its well-performing salespeople with membership in its prestigious 100-points club (CPC). Nonfinancial awards are especially helpful in building morale and aspirations.

Subjective criteria may be used for measuring other work that a salesperson performs. Some companies use an evaluation form, such as the one shown in Exhibit 12-3 which is used by a paper manufacturer. The evaluation form reflects a salesperson's personality, attitude, and habits on the job as well as in interactions with associates and the company. In all, there are eleven criteria rated on a scale from 0 to 10. Salespeople who score high (i.e., come out as outstanding) may be given awards in recognition of their performances. Awards may also be instituted for those in the excellent category.

What should be done about the salespeople who repeatedly fail to perform according to standards? Miner suggests that, first, the underlying reasons for failure should be established. These may fall into the following categories: lack of intelligence and job knowledge, emotional problems, lack of motivation, physical disorders, family problems, problems with the groups at work, mistakes

---

[36]Fred E. Webster, Jr., "Rationalizing Salesmen's Compensation Plans," *Journal of Marketing* (January, 1966), pp. 55–58, as quoted in G. David Hughes, *Marketing Management* (Reading, MA: Addison-Wesley Publishing Co., 1978), p. 393.

EXHIBIT 12-3 Salesperson Evaluation Form

Performance Criteria	Point Award*				
	10 Out- standing	8 Excellent	5 Average	2 Poor	0 Unsatis- factory
1. Personal Habits (Appearance, absentee record, punctuality, etc.)					
2. Administrative Management (Timeliness, thoroughness, promptness of correspondence and other details involving cus- tomers and internal company. Does salesperson plan time wisely)					
3. Attitude (Overall, to company and to others—Is he or she leader type)					
4. Continuing Education (Effort toward a better under- standing of the business, its technology, the business envi- ronment, etc.—as evidenced by continuing education efforts— both within and outside the company)					
5. Outside Activities (Within the business such as graphic arts organizations, salespeople's associations, and/or community or other affairs that relate to his or her standing and impor- tance within the industry or community and enhance both the salesperson's personal image and the company's)					
6. Customer Feedback (What do the customers say about the salesperson—has he or she impressed them sufficiently to war- rant a compliment; while unsol- icited, they are of most value, the regional manager will prob- ably want to solicit feedback where it is not forthcoming)					
7. Care Of Company Property & Finances (What is the record in regard to company cars, the wiseness of expenditures on expense ac- count; the settlement of R&A's, etc.)					

	Point Award*				
Performance Criteria	**10** **Out-** **standing**	**8** **Excellent**	**5** **Average**	**2** **Poor**	**0** **Unsatis-** **factory**
8. Sales Training, Customer Education, etc. (What is the track record in sales meeting-number and effective- ness; what other education or training has salesperson inaugurated for customers; how effective is he or she before these groups; manner and content of presentation)					
9. Specifications Effort (What is the extent and effec- tiveness of the salesperson's specifications efforts. Is he or she spending time conscien- tiously and aggressively in this area. If possible, measure re- sults)					
10. Market Development (Addition of new merchants or customers; improvements in ex- isting)					
11. Merchandising Ability (The extent and creativity with which salesperson uses advertising, promotional and public rela- tions tools, and products de- veloped within the company; or those that he or she has developed alone or in conjunction with a merchant or customer)					

*11 award categories were established with points that ranged from 0 to 10. That meant 110 points were possible to achieve. If $30 a point was awarded as bonus, an average performance warranted 55 points × $30 = $1,650 as bonus award, while an outstanding rated $3,300. In order to further award the top performers, there was an additional cash award to top 5 or 10 salespeople, i.e.,

#1—$3000
#2—$2000
#3—$1500
#4—$1000
#5—$ 500

Source: Subhash C. Jain and Iqbal Mathur, *Cases in Marketing Management* (Columbus, OH: Grid Publishing, 1978), pp. 371–372.

on the part of the company, and conflict with societal values and situational forces.[37]

After investigating the reasons for someone's poor performance, the sales strategist should take action to correct the situation, such as training, professional help, or transfer. If the company cannot do anything to add to the performance of a salesperson, dismissal may be the appropriate solution.

Supervision. Despite the best efforts in selecting, training, and compensating, salespeople may not perform as expected. Supervision is important to ensure that salespeople provide the services expected of them. Supervision is defined in a broader sense to include assignment of territory to a salesperson, control over his or her activities, and communication with the salesperson in the field.

Assignment. Salespeople are assigned to different geographic territories. An assignment requires solving two problems: 1) forming territories so that each is as much alike as possible in business potential, and 2) assigning territories so that each salesperson is able to realize his or her full potential. Territories may be formed by analyzing customers' locations and the potential business they represent. Customers can be categorized as having high, average, or low potential. Further, probabilities in terms of sales can be assigned to indicate how much potential is realizable. Thus, a territory with a large number of high-potential customers with a high probability of buying may be smaller in size (geographically speaking) than a territory with a large number of low-potential customers with a low probability of buying.

Matching salespeople to the territories should not be difficult once the territories have been laid out. Regional preferences and the individual affiliations of the salespeople require that employees be placed where they will be happiest. It may be difficult to attract salespeople to some territories, while some places may be in great demand. Living in big metropolitan areas is expensive and not always comfortable. Similarly, people may avoid places with poor weather conditions. It may become necessary to provide extra compensation to salespeople assigned to unpopular places.

Control. Although salespeople are their own bosses in the field, the manager must keep informed of their activities. To achieve that control, a system must be evolved for maintaining communication with employees in the field, for guiding their work, and for employing remedial methods if performance slackens. Firms use different types of control devices. Some companies require salespeople to fill in a call form giving all particulars about each visit to each customer. Some require their salesmen to submit weekly reports on the work performed during the previous week. Salespeople may be asked to complete several forms about

---

[37]John B. Miner, *Management of Ineffective Performance* (New York: McGraw-Hill Bk. Co., 1972).

sales generated, special problems they face, market information collected, and so on. Using a good reporting system to control the sales force should have a positive influence on performance.

Communication. Management communicates with salespeople through periodic mailings, regional and national conferences, and telephone calls. There are two areas of communication in which management needs to be extra careful to maintain the morale of good salespeople: 1) in representing the problems of the field force to people at the headquarters, and 2) in giving patient consideration to the salespeople's complaints. A sales manager serves as the link between the people in the field and the company and must try to bring their problems and difficulties to the attention of top management at the head office. Top management, not being fully aware of the operations in the field, may fail to appreciate the problems. It is, therefore, the duty of the sales manager to keep the top management fully posted about field activities and secure for the salespeople their favors. For example, a salesperson in a mountainous area may not be able to maintain the work tempo during the winter due to weather conditions. Management must consider this factor in reviewing the salesperson's work. There may also be occupational or personal problems bothering the salespeople, and it is the manager's duty to stand by and help.

Close rapport with the salespeople and patient listening can be very helpful in recognizing and solving the salespeople's problems. More often than not, a salesperson's problem is something the company can take care of with a little effort and expenditure if it is only willing to accept such responsibility. The primary thing, however, is to know the salesperson's mind. This is where the role of the supervisor comes in. It is said that the sales manager should be as much a behaviorist for solving salespeople's problems as the latter should be for handling customer's problems.

SUMMARY

Promotion strategies are directed toward establishing communication with the customers. Three types of promotion strategies may be distinguished. Advertising strategies are concerned with communication transmitted through mass media. Personal selling strategies refer to face-to-face interaction with the customer. All other forms of communication, such as sampling, demonstration, cents off, contests, etc., are known as sales promotion strategies. There were two main promotion strategies which were examined in this chapter. The first was the promotion-expenditure strategy, which deals with the question of how much may be spent on the overall promotion. The second was the promotion-mix strategy, which specifies the roles which the three ingredients of promotion (i.e., advertising, personal selling, and sales promotion) play in promoting a business.

Discussed also were two advertising strategies. The first is media-selection strategy, which focuses on the choice of different media to launch an ad campaign.

The second is advertising-copy strategy, which deals with the development of appropriate ad copy to convey the intended message. The personal selling strategies examined here were selling strategy and sales-motivation-and-supervision strategy. The selling strategy emphasizes the approach that may be adopted to interact with the customer (i.e., who may call on the customer, whom to call on in the customer organization, when, and how frequently). The sales-motivation-and-supervision strategy is concerned with the management of the sales force and refers to such issues as sales compensation, nonfinancial incentives, territory formation and salespeople assignment, control, and communication.

Examples from marketing literature were cited to illustrate the practical application of each strategy.

DISCUSSION QUESTIONS

1. Outline promotion objectives for a packaged food product, a small appliance, and a stereo system in assumed market segments.
2. Develop a promotion-expenditure strategy for a household computer to be marketed through a large retail chain.
3. Will promotion-expenditure strategy for a product in the growth stage of the product life cycle be different from that for a product in the maturity stage? Discuss.
4. How may a promotion budget be allocated among advertising, personal selling, and sales promotion? Can a simulation model be developed to figure out optimum promotion mix?
5. Illustrate with the help of an example how linear programming may be used in media selection.
6. Is comparison advertising socially desirable? Comment.
7. Should the media decision be made before or after the copy is first developed? Discuss.
8. Are emotional or rational appeals more effective? Are emotional appeals relevant for all consumer products?

Part Three
Product Portfolio Management

CHAPTER 13 – Developing a Product Portfolio

Chapter 13
Developing a Product Portfolio

All men can see these tactics whereby I conquer, but what none can see is the strategy out of which victory is evolved.

Sun Tzy

The previous chapters dealt with strategy development for individual product/market segments. Different product/market strategies must ultimately be judged from the viewpoint of the total organization before being implemented. In today's environment most companies operate with a variety of products/markets. Even if a company is primarily involved in a single broad business area, it may actually be operating in multiple product/market segments. From a strategy angle, the different products/markets or businesses of a company may have different roles to play. This chapter is devoted to the analysis of the different businesses of an organization so that each may be assigned the unique role for which it is suited, thus maximizing the long-term growth and earnings of the company.

Years ago Peter Drucker suggested classifying products into six categories which reveal whether the potential for future sales growth is present. These are: tomorrow's bread winners, today's bread winners, products capable of becoming net contributors if something drastic is done, yesterday's breadwinners, the "also rans," and the failures. Drucker's classification provides an interesting scheme for determining whether a company is developing enough new products to ensure future growth and profits.

Usually a company discovers that some of its products are competitively well placed, while others are not. Since resources, particularly cash resources, are limited, not all products can be treated alike. In other words, strategically different products must be treated differently. In this chapter three different frameworks are presented to enable management to select the optimum combination of individual product/market strategies from a spectrum of possible alternatives and opportunities open to the company, still satisfying the resource limitations within which the company must operate.

The first framework to be discussed, product life cycle, is a tool which many marketers have traditionally used to formulate marketing strategies for different products. The second framework was developed by the Boston Consulting Group and is commonly called the product portfolio approach. The third one, the multifactor portfolio approach, owes its development to the General Electric Company.

PRODUCT LIFE CYCLE (PLC)

Products tend to go through different stages, each stage being affected by different competitive conditions. These stages require different marketing strategies at different times if sales and profits are to be efficiently realized. The length of a product's life cycle is in no way a fixed period of time. It can last from weeks to years, depending on the type of product. The discussion of PLC in most texts portrays the sales history of a typical product as following an S-shaped curve. The curve is divided into four stages known as introduction, growth, maturity, and decline. (Some authors have included a stage called saturation.) Exhibit 13-1 illustrates a typical PLC curve showing the relationship between profits and corresponding sales throughout the product life cycle.

EXHIBIT 13-1   Product Life Cycle

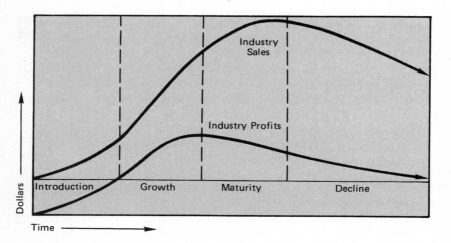

Introduction is the period during which initial market acceptance is in doubt; thus, it is a period of slow growth. Profits are almost nonexistent due to high marketing and other expenses. Setbacks in the product's development, manufacturing, and market introduction exact a heavy toll, but survivors enjoy a period of rapid *growth.* During this period there is substantial profit improvement. During the next stage, *maturity,* there is intense rivalry for a mature market which might be limited to replacements and new population. This leads to a proliferation of sizes, colors, attachments, and other product variants. Battling to retain the company's share, each marketer steps up persuasive advertising, opens new channels of distribution, and grants price concessions. Unless new competitors are obstructed by patents or other barriers, entry is easy. Thus, maturity is a period when sales growth slows down and profits peak and then start to decline. Finally, there is the *decline* period. Though sales and profits continue their downward trend, the declining product is not necessarily unprofitable. Some of the competition may have been removed by this stage. Customers who remain committed to the old product may be willing to use standard models, pay higher prices, and buy at selected outlets. Promotional expenses can also be retrenched.

PLC is a useful concept which may serve as an important aid in marketing planning and strategy. A concept familiar to most marketers, it is given a prominent place in any marketing textbook. Despite all this, its use in practice remains limited. This is due partly to the lack of normative models available for its application and partly to the vast amount of data needed for, and subjectivity involved in, its use in practice. As a matter of fact, the PLC concept has many times been criticized for its lack of relevance to businesspeople. Years ago Buzzell remarked: "There is very little empirical evidence to show how the life cycles operate and how they are related to competition and marketing strategy."[1] A few years ago, Dhalla and Yuspeh challenged the whole concept of product life cycle. They contend that PLC has led many companies to make costly mistakes and pass up promising opportunities.[2] Such criticism of PLC may, in effect, be attributed to the lack of a research base on the subject. As Levitt has said:

> Most alert and thoughtful senior marketing executives are by now familiar with the concept of the product life cycle. Even a handful of uniquely cosmopolitan and up-to-date corporate presidents have familiarized themselves with this tantalizing concept. Yet a recent survey I took of such executives found none who used the concept in any strategic way whatever and pitifully few who used it in any kind of tactical way. It has remained—as have so many fascinating theories in economics, physics, and sex—a remarkably durable but almost totally unemployed and seemingly unemployable piece of professional baggage whose presence in the rhetoric of professional discussions adds a much-coveted but apparently unattainable legitimacy to the idea that marketing management is somehow a profession.

---

[1]Robert D. Buzzell, "Competitive Behavior and Product Life Cycles," in John S. Wright and Jac L. Goldstucker (eds.), *New Ideas for Successful Marketing* (Chicago, IL: American Marketing Association, 1966), p. 47.
[2]Nariman K. Dhalla and Sonia Yuspeh, "Forget the Product Life Cycle Concept," *Harvard Business Review* (January-February, 1976) pp. 102–109.

The concept of the product life cycle is today at about the stage that the Copernican view of the universe was 300 years ago: a lot of people know about it, but hardly anybody seems to use it in any effective or productive way.[3]

While Levitt's criticism is very penetrating, many academicians and practitioners feel that even in its present stage of development, PLC has proved to be remarkably durable because it has been valuable to those who know how to use it. Smallwood claims:

The product life cycle is a useful concept. It is the equivalent of the periodic table of the elements in the physical sciences. The maturation of production technology and product configuration along with marketing programs proceeds in an orderly, somewhat predictable course over time with the merchandising nature and marketing environment noticeably similar between products that are in the same stage of their life cycle. Its use as a concept in forecasting, pricing, advertising, product planning, and other aspects of marketing management can make it a valuable concept, although considerable amounts of judgment must be used in its application.[4]

One caution which is in order in using PLC is to keep in mind that not all products follow the typical life cycle pattern indiscriminately. According to Kotler, a product may be conceived as a product class (cola drink), a product form (diet cola), and a brand (Tab). Among these, the PLC concept is most relevant for product forms.[5] Despite criticism and limitations, it is important not to lose sight of the PLC concept of basing marketing strategies on the position of a product in its life cycle.

Locating Products in Their Life Cycles

The easiest way to locate a product in its life cycle is to study its performance, competitive history, and current position and match this information with the characteristics of a particular stage of the life cycle. Analysis of past performance of the product will include:

1. Examination of sales-growth progression since introduction
2. Any design problems and technical bugs which need to be sorted out
3. Sales and profit history of allied products (those similar in general character or function as well as those directly competitive)

---

[3]Theodore Levitt, "Exploit the Product Life Cycle," *Harvard Business Review* (November-December, 1965), p. 81.
[4]John E. Smallwood, "The Product Life Cycle: A Key to Strategic Marketing Planning," *MSU Business Topics* (Winter, 1973), p. 35.
[5]Philip Kotler, *Marketing Management* (Englewood Cliffs, NJ: Prentice-Hall, 1976), pp. 232–233.

4. Number of years the product has been on the market
5. Casualty history of similar products in the past

The review of competition will focus on:

1. Profit history
2. Ease of entry with which other firms can get into the business
3. Extent of initial investment needed to enter the business
4. Number of competitors and their strengths
5. Number of competitors which left the industry
6. Life cycle of the industry
7. Critical factors for success in the business

Additionally, current perspectives may be reviewed to gauge whether sales are on the upswing, have leveled out for the last couple of years, or are heading down; whether any competitive products are moving up to replace the product under consideration; whether customers are becoming demanding vis-a-vis price, service, or special features; whether additional sales efforts are necessary to keep the sales going up; and whether it is harder to sign up dealers and distributors.

The above information on the product may be related to the characteristics of the different stages of the product life cycle as discussed above; the PLC stage with which the product perspectives match will indicate the position of the product in its life cycle. Needless to say, the whole process is highly qualitative in nature, and managerial intuition and judgment will bear heavily on the final placement of the product in its life cycle.

A slightly different approach for locating a product in its life cycle has been recommended by Clifford. He suggests the use of past accounting information for the purpose. Listed below are Clifford's steps which may be followed to position a product in its life cycle:

1. Develop historical trend information for a period of three to five years (longer for some products). Data included will be unit and dollar sales, profit margins, total profit contribution, return on invested capital, market share, and prices.
2. Check recent trends in the number and nature of competitors; number and market-share rankings of competing products, and their quality and performance advantages; shifts in distribution channels; and relative advantages enjoyed by products in each channel.
3. Analyze development in short-term competitive tactics such as competitors' recent announcements of new products or plans for expanding production capacity.
4. Obtain (or update) historical information on the life cycles of similar or related products.
5. Project sales for the product over the next three to five years, based on all the information gathered, and estimate an incremental profit ratio for the product during each of these years (the ratio of total

direct costs—manufacturing, advertising, product development, sales, distribution, etc.—to pretax profits). Expressed as a ratio— e.g., 4.8 to 1 or 6.3 to 1—this measures the number of dollars required to generate each additional dollar of profit. The ratio typically improves (becomes lower) as the product enters its growth period; begins to deteriorate (rise) as the product approaches maturity; and climbs more sharply as it reaches obsolescence.

6. Estimate the number of profitable years remaining in the product's life cycle, and—based on all the information at hand—fix the product's position on its life-cycle curve: 1) introduction, 2) early or late growth, 3) early or late maturity, or 4) early or late obsolescence.[6]

Developing a Portfolio

The current product-life-cycle positions of different products may be determined by following the above procedure, and the net results (i.e., the cash flow and profitability) of these positions may be computed. Similar analyses may be performed for a future time period. The difference between the current and future positions will indicate what results management may expect if no strategic changes are made. These results may be compared with corporate expectations to determine the gap. The gap can be filled either by making strategic changes to extend the product life cycle of a product, or by bringing in new products through research and development or acquisition. The above procedure may be put into operation by following the steps given below:

1. Determine what percentages of the company's sales and profits fall within each phase of the product life cycle. These percentage figures indicate the present life-cycle (sales) profile and the present profit profile of the company's current line.

2. Calculate changes in the life-cycle and profit profiles over the past five years, and project these profiles over the next five years.

3. Develop a target life-cycle profile for the company and measure the company's present life-cycle profile against it. The target profile, established by marketing management, specifies the desirable share of company sales that should fall within each phase of the product life cycle. It can be determined by industry obsolescence trends, the pace of new-product introduction in the field, the average length of product life cycles in the company's line, and top management's objectives for growth and profitability. As a rule, the target profile for growth-minded companies whose life cycles tend to be short will call for a high proportion of sales in the introductory and growth phases.

---

[6]"Managing the Product Life Cycle," Donald K. Clifford, Jr., *The McKinsey Quarterly*, Spring, 1965.

With these steps completed, management can assign priorities to such functions as new-product development, acquisition, and product-line pruning, based on the discrepancies between the company's target profile and its present life-cycle profile. Once corporate effort has been broadly allocated in this way among products at various stages of their life cycles, marketing plans can be detailed for individual product lines.[7]

Exhibit 13-2 lists typical strategic alternatives for a product which a firm may pursue in its different life cycle stages. Actual choice of strategies will rest on the objective set for the product, the nature of the product, and environmental characteristics operating at the time. For example, in the introductory stage in which a new product is launched without any competition and the firm may have spent huge amounts of funds on research and development, the firm may pursue a high price-low promotion strategy (i.e., skim the cream off the top of the market). As the product gets established and enters the growth stage, the price may be cut to bring new segments within the fold. This reflects the type of strategic perspective followed by Texas Instruments for its digital watches.

On the other hand, if the product is introduced into a market where there is already a well-established brand, the firm may follow a high price-high promotion strategy. Seiko, for example, introduced its digital watch with a high price and heavy promotion among well-to-do buyers without any intention of competing against Texas Instruments head on.

Of the four stages, the maturity stage of the life cycle offers the greatest opportunity to shape the duration of a product's life cycle. These critical questions must be answered: Why have sales tapered off? Has the product really approached obsolescence because of a superior substitute or a fundamental change in consumer needs, can obsolescence be attributed to management's failure to identify and reach the right consumer needs, or has a competitor done a better market job? The answer is crucial if an appropriate strategy is to be employed to strengthen the product's position. For example, the product may be redirected on a growth path through repacking, physical modifications, repricing, appeals to new users, the addition of new distribution channels, or the use of some combination of marketing strategy changes. The choice of a right strategy here can be extremely beneficial since a successfully revitalized product offers a higher return on management time and funds invested than does a new product.

PORTFOLIO MATRIX

A good planning system must guide the development of strategic alternatives for each of the company's current businesses and new business possibilities. It must also provide for management's review of these strategic alternatives and for the corresponding resource allocation decisions. The result is a set of approved

---

[7]*Ibid.*, p. 226.

EXHIBIT 13-2 Product-life-cycle Strategies

Introduction Stage	Growth Stage	Maturity Stage	Decline Stage
Different combinations of product, price, promotion, and distribution strategies. For example, the following are alternate strategies using price/promotion combinations: 1. High price/high promotion 2. High price/low promotion 3. Low price/heavy promotion 4. Low price/low promotion	1. Product improvement: addition of new features and models 2. Development of new market segments 3. Addition of new channels 4. Selective demand stimulation 5. Price reductions to vie for new customers	1. Search for new markets and new and varied uses for the product 2. Improve product quality through promoting distinguished product characteristics, and features and style improvement 3. New marketing mix perspectives; for the leader firm this will imply either innovation of a new product or market fortification by following multibrand strategy, or engaging in price-promotion war against the weaker members of the industry; the non-leader firm may seek a differential advantage to find a niche in the market either through product or promotional variable.	1. Continuation of current product/market mix perspectives 2. Concentration of business in selective markets 3. Divestment

Source: Philip Kotler, *Marketing Management: Analysis, Planning and Control*, 3rd ed., © 1976, pp. 236, 237, 242. Reprinted by permission of Prentice-Hall, Inc., Englewood Cliffs, New Jersey.

business plans which, taken as a whole, represent the direction of the firm. This process starts with, and its success is largely determined by, the creation of sound strategic alternatives.

The top management of a multibusiness firm cannot generate these strategic alternatives. They must rely on the managers of their business ventures and on their corporate development personnel. However, they can and should establish a conceptual framework within which these plan alternatives can be developed. One such framework is the portfolio matrix associated with the Boston Consulting Group (BCG). Briefly, the portfolio concept is used to establish the best mix of businesses in order to maximize the long-term earnings growth of the firm.

The portfolio concept addresses the issue of the potential value that a particular business has for the firm. This value has two variables: first, the potential for generating attractive earnings levels now; and second, the potential for growth, or in other words, for significantly increased earnings levels in the future. The portfolio concept holds that these two variables can be quantified. Current earnings potential is measured by comparing the market position of the business to that of its competitors. Empirical studies have shown that profitability is directly determined by relative market share. There are some types of businesses, however, in which the economics do not respond significantly to scale, and other factors are important determinants of return. In such cases the terminology for the earnings-potential yardstick may be changed from "market share" to "market leadership."

Growth potential is measured by the growth rate of the market segment in which the business competes. Clearly, if the segment is in the saturation or decline stage of its life cycle, the only way the business can increase its market share is by taking volume away from competitors. While this is sometimes possible and economically desirable, it is usually expensive, it leads to destructive pricing and erosion of profitability for all competitors, and it ultimately results in a market which is ill served. On the other hand, if a market is in its rapid growth stage, the business can gain share by preempting the incremental growth in the market. So if these two dimensions of value are arrayed in matrix form, we have the basis for a business classification scheme. This is essentially what the Boston Consulting Group portfolio matrix is. Each of the four business categories tends to have specific characteristics associated with it. The two quadrants corresponding to high market leadership have current earnings potential, and the two corresponding to high market growth have growth potential.

Exhibit 13-3 shows a matrix with its two sides labeled as "product sales growth rate" and "relative market share." The area of each circle represents its dollar sales. The market-share position of each circle is determined by its horizontal position in the exhibit. Each circle's product sales growth rate (corrected for inflation) in the market in which it competes is shown by its vertical position.

With regard to the two axes of the matrix, the relative market share is plotted on a logarithmic scale in order to be consistent with the experience curve effect, which implies that profit margin or rate of cash generation differences between

EXHIBIT 13-3   Product Portfolio Matrix

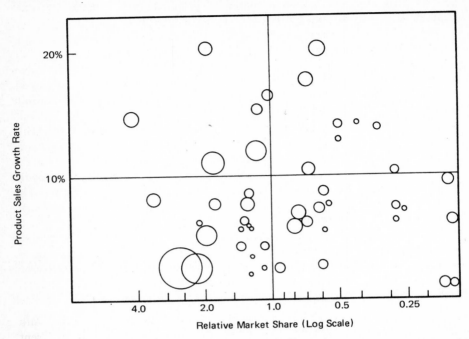

Source: Bruce D. Henderson, "The Experience Curve Reviewed: IV. The Growth Share Matrix or the Product Portfolio" (Boston: The Boston Consulting Group, Inc., 1973), Perspectives No. 135.

two competitors tends to be proportionate to the ratio of their competitive positions. A linear axis is used for growth, for which the most generally useful measure is volume growth of the business concerned; in general, rates of cash use should be directly proportionate to growth.

The lines dividing the matrix into four quadrants are arbitrary. Usually high growth is taken to include all businesses growing in excess of 10 percent annually in volume terms. The line separating areas of high and low relative competitive position is set at 1.0.

The importance of growth variables for strategy development is based on two factors. First, growth is a major influence in reducing cost by gaining experience or building market share. It is easier to gain market share in a growth market than in a low-growth situation. Second, growth provides opportunity for investment, i.e., for sinking cash into a business which returns even larger amounts of cash later. The relative market share affects the rate at which the business will generate cash. The stronger the relative-market-share position of a product, the higher the margins it will have, due to the experience effect.

EXHIBIT 13-4   Matrix Quadrants

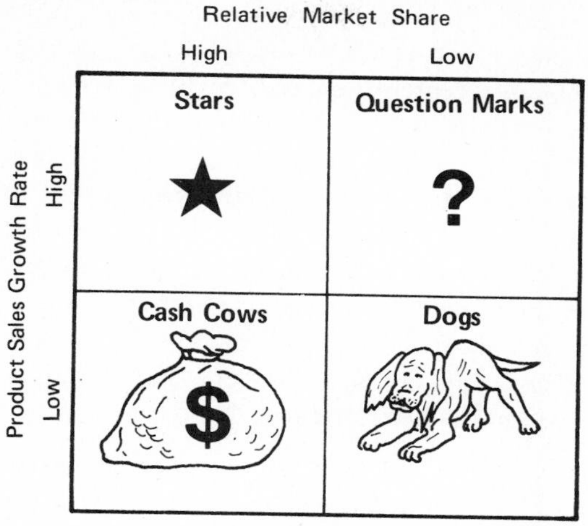

Source: The Boston Consulting Group, Inc., 1970.

Classification of Businesses

Using the two dimensions discussed above, one can classify businesses into four categories (see Exhibit 13-4). Businesses in each category exhibit different financial characteristics and offer different strategic choices.[8]

Stars. High-growth market leaders are called *stars*. They generate large amounts of cash, but the cash they generate from earnings and depreciation is more than offset by the cash that must be put back into these businesses in the form of capital expenditures and increased working capital. Such heavy reinvestment is necessary to fund the capacity increases and inventory and receivable investment that go along with market share gains. Thus, star products represent probably the best profit opportunity available to a company, and their competitive position must be maintained. If a star's share is allowed to slip because the star has been used to provide large amounts of cash in the short run or because of cutting back on investment and raising prices (creating an umbrella for competitors), the star will ultimately become a dog.

The ultimate value of any product or service is reflected in the stream of cash it generates net of its own reinvestment. For a star, this stream of cash is in the future, sometimes the distant future, and to obtain real value, the stream of cash must be discounted back to the present at a rate equal to the return on alternative

---

[8]See Bruce D. Henderson, *Henderson on Corporate Strategy* (Cambridge, MA: Abt Associates, 1979).

opportunities. It is the future payoff of the star that counts, not the present reported profit.

Lone Star Industries, Inc., provides an example of how a company attempts to take care of its star. The company's two main businesses were building-materials outlets, ranging from wholesale centers that catered to professional homebuilders to retail stores selling mostly to do-it-yourselfers, and cement manufacturing operations. Both businesses happened to be in the star category, but the company, as a matter of strategy, decided that it could not afford to support both the stars. Therefore, it harvested the former. In doing so, it parted with 40 percent of the $1.1 billion in sales in 1978. Simultaneously, the company planned a $300 million expansion of the cement business. Lone Star explained it in this manner: "The company could not afford rapid growth campaigns for both businesses. So we are going with cement. It is the business Lone Star managers are most familiar with and where we see the better returns."[9]

Cash Cows. Cash Cows are characterized by low growth and high market share. They are net providers of cash. Their high earnings coupled with their depreciation represent high cash inflows, while they need very little in the way of reinvestment. Thus, these products generate large cash surpluses which help to pay dividends and interest, provide debt capacity, supply funds for R & D, meet overheads, and also make cash available for investment in other products. Thus, cash cows are the foundation on which everything else depends. These products must be protected. Technically speaking, a cash cow has a return on assets which exceeds its growth rate. Only if that is true will the cash cow generate more cash than it uses. For the NCR company, the mechanical cash register business is a cash cow. The company still maintains a dominant share of this business even though growth in the midst of electronic cash registers has slowed down. The company uses the surplus cash from the mechanical cash registers to develop electronic machines with a view to creating a new star. Likewise, the tire business can be categorized as a cash cow for the Goodyear Tire & Rubber Company. The industry is characterized by slow market growth, and Goodyear has a major share of the market.

Question Marks. Products which are in a growth market but have a low share are categorized as *question marks.* Because of growth, these products require more cash than they are able to generate on their own since they have a low share of the market. If nothing is done to change its market share, the question mark will simply absorb large amounts of cash in the short run and later, as the growth slows down, become a dog. Thus, unless something is done to change its perspective, a question mark remains a cash loser throughout its existence and ultimately becomes a "cash trap."

---

[9]"Lone Star Industries: Selling the Source of One-third Its Profits," *Business Week* (May 28, 1979), p. 79.

What can be done to make a question mark more viable? One alternative is to gain share increases for it. Since the business is growing, it can be funded to dominance so that it may become a star, and later a cash cow when growth slows down. This strategy is a costly one in the short run. An abundance of cash must be infused into the question mark in order for it to win a major share of the business, but in the long run this is the only way of developing a sound business from the question mark stage. The other strategy is to divest the business. Outright sale is more desirable. But if this does not work out, a firm decision must be made not to invest further in the business, and the business must be allowed simply to generate whatever cash it can while none is reinvested.

For both General Electric Co. and RCA Corp., the computer business was a question mark. Both giants ultimately decided to quit this business. Although the market was growing rapidly, the major competitor (i.e., IBM) was so well established that to grow at a faster rate than IBM, G.E. (as well as RCA) would have needed to invest rather heavily in computer operations. An examination of the investment needed and the potential long-term cash expected showed that it was not a good business to be in.

Dogs. Products with low market share and positioned in a low-growth situation are called *dogs*. Their poor competitive position condemns them to poor profits. Because growth is low, there is little potential for gaining sufficient share to achieve a viable cost position. Usually they are net users of cash. Their earnings are low, and the reinvestment required just to keep the business together eats its cash inflow. The business, therefore, becomes a "cash trap" which is likely to regularly absorb cash unless further investment in the business is rigorously avoided. An alternative is to convert dogs into cash if there is an opportunity to do so. B.F. Goodrich Co. found its tire business in the dog category. With a No. 4 position in the market and in a period of slow growth, its return on sales in tires and related products had averaged 3.8 percent during 1971–76. The company decided to milk this business to finance potential stars such as its chemicals and plastics business.[10]

Exhibit 13-5 summarizes the investment earnings and cash flow characteristics of stars, cash cows, question marks, and dogs. Also shown are viable strategy alternatives for products in each category.

Strategy Implications

In a typical company there are products scattered in all four quadrants of the portfolio matrix. The appropriate strategy for products in each cell is briefly mentioned in Exhibit 13-5. The first goal of a company should be to secure a position with cash cows but to guard against the frequent temptation to reinvest in them excessively. The cash generated from cash cows should first be used to support those stars which are not self-sustaining. The surplus cash may be used

---

[10]"Goodrich's Cash Cow Starts to Deliver," *Business Week* (November 14, 1977), p. 78.

EXHIBIT 13-5 Characteristics and Strategy Implications of Products in the Strategy Quadrants

Quadrant	Investment Characteristics	Earning Characteristics	Cash-flow Characteristics	Strategy Implication
Stars	—Continual expenditures for capacity expansion —Pipeline filling with cash	Low to High	Negative cash flow (net cash user)	Continue to increase market share. If necessary, at the expense of short-term earnings.
Cash Cows	—Capacity maintenance expenditures	High	Positive cash flow (net cash contributor)	Maintain share and cost leadership until further investment becomes marginal.
Question Marks	—Heavy initial capacity expenditures —High R & D costs	Negative to Low	Negative cash flow (net cash user)	Assess chances of dominating segment. If good, go after share. If bad, redefine business or withdraw.
Dogs	—Gradually deplete capacity	High to Low	Positive cash flow (Net cash contributor)	Plan an orderly withdrawal so as to maximize cash flow.

to finance selected question marks to dominance. Any question mark which cannot be funded should be divested. A dog may be restored to a position of viability by shrewdly segmenting the market; i.e., rationalizing and specializing the business into a small niche which the product concerned may dominate. If this is not practical, a firm should manage the dog for cash; i.e., cut off all investment in the business and liquidate it when an opportunity develops.

Exhibit 13-6 shows the consequences of an incorrect strategic move. For example, if a star is not appropriately funded, it will become a question mark, and finally a dog (disaster sequence). On the other hand, if a question mark is provided adequate support, it may become a star, and ultimately a cash cow (success sequence).

There are two strategic questions that top management needs to answer: How promising is the current set of businesses with respect to long-term return and growth? Which business should be developed? maintained as is? liquidated? Following the portfolio approach discussed above, a company needs a cash-

EXHIBIT 13-6   Product Portfolio Matrix: Strategic Consequences

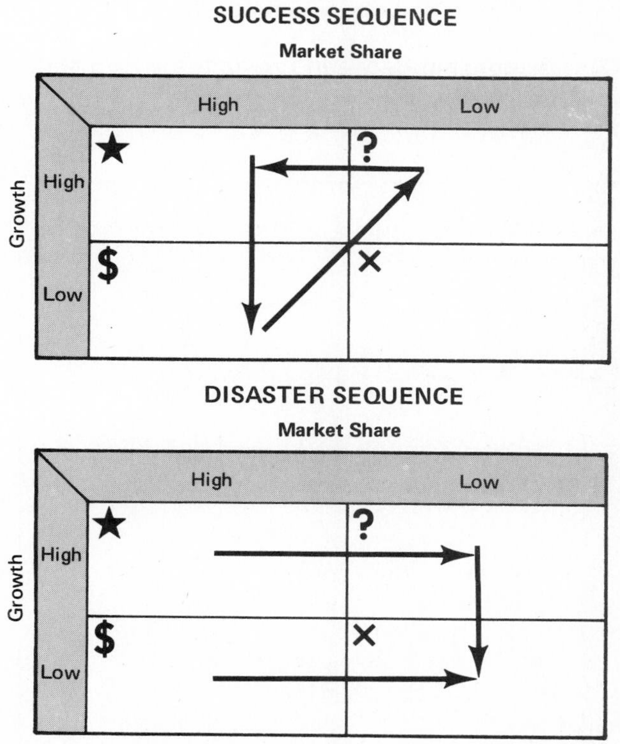

Source: Bruce D. Henderson, "The Product Portfolio" (Boston: The Boston Consulting Group, Inc., 1970). Perspectives No. 66.

balanced portfolio of businesses, i.e., cash cows and dogs, to throw off sufficient cash to fund stars and question marks. There should be an ample supply of question marks to ensure long-term growth and businesses with return levels appropriate to their matrix position. In response to the second question, the capital budgeting theory requires the lining up of capital project proposals, assessment of incremental cash flows attributable to each project, computation of discounted rate of return of each, and approval of the project with the highest rate of return until available funds are exhausted. But the capital budgeting approach misses the strategic content; i.e., how to validate the assumptions of volume, price, cost, and investment and how to eliminate the natural biases. This problem is solved by the portfolio approach.

Product Portfolio and Product Life Cycle

The product-portfolio approach propounded by the Boston Consulting Group may be related to the familiar product-life-cycle approach by letting the introduction stage begin in the question mark quadrant; growth starts toward the end of this quadrant and continues well into the star quadrant. Going down from the star to the cash cow quadrant, the saturation stage begins. The decline is positioned between the cash cow and dog quadrants (see Exhibit 13-7).

EXHIBIT 13-7   Relationship Between Product Portfolio Matrix and Product Life Cycle

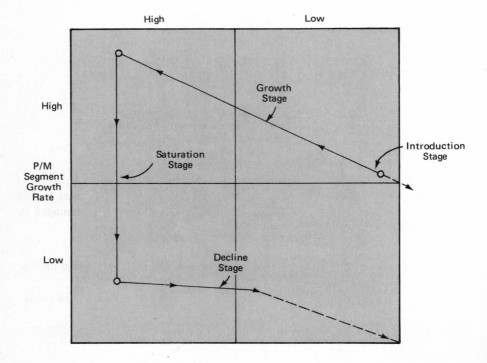

Ideally a company should enter the product/market segment in its introduction stage, gain market share in the growth stage, attain a position of dominance when the product/market segment enters its saturation stage, maintain this dominant position until the product/market segment enters its decline stage, and then determine the optimum point for liquidation.

Balanced and Unbalanced Portfolios

Exhibit 13-8 gives an example of a *balanced portfolio*. With two (actually three) cash cows, this company is well positioned with stars to provide growth

EXHIBIT 13-8   Illustration of a Balanced Portfolio

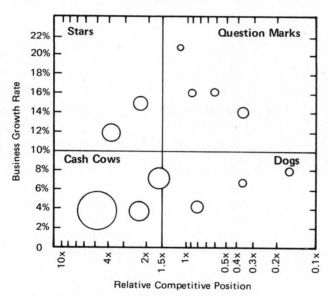

Source: The Boston Consulting Group, Inc., 1973.

and to yield high cash returns in the future when they mature. The company has four question marks, two of which offer a good opportunity to emerge as stars at an investment which the cash cows should be able to support (based on the area of the circles). The company does have dogs, but they can be managed in order to avoid drain on cash resources.

Unbalanced portfolios may be classified into four types:

1. Too many losers (due to inadequate cash flow, inadequate profits, and inadequate growth)
2. Too many question marks (due to inadequate cash flow and inadequate profits)
3. Too many profit producers (due to inadequate growth and excessive cash flow)

4. Too many developing winners (due to excessive cash demands, excessive demands on management, and unstable growth and profits)[11]

Exhibit 13-9 illustrates an *unbalanced portfolio.* The company has just one cash cow, three question marks, and no stars. Thus, the cash base of the company is actually inadequate to support question marks. The company may allocate the available cash among all question marks in an equal proportion. Dogs may also be given occasional cash nourishment. If the company continues its current strategy, it may find itself in a dangerous position in five years, particularly when the cash cow moves closer to being a dog. To take corrective action, the company must face the fact that it cannot support all the question marks. It must choose one or maybe two of the three question marks and fund them adequately to move them into star positions. Besides, disbursement of cash in dogs should be totally prohibited. In brief, the strategic choice for the company, considered in portfolio terms, is obvious. It cannot fund all question marks and dogs equally. The portfolio matrix focuses on the real fundamentals of the businesses and their relationships to each other within the portfolio. It is not possible to develop effective strategy in a multiproduct, multimarket company without considering the mutual relationships of different businesses.

Conclusion

The portfolio approach provides for the simultaneous comparison of different products. It also underlines the importance of cash flow as a strategic variable. Thus, when continuous long-term growth in earnings is the objective, it is necessary to identify high-growth product/market segments early, develop businesses, and preempt the growth in these segments. If necessary, short-term profitability in these segments may be foregone to ensure achievement of the dominant share. Costs must be managed to meet experience effect standards. The appropriate point at which to shift from an earnings focus to a cash-flow focus must be determined and a liquidation plan for cash-flow maximization established. A cash-balanced mix of businesses should be maintained.

There are many companies worldwide that have used the portfolio approach in their strategic planning. The first company to use this approach was the Norton Co. in the late 1960s. Since then, many large corporations have reported following this approach. Among them are Mead, Borg-Warner, Eaton, and Monsanto.

This approach, however, is not a panacea for strategy development. In reality, many difficulties limit the workability of this approach. These difficulties are listed below:

---

[11]C.W. Hofer and M.J. Davoust, *Successful Strategic Management* (Chicago: A.T. Kearney, Inc., 1977), p. 52.

EXHIBIT 13-9 Illustration of an Unbalanced Portfolio

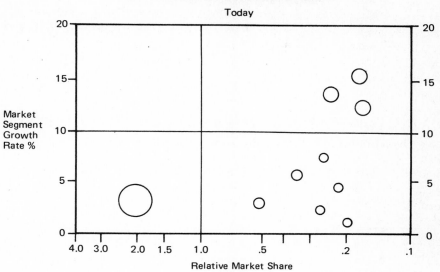

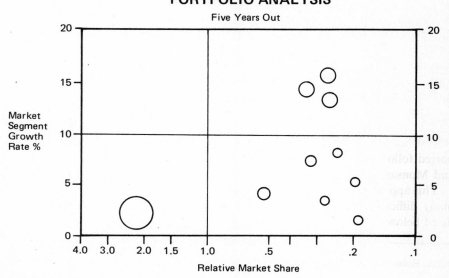

1. Overinvesting in low-growth segments (lack of objectivity and "hard" analysis)
2. Underinvesting in high-growth segments (lack of guts)
3. Misjudging the segment growth rate (poor market research)
4. Not achieving market share (due to market strategy, improper sales capabilities, or improper promotion)
5. Losing cost-effectiveness (lack of operating talent and control system)
6. Not uncovering emerging high-growth segments (lack of corporate development effort)
7. Unbalanced business mix (lack of planning and financial resources)

Thus, the portfolio concept should be used with great care.[12]

MULTIFACTOR PORTFOLIO MATRIX

The two-factor portfolio matrix discussed above provided a useful approach for reviewing the role that different products play in a company. Generally, however, the growth rate-relative market share matrix approach leads to many difficulties. At times, factors other than market share and growth rate may bear heavily on the cash flow, which is the mainstay of this approach. Some managements may consider return-on-investment a more suitable criterion than cash flow for making investment decisions. Further, this approach does not address itself to major investment decisions between dissimilar businesses. The above difficulties can lead a company into too many traps and errors. For this reason many companies (such as General Electric Co. and the Shell Group) have developed a multifactor portfolio approach.

Exhibit 13-10 illustrates the General Electric matrix. This matrix has two sides, labeled "industry attractiveness" and "business strengths." The two dimensions of the matrix have been based on a variety of factors. It is this multifactor characteristic which differentiates this approach from the one discussed in the previous section. The General Electric Company, for example, used the following factors to measure industry attractiveness and business strengths:

Industry Attractiveness	Business Strengths	
Size	Size	Technology position
Market growth, pricing	Growth	Strengths/Weaknesses
Market diversity	Share	Image
Competitive structure	Position	Pollution
	Profitability	People
	Margins	

[12]See George S. Day, "Diagnosing the Product Portfolio," *Journal of Marketing* (April, 1977), pp. 29–38.

EXHIBIT 13-10 Multifactor Portfolio Matrix

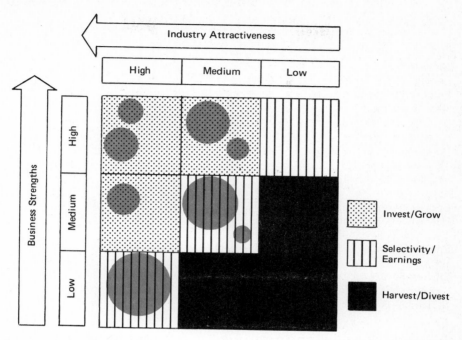

Source: *Maintaining Strategies for the Future Through Current Crises* (Fairfield, CT: General Electric Co., 1975).

These factors are only suggestive in nature; another company may adopt a different list. As a matter of fact, General Electric added the following factors later on to accommodate environmental shifts:

Industry Attractiveness	Business Strengths
Inflation vulnerability	Investment utilization
Cyclicality	Ventures
Customer financials	Vertical integration
Energy impact	Productivity

Rothschild recommends taking into consideration the following factors in measuring both "industry environment" (industry attractiveness) and "our position" (business strengths): market, competition, financial and economic factors, technological factors, sociopolitical factors, and overall factors. Each factor may be treated equally or assigned a different weight.[13] Exhibits 13-11 and 13-12 illustrate how the factors may be weighed and a final industry attractiveness and

---

[13]William E. Rothschild, *Putting It All Together* (New York: AMACOM, 1976), pp. 141–162.

EXHIBIT 13-11   Assessing Industry Attractiveness

Criteria	Weights*	×	Rankings**	=	Weighted Rank
Size	.15		4		.60
Growth	.12		3		.36
Pricing	.05		3		.15
Customer financials	.10		5		.50
Market diversity	.05		2		.10
Demand cyclicality	.05		2		.10
Expert opportunities	.05		5		.25
Competitive structure	.05		3		.15
Industry profitability	.20		3		.60
Inflation vulnerability	.05		2		.10
Value added	GO		4		–
Capital intensity	GO		4		–
Raw material availability	GO		4		–
Technological role	.05		4		.20
Energy impact	.08		4		.32
Social	GO		4		–
Environmental	GO		4		–
Legal	GO		4		–
Human	GO		4		–
	1.00		1 to 5		3.43

*Some criteria may be of a GO/NO GO type. For example, many *Fortune 500* firms would probably not invest in industries viewed negatively by society even if it were legal and profitable to do so.

**"1" denotes very unattractive; "5" denotes very attractive

Source: "Conceptual Constructs for Formulating Corporate and Business Strategies," a case prepared by Charles W. Hofer, Stanford University, 1977, p. 6. Reprinted from *Stanford Business Cases 1977* with permission of the Publishers, Stanford University Graduate School of Business, © 1977 by the Board of Trustees of the Leland Stanford Junior University.

competitive position (business strengths) score computed. Management may establish cutoff points for high, medium, and low industry attractiveness and competitive position scores.

It is worthwhile to mention that the development of the multifactor matrix discussed above may not be as easy as it appears. The actual analysis required may take considerable amounts of foresight and experience and many, many days of work. The major difficulties lie in identifying the relevant factors, relating the factors to industry attractiveness and business strengths, and weighing the factors.[14]

[14]Derek F. Abell and John S. Hammond, *Strategic Market Planning* (Englewood Cliffs, NJ: Prentice-Hall, 1979), pp. 211–227.

Strategy Development

The overall strategy for a business in a particular position was illustrated in Exhibit 13-10. The area of the circle refers to the business' sales. Investment priority is given to products in the "high" area (upper left), where a stronger position is supported by the attractiveness of an industry. Along the diagonal, selectivity is desired to achieve a balanced earnings performance. The businesses in the "low" area (lower right) are the candidates for harvesting and divestment.

EXHIBIT 13-12   Assessing Competitive Position

Criteria	Weights*	×	Rankings**	=	Weighted Rank
Market share	.10		5		.50
SBU growth rate	X		3		–
Breadth of product line	.05		4		.20
Sales/distribution effectiveness	.20		4		.80
Proprietary & key account effectiveness	X		3		–
Price competitiveness	X		4		–
Advertising & promotion effectiveness	.05		4		.20
Facilities location & newness	.05		5		.25
Capacity and productivity	X		3		–
Experience curve effects	.15		4		.30
Value added	X		4		–
Investment utilization	.05		5		.25
Raw materials cost	.05		4		.20
Relative product quality	.15		4		.30
R & D advantages/position	.05		4		.20
Cash throwoff	.10		5		.50
Caliber of personnel	X		4		–
Organizational synergies	X		4		–
General image	X		5		–
	1.00		1 to 5		4.30

*For any particular industry, there will be some factors that, while important in general, will have little or no effect on the relative competitive position of firms within that industry.

**"1" denotes a very weak competitive position; "5" denotes a very strong competitive position

Source: "Conceptual Constructs for Formulating Corporate and Business Strategies," a case prepared by Charles W. Hofer, Stanford University, 1977, p. 6. Reprinted from *Stanford Business Cases 1977* with permission of the Publishers, Stanford University Graduate School of Business, © 1977 by the Board of Trustees of the Leland Stanford Junior University.

A company may position its products or businesses on the matrix to study their present standing. Forecasts may be made to examine the direction different businesses may go in the future, assuming no changes are made in the strategy. The future perspectives may be compared to the corporate mission to identify gaps between what is desired and what may be expected if no measures are taken now. The gap filling will require making strategic moves for different businesses. Once strategic alternatives for an individual business have been identified, the final choice of a strategy will be based on the scope of the overall corporation vis-a-vis the matrix. For example, the prospects for a business along the diagonal may appear good, but this business cannot be funded in preference to a business in the "high-high" cell. Generally a company in devising future strategy would like to have a few businesses on the left to provide growth and furnish potential for investment and a few on the right to generate cash for investment in the former. The businesses along the diagonal may be selectively supported (based on resources) for relocation on the left. If this is not feasible, they may be slowly harvested or divested.

For an individual business there can be four strategy options: investing to maintain, investing to grow, investing to regain, and investing to exit. The choice of a strategy will depend on the current position of the business in the matrix (i.e., toward the high side, along the diagonal, or toward the low side) and its future direction, assuming the current strategic perspective continues to be followed. If the future appears undesirable, a new strategy for the business will be called for.

The analysis of the present position of the matrix may not pose any problem. At General Electric, for example, there was little disagreement on the position of the business.[15] The mapping of future direction, however, may not be easy. A rigorous analysis will have to be performed taking into account the environmental shifts, competitors' perspectives, and internal strengths and weaknesses.

The four strategy options are shown in Exhibit 13-13. Strategy to maintain the current position (strategy 1 in the exhibit) may be adopted if, in the absence of a new strategy, erosion is expected in the future. Thus, investment will be sought to hold the position, hence the name *invest-to-maintain strategy.* The second option is the *invest-to-grow strategy.* Here, the product's current position is perceived as less than optimum vis-a-vis industry attractiveness and business strength. In other words, considering the opportunities furnished by the industry and the strength exhibited by the business, the current position is considered inadequate. The growth strategy is adopted with the aim of shifting the product position upward and/or toward the left. Movement in both directions is an expensive option with high risk.

The *invest-to-regain strategy* (strategy 3 in Exhibit 13-13) is an attempt to rebuild the product or business to its previous position. Usually when environment (i.e., industry) continues to be relatively attractive, but the business position

---

[15]*Organizing and Managing the Planning Function* (Fairfield, CT: General Electric Co., no date).

EXHIBIT 13-13 Strategy Options

1. Invest to Maintain

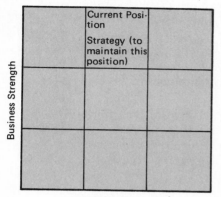

Industry Attractiveness

2. Invest to Grow

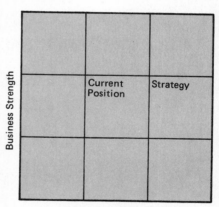

Industry Attractiveness

3. Invest to Regain

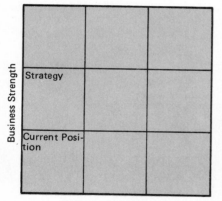

Industry Attractiveness

4. Invest to Exit

Industry Attractiveness

has slipped due to some strategic mistake in the past (e.g., premature harvesting), it may be decided to revitalize the business through new investments. The fourth and final option, the *invest-to-exit strategy,* is directed toward leaving the market through harvesting or divesting. Harvesting amounts to making very low investments in the business so that in the short run the business will secure positive cash flow and in a few years die out. (With no new investments, the position will continue to deteriorate.) Alternatively, the whole business may be *divested,* i.e., sold to another party on a one-time deal. Sometimes small investments may be made to maintain the viability of the business if divestment is desired but there is no immediate suitor. In this way the business can eventually be sold at a higher price than would have been possible right away.

Unit of Analysis

The framework discussed above may be applied to either a product/market or a strategic business unit. As a matter of fact, it may be equally applicable to a much higher level of aggregation in the organization, such as a division or a group. Of course, at the group or division level, it may be very difficult to measure industry attractiveness and business strength positions unless the group or division happens to be in one business.

In the scheme followed in this book, the analysis may be performed first at the product/market level and then at the SBU level. Finally, all SBUs may be simultaneously positioned in the matrix to determine a corporate-wide portfolio.

Directional Policy Matrix

A slightly different technique, the *directional policy matrix,* is popularly used in Europe. It was initially worked out at the Shell Group but later on caught the fancy of many businesses across the continent. Exhibit 13-14 illustrates a directional policy matrix. The two sides of the matrix are labeled "business sector prospects" (industry attractiveness) and "company's competitive capabilities" (business strengths). The business sector prospects are categorized as unattrac-

EXHIBIT 13-14   Directional Policy Matrix

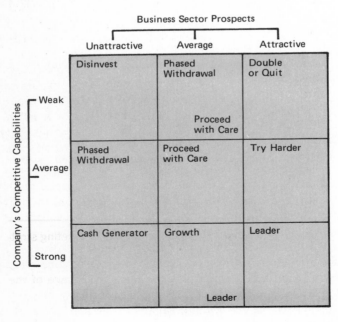

tive, average, and attractive, while the company's competitive capabilities are categorized as weak, average, and strong. Mentioned within each cell is the overall strategy direction for a business depicted by the cell. The consideration of factors used to measure business sector prospects and a company's competitive capabilities follows the same logic and analyses discussed above.

SUMMARY

A diversified organization needs to examine its widely different businesses at the corporate level (to see how they fit within the overall corporate purpose) and to come to grips with the resource allocation problem. The portfolio approaches described in this chapter help management determine the role which each business plays in the corporation and allocate resources accordingly.

Three portfolio approaches are discussed here: product life cycle, growth rate-relative market share matrix, and multifactor matrix. The product-life-cycle approach indicates what the life status is of different products and whether the company has enough viable products to provide desired growth in the future. If the company lacks new products with which to generate growth in coming years, investments may be made in new products. If growth is hurt due to the early maturity of promising products, the strategic effort may be directed toward extension of their life cycles.

The second approach, the growth rate-relative market share matrix, suggests locating products or businesses in a matrix with relative market share and growth rate as its dimensions. The four cells in the matrix, whose positions are based on whether growth is high or low and whether relative market share is high or low, are labelled as stars, cash cows, question marks, and dogs. The strategy for a product or business in each cell, which is primarily based on the business' cash-flow implications, is outlined.

The third approach, the multifactor matrix, again uses two variables (i.e., industry attractiveness and business strengths) to develop a 2×2 matrix. These two variables, however, are based on a variety of factors, hence the name multifactor matrix. Here again, a desired strategy for a product/business in each cell is recommended. The focus of the multifactor matrix approach, however, is on the return-on-investment implications of strategy alternatives, rather than on cash flow like the growth rate-relative market share matrix approach.

DISCUSSION QUESTIONS

1. What purpose may a product portfolio serve in the context of marketing strategy?
2. How may the position of a product in its life cycle be located?
3. What is the strategic significance of products in the maturity stage of the product life cycle?
4. What is the meaning of relative market share?

5. How does the experience curve concept fit into the growth rate-relative market share portfolio scheme?
6. What sequence should products follow for success? What may management do to insure this sequence?
7. What factors may a company consider to measure industry attractiveness and business strengths? Should these factors vary from one business to another in a company?
8. Illustrate how industry attractiveness and business strengths may be weighed.
9. What is the basic difference between the growth rate-relative market share matrix approach and the multifactor matrix approach?

Part Four
Organization and Control

CHAPTER 14 – Strategy-related Tools and Techniques

CHAPTER 15 – Strategy-related Models

CHAPTER 16 – Organizational Structure

Chapter 14
Strategy-related Tools and Techniques

A small jump is easier than a large one, but no one wishing to cross a wide ditch would cross half of it first.

Carl Von Clausewitz

Strategy development is by no means an easy job. Not only must decisionmakers review a variety of inside factors, but they must also incorporate the impact of environmental changes in order to work out a viable strategy. Strategists have become increasingly aware that the old way of "muddling through" is not adequate for taking care of the complexities involved in designing a future for the corporation. The 1970s were especially difficult years, the uncertainties and dilemmas of the end of the decade portraying the shape of things to come in following years.

Economic uncertainty, shortages of energy and basic raw materials, leveling off of productivity, international competition, tight money and inflation, political upheavals, and environmental problems pose new challenges which corporations will have to cope with in the 1980s when planning out their strategies. There is, therefore, a need for systematic procedures for formulating strategy. This chapter discusses selected systems or tools and techniques which serve as aids in strategy development.

A *tool* or *technique* may be defined as an instrument which serves as an aid in searching, screening, analyzing, selecting, and implementing strategies. Since marketing strategy interfaces with and/or affects the perspectives of the entire corporation, the tools and techniques of the entire management science can be considered relevant here. In this chapter, however, only four tools or frameworks which have direct application in working out marketing strategies are dealt with. Thus, discussed in this chapter are experience curves, the delphi method, scenario building, and techniques for evaluating investment proposals.

EXPERIENCE CURVE CONCEPT

Experience shows that practice makes perfect. It is common knowledge that beginners are slow and clumsy and that with practice they generally improve to the point where they can reach their own permanent levels of skill. As anyone

437

with business experience knows, the initial period of a new venture or expansion into a new area will frequently not be profitable for some time. Many factors— such as making the name known to potential customers—are often cited as reasons for this. In brief, even the most unsophisticated business person acknowledges that experience or learning leads to improvement. Unfortunately the significance of experience is realized only in abstract terms, and its implications for strategy formulation are hardly ever considered. For example, managers in a new and unprofitable situation tend to think of experience in vague terms without ever analyzing it in terms of cost. This statement applies to all the functions of a business except production management, where cost improvements are commonly sought.

As growth continues, we anticipate greater efficiency and more productive output. But how much improvement can one reasonably expect? Generally management makes an arbitrary decision to ascertain what output reflects the optimum level. Obviously in the great majority of situations, this decision is mainly based on pure conjecture. Ideally, however, one should be able to take previous historical data to predict the cost-volume relationship and learning patterns. Many companies have, in fact, developed their learning curves, but only in the area of production or manufacturing, where tangible data is readily available and most variables can be quantified.

A few years back, the Boston Consulting Group observed that the concept of experience is not limited to production alone. The experience curve concept tends to embrace almost all cost areas of a business:

> Unlike the well-known "learning curve" and "progress function," the experience curve effect is observed to encompass all costs—capital, administrative, research and marketing—and to have transferred impact from technological displacements and product evolution.[1]

In the rest of this section the application of the experience curve tool to marketing will be examined.

Historical Perspective

The experience effect was first observed in the aircraft industry. Since in this industry the expense incurred in building the first unit is exceptionally high, any reduction in the cost of succeeding units is readily apparent and becomes extremely pertinent in any management decision regarding future production. The phenomenon of an experience pattern in a manufacturing operation was first developed by the commander of Wright Patterson Air Force Base in Dayton, Ohio, around 1925. It was observed that an "80% air frame curve" could be developed in the manufacture of airplanes. This curve depicts a 20% improvement every time production doubles (i.e., the fourth unit requires 80% as much

---

[1]*Perspective on Experience* (Boston: Boston Consulting Group, 1970), p. 1.

time as the second unit, and so on).[2] Studies of the aircraft industry suggest that this rate of improvement seems to prevail consistently over the range of production under study—hence the label "experience" is applied to the curve. Even though this fact was fairly well established in the aircraft industry, it was not until eleven years later, 1936, that T.D. Wright published the first account of this concept.[3]

Implications

Although the significance of the experience curve concept is corporate-wide, it bears most heavily on the setting of marketing objectives and the pricing decision. As already mentioned, according to the experience curve concept, all costs go down as accumulated experience increases. Thus, if a company acquired a higher market share, its costs would decline, enabling it to reduce prices. The lowering of prices would enable the company to acquire a still higher market share. The process is unending as long as the market continues to grow. But as a matter of strategy, the company may be wise, while aiming at a dominant position in the industry, to stay short of raising the eyebrows of the Antitrust Division of the U.S. Department of Justice.

During the growth phase, the company would keep making the desired profit. But in order to provide for this growth, the company would need to reinvest the profits. In fact, further resources might need to be diverted from elsewhere to support such growth. Once the growth comes to an end, the product would make available huge cash throw-offs which could be invested in the growth of a new product.

The Boston Consulting Group (BCG) claims that in the case of a second product, the accumulated experience of the first product should provide an extra advantage to the firm in reducing costs. However, experience is transferable only imperfectly. There is a transfer effect between identical products in different locations, but the transfer effect between different products only occurs if the products are somewhat the same (e.g., belong to the same family). This is true, for instance, in the case of the marketing-cost component of two products which are distributed through the same trade channel. Even in this case, however, the loss of buyer "franchise" can result in some lack of experience transferability. Exhibit 14-1 presents a diagram of the implications of the experience concept.

Some of BCG's claims about the experience effect are hard to substantiate— in fact, may even be disputed—until enough empirical studies have been done on the subject. But even in its simplest form the concept adds new importance to the market-share strategy.

---

[2]W.B. Hirschmann, "Profit from the Learning Curve," *Harvard Business Review* (January–February, 1964), pp. 125–139.
[3]T.D. Wright, "Factors Affecting the Cost of Airplanes," *Journal of Aeronautical Science* (February, 1936), pp. 122–128.

EXHIBIT 14-1   Schematic Presentation of Implications of the Experience
                     Concept

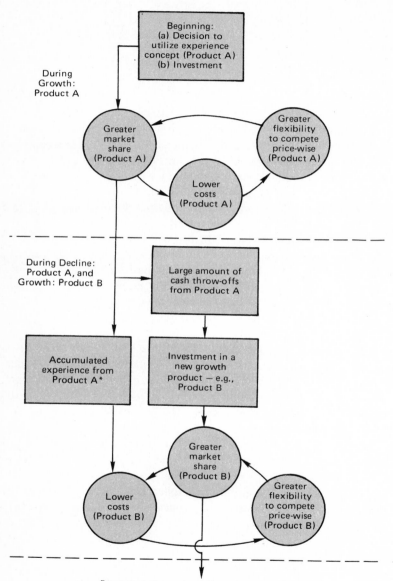

Process continues through successive products

*An assumption is made here that Product B is closely related to Product A.

Source: Subhash C. Jain, "Translating Experience into Growth," *Managerial Planning*
(March/April, 1975), p. 2.

Conceptual Framework for Marketing Application

The application of the experience curve principle requires sorting out various marketing costs and projecting their behavior for different sales volumes. It is hoped that the analyses will show a close relationship between the increase in cumulative sales volume and the decline in costs. The widening gap between volume and costs establishes the company's flexibility in cutting prices in order to gain higher market share.

The decline in costs is logical and occurs for reasons such as the following:

1. Economies of scale (e.g., lower advertising media cost)
2. Increase in efficiency across the board (e.g., ability of the salesperson to reduce time per call)
3. Snowball effect of popularity among customers (e.g., a customer reasoning, "If everyone is buying that, why don't I?")
4. Greater use of company-operated, instead of rented, facilities (e.g., company-owned warehouse and trucks)

Conceivably, four different techniques can be used to project the cost at different levels of volume: regression, simulation, analogy, and intuition. Since historical information on growing products may be lacking, the regression technique may not go very far toward the projection of costs in future years. Simulation is a possibility, but it continues to be rare in practice since it is strenuous. Drawing an analogy between the subject product and the one that has matured perhaps provides the most feasible means of projecting various marketing costs as a function of cumulative sales. But analogy alone may not suffice. Like any other managerial decision, therefore, analogy may have to be combined with intuition.

The cost characteristics of experience curves can be observed in all types of costs, whether they are labor costs, advertising costs, overhead costs, marketing costs, development costs, or manufacturing costs. Thus, marketing costs, as well as those for production, R&D, accounting, service, etc., should be combined to see how the total cost varies with volume. Further, total costs over different ranges of volume should be projected while considering the company's ability to finance an increased volume of business, risk proneness, and relations with the Antitrust Division.

Each element of cost included in the total cost may have a different slope on a graph. The aggregation of these elements will not necessarily produce a straight line on logarithmic coordinates. Thus the cost-volume relationship curve is necessarily an approximation of a trend line. Also, the cost derivatives of the curve are not based on accounting costs, but on the accumulated cash input divided by the accumulated end-product output. The cost decline of the experience curve is the rate of change in that ratio.

The management should establish a market share objective which projects well into the future. Pre-estimates should be made of the timing of price cuttings in order to achieve designated market share. If at any time a competitor happens to challenge the firm's market share position, the firm should go all out to protect its market share and never surrender it without an awareness of its value. Needless to say, the perspective of the entire corporation will have to be changed if the gains expected out of the market share strategy are to become a reality. Thus, proper coordination among different functions becomes essential for the timely implementation of related tasks.

Prerequisites for Application

While the experience effect is independent of the life cycle, of growth rate, and of initial market share, as a matter of strategy, it is safer to base one's move on experience when the following conditions are operating: 1) the product is in the early stages of growth in its life cycle; 2) no one competitor holds a dominant position in the market; 3) the product is not amenable to nonprice competition —e.g., emotional appeals, packaging. Since the concept demands taking a big offensive in which the battle might last many years, a well-drawn, long-range plan should be in existence. The top management should be capable of undertaking risks and going through the initial period of fast activity involved in sudden moves to enlarge the company's operations; the company should also have enough resources to support the enlargement of operations.

Barriers to Application to Marketing

The experience effect has been widely accepted in the aircraft industry, and some application can also be found in the petroleum industry and maintenance-related areas. The application of this concept to marketing is minimal. The following reasons are given for this:

1. Skepticism that improvement can continue.
2. Difficulty with the exact quantification of different relationships in marketing.
3. Not being able to recognize experience patterns even though they are already occurring.
4. Lack of awareness that the improvement pattern can be subjectively approximated and that the concept can apply to groups of men or crews, as well as to individual performance across the board in different functions of the business.
5. Future technological advances, which can badly distort any historical data.
6. Current accounting practices which may make it difficult to segregate costs adequately.

Despite these obstacles, however, the concept is too exciting for one to give up striving for its smooth application to marketing.

Conclusion

The acceptance of the experience curve concept leads naturally to recognizing the importance of gaining and sustaining market share. The linkage is direct. Increases in relative volume result in increases in relative experience; increases in relative experience result in cost advantages over less-experienced competitors.

Strategy is based upon competitive differences. If the experience curve permits you to confidently predict that one competitor can and should have a lower cost than another one, then the experience curve also permits you to predict that the low-cost competitor can and should displace the higher-cost competitor if it provides identical products to identical customers with identical values at identical margins.

The long-term profitability of a product is related to the producer's ability to increase and hold the market share and to the amount that must be spent in doing so. There is, in fact, a conceptually best market share for each product. This "target" share is that which provides the greatest long-term value, which is measured in terms of the present worth of all future cash flows related to the product.[4]

Assume that a business unit has a cost-experience curve for one of its products and can make assumptions regarding the product's industry growth rate and the manner in which price will decline with industry experience. This information is sufficient to project the future cash flows of the product under the assumptions of maintaining current market share and increasing share to any specified level. From this, the incremental cash flows attributable to the share increase can be determined, and the present value of these incremental cash flows can be computed with the use of the discounted cash-flow technique. This present value can then be balanced against the estimated cost of obtaining the increase in market share. This cost typically takes the form of "expensed investments" for price reduction or such nonprice inducements as improved quality or service. When the values of specific share increases are traded off against the costs of achieving them, the highest attainable market share which justifies the cost can be determined. Plans may then be developed for acquiring this target share. The type of analysis described above can be very useful in developing product/market strategy.[5]

Increasing market share is proportionately much easier, less costly, and more profitable with products having higher growth rates. Growth rates higher than that of the economy, however, cannot be sustained indefinitely. The industry growth rate for all products eventually must slow down. Because it is difficult to gain share in slow-growth markets, the objective of a producer in a rapidly growing market must be to achieve cost dominance. The competitor who has the lowest unit cost when growth subsides is in a nearly impenetrable position.

Achieving cost dominance requires a long-term perspective. Cash spending for capacity may exceed earnings until the growth rate declines. If it is a true growth product, however, the future cash inflows for the dominant producer will have a present worth far higher than the current cash outflows.

Once growth slows down, the strategy of the dominant producer may simply be to retain its dominance at the least cost. The producer can do so by continuing

---

[4]See Paul N. Bloom and Philip Kotler, "Strategies for High Market-Share Companies," *Harvard Business Review* (November–December, 1975), pp. 63–72.
[5]"Experience Curves Applied to Product Strategy," an informal statement by the Boston Consulting Group, 1969.

to achieve the full cost-reduction potential of the experience gains and by making undesirable investments in increased share on the part of the competitors. If, instead, the high-market-share producer in a slow-growth market fails to maintain the industry norm of cost reduction (by failing to continue product development or process improvement), the producer will gradually relinquish its dominance.

Even if the high-share producer remains cost-effective, infringement on its dominance will be invited if the market is allowed to be viewed by current or potential competitors as an attractive one for significant investment. This will occur if the producer holds a price umbrella which makes the product particularly profitable for the less-experienced competitors despite their higher unit cost levels or if the producer gives the competitors reason to believe that it will not protect its dominant position.

One of the dominant producer's main weapons against such infringement is price or, equivalently, nonprice inducements. The objective of the pricing strategy must be to find the balance between getting the highest possible profit and maintaining market share and, hence, the cost advantage and the stability of the market. The concepts and techniques of the experience curve analysis can be invaluable in helping the dominant producer find this balance.

A sound strategy for the dominant producer is to keep the constant dollar price, as plotted on its experience curve graph, parallel to the cost curve and at a height where the profitability of the strongest competitor is just tolerable. This strategy, however, should be tempered by an assessment of the competition. If the less-experienced competitor, for example, is viewed by the dominant producer as less competent in terms of seeing the strategic advantage of increased share, having a lower appraisal of the market's potential, or having inadequate resources to commit to buying an increased share, then the dominant producer may be able to maintain a higher price without risking market share erosion. Similarly, if the dominant producer can convince the competitor that attempts to increase share would be aggressively countered, this is also reason to set a higher price than would otherwise be set.

The approach to price strategy vis-a-vis the experience curve concept is significantly different from traditional pricing theory. The traditional approach is to lower the price only if unit margin times volume (considering price sensitivity) will be increased. This approach emphasizes short-term profitability and ignores both the experience effect and competition. The dominant producer who follows it is susceptible to the competitor who is willing to sacrifice short-term profit by reducing price in return for increased market share and the resulting greater long-term profits.

It can be seen that once industry growth slows down, marginal producers are virtually at the mercy of the leader. If the leader is and has been cost-effective and follows a pricing strategy which makes investment in increased share undesirable for its competitors, there are only three alternatives open to the other producers: 1) to be satisfied with a marginal return, 2) to find a product/market segment for concentration in which there is a good chance for dominance, or 3) to get out of the market entirely.

The strategy-development activity of the smaller competitor in a slower-growth market must begin with an assessment of the dominant producer. The types of questions to be asked are: Is the dominant producer losing cost-effectiveness? Has it raised a price umbrella? How quickly, if at all, could it meet a price cut or nonprice inducements? In view of the total product mix, how important is the dominant producer's current profitability in regard to this product? The answer to such questions should form the basis for a decision as to whether attempting to displace the leading producer on a broad scale is worthwhile.

If the smaller producer concludes that the industry leader is not vulnerable in terms of the total product/market, the former should explore the possibility of concentrating all of its resources on those segments which maximize its strengths while minimizing those of the leader. The process of segmentation is one of making explicit choices from among the various product characteristics and customer requirements within the total market on which to focus the attempt for dominance.

The smaller competitor's decision as to whether and where to concentrate should be based on an assessment of its functional skills (development, production, marketing, distribution, etc.) relative to the market leader and of the importance of these skills in serving specific market segments. An analysis to determine in which skill areas the producer is most experienced and, hence, most likely to have a cost advantage will facilitate the decision.

This same segmentation strategy may be desirable for the smaller producer in a high-growth market if it is determined that competing with larger producers on a broad scale is unlikely to result in dominance before the industry growth subsides. If successful segmentation is not possible, the best strategy for the smaller producer in the high-growth market is to withdraw.

To summarize, the experience curve concept leads to the conclusion that all producers must achieve and maintain the full cost-reduction potential of their experience gains if they hope to survive. Furthermore, the experience framework has implications for strategy development, as shown in Exhibit 14-2. The appendix at the end of this chapter describes the experience curve construction procedure, showing how the relationship between costs and accumulated experience can be empirically developed.

EXHIBIT 14-2   Experience Curves: Strategy Implications

| | | Market Power | |
		High	Low
Industry Growth Rate	**High**	Continue to invest in increased market share up to "target" level.	Assess competition; then either invest heavily in increased share, segment market, or withdraw.
	Low	Obtain highest possible earnings consistent with maintaining market share.	Assess competition; then either challenge, segment market, or withdraw.

DELPHI TECHNIQUE

The Delphi technique consists of a refined method of making forecasts based on expert opinion. The technique was named after Apollo's oracle at Delphi. Traditionally expert opinions were pooled in a committee situation. The Delphi technique has been developed to show up the weaknesses of the traditional committee method. Wedgewood lists some of the problems that occur when issues are discussed in committees:

1. The influence of a dominant individual.
2. The introduction of a lot of redundant or irrelevant material into the committee workings.
3. Group pressure which places a premium on compromise.
4. It is a slow, expensive, and sometimes painful way to reach a decision.
5. The difficulty of holding members accountable for the actions of the group.[6]

All of the above factors provide certain psychological drawbacks to people in face-to-face communication situations. Often the most popular solution, instead of the best one, prevails since people like to conform.

The Delphi method attempts to overcome the problems of committees. Under this method, a staff coordinator questions selected individuals on various issues. The following is a sample of questions asked:

1. The probability of a future event occurring. Example: By what year do you think there will be widespread use of robot services for refuse collection, as household slaves, as sewer inspectors, etc.?
   a. 1980   b. 1990   c. 2000   d. 2010
   e. 2020   f. 2030   g. 2040   h. 2050
2. How desirable is the event in question 1?
   a. needed desperately   b. desirable   c. undesirable but possible
3. What is the feasibility of the event in question 1?
   a. highly feasible   b. likely   c. unlikely but possible
4. What is your familiarity with the material in question 1?
   a. fair   b. good   c. excellent

The coordinator compiles the responses, splitting them into three groups: lower, upper, and inner. The division of the three groups may vary from one investigation to another. Frequently, however, the lower and upper groups are 10 percent each, while the inner group takes the remaining 80 percent. When a person makes a response in either the upper or lower group, it is customary to ask him or her the reasons for the "extreme" opinion.

---

[6]H.C. Wedgewood, "Fewer Camels, More Horses: Where Committees Go Wrong," *Personnel* (July–August, 1967), p. 64.

In the next round the respondents are given the same questionnaire along with a summary of the results of the first round. The data feedback includes the majority consensus and minority opinion. During the second round the respondents are asked to specify by what year the particular product or service will come to exist with 50 percent probability and 90 percent probability. Results are once again compiled and fed back. This process of repeating rounds can be continued indefinitely. However, rarely has any research to date been conducted past the sixth round.

The Delphi technique is gradually becoming important for long-range forecasting. The Rand Corporation has done extensive research on the technique.[7] The Delphi technique has been primarily used to predict future events objectively. In 1970, according to *Business Week,* about 50–100 corporations were using this technique for forecasting purposes.[8] Since then, many more corporations must have begun to use the technique.

Some of the advantages of the Delphi technique are listed below:

1. It is a rapid and efficient way to gain objective information from a group of experts.
2. It involves less effort for a respondent to answer a well-designed questionnaire than to participate in a conference or write a paper.
3. It can be highly motivating for a group of experts to see the responses of knowledgeable persons.
4. The use of systematic procedures applies an air of objectivity to the outcomes.
5. The results of the Delphi exercises are subject to greater acceptance on the part of the group than are the consequences arrived at by more direct forms of interaction.[9]

Delphi Application

Change is an accepted phenomenon in the modern world. Change coupled with competition makes it necessary for a corporation to pick up the trends in the environment and determine their significance for company operations. Then in the light of the changing environmental situation, the corporation must evaluate and define strategic posture in order to be able to face the future boldly. Two types of changes can be distinguished: cyclical and developmental. A cyclical change is repetitive in nature; managers usually develop routine procedures to meet these changes. A developmental change is innovative and irregular; having no use for the "good" old ways, it abandons them. The developmental change appears on the horizon so slowly that it may go

---

[7]Norman C. Dalkey, *The Delphi Method: An Experimental Study of Group Opinion* (Santa Monica, CA: Rand Corp., 1969).
[8]"Forecasters Turn to Group Guesswork: Delphi Technique," *Business Week* (March 14, 1970), p. 132.
[9]Dalkey, *op. cit.,* pp. 16–17.

unrecognized or ignored until it becomes an accomplished fact with cancerous effects. It is this latter category of change which assumes importance in the context of strategy development. The Delphi technique can be fruitfully used to analyze developmental changes. Functionally, a change may fall into one of the following categories: social, economic, political, or technological. The Delphi technique has been used by organizations to study emerging perspectives in all these areas.

An Illustration

The use of the Delphi technique is demonstrated here in studying the impact of emerging socio-economic-political trends on the department store industry. The example to be used here is based on a project with which the author was involved as a consultant. A set of 31 social trends that were found profoundly prevalent by Daniel Yankelovich, Inc., as shown in Exhibit 14-3, were used here. A list, as shown in Exhibit 14-4, of areas of concern to department store executives (i.e., those areas having a direct bearing on the shopping behavior of the department store customers) was prepared.

The panel for the study consisted of 11 retailing executives in an Ohio metropolitan area. Before the panel was approached, however, a sample run was conducted using 28 students in the retailing class of a local university. Exhibit 14-5 shows the instructions for the questionnaire that was used. It should be noted that each prediction had to be rated on a scale ranging from 0 to 1 for its desirability, feasibility, and probability of occurrence. The panel responses on each round were sorted into lower, inner, and upper groups, as is shown below Exhibit 14-5.

The percentage of respondents falling into each category on every variable (i.e., desirability, feasibility, probability of occurrence, and time of occurrence) for a prediction was fed back to the panel members on the completion of the first round. The respondents were asked to complete the same questionnaire in the second round after they had had a chance to digest the findings of the first round. This process continued for as many as four rounds.

The process could have been continued further. But results of a comparison of round 3 with round 4 were statistically insignificant (results were significant between rounds 1 and 2 and rounds 2 and 3.) Thus, there was no point in carrying on further. In other words, by conducting tests of significance (i.e., analysis of variances between two rounds), it can be determined whether it is worthwhile to undertake another round. Exhibit 14-6 shows a sample of the results obtained in the three rounds.

Tabulation of data obtained in the first round provided a long list of 37 changes in the area of concern in this study. After attrition and the screening out of irrelevant, trivial, and duplicate changes among those mentioned initially, in the final round 23 meaningful retailing predictions came out, which are listed in Exhibit 14-7. In presenting the final results, meaningful labels were assigned to the groupings as illustrated.

EXHIBIT 14-3   Social Trends

PSYCHOLOGY OF AFFLUENCE TRENDS, reflecting the increasing assumption that the essentials of economic survival are assured, leading to a focus on having more or doing more to improve the quality of living.

Part I.   Trend   1. Personalization
                                       2. Physical Self-Enhancement
                                       3. Physical Fitness and Well-Being
                                       4. Social/Cultural Self-Expression
                                       5. Personal Creativity
                                       6. Anti-Materialism
                                       7. Meaningful Work

ANTI-FUNCTIONALISM TRENDS, reflecting reaction to the emphasis on the functional and "scientific," seen as leading to drabness and boredom in everyday life.

Part II.   Trend   8. Mysticism
                                       9. Sensuousness
                                      10. New Romanticism
                                      11. Introspection
                                      12. Novelty and Change
                                      13. Beauty in the Home

REACTION AGAINST COMPLEXITY TRENDS, reflecting the belief that life has become excessively complicated, that the individual has lost control of his destiny, and that there is much to be gained by returning to a more natural and more simple style of life.

Part III.   Trend 14. Return to Nature
                                      15. Simplification
                                      16. Anti-Bigness
                                      17. Scientism and Technocracy
                                      18. Ethnic Orientation
                                      19. Local Community Involvement

TRENDS RELATED TO THE WEAKENING OF THE "PROTESTANT ETHIC," reflecting questioning of a value system, termed the "Protestant Ethic" by sociologists, which, put very simply, is based on the belief that ambition, striving, hard work, self-sufficiency, self-denial, and other familiar virtues will lead to a successful life.

Part IV.   Trend 20. Living for Today
                                      21. Hedonism
                                      22. Away From Self-Improvement
                                      23. Noninstitutional Religion
                                      24. Liberal Sex Attitudes
                                      25. Blurring of the Sexes
                                      26. Acceptance of Drugs

TRENDS REFLECTING PERMISSIVENESS IN CHILD REARING, deriving from the psychological guidelines which have been widely used in the upbringing of our current youth population. These guidelines were based largely on concern about the negative aftereffects of a rigid, demanding, punishment-oriented childhood.

Part V.   Trend 27. Anti-Hypocrisy
                                      28. Rejection of Authority
                                      29. Tolerance for Chaos and Disorder
                                      30. Female Careerism
                                      31. Familism

Source: D. Yankelovich, Inc.

EXHIBIT 14-4   Aspects of the Department Store Industry That Are of
Special Interest

A. Products
 1. Women's better dresses
 2. Housedresses and undergarments
 3. Children's clothing
 4. Men's socks and shirts
 5. Furniture
 6. Large appliances
 7. Towels, sheets, blankets, and spreads
 8. Kitchen utensils and small electrical appliances
B. Telephone shopping
C. Downtown vs. suburban (shopping center) shopping
D. Competition, such as from a discount store
E. Shopping motivations: convenience, fun, etc.
F. Nature and scope of services such as charge accounts, delivery, gift wrapping,
 sales clerks, etc.
G. Mail-order shopping
H. Fashion
I. Store decor
J. Advertisements and other aspects of promotion
K. Time preferences in shopping
L. Significance of comparison shopping, bargain hunting, impulse buying, brows-
 ing through the store, etc.

The most prominent trends (i.e., those most desirable, most highly feasible,
and most likely to occur in the immediate future) that the panel predicted are the
following:

 1. Checkless shopping
 2. Market for natural products
 3. Door-to-door selling
 4. Cooperative stores
 5. Outfitting
 6. International shopping
 7. Store guarantee
 8. Common products for men and women

Needless to say, the significance of these trends, if in fact they do occur, will be
great for the department store industry. Their impact must be considered in
designing corporate strategy.

Other Uses of the Delphi Technique

The Delphi technique has great potential. It has so far been used mainly for
predicting distant and abstract changes. Occasionally it has also been used
for forecasting short-term sales and determining optimum bid price. As work
on the technique continues, perhaps many more applications of it will be

EXHIBIT 14-5   Delphi Study Questionnaire: Future Perspectives of Retailing

1. A well-known consulting organization has recognized 31 socio-economic trends which it claims would have far-reaching impact on people's life-style. These trends are listed on the enclosed sheet. Our purpose here is to study the significance of these trends on the department store industry (especially the aspects listed on the enclosure, but not necessarily limited to them).

2. Please read and ponder over the trends and indicate below in column 1 all anticipated changes expected in the sphere of the department store industry. For each change, indicate the source—e.g., the particular trend(s) which lead you to such an anticipation. Then evaluate each projected change with respect to the four factors at the right in view of the total environment as you see it.

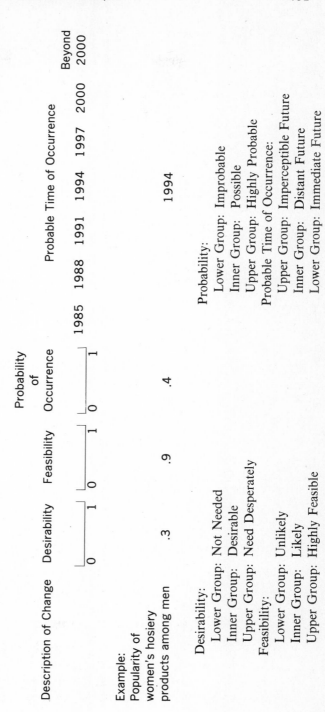

Description of Change	Desirability	Feasibility	Probability of Occurrence	Probable Time of Occurrence
				1985 1988 1991 1994 1997 2000 Beyond 2000
Example: Popularity of women's hosiery products among men	.3	.9	.4	1994

Desirability:
    Lower Group: Not Needed
    Inner Group: Desirable
    Upper Group: Need Desperately
Feasibility:
    Lower Group: Unlikely
    Inner Group: Likely
    Upper Group: Highly Feasible

Probability:
    Lower Group: Improbable
    Inner Group: Possible
    Upper Group: Highly Probable
Probable Time of Occurrence:
    Upper Group: Imperceptible Future
    Inner Group: Distant Future
    Lower Group: Immediate Future

EXHIBIT 14-6   Sample Results of the Delphi Technique (Three Rounds)

Percentage Responses

Prediction		Desirability			Feasibility			Probability of Occurrence			Probable Time of Occurrence		
		Not Needed	Desirable	Needed Desperately	Un-likely	Likely	Highly Feasible	Improbable	Possible	Highly Probable	Imperceptible Future	Distant Future	Immediate Future
1. Twenty-four-hour shopping	Round 1	75	20	5	38	40	22	57	28	15	55	30	15
	Round 2	58	35	7	49	38	13	44	47	9	62	27	11
	Round 3	43	46	11	54	35	11	29	62	9	69	21	10
2. New role of a salesclerk: "a doctor in waiting"	Round 1	27	45	28	40	33	27	32	56	12	38	44	18
	Round 2	31	58	11	45	39	16	28	62	10	26	52	22
	Round 3	28	63	9	48	42	10	21	70	9	3	68	29

EXHIBIT 14-7   Predictions: Retailing

1. Twenty-four-hour shopping
2. New role of salesclerk: "a doctor in waiting"
3. Shops for different moods
4. Declining market for "artificial" products
5. Checkless shopping
6. Growth through vertical integration
7. Increased emphasis on door-to-door selling
8. Computerized shopping
9. High-rise shopping centers
10. Recyclable clothes
11. Personal wear adjustable with physical growth
12. Universal merchandise standards
13. Rise of holding companies
14. Shopping across national boundaries
15. Frequent changes in store decor
16. Intellectual advertising
17. Customer's cooperative stores
18. Store's guarantee on merchandise
19. Trade-ins for unconventional merchandise
20. New forms of common products for men and women
21. Matching brands to moods and occasions
22. Temperature-proof clothes
23. Computerized service: what outfit to wear

developed, and it will be safe to say that the Delphi method can be used to determine the value of any uncertain event. Even if the event happens to be completely unknown, at least initial insights can be gained into it (what statisticians call *prior distribution*). Then as more information becomes available, the original predictions can be revised with the use of statistical techniques such as the Bayes Theorem.

Comments

The following are the points which become relevant in using the Delphi method:

1. Choice of panel members
2. Number of people in a panel
3. Number of rounds to be repeated
4. Impact of interactive variables

The choice of panel members should be related to the purpose for which the Delphi technique is employed. If the purpose is to make broad predictions, an interdisciplinary team of experts would be most appropriate. On the other hand, if the forecast deals with a specific industry, persons supposedly knowledgeable about the industry should be preferred. But if the forecast is concerned with the company's perspective, the in-house experts should comprise the panel. This rule of thumb is fine. But, as can be imagined, most people, while having some insights into related fields, are most knowledgeable in a few areas. It is a good idea, therefore, to choose people who rate highly on the relevant factors. Exhibit 14-8 provides the appropriate qualification mix of experts for different types of forecasts. As may be recalled, the study discussed earlier was concerned with forecast 3 in Exhibit 14-8. For that study the experts, according to the scheme presented in Exhibit 14-8, should have the following backgrounds: They should be very good informal generalists, have widely diversified and interdisciplinary experience, have high creative conjecturing ability, etc.

As far as the size of the panel is concerned, experiments at Rand Corporation have shown a positive correlation between reliability of results and size of the panel. In other words, the error goes down with every increase in the size of the panel. For example, the error factor decreases from 1.2 in a one-man panel to .6 at panel size 9. In fact, the error continues to decline even at size 29. The Rand study does not pinpoint the exact desirable size for a panel. However, certain generalizations can be made. The minimum size should be somewhere between 9 to 11, while it is helpful for the sake of reliability to go as high as 30. There are organizations, however, which have used panels of 140 people.[10]

The question of the number of rounds that should be tried in an experiment has already been discussed above. Briefly, however, another additional round should be carried on as long as the variances of the results of the previous two rounds are statistically significant. Once the improvement in results from the previous round is marginal (as proved by the analysis of variance), an additional round is unnecessary. The outcome of the last round need not be used as a final result, but would be of interest for proving that no further significant improvements in the results are possible.

One drawback of the Delphi method is that each trend is given unilateral consideration on its own merits. Thus, using the Delphi method, one may end up with conflicting forecasts; i.e., one trend may suggest that something will happen, while another may lead in the opposite direction. To resolve this problem, another forecasting technique called the *cross-impact matrix* has been used by some researchers. With this technique the effects of potential interactions among items in a forecast set of occurrences can be investigated. If the behavior of an individual item is probable, (i.e., if it varies positively or negatively with the occurrence or nonoccurrence of other items), the cross-impact effect is present. Thus, using the cross-impact matrix method, it can be determined whether the predicted event will have an enhancing or inhibiting influence upon each of the other events affected.

---

[10]Harper Q. North and Donald L. Pyke, "Probes of the Technological Future," *Harvard Business Review* (May–June, 1969), p. 68.

EXHIBIT 14-8   Important Factors in the Selection of a Panel of Experts

Specific Corporate Orientation to the Future	Empirical Data	Judgment			Diversity of Participants		Imagination	
		Specialized Expertise	Less Specialized Expertise	Informal Generalists	Close to Specialized Fields and Interests	Widely Diversified and Interdisciplinary	Extrapolative	Creative Conjecture
1. Broadened applications of existing technologies	high	high	high	low	high	low	high	medium
2. New alternatives evolving from existing knowledge	medium	medium to high	high	medium	medium	medium	medium	medium
3. New alternatives evolving from new knowledge derived from trends of research, analysis, and social developments	low	medium	high	high	medium to low	high	medium to low	high
4. New alternatives evolving from new knowledge derived from responsible, educated conjecture	low	medium to low	high	high	low	high	low	high
5. New alternatives from creative conjecture not discernable from any existing knowledge	low	low	high	high	low	high	low	high

Source: Robert M. Campbell and David Hitchin, "The Delphi Technique: Implementation in the Corporate Environment," in Subhash C. Jain and Surendra Singhvi, *Essentials of Corporate Planning* (Oxford, OH: Planning Executives Institute, 1973), p. 306.

SCENARIO BUILDING

Traditionally plans for the future were developed on a single set of assumptions. This was alright during times of relative stability. But in the 1980s, as the turbulent years of the 1970s have shown, it may not be desirable to commit the organization to the "most probable" future alone. It is equally important to make allowances for unexpected or less probable future trends which may seriously jeopardize the strategy. One way to focus on different futures within the planning process is to develop scenarios, then design the strategy so that it has enough flexibility to accommodate whatever future occurs. In other words, by developing multiple scenarios of the shape of things to come, a company can make a better strategic response to the future environment. A *scenario* may be defined as a synopsis of the plot of a drama dealing with certain aspects of the future which depicts potential actions and events in a likely order of development, beginning with a set of conditions which describe a current situation or set of circumstances. In addition, scenarios depict a possible course of evolution in a given field. The two stages in scenario building can be labeled as "identification of changes" and "evolution of programs."

Changes are picked up in the environment and can be grouped into two classes: 1) scientific and technological and 2) socio-economic-political. Chapter 3 on environmental scanning dealt with the identification of these changes. This identification should be done by taking into consideration the total environment and its possibilities: What changes are taking place? What shape will they take in the future? How are other areas related to the changes? What effect will the changes have on other related fields? What opportunities and threats are likely?

The scenario should be developed without any intentions of it being a prediction of the future. It should be a time-ordered sequence of events bearing a logical cause-and-effect relationship to each other. The objective of a scenario exercise should be to clarify certain phenomena and/or study the key points in a series of developments in order to evolve new programs. One can follow an inductive or a deductive approach in building a scenario. The deductive approach, which is predictive in nature, studies the broader changes and analyzes the impact of each change on the company's existing lines, at the same time generating ideas about new areas which seem feasible. Under the inductive approach, the future of each product line is simulated by exposing its current environment to various changes foreseen in the future. Through a process of elimination those changes which bear relevance to one's business can be studied more deeply for possible action. Both approaches have their merits and limitations. The deductive approach, however, is much more demanding since it calls for proceeding from unknowns to specifics. At different levels in the organization both approaches have some contribution to make. At the strategic level, the deductive approach of building a scenario is likely to be more useful. In operations planning, however, the inductive approach is likely to prove more useful.

Exhibit 14-9 describes how scenarios are constructed at the General Electric Company. Scenarios are not a set of random thoughts, but logical conclusons based on past behavior, future expectation, and the likely interactions of these two. As a matter of fact, a variety of analytical techniques (i.e., the Delphi method, trend-impact analysis, and cross-impact analysis) are used at G.E. to formulate scenarios.

Scenarios may be analyzed following Linneman and Kennell's ten-step approach, which is stated below:

1. Identify and make explicit your company's mission, basic objective, and policies.
2. Determine how far into the future you wish to plan.
3. Develop a good understanding of your company's points of leverage and vulnerability.
4. Determine factors that you think will definitely occur within your planning time frame.
5. Make a list of key variables that will have make-or-break consequences for your company.
6. Assign reasonable values to each key variable.
7. Build scenarios in which your company may operate.
8. Develop a strategy for each scenario which will most likely achieve your company's objectives.
9. Check the flexibility of each strategy in each scenario by testing its effectiveness in the other scenarios.
10. Select—or develop—an "optimum response" strategy.[11]

EVALUATION OF INVESTMENT PROPOSALS

Investment proposals can be evaluated by using profitability criteria. Various profitability measures are discussed below.

Payback Period

This is perhaps the simplest method used to rank projects for allocating limited resources. The ranking criterion used in this method is the number of years a project will take to return the original investment. Usually companies establish a break-off point, such as three or five years, when ranking projects. Thus, if three years is the criterion, only projects that will return investment in less than three years are accepted. The ones exceeding that three-year period are rejected. If there are more projects meeting the criterion than can be approved due to limitation of resources, the projects promising to return investment most quickly are chosen.

---

[11]Robert E. Linneman and John D. Kennell, "Shirt-sleeve Approach to Long-range Plans," *Harvard Business Review* (March–April, 1977), pp. 141–151.

EXHIBIT 14-9   Scenario-building Method at General Electric Company

Prepare Background
- Assess overall environmental factors for the industrial sector under investigation
  - Demographic and life-style
  - General business and economic
  - Legislative and regulatory
  - Scientific and technological
- Develop crude "systems" model of the industry

Select Critical Indicators
- Identify the industry's key indicators (trends)
- Undertake literature search to identify potential future events impacting the key trends
- Nominate Delphi panel participants whose expert opinion is credible in evaluating the industry's future

INDICATOR:
Potential Future Events
Experts on Indicator

Establish Past Behavior For Each Indicator
- Establish the historical performance for each indicator
- Enter this data into the data base of the TIA program
- Analyze reasons for past behavior of each trend
  - Demographic & social
  - Economic
  - Political & legislative
  - Technological
- Construct Delphi panel interview artifact

Value
1950   1975

Verify Potential Future Events
- Interrogate Delphi panel
- Evaluate past trends
- Assess the potential impact of future events
- Assess the probability of future events
- Forecast future values
- Specify and document assumptions for forecasts
- Specify and document rationale for projected values

Forecast Each Indicator
- Operate the TIA and CIA programs on the literature search and Delphi output to establish the range of future values

Historical & Projected Value
1950   1990
(TIA)

(CIA)

	CO₂ Causing Climate Change	OPEC Doubling Prices	Industrial ZPG Climate Change	BTU Cleaning Percentage	Bursting 250 Agreement
Wild Card Events	Interdependence Events Most Impacted				
Development of Fusion	+	+	−	−	−
Cost-effective Oil Shale	+	+	−	−	−
Economic Synthetics from Coal	+	−	−		
Clean Combustion of Coal	+	+	−		
Conservation Ethic	+	−	−		

- Analyze forecast results

Write Scenario(s)

Note: TIA = Trend-impact analysis; CIA = Cross-impact analysis.
Source: General Electric Company.

The payback method has one serious limitation. It ignores the time value of money. There are projects which take big doses of investment and are slow to return, but total return from them can be several times the original investment. If they are judged strictly on the basis of the payback method, they may be rejected.

Return on Investment (ROI):

The return on investment can be computed by using as a base the average net income from a project during its life and the gross original investment:

$$ROI = \frac{\text{average net income during life}}{\text{gross original investment}}$$

If the computed ROI on a project is higher than the target return on investment, the project will be accepted. Some companies, instead of gross original investment, use *net investment* (gross assets minus current liabilities minus depreciation reserves). The primary advantages of ROI are: 1) its simplicity and 2) management's familiarity with it (since it is frequently used in the context of other operational matters). However, ROI does not reflect the time value of money, and this disadvantage is compounded when cash flows are uneven.

To illustrate the return-on-investment method, let us consider a company which buys an old machine for $13,560. The machine will produce a product which will provide $2080 in annual profits for six years. The salvage value of the machine at the end of the sixth year will be zero. Then the return on investment will be:

$$\frac{\dfrac{(\$2,080)(6)}{6}}{\$13,560 + 0} = \frac{2,080}{13,560} = 15.34\%$$

Present-value Method

In its simplest form, the present-value method entails computing the present value of expected cash flows discounted at the cost of capital or target rate of return and comparing it with the cost of the project. The project is considered acceptable if the difference is positive and rejected if negative. A positive difference shows that the project will earn more than the discount rate. If the investments in a project are made in different time periods, it is preferable to have the return from the project reduced to its present value also. Essentially, the present value represents the net cumulative value of a project's cash outflows and inflows discounted at a stated rate of interest.

The present-value approach, like the discounted-cash-flow-return-on-investment method discussed below, assumes immediate reinvestment of funds at the discount rate. Thus, it avoids the distortion of projects which have either very high or low rates of return. Besides, the present values of all projects may be totaled to give an overall measure of profitability. However, when one compares present values for different projects, these values must be related to the size of the respective project investments in order to provide meaningful project comparisons.

Discounted Cash Flow Rate of Return (Internal Rate of Return)

It is simple arithmetic that $1,000 deposited in a savings account at five percent interest will be worth $1,050 at the end of the first year, $1,102.50 at the end of the second year, etc. Discounting implies the same basic concept with a different twist: How much would have to be deposited today at five-percent compound interest in order for it to be worth $1,000 in one year? The compounded amounts show the future values of $1,000 at the end of each year, while the discounted figures represent today's value of $1,000 to be received at the end of the year. Thus the dollar which will not be received for five years is worth only $.78 today. In other words, $.78 must be invested today in order to receive $1 at the end of five years at five percent interest. What has been done here is to equate the present value of future cash flows to the cost of investment. The rate of interest which does that is the discounted cash flow rate of return.

The *discounted cash flow rate of return,* or *internal rate of return,* is the interest rate that discounts future cash receipts from a project down to a present value equal to the cash disbursements required by the project. In other words, it is the maximum rate of interest which can be paid for a project's capital requirements while still recovering the original project investment.

Under this method, the decreasing capital investment in the project is related to its expected cash flows. Alternatively, the investment is reduced by cash inflows so that the average investment is about one half of the original investment.

The discounted cash flow return on investment must be found by trial and error. To begin with, an interest rate must be assumed. Taking this rate of interest, the cash flows from an investment should be reduced to their present value. The present value should be compared with the investment (cost incurred on a project). If the present value and investment are almost equal, the assumed rate of interest will be the discounted cash flow return on investment. If the present value exceeds the investment, a new rate of interest which is higher than the previous one should be assumed and the above process repeated. However, if the present value is lower than the investment, an interest rate lower than the earlier interest rate should be assumed, and once again present value should be computed to see how it compares with the investment. This process (assuming interest rate and comparing present value to investment) should continue until present value is almost equal to investment. The rate of interest at which this happens will be the desired rate of return. Exhibit 14-10 shows the computation of the discounted cash flow rate of return or internal rate of return for two projects, A and B. In the first instance, present values for two projects have been computed at an assumed four-percent rate of interest. In the case of both the projects, the present value exceeds the investment. Therefore, a higher interest rate should be assumed,

EXHIBIT 14-10   Computation of Discounted Cash Flow

Year	Cash Outflow	Cash Inflow PROJ. A	Cash Inflow PROJ. B	Present Value at 4 Percent			Present Value at 10 Percent			Present Value at 15 Percent			Present Value at 20 Percent		
				Interest Factor	A	B	IF	A	B	IF	A	B	IF	A	B
1	$5000	$2500	$500	.96	$2400	$ 480	.91	$2275	$ 455	.87	$2175	$435	.83	$2075	$415
2		2000	1000	.92	1840	920	.83	1660	830	.76	1520	760	.69	1380	690
3		1500	1500	.89	1335	1335	.75	1125	1125	.66	990	990	.58	870	870
4		500	2000	.85	425	1700	.68	340	1360	.57	285	1140	.48	240	960
5		—	2500	.82	—	2050	.62	—	1550	.50	—	1250	.40	—	1000
6		—	3000	.79	—	2370	.56	—	1680	.43	—	1290	.33	—	990
					6000	8855		5400	7000		4970	5865		4565	4925
CASH OUTFLOW					5000	5000		5000	5000		5000	5000		5000	5000
NET PRESENT VALUE					$1000	$3855		$ 400	$2000		$ (30)	$865		$(435)	$ (75)

say, 15 percent, and the present values at that rate computed. It is noticed that for project A at a 15 percent rate of interest, present value and investment are almost equal, while for project B at 20 percent interest, the two match. Thus, the internal rate of return for project A is 15 percent, while for project B it is 20 percent.

The internal rate of return should be compared with the company's cost of capital. If the former exceeds the latter, the project will be accepted. If there are more projects in which the internal rate of return is higher than the cost of capital, and if resources won't permit accepting all of them, then the ones showing larger differences between internal rate of return and cost of capital will be accepted, starting from the top.

The discounted-cash-flow-rate-of-return method is credited with providing the true yield from a project. However, it is based on an implicit assumption which is often missed in using this method. This assumption is that the firm is in a position to reinvest cash throw-offs from a project immediately on their receipt. If reinvestment opportunity is lacking, the discounted cash flow will be different.

Present-value Index (Profitability Index)

The *present-value index,* or *profitability index,* is the ratio of the cumulative present value of cash inflows divided by the cumulative present value of cash outflows. An index of exactly 1 signifies that the project earns at the discount rate. An index of less than 1 shows an earning rate which is lower than the discount rate. An index exceeding one denotes a higher rate of earnings.

In addition to advantages attributed to present value, the profitability index provides a basis for comparing different projects since it relates cash inflows to the project investment. It is, therefore, the most useful single guide for the financial ranking of different projects.

Risk Analysis

The attractiveness of a proposed investment is not only dependent upon its anticipated financial returns, but also upon the degree of risk involved; i.e., the possibility of loss or of lower-than-estimated results. It is true, of course, that as risk increases, the expected financial return should increase sufficiently to compensate for it. The assessment of risk, however, is the most difficult task in the evaluation process. The difficulty lies not only in projecting return on investment for any given set of assumptions, but also in developing proper assumptions and estimating their impact. Each assumption involves some degree of uncertainty, and the combined uncertainties may reach critical proportions.

Most frequently the economic analysis of a project takes into consideration only a single most likely set of profit projections and, consequently, does not necessarily assess risk. For example, there may actually be only a 20 percent chance that the "single best estimate" will occur and an 80 percent chance of either higher or lower returns. This "single best estimate" may suffice for the majority of projects since management knowledge and experience may enable an adequate subjective judgment on the degree of risk to be made. However, a conscious assessment of risk should be made for every proposed project; this assessment may range from an informal subjective appraisal to a comprehensive evaluation employing advance sampling and mathematical techniques. The following are the factors critical to the success of a project:

1. Marketing (price-volume relationship, product's competitive strengths and weaknesses, product mix, etc.)
2. Technological or processing factors (manufacturing costs, raw materials, payroll cost, and utilities)
3. Capital cost

Risk analysis is essentially a method of dealing with the problem of uncertainty. Uncertainty usually affects most of the variables which are combined to obtain a cost estimate, a financial return, or any other indicators which may be used to evaluate a project. Sometimes this uncertainty can be dealt with by combining values for all input variables, chosen in such a way that they yield a conservative estimate for the result of the analysis. In other cases the best-estimate value may be selected (that is, the value which is most likely to be achieved). Each of these approaches implies a decision: the first, to look at the project with a conservative eye, and the second, to disregard the consequences of any variation around the best-estimate value. Both can lead to biased decisions. For example, if only conservative estimates of the variables are combined, the final result is likely to be "over-conservative."

On the other hand, the use of only best-estimate values fails to take into account the fact that some values of the variables might vary substantially in the final computation; thus, basing a decision on a single value may lead to more risk than one intended.

The purpose of risk analysis is to eliminate the need to restrict one's judgment to a single optimistic, pessimistic, or "best" evaluation by carrying throughout the analysis a complete judgment on the possible range of each variable and on the likelihood of each value within this range. At each step of the analysis, these judgments are combined at the same time as the variables themselves are combined. As a result, the product of the analysis is not just a single value, but a judgment on the likelihood of each value within this range.

Risk analysis is expensive and time consuming. Thus, detailed analysis may be undertaken only selectively. One chemical company executive notes that it took two worker-months and $10,000 in expenses to analyze the risk on a $100 million project back in 1974. Sensitivity analysis and simulation are two important techniques for evaluating risks.

Sensitivity Analysis. Sensitivity analysis measures the effect of changes in selling prices, sales volume, elements of operating cost, and investment upon project profitability and rate of return. While sensitivity analysis does not determine probability or risk as such, it is particularly useful for indicating those factors which are critical to a project's success or failure and highlighting areas where further study or analysis would be desirable. Sensitivity analysis followed by managerial intuitive judgment is frequently sufficient for risk evaluation.

Simulation. *Simulation* provides insights into an operation by highlighting the mode and extent of various effects of the underlying variables; this is possible by reproducing in miniature form the characteristics of a system too complex to be analyzed otherwise. It is possible to build a corporate financial model and then use it to evaluate the risk of a particular financial decision. For example, the impact of a change in the proportion of profits paid out as dividends on cash, growth, market value of stock, and so on can be noted. Simulation is an interesting and comparatively easy technique for studying the impact of a change on some variables. The difficult part, however, is to build a model encompassing the various ingredients of a system. A number of large corporations have developed corporate financial models.

In addition to sensitivity analysis and simulation, there are various techniques, both statistical and nonstatistical, which are useful aids in the various phases of project analysis and evaluation. Among these are linear programming, correlation analysis, decision trees, the learning curve, and game theory.

SUMMARY

This chapter discusses a variety of tools and techniques for the planning and analysis of strategic issues. These include the experience curve concept, the Delphi technique, scenario building, and evaluation of investment proposals. Most of these techniques require data inputs both from within the organization and from outside. Each tool or technique has been examined for its application and usefulness. In some cases procedural details for using a technique have been illustrated by means of examples from the field. Of the many techniques dealt with in this chapter, the experience curve concept is the most far reaching from the viewpoint of marketing strategy.

DISCUSSION QUESTIONS

1. Explain the relevance of experience curves in formulating pricing strategy.
2. The experience curve concept seems to suggest that antitrust laws are dysfunctional. Comment on this.
3. Discuss how the Delphi method may be used to generate innovative ideas for new types of channels for distributing automobiles.
4. Develop a scenario on the use of the automobile, assuming acute shortages and high prices for gasoline in the 1980s.
5. Explain how the internal-rate-of-return method is superior to the return-on-investment method for evaluating investment proposals.
6. Examine the significance of risk analysis in determining the attractiveness of an investment proposal.

APPENDIX: EXPERIENCE CURVE CONSTRUCTION

The experience curve concept can be used as an aid in developing marketing strategy. The curve construction procedure discussed below describes how the relationship between costs and accumulated experience can be empirically developed.

The first step in the process of constructing the experience curve is to compute experience and accumulated cost information. *Experience* for a particular year is the accumulation of all volume up to and including that year. It is computed by adding the year's volume to the experience of the previous years. *Accumulated cost (constant dollars)* is the total of all constant costs incurred for the product up to and including that year. It is computed by adding the year's constant dollar cost to the accumulated costs of the previous years. A year's constant dollar cost is the real dollar cost for that year, corrected for inflation. It is computed by dividing the cost (actual dollars) by the appropriate deflator.

The second step is to plot the initial and annual experience/accumulated cost (constant dollars) data on log-log graph paper (see Exhibit 14-A). It is important that the experience axis of this graph be calibrated so that its point of intersection with the accumulated cost axis is at 1 unit of experience. The accumulated cost axis may be calibrated in any convenient manner.

The next step is to fit a straight line to the points on the graph, which may be accomplished by using the least-squares method (Exhibit 14-A). It is useful at this point to stop and analyze the accumulated cost diagram. In general, the closer the data points are to the accumulated-cost curve, the stronger is the evidence that the experience effect is present. Deviations of the data points from the curve, however, do not necessarily disprove the presence of the experience effect. If the deviations can be attributed to heavy investments in plant, etc. (as is common to very capital-intensive industries), the experience effect still holds, but in the long run (since in the long run the fluctuations are averaged out). If, on the other hand, significant deviations from the line cannot be explained as necessary periodic changes in the rate of investment, then the presence of the experience effect, or at least its consistency, is open to question. In Exhibit 14-B there is one deviation (see point X) that stands out as significant. If this can be ascribed to heavy investment (in plant, etc.), the experience effect is still viable here.

The next step in the process of constructing the experience curve is to calculate the intensity of the product's experience effect. *Intensity* is the unit-cost-reduction percentage achieved each time the product's experience is doubled. As such, it determines the slope of the experience curve. To compute the intensity from the accumulated cost curve, arbitrarily select an experience level on the experience axis (e.g., point E_1 in Exhibit 14-C). Draw a line vertically up from E_1 until it intersects the accumulated-cost curve. From that point on the curve, draw a line horizontally left until it intersects the accumulated cost axis. Read the corresponding accumulated cost (A_1) from the scale. Follow the same procedure for

EXHIBIT 14-A   Accumulated Cost Diagram

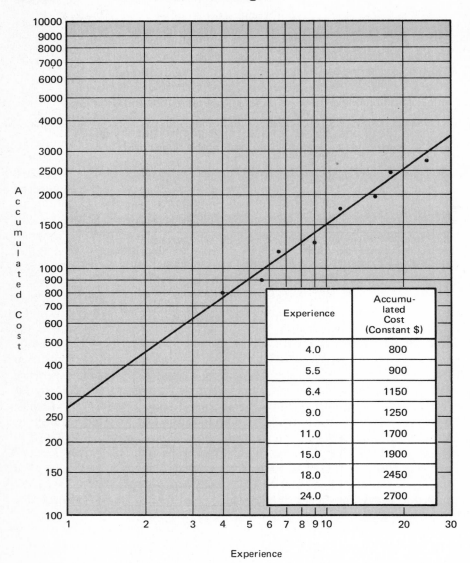

Experience	Accumulated Cost (Constant $)
4.0	800
5.5	900
6.4	1150
9.0	1250
11.0	1700
15.0	1900
18.0	2450
24.0	2700

Experience

experience level E_2, where E_2 equals E_1 times 2, to obtain A_2. Divide A_2 by A_1, divide the result by 2, and subtract the second result from the number 1. The final answer is the product's intensity. With the information given in Exhibit 14-C, the intensity works out to be 16.7 percent:

$$1 - \left(\frac{2500}{1500} \times \frac{1}{2}\right) = .167 = 16.7\%$$

EXHIBIT 14-B   Interpretation of Deviations from Accumulated Cost Curve

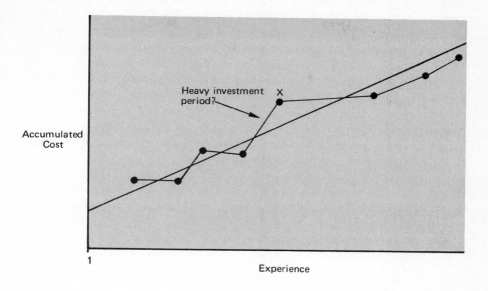

EXHIBIT 14-C   Product Intensity Computation

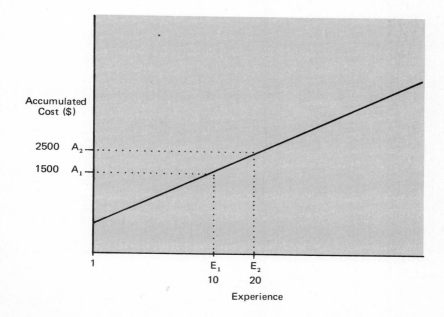

When the intensity has been computed, the slope of the experience curve is determined. However, as shown in Exhibit 14-D, this in itself is not sufficient for constructing the curve. This is because all of the lines in Exhibit 14-D, since they are parallel, have the same slope and represent the same intensity. To construct the experience curve, it is necessary to find a point (C_1) on the unit cost axis. This can be achieved in the following manner. Find the "intensity multiplier" corresponding to the product's intensity from the charts specially prepared for the purpose (Exhibit 14-E). If the intensity falls between two values in Exhibit 14-E, the appropriate intensity multiplier should be determined by interpolating between the two closest intensity multipliers from the exhibit. Read the value on the accumulated cost axis where the curve intersects that axis. Multiply this value by the intensity multiplier. The result is C_1.

The intensity was calculated above as 16.7%. By using Exhibit 14-E, the corresponding intensity multiplier can be interpolated as approximately 0.736. As shown in Exhibit 14-A, the accumulated cost at the point of intersection can be read as approximately $260. Multiplying $260 by 0.736 yields a C_1 of $191. The experience curve can now be plotted on log-log graph paper. Position C_1 on the unit cost axis. Multiply C_1 by the quantity (1 - intensity) to obtain C_2:

$$\$191\ (1-0.167)=\$159$$

Locate C_2 on the unit-cost axis. Find the point of intersection (y) of a line drawn vertically up from 2 on the experience axis and a line drawn horizontally right

EXHIBIT 14-D   Slopes of Parallel Lines

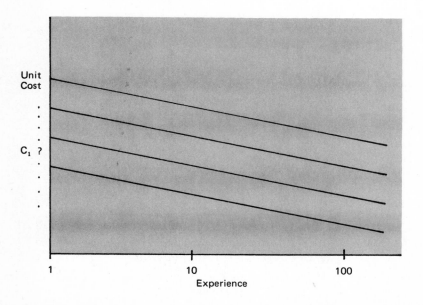

EXHIBIT 14-E   Intensity Multipliers

Intensity	Intensity Multiplier	Intensity	Intensity Multiplier
5.0%	.926	20.5%	.669
5.5	.918	21.0	.660
6.0	.911	21.5	.651
6.5	.903	22.0	.642
7.0	.895	22.5	.632
7.5	.888	23.0	.623
8.0	.880	23.5	.614
8.5	.872	24.0	.604
9.0	.864	24.5	.595
9.5	.856	25.0	.585
10.0	.848	25.5	.575
10.5	.840	26.0	.566
11.0	.832	26.5	.556
11.5	.824	27.0	.546
12.0	.816	27.5	.536
12.5	.807	28.0	.526
13.0	.799	28.5	.516
13.5	.791	29.0	.506
14.0	.782	29.5	.496
14.5	.774	30.0	.485
15.0	.766	30.5	.475
15.5	.757	31.0	.465
16.0	.748	31.5	.454
16.5	.740	32.0	.444
17.0	.731	32.5	.433
17.5	.722	33.0	.422
18.0	.714	33.5	.411
18.5	.705	34.0	.401
19.0	.696	34.5	.390
19.5	.687	35.0	.379
20.0	.678	35.5	.367

from C_2 on the unit-cost axis. Draw a straight line through the points C_1 and y. The result is the product's experience curve (Exhibit 14-F).

The application of the experience curve concept in marketing strategy requires the forecasting of costs. This can be achieved by using the curve above. To accomplish this, determine the current cumulative experience of the product. Add to this value the planned cumulative volume from the present to the future time point. The result is the planned experience level at that point. Locate the planned experience level on the experience axis of the graph. Move vertically up from that point until the line extension of the experience curve is reached. Move horizontally left from the line to the unit-cost axis. Read the estimated unit-cost value from the scale. The unit cost obtained above is expressed in constant dollars, but can be converted to an actual-dollar cost by multiplying it by the projected inflator for the future year.

Cost forecasts can also be used to determine the minimum rate of volume growth necessary to offset an assumed rate of inflation. For example, with an assumed inflation rate of 3.8%, a producer having an intensity of 20% must realize a volume growth of approximately 13% per year in order to just maintain his unit cost in real dollars. Should growth be slower, or should full cost-reduction potential not be realized, the producer's unit cost would rise.

Competitor cost is one of the most fundamental, yet elusive, information needs of the producer attempting to develop marketing strategy. The experience curve concept provides a sound basis for estimating the cost positions of competitors as well. With certain assumptions, the competitors' curves can be estimated.

EXHIBIT 14-F Experience Curve Estimation

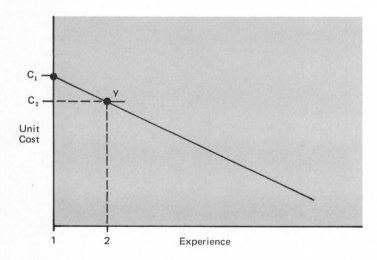

Chapter 15
Strategy-related Models

The Red Queen said: "Now, here, it takes all the running you can do to keep in the same place. If you want to get somewhere else, you must run at least twice as fast as that."

Lewis Carroll
Alice in Wonderland

The previous chapter examined a variety of tools and techniques which may be employed to simplify the task of strategy formulation and implementation. This chapter deals with specific models which can be used in various phases of the strategic planning effort. The techniques are aids which have applications in different management areas. The models which will be discussed in this chapter are used for specific decisions. For example, one model may be used to evaluate different pricing strategies, while another model may be utilized to determine the optimum product-mix strategy. The models are an attractive and viable alternative to informal ad hoc decision making.

Management scientists have made tremendous progress in the development of formal managerial models and in the application of information-processing technology. This success gives hope that we may also be able to improve upon the complex task of systematizing the strategic planning activity by extending the use of models.

As a matter of fact, the progress in this direction is already visible. The PIMS (profit impact of market strategy) model, which is discussed in this chapter, is an example. Other models included here are models for measuring sustainable growth, marketing simulation, trend-impact analysis, cross-impact analysis, a product model, a pricing model, and a model to speculate about the future. The selected models presented in this chapter are but a handful of managerial models which appear to have a direct relevance to strategic planning. These represent an attempt to describe the complex interrelationships among an organization's financial, marketing, and production activities in terms of a set of mathematical and logical relationships which have been programmed into a computer.

PROFIT IMPACT OF MARKET STRATEGY (PIMS)

The PIMS program was initiated in 1972 at the Marketing Science Institute, a nonprofit organization associated with the Harvard Business School, to determine the profit impact of market strategies. As a matter of fact, the initiation of this program is ascribed to the General Electric Company. Back in 1960, the vice-president of marketing services at G.E. authorized a large-scale project (titled PROM, for "profitability optimization model") to examine the above question. Several years of effort finally produced a computer-based model that identified the major factors responsible for a great deal of the variation in return on investment. Since the data used in the model came from diverse markets and industries, it is often referred to as a "cross-sectional" model. Even today cross-sectional models are popularly used at G.E.

The scope of the PIMS program increased so much and its popularity gained such momentum that a few years ago its administration moved to the Strategic Planning Institute, a new organization established for PIMS.

The PIMS program is based on the experience of more than 100 companies in more than 1000 "businesses." "Business" is synonymous with "strategic business unit" (SBU) and is defined as an operative unit which sells a distinct set of products to an identifiable group of customers in competition with a well-defined set of competitors. Essentially, PIMS is a cross-sectional study of the strategic experience of profit organizations. The information on experience has been gathered from the businesses in the form of about 100 pieces of data supplied by them in a standardized format. The gathered information deals with such items as:

1. Market served (in terms of growth, stability, etc.)
2. Competitive environment (number and size of competitors and customers)
3. Position of the business (market share, comparative product quality, comparative price, etc.)
4. Strategy employed (changes in position, discretionary budget allocations, product quality, etc.)
5. Operating results obtained (profit, cash flow, etc.)[1]

Overall Results

The PIMS project (Phases I and II) indicated that the profitability of a business is affected by 37 basic factors. These factors explained the more than 80 percent profitability variation among the businesses studied. Of the 37 basic factors, six proved to be of primary importance (Exhibit 15-1). Among these six factors,

---

[1]See Sidney Schoeffler's speech delivered at the Strategic Planning Conference at Indiana University, November, 1975.

EXHIBIT 15-1   ROI and Key Profit Influences

Return on investment (ROI):
The ratio of net pretax operating income to average investment. Operating income is what is available after deduction of allocated corporate overhead expenses but before deduction of any financial charges on assets employed. "Investment" equals equity plus long-term debt or, equivalently, total assets employed minus current liabilities attributed to the business.

Market share:
The ratio of dollar sales by a business, in a given time period, to total sales by all competitors in the same market. The "market" includes all of the products or services, customer types, and geographic areas that are directly related to the activities of the business. For example, it includes all products and services that are competitive with those sold by the business.

Product (service) quality:
The quality of each participating company's offerings, appraised in the following terms: What was the percentage of sales of products or services from each business in each year which were superior to those of competitors? What was the percentage of equivalent products? Inferior products?

Marketing expenditures:
Total costs for sales force, advertising, sales promotion, marketing research, and marketing administration. The figures do not include costs of physical distribution.

R&D expenditures:
Total costs of product development and process improvement, including those costs incurred by corporate-level units which can be directly attributed to the individual business.

Investment intensity:
Ratio of total investment to sales.

Corporate diversity:
An index which reflects 1) the number of different 4-digit Standard Industrial Classification industries in which a corporation operates, 2) the percentage of total corporate employment in each industry, and 3) the degree of similarity or difference among the industries in which it participates.

Source: Reprinted by permission of the *Harvard Business Review*. Exhibit from "Impact of Strategic Planning on Profit Performance" by Sidney Schoeffler, Robert D. Buzzell, and Donald F. Heany (March–April, 1974), p. 140. Copyright © 1974 by the President and Fellows of Harvard College. All rights reserved.

investment intensity ranked first and market share ranked second (in terms of their impact on profitability).

The PIMS program actually has two models; in addition to the one for predicting ROI, it also has a model for predicting cash flow. The latter model shows that a large variance in cash flow among businesses is explained by 19 factors. Some of the variables in the cash-flow model were also found to be salient in the ROI model. The PIMS study may be defended on the grounds that it is necessary to learn about strategy from experience—something which requires diversity. From this diverse experience have been derived "principles" which are usually expressed in the form of a 3×3 matrix (3 levels of each of three variables with ROI as the criterion). For example, Exhibit 15-2 shows that low market share combined with high investment intensity leads to a very poor return on investment, and vice versa.

EXHIBIT 15-2   Impact of Strategic Planning on Profit
                Performance: Investment Intensity
                and Market Share

Investment Intensity	Market Share		
	Under 12%	12%–26%	Over 26%
Under 45%	21.2%	26.9%	34.6%
45%–71%	8.6	13.1	26.2
Over 71%	2.0	6.7	15.7

Source: Reprinted by permission of the *Harvard Business Review.* Exhibit from "Impact of Strategic Planning on Profit Performance" by Sidney Schoeffler, Robert D. Buzzell, and Donald F. Heany (March–April, 1974), p. 143. Copyright © 1974 by the President and Fellows of Harvard College. All rights reserved.

Relevance of the Program

Not only does the PIMS program provide interesting insights into relationships among crucial variables in a business setting, but it can also be used by a business seeking strategy guidance. In 1977 the PIMS program began providing four different sets of output reports to participating businesses: the par report, the cash-flow par report, the strategy sensitivity report, and the optimum strategy report. The first two reports analyze the performance of a business in the last three years and evaluate the contribution of a number of factors to its return on investment and cash flow. The third report predicts the outcome of various strategic moves for both the long and the short run.

Exhibit 15-3 shows an example of a par report. The par ROI shown here is 26.3%, while the average ROI of all PIMS businesses is 16.7%. The former figure represents the return normally expected from an average management team with average luck. The net difference between the average ROI and the PIMS par ROI for the business under consideration is called the "impact of

EXHIBIT 15-3   Sample PIMS Report: Par Return on Investment (Pretax)
1972–1974

Par return on investment is an estimate of the pretax return on investment (ROI)
that in 1972–74 was normal for businesses facing market and industry conditions
equivalent to those of your business and occupying a similar market position.

For Business No. 87041, Pretax

Par ROI 26.3%
Actual ROI 25.4

Impact on Par ROI of the Factors by Category

Par ROI equals the sum of the total impact and the average ROI of all businesses
in the PIMS data base.

Category	Impact on Par ROI (Pretax)%
Attractiveness of business environment	3.1
Strength of your competitive position	0.1
Differentiation of competitive position	1.2
Effectiveness of use of investment	13.4
Discretionary budget allocation	−6.8
Company factors	−1.2
Change/action factors	−0.2
Total impact	9.6
Average ROI, all PIMS businesses	16.7
Par ROI, this business	26.3%

Source: From Derek Abell, "Tex-Fiber Industries—Petroloid Products Division (D)," 9-577-
040, Harvard Business School, p. 3. Copyright © 1976 by the President and
Fellows of Harvard College. Reproduced by permission.

strategic factors on par ROI." Thus, for the business analyzed in Exhibit 15-3,
the impact works out to be 9.6 percent (i.e., 26.3 − 16.7). This is explained by
the 7 categories of 35 factors. The actual factors included in these categories are
listed in Exhibit 15-4.

A sample of a cash flow par report is shown in Exhibit 15-5. The average cash
flow for all PIMS businesses was 2.0 percent, while the cash flow par for the
business studied here was 0.3 percent. The difference, − 1.7 percent, is explained
by the 19 factors listed in Exhibit 15-5.

EXHIBIT 15-4   Sample PIMS Report: The Impact on Par ROI of Each Factor in the Par Profit Equation (Points of ROI)

	Base Period Values For:			Impact of Factor	
Factors	All PIMS Businesses	This Business	This Type of Business	on ROI	Par (%)
Attractiveness of Business Environment					3.1
Industry (sic) growth, long-run	8.0	21.3	8.2	3.2	
Market growth, short-run	5.9	21.4	5.9	1.4	
Industry exports (% totl shpts)	7.6	0.0	9.6	−1.1	
Sales direct to end user (%)	51.0	60.0	64.5	−0.4	
Strength of Your Competitive Position					0.1
Your market position	22.5	20.5	24.2	−0.1	
Share of 4 largest firms (SIC)	51.6	72.0	52.1	0.6	
Instability of your mkt share	2.9	0.9	3.3	1.1	
Buyer fragmentation index	13.6	15.0	13.8	−1.5	
Differentiation of Competitive Position					1.2
Price relative to competition	2.7	3.0	2.7	−1.2	
Relative pay scale	6.4	6.0	6.4	−0.4	
Product quality	23.2	0.0	24.7	1.1	
New product sales (% totl sales)	12.1	20.0	12.1	0.6	
Manufacturing costs/sales	30.7	22.0	33.6	1.1	
Effectiveness of Use of Investment					13.4
Investment intensity	63.8	61.9	71.3	−12.1	
Fixed capital intensity	57.5	78.2	61.2	−0.5	
Receivables/sales	14.4	12.9	14.9	0.2	
Vertical integration	58.8	81.4	60.1	17.5	
Capacity utilization	75.7	113.7	75.9	5.4	
Raw & in proc.invent./purchase	33.2	35.2	39.3	0.2	
Sales/employees	47730.	50077.	42860.	2.7	
Discretionary Budget Allocation					−6.8
Mktg less sales forc exp/sales	4.1	14.6	3.0	−7.8	
R&D expenses/sales	2.9	4.8	3.4	1.1	
Company Factors					−1.2
Corporate payout (%)	62.0		63.2	−0.0	
Degree of corp diversification	2.1		2.3	−1.2	
Corporate size	1588.0		1431.0	0.0	
Growth rate of corporate sales	10.1		10.3	0.0	

Change/Action Factors

					−0.2
Change in your market share	2.3	−3.4	3.1	−0.7	
Change in product quality	3.2	0.0	3.3	−0.0	
Change in price index	2.9	13.0	2.3	0.2	
Competitive market activity	0.1	−6.5	0.1	−0.0	
Change in capital intensity	−3.3	−22.7	−4.3	−0.7	
Change in vertical integr (%)	0.5	−9.2	0.3	0.6	
Point change adv & prom/sales	−0.1	−1.9	−0.1	−0.7	
Change in sales forc exp/sales	−0.3	−0.8	−0.3	−0.4	
Point change return on sales	1.1	0.2	1.3	1.4	

Notes

1. Components of "your market position" impact:

Your market share	22.5	20.5	24.2
Your market share/share big 3	54.3	37.0	58.8

2. Components of "investment intensity" impact:

Investment/sales	63.8	61.9	71.3
Investment/(value added −.5ni)	120.0	82.5	125.3

3. Only the combined net effect of "investment intensity," "vertical integration," and "sales/employees" should be given an interpretation, not the individual impacts:

$$-12.14 + 17.48 + 2.68 = 8.03$$

4. Interpretation of relative scales:

"Price relative to competition"   "relative pay scale"
  if "2" your price is higher   if "4" your pay scale is lower
    "4"   lower   "8"   higher

Column 3, the means for this type of business (industrial), is for reference only and is not used to calculate the impacts except when used to replace missing data (noted with an *). Company factors are not shown for reasons of data security.

Source: From Derek Abell, "Tex-Fiber Industries—Petroloid Products Division (D)," 9-577-040, Harvard Business School, pp. 4–5. Copyright © 1976 by the President and Fellows of Harvard College. Reproduced by permission.

A strategy sensitivity report is shown in Exhibit 15-7. This report is based on the strategy move of "no planned change." It was prepared assuming the "most likely" environment, as enumerated in Exhibit 15-6. For the strategy sensitivity report, the model based the forecast of trends in the market environment and in the cost structure on the firm's recent performance. This forecast was then used to predict future performance. Although the strategy sensitivity report shown in Exhibit 15-7 is based on the strategy of "no planned change," the model could be used to spell out the likely impact of various changes in the strategy; i.e., market share, degree of vertical integration, and investment intensity could be varied and the probable outcomes of such moves could be examined.

Finally, the optimum strategy report is concerned with isolating a particular combination of strategic moves which optimize a particular criterion (e.g., profit, cash, or growth). This, again, is based on the past experience of others in similar situations.

PIMS operates from the premise that certain structural factors (e.g., market position, capital intensity, etc.) of a business influence, if not determine, the return of that business. The PIMS approach is to gather data on as many actual

EXHIBIT 15-5   PIMS Cash Flow Par Report

	PIMS Mean	This Business	Impact	Change of	Sensitivity Changes Impact by
Decision Use of Cash			−2.6		
1 Market share growth rate	3.2	−1.7	2.5	2.00	−1.02
2 Marketing expense growth rate	10.3	25.3	−1.6	2.00	−0.22
3 New product sales (% tot sales)	13.1	20.0	−1.0	5.00	−0.96
4 R&D expense/sales	2.4	4.8	−1.2	0.50	−0.34
5 Marketing expense/sales	10.3	18.1	−1.2	2.00	0.11
Change in Investment/Sales			3.6		
6 Point change investment/sales	−4.7	−7.3	3.6	2.00	−2.38
Forced Use of Cash			−7.0		
7 Real market growth, short run	8.2	21.7	−7.3	2.00	−1.07
8 Selling price growth rate	6.4	6.5	−0.1	1.00	−0.75
9 Industry (SIC) growth, long run	9.3	19.4	0.4	1.00	0.04
Strength of Competitive Position			−0.8		
10 Market share	23.3	20.5		5.00	1.23
Relative market share	60.6	37.0			
Differentiation from Competitors			−0.5		
11 Price relative to competition	1.030	1.000	0.0	0.01	−0.01
12 Relative product quality	23.5	0.0	−0.1	5.00	0.15
13 Price diff from competitors	0.040	0.000	−0.5	0.01	0.13
Capital and Production Structure			5.6		
14 Investment/sales	58.3	61.9	−2.3	5.00	−1.04
15 Vertical integration	59.8	82.5	5.8	2.00	0.62
16 Value added per employee	29.3	40.3	0.5	5.00	0.11
17 Capacity utilization	80.6	113.7U	1.7	5.00	0.00
18 Replacement value/GBV of P&E	185.4	180.0	−0.1	10.00	0.11
19 Employees unionized (%)	51.3	50.0	0.1	5.00	−0.08

Footnotes
(U) Capacity utilization compressed to upper limit of 110.0
Source: From Derek Abell, "Tex-Fiber Industries—Petroloid Products Division (D)," 9-577-040, Harvard Business School, p. 11. Copyright © 1976 by the President and Fellows of Harvard College. Reproduced by permission.

business experiences as possible and to search for those relationships which appear to have the most significant effect on the ROI. A model of these relationships is then developed so that an estimate of a business' ROI can be made from the structural factors describing the business. Obviously the PIMS conceptual framework must be modified on occasion in the real world. For example, the repositioning of the structural factors may be impossible and the costs of doing so may be prohibitive. Besides, actual performance may reflect some element of luck or some unusual event. Additionally, the results may be in-

EXHIBIT 15-6   PIMS Strategy Sensitivity Report: Version
002C (611010) –5 Summary

"Most Likely" Environment
Key Assumptions

	1975–78	1978–84
Industry sales growth rate	10.0%	12.0%
Annual change in selling price	5.0%	3.0%
Annual change in wage rates	8.0%	
Annual change in material cost	8.0%	
Annual change in plant cost	8.0%	6.0%
Time discount rate	10.0%	
Capital charge rate	0.0%	
Tax rate	50.0%	
Dividend payout rate	0.0%	
"Quantum" of additional capacity	2.0%	
Targeted capacity utilization	113.0%	
Annual depreciation rate	12.0%	

Deviations from:	Actual Historical	Assumed Future
Par ROI	−1.3	−1.3
Delta ROI	−3.0	0.0

Source: From Derek Abell, "Tex-Fiber Industries—Petroloid Products Division (D)," 9-577-040, Harvard Business School, p. 12. Copyright © 1976 by the President and Fellows of Harvard College. Reproduced by permission.

fluenced by the transitional effect of a conscious change in strategic direction. Despite these reservations, the PIMS framework can be beneficial in the following ways:

1. It provides a realistic and consistent method for establishing potential return levels for individual businesses.
2. It stimulates managerial thinking as to the reasons for deviations from par performance.
3. It provides insight into strategic moves which will improve the par ROI.
4. It encourages a more discerning appraisal of business unit performance.

GROWTH POTENTIAL

Growth is a common objective of business organizations. Growth requires resources; therefore, adequate management of corporate resources constitutes an important part of a strategic planning process. Zakon has said:

EXHIBIT 15-7   PIMS Strategy Sensitivity Report: Version
               002C (611010) –5 Details

STRATEGY MOVE: NO PLANNED CHANGE

	Recent Position (1972–74)	During Strategy Implementation (1977)	New Steady-State Position (1979)	New Long-Term Position (1984)
Net sales (current $)	476.4	643.0	803.3	1415.7
Net income	74.7	101.4	128.1	225.1
Average investment	294.8	345.3	472.6	862.4
Net cash flow	9.3	33.8	0.4	34.6
Return on investment	25.4%	29.4%	27.1%	26.1%
Return on sales	15.7%	15.8%	15.9%	15.9%
FACTORS				
Competitive Position:				
Market share	20.5	20.8	21.1	21.1
Relative market share	37.0	37.7	38.3	38.3
Relative price index	3.0	3.1	3.0	3.0
Product quality	0.0	−12.5	−3.0	−3.0
Use of Investment:				
Investment/value added	82.5	73.0	78.6	81.3
Investment/sales	61.9	53.7	58.8	60.9
Fixed capital intensity	78.2	68.7	71.2	74.1
Net book/gross book value	52.9	49.6	54.0	54.7
Value added/sales	81.4	79.9	81.4	81.4
Working capital/sales	20.5	19.6	20.4	20.4
Capacity utilization	113.7	112.8	111.5	113.0
Sales/employees	50077.	50671.	53431.	61648.
Budget Allocations:				
Marketing expenses/sales	18.1	17.8	18.1	18.1
R&D expenses/sales	4.8	4.0	4.8	4.8

PERFORMANCE MEASURES:

Discounted net income 10yr	816.2
Discounted cash flow 10yr	99.7
Average net income 3yr	92.5
Discounted cash flow yield rate 10yr	15.1%
Average return on invest -ment 5yr	27.9%

Source: From Derek Abell, "Tex-Fiber Industries—Petroloid Products Division (D)," 9-577-040, Harvard Business School, p. 14. Copyright © 1976 by the President and Fellows of Harvard College. Reproduced by permission.

Most importantly, in an environment where the perception of a corporation's worth—and hence the long-run interests of its shareholders—is largely in terms of growth, the chief financial officer possesses what for many firms are the most potent strategic weapons. The firm that grows the fastest is the one which generates enough money to add to its assets at the fastest rate. The firm that grows the fastest is the one which sustains the highest rate of return on its equity capital (and reinvests these funds). The firm that grows the fastest is the one that brings to bear the greatest force of resources in the face of its competitors.[2]

Resources for growth can be generated either internally or externally. Internally, resources are provided through retention of earnings. The amount of earnings that can be plowed back is a function of dividend payout. Among the two external sources, debt capital costs less than equity capital. But a corporation cannot use debt indiscriminately for a variety of reasons, an important one being the unwillingness of management to accept the risk attached to a high debt ratio. Interest on debt is a fixed expense which must be appropriated regardless of the company's profit position. Thus, when times are bad and profits low, debt further aggravates the situation by absorbing profits or by further increasing losses. Finally, there are limits to the amount of debt which a corporation can raise. As far as equity is concerned, new issues of stock may dilute existing stockholders' equity, and there is a point beyond which the corporation cannot hurt the stockholders' interest. Besides, money market conditions may not be favorable enough for the corporation to raise money by issuing stock. In essence, then, in order to maximize its growth, a company needs to sustain the optimum mix of strategic resources. This, of course, varies according to place, time, and amounts involved.

The sustainable growth rate for a company can be determined to an extent by the rate at which it can generate funds for investment in growth businesses and by the return it can expect to earn on these funds. Usually retained earnings, debt, and new equity constitute the sources of funds. The availability of funds depends upon dividend payout and capital turnover. Finally, rate of return and the risk characteristics of investment projects will determine the effectiveness of their use. Thus, a company's perspectives regarding debt, dividend, and rate of return underlie the growth rate the company can sustain.

The relationship between debt, dividend, and rate of return and their impacts on corporate growth can be studied with reference to the following formula:

---

[2]Alan Zakon, *Growth and Financial Strategies* (Boston: Boston Consulting Group, 1968), p. 3.

$$g = \frac{D}{E}(r-i)p + rp \qquad \text{where} \quad \begin{aligned} g &= \text{rate of growth in earnings} \\ D &= \text{debt} \\ E &= \text{equity} \\ i &= \text{interest rate} \\ r &= \text{return on assets} \\ p &= \text{percent of earnings retained}[3] \end{aligned}$$

Hypothetical data can be used to find the growth rate for a hypothetical company, as follows:

$$
\begin{aligned}
D &= 10.0 \text{ million} & p &= 50\% \\
E &= 10.0 \text{ million} & i &= 6\% \\
r &= .7/10 = .07
\end{aligned}
$$

$$g = \frac{10}{10}(.07 - .03)(.5) + (.07)(.5) = 5.5\%$$

Thus, for the hypothetical company discussed here, the sustainable growth rate comes out to be 5.5 percent. To achieve the highest achievable growth, it is necessary to combine rate of return, debt, and dividends in an optimum fashion. While a firm should work out its own optimum mix of strategic resources, it is unwise to emphasize one factor at the expense of others since this can put a major burden on corporate performance. To elucidate the point, let us compute the effect of a ten percent change in each variable at a time, holding the others constant. This is shown in Exhibit 15-8. The changes in each of these variables affect growth differently, earning power being the most effective. But a positive change in earning power cannot be achieved at the discretion of management. Next to earning power is the plowing back of earnings, which seems to have an impact almost equal to earnings on growth. As far as the debt-equity ratio is concerned, small increases in leverage don't make much difference. Thus, in order to have a noticeable effect on growth because of leverage, the increase in debt must be substantial. The changes in interest rate do not seem to be very influential. In practice, the position of these variables must be set in combination with each other so that growth can be maximized at the discretion of management by alternating the values of different variables. The technique of computer simulation can be used to figure out the optimum combination. Having discovered the maximum growth that is achievable with the given inputs, the management can specify the measurement objectives (i.e., return on investment, return on stockholders' equity, and the pretax profit desired).

MARKETING SIMULATION

The purpose of simulation is to provide insights into an operation by highlighting its crucial variables and the mode and extent of their interactions. Under-

---

[3]*Ibid.*, p. 10.

EXHIBIT 15-8   Impact of Different Variables on Growth

Variable	Growth Rate	Change in Growth in Response to a 10% Change in Variable
Earning Power		
6.3%	4.80%	
7.0%	5.50%	
7.7%	6.20%	12.7%
Interest Rate		
3.3%	5.35%	
3.0%	5.50%	
2.7%	5.65%	2.7%
Debt-equity Ratio		
0.9:1.0	5.30%	
1.0:1.0	5.50%	
1.1:1.0	5.70%	3.6%
Earning Retention		
45.0%	4.95%	
50.0%	5.50%	
55.0%	6.05%	10.0%

standing the ingredients of a system helps in the construction of a laboratory model of the system by allowing the ranking of variables by importance. In brief, simulation permits the evaluation of the outcomes of alternative strategies in a laboratory situation, thus assisting in the choice of a right strategy.

A number of companies are known to have worked out corporate simulation models. George Gershefski's research in the area is a classic example of total corporate simulation.[4] Most of these models are financially oriented; our concern here, however, is with marketing simulation, which is much more complex. This is because simulation requires the quantification of all the variables at work in a marketing situation, which may not be easy. One must know how and to what extent the different variables affect customers' behavior both individually and in

---

[4]George W. Gershefski, "Building a Corporate Financial Model," *Harvard Business Review* (July–August, 1969), pp. 61–72.

interaction with other variables. The absence of a theoretical framework in marketing makes it necessary to make a variety of assumptions in constructing a model; justification of these assumptions becomes a difficult task. Thus, despite the many advantages that the simulation technique offers, its use in marketing remains limited.[5] An example of marketing simulation is the system developed by the Hendry Corporation, which includes a series of models that deal with market share, sales volume, and profit results, based on such inputs as the levels of advertising expenditures, prices, and distribution. A hallmark of Hendry simulation is its emphasis on sets of brands and products and sets of consumers themselves who define the structure of competition with their purchasing and brand-switching behavior. The focus of this simulation, therefore, is on the nature of interacting elasticities in the marketplace. One of the Hendry models is concerned with the impact of changes in product prices and expenditures of advertising on the market share and on return on marketing expenditures. This model, called Hendro Dynamics, can be used to set an optimum advertising and price level. Another Hendry model deals with the vulnerability of current brands to the introduction of a new one. This model requires dividing the market into a set of mutually exclusive and exhaustive segments. Each of these segments is treated as a distinct market, and consumer behavior within each segment is described by a heterogeneous, multinomial probability model. This model provides valuable information needed for new-brand introduction in the given segment (especially information on cannibalization).[6]

Discussed below is an example of total marketing simulation which illustrates the construction of a simulation model. Exhibit 15-9 gives a symbolic outline of the simulation model. This model was built for a consumer product. The rationale of the model is based on who the customer is (with respect to status and residence), where the customer stands with respect to the states of buyer behavior, and his or her perceived need for the product. This need leads the customer to a purchase decision and eventually to a purchase.

The model emphasizes the states of buyer behavior and stages of action. The states of buyer behavior are awareness, knowledge, liking, preference, and conviction.[7] Stages of action are felt need, purchase decision, and actual purchase. States of behavior need not be sequential, while stages of action must be. Relationships are built around each state of behavior and stage of action as affected by intercompany and intracompany variables. Simulation of these relationships in a system provides the output.

---

[5]The following is perhaps the single most important study on total marketing simulation: Arnold E. Amstutz, *Computer Simulation of Competitive Market Response* (Cambridge, MA: Mass. Inst. of Technology Press, 1967).

[6]*Hendro Dynamics: Fundamental Laws of Consumer Dynamics* (New York: Hendry Corp., 1970). See also M.V. Kalwani and Donald G. Morrison, "A Parsimonious Description of the Hendry System," *Management Science* (January, 1971), pp. 467–477.

[7]See Robert J. Lavidge and Gary A. Steiner, "A Model for Predictive Measurements of Advertising Effectiveness," *Journal of Marketing* (October, 1961), p. 61.

EXHIBIT 15-9 Overview of Variables in the Simulation Model

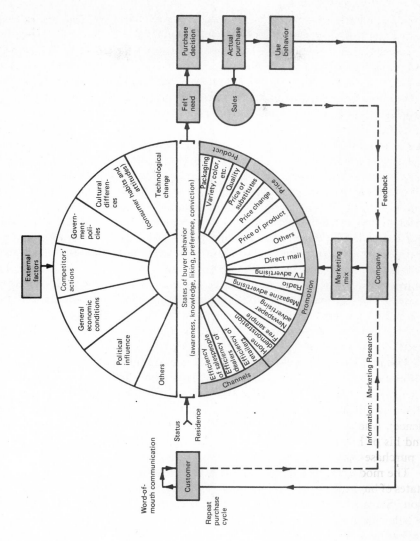

Customers are segmented on the basis of residence and status. Residence can be rural or urban; only urban customers qualified as subjects for this simulation. They were segmented on the basis of income into four status groupings; of these groupings, only the top three were considered for the purpose of this model.

The ingredients of the marketing mix—product, price, promotion, and distribution—included in the model are self-explanatory. The variables included under each ingredient differ, of course, from product to product. For example, technical journals are not considered here since this simulation is built for a consumer product. External factors have been included in the model only in rough terms. Their effects differ depending on the customer and product.

Two approaches are available for recreating the existing marketing conditions for the computer. The first approach is to measure the existing marketing conditions and substitute these in the simulation program. In following this approach, since some of the parameters cannot be measured, reasonable assumptions must be made about their values. The second approach is to let the simulation start from an initial condition of zero. In other words, the computer simulation starts from the period prior to product introduction. The values of the external factors are supplied. The actual performance is compared with the performance simulated by the computer, and necessary changes are made in the model relationships to reduce the gap between actual and simulated performance. In this manner the actual conditions can be created in the computer. The latter approach was followed in this model.

As the general model was being built and computerized, its validity was tried against a consumer product: frozen yogurt. The relationships developed in the general model were reworked on the basis of information obtained from company executives concerning the various types of marketing activities of the product. To fill the information gaps, a consumer survey was done whereby 300 randomly sampled interviews were completed. The impact of advertising on various states of buyer behavior was measured through a simulated advertising experiment. All this information was used to develop final relationships.

As an example of one relationship, the degree of awareness (DA) at the current time (t) was found to be a function of the degree of awareness at a previous time (t-1). This can be expressed mathematically as:

$$DA_t = f\,[DA_{t-1}]$$

The degree of awareness was also found to be a function of the following factors:

1. Competitors' action (ICA)
2. Word-of-mouth communication (WOM)
3. Retailers' efficiency (REEFE)
4. Demonstration (ADHD)
5. Free sample (ADFS)
6. Newspaper advertising (ADNP)
7. Magazine advertising (ADMG)

8.   Direct-mail advertising (ADDM)
9.   Television advertising (ADTV)

In a similar manner, relationships were developed for knowledge, degree of liking, preference, conviction, felt need, purchase decision, word-of-mouth messages, and channel efficiency. These relationships together constituted the model.

The model was computerized and run with the past input data supplied by the company. The variation between the actual and predicted sales was minor and could be explained by the fact that during the time covered, gasoline shortage made deliveries difficult, with the result that supplies became deficient. After it was agreed upon that the variation between actual and predicted sales was within acceptable limits, different sets of inputs were run to determine the effects on sales of changes in the ingredients of the marketing mix. For example, a run was made with three alternatives: 1) allocating more funds for advertising, 2) spreading advertising throughout the year, and 3) maintaining the status quo. It was found that spreading advertising throughout the year would be the most attractive alternative. Thus, by feeding the model with different inputs or alternative strategies, one could determine the best course of strategy to adopt.[8]

TREND-IMPACT ANALYSIS

Trend-impact analysis is a technique developed by the Futures Group, Inc., a consulting firm, for projecting future trends from information gathered on past behavior. The uniqueness of this method lies in its combination of statistical methods and human judgment. If the future is predicted on quantitative data alone, it fails to take into account the impact of unprecedented future events. On the other hand, human judgment provides only subjective insights into the future. Therefore, since both human judgment and statistical extrapolation have their shortcomings, they should both be taken into consideration when predicting future trends.

In trend-impact analysis (TIA), past history is first extrapolated with the help of a computer. Then the judgment of experts is used (usually by means of the Delphi technique) to specify a set of unique future events which may have a bearing on the phenomenon under study and to indicate how the trend extrapolation would be affected by the occurrence of each of these events. The computer then uses these judgments to modify the trend extrapolation. Finally, the experts review the adjusted extrapolation and modify the inputs in those cases in which the input appears unreasonable.[9]

To illustrate the TIA method, let us consider the case of the average cost of a prescription in the 1980s. As shown in Exhibit 15-10, the statistical extrapola-

---

[8]Based on Jay Satia and Subhash C. Jain, "A Simulation Model of a Total Marketing System" (working paper, Dayton, OH: Univ. of Dayton, 1970).
[9]See "Trend Impact Analysis," reference paper of The Futures Group, Glastonbury, CT.

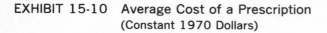

EXHIBIT 15-10   Average Cost of a Prescription
(Constant 1970 Dollars)

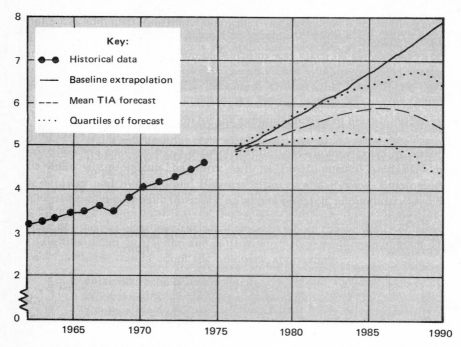

Source: Pharmaceutical PROSPECTS, a service of The Futures Group and IMS America, Glastonbury, CT (1975).

tion based on historical data shows that this cost will rise to $8 by 1990. The events considered relevant here are shown in Exhibit 15-11. The first event, i.e., the abolition of all drug product brand names, is indicated to have a 10 percent probability of occurring by 1985 and a 15 percent probability of occurring by 1990. If this event does occur, it is expected that its first impact on the average cost of a prescription will begin two years after its occurrence. The maximum impact will occur after five years and will be a 20 percent reduction in the average price. The steady-state impact is judged to be the same as the maximum impact.

The combination of these events, probabilities, and impacts with the baseline extrapolation leads to a forecast markedly different from the baseline extrapolation (see Exhibit 15-10). The curve even begins to decline in 1987. The uncertainty is indicated by quartiles about 18 percent above and below the mean forecast. (The quartiles indicate the middle 50 percent of future values of the curve, with 25 percent lying on each side of the forecast curve.) The uncertainty shown by these quartiles results from the fact that many of the events that have large impacts have relatively low probabilities.

EXHIBIT 15-11   Events Used in Trend-impact Analysis of Average Cost of a Prescription

Event	Estimated Probability by Years Shown		Years to First Impact	Years to Maximum Impact	Maximum Impact	Years to Steady-state Impact	Steady-state Impact
1. Abolition of all drug product brand names; standard abbreviations for generic names.	.10	1985	2	5	−.20	5	−.20
	.15	1990					
2. Drug reimbursement in all federally funded health programs based on Maximum Allowable Cost.	.75	1976	5	5	−.15	5	−.15
	.75	1990					
3. Removal of all federal and state restrictions on prescription-price advertising.	.20	1980	0	2	−.10	2	−.10
	.60	1990					
4. Decrease in the average size of prescription by 20 percent.	.10	1985	0	2	−.10	2	−.10
5. Comprehensive health care package initiated, federally run, federally subsidized.	.50	1980	2	10	−.10	10	−.10
	.50	1990					
6. Period of patent protection reduced to five years after market introduction of product.	.40	1984	5	15	−.15	20	−.05
	.45	1990					
7. Economic recession (similar to late 1950s).	.30	1980	0	2	−.10	3	0
	.35	1990					
8. Federal and state legislation to allow para-professionals to perform more drug-dispensing duties.	.25	1984	5	5	−.05	5	−.05
	.50	1990					
9. Antisubstitution laws repealed in most states.	.44	1985	1	10	−.05	10	−.05
10. Semiautomated drug dispensing equipment for use by pharmacists.	.50	1980	2	10	−.02	10	−.02
	.65	1985					
11. Number of prescriptions per user increases 10 percent over 1973 levels.	.40	1980	1	10	+.05	10	+.05
	.50	1990					

Source: Pharmaceutical PROSPECTS, a service of The Futures Group and IMS America, Glastonbury, CT (1975).

At this juncture it is desirable to determine the sensitivity of these results to the individual estimates upon which they are based. For example, one might raise valid questions about the estimates of event probability, the magnitude of the impacts used, and the delay time associated with these impacts. Having prepared these data in a disaggregated fashion, one can very easily vary such estimates and view the change in results. It may also be observed that intervention policies, whether they are institutional (such as lobbying, advertising, or new marketing approaches) or technological (such as increased R & D expenditures), can be viewed as a means of influencing the event probabilities or impacts.

Suppose, for example, a certain pharmaceutical company were in a position to lobby for the immediate removal of restrictions on prescription advertising (see event 3 in Exhibit 15-11), or suppose an analyst thought that there was a more than 20 percent likelihood that these restrictions would be removed in 1980. In each case, knowledge of the sensitivity of the forecast to the removal of advertising restrictions would be useful. This sensitivity can be tested by raising the probability of this event from .20 (in 1980) to .90. It is found that the sensitivity of the forecast to an early occurrence of this event would be mainly during the 1975–1985 period. During this period the forecast is reduced by about seven percent, and the quartiles are similarly reduced. By 1990, however, when the probability of the event has already reached .60 in the first forecast, the difference is slight. The sensitivity of the forecast to each of the other events, or combinations of events, can be determined in a similar manner.

TIA can be used not only to improve forecasts of time series variables, but also to study the sensitivity of these forecasts to policy. Of course, any policy considered should attempt to influence as many events as possible, rather than one as in this example. Realistically, corporate actions often have both beneficial and detrimental possibilities since they may increase both desirable and undesirable possibilities. The use of TIA can make such uncertainties more clearly visible than is possible with traditional methods.

CROSS-IMPACT ANALYSIS

Cross-impact analysis is a technique used for examining the impacts of potential future events upon each other. It indicates the relative importance of specific events, identifies groups of reinforcing or inhibiting events, and unfolds relationships between events which appear unrelated. In brief, cross-impact analysis provides a future forecast, making due allowance for interacting forces having a bearing on the shape of things to come.

Essentially, this technique consists of selecting a group of five to ten people to serve as project participants. They are asked to specify critical events having any relationship with the subject of the project. For example, in a marketing project the events may fall into any of the following categories:

1. Corporate objectives and goals
2. Corporate policy and strategy

3.   Markets or customers (potential volume, market share, possible strategies of key customers, etc.)
4.   Competitors (product, price, promotion, and distribution strategies)
5.   Overall competitive strategic posture, whether aggressive or defensive
6.   Internally or externally developed strategies which might affect the project
7.   Legal or regulatory activities having favorable or unfavorable effects
8.   Other social, demographic, or economic events

The initial attempt presumably generates a long list of alternatives which should be consolidated into a manageable size (e.g., 25–30 events) by means of group discussion, concentrated thinking, elimination of duplications, and refinement of the essence of the problem. It is desirable for each event to contain one and only one variable, thus avoiding the double counting of impacts. The selected events are represented in an "n × n" matrix for developing the estimated impact of each event on every other event. This is done by selecting a specific event, assuming that it has already occurred and that it will have an enhancing, an inhibiting, or no effect on other events. The impacts, if desired, may be weighed. The project coordinator seeks the impact estimates from each project participant individually and displays the estimates in the matrix in a consolidated form. The individual results, in summary form, are presented to the group. The project participants vote on the impact of each event. If the spread of the votes is too wide, the coordinator will ask those voting at the extremes to justify their positions. The participants are encouraged to discuss differences in the hope of clarifying the problem. Another voting takes place. During the second round of voting, the opinions usually converge, and the median value of the votes is entered in the appropriate cell in the matrix. This procedure is repeated until the entire matrix is complete.

In the process of matrix completion, the review of occurrences and interactions identifies those events which are strong actors and significant reactors and provides a subjective opinion on their relative strengths. This information then serves as an important input in formulating strategy.

The use of cross-impact analysis may be illustrated with reference to a study concerned with the future of U.S. automobile component suppliers. The following were the events set forth:*

1.   Motor vehicle safety standards which come into effect between 1974 and 1978 will result in an additional 260 lbs. of weight for the average-sized U.S. car.
2.   The 1978 NO_x emissions regulations are relaxed by the EPA.
3.   The retail price of gasoline (regular grade) is $1.00 per gallon.

---

*This illustration was developed before the 1979 gas price increases.

4.   U.S. automakers introduce passenger cars which will achieve at least
     32 mpg under average summer driving conditions.

These events are arranged in matrix form as shown in Exhibit 15-12. The arrows
show the direction of the analysis. For example, the occurrence of event A would
likely bring more pressure to bear upon regulatory officials, so event B would be
more likely to occur. Therefore, an enhancing arrow is placed in the cell where
row A and column B intersect. Moving to column C, it is not expected that the
occurrence of event A would have any effect on event C, so a horizontal line is
recorded in this cell. It is judged that the occurrence of event A would make event
D less likely to occur, and an inhibiting arrow is placed in this cell. If event B
were to occur, the consensus is that event A would be more likely, hence the
enhancing arrow. Event B is not expected to affect event C, but would make event
D more likely. The cells are completed in accordance with these judgments.
Similar analyses for events C and D complete the matrix. The completed matrix
shows the direction of impact of rows (actors) upon columns (reactors). An
analysis of the matrix at this point reveals that reactor C has only one actor (event
D) since there is only one reaction in column C. If the interest is primarily in event
D, column D should be studied for actor events. Then each of those actor events
should be examined to determine what degree of influence, if any, it is possible
to have on these actors in order to bring about event D.

Next, the impacts should be quantified to show linkage strengths (i.e., to
determine how strongly the occurrence or nonoccurrence of one event would
influence the occurrence of each of the other events). To assist in quantifying the
interactions, a subjective rating scale such as the one shown below may be used.

Voting Scale	Subjective Scale	
+8	Critical: essential for success	
+6	Major: major item for success	
+4	Significant: positive, helpful, but not essential	Enhancing
+2	Slight: noticeable enhancing effect	
0	No Effect	
−2	Slight: noticeable inhibiting effect	
−4	Significant: retarding effect	Inhibiting
−6	Major: major obstacle to success	
−8	Critical: almost insurmountable hurdle	

Consider the impact of event A upon event B. It is felt that the occurrence of
event A would significantly improve the likelihood of occurrence of event B. Both

EXHIBIT 15-12   Basic Format for Cross-impact Matrix

If This Event Were to Occur	Then the Impact upon This Event Would Be			
	A	B	C	D
A MVSS ('74 through '78) require 260# additional weight for "average" U.S. auto.	✕	←	|	→
B 1978 NO$_x$ emissions requirements are relaxed by EPA.	←	✕	|	←
C Retail price of gasoline is $1.00/gallon.	→	←	✕	←
D U.S. automakers introduce cars capable of 32 mpg in average summer driving.	←	→	→	✕

CODE: ← = enhancing

   — = no effect

   → = inhibiting

Source: *A Guide to Cross-Impact Analysis* (Cleveland, OH: Eaton Corp., no date).

the direction and degree of enhancing impact are shown in Exhibit 15-13 by the +4 rating in the appropriate cell. Event A's occurrence would make event D less likely; therefore, the consensus rating is −4. This process is continued until all interactions have been evaluated and the matrix is complete. There are a number of variations on the quantification techniques. For example, the subjective scale could be 0 to 10, rather than −8 to +8 as shown in the above example.

Yet another technique involves the use of probabilities of occurrence. If the probability of occurrence of each event is assessed before the construction of the matrix, then the change in that probability can be assessed for each interaction. As shown in Exhibit 15-14, the probabilities of occurrence can be entered in an information column preceding the matrix. Next, the matrix is constructed in the conventional manner. Consider the impact of event A on the probable occurrence of event B. It is judged to be an enhancing effect, and the consensus is that the probability of occurrence of event B will change from 0.8 to 0.9. The new probability is, therefore, entered in the appropriate cell. Event A is judged to have no effect upon event C; therefore, the original probability, 0.5, is unchanged. Event D is inhibited by the occurrence of event A, and the resulting probability of occurrence is lowered from 0.5 to 0.4. The occurrence of event B will increase the probability of occurrence of event A from 0.7 to 0.8. Event B has no impact upon event C (0.5, unchanged), and will increase the probability of event D to 0.7. This procedure is followed until all of the cells are completed.

An examination of the matrix at this stage reveals several important relationships. For example, if we wanted event D to occur, then the most likely actors would be events B and C. We would then examine columns B and C to determine what actors we might influence. Often, influences which bring about the desired results at the critical moment are secondary, tertiary, or beyond. In many instances the degree of impact is not the only important information to be gathered from a consideration of interactions. The time relationships are often very important and can be shown in a number of ways. For example, in Exhibit 15-14, time information has been added within parentheses. It shows that if event A were to occur, it would have an enhancing effect upon event B, raising B's probability of occurrence from 0.8 to 0.9; this enhancement would occur immediately. If event B were to occur, it would raise the probability of occurrence of event D from 0.5 to 0.7; it would take two years to reach the probable time of occurrence of event D.[10]

SPECIAL-PURPOSE MODELS

Many companies develop models to find solutions to specific strategic problems. These models may be directed toward a particular area, such as product, price, promotion, or distribution, or toward the entire corporation. Discussed

---

[10]*A Guide to Cross-impact Analysis* (Cleveland, OH: Eaton Corp., no date).

EXHIBIT 15-13 Cross-impact Matrix Showing Degrees of Impact

If This Event Were to Occur		Then the Impact upon This Event Would Be			
		A	B	C	D
A	MVSS ('74 through '78) require 260# additional weight for "average" U.S. auto.	✕	+4	0	-4
B	1978 NOx emissions requirements are relaxed by EPA.	+2	✕	0	+4
C	Retail price of gasoline is $1.00/gallon.	-4	+4	✕	+2
D	U.S. automakers introduce cars capable of 32 mpg in average summer driving.	+2	-2	-2	✕

Source: *A Guide to Cross-Impact Analysis* (Cleveland, OH: Eaton Corp., no date).

EXHIBIT 15-14   Cross-impact Matrix Showing Interactive Probabilities of Occurrence

If This Event Were to Occur	Having This Probability of Occurrence	Then the Impact upon This Event Would Be			
		A	B	C	D
A MVSS ('74 through '78) require 260# additional weight for "average" U.S. auto.	0.7	✕	0.9 (immed.)	0.5	0.4 (immed.)
B 1978 NO_x emissions requirements are relaxed by EPA.	0.8	0.8 (immed.)	✕	0.5	0.7 (+ 2 yrs.)
C Retail price of gasoline is $1.00/gallon.	0.5	0.6 (+1 yr.)	0.9 (+1 yr.)	✕	0.7 (+2 yrs.)
D U.S. automakers introduce cars capable of 32 mpg in average summer driving.	0.5	0.8 (immed.)	0.6 (immed.)	0.4 (+1 yr.)	✕

Source: *A Guide to Cross-Impact Analysis* (Cleveland, OH: Eaton Corp., no date).

below, for illustration purposes, are three models: one each in the areas of product strategy and pricing strategy and the third one a forecasting model.

Product-line-strategy Model[11]

The product-line-strategy model delineates information on a product's sales, market share, and profit position, showing both current and past trends. This information may be summarized in a matrix. For example, Exhibit 15-15 shows

EXHIBIT 15-15   Product Evaluation Matrix: A Hypothetical Example Tracing Two Products over Three Years

Company Sales		Decline			Stable			Growth		
Industry Sales	Profita-bility Market Share	Below Target	Target	Above Target	Below Target	Target	Above Target	Below Target	Target	Above Target
Growth	Leading									
Growth	Average								A 74	A 75
Growth	Marginal				A 73					
Stable	Leading									
Stable	Average									
Stable	Marginal									
Decline	Leading									
Decline	Average	B 74			B 73					
Decline	Marginal	B 75								

Source: Yoram Wind and Henry J. Claycamp, "Planning Product Line Strategy: A Matrix Approach," *Journal of Marketing* (January, 1976), p. 5.

the history of two hypothetical products for three years. As the exhibit shows, product A was in the growth stage of the industry for the years 1973–1975. As far as the company is concerned, it moved from a stable to a growth position during the period 1973–1974, and at the same time its market share position changed from marginal to average. Finally, the profit position of the product consistently improved, i.e., from below target to target or above target. Product B, however, presented a sad situation. In the years 1973–1974 its sales moved down from a stable to a declining position, thus matching the industry sales status. Its market share eroded, too (i.e., from average to marginal); profitability, however, continued to be on target in 1975.

---

[11]Adapted from Yoram Wind and Henry J. Claycamp, "Planning Product Line Strategy: A Matrix Approach," *Journal of Marketing* (January, 1976), pp. 2–9.

The next step in this model is to forecast a product's sales, market share, and profitability, assuming no change in either the environment or the company's perspectives. See the first eight columns of the upper portion of Exhibit 15-16 (i.e., current position and unconditional projection for the products labeled 1 and 2). Conditional forecasts must also be made, as indicated by the last four columns of the upper portion of Exhibit 15-16. These are sales, market share, and profit forecasts under a variety of marketing strategies. In other words, sales, market share, and profit results with different strategic perspectives should be determined

EXHIBIT 15-16   **Incorporating Sales, Market Share, and Profit Forecasts into the Product Evaluation Matrix: A Hypothetical Example**

	Current Position (C)				Unconditional Projection (P)				Conditional Forecast (CF)			
Product	Industry Sales	Company Sales	Market Share	Profita-bility	Industry Sales	Company Sales	Market Share	Profita-bility	Industry Sales	Company Sales	Market Share	Profita-bility
1	Decline	Decline	Average	Below Target	Decline	Decline	Average	Below Target	Decline	Decline	Marg.	Target
									Decline	Stable	Average	Below Target
2	Stable	Decline	Average	Target	Stable	Stable	Average	Above Target	Stable	Stable	Dom.	Target

		Decline			Stable			Growth		
Company Sales →	Profita-bility	Below Target	Target	Above Target	Below Target	Target	Above Target	Below Target	Target	Above Target
Industry Sales ↓	Market Share									
Growth	Dominant									
	Average									
	Marginal									
Stable	Dominant					2 CF				
	Average		2 C			2 P				
	Marginal									
Decline	Dominant									
	Average	1 C 1 P	1" CF							
	Marginal	1' CF								

Key: 1, 2 products. C = current; P = projected position.
CF = expected position based on results of a conditional forecast analysis.

Source: Yoram Wind and Henry J. Claycamp, "Planning Product Line Strategy: A Matrix Approach," *Journal of Marketing* (January, 1976), p. 5.

and the results of the best strategy used here. When there is no single best strategy on all counts, the best strategy for each objective should be incorporated into the analysis. Thus, in the lower portion of Exhibit 15-16, for product 2 there is one conditional forecast, while for product 1 there are two best alternatives. Along with the conditional forecast, the current position and unconditional projection for each product are also shown.

Product 1 is in bad shape, according to Exhibit 15-16: In a declining industry, it has declining sales with below-target profitability and average market share. If the current strategy is continued in the future, its situation is unlikely to change. There are two different types of strategic alternatives from which the management may choose in seeking some improvement in the performance of product 1. The first alternative ($1'_{CF}$) will enable the product to improve its profitability to the target level, but its market share will further decline to a marginal level, and it will continue to be in a declining industry with declining sales. Following the second alternative ($1''_{CF}$), however, sales can be improved from a decline level to a stable level, but profitability and market share will remain where they are. Briefly, then, the management must choose between opting for higher sales or higher profitability for product 1 as a part of the total company perspectives.

Product 2 presents a simpler case than product 1. If the present strategy continues in the future, the current position will be maintained, except for the fact that the level of product sales will improve from a decline to a stable status. But if a new strategy is adopted, market share performance along with sales will improve.

The matrix approach discussed above provides a useful way to diagnose a product's past and current status on important measures of performance, i.e., sales, market share, and profitability. It also helps in the easy comprehension of trade-offs between alternative strategies for the future. The approach, if required, can be further refined by bringing in additional analysis. For example, competitive structure and the effectiveness of the marketing effort can be diagnosed and incorporated within the framework.

Framework-for-pricing-strategy Model[12]

The framework-for-pricing-strategy model is relevant in industrial pricing situations. It examines the determinants of "strength" in the industrial environment, then continues to refine this evaluation by adding an environmental dimension. The combination forms a matrix of parameters for choosing the specific pricing strategy and tactics. The model follows the following steps:

1. Measures buyer's and seller's strengths
2. Assigns buyer and seller to strategic quadrangles

---

[12]Adapted from Subhash C. Jain and Michael V. Laric, "A Framework for Strategic Industrial Pricing," *Industrial Marketing Management,* Vol. 8 (1979), pp. 75–80.

3. Evaluates needs for product/sale and categorizes them
4. Determines which pricing strategy and what tactics to follow in selling (i.e., develops the pricing matrix)
5. Incorporates environmental impact into the pricing matrix
6. Selects most appropriate price

Buyers and sellers can be differentiated by means of a number of criteria. Buyers can be differentiated on the basis of their bargaining power, which depends on factors such as their size, potential sales, etc. Sellers can be differentiated on the basis of their bargaining power, which depends on their products' quality, uniqueness, design, etc. Their relative strengths are a function of these differences. The strengths of both buyers and sellers are measured in relative terms (i.e., the buyer's strength is relative to the seller's for a given product). The relationships between buyers and sellers can change over time and from one product to another.

A buyer's strengths are determined by looking at several characteristics of the buyer's firm and comparing them to the rest of the industry. These characteristics include: 1) size of organization (as compared to industry average), 2) sales potential, 3) size of past purchases from the seller, and 4) whether the buyer is a new customer.

After the buyer's strength is evaluated on each of the four criteria, an overall measure of strength/weakness is derived for the buyer. A sample measurement of a buyer's strengths is shown in Exhibit 15-17. Each criterion is first rated on

EXHIBIT 15-17   Sample Measurement of Buyer's Strengths

Strength Criteria	Scale Value (Range 1–10)	Weights	Total Score
1. Organization's size	9	3	27
2. Sales potential	7	2	14
3. Size of past purchases	3	4	12
4. Desirability of maintaining the customer (repeat purchases)	8	5	40
TOTAL			93

Total possible score = 140.
Percentage score = $\frac{93}{140} \times 100 = 66.4\%$.

Source: Subhash C. Jain and Michael V. Laric, "A Framework for Strategic Industrial Pricing," *Industrial Marketing Management*, Vol. 8 (1979), pp. 75–80.

a scale of 1–10 (weak-strong). Then weights are assigned to each criterion. The total score for each criterion is derived by multiplying the scale value by the weight for each criterion; adding these four figures gives the total score of the four criteria. By using a similar procedure, the seller's strengths may also be measured (Exhibit 15-18).

EXHIBIT 15-18   Sample Measurement of Seller's Strengths

Strength Criteria	Scale Value (Range 1–10)	Weights	Total Score
1. Delivery service	4	3	12
2. Company image	6	3	18
3. Product quality	3	2	6
4. After-sales services	5	2	10
5. Trade-in policy	6	1	6
6. Price	8	2	16
TOTAL			68

Total Possible Score = 130.

Percentage Score = $\dfrac{68}{130} \times 100 = 52\%$.

Source: Subhash C. Jain and Michael V. Laric, "A Framework for Strategic Industrial Pricing," *Industrial Marketing Management,* Vol. 8 (1979), pp. 75–80.

Four different bases were mentioned in classifying buyers as strong or weak; six different bases classify sellers' strength. There are a number of other variables which can be used to differentiate between buyers and sellers. But even with the limited number of classifying variables, there are 16 possible types of buyers with varying characteristics (2^4). Similarly, there are 64 possible types of sellers (2^6). Classification of buyers and sellers into so many categories may seem impractical. However, with some experience, an executive familiar with the clients and industry may be able to shorten the criteria listing.

The two overall score numbers are used to locate the positions of the seller and the buyer in the pricing strategy quadrangle. Exhibit 15-19 shows such a quadrangle. An industrial seller can use one of four different pricing strategies: negotiated strategy, dictatorial strategy, defensive strategy, or gamesmanship strategy. A negotiated strategy is one in which both parties have a close match of strengths. Here the buyer and the seller negotiate a price which is fair to both since both are equally strong. A dictatorial strategy is used when the buyer is weak. Here the seller will try to set the price which is most favorable to him or her with an attitude of "take it or leave it." A defensive strategy is viable when a customer has strengths which the seller cannot match. A gamesmanship strategy is applicable when both parties are weak. In such a situation the two parties play "hide and seek" in agreeing on a price. Using the strength scores computed above, the buyer and seller are located at point A, which is in the negotiations quadrangle. Both are relatively strong, and the price is likely to be negotiated. Once it is determined which strategy is to be followed, different tactical levels may be considered.

Although the buyer and seller generally negotiate price, particular agreement depends on their positioning with respect to the need for a given product/service in a given time context. A buyer's need for the product in question can be

EXHIBIT 15-19   Pricing Strategy Quadrangle

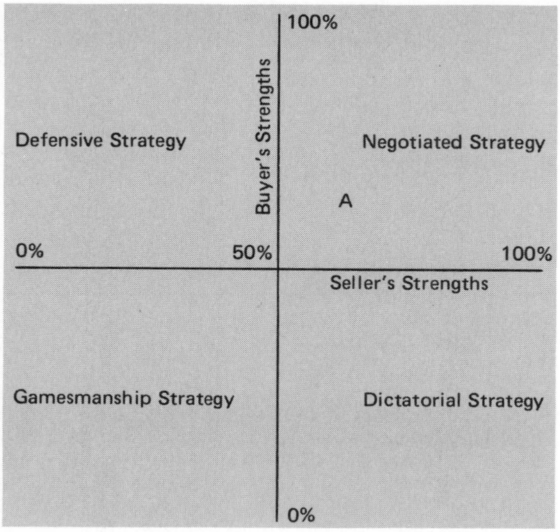

Source: Subhash C. Jain and Michael V. Laric, "A Framework for Strategic Industrial Pricing," *Industrial Marketing Management,* Vol. 8 (1979), pp. 75-80.

classified as acute, moderate, or marginal. An acute need exists, for example, when a product must replace a defective component in a machine which supplies an assembly line. In this case the buyer's manufacturing process depends on the product, and he is not likely to be price sensitive. A moderate need is one which, while not immediate, must be taken care of within a span of a few days. The buyer may indulge in a search before finalizing the order. A marginal need is exemplified by a manufacturer searching for something needed, say, ten months from now. In this case the manufacturer has ample time to locate and price an acceptable vendor. The search has only a marginal impact on day-to-day operations, giving the manufacturer sufficient time for shopping around and increasing its price sensitivity.

Just as the buyer must classify the need for a product, the seller must classify the need for a product sale. Acute, moderate, and marginal needs for products or sales occur in every strength category. An acute need for a product sale can exist when the company is in dire need of working capital and the sale would be instrumental in securing a bank loan. Similarly, if the product in question is a prototype for the buyer and is likely to generate repeat orders, the seller's need for a sale could be defined as acute. If, on the other hand, there is a big backlog and the buyer is not interested in the particular seller for any repeat orders, the need for the product sale may be classified as marginal.

Exhibit 15-20 shows a pricing tactics matrix, which classifies the buyer's and seller's needs into need categories. When the buyer's need is stronger than the seller's, the buyer is apt to yield to the seller on price matters. Cells 1, 2, and 4

EXHIBIT 15-20   Pricing Tactics Matrix

Buyer	Seller		
	Marginal Need	**Moderate Need**	**Acute Need**
Acute Need	1. Seller is in complete control	2. Seller has leeway	3. Neutral ground
Moderate Need	4. Seller has leeway	5. Neutral ground	6. Buyer has leeway
Marginal Need	7. Neutral ground	8. Buyer has leeway	9. Buyer is in complete control

Price elasticity of demand is inversely related to the acuteness of need. When the need is marginal, price elasticity is high, and conversely, when the need is acute, price elasticity is low.

Source: Subhash C. Jain and Michael V. Laric, "A Framework for Strategic Industrial Pricing," *Industrial Marketing Management,* Vol. 8 (1979), pp. 75–80.

show this situation. If both buyer and seller have the same degree of need (cells 3, 5, and 7), neither of them can dictate price. If the seller needs to sell more than the buyer needs to buy (cells 6, 8, and 9), then the buyer is likely to have an upper hand. In cell 8, for example, the buyer is looking for a marginally needed product whose sale is of moderate importance to the seller. Thus, the buyer has leeway in the negotiations.

Exhibit 15-21 incorporates the tactical considerations with the strategic ones. Each quadrangle is divided into a 3 × 3 matrix based on the need for the product purchase (from the buyer's point of view) and sale (from the seller's point of view). In the negotiated strategy quadrangle (upper right), the seller has more leeway than the buyer in areas designated by A. The buyer has more leeway in areas designated by C. Thus, if the strength interaction of the buyer and seller takes place at point 3, the seller is positioned to pursue a negotiated strategy with leeway over the buyer. The above analysis, however, is not enough to arrive at a price. The pricing decision is also influenced by a number of environmental factors which must be accounted for.

Thus far no mention has been made of the seller's industry and competitors. Several important factors must be considered in making a pricing decision: 1) degree of competition, 2) ease of entry, 3) competitors' clout, 4) industry growth prospects, and 5) technological threats to the industry. The impact of these environmental factors on a pricing decision may be computed as shown in Exhibit 15-22. The procedure is essentially the same as the one employed in deriving the buyer's and seller's strengths.

Marketing management should decide on the interpretation of the impact score. For example, a score of 75 percent or more may be considered as an indication of an unfavorable environment, a score between 50 percent and 75 percent may be taken as an indication of moderate environmental impact; and a

EXHIBIT 15-21   Pricing Strategy Quadrangle with Different Tactical Considerations

		Acute Need	Moderate Need	Marginal Need	Acute Need	Moderate Need	Marginal Need
		Defensive Strategy Quadrangle			Negotiated Strategy Quadrangle		
Strong Buyer	Acute Need	I	I	H	100% C	C	B
	Moderate Need	I	H	G	C	B	A
	Marginal Need	H 0%	G	G	B 50%	(3) A Seller's Strengths	A 100%
Weak Buyer	Acute Need	L	L	K	F	F	E
	Moderate Need	L	K	J	F	E	D
	Marginal Need	K	J	J	E 0%	D	D

(Vertical axis: Buyer's Strengths. Horizontal axis: Seller's Strengths.)

Gamesmanship Strategy Quadrangle   Dictatorial Strategy Quadrangle

Negotiated Strategy Quadrangle: A, seller has leeway; B, neutral ground; C, buyer has leeway. Dictatorial Strategy Quadrangle: D, seller is in complete control; E, seller will exert major influence; F, seller can tilt the balance. Defensive Strategy Quadrangle: G, buyer can tilt the balance; H, buyer will exert major influence; I, buyer is in complete control. Gamesmanship Strategy Quadrangle: J, buyer is weak; K, neutral ground; L, seller is weak.

Source: Subhash C. Jain and Michael V. Laric, "A Framework for Strategic Industrial Pricing," *Industrial Marketing Management,* Vol. 8 (1979), pp. 75-80.

score of less than 50 percent may signify favorable environmental climate for pricing.

To arrive at a price, the pricing strategy and tactics position and environmental analysis may now be combined in a matrix as shown in Exhibit 15-23. This matrix spreads out the pricing strategy quadrangle (Exhibit 15-21) into 12 columns, each column having three environmental impact levels. Each resulting letter/number combination shows the price level which should be charged by the seller, given a particular combination of strategy and buyer/seller strength. The numbers 1, 2, and 3 refer to high, average, and low price levels, respectively. Taking industry practices into consideration, however, one can be more specific. For example, high price may refer to a price giving over 20 percent return on investment, moderate price may refer to 15–20 percent return, and low price may indicate aiming at less than 15 percent return.

General Electric's Futurscan[13]

Essentially, Futurscan (FSCAN) is a model used to systematically speculate about alternative contingencies and their impact upon the future business environment. It was developed in the mid-1970s by the General Electric Company

---

[13]Excerpted from a General Electric pamphlet on Futurscan.

EXHIBIT 15-22   Measurement of the Impact of Environmental Factors on Pricing

Factors	Impact on Pricing Decision Score 1___10 Low	High	Weights	Total Impact Score
1. Degree of competition	5		3	15
2. Ease of entry	3		2	6
3. Competitor's clout	6		3	18
4. Industry growth rate prospects	5		3	15
5. Technological threats	3		1	3
TOTAL				57

Total possible score = 120.

Percentage score = $\frac{57}{120} \times 100 = 47.5\%$.

Source: Subhash C. Jain and Michael V. Laric, "A Framework for Strategic Industrial Pricing," *Industrial Marketing Management,* Vol. 8 (1979), pp. 75–80.

EXHIBIT 15-23   Choosing a Specific Price Level

Environmental Impact	Pricing Strategy and Tactics Combination											
	Negotiated Strategy			Dictatorial Strategy			Defensive Strategy			Gamesman-ship Strategy		
	A	B	C	D	E	F	G	H	I	J	K	L
Favorable	A1	B1	C1	D1	E1	F2	G3	H3	I3	J1	K1	L2
Moderate	A1	B1	C2	D1	E2	F3	G3	H3	I2	J1	K2	L3
Unfavorable	A1	B2	C2	D2	E3	F3	G3	H2	I2	J2	K3	L3

1, High; 2, Average; 3, Low.

Source: Subhash C. Jain and Michael V. Laric, "A Framework for Strategic Industrial Pricing," *Industrial Marketing Management,* Vol. 8 (1979), pp. 75–80.

in its efforts to forecast the future of the electric energy demand. Currently it is available to other companies over General Electric's Information Service Business Division Timeshare Network as a tool for analyzing the future business environment. A primary feature of the FSCAN system is that it gets all the assumptions out in the open. It does this by stating them in terms of potential future events and casting them in a framework of alternative scenarios in which they provide a realistic basis for contingency planning.

Two unique features set FSCAN apart from all other forecasting techniques. First, forecasts are stated in terms of probability, such as 30 percent probability (not too likely) by the year 1985 or 80 percent probability (very likely) by the year 1990. This expresses a realistic view of the world, especially the world of today, in which the manager admits that he or she does not know *the* future but is willing to place shrewd bets on the likelihood of *a* particular future as long as its development can be traced and early warning about its possible dislocation can be received. The second unique feature of FSCAN is that forecasts are continually monitored and updated. In this way the manager does receive early warnings of possible dislocations among social, economic, political, and technological developments which may affect company strategies.

FSCAN contains four basic modules which can be used separately or in concert: a data base, trend-impact analysis, cross-impact analysis, and the probabilistic system dynamics modeling capability.

The FSCAN data base contains events which may trigger alternative futures. To identify these events, FSCAN relies on two sources: a continuing literature search and a highly structured interview procedure. In the literature search, a reader network and an automated index regularly search some 5,000 periodicals, reports, and publications for pertinent event forecasts and updates. But of all the techniques discussed here, unique to FSCAN is the Delphi technique, which collects informed judgments in face-to-face settings. An FSCAN Delphi panel is typically comprised of three types of individuals: first, the expert (i.e., the individual who sees the trees but not necessarily the woods); second, the wise person (i.e., the individual who sees the forest but not necessarily the individual trees); and third, the linkage respondent, who is capable of bringing both views together into a systemic or holistic picture. Specifically, Delphi panelists express their opinions concerning the likelihood, timing, and impact of future events. In addition to a sampling of conventional thinkers, there is also an assortment of mavericks. These are the independent thinkers who are not afraid to advocate generally unaccepted ideas. Herein lies one of the most important features of the FSCAN system: its ability to display consensus at the same time as it preserves and even highlights dissension.

The second FSCAN module is trend-impact analysis (TIA), where event content is brought to bear on specific trends. Trend-impact analysis specifies a range of alternative futures for a given trend and thus permits preliminary and cost-effective sensitivity testing. This in turn suggests which potential events should be emphasized in the planning/decision-making process.

The third module is cross-impact analysis (CIA). Cross-impact analysis takes into account the "spillover" effect events have upon each other. It acknowledges that events can do more than move a given trend line up or down. They can also trigger other events, thus altering the total business environment. These are the events to watch for, and it is these events which cross-impact analysis highlights.

The fourth and final module is the probabilistic system dynamics modeling capability (PSD). At its core, PSD is a system dynamics model of the interactions among various sectors or subsectors of the economy. But the model has been modified to handle the probable impact of potential future events. When this content is introduced, the whole structure of the model may change. Thus, by serving as a replica of the real world, the PSD modeling capability describes alternative futures which are both explicit and internally consistent. As a result, the manager is able to position contingency plans in the context of an array of realistic alternative futures.

While FSCAN does not make the future less uncertain, it does help to make the future more manageable. It encourages the manager to think in terms of what may make the future different from the past. In this way, it enables the manager to explicitly account for these differences when planning. Thus, for the manager who cannot afford a planning standoff, FSCAN performs the indispensable service of getting all assumptions out in the open where they can be tested and evaluated. In the process, FSCAN accomplishes something even more valuable: It demonstrates that few events (hence, few futures) are totally unmanageable. It demonstrates that events shown to have a desirable impact may be encouraged, while events shown to have an undesirable impact may be delayed or prevented. By using FSCAN, the manager does not have to wait passively for the future to occur, but instead can speculate about what may occur and even intervene in the interests of the most desirable future.

SUMMARY

This chapter presents a variety of models which should be helpful in different aspects of strategy formulation and implementation. Among these is PIMS (profit impact of market strategy), a project which entails a cross-sectional study of the strategic experience of a large number of businesses. Also examined in this chapter is a model which may be utilized to figure out the sustainable growth of a business. Another model deals with the simulation of the entire marketing system. This model is useful for determining a viable marketing mix for a product/market configuration. An additional two models, trend-impact analysis and cross-impact analysis, are used to project future trends and to determine the cross impact of these trends on each other. The chapter ends with three special-purpose models, one each on product, pricing, and environmental monitoring.

DISCUSSION QUESTIONS

1. Explain how PIMS judgments can be useful in developing marketing strategy.
2. Experience curves and the PIMS model both seem to imply that market share is an essential ingredient of a winning strategy. Does that mean that a company with a low share of the market has no way of running a profitable business?
3. Describe how par reports may help a business in its strategic decision making.
4. Explain how the amount paid out in the form of dividends affects the growth potential of a business.
5. Explain the use of cross-impact analysis with reference to an emerging trend: the use of computers in households. Make appropriate assumptions.
6. What factors hinder the use of simulation models in marketing?

Chapter 16
Organizational Structure

Whatever action is performed by a great man, common men follow in his footsteps, and whatever standards he sets by exemplary acts, all the world pursues.

Bhagavad Gita

A strategic planning system should provide answers to two basic questions: what to do and how to do it. The first question refers to a selection of strategy, and the second to organizational arrangements. An organization must have not only a winning strategy to pursue, but also a matching structure to facilitate its implementation. The emphasis in most of the preceding chapters has been on strategy formulation. This last chapter is devoted to building a viable organizational structure to administer the strategy.

William Durant, the founder of General Motors, had a winning strategy: "a car for every pocket and taste." Despite this superb strategy, General Motors in its early history ran into problems because a matching structure did not accompany the strategy. Alfred Sloan discovered the missing link (i.e., the lack of an appropriate structure to match Durant's strategy) in General Motors' strategic perspective and restructured the company around the concepts of decentralization and the profit center. How General Motors continued to grow and eventually emerged as the world's largest corporation is history.[1]

The structural response to implementing strategic planning is discussed here with reference to two different companies, General Electric and Texas Instruments. Also mentioned are the emerging trends for strategic integration at the top. The roles of the chief executive officer and the strategic planning staff are examined. Finally, the impact of strategic planning on marketing organization is studied.

---

[1]See Alfred D. Chandler, Jr., *Strategy and Structure: Chapters in the History of the Industrial Enterprise* (Cambridge, MA: Mass. Inst. of Technology Press, 1962) and Alfred P. Sloan, Jr., *My Years with General Motors* (New York: Doubleday & Co., 1964).

STRATEGY AND STRUCTURE

Traditionally corporations have been organized with a strong emphasis on pursuing and achieving established objectives. Such organizations adapt well to growing internal complexities and provide adequate incentive mechanisms and systems of accountability to support objectives. However, they fail to provide a congenial environment for strategic planning. For example, one of the organizational capabilities needed for strategic planning is that of modifying or redefining the objectives themselves so that the corporation is prepared to meet future competition. The traditional organizational structure resists change, and this is why a new type of structure is needed for strategic planning. Mainer explains this point as follows:

> The crux of the matter is that the behavioral requirements of planning as a management task are often different from, or in conflict with, the processes and content of management work normally prevalent in the organization. Thus, it is quite possible that an organization optimally geared to the pursuit of established objectives may be less than optimally prepared to work on the evaluation and adoption of new objectives or strategies. To a very real extent, planning is a new kind of management activity.[2]

Exhibit 16-1 differentiates the characteristics of operational management (i.e., the traditional organization with emphasis on the achievement of established objectives) and strategic planning. By and large, operational management works in known territory and is concerned with immediate issues. Strategic planning, however, stresses unfamiliar perspectives and is oriented toward the future.

Allen, who has done empirical work in the area of organizational changes, provides interesting insights into the subject. He studied organizational changes in 40 American corporations between 1970 and 1974 and found that while traditional organizational structures have not been modified to any large extent, corporations have made changes in processes and systems to accommodate strategic planning.[3] These changes are described below with reference to two large corporations: Texas Instruments and General Electric.

Texas Instruments' OST System[4]

Because of its calculators and digital watches, Texas Instruments Incorporated (T.I.) is well known today. The company has grown over the years at an average

---

[2]Robert Mainer, "The Impact of Strategic Planning on Executive Behavior," a special commentary (Boston: Boston Consulting Group, 1968), pp. 4–5.

[3]Stephen A. Allen, "A Taxonomy of Organizational Choices in Divisionalized Companies," working paper (Lausanne, Switz.: IMEDE, 1976).

[4]Discussion on Texas Instruments' OST system is based on executive speeches available from the company. See also "Texas Instruments Incorporated" in Peter Lorange and Richard F. Vancil, *Strategic Planning Systems* (Englewood Cliffs, NJ: Prentice-Hall, 1977), pp. 338–361.

EXHIBIT 16-1   Organizational Characteristics

Operational Management	Strategic Planning
1. Concerned with goals derived from established objectives.	1. Concerned with the identification and evaluation of new objectives and strategies.
2. Goals usually have been validated through extensive past experience.	2. New objectives and strategies can be highly debatable; experience within the organization or in other companies may be minimal.
3. Goals are reduced to specific sub-goals for functional units.	3. Objectives usually are evaluated primarily for corporate significance.
4. Managers tend to identify with functions or professions and to be preoccupied with means.	4. Managers need a corporate point of view oriented to the environment.
5. Managers obtain relatively prompt evidence of their performance against goals.	5. Evidence of the merit of new objectives or strategies is often available only after several years.
6. Incentives, formal and social, are tied to operating goals.	6. Incentives are at best only loosely associated with planning.
7. The "rules of the game" become well understood. Experienced individuals feel competent and secure.	7. New fields of endeavor may be considered. Past experience may not provide competence in a "new game."
8. The issues are immediate, concrete, and familiar.	8. Issues are abstract, deferrable (to some extent), and may be unfamiliar.

Source: Robert Mainer, "The Impact of Strategic Planning on Executive Behavior," a special commentary (Boston: Boston Consulting Group, 1968), pp. 4–5.

compound rate of 25 percent annually, reaching $2.5 billion in sales in 1978. Over the same period profits have grown at a rate of 24 percent.

Exhibit 16-2 shows the traditional organizational structure at T.I. The company is divided into four groups supported by four staff departments. The groups break down further into divisions, which in turn divide into product-customer centers. There are a total of 77 product-customer centers (PCCs). The PCCs operate like complete small business organizations, each having its own profit responsibility. Each PCC manager has decentralized responsibility for the creation, manufacturing, and marketing functions for products serving a particular class of customers in a specific product area. The range of a PCC business may be between $1 million and $80 million in sales.

Basically, the PCC environment has a short-term emphasis. Traditionally long-term planning at T.I. was carried out by top management, with the group and division managers serving as communicators between PCCs and top management. The traditional structure worked well until the early 1960s, when certain developments in the semiconductor field and the loss of some government business led T.I. to change its strategic perspective. The traditional structure posed some problems for the pursuit of new strategic directions. For example, in many cases one PCC duplicated the staff work of other PCCs. Each PCC operated to maximize its own benefits without any concern for the corporation as a whole— a typical characteristic of a decentralized unit. New ideas were keyed to current strengths and were mostly incremental in nature. In short, there was a lack of synergistic effort.

The OST (objectives, strategies, and tactics) system was created to offset the above problems and to provide an aggressive perspective for facing the future. The system was established to supplement, not replace, the traditional organization. Having complete budgetary responsibility, the PCCs continue to be the operating units for implementation of plans. The OST system is meant for strategic planning (including resource allocation).

Exhibit 16-3 presents the OST system. At the top is the corporate objective, which refers to 1) the economic purpose of the company; 2) product, market, and technical goals; 3) responsibilities to employees, share owners, community, and society; and 4) financial goals. The corporate objective is supported by a set of nine business objectives, each of which is expressed in the following terms:

1. *Scope* (a business charter which establishes the boundaries of the business, appraises the potential opportunities in the business, and studies the technical and market trends and the overall competitive structure of industry serving the business)
2. *Performance measures* (sales, profit, return on assets, and served available market penetration for five and ten years ahead)
3. *Market and product goals* (served available market projections by product and percentage penetration by product)
4. *Technical goals* (technical constraints and innovations required)
5. *Critique* (competitive evaluation, threats and contingencies, and market shifts)

EXHIBIT 16-2   Texas Instruments Inc.: Traditional Organization (1970)

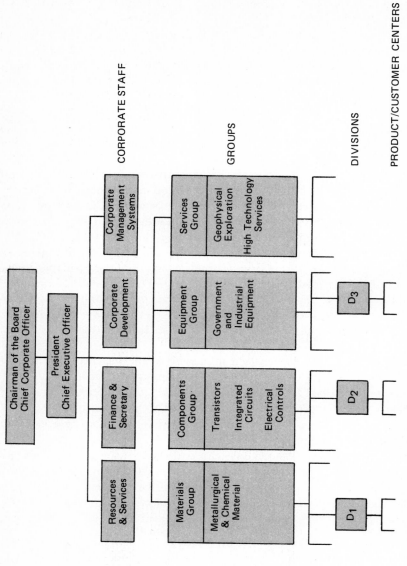

Source: Grant A. Dove, "The OST System of Texas Instruments Incorporated," an address made to the London Graduate School of Business Studies, May 22, 1970.

EXHIBIT 16-3   Texas Instruments Inc.: The OST System

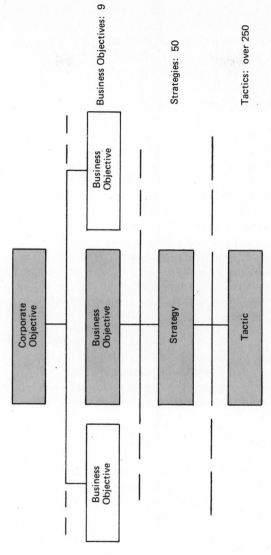

Source: Grant A. Dove, "The OST System of Texas Instruments Incorporated," an address made to the London Graduate School of Business Studies, May 22, 1970.

The business objectives for a company using the OST system are stated by the top management and the corporate development. Objectives which pertain to an industry (e.g., the auto industry) or a geographic area (e.g., Latin America) often cut across groups and divisions. For each objective an objective manager, who may be a group or division manager, is appointed. In other words, an executive in the traditional organization has an additional responsibility in the OST system. The objective manager for the auto industry, for example, may be the components group executive since most of the sales for this industry come from integrated circuits. When a manager has dual responsibility, about one fourth of the manager's time is spent on strategy-related work and the remaining three fourths of the time on the responsibilities to the product line or on short-run profit performance.

At the next level in the OST system is the strategy statement, which describes in detail the environment of the business opportunity to be pursued in support of the objective. Normally there are several strategies for supporting an objective. For example, in the auto industry the company may have one strategy involving automobile electronics, one involving material applications, and perhaps one for safety systems. The strategy looks ahead a number of years (normally five to ten) and defines intermediate checkpoints along the way so as to provide milestones against which to judge progress. Each strategy is defined by taking the following factors into consideration:

1. Strategy statement (opportunity environment, required innovations, competitive actions, contingencies, and major commitments)
2. Major long-range checkpoints
3. Contribution to and/or possible impact on the objective
4. Probability of success

Texas Instruments has over 60 strategies throughout the company.

There is a strategy manager for each strategy. In the auto industry, the strategy manager for automobile electronics may be a division manager in the components group (see D_2 in Exhibit 16-2); the strategy manager for material applications may be a division manager in the materials group (D_1). In addition, the safety-systems strategy manager may come from the equipment group (D_3). Thus, the group executive of the components group has an additional responsibility for strategic planning as an objective manager. For the latter responsibility this executive has three strategy managers reporting to him. One of these strategy managers (i.e., D_2) also reports to him for short-term performance. But D_1 and D_3 report only as strategy managers. For short-term performance they report to other group executives. In brief, each manager has the two responsibilities of short-term performance under the traditional structure and strategy-oriented performance under the OST system. For these two responsibilities a manager may report to the same executive or to two different executives. In about one fourth of the cases, there are cross-group and cross-divisional objectives and strategies. The objective manager is expected to identify strategies throughout the company and integrate them into a strategic plan for the objective.

For each strategy there are several tactics (over 250 for the company as a whole), and for each of them a tactical action program (TAP) is developed. A TAP is a detailed action plan of the steps necessary for reaching the major or long-range checkpoints defined by the strategy. A TAP is normally a short-term program ranging in length from six to eighteen months. Each tactic is assigned to a product/customer center (PCC) manager; the resources required for its implementation are defined, and a time schedule for completion is established. PCC managers may cut across group and division lines. Progress on the status of the tactic is reported monthly. Thus, strategic planning and its implementation are linked since the same people operate in both modes.

The relation between a strategic mode and an operating mode within the same organization, as practiced at T.I., may be illustrated in the form of a matrix, as shown in Exhibit 16-4. It must be noted that there are not two separate and distinct organizations; there is a single organization with clearly defined responsibilities for both the strategic and the operating modes.

For example, one of the roles of a strategy manager, as indicated in Exhibit 16-4, is to identify the TAPs required (represented by X's) and to pull them together from across the company into a coordinated strategic plan. Sometimes the strategy manager may also be the manager of a product-customer center (PCC), especially if there is one PCC which occupies a dominant position in the strategy. Almost invariably the strategy or tactic manager will also have an operating role to play. Only rarely does the strategy manager or tactic manager serve only in a strategy role. Dove explains the manager's roles as follows:

> To understand how this works, let's look at the differences between what we would call operating investments and strategic investments. Suppose that you were an operating manager and were concerned only about short-term profit and loss goals. The investments you would make would tend to be only those necessary for current operations, those required to meet your current commitments. In other words, you probably would invest about what was necessary to maximize the year-ahead results.
>
> Now, on the other hand, suppose you were a strategy manager concerned mainly with long-term goals. First—let's face it—your investments would be completely discretionary to current operations; that is, we can choose not to undertake them at all. They are always avoidable or postponable, but they are key to our long-term growth.
>
> Now, with these definitions in mind, let us say you are a young manager somewhere within one of the company's product-customer centers. You might be in Research, or Manufacturing, or Marketing, or any area, but let's say you are performing a line function within your center and a large measure of your day-to-day responsibility is the profitability of that center. Suppose that you thought you could see the possibility for a new business entry for T.I., or possibly for a major impact on one of the existing strategies. You are excited about the proposal and would like to spend more time digging into the possibilities of its success. The

EXHIBIT 16-4   Texas Instruments Inc.: Relationship Between Strategic and Operating Modes

(a) Organization Matrix
OST/Operating

O	S	T		Group 2						Group 1
				Division A			Division B			
			PCC	PCC	PCC	PCC	PCC	PCC	PCC	
		1	X							
		2	X							
	A	3			X					
		4					X			
1		5							X	
		1			X					
	B	2			X					
		3	X							

(b) Dual Organizational Roles

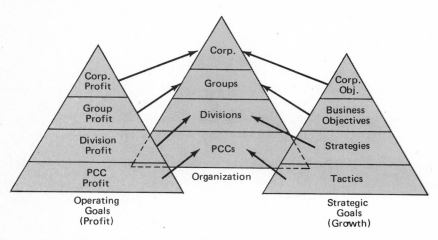

| Operating Goals (Profit) | Organization | Strategic Goals (Growth) |

Source: Grant A. Dove, "The OST System of Texas Instruments Incorporated," an address made to the London Graduate School of Business Studies, May 22, 1970.

problem is that every minute you give to this idea is a minute you have not given to your product-customer center. In a way, this might be considered wasteful. In many organizations, short-term pressures for operating profits might completely block your efforts. This would be a very frustrating and demotivating experience. You might soon learn to avoid wasting time on such innovative thinking. But in terms of future business growth, these are precisely the kinds of ideas the organization needs to stay alive. This is the activity we are attempting to institutionalize through the OST system. How does this come about?

Through the OST overlay, we have a goal structure for strategic activities as well as operating activities. Not only can we measure profit and loss performance operationally, but we also can allocate resources through the OST structure and measure our progress toward these strategic goals. Now your new idea has a home. It can be given resources for further development and, if the progress warrants, heavier support later. A number of outcomes are possible. Your idea might develop as a tactic. Or it might be big enough to stimulate an entire strategy. Or it might even be the catalyst which would lead to a new major corporate goal at the objective level. Whatever the case, your idea would be clearly a part of the OST structure and would be recognized and supported by deliberate choice. It won't have to be bootlegged or dropped completely through the crack.[5]

The OST cycle begins in the spring of each year with the Strategic Planning Conference. About 400 managers from T.I.'s worldwide operations attend this meeting along with corporate officers and board members. Each business objective manager presents his current assessment of opportunities and redefines the long-range goals. His position is supported by presentations from his key strategy managers, who define their business directions and goals and the resources required for each of these. By the end of the second quarter, the plans are appraised, goals reviewed, and corrective action defined. In the third quarter the corporate OST expenditure level for the forthcoming year is defined, and the Corporate Development Committee allocates funds to each business objective according to its growth opportunities, competitive status, and progress made in the execution of its plans. The objective and strategy managers define their tactical programs, rank them in order of importance, and, after several iterations, present them to the Corporate Development Committee for approval. During the process of this approval, tactical programs may be reoriented and funds shifted between objectives. Thereafter, during the course of the year, the business objective managers are encouraged to continually appraise the progress of their programs and shift funds as necessary.

For the first five years of OST implementation, although plans were developed and action programs defined, there was no control on the extent of resources being used on a current basis. In order to close this loophole and control the resources

---

[5]Grant A. Dove, "The OST System of Texas Instruments Incorporated," an address made to the London Graduate School of Business Studies, May 22, 1970, pp. 22–23.

actually being applied to the strategic program, the expense budgets were divided into operating and strategic expenses.

A strategic expense is directed toward the attainment of long-term perspectives. It is project oriented (not level-of-effort oriented); that is, it must have a beginning and an end as well as milestones in between. Most of all, it is directed toward optimizing long-term results. An operating expense, on the other hand, is necessary for current operations. It is required to meet operational goals and should optimize year-end results.

The OST system has worked well for T.I. The company has developed an appropriate compensation structure which measures both strategic and operating performances. Over the years a variety of adjustments have been made to resolve difficulties. Despite that, many problems still remain. For example, the drainage of strategic resources to meet short-term problems continues to be a difficulty. Another problem is the quality of longer-range quantitative data available for developing strategies and tactics. Besides this, there are the occasional conflicts which arise because managers have multiple bosses. Also, there are arguments that detailed project planning is an over-regimented approach. Another problem often arises, ironically as a result of the success of the OST system. Often more tactical action programs or good ideas are generated than can be undertaken in a given year. This means that many well-developed proposals fall below the funding-approval line. This is a major disappointment to the individuals who have worked very hard to formulate these proposals.

General Electric Company's Strategic Business Unit Structure[6]

G.E.'s line organization, as well as its strategic business unit setup, is shown in Exhibit 16-5. The company has a chairperson and chief executive officer, three vice-chairpersons, and nine major product groups with a number of divisions and departments within each group. To superimpose a strategic business planning process on the existing structure, G.E. established basic planning blocks which it refers to as "strategic business units" (SBUs). The SBU is defined as a unit whose manager has complete responsibility for integrating all functions involved in a strategy against an identifiable external competitor. The SBUs are at various levels and of various sizes. Some at the group level have sales in excess of $1.5 billion. Each business unit has a strategic plan, and resource allocation among SBUs is at the corporate level.

G.E.'s SBUs are similar to the strategies at T.I. Like the OST system, the SBU structure is intended for strategic planning, while the line organization is oriented toward short-term operations and control. In 1978 G.E. had 49 SBUs. Six of these were managed by group executives, twenty-two by division managers, and

---

[6]Discussion on G.E. is based on executive speeches available from the company. See also "G.E.'s New Strategy for Faster Growth," *Business Week* (July 8, 1972), pp. 56–57.

EXHIBIT 16-5 General Electric Co.: Line Organization and Strategic Business Units

Line Organization

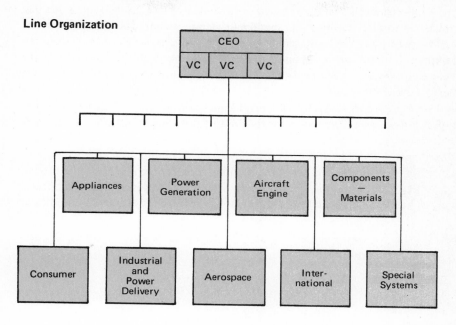

Strategic Business Units

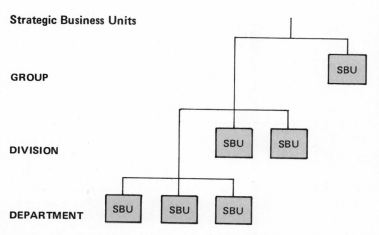

Source: *Maintaining Strategies for the Future Through Current Crises* (Fairfield, CT: General Electric Co., 1975).

twenty-one by department managers. The SBU's level is determined by whether the SBU is cross-departmental or cross-divisional and by the size of the business.

G.E. also changed its corporate staff from a functional organization to one that emphasizes administration under one senior vice-president. The planning activity was formerly staffed by four senior vice-presidents. Under the new system the administration and coordination of functions was taken off the shoulders of the chief executive officer. The corporate executive staff was strengthened so as to be able to advise the CEO on key decisions. An executive board made up of a vice-chairperson and the senior vice-presidents was organized for each group. The board functions as a mechanism for the continual review of operations and plans within each group.

As shown in Exhibit 16-6, Corporate Strategic Planning, headed by one of the four senior vice-presidents, has three sections: Environmental Analysis, Corporate Strategy and Systems, and Business Strategy and Review. Environmental Analysis handles economic forecasts, economic research, and industry studies; it

EXHIBIT 16-6   General Electric Co.: Corporate Strategic Planning Organization

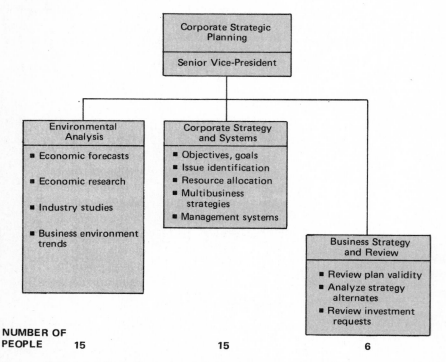

Source: *Maintaining Strategies for the Future Through Current Crises* (Fairfield, CT: General Electric Co., 1975).

also follows up and advises on business, social, and legal trends that may lead to future legislation. Corporate Strategy and Systems deals with company objectives and goals, issue identification, and resource allocation strategies which may involve a number of businesses and management systems. The particular emphasis here is on the corporate plan. The third component, Business Strategy and Review, reviews the validity of the plans as they are submitted by each of the SBUs. This department analyzes alternate strategies and reviews specific investment requests to make certain they conform to the approved strategy of the business. In 1978 there were 36 professionals in these three departments.

In the SBUs themselves, about 44 lead planners were identified and appointed. Additionally, some 123 staff members were added to the SBUs. The turnover among SBU planners is high. For example, the turnover for ten group-level planners was 100 percent in three years, mostly because of promotions. Fifty percent of the other planners in the company also turned over in that time. This is perceived as evidence that an individual planner's performance is relatively easy to assess in a short period of time.

It must be emphasized that it is the line manager's responsibility to develop a strategy for the business. The staff members are merely assistants. This is true at both the corporate and P&L center levels. G.E. undertook an extensive operation to train its planners. The top 320 executives attended a four-day orientation session organized internally. More extensive training was given to strategic planners in a two-week strategic planning workshop, and an audiovisual program described the basics to 10,000 people in the company.

The matter of motivating managers to keep a balanced view of short-term problems and future opportunities was also considered. The critical issue was, "On what basis do managers get promoted or rewarded?" One can have elegant strategic plans, but if managers are rewarded on short-term results alone, then plans for the future will not be considered along with short-term actions.

G.E.'s strategy for motivating managers is depicted in Exhibit 16-7. Managers received clear instructions as to their strategic assignments, and the incentive compensation program was modified to reflect these strategic assignments. As shown in Exhibit 16-7, the entrepreneurial managers are now aligned with the growth businesses, the more sophisticated, critical managers with businesses where great selectivity is needed, and the more solid, experienced managers with the tough cost-control and investment-reduction tasks in the weaker businesses. Bonuses to these different groups of businesses were duly adjusted, with low emphasis on current results in the invest/grow type of business.

Shown in Exhibit 16-8 are some of the financial measures of current performance—income compared with the previous year and income compared with budget. Also mentioned are the performance factors concerned with future benefits: performance in building manpower, in developing facilities, in designing and executing programs for market or product development, and in strengthening the strategy of the business. There are additional criteria to cover unforeseen events or unique contributions.

EXHIBIT 16-7   General Electric Co.: Managerial Incentive Compensation

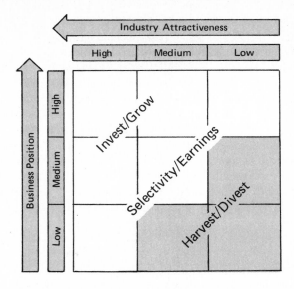

Portfolio Category	Manager's Key Characteristics	Weighting of I.C. Based On	
		Current Results	Future Benefits
Invest/Grow	Entrepreneur	Low	High
Selectivity/ Earnings	Sophisticated/ Critical	← Balanced →	
Harvest/Divest	Solid/Experienced	High	Low

Source: *Maintaining Strategies for the Future Through Current Crises* (Fairfield, CT: General Electric Co., 1975).

In the growth businesses only 40 percent of a manager's bonus award depends on current financial results; the predominant portion depends on the manager's performance in building the future of the business. The proportion is reversed when the role of the business is to produce short-term results. In the harvest/divest business, 72 percent of the bonus depends on the manager's short-term financial results.

The planning system at General Electric gives each business a firm role in the overall company picture, defining that role and paying for it. The planning system is based on the premise that at the corporate level one cannot know enough about every business to develop its strategy. Nor can a manager set goals effectively alone; the manager needs someone to augment his or her efforts. That is what is done at the corporate level.

EXHIBIT 16-8   General Electric Co.: Matching Performance Factors to Business Portfolio Position

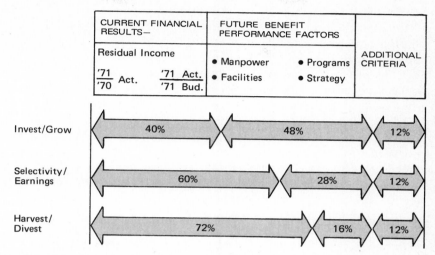

Source: *Maintaining Strategies for the Future Through Current Crises* (Fairfield, CT: General Electric Co., 1975).

INTEGRATION AT THE TOP

In today's environment the chief executive officer cannot handle alone the various demands that are made on his time. To ensure top-level involvement in strategic planning, companies have adopted two types of organizational changes, which are examined here. The first of these is the formation of the office of chief executive officer, and the other is the creation of a sector-executive position.

CEO Office

A large number of companies now have an office of the chief executive officer (CEO office) rather than just one chief executive officer (CEO). The term "office" implies here that more than one executive is designated to the chief executive office. For example, at Mead Corporation the CEO office includes the chairperson of the board (who is also the chief executive officer), the vice-chairperson, and the president. The vice-chairperson is responsible for strategic planning, while the president looks after the operations. This type of structure permits the chief executive officer to draw a proper balance between operations and strategy while it also frees the CEO for interaction with the outside world.

A recent example of the creation of the CEO office (sometimes also referred to as the office of the president) is provided by the Itel Corp. of San Francisco, a company which leases computer and transportation equipment. After many successful years, the company was faced with a variety of problems in 1979. On analysis it was realized that, among other things, Itel had a one-person management structure. To remedy this situation, the company established an office of the president, which included three additional executives. It was anticipated that this would change the style of management and control for the better and create checks and balances that did not exist before.[7]

Conceptually, an activity needs to be integrated at the top when it is spread across the company in many groups and divisions and its coordination is scattered throughout the organization. The number of executives in the CEO office may vary from two to five. The responsibilities assigned to individuals depend on their backgrounds and interests. Operational, strategic, international, and government responsibilities are among the duties which may be assigned to executives in the CEO office. People who constitute the CEO office are expected to visualize things from the total corporate viewpoint. Their individual performances and rewards are based on the performance of the entire corporation. Large companies with established planning systems often have an executive in the CEO office who is responsible for strategic planning. In this way top management is able to play the key role required for successful strategic planning.

Sector Organization

In some corporations a new level has been created between the chief executive officer and the group managers. This has been achieved by forming clusters of groups which are interdependent in their work and relatively independent of other groups not in their cluster. For example, G.E. recently added five sector executives, each of whom is in charge of a sector. One of the sectors is concerned with consumer products and services. Thus, all groups doing business in the consumer sector of the economy, as opposed to those selling to industry or the government, report to the executive in charge of the consumer sector. The new level of management at G.E. was installed just below the corporate executive office. Group heads who formerly reported to the executive office now report to a sector executive, who in turn reports to one of the two vice-chairpersons. G.E.'s 49 strategic-business-unit heads also report to sector executives. Previously strategic plans for each SBU had to be reviewed by the top office. Now the executive office sees only the sector plans, which are summaries of all the SBU plans. G.E.'s five sectors are: 1) Consumers Products and Services, 2) Power Systems, 3) Technical Systems and Materials, 4) Industrial Products and Components, and 5) International Operations. Each sector executive at G.E. absorbed many chief executive functions in the company reorganization.[8]

The sector concept has also been adopted by the American Can Company. The company appointed five of its ten senior vice-presidents to the position of sector executive. The five sectors at American Can are: 1) Packaging; 2) Consumer

---

[7]"How Itel Shook Off One-Man Management," *Business Week* (July 9, 1979), p. 28.
[8]"G.E.'s New Billion-Dollar Small Businesses," *Business Week* (December 19, 1977), pp. 78–79.

Products; 3) Technology and Development (including recovery systems and chemicals); 4) Specialty Wholesaling and Retailing, and 5) International Business.[9] Similarly, W.R. Grace & Co. has established four new sector executive positions.

The sector arrangement is considered a vehicle for cross-fertilization. Corporate-wide trade-offs in capital, technology, and human resources can be dealt with at the sector level without creating any suspicions at the group or division levels. Additionally, the sector structure relieves the chief executive officer of strategic planning responsibility, thus permitting the CEO to get involved in external matters. As a matter of fact, the sector executives become the representatives for an industry insofar as the company's participation in the industry is concerned. This is a function people traditionally expected the chief executive officer to dominate. Thus, sector organization is a way of developing institutional leadership.

ROLE OF THE CHIEF EXECUTIVE

The chief executive officer (CEO) of a company is the chief strategist. We will examine here the major responsibilities of the CEO's role in strategic planning.

The CEO communicates the importance of strategic planning to the organization. Personal commitment on the part of the CEO to the significance of planning must not only be highly visible, but also be consistent with all the other decisions the CEO makes to influence the work of the organization. To be accepted within the organization, the strategic planning process needs the CEO's support. People accustomed to short-term orientations may resist the strategic planning process, which requires different methods. But the CEO can set an example for them by adhering to the planning process. Essentially, the CEO is responsible for creating a corporate climate which is conducive to strategic planning. The CEO can also set a future perspective for the organization. One CEO remarked:

> My people cannot plan or work beyond the distance of my own vision. If I focus on next year, I'll force them to become preoccupied with next year. If I can try to look five to ten years ahead, at least I'll make it possible for the rest of the organization to raise their eyes off the ground immediately in front of them.[10]

The CEO should focus attention on the corporate purpose and approve strategic decisions accordingly. To perform these tasks well, the CEO should support the staff work and analysis upon which his or her decisions are based. Along the same lines, the CEO should ensure the establishment of a noise-free communications network in the organization. Communications should flow downward from

---

[9]"Canco Adds a Rung to Its Executive Ladder," *Business Week* (April 30, 1979), p. 25.
[10]Robert Mainer, "The Impact of Strategic Planning on Executive Behavior," a special commentary (Boston: Boston Consulting Group, 1968), p. 24.

the CEO with respect to organizational goals, aspirations, and values of top management. Similarly, information about risks, results, plans, concepts, capabilities, competition, and the environment should flow upward.

Concern for the future may require a change in organizational perspectives. The CEO should not only perceive the need for a change, but also be instrumental in making it happen. Change, however, is not easy since past success provides a strong motive for continuing the status quo. As long as the environment and competitive behavior do not change, the past perspectives are fine. However, as the environment undergoes a shift, changes in policies and attitudes become essential. It is here that the CEO must rise to the occasion and not only initiate change, but also encourage others to accept it and adapt to it. Here, the timing of the change may perhaps be more important than the change itself. The need for change must be realized before the optimum time for it has passed so that competitive advantage and flexibility are not lost.

The difference between managers and leaders must be pointed out here. Managers keep things running smoothly, while leaders provide longer-term direction and thrust.[11] Successful strategic planning requires that the CEO be a good leader. In this capacity the CEO should:

1. Gain complete and willing acceptance of his leadership.
2. Determine those business goals, objectives, and standards of behavior which are as ambitious as the potential abilities of the organization will permit.
3. Introduce these objectives and motivate the organization to accept them as their own. The rate of introduction will be the maximum consistent with continued acceptance of leadership. Because of this need for acceptance, the new manager must always go slowly, except in emergencies. In emergencies the boss must not go slowly if he is to maintain leadership.
4. Change the organizational relationships internally as necessary to facilitate both the acceptance and attainment of the new objectives.[12]

ROLE OF THE STRATEGIC PLANNER

A strategic planner is a staff person who assists line executives in their planning efforts. Thus, there may be a corporate strategic planner working closely with the chief executive officer. A strategic planner may also be attached to an SBU. This section examines the role that the planner plays in an organization's strategic planning process.

---

[11]See Abraham Zalezink, "Managers and Leaders: Are They Different?" *Harvard Business Review* (May–June, 1977), pp. 67–78.
[12]Bruce D. Henderson, *Henderson on Corporate Strategy* (Cambridge, MA: Abt Associates, 1979), p. 54.

The planner conceptualizes the planning process and helps translate it for line executives who actually do the planning. As part of this function, the planner works out a planning schedule and may develop a planning manual. He or she may also design a variety of pro forma forms, charts, tables, etc., which may be used to collect, analyze, and communicate planning-oriented information. The planner may also serve as a trainer in orienting line managers to strategic planning.

The planner generates innovative ways of performing difficult tasks and educates the line management in the new techniques and tools needed for an efficient job of strategic planning. The planner also coordinates the efforts of other specialists (i.e., marketing researchers, systems persons, econometricians, environmental monitors, and management scientists) with those of the line management. In this role the planner exposes managers to the newest and most sophisticated concepts and techniques in planning.

The planner serves as an adviser to the head of the SBU. In matters of concern, the head of the planning unit may request the planner to undertake a study and resolve the issue. For example, the corporate strategic planner, who may report to the vice-chairperson of the board, may be asked to evaluate the wisdom of developing a corporate-wide financial model. The planner may also be asked to recommend a way to sell other executives on the usefulness of such a model. Similarly, the SBU head may seek the advice of the SBU strategic planner in such matters as deciding whether private branding should be accepted so as to increase market share and gain experience, or whether it should be rejected for eroding the quality image of the brand.

Another key role that the planner plays is that of evaluator of strategic plans. For example, strategic plans of various SBUs are submitted to the corporate executive in charge of strategic planning. The latter may ask his or her planner to develop an evaluation system for the SBUs' plans. In addition, the planner may also be asked to express an opinion on strategic issues or to evaluate different product/market plans.

The planner may also be involved in integrating different plans. For example, the planner may integrate different product/market plans into an SBU strategic plan. Similarly, the SBUs' plans may be integrated by the corporate strategic planner from the perspectives of the entire corporation. For example, if the company uses the growth rate-relative market share matrix (see Exhibit 13-4) to judge plans submitted by different businesses, the planner may be asked not only to establish the position of these businesses on the matrix, but also to furnish a recommendation on such matters as which of two question marks (businesses in the high-growth-rate, low-market-share quadrant of the matrix in Exhibit 13-4) should be selected for additional funding. The planner's recommendation on such strategic issues helps in the crystallization of executive thinking.

Matters of a nonroutine nature may be assigned to the planner for study and recommendation. For example, the planner may head a committee to recommend structural changes in the organization. The committee that recommended sector organization at General Electric was headed by the corporate senior vice-president of strategic planning.

Obviously the job of strategic planner is not an easy one. The strategic planner must:

1. Be well versed in theoretical frameworks relevant to planning, at the same time realizing their limitations as far as practical applications are concerned.
2. Be capable of making a point with conviction and firmness and at the same time be a practical politician who can avoid creating conflict in the organization.
3. Maintain a working alliance with other units in the organization.
4. Command the respect of other executives and managers.
5. Be a salesperson who can help managers accept new and difficult tools and techniques.

In short, a planner needs to be a jack-of-all-trades.

EFFECT OF STRATEGIC PLANNING ON MARKETING ORGANIZATION

The focus of this section is on the impact of strategic planning on the marketing organization in a company. Unfortunately a dearth of research on the subject limits the discussion here to speculations and a recent unpublished study.

It is generally believed that the only marketing decision which has strategic content is the one concerned with product/market perspectives. As far as other marketing decisions are concerned, while they may occasionally have strategic elements, they are mainly operational in nature; i.e., they deal with short-term performance. Product/market decisions, however, being the most far-reaching in nature as far as strategy is concerned, are frequently made by top management. Thus, the product/market decisions having been taken, marketing organization is relegated to making operating decisions. In brief, strategic planning inroads tend to lower marketing's status in the organization. Kotler explains it as follows:

> And as strategic planning takes hold, it will force a repositioning of marketing within the firm. If anything, it threatens to demote marketing from a strategic to an operational function. Instead of marketing being in the driver's seat, strategic planning has moved into the driver's seat. Marketing has moved into the passenger seat and in some companies into the back seat.[13]

---

[13]Philip Kotler, "The Future Marketing Manager," in Betsy D. Gelb (ed.), *Marketing Expansion in a Shrinking World: 1978 Business Proceedings* (Chicago: American Marketing Assoc., 1978), p. 3.

Rich did a study to examine if indeed strategic planning has relegated the marketing function to a lower status in the organization.[14] Although his study is limited to one industry, i.e., 20 U.S. forest-products companies, he feels his findings represent a general trend among all industrial companies. Rich had done a similar study in the early 1960s to determine the role of marketing in forest-products companies. Thus, his current study provides an opportunity for examining the changes which have taken place in the role of marketing since the 1960s.

Exhibit 16-9 shows the typical role of marketing in a large forest-products company in the 1960s. A vice-president of marketing reported directly to the president, who was also the chief executive officer. There were a variety of functions included in the marketing department, the progress of each of which was reported to the marketing vice-president. Under the general sales manager were the product managers and regional sales managers. The product managers carried such titles as sales manager - lumber, sales manager - plywood, etc., and had functional authority over the sales force in matters concerning their product lines. Regional sales managers had administrative authority over the salespeople. Promotion and marketing research were controlled by the director of market development.

This typical forest-products company was organized functionally on the whole. However, at that time a trend was emerging toward divisionalized organization. As a matter of fact, by the late 1960s the above company had expanded its line and set up two divisions (the Pulp and Paper Division and the Lumber and Wood Products Division).

The 1979 study shows that with the emergence of strategic planning the status of marketing has declined. In none of the twenty companies that Rich studied did he find a marketing vice-president having the stature of the one shown in Exhibit 16-9, who reported to the chief executive officer. Rich noted:

> The highest level at which most marketing executives were found was just under the head of a strategic business unit, be it at the group or at the division level. Those few marketing executives who were found up at the corporate level tended to be one of three types. The first type was a "V.P., Distribution Division" and was found in companies with strong captive distribution systems. His job was overseeing the distribution, usually at the wholesale level, of all or some of the products of the company's mills. Sometimes he drew on outside sources of supply as well. The second type carried a title such as "Manager of Marketing Planning" and reported to a "Director of Strategic Planning" who came under the CEO. The third type, sometimes carrying the title "Marketing Services Manager," reported to the president or executive vice-president,

---

[14]The following discussion is indebted to Stuart U. Rich, "Organization Structure and the Marketing Function in Forest Products Companies," a paper presented at the AMA Western Marketing Educators' Conference, San Jose, CA, April 20, 1979.

EXHIBIT 16-9   Typical Organizational Structure of a Forest-products Company in the 1960s

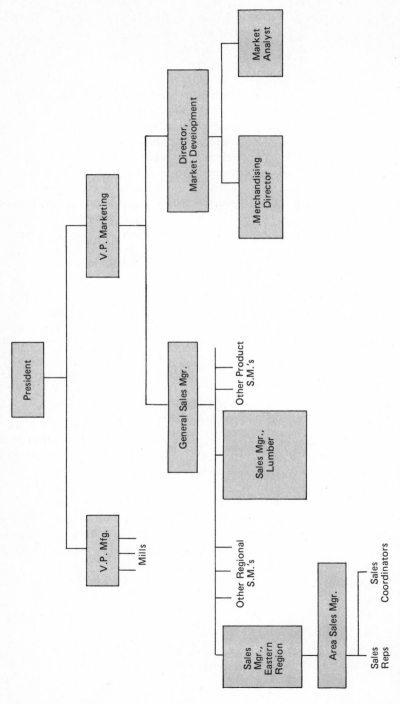

Source: Stuart U. Rich, "Organization Structure and the Marketing Function in Forest Products Companies," a paper presented at the A.M.A. Western Marketing Educators' Conference, San Jose, CA, April 20, 1979.

but his duties were confined mainly to handling important national accounts, that is, large customers who bought from many different divisions of the company. Such national account sales managers, however, were more likely to be found down at the group level.[15]

The highlights of Rich's study may be summarized separately for different companies, depending upon whether their SBUs are at the divisional level, the group level, or at both levels. Exhibit 16-10 shows the organization chart of a company having SBUs at the divisional level. Given here are the details of the Consumer Products SBU and the Printing Papers SBU. The highest ranking marketing officer in the Consumer Products SBU is the director of marketing. He has two marketing managers reporting to him: one for toilet tissue and facial tissue and the other one for towels and napkins. Marketing managers are responsible for promotional programs and sales forecasts. Reporting to marketing managers are a number of product managers responsible for the sales, market shares, and profitability of their brands within these product lines, similar to brand managers at Procter & Gamble. Obviously this SBU has a large marketing staff.

The Printing Papers SBU has a marketing manager and a sales manager. The former is in charge of advertising and research programs in addition to serving as a general administrative assistant to the SBU head. The product manager reporting to the marketing manager works with the mills on product quality and the customers to keep up with technical innovations. The sales manager supervises the sales force and customer service and takes care of production planning and scheduling.

The organizational structure of a company with SBUs at the group level is illustrated in Exhibit 16-11. The group-level SBUs in this company are headed by senior vice-presidents. They were brought together into two group clusters: 1) Paper and Related Businesses, and 2) Wood Products and Related Businesses. Each cluster is headed by an executive vice-president.

The Paper group was split into two subgroups: Fine Papers and Commodity Papers. Each subgroup is headed by a vice-president of marketing and sales. Reporting to each vice-president are marketing managers and general sales managers of different businesses in that subgroup. Marketing managers are responsible for product planning, promotion, pricing, market research, market development, merchandising programs, and customer technical service. General sales managers supervise the sales force with the help of regional and district sales managers.

Shown in Exhibit 16-12 are SBUs at both group and divisional levels. The White Papers group illustrates a group-level SBU, while the Folding Carton business constitutes a division-level SBU. The White Papers SBU is headed by

---

[15]Rich, *op. cit.*, pp. 5–6.

EXHIBIT 16-10 Typical Organizational Structure of a Forest-products Company with SBUs at the Divisional Level

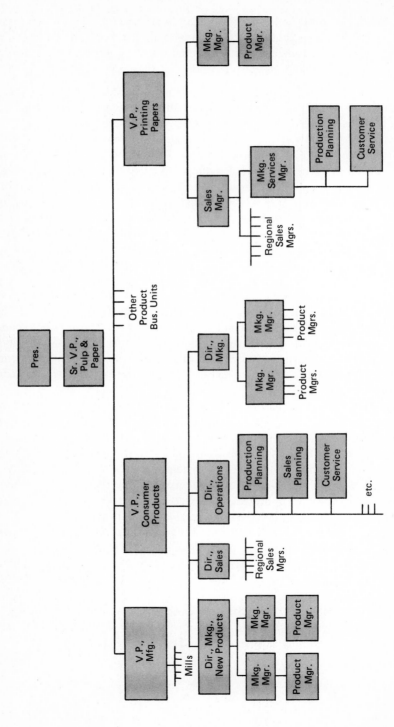

Source: Stuart U. Rich, "Organization Structure and the Marketing Function in Forest Products Companies," a paper presented at the A.M.A. Western Marketing Educators' Conference, San Jose, CA, April 20, 1979.

EXHIBIT 16-11   Typical Organizational Structure of a Forest-products Company with SBUs at the Group Level

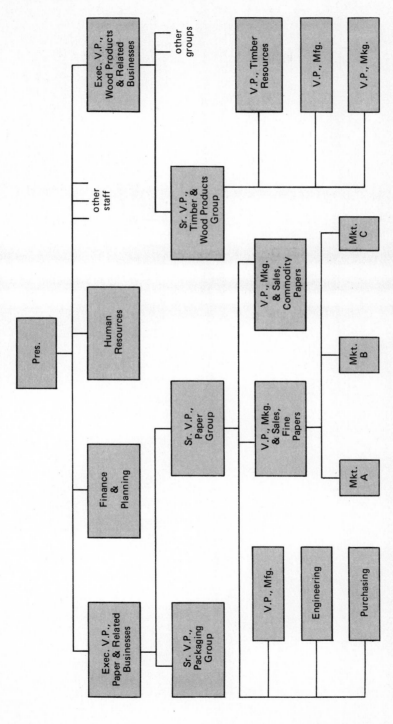

Source: Stuart U. Rich, "Organization Structure and the Marketing Function in Forest Products Companies," a paper presented at the A.M.A. Western Marketing Educators' Conference, San Jose, CA, April 20, 1979.

EXHIBIT 16-12   Typical Organizational Structure of a Forest-products Company with SBUs at Group and Divisional Levels

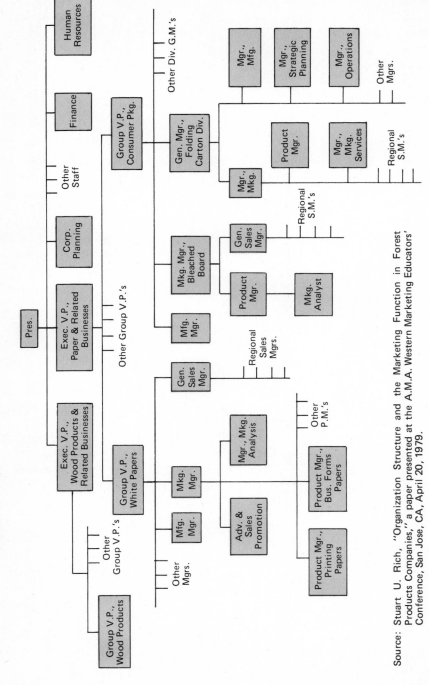

Source: Stuart U. Rich, "Organization Structure and the Marketing Function in Forest Products Companies," a paper presented at the A.M.A. Western Marketing Educators' Conference, San Jose, CA, April 20, 1979.

a vice-president who has a marketing manager and a general sales manager reporting to him. The marketing manager is responsible for developing and implementing a marketing plan for the whole White Papers line, reviewing and monitoring the implementation of the plans of the product managers under him, recommending to the group vice-president pricing strategies and capital expenditures, and supervising the manager of marketing financial planning (not shown in the exhibit). The general sales manager supervises the sales force and develops sales budgets and sales profit plans.

The division-level SBU in the same company, the Folding Carton Division, is headed by a general manager who has authority over a marketing manager and a manufacturing manager. The marketing manager has a range of duties similar to those of both the marketing manager and the general sales manager in the White Papers SBU.

One of the purposes of this chapter has been to examine adjustments and changes in marketing organization to accommodate strategic planning. The major structural change has revolved around the formation of strategic business unit (SBU). A strategic business unit in an organization can be constituted at the group level, at the divisional level, or at both the group and divisional levels. Rich's study shows that regardless of the level at which the SBU is established, it has a deteriorating effect on marketing organization. For example, at the corporate level the marketing function has declined in importance. In companies that have formalized strategic planning, there may not be senior marketing vice-presidents directly reporting to the chief executive officer. This means that as strategic planning makes inroads into companies, marketing people may have less opportunity to be among the senior executives.

At the same time, however, Rich notes that with the emergence of strategic planning, particularly in organizations that have adopted the SBU concept, marketing has become a more pervasive function than it was before. A marketing vice-president or director of marketing is found directly under the SBU head. Marketing and sales managers are involved mainly in day-to-day operations and occasionally in the strategic planning of the SBU. Thus, while marketing positions at the corporate level may have vanished, the marketing function still plays a key role in the running of a corporation, particularly in the day-to-day operations.

In summing up, Kotler predicts the following about the future of marketing management.

1. The marketer's job will be harder than ever in the 1980s because of the tough environment.
2. The strategic planner will provide the directive force to the company's growth, not the marketer.
3. The marketer will be relied on to contribute a great deal of data and appraisal of corporate purposes, objectives and goals, growth decisions, and portfolio decisions.

4. The marketer will assume more of an operational and less of a strategic role in the company.
5. The marketer will still have to champion the customer concept because companies tend to forget it.[16]

SUMMARY

It is not enough for an organization to develop a sound strategy. It must at the same time structure the organization in a manner that will ensure the implementation of the strategy. This chapter examines how the latter task, i.e., the matching of organizational structure to strategy, may be accomplished.

Inasmuch as strategic planning is a recent activity in most corporations, no basic principles have been developed on the subject. As a matter of fact, little academic research has been reported in this area. In spite of this, the structuring of an organization to accommodate strategic planning is illustrated here with reference to two pioneering companies in the field. Thus, discussed in this chapter are Texas Instruments' objective, strategy, and tactics (OST) system and General Electric's strategic business unit structure.

Also discussed is the integration of strategic planning at the level of the chief executive officer. In this area two recent developments, the CEO office and the position of sector executive, are examined. The roles of chief executive officer and strategic planner, both at the corporate and SBU levels, are discussed in the context of strategic planning activity.

The final section of this chapter focuses on the implications of the inroads of strategic planning for marketing organization. The discussion here is primarily based on a recent study of twenty forest-products companies. It is concluded that marketing may be losing some of its status in the organization. The position of vice-president of marketing at the corporate level may vanish. While marketing does provide inputs for strategic decisions, most marketing positions may be oriented to operations rather than to strategy.

DISCUSSION QUESTIONS

1. Why is it that traditional organizational structures may not be suited for strategic planning?
2. Discuss the main features of Texas Instruments' OST system. Does it have a matrix form of organization?
3. How did General Electric Company create the SBU organization? What are its major characteristics?

---

[16]Philip Kotler, "The Future Marketing Manager," in Betsy D. Gelb (ed.), *Marketing Expansion in a Shrinking World: 1978 Business Proceedings* (Chicago: American Marketing Assoc., 1978), p. 5.

4.   Between the OST system and the SBU organization, which one is more productive? Why?
5.   How did General Electric Company adjust its compensation package for its people managing different types of businesses (i.e., the invest/grow, selectivity/earnings, and harvest/divest types)?
6.   What is the significance of the CEO office for strategic planning?
7.   What is a sector organization? What impact does it have on strategic planning?
8.   What are the conclusions of the Rich study on the impact of strategic planning on marketing organization?
9.   How far may Rich's conclusions be applied to other industries?
10.   What are the chances of strategic planning succeeding in a company whose chief executive is not interested in it and delegates the task to staff people?
11.   How does the role of a strategic planner at the corporate level differ from the role of a planner with the strategic business unit?

Case A

Wilmington Corporation

In June 1975, executives in the Consumer Products Division of the Wilmington Corporation were considering the introduction of a range of cook and bake-ware products made from a glass-ceramic material. The sole existing producer of pressed glass-ceramic cookware, Corning Glass Works, held a patent on the product which was due to expire in January 1977. Corning's product range, marketed under the trade name of CORNING WARE®[1] cookware, was considered to be well established and held a strong position in the marketplace. While Wilmington did not have detailed figures on CORNING WARE® sales or profits, it was felt that this line provided a sizeable proportion of the sales and profits of Corning's Consumer Products Division. The expiration of Corning's patent in 1977 would remove a major barrier to entry into the glass-ceramic market. In anticipation of this event, Wilmington had already developed the technology to produce a product comparable in quality and performance to CORNING WARE® cookware.

The investigation of Wilmington's possible entry into the glass-ceramic market was the responsibility of a three-man task force appointed in March 1975 by Mr. Thomas Alstone, Marketing Vice President for the Consumer Products Division. The task force included as its members Mr. F. Henderson Bruit, Product Manager for Wilmington's Country Squire line, Mr. John P. Middle, a market analyst from the Market Research Department, and Mr. Allen S. Stern, an engineer from the manufacturing staff. In his initial discussions with the task force, Mr. Alstone had indicated that their final report should include:

1. a detailed study of the glass-ceramic market;
2. a recommendation as to whether or not Wilmington should enter the market; and
3. if yes, detailed plans for entry.

---

[1]CORNING WARE® is a registered trademark of Corning Glass Works.

Mr. Alstone felt that fairly heavy capital expenditure would be required for the glass-ceramic project and he knew that the plans would have to be placed before the New Products Review Committee and the Capital Expenditure Review Committee before any final decisions could be made. Preliminary estimates had shown that a twelve-month period would be required to develop the facility to produce glass-ceramic products. Some existing facilities at Wilmington's Marygold, New York plant were being phased out and could be converted to production of glass-ceramic products at a lower capital cost than would be required to construct a completely new manufacturing plant. Mr. Alstone felt that a decision about whether or not to enter the glass-ceramic business had to be made as soon as possible, and if the company were to go ahead, further decisions about plant size and capital expenditure should follow fairly quickly.

In his preliminary discussions with the engineering staff, Mr. Alstone had been assured that Wilmington was capable of producing a product at least as good as CORNING WARE® cookware. He had been shown some laboratory samples which were very similar to CORNING WARE® in material and weight, though their shape and appearance were somewhat different.

COMPANY BACKGROUND

Wilmington Corporation was a large, diversified manufacturer of glass and glass-related products. The company was started in 1901 to manufacture glass tumblers, and had grown in sales to $510 million per year by 1974. (See Exhibit A-1 for a ten-year statistical history of the company.) The major share of this growth had come from expansion of company operations in the glass industry. Currently, the company had twenty-one plants in operation: seventeen in the United States; two in Canada and one each in Germany and Brazil. Although the company marketed its products in seventy-five countries, 76% of its sales came from the United States and Canada. Wilmington divided its business into four major areas—consumer products, packaging, commercial products and technical. Exhibit A-2 shows the net sales and income before taxes of the company's major lines of business.

While the Consumer Products Division had always been an important part of the company's business, the Packaging Division had provided the major share of the growth and earnings in the 1960s. During the late sixties, however, the glass packaging industry's growth was slowed by growth in the use of plastic materials. As a result, both sales and earnings from packaging declined. The company did try to enter the plastic packaging business by acquiring two plastic packaging companies in the United States and one in Canada. The Canadian plant was moderately successful, but both the United States plastics operations had failed to make money.

The Consumer Products Division

The company manufactured over 2,000 different items in its Consumer Products Division. These were sold both as individual pieces, which were shipped to

EXHIBIT A-1   Wilmington Corporation: Ten-Year Financial Summary,
1965–1974

	1974	1973	1972	1971
Operations				
Net sales	$509,975,200	$455,493,300	$422,242,800	$387,705,500
Costs and expenses:				
Cost of products sold	423,283,900	366,793,000	331,191,000	303,253,900
Selling and administrative	48,993,500	44,296,800	40,311,100	36,604,600
	472,277,400	411,089,800	371,502,100	339,858,500
Income from operations	37,697,800	44,403,500	50,740,700	47,846,900
Other income	1,984,200	1,713,600	1,338,900	959,200
Interest expenses	(2,418,500)	(1,755,800)	(1,511,400)	(1,428,200)
Income before income tax	37,263,500	44,361,300	50,568,200	47,377,900
Net income	17,032,300	21,124,700	24,832,400	23,613,900
Financial Position Data				
Working capital	97,556,400	95,969,300	93,209,600	85,098,000
Property, plant and equipment	288,970,200	270,854,700	249,155,500	232,867,700
Accumulated depreciation	127,883,400	116,048,000	103,783,100	97,696,600
Long-term debt	22,009,400	24,468,800	23,919,100	24,837,400
Common stockholders' equity	223,614,500	214,913,500	203,887,100	185,718,200
Statistics				
Property, plant and equipment expenditures	24,679,800	24,661,200	24,025,800	17,538,500
Depreciation expense	15,673,500	14,863,200	13,273,600	12,964,700
Weighted average no. of common shares	8,489,195	8,705,625	8,701,510	8,666,405
No. of common stockholders	10,253	10,114	9,139	8,522
No. of employees	18,489	19,109	18,116	17,868

retailers in bulk, as well as in sets. The sets were mostly sold in gift packs, though company research showed that a number of the so-called gift sets were used by the purchasers in their own home or given to a person in the same house.

The product range had initially started with drinking glasses, but had been expanded over the years to include dinnerware, decorative items, giftware, ovenware and a great variety of miscellaneous glass pieces. A description of the product range is presented in Exhibit A-3. Traditionally the company had concentrated in the low price, high volume end of the market, and competed by offering "good value for the money." The product range was subsequently broadened, however, to include a number of middle price range pieces as well.

The company used a great variety of styles and designs in its glassware, but the bulk of them tended to be either traditional or "popular." Some of its lines were promoted as being "modern," but these lines represented only a small proportion of total sales, and did not fare well in competition with imported glassware. Generally speaking, each product was offered in three or four colors or designs. Wilmington executives believed that few consumers recognized the name Wilmington or associated it with any of the products in their line.

Though not highly innovative in the application of technology to consumer glassware manufacture, the company did monitor consumer tastes and preferences quite closely. Product development activities were guided by analysis of this

1970	1969	1968	1967	1966	1965
$363,824,800	$344,655,800	$290,852,600	$265,016,400	$249,283,300	$212,013,600
281,590,700	256,711,200	219,946,500	210,975,000	195,869,800	172,495,400
34,547,200	32,230,500	29,758,700	26,055,900	24,638,800	19,746,100
316,138,000	288,941,700	249,705,200	237,030,900	220,508,600	192,241,500
47,686,900	55,714,100	41,147,400	27,985,500	28,774,700	19,772,100
1,625,500	1,801,800	2,089,600	1,301,700	1,340,100	596,900
(1,531,200)	(1,503,900)	(1,377,400)	(1,341,400)	(959,200)	—
47,781,200	56,011,900	41,859,700	27,945,800	29,155,600	20,369,000
24,246,700	29,207,700	21,693,000	13,127,200	13,499,500	9,374,800
73,385,400	68,383,400	68,599,300	62,911,200	59,439,700	39,951,200
223,824,200	206,581,000	176,704,500	158,342,000	144,768,000	117,945,300
92,596,600	85,791,700	77,918,300	69,986,600	65,072,800	57,724,300
26,255,700	26,961,800	26,289,200	26,286,700	24,817,500	—
170,181,200	155,210,000	133,627,400	118,527,200	108,682,100	93,215,800
22,845,800	33,584,300	20,558,800	16,951,600	24,193,400	14,902,900
12,119,600	11,082,300	9,598,200	8,117,800	6,630,000	5,304,700
8,652,421	8,595,710	8,502,468	8,476,516	8,440,523	7,376,960
8,140	7,614	7,350	7,921	7,954	8,337
18,240	18,240	17,496	16,875	16,441	15,262

EXHIBIT A-2   Wilmington Corporation: Sales and Income Before Taxes

	Percentage				
	1970	1971	1972	1973	1974
Net Sales:					
Consumer Products	25%	27%	29%	30%	30%
Packaging	57	56	55	54	54
Commercial	12	11	10	10	10
Technical	6	6	6	6	6
Total net sales	100%	100%	100%	100%	100%
Income Before Taxes:					
Consumer Products	37%	44%	44%	51%	51%
Packaging	44	40	40	34	34
Commercial	12	8	7	7	7
Technical	7	8	9	8	8
Total income before taxes	100%	100%	100%	100%	100%

research data, as well as through preference testing of new products at both the regional and national levels. Before products were put into distribution, they were generally test marketed; after the test market, the company often conducted

EXHIBIT A-3   Wilmington Corporation Consumer Products Division: Product Range, 1974

	No. of designs/ decorations/colors	No. of sizes/ items	Total no. of pieces
1. Mugs and bowls	9	3	27
2. Decorated mugs	9	3	27
3. Ovenware	10	11	31
4. Ovenware gift sets	5	12	20
5. Mixing bowls	4	3	11
6. Mixing bowl gift sets	8	12	40
7. Kitchen aids	4	10	10
8. Dinnerware gift sets	7	12	184
9. Serving dish gift sets	4	6	31
10. Table server gift sets	2	8	16
11. Salad gift sets	4	3	12
12. Salt and pepper shakers	4	2	8
13. Salt and pepper gift sets	4	2	8
14. Punch gift sets	5	5	25
15. Chip'n dip gift sets	7	3	21
16. Decorated novelty gift	35	97	435
17. Decorated cocktail ware	24	6	78
18. Glass/refreshment	13	14	122
19. Decorated glasses	2	14	38
20. Cocktail glasses	5	11	60
21. Miscellaneous drinking	19	12	201
22. Decorative glasses	5	7	42
23. Cut glass	6	12	72
24. Beer glasses and mugs	16	3	49
25. Brandy snifters	1	12	12
26. Whiskey glasses	1	12	12
27. Wine and decanter sets	7	6	54
28. Beverage gift sets	9	4	42
29. Refreshment gift sets	5	4	31
30. Decorated gift sets	26	81	312
31. Decorated cocktail gift sets	3	18	31
32. Decorated juice gift sets	2	5	12
33. Dinnerware	7	12	184
34. Accessories for dinnerware	4	27	208
35. Serving dishes	4	11	31
36. Punch cups	5	2	7
37. Fountainware	7	12	12
38. Terrarium	3	3	3
39. Imaginarium gift sets	3	3	3
40. Vases and planters	6	36	42
41. Ash trays	38	54	54
42. Storage jar gift sets	4	5	20
43. Storage jars	21	32	38
44. Fish bowls	5	14	14
45. Miscellaneous ornaments	12	12	12
46. Candleholders	5	14	14
47. Ashtray gift sets	8	13	13
48. Snack and buffet gift sets	4	2	8
49. Lazy susan gift sets	2	3	66
50. Miscellaneous gift sets	12	12	12

Note: There was considerable overlap between pieces offered individually and in sets. The total number of different pieces manufactured by Wilmington was a little over 2,000.

post-test follow-up research with consumers to find out how well the product performed in actual use and whether consumers were satisfied with it.

Distribution

The Consumer Products Division distributed its products direct to retailers in major market areas through 15 field offices in 43 states. Each field office consisted of a district sales manager with a staff of three to five salesmen, two or three sales promotion assistants and clerical staff. In addition, the national account sales manager and a staff of ten salesmen handled sales to large multiple-unit retailers, mail order houses, premium companies and government. The sales force called regularly on the retail trade to book orders, arrange sales promotion and displays in stores, and handle routine customer problems. The Consumer Products Division operated fifteen distribution centers, six at plants where the products were produced, and the other nine at key distribution locations.

The company serviced about 13,000 retail outlets through its direct distribution network, plus 175 national accounts which accounted for about 9,000 locations. In addition, the company had a network of 87 wholesalers to service those areas which were uneconomical to call on directly. It was estimated that these wholesalers serviced about 10,000 additional outlets, though they accounted for only 11% of sales. The breakdown of sales by type of outlet is shown in Exhibit A-4.

Wilmington's suggested list prices provided the retailer with average margins of approximately 42 per cent. However, because of differences among suggested trade margins for various items in the Wilmington line, as well as regular discounting from list on certain more standard products, substantial variation existed in the actual margins received.

EXHIBIT A-4   Wilmington Corporation Consumer Products Division: Estimated Breakdown of Sales by Type of Outlet, 1974

	No. of Outlets	%	$ Million	%
Department Stores	3840	12	32.1	21
Supermarkets	9280	29	18.4	12
Discount Stores	5420	17	36.5	24
Hardware Stores	6440	20	16.8	11
Chain Stores	2540	8	12.2	8
Premium	660	2	10.7	7
Institutional	1600	5	6.1	4
Government	1290	4	12.3	8
Mail Order	300	1	6.2	4
Others	630	2	1.7	1
Total	32,000	100%	153.0	100%

Source: Company records.

544	Case A	Wilmington Corporation

Typically, Wilmington spent between 1% and 2% of sales on advertising and sales promotion activities. The bulk of these funds went to support in-store display and merchandising activities. Advertising expenditures were confined to the few branded products within the Wilmington line.

Country Squire Product Line

The first line of heat-resistant glass cook and bakeware was launched by Corning in 1915. The product, branded PYREX® ware,[2] was protected by strong patents which were ultimately extended until 1957. When the patent for PYREX® ware expired, Wilmington considered the introduction of a range of heat-resistant glass bakeware similar to PYREX® ware. However, the management of the company was reluctant to make the investment in the new technology for a product which was somewhat different from the rest of its range. The company had a large range of glass products at the time, but none of them were suitable for cooking or baking. While the company hesitated, American Glass introduced its Blue Flame range of heat-resistant glass bakeware at 20%–25% below PYREX® ware prices. This was followed by Ajay Corporation with a similar range. By this time, Wilmington was convinced that there was a good opportunity for it to add a line of heat-resistant glass ovenware to its line. It developed the Country Squire line of opal ovenware which was made available in four colors and two decorations. Later, the company added a range of clear glass items to the Country Squire line.

Wilmington experienced some difficulty in obtaining distribution for the Country Squire line. By the time the product was ready for distribution, both American Glass and Ajay Corporation had achieved substantial distribution. Most stores were already carrying one or two lines and were reluctant to add a third. Exhibit A-5 shows the market penetration of Country Squire.

EXHIBIT A-5   Market Shares, Heat-Resistant Glass Bakeware

	1957	1958	1959	1960	1961	1965	1974
PYREX® ware	98%	90%	83%	71%	60%	61%	58%
American Glass	2	8	12	18	19	18	18
Ajay Corporation	—	2	4	7	11	12	13
Country Squire	—	—	1	4	9	8	8
Others	—	—	—	—	1	1	3
	100%	100%	100%	100%	100%	100%	100%

THE HOUSEWARES INDUSTRY

The housewares industry was reported to have retail sales in the order of $14 billion per year in 1973. A fairly common breakdown of the industry is shown in Exhibit A-6.

---

[2]PYREX® ware is a registered trademark of Corning Glass Works.

EXHIBIT A-6   Breakdown of the Housewares Industry, 1973

	Manufacturer's Shipments (in $ millions)
Small electrics	$3,033
Serving/buffet	1,127
Cook and bakeware	1,040
Outdoor	433
Bath and closet	260
Kitchen tools and gadgets	173
Others	2,601
Total	$8,667

Source: National Housewares Manufacturers Association, Seventh Annual Survey of Housewares Manufacturers, 1973.

The industry was highly fragmented. More than 1,500 firms produced houseware products and over 60% of these firms had sales of less than $5 million per year. However, several of the largest U.S. corporations had a stake in the housewares business, including General Electric's Consumer Products Division, the Hardware Division of American Home Products Corporation, National Presto Industries, Inc. and General Housewares, Inc.

The growth of the industry is illustrated in the figures on total industry shipments shown in Exhibit A-7.

EXHIBIT A-7   Manufacturers' Shipments of
Housewares, 1966–1973

1966	$4,035 million
1967	4,535
1968	5,700
1969	5,475
1970	5,400
1971	6,135
1972	7,061
1973	8,667

Source: National Housewares Manufacturers Association, various reports and publications.

It was generally believed that the sale of housewares was related to the rate of family formation. This had been running at approximately two million households per year since 1970, and was expected to continue at about this level into the early 1980s. One observer of the industry commented:

> Young housewives tend to stock up on pots and pans and other kitchen paraphernalia even before they get married, and housewares were traditionally regarded as good gifts for weddings and showers.

Industry growth was attributed in part to the rapid introduction of new products. New products seldom tended to originate from fundamental technological breakthroughs, however. Rather, the industry appeared to concentrate on the use of innovative materials, design and color to introduce newness into its products. Corning's original breakthrough in heat-resistant glass, and later pressed glass-ceramic, were included with Du Pont's nonstick Teflon among the few fundamental technological changes in the industry.

There appeared to be definite fashion trends in color and design, analogous in many ways to fashion trends in the clothing industry. Observers attributed these partly to trends in the development of consciousness about kitchen decor and color coordination. Housewives were encouraged to plan the appearance of their kitchens because this was a room where they and the rest of the family spent a great deal of time. This had introduced a fashion element into the cook and bakeware market. The color and decor of kitchen utensils had thus become an important purchase consideration. The cook and bakeware industry expended a considerable amount of effort in tracking and predicting these trends. The trade literature devoted considerable space to identifying the latest "in color," as indicated by the following two extracts:

> Color is still a tricky point. While avocado continues to be the number one seller, red and harvest are still vying for the number two spot. It looks like red will come out ahead of harvest, but harvest may prove somewhat harder to knock out of the running than earlier anticipated. Blue is still being talked about as a potentially strong seller, and spring selling may make or break the talk about blue.[3]

> One noticeable product trend was heavy emphasis on color. Floral designs were splashed on everything from cookware and toilet-seat covers to pastry servers. "Our market research tells us the fashion concept is extremely important," noted Corning's Stemski.[4]

The industry was to some extent less affected by general business conditions than most other industries, as indicated by the following abstract from *Barron's:*[5]

> While many a business is suffering recession pains, the housewares trade is booming. Reason: sales are benefiting from more leisure time, higher discretionary income, and the willingness of customers to continue buying reasonably priced products, while holding back on such big ticket items as refrigerators and stoves.

---

[3]*Merchandising Week,* December 14, 1970, p. 23.
[4]*Business Week,* January 22, 1972, p. 14.
[5]*Barron's,* November 30, 1970, p. 12.

The Cook and Bakeware Industry

In general, cookware is used for range top cooking and bakeware products are used only for baking in the oven. Exact sales figures for the total cook and bakeware industry were not available and only rough estimates could be made. In 1973, the National Housewares Manufacturers Association estimated that the annual sales of the cook and bakeware industry were about $1,040 million and were growing at the rate of 5.3% per year. In 1972, the Metal Cookware Manufacturers Association estimated that shipments of metal cookware had reached an estimated $431 million and were growing at the rate of 4% per year. From these and other sources, Wilmington produced the estimated breakdown of industry sales by type of material shown in Exhibit A-8.

EXHIBIT A-8   Estimates of Manufacturers' Shipments of Cook and Bakeware, 1974

	Cookware	Bakeware
	(Percent of total sales)	
Stainless steel	23%	6%
Glass/heat-resistant glass	17	25
Aluminum	13	14
Cast iron	8	15
Porcelain clad metal	15	24
Stoneware*	9	6
Copper	5	—
Others	10	10
Total	100%	100%

*Recently several manufacturers had begun to sell "stoneware dinnerware" in supermarkets. Some sets contained casseroles in addition to place settings. These casseroles were promoted in supermarket-sponsored advertising as "freezer-to-oven-to-table" items. In Mr. Alstone's judgment their quality was inferior to heat-resistant glass products of the Country Squire type.

It was generally acknowledged in the industry that a considerable proportion of sales were purchased by the customer as gifts, but Wilmington executives did not have figures on the proportion of gifts within each product or material category. They felt that gift purchasing was more common for the higher priced products, while the lower priced products were typically bought for the consumer's own use.

Data were also collected to provide an estimate of cookware and bakeware sales by major product type. These are shown in Exhibit A-9.

Wilmington executives felt that the breakdown for CORNING WARE® cookware was different from the figures in Exhibit A-9, but they did not have accurate figures to back this up.

EXHIBIT A-9   Estimated Breakdown of Cook and Bakeware Market by
Product Type, 1974

	Percent of Total Sales	
Cookware		
Casseroles (1½ qt. or larger)	19%	
Frying pans	15	
Saucepots (below 1½ qts.)	8	
Subtotal		42%
Bakeware		
Pans	11%	
Baking dishes	13	
Baking trays	4	
Special items	2	
Subtotal		30%
Measuring and Mixing		
Bowls	11	
Cups	4	
Subtotal		15%
Miscellaneous	13	13%
Total		100%

General Environmental Trends

Home cooking habits in the U.S. were being influenced by several trends in the general environment. On the one hand, the popularity of convenience foods had reduced the amount of time that the average housewife spent on meal preparation, particularly when combined with the impact of kitchen gadgets and appliances in the cooking process. On the other hand, there had been a surge of interest in ethnic, specialty and gourmet foods, evidenced by the popularity of cookbooks on these subjects. The popularity of these foods had created demand for more, and often specialized, cooking utensils. *Barrons* reported:

> The latest trend to catch the imagination of housewives—and the marketing managers of the industry—is so-called gourmet cooking. Popular television shows like Julia Child's workmanlike French Chef and the good natured Galloping Gourmet, Graham Kerr, have spurred interest in the "joy of cooking." Best selling cookbooks are doing likewise. To cash in on the trend, West Bend is offering French-style skillets. Others are rushing out with fondue sets in every shade of the rainbow. Many new entries allow food to be cooked and served from the same utensils at the table—sort of a rich man's TV dinner.

To the Tube

Just as television is whetting the appetites of would-be Cordon Bleu chefs, it also is becoming more popular as a medium for selling housewares. APL, for example, has gone on the air to promote its line of "Superseal" air-tight, food storage containers. The firm already advertises in selected TV markets and will go national next year.[6]

Merchandise Week reported:

> The metal cookware industry . . . has accepted the challenge of homemakers who prepare more than 45 million custom prepared meals daily, to provide glamorous cooking utensils of top quality with color, no-stick, easy-to-clean pans, with a purpose.
>
> For the first time, stores can offer fashion colors and a choice of styles to customers who prefer stainless steel. But some buyers have doubts, believing consumers will, in the words of one buyer, choose "Farberware to cook in and Copco to serve in"—or, in other words, prefer the decorative look of enameled cast iron to enameled stainless steel.[7]

Further, more and more meals were being eaten outside the home. A recent *Business Week* article reported that by 1980 two out of every three meals would be eaten out. The impact this would have on cookware purchase decisions was uncertain.

Finally, cooking technology also appeared to be undergoing some changes. This had been marked by the introduction of flat top stoves and microwave ovens.[8] Microwave oven sales exceeded 900,000 units in 1975 and amounted to approximately $360 million. This represented a growth of 25 per cent and 63 percent over 1974 and 1973 respectively. Since metal cookware was not suitable for use with these new ovens, some observers foresaw the possibility of a substantial change in cook and bakeware purchases in the future.

CORNING GLASS WORKS

Corning Glass Works ranked 190th in the *Fortune 500* 1974 listing of the largest manufacturing companies in the United States. Its 1974 sales exceeded $1,051 million, of which some 68 per cent were in the United States. Consumer products accounted for 25 per cent of the company's sales, electrical and electronic products for 44 per cent, and "technical" and other products for the remaining 31 per cent. The company depended heavily on sales to industrial customers. Among the most important were manufacturers of television tubes who bought glass blanks from Corning.

The Consumer Products Division

The Consumer Products Division handled the manufacture and marketing of the PYREX® ware and CORNING WARE® ranges of cook and bakeware,

---

[6]*Barrons,* November 30, 1970, p. 12.
[7]*Merchandise Week,* November 9, 1970, p. 21.
[8]A flat top stove is a cooking range with a flat sheet over the top of individual burners.

the CORELLE® Livingware[9] range of tableware, the Electromatics range of small electrical appliances, a range of domestic major appliances such as stoves, and some miscellaneous products including decorative glassware. The world-renowned Steuben range of crystal glassware was handled by another division. The marketing staff of the Consumer Products Division was divided into two sections. One handled PYREX® ware, CORNING WARE® and CORELLE® and generally distributed its products through a chain of wholesale distributors who in turn sold to the retail stores. The other section handled all the other products and sold through a variety of distribution methods, as appropriate.

The PYREX® ware line of heat-resistant glass cook and bakeware had been launched by Corning in 1915. It was promoted on the basis of a combination bake and serve utensil—strong and heat resistant enough to bake products in an oven and yet goodlooking enough to serve on the table. PYREX® ovenware was not recommended, however, for range top cooking and could not be heated directly on a flame. PYREX® ware was protected by patents and until the expiration of its patents in 1957 enjoyed an unchallenged position in the market for glass cookware. Wilmington executives estimated that by 1975 PYREX® ware still accounted for between 10 per cent and 15 per cent of the Consumer Products Division's sales.

CORNING WARE®

CORNING WARE® cookware was introduced to the United States market with nationwide distribution in 1959. Manufactured from pressed glass-ceramic, trademarked PYROCERAM®,[10] it not only had a superior appearance to PYREX® ware, but also was suitable for range top cooking. There was some research evidence, however, that some consumers did not recognize this functional distinction between the two products and thought of CORNING WARE® cookware as merely being a superior type of oven-to-table ceramic-glass product.

Only rough estimates were available of CORNING WARE® sales, since the company did not publish these figures. The 1974 Annual Report of the company indicated that sales of consumer products was $235 million for that year. Industry sources estimated that about half of these sales were of housewares products, and about half of the houseware sales were CORNING WARE®. However, since some of the CORNING WARE® brand products were part of the Electromatic range of small electrical houseware products, the sales of cook and bakeware under the CORNING WARE® label were somewhat less than total CORNING WARE® sales. One trade source estimated that the Electromatics represented

---

[9]CORELLE® Livingware is a registered trademark of Corning Glass Works.
[10]PYROCERAM® is a registered trademark of Corning Glass Works.

12% of the sales of housewares for Corning. Based on overall industry trends and their own perception of CORNING WARE® products' market acceptance, Wilmington executives estimated that CORNING WARE® had probably doubled its unit sales over the previous seven years.

Product Line

The CORNING WARE® product line consisted of twenty-four individual pieces, ranging from the one-quart covered saucepan to the four-quart saucepot (see Exhibit A-10). In addition, items were combined into sets; Corning currently offered ten such sets. The company also made available several accessories, such as handles, as well as spare parts and replacement of broken items.

The product line was fairly narrow by industry standards (see Exhibit A-11); only one basic color and two types of decoration were available (see Exhibit A-12). The available decorations were the traditional Cornflower Emblem which was closely associated with the CORNING WARE® name, and the Spice O' Life® which was available in all the sets and in a limited number of individual pieces. Up to 1970, only the Cornflower Emblem was available. In that year, the company introduced the Floral Bouquet design. According to industry reports, CORNING WARE® sales grew 24 per cent over the previous year and the new design accounted for 14 per cent of total CORNING WARE® sales.

Spice O' Life® was introduced in the second half of 1972, and demand for this decoration grew so fast that the company discontinued the Floral Bouquet in June 1974. This decision was apparently taken in order to be able to produce the Spice O' Life® design in sufficient quantities. Reports indicated that CORNING WARE® sales had grown 27 per cent over the previous year, with Spice O' Life® attaining 46 per cent of the total. There were trade rumors that the company was planning to introduce a third decoration in the middle of 1975.

Wilmington estimated that over 60 per cent of CORNING WARE® was sold in sets, and the remainder was sold as single pieces. The company felt that the majority of the sets were bought for gifts and that gift purchasing accounted for a large part of the sales of single pieces as well. Some sales were for accessories and replacement of broken parts.

Pricing

Retail prices of CORNING WARE® products were near the top end of cook and bakeware products though they were lower than those of the top quality stainless steel and enamel ware. The prices of PYREX® ware were much lower than CORNING WARE®, as shown in Exhibit A-13.

The Wilmington task force studied the history of CORNING WARE® prices and concluded that Corning had kept prices relatively stable with only four major increases between 1958 and 1974. CORNING WARE® prices

EXHIBIT A-10 Extract From Corning's Suggested Retail Price List, 1975

Catalog Number	Description	Price Each	Pieces Per Pack	Packs Per Shipper	Weight Per Shipper	Price Per Shipper
A-1	1-Qt. Covered Saucepan—Cornflower Emblem	$7.95	1	3	9 lbs.	$23.85
A-1-8	1-Qt. Covered Saucepan—Spice O'Life™ design	8.95	1	3	9 lbs.	26.85
A-1½	1½-Qt. Covered Saucepan—Cornflower Emblem	8.95	1	3	10 lbs.	26.85
A-1½-8	1½-Qt. Covered Saucepan—Spice O'Life	9.95	1	3	10 lbs.	29.85
A-2	2-Qt. Covered Saucepan—Cornflower Emblem	9.95	1	3	13 lbs.	29.85
A-2-8	2-Qt. Covered Saucepan—Spice O'Life	10.95	1	3	13 lbs.	32.85
A-3	3-Qt. Covered Saucepan—Cornflower Emblem	11.95	1	3	17 lbs.	35.85
A-3-8	3-Qt. Covered Saucepan—Spice O'Life	12.95	1	3	17 lbs.	38.85
A-5	5-Qt. Covered Saucepot—Cornflower Emblem	16.95	1	3	25 lbs.	50.85
A-5-8	5-Qt. Covered Saucepot—Spice O'Life	17.95	1	3	25 lbs.	53.85
A-8	1½-Qt. Covered 8" Skillet—Cornflower Emblem	9.95	1	3	12 lbs.	29.85
A-8-8	1½-Qt. Covered 8" Skillet—Spice O'Life	10.95	1	3	12 lbs.	32.85
A-10	2½-Qt. Covered 10" Skillet—Cornflower Emblem	11.95	1	3	20 lbs.	35.85
A-10-8	2½-Qt. Covered 10" Skillet—Spice O'Life	12.95	1	3	20 lbs.	38.85
A-84	4-Qt. Covered Saucepot—Cornflower Emblem	14.95	1	3	23 lbs.	44.85
A-84-8	4-Qt. Covered Saucepot—Spice O'Life	15.95	1	3	23 lbs.	47.85
A-115-S	Dollar Days Special complete with covered 1-Qt. saucepan and 10" skillet—Cornflower Emblem	12.95	1 set	2 sets	20 lbs.	25.90
A-115-8-S	Dollar Days Special complete with covered 1-Qt. saucepan and 10" skillet—Spice O'Life	13.95	1 set	2 sets	20 lbs.	27.90

Number	Description				Weight	
A-300	Kitchen Starter Set complete with 1½-Qt. and 2-Qt. covered saucepans and 10" covered skillet—Cornflower Emblem	22.88	1 set	1 set	15 lbs.	22.88
A-300-8	Kitchen Starter Set complete with 1½-Qt. and 2-Qt. covered saucepans and 10" skillet—Spice O'Life	25.88	1 set	1 set	15 lbs.	25.88
A-300-P	Kitchen Starter Set with Bonus Value complete with 1½-Qt. and 2-Qt. covered saucepans, 10" covered skillet, and a 9" pie plate—Cornflower Emblem	22.88	1 set	1 set	17 lbs.	22.88
A-300-8-P	Kitchen Starter Set with Bonus Value complete with 1½-Qt. and 2-Qt. covered saucepans, 10" covered skillet, and an undecorated 9" pie plate—Spice O'Life	25.88	1 set	1 set	17 lbs.	25.88
A-500	Chef Master Set complete with 1-Qt. and 2-Qt. covered saucepans, 4-Qt. saucepot, 8" and 10" skillets—Cornflower Emblem	39.88	1 set	1 set	27 lbs.	39.88
A-500-8	Chef Master Set complete with 1-Qt. and 2-Qt. covered saucepans, 4-Qt. saucepot, 8" and 10" skillets—Spice O'Life	44.88	1 set	1 set	27 lbs.	44.88
A-700	Great Cook's Set complete with 1-Qt. saucepan bowl with plastic storage cover, 1½-Qt. and 3-Qt. covered saucepans, 8" and 10" covered skillets, 6-Cup teapot, and two 1¾-Cup petite pans with two plastic storage covers—Cornflower Emblem	44.88	1 set	1 set	26 lbs.	44.88
A-700-8	Great Cook's Set—Spice O'Life	49.88	1 set	1 set	26 lbs.	49.88
P-4	1½-Qt. Covered Baking Dish (7"×5½"×3")—Cornflower Emblem	7.95	1	3	10 lbs.	23.85
P-4-8	1½-Qt. Covered Baking Dish (7"×5½"×3")—Spice O'Life	8.95	1	3	10 lbs.	26.85

Catalog Number	Description	Price Each	Pieces Per Pack	Packs Per Shipper	Weight Per Shipper	Price Per Shipper
P-19	13″ Serving Platter with spatter shield—Cornflower Emblem	$11.95	1	3	11 lbs	$35.85
P-20	1¾-Qt. Party Buffet with cover and candlewarmer—Cornflower Emblem	12.95	1	3	13 lbs	38.85
P-21	13″ Roaster with rack—Cornflower Emblem	12.95	1	3	13 lbs.	38.85
P-21-8	13″ Roaster with rack—Spice O'Life™ design	13.95	1	3	13 lbs.	41.85
P-34	5-Qt. Dutch Oven with cover and rack—Cornflower Emblem	15.95	1	3	20 lbs	47.85
P-40	2½-Qt. Royal Buffet with cover and candlewarmer—Cornflower Emblem	14.95	1	3	18 lbs.	44.85
P-42	1¾-Cup Petite Pan Set (set of 4 pans and 4 plastic covers)—Cornflower Emblem	10.95	1 set	3 sets	10 lbs	32.85
P-42-8	1¾-Cup Petite Pan Set (set of 4 pans and 4 plastic covers)—Spice O'Life	12.95	1 set	3 sets	10 lbs	38.85
P-43	2¾-Cup Petite Pan Set (set of 2 pans and 2 plastic covers)—Cornflower Emblem	6.95	1 set	3 sets	7 lbs.	20.85
P-43-8	2¾-Cup Petite Pan Set (set of 2 pans and 2 plastic covers)—Spice O'Life	8.95	1 set	3 sets	7 lbs.	26.85
P-46	1¾-Cup Petite Pan—Cornflower Emblem	2.95	6	3	14 lbs.	53.10
P-64	1-Qt. Covered Saucemaker—Cornflower Emblem	6.95	1	3	9 lbs.	20.85
P-76	15½″ Open Roaster with 2-section wire rack—Cornflower Emblem	16.95	1	3	16 lbs.	50.85

Code	Description					
P-100	Menu-ette Set complete with 1 and 1½-Pt. covered saucepans and 6½" covered skillet—Cornflower Emblem	12.88	1 set	3 sets	18 lbs.	38.64
P-100-8	Menu-ette Set—Spice O'Life	15.88	1 set	3 sets	18 lbs.	47.64
P-104	6-Cup Teapot—Cornflower Emblem	9.95	1	3	5 lbs.	29.85
P-104-8	6-Cup Teapot—Spice O'Life	10.95	1	3	5 lbs.	32.85
P-146	6-Cup Percolator—Cornflower Emblem	12.95	1	3	10 lbs.	38.85
P-146-8	6-Cup Percolator—Spice O'Life	13.95	1	3	10 lbs.	41.85
P-149	10-Cup Percolator—Cornflower Emblem	14.95	1	3	11 lbs.	44.85
P-149-8	10-Cup Percolator—Spice O'Life	15.95	1	3	11 lbs.	47.85
7186-FP	Filter Paper for P-186-N, pk of 100	2.95	1 pk	6	6 lbs.	17.70
P-250	Baker's Helper Set complete with 9" Pie Plate, 2-Qt. Loaf Dish, Square Cake Dish and 1½-Qt. Covered Baking Dish—Cornflower Emblem	18.88	1 set	1 set	11 lbs.	18.88
P-250-8	Baker's Helper Set complete with 9" undecorated Pie Plate, 2-Qt. Loaf Dish, Square Cake Dish and 1½-Qt. Covered Baking Dish—Spice O'Life	21.88	1 set	1 set	11 lbs.	21.88
P-309	9" Pie Plate—Cornflower Emblem	3.95	1	4	8 lbs.	15.80
P-315	9" × 5" × 3", 2-Qt. Loaf Dish—Cornflower Emblem	5.95	1	3	8 lbs.	17.85
P-315-8	9" × 5" × 3", 2-Qt. Loaf Dish—Spice O'Life	6.95	1	3	8 lbs.	20.85
P-322	8" × 8" × 2", Square Cake Dish—Cornflower Emblem	7.95	1	3	11 lbs.	23.85
P-322-8	8" × 8" × 2", Square Cake Dish—Spice O'Life design	8.95	1	3	11 lbs.	26.85

Catalog Number	Description	Price Each	Pieces Per Pack	Packs Per Shipper	Weight Per Shipper	Price Per Shipper
P-332	12" × 7½" × 2", 2¾-Qt. Oblong Baking Dish—Cornflower Emblem	$ 9.95	1	3	12 lbs.	$29.85
P-332-8	12" × 7½" × 2", 2¾-Qt. Oblong Baking Dish—Spice O' Life™	10.95	1	3	12 lbs.	32.85
P-423	Petite Fours 2 ea. 1¾-Cup and 2¾-Cup Petite Pans with 2 plastic covers and 2 glass covers—Cornflower Emblem	8.88	1 set	1 set	5 lbs.	8.88
P-423-8	Petite Fours 2 ea. 1¾-Cup and 2¾-Cup Petite Pans with 2 plastic covers and 2 glass covers—Spice O' Life	11.88	1 set	1 set	5 lbs.	11.88
P-81	1-Pt. Menu-ette Saucepan with Cover—Cornflower Emblem	4.50	1	3	6 lbs.	13.50
P-81-8	1-Pt. Menu-ette Saucepan with Cover—Spice O'Life	5.50	1	3	6 lbs.	16.50
P-82	1½-Pt. Menu-ette Saucepan with Cover—Cornflower Emblem	5.50	1	3	7 lbs.	16.50
P-82-8	1½-Pt. Menu-ette Saucepan with Cover—Spice O' Life	6.50	1	3	7 lbs.	19.50
P-83	6½" Menu-ette Skillet with Cover—Cornflower Emblem	5.50	1	3	7 lbs.	16.50
P-83-8	6½" Menu-ette Skillet with Cover—Spice O' Life	6.50	1	3	7 lbs.	19.50

EXHIBIT A-11   Range of Products Sold—Cook and Bakeware, 1975

Company/Brand	Number of Individual Pieces	Number of Sets	Number of Colors	Number of Decorations
CORNING WARE®	24	10	1	2
PYREX® ware	56	20	5	4
Wilmington's Country Squire	31	13	7	2
American Glass (heat-resistant glass line)	15	5	5	3
Ajay Corporation (heat-resistant glass line)	20	—	2	6

Source: Catalogues of the companies concerned, 1975.

had kept up with inflation, and gained ground somewhat in the last few years. A summary history of CORNING WARE® prices is presented in Exhibit A-14.

Distribution

Corning used a two-level distribution system for its PYREX® ware, CORN-ING WARE® and CORELLE® product lines: the company sold directly to a network of 350 independent distributors who, in turn, sold to retailers. The Corning sales force sold to and serviced the distributors and in addition, assisted at the retail level, mainly by doing in-store displays, promotion and merchandising. Over the years, the company had managed to build up a strong network of loyal, competent distributors in most marketing areas. The typical Corning distributor was financially sound and a major force in the housewares trade in the area in which he operated. This strong distribution network was considered a major factor in Corning's competitive position.

Although Wilmington executives knew that CORNING WARE® products were broadly distributed in many different types of stores, they had little idea of the exact extent of this coverage or its effectiveness. As a result a group of MBA students were commissioned to do a trade survey of both PYREX® ware and CORNING WARE® distribution. This involved a retail store audit as well as interviews with store buyers. An extract from the student report is presented in Appendix A-1. Wilmington executives did know, however, that Corning had developed particularly strong relationships with Sears, as well as other large chains such as Montgomery Ward and J. C. Penney Co. It had been rumored in the trade that Corning was about to embark on the production of a special pattern to be distributed by Sears through all of its outlets in North America. Sears was known to be a major outlet for CORNING WARE® as well as PYREX® and CORELLE® products.

EXHIBIT A-12   CORNING WARE® Patterns

Cornflower

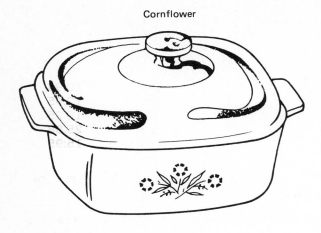

Spice O' Life

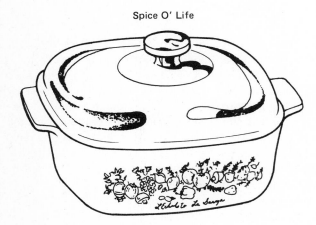

   According to industry sources, Corning was reputed to have a reputation in the trade of "selling itself": it had a strong brand name, a high reputation for quality, and was manufactured by a well-known company.

   Up to 1974, trade margins were guaranteed by Corning's fair trading rules. The company set the retail prices for all its CORNING WARE®, PYREX® and CORELLE® products and generally speaking managed to get the retail trade to maintain these prices. It sold the products to its wholesale distributors at 52½% discounts from retail price and expected the wholesaler to sell to the retailer at 40% discount from retail price.

EXHIBIT A-13   Comparison of PYREX® and CORNING WARE® Retail
Prices—Selected Items, 1975

	Unit	PYREX®	CORNING WARE®	
			Cornflower	Spice O'Life®
1 qt. covered casserole	ea.	$2.29	$ 7.95	$ 8.95
1½ qt. covered casserole	ea.	2.59	8.95	9.95
2 qt. covered casserole	ea.	2.99	9.95	10.95
3 qt. covered casserole	ea.	3.99	11.95	12.95
Baking dish	ea.	1.89	9.95	10.95
3 pc. Bake set	set	8.95	22.88	25.88
4 qt. Saucepot	ea.	9.95	14.95	15.95

EXHIBIT A-14   Inflation Adjusted Pricing for CORNING WARE® 1½-Qt.
Saucepan at Retail

Year	Price	Consumer Price Index	Inflation Adjusted Price Level
1958	$4.50	$ 86.6	$5.20
1959	4.50	87.3	5.15
1960	4.50	88.7	5.07
1961	4.50	89.6	5.02
1962	4.50	90.6	4.97
1963	4.50	91.7	4.91
1964	4.50	92.9	4.84
1965	4.50	94.5	4.76
1966	4.95	97.2	5.09
1967	4.95	100.0	4.95
1968	4.95	104.2	4.75
1969	5.95	109.8	5.42
1970	5.95	116.3	5.12
1971	5.95	121.3	4.91
1972	6.50	125.3	5.19
1973	6.50	133.1	4.88
1974	7.95	147.7	5.38

In January 1974, Corning discontinued its practice of fair trading at the wholesale level and permitted each wholesaler to set his own price to the retailer. While this move apparently caused some concern among distributors and large department store buyers, there was very little change in the market situation as a result of this move.

In April 1975, Corning discontinued its retail fair trade policy and allowed each retailer to set its own price for CORNING WARE®, PYREX® and CORELLE® products. This move was followed by substantial discounting by some retailers. *Business Week* reported that, in Massachusetts, Corning products began selling at discounts of 20 per cent to 40 per cent.[11] It was, however, too early for Wilmington to assess the full impact of this move.

Advertising and Promotion

Although no exact figures were available, Wilmington executives estimated that Corning typically spent between 2% and 3% of sales on advertising and promotional expenses. These percentages appeared to apply to both the PYREX® and CORNING WARE® lines with the split between advertising and promotion being approximately 50/50.

Advertising was primarily national in scope, with women's service magazines and TV being used. The bulk of the sales promotion for CORNING WARE® was tied in with the company's cooperative program for retailers. This consisted of special displays, company designed promotions operated through stores, and advertising assistance. The company introduced these programs to the trade at the housewares shows organized by the National Housewares Manufacturers Association in Chicago in January and July of each year. The company made elaborate arrangements for participation in these shows. The plans for CORN-ING WARE® for the first half of 1975 are presented in Exhibit A-15.

EXHIBIT A-15   Extract from Wilmington Corporation Report on Plans for Sales Promotion and Advertising of CORNING WARE® for the First Half of 1975

This report was prepared on the basis of a visit to the Corning stand at the Chicago Housewares Show in January 1975. It covers plans for the first half of fiscal year 1975 for CORNING WARE®:

1. Gift Promotion—which consisted of the following:
   a. A full color two-page advertisement in the Sunday supplements of April 27, 1975 that would reach about 80% of the U.S. households.
   b. Local advertising aids that helped retailers tie in with local newspaper advertisements, radio spots and store announcements.
   c. A four-page full color enclosure provided free by Corning for retailers to insert into their direct mail advertisements or with bills, etc.
   The entire promotion was built around the theme, "Corning—Gifts That Make Life Easier," and featured PYREX® Ware and CORELLE® Livingware in addition to CORNING WARE®. It helped to position CORNING WARE® in the high quality, gifting end of the cook and bakeware market where its slightly higher prices made sense.
2. In-store displays—Corning salesmen would assist and encourage stores to set up shelves with special CORNING WARE® displays. Retailers were to be provided with full color brochures with suggestions for shelf displays running from eight feet to twenty-four feet as well as six foot end cap displays. They were

---

[11]*Business Week,* April 21, 1975, p. 38.

also to be provided with special printed set organizers for displaying the individual sets. Eight such set organizers were available.

3. Dollar Day Special—This was a set containing a ten-inch covered skillet and a one quart covered saucepan which sold for $1.00 more than the regular price of the skillet. The consumer paid $13.95 for a set which would cost $21.95 if purchased separately, a saving of $7.95. The sets were specially packed and labelled and Corning would supply stores with ads to insert in local newspapers at the store's expense.

4. Kitchen Starter Set—A similar promotion in which the consumer got a free nine-inch pie plate and a savings of $7.97 to make a total savings of $11.92. Supported with full color ad in the April/May issue of *Reader's Digest.*

5. Cookware Set—Corning would provide stores with ads to promote cookware sets—at the store's expense.

6. New Spice O'Life® ads to promote new items in the Spice O'Life® range—at the store's expense.

THE WILMINGTON TASK FORCE

The task force began its assignment by collecting information from a variety of sources. Production and capital costs estimates were easy to gather because a great deal of the engineering data was already available in the company. These figures were confirmed by discussion with equipment and raw material suppliers, trade association data and technical literature.

Capital and Cost Estimates

Estimates of the cost of converting existing facilities, new capital equipment, start-up, and front end costs indicated that a capital investment of $10 million would be necessary to set up a production facility with a capacity of about 75% of Corning's current production. This was considered the minimum economic plant size. A completely new production facility was estimated to cost $15 million. Preliminary estimates also indicated that total manufacturing overheads for either plant would amount to $2 million per year (exclusive of depreciation). The variable costs of production for the two-quart casserole, a typical item of the proposed product line, were estimated to be as shown in Exhibit A-16. It was believed that these variable cost levels could be attained within six months of

EXHIBIT A-16   Variable Cost for a Two-Quart
              Saucepan with Decal
              Decoration

Raw material	$ .23
Direct labor	.73
Packing and cover	.70
Freight	.62
Other	.48
Total variable cost	$2.76

start-up provided the plant was running at more than 30 per cent capacity. Wilmington executives guessed that equivalent costs for Corning might be lower than these because of their greater experience, but they had no way of knowing exactly how low they might be.

Product Line

Several decisions had to be made about the proposed product line. Four possibilities were considered by the task force:

Alternative A: "Me too" line. Similar to existing CORNING WARE®, i.e., "square" shape, white color, decorations similar to the Cornflower Emblem and Spice O' Life®.

Alternative B: Similar shape to above, but in solid "fashion" colors, some dark and some pastel.

Alternative C: Round shapes, solid colors, some dark and some pastel.

Alternative D: Round shapes with all-over floral and/or geometric patterns.

Samples of these four types were made up in the company's Development Laboratories and were reviewed by the task force and other marketing and sales personnel. Since opinion on these alternatives was divided, the task force decided to conduct consumer research to evaluate the alternatives. This research, consisting of focus group interviews with panels of housewives, was conducted in February 1975. An extract from the findings of this study is contained in Appendix A-2.

In evaluating the impact of design on sales, the task force reported:

> There is considerable evidence that varying the traditional CORNING WARE® design could expand sales volume. Specifically by changing the shape from rectangular to round the market could be expanded by increasing the number of ways in which the consumer would want to use glass-ceramic products. When consumers at our focus group interviews discussed CORNING WARE®, some considered the product oven and table ware. When exposed to a round version they indicated they would also use it as a saucepan for range top cooking.

Proposed Prices

The task force was considering three alternative price ranges for the new product line:

A. About the same as CORNING WARE® products
B. 5–10% lower—i.e., shallow price cuts
C. 20–25% lower—i.e., deep price cuts

The first alternative was rejected as impractical. The task force felt that since Wilmington would be facing an established competitor who had had patent protection for 18 years in a fairly mature market, it would have to offer the consumer a better deal before a switch could be expected.

The choice then boiled down to whether the task force should recommend a shallow or deep price cut. The shallow cut was obviously attractive in that it would permit the product line to deliver a better contribution. This contribution would fall substantially if the firm chose a deep price cut; on the other hand, it was recognized that a shallow price cut might not give the consumer sufficient incentive to switch, and the resultant sales volume would be too small to justify entry. In its analysis of the price factor, the task force reported:

> That price is an important factor is evident from the consumer research. Fifty-nine per cent of consumers expected cookware to be inexpensive, yet our research shows that CORNING WARE® cookware is considered to be expensive. Twenty-eight per cent of the nonowners say that they do not, in fact, own it because it is too expensive. Industry research shows that 26 per cent of all consumers purchase bakeware on price alone. Lowering the price may also have an indirect effect on the potential uses of the product. In our focus group interviews it became apparent that most consumers considered CORNING WARE® to be a serving vessel, while when it was presented at a lower price consumers saw it as a saucepan. Thus, lowering the price allowed the product to compete in an entirely different market.

Proposed Distribution

CORNING WARE® cookware was sold mainly in department stores, national chains, discount stores, hardware stores and specialty stores. It was generally not sold in supermarkets, although PYREX® ware and other heat-resistant glass products were available in a number of supermarkets. Wilmington estimated that its present direct distribution system had managed to put its Country Squire range into 35% of the supermarkets and 75% of the stores where Corning products were available.

Wilmington was debating whether to use its own direct distribution system for the new product or to set up a chain of wholesalers similar to Corning's two-tiered distribution system. Most management personnel were in favor of using the company's direct distribution; even though several felt that the quality of service to the retail trade provided by independent wholesalers was superior to the company's system. In support of this position they noted that Corning had a high degree of loyalty with key wholesalers, and Wilmington might have to content itself with marginal distributors.

Further, Wilmington had to decide whether to extend distribution to supermarkets; it was unclear how much sales would result from supermarket distribution. On the other hand, the absence of CORNING WARE® from the supermarket shelves was looked upon as an opportunity for Wilmington.

The national sales manager was asked to prepare estimates of how well the Wilmington sales force would be able to achieve distribution for the new product. His report indicated that at least 25% of the retail outlets served by Wilmington might be persuaded to carry the product at the time of the product launch because of the good relations that Wilmington enjoyed with the retail trade. This could perhaps be increased to about 40% in three months after launch. After that, he indicated that "progress would depend on how the consumer accepts our product."

Sales Promotion and Advertising

It was believed that the new line would require heavy sales promotion and advertising in order to compete with the well-established and highly regarded CORNING WARE® brand name and image. A somewhat arbitrary figure of $700,000 was agreed upon as the recommended budget for advertising and promotion, partly because the task force felt that Wilmington management would not be willing to spend a larger amount on a new product line.

The task force then addressed itself to the problem of finding the optimal method of spending this money. This boiled down to three alternatives:

A. Spend most of the money on a media advertising campaign, with a small back-up budget for sales promotion.
B. Spend about equal amounts on advertising and sales promotion.
C. Develop a heavy sales promotion campaign, particularly at launch, and spend a smaller amount of money on media advertising.

In addition, the task force intended to develop a cooperative advertising campaign in which Wilmington would provide designs and advertising materials and the trade would pay for media space costs. It was expected, however, that trade support for such a program would be only marginal, since the trade was usually reluctant to invest its own funds in promoting a new product or brand. Therefore, the coop program did not figure heavily in the preliminary plans.

Other Factors

Mr. F. Henderson Bruit conducted a brief study of what he believed to be analogous situations in the housewares industry to find out what happened when a patent expired or competitors entered a market which had been dominated by one producer. A summary of his findings is presented in Appendix A-3.

The task force was grappling with two additional sets of unknown factors. First, there was a question as to whether other firms would attempt to bring out glass-ceramic lines after the expiration of the patent. The task force felt that it would have to take into account the potential impact of these entries on Wilmington's entry. A crucial element in this problem was the question of timing. It was felt that the timing and success or failure of the first entrant would have a bearing on both the strategy and success of other entrants. If the first entrant was highly successful or a conspicuous failure, this might cause other firms to change their plans.

The task force could not gather any substantial information about the plans of other potential competitors. It believed that Ajay Corporation was studying the possibility but it had no information about the direction of their efforts. Ajay had a reputation in the industry as a manufacturer of high quality glass ware and table ware and distributed its products broadly through department stores, discount stores, variety stores, and home furnishings specialty outlets. Although it was felt unlikely, the task force believed that there was also some possibility of either a Japanese or European entry into the glass-ceramic cook and bakeware market if the market potential proved to be substantial.

The other set of unknowns that the task force had to consider was the possible moves by Corning to protect its market for CORNING WARE® cookware. These moves could be made either before, during or after the expiration of Corning's patent. The task force felt that the most likely move by Corning would be a lowering of price. It was felt that a factory price cut of 5% would do little harm to the profitability of the line for Corning. Accompanied by the drop in trade margins due to the abandonment of fair trading this could result in a substantial drop in consumer prices. On the other hand, a deep price cut of around 20% would probably have a large impact on the profitability of the line for Corning, and was therefore deemed to be unlikely.

Further, if Corning chose not to drop prices, Wilmington executives were concerned that they might impede and perhaps destroy a potential competitor by heavy sales promotion and advertising at the time of a competitor's launch.

Finally, there was the possibility that Corning would consider its position so secure that it would choose to do nothing before or during the launch of the competitor and would react only if it found that that competitor was making substantial inroads into its market.

APPENDIX A-1: EXTRACT FROM STUDENT TRADE SURVEY CONDUCTED ON CORNING WARE® AND PYREX® WARE ON ONE MAJOR METROPOLITAN AREA

Introduction

This study was conducted through retail store audits and telephone interviews with buyers in a sample of twenty-one stores in the Boston metropolitan area. The sample consisted of five department stores, four discount stores, six variety stores, four hardware stores and two supermarkets. About one-third were located in downtown areas, one-third in nearby suburban shopping centers and the rest in small adjacent towns.

The survey attempts to evaluate retailer merchandising of CORNING WARE® and PYREX® ware with respect to stock conditions, display, promotion and pricing. Attention was focused on the five most popular CORNING WARE® items and six most popular PYREX® ware items. Stores that carried four or five items (5–6 PYREX® ware items) were considered well stocked; two or three moderately stocked (3–4 PYREX® ware items); and one or two, poorly stocked. The final determination of the stock condition took into consideration the amount of stock in other items in the product line.

The display ratings reflected our opinion of shelf condition (neatness or otherwise), shelf location and general appearance. The promotion category indicates the presence of either point-of-purchase displays or sales promotions.

Finally, the selling prices column compares retailer prices with list prices or, in the case of PYREX® ware, comparison between the mean prices of the items in the twenty-one stores and the particular store in question.

The overall results of the retail store audit are tabulated on the next two pages.

Store Buyer Attitudes

Houseware buyers were contacted to determine their attitudes toward CORNING WARE® cookware and the distribution process that places CORNING WARE® on their shelves. A summary of the attitudes of buyers from Jordan Marsh, Kresge, Zayre, Bradlees, Tags, and Lechmere is contained below.

Product Characteristics

The buyers placed special emphasis on the brand image of CORNING WARE® products stating that it would be virtually impossible to compete with the product's design and quality. CORNING WARE® products' competitive strength, tenure in the market, and its well-scheduled promotion and advertising campaign have created a formidable brand name and image. The buyers' universal faith in the strength of CORNING WARE® has been reinforced by PYREX® ware successes, and the realization that consumer awareness pulls the product through the distribution channels.

The buyers feel that no company could provide the same quality and brand name product. Confronted with the question of carrying a CORNING WARE® type product at a reduced price, the majority of the buyers indicated a willingness to carry such a line only if the price reduction was substantial (15%–20%), and most importantly, if the product's quality was acceptable.

All buyers predicted that CORNING WARE® cookware would maintain market share if a new product was introduced, yet none, with the exception of the local hardware retailer, would rule out the possibility of taking on such a brand.

Distribution

All buyers were enthusiastic about the service they had been receiving from the two-tiered distribution system. All were especially content not to carry excess inventory in recessionary times. The buyers of a large, national chain agreed that the local wholesalers provided a much quicker response to their needs than the bureaucracy of a central office. Orders were being filled quite adequately for PYREX® ware and CORNING WARE®, but the buyers were a little disgruntled with the lack of CORELLE® Livingware. Finally, the services provided by the local distributors (order taking and shelf service) were excellent; the buyers did not want to sacrifice this amenity.

CORNING WARE®

Company	Stock Conditions			Display		Promo		Price		
	Well	Mod	Poor	Good	Poor	Yes	No	List	Above	Below
Department										
Jordan Marsh (Bos)	X			X		X		X		
Jordan Marsh (Burl)		X		X		X		X		
Sears (Camb)	X			X		X		X		
Sears (Burl)	X			X		X		X		
Coop	X			X		X		X	X	
Discount										
Lechmere (Camb)	X			X			X			X
Zayre (128)			X	X		X				X
Bradlees (Wob)		X		X			X			X
Turnstyle (Walt)		X			X		X	X		
Variety										
Woolworth (Bos)		X			X		X	X		
Woolworth (Camb)		X			X		X	X		
Woolworth (Harv)		X			X		X			X
Kresge (Bos)			X		X		X	X		
Kresge (Camb)	NONE									
WT Grant (Bos)			X		X		X	X		
Grocery										
Stop and Shop (Walt)	NONE									
Broadway Super	NONE									
Hardware										
Almys (Camb)	X			X			X	X		
Tags (Camb)		X		X		X		X		
Dickson Bros (Camb)		X			X		X	X		
Pharmacy Super (Camb)			X	X		X		X		

PYREX® WARE AND COMPETITION

Company	Well	Mod	Poor	Good	Poor	Yes	No	Medium	Above	Below
	Stock Conditions			**Display**		**Promo**		**Price***		
Department										
Jordan Marsh (Bos)	X			X		X		X		
Jordan Marsh (Burl)	X			X		X		X		
Sears (Camb)			X	X		X		X		
Sears (Burl)	X			X		X				X
Coop	X				X		X	X		
Discount										
Lechmere (Camb)		X		X			X			X
Zayre (128)		X			X	X		X		
Bradlees (Wob)		X		X			X	X		
Turnstyle (Walt)		X		X			X		X	
Variety										
Woolworth (Bos)		X		X			X		X	
Woolworth (Cent)	X			X			X	X		
Woolworth (Harv)			X	X			X	X		
Kresge (Bos)	X			X			X	X		
Kresge (Camb)	no Pyrex			X			X			X
WT Grant (Bos)		X								
Grocery										
Stop and Shop (Walt)			X	X		X				X
Broadway Super		X		X			X		X	
Hardware										
Almys (Camb)		X		X		X				X
Tags (Camb)	X			X		X				X
Dickson Bros (Camb)	X			X			X			X
Pharmacy Super (Camb)			X	X			X			

*In stores which carried both Pyrex and competitive products, the latter were invariably priced lower than Pyrex.

The only buyers who expressed any interest in a direct system predicated their remarks on the state of the economy; that is only with a booming economy where products were literally "jumping off those shelves" would they prefer to switch systems.

Although the decision to carry a brand to compete with CORNING WARE® cookware would be made at a central headquarters level, the buyers (who are an important input in the decision making process) say that CORNING WARE® is very strong. No company could compete on image, brand, or quality. Only a price reduction would provide incentive for the stores to consider carrying the product.

APPENDIX A-2: EXTRACT FROM REPORT ON FOCUS GROUP INTERVIEWS

Focus Group Interviews were conducted with six different panels, each one consisting of approximately ten housewives. Participants were selected on the following basis:

Group Number	Social Group	Ownership of CORNING WARE®
1	white collar	no
2	white collar	yes
3	blue collar	no
4	blue collar	yes
5	working women	no
6	working women	yes

The moderator was instructed to first lead the group into a general discussion of cook and bakeware and then focus the discussion on oven-to-table and stove-to-table products. The groups were then shown four sets of samples, as follows:

Set 1: Similar to existing CORNING WARE® cookware, i.e., square shape, blue decoration

Set 2: Similar to CORNING WARE® in shape, but in solid colors, some dark and some pastel

Set 3: Round shape, in solid colors, both dark as well as pastel

Set 4: Round shape, in white with all-over floral designs and geometric patterns.

The order in which the sets were shown to each group was rotated systematically to eliminate the end-bias effect. In addition, two price levels were exhibited, one about the same as Corning's current prices and the other 25% lower. Prices were attached to the bottom of each piece and the interviewees were allowed to handle the items before discussing them.

Attitudes Toward CORNING WARE® Cookware

A majority of CORNING WARE® owners (73%) had received the product as a gift, and did not add to the sets once they received them. When asked why, most respondents said that they preferred to buy less costly products, such as PYREX® ware and other brands for their own use. The respondents did not think of CORNING WARE® cookware as being a different class of product from heat-resistant glass products, but rather thought of it as more expensive and higher quality. Many respondents were not aware that CORNING WARE® could be used on top of the range.

Most purchases of CORNING WARE® cookware were for gifts; only 19% of the respondents reported buying CORNING WARE® for their own use. The most commonly reported reasons for buying CORNING WARE® as a gift were its high quality, brand name and reputation, colors and design, and warranty. Purchases of CORNING WARE® were usually planned in advance (87% vs. 13%).

Reaction to Set 1—CORNING WARE® Imitation. The groups generally characterized this set as being "like CORNING WARE®." The general reaction was that if they were to purchase this type of product, they would prefer to buy CORNING WARE® because of its brand name, reputation and warranty. Most of the respondents said that they would prefer CORNING WARE® cookware if the price was the same; a few indicated that they might buy the new set at the 25% lower price, provided it carried a guarantee like CORNING WARE® and was made by a well-known company. However, most respondents said that the brand name was more important than the price differential, particularly if they were buying a gift. Several respondents said that the cheaper price version might be PYREX® ware, and a few of these said that they would buy it for themselves, but not as a gift.

Reaction to Set 2—Solid Color, Corning Shape. Most respondents thought that this set was PYREX® ware. The general reaction was that this set looked "cheap" and "gaudy." They thought that it was definitely inferior to CORNING WARE® and would only buy it at a lower price. Among those who indicated that they would buy, the most commonly stated reason was that it "suited the color scheme" of their kitchen. There was a slightly greater preference for the dark colors among the blue collar and professional families, while the white collar and working women appeared to prefer the pastel colors. Most respondents who said that they might buy the product said that they would buy it for their own use, but would prefer CORNING WARE® for gifts. Owners of CORNING WARE® were less inclined to buy this product than nonowners.

Reaction to Set 3—Solid Colors, Round Shape. The reaction to this set was similar to Set 2, except that a number of respondents who thought they might buy the product said that these products could be used on top of the stove because they were shaped like a pot. A number of respondents said that this set looked very similar to PYREX® mixing bowls. When asked whether they would use this product for baking, most respondents said that it was not suitable because of the round shape and the colors. The proportion of respondents who said they might buy the product was highest among the blue collar workers.

Reaction to Set 4—Decorated, Round Shape. The reaction to this set was mixed—some liked the patterns and said they would buy it, while others did not like the patterns for a variety of reasons. Most of the respondents who said they would buy it also said they would use it themselves for everyday use. There was some resistance to price at the CORNING WARE® level: most respondents said they would buy it only if the price was cheaper. On the whole, more respondents appeared to like this set than dislike it. The floral pattern was preferred to the geometric designs which were said to look "too much like metal utensils." However, for gifts, most people said they would prefer CORNING WARE® products.

APPENDIX A-3: SUMMARY OF TASK FORCE INVESTIGATION OF OTHER HOUSEWARES MARKETS

In attempting to assess the share of market that Corning might be expected to lose to an aggressive competitor, we investigated the market structure of a number of rather mature markets within the general housewares industry. In these markets a strong nationally advertised brand commands a premium price despite the existence of lower priced substitutes. A summary description of these "two-tiered" markets follows:

1. Plastic Housewares (exclusive of Tupperware type storage containers)

	SOM	Price	Distribution
Rubbermaid	.65	1.00	2-step intensive
Festival	.15	.70	direct
Sterilite	.08	.66	direct to national chains, manufacturers reps.
Eagle	.06	.66	direct to discounters, chains
Loma	.06	.66	direct, manufacturers reps.

Source: Wilmington estimates.

Price promotions in this category are extremely effective. Often, different products are grouped in sets, and sold at prices nearer to 50% of Rubbermaids. These sets are designed for retailers' purchase, *not* for ultimate consumer purchase.

2. Tupperware

	SOM	Price	Distribution
Tupperware	.70	1.00	home party selling
Rubbermaid	.12	.75	85% distribution, 15% party
Eagle	.10	.75	direct, mainly supermarkets
Republic Molding	.08	.75	direct, mainly supermarkets

Source: Wilmington estimates.

The price differential may be substantially greater than the indicated 75% in some cases. What is particularly significant is that Tupperware, in response to several entrants in the late sixties, *did not* lower prices. Their basic response has been to add new products, further differentiating through design. Apparently, the new entrants in this market did "cherry pick," typically coming in with the most popular fifteen or so items in the product line.

3. Ekco (gadgets only)

Many competitors abound in the gadget segment of Ekco's market. The overall market structure looks approximately as follows:

	SOM	Price	Distribution
Ekco	.40	1.00	Direct
Kenberry	.15	.80	Through distributors
Tasco	.15	.80	Through distributors
Elpo	.10	.80	Through distributors
Foley	.10	.80	Through distributors
Others	.10	.80	Through distributors

Source: Wilmington estimates.

It appears that Ekco's competitors try to fill in the gaps that Ekco leaves for them, rather than competing directly. Indeed in a few audits, directly competitive products could be found for only 20–25% of the Ekco line.

Case B

Colonial Manor Hospital

Colonial Manor was a successful private hospital in Florence, Alabama. In late 1976, Mr. Robert L. Kidd, the chief administrative officer of the hospital, felt that time was ripe for launching a systematic marketing effort for the purpose of expanding the hospital's business so that the various facilities could be fully utilized. The urgency for such systematic and planned marketing effort was keenly felt because of several developments in the health care industry in general and competitive developments in the area in particular. In December, 1976, Mr. Kidd was in the process of reviewing the operations of the hospital and drafting a developmental plan incorporating his ideas and suggestions for more effective marketing of the various health care services provided by the hospital. He felt that the hospital should develop both out-patient and in-patient business to fully utilize the hospital service capacity and increase the overall earnings of the hospital. These two types of services (out-patient and in-patient), according to Mr. Kidd, though interrelated, required separate marketing strategy and efforts to achieve the overall objectives of the hospital.

BACKGROUND

Colonial Manor Hospital was a 100-bed medical-surgical hospital located in Florence, Alabama. Owned by Humana Incorporated of Louisville, Kentucky, the hospital is one of two investor-owned hospitals in the Quad City area; the other was Shoals Hospital in Sheffield, Alabama. There were also two county hospitals, Colbert County, in Tuscumbia, Alabama and Eliza Coffee Memorial, in Florence, Alabama. Exhibit B-1 shows the location of the Colonial Manor Hospital.

These four hospitals served a trade area of approximately 120,000 people. Colbert County and Shoals served Colbert County with a population of 50,000, while Eliza Coffee Memorial Hospital and Colonial Manor Hospital served Lauderdale County with a population of approximately 70,000 people. Assum-

This case is printed here with the permission of Professor C.P. Rao of the University of Arkansas at Fayetteville and Associate Professor Gerald Crawford of the University of North Alabama.

EXHIBIT B-1   Geographic Location of the Hospital

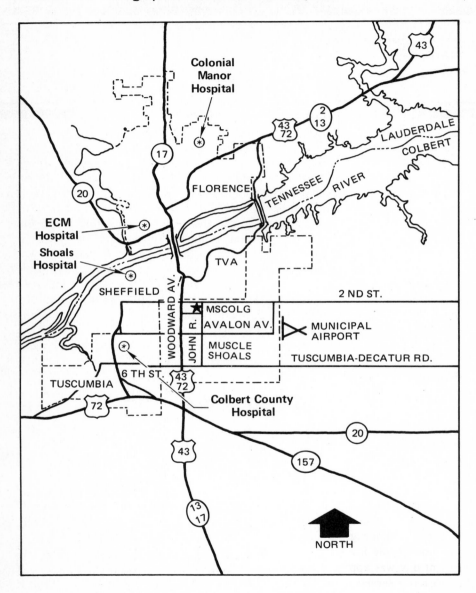

ing a stable growth rate of the area, the population for Florence and Lauderdale
county was expected to be approximately 38,500 and 72,900 by 1980. Analysis
of age distribution in Lauderdale and Colbert counties in 1970 showed that 9.0
percent were 65 years or older and the median age was 28 years, compared to

27.1 for the state and 23.3 for the U.S. The birth and death rates for Lauderdale county were 15.4 and 8.9 respectively, which were lower than the national averages—17.5 and 9.5. The area was considered a medium-income area with 17.4 percent of families with incomes less than $3,000 and 10.9 percent above $15,000. Median family income was $7,608, which was higher than the state figure of $7,263.

Colonial Manor's major competition came from Eliza Coffee Memorial Hospital since most physicians practiced in only one county. Colonial Manor was the smaller of the two with 100 beds while Eliza Coffee Memorial had 296 beds. Both were expanding their facilities and the number of licensed beds; Colonial Manor to 155 beds, and Eliza Coffee Memorial to 392 beds (see Exhibit B-2 for comparison). Renovation and additional construction at both hospitals began in

EXHIBIT B-2   Comparison of Lauderdale County Hospitals

	Eliza Coffee	Colonial Manor
Present number of licensed beds:	296	100
Beds under construction to be completed in 1976:	96	55
Total Beds 1976:	392	155
Room Rates:		
Private	$ 58	$ 64
Semi-Private	48	51
ICU/CCU	115	115
Average Occupancy*	85%	89%

*Acceptable occupancy is considered between 80–85%.
Source: Hospital records.

late 1973 and were scheduled for completion in early 1976. Coffee Memorial had a physical therapy wing which was affiliated with the crippled children's program, a regional mental health center, and was also the primary community emergency center.

Colonial Manor, established in 1969, was generally considered the most elite because of its location and newer facilities and therefore had been able to charge higher rates. The higher rates were necessary since the privately owned institution was not eligible for grants and was subject to taxation. Average revenue per patient day was approximately $135.00 (see Exhibit B-3).

Florence served as the trade and service center of northwest Alabama extending into southern Tennessee and northeastern Mississippi. It was also an educational center for the region since it was the site of the University of North Alabama. It was considered the "bedroom" community for the executive-level people employed by the industries located in the area south of the Tennessee River. Some of the industries in the area included Reynolds Metal,

EXHIBIT B-3   Comparative Profiles of Colonial Manor and Typical
              Competitor in the Area—Facilities and Rates

FACILITIES

Colonial Manor	Typical Competitor
1. Newer and more attractive physical plant	Older, less attractive
2. Excellent parking facilities	Little or no parking area
3. More specialists	Fewer specialists
4. More and better equipment in operating room	Less and older equipment
5. Higher standards	Lower standards
6. Better trained staff	Less trained staff

RATES

Service	Colonial Manor	Typical Competitor
1. Emergency room (First 30 minutes)	$ 9.00	$ 7.50
2. Patient rooms (per day)		
private	$69.00	$58.00
semi-private	$53.00	$48.00
3. Intensive care (per day)	$130.00	$120.00
4. Operating room (First Hour)	$85.00	$75.00
5. Chest X-ray	$30.00	$25.00

Source: Hospital records.

TVA, Union Carbide, textile plants, Ford Motor Company, and fertilizer plants.

Florence was also the center for health care for the whole region including southern Tennessee and northeast Mississippi (see Exhibit B-4). The medical staff had grown from 52 in 1969 to 78 in 1975 and represented many specialists which drew patients from the entire region. In 1975, two new physicians came to Florence to join the Colonial Manor staff—one was a urologist and the other an internist. Another physician also expressed interest in coming to the area.

Colonial Manor did most of the orthopedic work in the community, due to the concentration of orthopedic surgeons on the staff. Pediatric work was increasing especially with the addition of a specialist to the staff. Increased activity in this area was expected to continue with the impending arrival of the urologist who wanted to concentrate on pediatric urology. The facilities utilization statistics at Colonial Manor are given in Exhibit B-5.

There are currently 78 physicians in Lauderdale County, which was almost the one physician per one thousand population usually regarded as necessary. The

EXHIBIT B-4   Geographic Admissions Summary

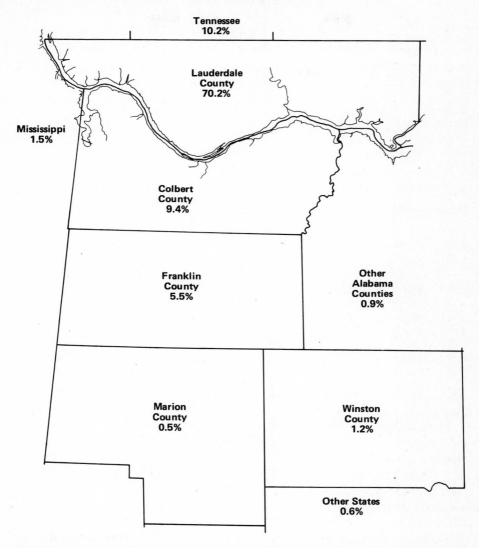

majority of the 78 physicians were on the medical staff of both hospitals and had admitting privileges to both (see Exhibit B-6). During 1975 only 39 of the 78 licensed physicians in Lauderdale County admitted patients to Colonial Manor. Two reasons for this were:

1. Many physicians admitted all patients to only one hospital for their convenience.
2. Some physicians did not accept the private-hospital concept.

EXHIBIT B-5   Colonial Manor Hospital: Utilization Statistics

	1974	**1975 (through July)**
Admissions	3,925	3,960
Patient days	31,437	29,724
Average length of stay (No. of days)	8.0	7.5
Medical patient days	8,323	8,898
Surgical " "	6,250	5,916
Gynecology " "	1,074	939
Urology " "	1,136	1,193
Orthopedic " "	14,654	12,778
Pediatric " "	—	896

Utilization by Departments

Department	Inpatient (1)	Outpatient (2)	Total (3)	Outpatient % (2) as % of (3)
Physical Therapy				
7/73–6/74	38,287	8,413	46,700	21.2
7/74–6/75	31,129	6,952	38,081	17.9
Respiratory Therapy				
9/73–6/74	11,123	24	11,147	0.2
7/74–6/75	13,525	2	13,527	—
Emergency Room Visits				
9/73–6/74	640	2,222	2,862	77.6
7/74–6/75	1,071	3,467	4,538	76.4
X-Ray Treatments				
7/73–6/74	7,161	2,141	9,302	23.0
7/74–6/75	7,955	2,913	10,868	26.8
Laboratory Tests				
7/73–6/74	83,652	2,940	86,592	3.4
7/74–6/75	95,152	2,984	98,136	3.0
Surgery				
7/73–6/74	1,828	19	1,847	1.0
7/74–6/75	2,111	40	2,151	1.8

Source: Hospital records.

Of the 39 physicians who admitted to Colonial Manor Hospital, 18 contributed to 90% of the total admissions (see Exhibit B-7). This phenomenon could be attributed to the following two factors:

1. Thirteen of the physicians admitted exclusively to Colonial Manor. Eleven of these physicians were located in the Colonial Manor Professional Building adjacent to the hospital.
2. The other twenty-six physicians admitted only when admission was specifically requested by the patient or his family, or the physician

EXHIBIT B-6   Colonial Manor Hospital: Categories of the Medical Staff

Specialty	Active	Associate	Courtesy
Urology	1	1	1
Pathology	1		1
Surgery	3	1	5
Radiology	1	1	4
Ophthalmology	1		3
Orthopedics	5		
General medicine	4	4	7
Internal medicine	1	1	5
Neurosurgery	2		
Anesthesiology	1		2
OB/GYN			3
EENT			1
OB			1
GYN			1
Psychiatry			1
Pediatrics			4
Dermatology			2
General practice & general surgery		1	6
ENT		2	
TOTAL	20	11	47

According to the Article IV of the Hospital's Administrative Manual:

Section 1. The Medical Staff

The medical staff shall be divided into consulting, active, courtesy and associate groups.

Section 2. The Consulting Medical Staff

Subsection 1. The consulting medical staff shall consist of physicians of recognized professional ability who are active in the hospital or who have signified willingness to accept such appointment.

Subsection 2. In cases in which consultation is required by the rules of the hospital, these services may be given without charge.

Subsection 3. Membership on the consulting medical staff does not preclude membership on the active staff.

Section 3. The Active Medical Staff

Subsection 1. The active medical staff shall consist of physicians resident in the community who have been selected to transact all business of the medical staff and to attend patients in the hospital. Only those members of the active medical staff shall be eligible to vote and hold office; however, those members serving in associate status may be elected or appointed to office if the active staff so desires.

Subsection 2. Members of the active medical staff shall be required to attend medical staff meetings as provided in Article VII of these By-Laws.

Section 4. The Courtesy Medical Staff

The courtesy medical staff shall consist of those members of the medical profession eligible as herein provided for staff membership, who shall be privileged to admit private patients to the hospital. They are not eligible to vote or hold office.

Section 5. The Associate Staff

The associate staff shall consist of those new members who have been determined eligible for privileges. They shall be entitled to all rights and responsibilities accorded active members but shall serve in a probationary capacity under the surveillance of the active staff for a period of one (1) year. At the end of one (1) year, they shall be considered for active membership.

Source: Hospital records.

was consulting the patient's condition with one of the specialist in the Professional Building, or rooms were not available in the county hospital.

As can be seen from the data in Exhibit B-8, the Professional Building was greatly helpful to Colonial Manor to increase its market share since it was built in 1973. The use rate for Lauderdale County averaged 1248 patient days per thousand population over the last three years. Colonial Manor's "market share" for Lauderdale County increased over the past three years (1973–75) from 20.2% to 24.9% while Eliza Coffee Memorial's share declined from 73.3% to 66.2%.

According to some members of the medical staff of Eliza Coffee Memorial Hospital, when their patients desired to be admitted to Colonial Manor, it was due to the more attractive patient accommodations. Physicians at Colonial Manor often indicated that they admitted their patients to Colonial Manor Hospital because of better surgical accommodations and patients' requests.

In January, 1974, P.S.R.O.[1] standards were set by the Federal Government to regulate the length of stay and type of admissions for Medicare and Medicaid patients in the hospital. Although P.S.R.O. standards had not yet been implemented to date, plans were underway for implementation in the immediate future. Medicare and Medicaid patients made up about 22% of the total admissions at both hospitals. Due to these regulations occupancy rates were expected to decrease approximately 5% (see Exhibit B-9).

---

[1]Professional Standards Review Organization mandated by Section 249 F of Public Law 92-603, Sections 1151–1170 of the Social Security Amendments of 1972.

EXHIBIT B-7   Colonial Manor Hospital: Admitting Physicians Statistics

Physicians	Location	Specialty	1975 Admissions (1st 6 months)
Dr. A	Colonial Manor*	Orthopedic	355
Dr. B	Florence**	Orthopedic	285
Dr. C	Colonial Manor	Surgeon	278
Dr. D	Florence	General P.	251
Dr. E	Colonial Manor	Internist	244
Dr. F	Colonial Manor	ENT	240
Dr. G	Colonial Manor	General P.	203
Dr. H	Colonial Manor	Surgeon	188
Dr. I	Colonial Manor	ENT	120
Dr. J	Florence	Surgeon	106
Dr. K	Florence	Urology	92
Dr. L	Florence	Orthopedic	53
Dr. M	Eliza Coffee***	Neurosurgery	44
Dr. N	Florence	Orthopedic	44
Dr. O	Colonial Manor	Ophthalmology	36
Dr. P	Florence	GYN	29
Dr. Q	Eliza Coffee	Neurosurgery	26
Dr. R	Eliza Coffee	Surgeon	26
		Total	2,620
		Total Admissions	2,917

*Colonial Manor Professional Building
**Located downtown Florence approximately 1 mile from Eliza Coffee Memorial and 3 miles from Colonial Manor Hospital
***Eliza Coffee Memorial Professional Building
Source: Hospital records.

EXHIBIT B-8   Colonial Manor Hospital: Occupancy Chart

Year	% Occupancy
1969	65%
1970	81%
1971	80%
1972	71% **
1973	85% ***
1974	89%
1975	89%

**August 1972 increased to 100 beds.
*** 1973 Professional building was built.
Source: Hospital records.

EXHIBIT B-9   Regulatory Restrictions on In-patient Stay in Hospitals

From Blue Cross and Blue Shield of Alabama: 930 South 20th St., Birmingham, AL 35298

(Contents of this communication are pursuant to Public Law 89-97)

July, 1976

MEDICARE NEWSLINES NUMBER 76-7

TO: Hospital Utilization Review Committees

FROM: J. Frank Trucks, M.D., Medical Advisor

SUBJECT: Long Hospital Stays

In reviewing claims for overutilization, we are finding cases where patients are admitted to the hospital with such diagnosis as terminal carcinoma, etc., where the patients' condition is such that no definite treatment is or can be given.

In many cases these patients remain in the hospital for extended periods of time, probably in many cases, due to pressure from the family not to transfer them to a nursing home. We have a problem in these cases since the Medicare and Medicaid guidelines do *not* allow these patients hospital care.

We will appreciate it if you will contact the physicians on your staff and ask them to notify the patient or their families that this type of service is *non*-covered and that if they wish for them to remain in the hospital, they will have to assume liability for hospital costs.

We realize that aged people present a real problem when it comes to discharging them from the hospital after fractured hips, etc., against the wishes of the family or the patient and that physicians must consider repercussions if something happens to the patient shortly after discharge. However, under government guidelines they must be transferred to extended care facilities or lose their "free" status for hospitilization.

We ask for your cooperation in reducing these extended stays whether there is an acute or chronic condition. By doing this, the complaints from the patients, hospitals and physicians can be greatly reduced and all three will not lose payment for services rendered.

Your cooperation will be greatly appreciated and many of the complaints by recipients and providers can be eliminated.

JFT/cd

NOTICE OF PROSPECTIVE LIMIT APPLICABLE TO MEDICARE GENERAL *ROUTINE* SERVICE COSTS FOR MEDICARE FISCAL YEAR BEGINNING 6/1/76.

As you are aware, the Social Security Amendments of 1972 require that a prospective limitation be placed on the reimbursable costs for services rendered to Medicare beneficiaries. Regulations governing this section of the Social Security Act were published in the Federal Register dated June 6, 1974, under Part 405, Chapter III, Title 20 of the Code of Federal Regulations. A copy of these regulations was forwarded to providers on June 28, 1974.

A new Schedule of Limits on Hospital Inpatient General Routine Service Costs for hospitals with cost-reporting periods beginning on or after July 1, 1975 was published in the Federal Register dated Friday, May 30, 1975. A copy of these regulations and the accompanying schedule of cost limitations is attached.

We wish to inform you that, pursuant to these Regulations, and the accompanying revised schedule of cost limitations, Medicare reimbursement for the above service provided in your hospital during the identified fiscal period will not exceed $82.53 per patient day of general *routine* care. This is based on the limit established for Alabama, S.M.S.A., Group V bed size category 100 to 404.

The above calculation of the limit applicable to your hospital was based on the bed size currently available in our records. Should the number of your available beds differ or change from that bed size category established as of the start of the Medicare fiscal year indicated above, or should clarification of regulations indicate that special rules apply to bed size determination for purposes of these limitations, your limitation will be adjusted accordingly.

We trust this will assist you in your planning for the coming fiscal year.

Bill L. Wear
Administrative Manager
Medicare/Medicaid Reimbursement

BLW/kc

Enclosure

BLUE CROSS AND BLUE SHIELD OF ALABAMA

Colonial Manor was actively engaged in recruiting new physicians to the area. Plans for a new professional building would be fulfilled with the successful recruitment of four additional physicians. Two local physicians expressed serious interest in moving to the new proposed Professional Building.

Colonial Manor's long-range plans included the construction of 95 additional beds within the next ten years and construction of additional Professional Buildings as needed. These plans could only be materialized if Colonial Manor continued profitable operations and showed justification to the state of Alabama for the need of additional beds.

Although Colonial Manor enjoyed certain distinctive advantages with both the physicians and patients, with Eliza Coffee Memorial building new facilities there was a possibility of Colonial Manor losing these advantages. The majority of the physicians who were not located in the Professional Building at Colonial Manor were located close to Eliza Coffee Memorial Hospital.

MR. KIDD'S STRATEGY FOR DEVELOPING IN-PATIENT BUSINESS

An additional 147 patient beds would be available to the citizens and physicians in Lauderdale County in 1976. The P.S.R.O. program would decrease inpatient days in both hospitals by approximately 5%. Attracting additional physicians to the area would be handicapped because the county had almost reached its "quota" of one physician per one thousand persons.

Assumptions:

1. The Florence area would continue to grow and the need for physicians and hospital beds would continue.
2. Patients were admitted to the hospital where the physicians preferred to practice.

Colonial Manor's approach to meet the problem of a possible decrease in inpatient admissions needed to be physician oriented. The patient was the customer but the physician was the agent through whom the customer obtained the service. Physician satisfaction and patient satisfaction went hand in hand. Hence Colonial Manor should adopt the following approaches:

1. Increased professional relations.
2. Adoption of a physician recruitment program.
3. Increased services.

1. Increased Professional Relations

The majority of the 78 physicians in Lauderdale were on the Medical Staff at Colonial Manor. The potential for admission by all physicians was a possibility. The attitude of some physicians to admit only to the county hospital needs to be changed. This could be done through effective professional relations.

1. A monthly newsletter to all physicians on the Medical Staff should be started informing the physicians of the new equipment, types of services offered and newsworthy information.
2. When construction was completed all area physicians should be invited to tour the new facilities.
3. There should be personal contact by administration of the hospital to area physicians, encouraging them to use the hospital facilities.
4. Continuing education was essential to physicians. Offering conference space and establishing programs for continuing education should attract physicians who presently did not use the hospital.

2. Adoption of a Physician Recruitment Program

Additional office spaces adjacent to the hospital were essential for an ongoing physician recruitment program. Physicians recruited to the area, if located elsewhere, could be encouraged by Eliza Coffee Memorial Hospital to practice there if it was more convenient for the physician. Since the area almost had its "quota" of physicians, recruitment of new physicians to Florence would be difficult. Recruitment of new physicians should be limited to specialties which Colonial Manor did not have in its present professional building. These specialties were: Family Medicine, Internal Medicine, and Urology. Physician recruitment should not be limited to new physicians, offers should also be made to physicians in the area who would complement the other specialties of physicians in the hospital. Physicians already in the area would have established practices and add to the inpatient admissions of the hospital.

The recruitment program's major objectives should be:

1. Recruitment of physicians who would complement present specialties.
2. Recruitment of physicians who would admit to Colonial Manor Hospital exclusively.

Recommendations for physician recruitment:

1. Should be concentrated toward physicians presently in Lauderdale County who did not admit to Colonial Manor Hospital. Three reasons for this being:
   a. Number of physicians for Lauderdale County was almost adequate. Therefore, it would be harder to recruit new physicians to the area.
   b. Physicians already in Lauderdale County had established practices.
   c. It would cost less to contact physicians in Lauderdale County. To attract new physicians, advertisements would need to be placed in national publications, contact made with medical schools, and expense paid for physicians' visits.
2. Specialities that could not be filled locally should be attempted through state or national recruitment.
3. Incentives for attracting physicians needed to be provided. Recommended incentives were:
   a. Free rent in professional building for one year.
   b. Guaranteed cash receipts for a short period of time.
   c. Paid moving expenses.

These incentives, although somewhat expensive to the hospital, would be a wise investment in the long run and help the hospital meet its objectives. Average revenue per patient day at Colonial Manor was $135.00. If a new physician averaged 5 inpatients per day, for one year, this would mean an additional $246,000 in revenue for the hospital.

3. Increased Services and Further Differentiation

Additional services not available at the other hospital would allow Colonial Manor to attract area physicians.

1. Outpatient Surgery: Many surgeries for which patients were usually admitted could now be performed for outpatients. Although this would not increase inpatient days, this should attract additional physicians to the hospital.
2. Artificial Kidney: Internists in the area would find it hard not to admit patients or refer patients to a hospital with an artificial Kidney machine.
3. Open-heart Surgery: No hospital within a 150-mile radius of Florence performed open-heart surgery. Colonial Manor presently had physicians on staff capable of performing such surgery.

Other services not included which should be studied are a Pulmonary Laboratory and Gastric Laboratory. These additional services which might not be feasible at present would certainly be an added asset.

PLAN FOR INCREASING OUTPATIENT SERVICES

Government-supported programs, like Medicare, Medicaid, Crippled Children, indigent programs and others, paid hospitals on a cost basis. With new regulations limiting the number of days that a patient with a particular diagnosis could stay as an inpatient in the hospital, it was necessary that hospitals start a program of marketing outpatient services (see Exhibit B-10).

Hospitals faced another problem in that the Emergency Room and outpatient services often resulted in increased bad debts. Most insurance companies did not cover outpatient services and others only covered a percentage of the bill leaving a balance for the patients to pay. Hospitals had to strive hard to collect these small balances resulting in increased hospital costs.

Colonial Manor Hospital was also a private hospital liable for state and federal sales and property taxes, competing with city and county hospitals, not liable to pay taxes. It is necessary for Colonial Manor's rates to be higher.

Colonial Manor Hospital was located in a better neighborhood than other hospitals in the area and has the room to expand if necessary. Colonial Manor was in the process of acquiring a new scanner. According to Mr. Kidd, this would enable them to perform brain scans, liver scans and other related tests in their hospital and this would not only increase the inpatient load, but would also attract some outpatients to the hospital.

Mr. Kidd felt that recruiting five to six more doctors should enable the Colonial Manor to compete effectively even after Eliza Coffee Memorial expanded their bed capacity. "It is our belief that patients go to where doctors will prefer to practice and we work toward a doctors-oriented policy rather than a patient-oriented one. If we can please the doctor, we have pleased the patient in the process."

Strategy to Increase Out-Patient Business

1. Laboratory:

The laboratory had been operating at a profit margin of 37.5 percent and outpatient revenues in July 1975 made up 4.4 percent of total lab revenues.

EXHIBIT B-10   Limits on In-patient Costs by Government Regulations

On April 17, 1975, there was published in the Federal Register (40 FR 17190), a notice of proposed Schedule of Limits on Hospital Inpatient General Routine Service Costs For Hospitals With Cost-Reporting Periods Beginning On or After July 1, 1975. Section 1861 (v) (1) of the Social Security Act, as amended, permits the Secretary of Health, Education, and Welfare to set prospective limits on direct or indirect overall incurred costs of specific items or services or groups of items or services furnished by a provider, to be recognized as reasonable based on estimates of the cost necessary in the efficient delivery of needed health services.

1. The bulk of the comments dealt with the lowering of the limits to the 80th percentile. A number of commenters asserted that the limits were lowered to the 80th percentile only as a cost-cutting device, without consideration of the financial impact on providers or the possible reduction in the quality of care. Other commenters suggested that the lower limits based on the 80th percentile, with the accompanying lowering of the interim payment rate, would imperil the cash-flow position of many providers.

2. Comments were made that the effects of such factors as educational programs, patient mix, or scope of service on the hospital's inpatient general routine service cost were ignored in the revised classification system. These factors were not ignored, but were carefully considered before the revised classification system was issued. It is true that institutions which have educational programs may incur higher costs than institutions without educational programs. However, the classification variables in the new system cause teaching hospitals to be grouped together. The regulations (see 405.460 (f) (2)) provide that, where a provider can demonstrate that its costs exceed the applicable limit by reason of educational activities or by the special needs of the patients treated, an exception can be made to the application of the limit, to the extent that the added costs flow from approved educational activities, to the extent they are atypical (although reasonable) for providers in the comparison group, or flow from the provision of special needs of patients treated and are necessary in the delivery of needed health care.

3. A number of commenters appeared to be under the impression that the limits apply to *total* hospital inpatient costs per day. It should be understood that the Schedule of Limits presented herein applies only to the hospital inpatient general *routine* service costs, but does not apply to the costs of services furnished in special-care units or to the costs of ancillary services.

4. Some parties expressed the view that they have a lower average length-of-stay than comparable hospitals, due to the more intense services that they provide, and this results in their having a higher routine service cost per day. They believe hospitals with shorter length-of-stays result from differences in case mix or from the provision of more intensive ancillary services. Since the published limits pertain to general routine service costs, the application of the limits do not more adversely affect hospitals with a lower average length of stay.

5. A number of parties commented that the classification system and Schedule of Limits do not distinguish between whether a hospital is an old or new one. Thus,

a hospital with a new building and, therefore, with higher capital and interest costs, may have a higher routine cost per day than would other hospitals with older facilities.

Although a newer facility may have higher capital and interest costs than an older facility, a newer facility, generally, incorporates more advanced design concepts, which permit it to operate more efficiently than an older one and incur lower repair and maintenance costs. Thus, the different cost consequences of capital and interest costs, on one hand, and repair, maintenance, and operation of plant costs, on the other hand, are reasonably accounted for in the published limits.

Recommendations for the lab to increase its share of outpatient business:

1) Request that a Laboratory Consultant study the current lab situation and recommend action on some automated equipment for the hospital lab.
2) Pursue agreement with Pathologist relative to hematology work to be possibly done in the hospital.
3) Assign a sales representative to approach the nursing homes in Tri-Cities area and surrounding areas about doing lab work, employee physicals, infection control tests, and cultures for them.
4) Meet with new physicians coming into the area to acquaint them with lab facilities and procedures in order to encourage them to use the hospital, rather than getting their own equipment and personnel.

2. Radiology Department:

The Radiology Department faced competition primarily from the doctors, most of whom had their own equipment. There were four X-ray machines in the professional building adjacent to the hospital; most of the physicians had their own equipment when they moved into the professional building. The new physicians generally used the hospital radiology department.

The Radiology Department does about 200 procedures a month through the Emergency Room. The hospital had an agreement with the nearby nursing home and a new home under construction to do X-ray work.

The X-ray department also did some industrial employee physicals for those whose physicians had no equipment.

As a result of the expansion program, the increased patient load was expected to increase the department work load by approximately one-third, and the radiology department was being expanded accordingly.

The Radiology Department currently operated at a profit margin of 15.3 percent, and outpatient revenues comprised 19.3 percent of the total in July, 1975.

Recommendations to increase outpatient business for the Radiology department:

1) Pursue construction of second professional building near the hospital for easier access to the hospital Radiology Department.

2) Approach physicians on a one-to-one basis regarding outpatient radiology work. The new physicians should be encouraged to use the hospital, rather than investing in their own equipment. Older physicians who already operated their equipment should be encouraged not to replace it when their equipment was no longer usable. This should not be too difficult in light of increasing costs and possible state legislation requiring inspection and use of x-ray technicians, not just nurses, to operate equipment.

3. Physical Therapy Department:

The physical therapy department was performing the largest number of procedures in the county, largely because of the concentration of orthopedic surgeons on the medical staff.

The Colonial Manor department did far more procedures than the separate physical therapy wing at the Eliza Coffee Memorial.

Local schools had their own equipment for therapy of athletic injuries. Industries in the area sent their injured employees to Colonial Manor for their physical therapy needs.

The physical therapy department currently operated at a profit margin of 54.3 percent and outpatient revenues comprised 13.1 percent of total revenues.

Recommendations to increase outpatient business for the Physical Therapy department:

1) Contact nursing homes in the area to determine the market for physical therapy for their patients.
2) Contact area industries to determine interest in individual executive physical fitness programs developed by the physical and respiratory therapists. These programs would be developed with the cooperation of the physician who performed the annual physical examination.
3) Work with the Communications Department to develop outpatient brochures for physical therapy that would describe services and treatments and serve as pre-written prescriptions for the patients.

4. Respiratory Therapy Department:

In the past, outpatient respiratory therapy work was not actively sought because it was felt that there were not adequate personnel to handle such additional load. There was no commercial respiratory therapy service in the area, although some people did have their own home equipment. The nursing homes would be the prime places to start by offering respiratory therapy to patients in the nursing homes.

The Respiratory Therapy Department currently operated at a profit margin of 36.8 percent, but outpatient revenues had not been accurately recorded so it was not possible to measure the outpatient percentage.

Recommendations to increase outpatient business for the Respiratory Therapy Department:

1) Contact nursing homes and extended care facilities to determine their present supplier of the service.
2) Analyze the feasibility, in line with the capabilities of the department, of servicing nursing homes, and of providing service to homebound patients and of establishing a home-equipment rental service.
3) Possibly conduct clinics on maintenance and calibration of home equipment.
4) Work with the Communications Department to adapt standardized brochures describing the services which could also serve as a pre-written prescription and instructions for the patients.

5. Outpatient Surgery:

Outpatient surgery at Colonial Manor was limited by the lack of space, especially for recovering surgery patients. In the current expansion program, the surgical suite was being expanded and one operating room was being equipped for outpatient surgery with a recovery area.

Physicians had a positive attitude toward outpatient surgery and these procedures would probably increase after completion of construction of expanded facilities. The new urologist indicated that he would want to do some cystoscopies on an outpatient basis and the new ENT men will also be able to use this capability. With the increasing concentration on malpractice liability, many of the procedures that were now performed in the doctors' offices may be moved to the hospital setting.

The high occupancy rate at Colonial Manor and the expected increase in the number of physicians were likely to increase the use of the outpatient surgery at Colonial Manor.

Specific recommendations to increase outpatient surgery at Colonial Manor:

1) After discussions with the physicians, develop an organized program for outpatient surgery at Colonial Manor, including scheduling personnel, procedures to follow and separate charge structure etc.
2) Make a formal presentation to the medical staff on the potential of outpatient surgery, the benefits of the hospital setting over the office for minor procedures, and the program developed by Colonial Manor.

6. Central Supply

At present, there was no place in the area to buy medical supplies like slings, collars, dressings, braces, tennis elbow bands, etc. on an outpatient basis. There might be potential for setting up a separate outpatient services department which would sell these items including fitting by an ER nurse or attendant.

Other suggestions for increasing outpatient business:

1) Efforts to secure commitments from one or two more physicians for space in a new professional building be intensified in order to secure Executive Committee approval to proceed with this project. Another

professional building near the hospital would provide needed office space for physicians being recruited by Colonial Manor and a built-in market for the hospital lab and X-ray departments. Florence was a regional health center in the area and a second professional building could assist in making Colonial Manor the major regional health care facility.

2) Review the regional lab concept in relation to Colonial Manor and follow-up on procuring automated equipment for the hospital lab, especially automated hematology equipment since the competing lab did not have the latter. The increased work load generated by the additional beds could not be accomplished entirely normally. Given the size of the hospital and its high occupancy rate, the lab would be able to generate enough inpatient and outpatient business to justify some automation. Outpatient business could start going directly to the competing lab showing no increase in revenue for the hospital if the lab was not automated.

3) Develop a total outpatient surgery program for Colonial Manor, including setting up a separate charge structure. Presently, there was no other outpatient surgery program in Florence and with the high rates of occupancy of the hospitals, the concentration of health-care specialties in Florence, the increase in the number of physicians in the area, and the growing emphasis on utilization of outpatient services, this program would be highly successful.

4) On completing the construction of expanded facilities, groups to hold meetings in the hospital; for example, Weight Watchers, Future Nurses.

5) Sponsor public service clinics such as diabetes or cancer detection clinics; hypertension, obesity and venereal disease clinics; and pulmonary function tests.

6) Participate in Career Week by having the Director of Nurses and other department heads make presentations to area schools.

7) Maintain contact with area industries and contact any new industries to determine their health service needs. Consider issuing VIP cards to industry employees with their insurance information which would allow them to be admitted without a cash deposit. Work with staff physicians to develop an "Executive Physical" Package.

Case C
Johnston, Inc.

Bob Johnston, President of a children's high quality apparel firm, was concerned about his company's future strategy. Although his company was doing well, there were a number of unsettling industry trends. It wasn't as if there were one or two major problem areas; rather, discernible developments in the children's wear industry were unfocused and contradictory. Bob found it difficult, therefore, to assess his best future course of action in respect to such marketing issues as exclusive versus non-exclusive retail arrangements; the use, or combination, of such diverse retail outlets as specialty shops, department stores, mass merchandisers, catalog houses, and discounters; product line definition and price policies; the appropriate mix among selling, advertising, and promotional alternatives; and the very issue of growth—Was growth desirable and in what form?

It was not that doing business through the company's traditional outlets, specialty retailers, had ever been simple. Volatility in those channels was traditional; doing business with specialty merchants had been a constant challenge given the ever changing requirements of consumers, retail store buyers, merchandise managers, and store presidents. In a real sense, the country's general environmental changes in lifestyles, attitudes, and population priorities were magnified at the retail level. The desire of most successful retail managers was to be "relevant—exciting—in the lead."

Channel changes, needless to say, made it difficult for a smallish firm like Johnston's (less than $6,000,000 in sales) to adapt easily to new requirements. And they increased greatly the risks of growth. Johnston's size called for larger commitments to style, the spreading of an already thin management base, and even greater anticipation of future needs of the trade and consumers. Needless to say, it had always been a gamble in clothing to guess correctly the designs, fabrics, styles, and colors for presentation to the buyers. There was also the ever present concern that the styles and fabrics shown in the women's wear industry might not translate into consumer acceptance in children's clothing; or the re-

This case was written by Isabelle Schmid. Reprinted from *Stanford Business Cases 1979* with permission of the Publishers, Stanford University Graduate School of Business, © 1979 by the Board of Trustees of the Leland Stanford Junior University.

verse, that the women's industry would corner the supply of a specific, widely demanded fabric (such as corduroy).[1]

Thus it was natural for Bob to ask, "How should my company expand? Should we seek more volume from present customers, from wider geographic penetration, from new distribution, from product line extension (such as the recent additions of christening and layette garments), or from vertical integration into the channels? In fact, can there be much aggressive growth given the financial implications (heavier debt), the three-year breaking-in period for personnel and equipment in new plants, and the danger that size might tarnish the company's image of exclusivity?"

COMPANY HISTORY

Forty-eight seasons, or 16 years ago, Johnston began to produce an infant designer collection exclusively for Lord & Taylor, a well-known Fifth Avenue prestige retailer. The brand name Betti Terrell (Johnston's designer at the time) was adopted for this collection. As the line gained in popularity, Johnston began to look toward expanded distribution. Other retailers coveted the Betti Terrell designer collection due to Lord & Taylor's reputation in the fashion industry.

Under the franchise agreement, Johnston could not sell his Betti Terrell line to another store based in the same city. However, he could market an "open line," Little One. Because Betti Terrell was also limited to the infant line, Johnston introduced a third label, Fischel (Priscilla Fischel was Vice President for Sales, headquartered in New York), aimed at toddlers and 4–7 year-olds. These separate brand decisions reflected the historical importance and strength of Lord & Taylor to Johnston.

By 1977, Johnston had 800 active accounts, some franchised and some not. A third of the firm's sales came from 15 customers. There were five labels covering the following age categories: newborn, infant, toddler, girls 4–6 and girls 7–12. Each year, the company designed and manufactured about 1,200 styles, not including different sizes and colors. A summary of their current production revealed eight major lines as follows:

Types of Apparel Produced

1-piece. *Long*—B'alls, jiffies, j'alls, skipsuits, pants, etc.
1-piece. *Short*—Sunsuits, shortalls, bubbles, shorts, etc.
2-piece. *Long*—Overall sets, pant-suits, etc.
2- & 3-piece. *Short*—Shortall and shirt, skip and jacket, etc.
Coats, coat sets, jackets
Shirts, blouses, toys

---

[1]Women's and men's clothing was traditionally designed and manufactured ahead of children's, hence those cutters purchased fabrics first. These fabric purchases normally indicated the trend in clothing.

Dresses, jumpers, dress sets, etc.
Miscellaneous—Beachwear, bonnets, pram bags, bear suits, etc.

A small sample of some 1977 baby items is included in Exhibit C-1.

EXHIBIT C-1   Johnston, Inc.: Sample of Products

BETTI TERRELL DESIGNER COLLECTION
FOR BABIES
Designed by
CAROLYN HOGUE
Spring-Summer, 1977
In our 48th Season

JOHNSTON, INC.
P.O. BOX 15125
DALLAS, TEXAS 75201

FOR DELIVERY—SPRING—AS READY—COMPLETE MARCH 1
FOR DELIVERY—SUMMER—AS READY—COMPLETE MARCH 31
TERMS: 8/10 EOM

STYLE NO.	GARMENT	PRICE	SIZE
	"STRIPE IT FUN"		
	ESTIMATED SHIPPING DECEMBER 15 ON EARLY ORDERS, *COMPLETE MARCH 1*		
9188	GIRL POPOVER DRESS & PANTIES—sun popover in white precured b/c (65%KODEL/35%COT) with elastic neckline —angel wing sleeves—accents of green binding & orange tulip applique. Panties of bold stripe (50%AVRIL/50%COT) in green/orange/gold/white. SUGGESTED RETAIL—19.00 (50.0) WHITE STRIPE	$9.50	6-9-12-18
9619	GIRL SUN HAT—ruffle brim completely lined hat in bold stripe (50%AVRIL/50%COT) in green/orange/gold/white—white pique binding & bow. SUGGESTED RETAIL—8.00 (50.0) STRIPE	4.00	9-12-18
9158	SHORTALL—zip front shortall with half the back & half the front in white twill (65%KODEL/35%COT) and the other half in bold stripe (50%AVRIL/50%COT) in green/	6.25	6-9-12-18

orange/gold/white—stripe patch pockets on
white front.
    SUGGESTED RETAIL—12.50 (50.0)
WHITE/STRIPE

9624	SUN HAT—white twill sun hat with bright orange and green button trim. Could be worn by boy or girl. All fabrics 65%KODEL/35%COT. SUGGESTED RETAIL 8.00 (50.0) WHITE	$4.00	9-12-18
9189	GIRL SUN BUBBLE—in white precured b/c (65%KODEL/35%COT)—with orange tulip applique on bib—bold green/orange/gold stripe ruffling accents (50%AVRIL/50%COT). SUGGESTED RETAIL—12.50 (50.0) WHITE	6.25	6-9-12-18

The following table summarizes the label and age matrix:

Size Range

	NEWBORN (0–6 Mo.)	INFANT (6,9,12,18 Mo.)	TODDLER (2–4)	GIRLS (4–6)	GIRLS (7–12)
Franchise Labels	—	Betti Terrell	Fischel	Fischel	—
Open Labels	Johnston	Little One	Little One	Little One	Johnston

Low   STYLE AND PRICE SENSITIVITY   High

One explanation: the franchise line was granted to one store per city, whereas open labels could be purchased by any store.

Reproductions of the five major labels as well as some lesser ones are continued in Exhibit C-2.

Competition for Johnston was difficult to assess. There were, of course, a number of well regarded small firms—Florence Eiseman, Grace Company, Sylvia Whyte, Ruth of Carolina and Dorissa—but it was also true that the market was so diffuse that a small manufacturer like Johnston tended to ignore competition and just "go for a share." In reality, it was difficult to pinpoint specific competition. Very few firms, for instance, offered designer collections, although there were plenty of specialists (i.e., pants, skirts, swimsuits) for any particular type of clothing. Some operators were imitators or knock-off artists, who copied and sold at a discount. In a way, it was easy to break into the industry because start-up

EXHIBIT C-2 Johnston, Inc.: Labels

Fischèl®

MADE EXPRESSLY FOR
Neiman-Marcus
by Betti Terrell®

BETTI TERRELL
FOR
Lord + Taylor

Fischèl® FOR
Lord + Taylor
AT

LITTLE ONE®
by Johnston

Betti Terrell®
18-24 mo.

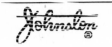
Johnston®

costs were relatively low. But it was difficult to gain credibility with store buyers as a new supplier. They valued economy, perhaps, but even more they had to be sure of delivery, quality, and follow-through. And buyers had long memories in these matters.

Johnston, Inc. had done reasonably well financially by comparison with its competition. For example, a reporting service (Robert Morris Associates) published in 1974 a composite index of 26 children's clothing manufacturers with sales under $10 million, which can be compared with Johnston's record:

	Robert Morris Associates	*Johnston*
ASSETS		
Cash	2.3	2
Receivables Net	33.1	46
Inventory Net	45.8	46
Other Current	3.6	—
Total Current	84.9	94
Fixed Assets Net	11.0	5
Other Non Current	4.1	1
Total	100.0	100
LIABILITIES		
Due Banks (short-term)	19.6	6
Due Trade	23.6	10
Income Taxes	2.3	—
Current Maturities LTDebt	.7	—
All Other Current	8.1	12
Total Current Debt	54.3	28
Long-Term Debt	5.6	—
Net Worth	40.1	72
Total	100.0	100

INCOME STATEMENT	*Robert Morris Group*
Net Sales	100.0
Cost of Sales	75.1
Gross Profit	24.9
All Other Expenses—Net	22.7
Profit B/T	2.2

Johnston stated that although his company's gross was significantly greater than industry average, profits were only slightly better due to high sales and design costs attributable to a designer's collection. Sales costs, including offices, showrooms, sales compensation, and samples, were 10% of sales.

ORGANIZATION AND PRODUCTION

Bob Johnston summarized his firm's key functions as design, production, marketing, and sales. Because of the nature of the business, all were interconnected around the concept of seasons.

From an overall point of view, Johnston had organized his operations as follows:

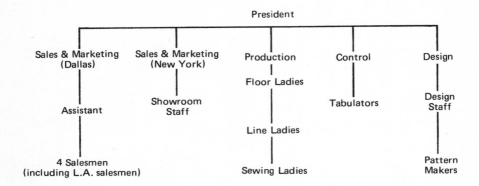

The key marketing/sales locations were in two major buying centers, New York and Dallas. Because of the firm's size, relationships among the various groups were much more informal than formal and circumscribed.

Design

The design function was directed by Carolyn Hogue, with a small staff of designers and pattern makers. Typical of her schedule and duties was the time-table for the 1978 Spring line for the labels Betti Terrell, Fischel, and Little One:

July–September 1977: Carolyn winnowed information from buyers, the company's showroom staff, other designers, and the fabric industry, as well as her own intuitions. She also previewed domestic and international fabric shows. Then, from five-yard sample swatches, she created five lines, styles within each line reflecting her feelings about what the line "needed" to present a well-balanced collection. These results were previewed by the top five Johnston executives. At this time, certain items were eliminated as not being "right" for the line in terms of price, design, and classification (classification meant grouping by type of garment, such as pant, dress, coverall). The surviving items were priced by the Controller. During this same period, the company forecasted the required yardage necessary to produce the number of garments it estimated would be sold. Samples for showrooms and salesmen were made.

October: The lines went into production.

October–November: Key retail buyers made garment selections at the plant and typically left specific orders. These key customers normally selected a few items as exclusives, for which they had to guarantee a minimum cut. On the basis of these early orders and buyer comments, the line was "put to bed." Delivery terms and prices were finalized and fabric purchases completed. Production of the remaining lines was finished.

December–March 1978: Repeat of the July–September schedule, for the Fall 1978 line.

Perhaps the best summary of the sales pattern can be shown as follows:

Sales Pattern: Fall 1976

Report #	Report Date	$\dfrac{Sales\ to\ Date—All\ Lines}{Total\ Season\ Sales}$ *(ratio)*
1	4/5/76	.30
2	4/13/76	.51
3	4/21/76	.64
4	4/29/76	.82
5	5/6/76	.91
6	5/13/76	.94
7	5/20/76	.97
8	5/27/76	.99
9	6/10/76	1.00
10	6/18/76	1.00
Final	8/5/76	1.00

These data refer to orders received, i.e., purchase orders from retail buyers, on a weekly basis. Notice the time periods required for the gradual accumulation of total sales. It is also evident that information on selling trends is difficult to read early in the selling season, when accumulated sales are limited.

Production

The basic rule was "first come, first served." That is, the buyer who first ordered received the first shipment. Moreover, second cuttings were seldom made. Consequently, if a buyer ordered too little, there was scant opportunity to ask for a subsequent factory run. This rule created an interesting buyer trade-off: sufficient orders versus ordering flexibility.

The first production steps consisted of making patterns and coordinating the cutting and sewing schedule with market demand. Separate bolts of fabric were distinguished from each other with care to guarantee matched coloring and shading. All pieces of a style were grouped and assigned to a production line.

These lines consisted of eight to eleven ladies, working sequentially on each garment as it passed through to the head of the line, where it emerged completed. This production technique contrasted to the "bundle" system, where each worker always performed the same operation and pieces were joined at the very end.

Johnston's technique sacrificed some efficiency for accuracy and flexibility, which was in keeping with the firm's need for small runs of many items, where schedules were tight and small margins called for minimum errors. Each line had a supervisor, who served as leader and adviser on the intricacy of the next garment coming through. The last production step included finishing details, inspection, pressing, hanging, and bagging.

Generally speaking, the Johnston manufacturing operation was a critical factor to success. Some of the sewing techniques were complex and unusual; yet the quality of the finished product was expected to be noticeably superior to that of competition—no loose threads, garments equally well finished inside and out, finished seams, and collars cut on the bias.

One of the key influences upon profit was inventory turnover; it was essential to hold inventories to a minimum and yet be responsive to the requirements of a seasonal market.

Production Constraints

Three requirements affected production constraints: the need to fully sell out all runs, a policy of no re-orders, and quality standards. Profits depended upon sold-out production runs which, in turn, were a function of plant capacity (both in-house and outside-contract) and fabric and trim availability. However, these constraints were relatively flexible at the beginning of each season. Once the rough sales forecast of the styles was determined, supplies purchased, and production schedules set, however, flexibility was greatly diminished. Notwithstanding, certain production adjustments were possible as sales information improved. Still, poor early information could lead to expensive wrong cuts.

Full production requirements were a function of small margins. Unused fabrics usually had to be sold off at a loss. Laying off employees was undesirable because of the company's dependence on the local work force and the general difficulty of finding skilled workers. Expanding production greatly beyond average plant capacity was only possible (short run) by contracting out various garments. In these cases, the question of quality was problematical. Within the greater Dallas area, nobody was able or willing to match Johnston's quality standards. Moreover, the time factor was critical. Usually about four to five extra weeks had to be allowed for outside production schedules. Given very tight production schedules, such flexibility was often unavailable.

In the long run, increased capacity was possible with the purchase of an existing plant, the construction of a new plant, or the development of additional contractors. In the case of a new plant, the learning curve was about three years.[2] Regardless of the choice, Johnston had two other considerations to keep

---

[2]Johnston could figure a contractor premium of 15–20% above factory labor; a $1,500 premium per operator above asset cost in the case of buying an existing plant; and $125,000 (or $2,500 per operator, assuming 50) if a plant were built.

in mind: the costs of servicing any additional financial debt and the ability to stimulate demand while maintaining the quality, reputation for uniqueness, and exclusivity presently attached to Johnston products.

Reorders were not in the plan. A request could be serviced if unsold stock was on hand, but Johnston would not cannibalize signed orders to the benefit of a more important customer. Although some production adjustment was possible, reorders were usually unavailable due to fabric limitations and tight schedules. Furthermore, reorders generally arrived after the production line had been shifted to producing for the next season. (Reorders came in after the merchandise had had a one-month selling time on the retail floor, or about two to four months after production was finished.)

The third production constraint was a function of quality standards. For three reasons, quality limited production:

1) Uniqueness of design, which caused an intricate production requirement;
2) Quality of workmanship and the shortage of properly skilled
   workers;
3) The logistical problem of on-time delivery of individual items and
   groups of items (an important dimension of supplier quality).

Marketing and Sales

As mentioned earlier, Johnston carried five labels: Betti Terrell, Fischel, Little One, Johnston, and Toymaker Designs. The target audience consisted of those consumers described as "middle-upper class, with understated tastes, preferring pastel towards bright colors, a city-type, and department or specialty store patron."

As we have noted, there was a wide variety of retail operations in the garment industry. But for a firm like Johnston's, with its high priced, exclusive lines, the only pertinent categories were specialty stores and department stores. In fact, Bob Johnston found it easier to talk about specialty stores (such as I. Magnin) and department stores (such as Macy's). When pressured to generalize how he saw the differences between these two types, he summarized as follows:

Department Stores	Area of Contrast	Specialty Stores
Tight	**Margins**	Higher
Volume	**Sales Orientation**	Higher gross
Sometimes buys for $10 less from a knock-off artist, such as a copy of Pierre Cardin produced in the Orient.	**Merchandise**	Insists on original label

Department Stores	Area of Contrast	Specialty Stores
Buys deep in one resource (like ½ of Johnston's output) and hence makes the product into a commodity ("you can buy it at the Emporium")	**Depth of Line**	Breadth in selective lines

The consumer was a different matter. In Johnston's opinion, the buying decision was normally made by either the mother or grandmother. Not until the teen years did one find strong user input into the buying decision. The decision-makers often had very different ideas about how they wanted to dress the offspring. The mother emphasized practicality: "Is it wash 'n wear, permanent press?" Grandmothers tended to overlook these features. Further value differences encompassed such dimensions as quality workmanship, colors, relevance to life style, and the image the garment should convey. In addition to these contrasts, geographical differences were significant in the American market. Chicago and New York favored classical, traditional styles, somber or pastel colors, and wool, corduroy, and light-weight cotton fabrics. The West and South were attracted to bright, "sun and sport" styles and colors, and materials which were adaptable to year-round wearing.

The characteristics of the consumer were difficult, therefore, to generalize. In this respect it is interesting to note remarks made during an interview with some Macy's children's wear buyers in June 1977:

> Young marrieds get quite practical when buying. They wouldn't buy a "way out" gift because it would reflect on the giver.

> The high end market is not shrinking; rather there is increasing concern with quality, durability, practicality, and style.

> The mother, after all, can't dress the little girl fancier than she is dressed.

> The grandmother is interested in the brand name. The mother is more interested in copying what "she" is like—a bit trendy, somewhat unique, but wash 'n wear.

> There are two kinds of customers—those who want their kids to look like miniature adults and those who want them to look like children.

An important part of the firm's strategy had to do with its overall image in the trade. The trade was, of course, Johnston's first level of customer. When asked to comment on "What does a retailer buy when he deals with Johnston?" the

President replied: "Exclusive designs that stand out on the rack; prompt, reliable deliveries; quality; a New York office that can facilitate the purchasing process enormously; longevity—a proven name; prestige customers; ethical behavior."

The interface between manufacturer and retailer was an important constraint, as well as opportunity, in the Johnston strategy. For example, one buyer made the following observation: "The real problem in the store is the fixtures and racks. They limit what you can do in presentation—what, in fact, can be displayed."

Not all department stores were interested in having a children's apparel department. Although a good department hopefully could generate store traffic and create long-term customers, the margins and ROI were average; the space could be better put to fast-moving merchandise; and total sales volume was relatively small (about 4½% of total store sales).

Because of the fundamental changes taking place in the channels, it was unclear to Johnston in 1977 whether major retailers would continue to carry and support major designer labels or try to revert to their earlier role of being fashion dictators—the "Fifth Avenue" tradition; whether they would be more insistent upon exclusive arrangements or willing to accept selected local competition. It is significant to note that in the Johnston Company, Carolyn was designer, merchandiser, and market researcher in that she maintained close contact with the key store accounts.

Pricing was another important ingredient of marketing strategy. Price levels were arrived at among the controller, the designer, and the New York showroom (in the person of Priscilla Fischel) and reflected history, competition, market trends, degree of risk inherent in a style, and season. For example, Spring-Summer items generally contributed more to the overall margins than labor-intensive winter clothing.

Typically, Johnston catered to the high end of the price segment. The normal procedure was to multiply a garment's cost by a factor to arrive at a selling price. This formula, of course, was not rigid, since it was necessary that after the retailer had added his mark-on, the eventual retail selling price still be in an appropriate "price line." The company had done little price experimentation. Bob explained that management instinctively believed that if the price were set too high, obviously all sales would disappear.

Selling strategy was premised upon the existence of three key purchase "points:" the factory, the showrooms, and the travelling sales force. A select few retailers came to the factory to purchase, indicating that these buyers were sure of their consumers and the appropriateness of the Johnston merchandise fit in terms of the preferred store "look." In short, these buyers purchased on the basis of their feelings and the historical record of the manufacturer, regardless of what the retail market shows offered as to design, price, fabric, or color.

The major apparel cities (New York, Chicago, Dallas, Los Angeles) offered "market weeks" in which buyers visited a number of manufacturer's showrooms and placed orders. These "markets" were seasonal, including Fall/Holiday, Spring/Summer. Department store buyers were of two types. "Key buyers" normally purchased about the same number of pieces. The others "shopped the market" seeking particular items with which to enhance their department. This second approach was not so much a "fill in the gap" approach as it was an attempt to give their departments a broader "look." The strategy, of course, was intended to increase the selection for the customer in order to foster store loyalty as well as to create a feeling of "theater." It was important, needless to say, to be competitive in these regards. It was not surprising that this second type of buyers was not very brand loyal. She/he would only buy in terms of specific look, price, color, and design.

The third sales point was the travelling sales force, the traditional channel for smaller store buyers. Due to increased travel costs and the great popularity of market shows, travelling salesmen were steadily diminishing in importance.

Store buyers had a number of criteria for buying, common among which were the following:

1. Does the line reflect "the look" I want?
2. Does the merchandise "jump off the rack?"
3. Does the line fit in with other merchandise I have purchased? Does it enhance my total department image?
4. Are the price points right for my department? (Is it too expensive? Not expensive enough?)
5. Will it be delivered when I want it?
6. Does the supplier have delivery credibility?
7. Does it fit into my departmental budget?
8. How much should I buy, for which stores, and which pieces of the collection?
9. Is the line confined?
10. Can I wait until the last minute to order so as to read the market better, to maximize my "open-to-buy," and to be flexible in case a new item, new designers, new look or color takes off in the market?
11. Is the merchandise convenient to handle? Does it have to be steamed first? Pre-ticketed? Supplied with hangers?

The manufacturer's showroom personnel, as well as salesmen, played a critical role, despite the implied dominance of the garments themselves. Many supplier intangibles, including integrity, dependability, workmanship, appropriateness of line, were inferred from the sales persons' behavior. Moreover, the field people recognized the inherent conflict between the tightness of the production schedule and the buyers' preferences to commit at the last minute. The trick was to balance the two so as to satisfy the customer while protecting the company. This was a selling role demanding understanding and interpersonal skills. It was a selling role that required sound communications between buyers, the New York office, other field personnel, and the plant. Feelings were as important as facts.

Advertising was a final key ingredient to Johnston's marketing strategy. It was not easy, in this regard, to decide the correct relative emphasis to place upon the consumer and the trade. Was pull or push more appropriate? Traditionally, Johnston had spent little on consumer advertising (about $20,000).[3] Management's assumption was that brand awareness among consumers was high, particularly among long-time Betty Terrell and Fischel customers. Therefore, the firm relied on the quality and design of the merchandise to move garments off the rack. Even among buyers, Johnston advertised infrequently, depending upon name reputation, to induce a visit to the showroom during market week. Co-op advertising with particular retail outlets was not considered feasible due to high cost and limited exposure. Each year, one or two half-page ads (@ $2,000) were run in *The New Yorker,* a reflection of the era when that magazine was read by Johnston's primary market.[4]

But management had important advertising concerns, particularly given brand proliferation in the markets. Should the advertising budget be redirected? Was it possible to increase brand awareness? Could a small company compete with the well known women's clothing designers who were entering the children's market? Or should the emphasis be placed upon retail buyer promotions, with price-off deals and co-op newspaper ads?

A brand campaign was not easy. If the attempt were made, it was not clear whether the emphasis should be placed upon "best sellers" (a standard, simple item) or "fashion" items. Should the message be directed at the mother or grandmother? Which aspect of the products should be mentioned—line, color, design, practicality, quality?

Finally, store contacts might be enhanced by spending money educating the selling personnel about merchandising techniques, including how to display the groups, how to coordinate the Johnston garments with those from other resources, and how to order appropriately.

Bob Johnston also considered the greater use of selected promotional techniques which would substitute value attributes for quality attributes. For example, spring sunsuits could be "offered at a special price due to surplus fabric and labor." In this offering, there would be no markdown money, advertising money, or rebates. But if the company made such offerings, even late in a selling season, would the result cannibalize the regular line? Would the firm lower the reputation of its name?

In recapping Johnston's marketing strategy, it is revealing to note Bob's answer to two questions:

1. What is your firm's uniqueness—your essential strength?
    "Complete designer collections with matching wardrobes, quality in design, product flexibility, and our inherent belief in good taste."

---

[3]This amount of advertising is deceptively low. Frequently, leading specialty and department stores will advertise in catalogs and newsprint the brand label in order to enhance their prestige among consumers.
[4]See Exhibit C-3.

EXHIBIT C-3   Johnston, Inc.: Advertisement

Betti Terrell®
By Johnston

My Friend Charlie on my clothes,
in my arms, and in my book.
Charlie Goes Fishin' sundress and
panties in white polyester/cotton
with blue edging and applique,
about $22. 9, 12 and 18 mos. sizes.
Stuffed bear, about $9. 32-pg.
"My Friend Charlie" book about $4.

*Godchaux's / Joseph Horne / Lord & Taylor
and other fine stores*

Johnston, Inc.
Box 15125, Dallas, Texas 75201

1 col. x 71 lines
Space & production cost $1453.00
New Yorker Magazine — 3-28-77

2. What are your company's goals and objectives?
"To survive; to grow within limits so as to maintain our niche; to do better by expanding present accounts and adding new ones; to increase in a timely manner our productive capacity; to optimize the impact of our salesforce by teaching them how to relate even better to customers."

GROWTH POSSIBILITIES

Bob Johnston liked to describe the prospects for growth as dependent upon four variables: design; production/organization; contact with the "rest of the world" (ROW); and image with store buyers. It was his philosophy that these four were interrelated and that growth was premised upon the proper balance among them.

Take, for example, a new design concept created by Carolyn and requiring increased production capability. For the design to succeed, it had to be accepted by the retail buyers, an acceptance based upon their reading of the "ROW" (i.e., the consumer market). Similarly, if the buyers "wanted" a particular design from a manufacturer in order to broaden their look, the "ROW" must be induced to want this design, and the plant must be made capable of producing it. The interdependence between manufacturer, buyer, and consumer was critical and delicate.

Growth, in Johnston's opinion, could be viewed a number of ways. In the first place, growth could be defined as increased revenue sufficient to cover inflated costs. Unfortunately, raising prices for this purpose was not always possible. In many markets, for example, there seemed to be some psychological price barriers. A $25 gift might be acceptable, but not one for $26. Hence, growth to cover costs might have to be obtained through volume and, therefore, lower unit costs.

Or growth might be more strategically oriented, such as "present products, expanded distribution." Such a move would probably entail maintenance of the multi-label format (namely, exclusive franchise lines and open lines) but selling to more outlets. The question would be how to accomplish this goal. If exclusiveness were the selling proposition, then expansion would only be possible by finding markets not already covered by stores presently carrying the line. This would basically require selling to smaller stores in areas outside the mainstream of department store operations, because most major cities already had at least one store carrying the Johnston franchise line. Moreover, selling to smaller stores involved greater risk and uncertainty. These markets represented a credit sensitive area of the market in which total quantities purchased were smaller. The mortality rate of small specialty stores was excessive. Thus, it would probably require that new sales rely heavily on the "open lines."

Unfortunately, certain key buyers who presently had the franchise felt very strongly about exclusives. They argued that their department's reputation was based primarily on image and uniqueness. They resented new franchises. Whether they would cease ordering Johnston garments if the firm expanded was unknown. (Of the top 15 buyers, at least three were adamant about retaining exclusivity.)

Or growth could come from product redefinition with the same or expanded distribution. Product redefinition might consist of shrinking to one label, reducing or expanding size availability, and reducing or expanding collection designs. Let's consider these separately:

One Label or Many

The issues introduced by this alternative were several. Would the firm's focus be on present customers or new ones? Would the concept be applied to present products or to new ones? What did "exclusivity" mean as department stores expanded from coast to coast? Did "exclusivity" matter to a customer? What effect would one label have on small shops which had positioned themselves on the concept of "uniqueness, originality, and exclusivity?" Would sales drop because fewer items were offered (consolidation of line with Betti Terrell for infants, toddlers, and kindergarten)? Would those customers who now bought from both the franchise and open lines buy less because all garments carried the same label? Was a buyer concerned with how many labels a department carried? If the lines were consolidated, and therefore the number of styles reduced, would the buyer purchase collection groups in greater depth or as sparingly as at present?[5] Would departments who presently carried the Fischel line and the Betti Terrell label experience a reduction in sales because of customer unfamiliarity with the name? Did customers buy labels? Store image? Store name?

Size Availability

As mentioned earlier, Johnston manufactured layette, infant, toddler, girls 4–6 and girls 7–12-year-old lines. Was it possible to further expand into the 7–12 size bracket in order to fill a need, expressed by various buyers, for elegant but "young looking" clothes (in contrast to most 7–12 sizes, which were miniature versions of the junior market)? The size of the market was hard to estimate. And there were important differences among retailers and users. For instance, the buying staff was generally different; the department was located in a different area on the children's floor; the child himself had more involvement in the buying decision (she/he wants the grown-up look); and the Johnston name was unfamiliar to consumer and retailer.

Collection Design

Johnston could eliminate certain designs from the line, by concentrating on dresses or sportswear, for example. However, the Johnston brand was essentially

---

[5]Carolyn designed several groups, each around a unique theme, integrating fabric, color, and style. Each group normally consisted of interchangeable dresses, skirts, pants, jackets, overalls, and boy's shortalls or overalls.

strong because the company manufactured a "total concept." If this concept were eliminated, then the company might lose buyers who purchased for this reason. And Johnston would find itself in direct competition with established children's clothing manufacturers who had always specialized. Usually these specialists' strong selling point was the "total look" composed of interchangeable dresses, pants, skirts, jackets, blouses, and matching brother-sister outfits. Thus, any change from the present "total" format would probably shift the buying patterns, both in stores and quantity purchased.

Case D
Sigtronics, Inc.

In such a diversified company, it is extremely difficult to properly allocate limited financial resources among what appear to be so many attractive investment opportunities. Unfortunately, there are no easy solutions, only difficult choices.

In the spring of 1978, Sandra Greenberg, Special Projects Analyst in the Corporate Planning Department of Sigtronics, Inc., a highly diversified manufacturing company based on the West Coast with 1977 sales of approximately $730 million and over 30 separate product divisions, was concerned with improving the methods by which "strategic expenditures" were allocated and spent within the company.

STRATEGIC EXPENDITURES

Strategic expenditures were considered to be those funds invested for the future position of the company. They were not those expenses necessary to manufacture and sell current products, but rather were "investments" made to improve the business(es) in the years ahead. Such "strategic expenditures" could be capital expenditures as well as expense items, but Greenberg's current interest was primarily in controlling strategic expenses. These were significant in that the company recently had been spending about $35 million a year in the strategic expense category, and in a typical year, such an amount was larger than either capital expenditures or after-tax profits.

Strategic expenses included a variety of improvements in capability which were considered crucial for the survival and success of a business. Illustrative of the types of projects which would qualify for categorization as strategic expenses were the following:

New product development
Improvement of existing products

This case was prepared by Professor Edwin A. Murray, Jr. of Boston University and is printed here with his permission.

New market development
Cost and operating expense reduction
Increase capital turnover
Advertise the company and its products
Marketing and distribution improvements

The effective management of strategic expenses was of major importance because they represented basically a reduction of current profits, and they could substantially affect the size, direction of growth, and future profitability of the company's various divisions. In general, management sought to control strategic expenditures so as to derive the maximum possible future benefit for the company. Whereas the capital investments were handled separately and consisted of after-tax dollars, the strategic *expense* items had in the past been mixed in with operating costs. However, if they were isolated for a typical division of Sigtronics, they would represent about 5% of the division's annual revenue. (In an "average" division, "product costs" would constitute about 60% of the division's sales, "operating costs" another 30%, and pre-tax profits would be approximately 5%.)

Division management traditionally had had wide discretion in trading off strategic expenses for current profits and *vice versa*. However, there were practical limits on the degree to which one could be foregone for the sake of the other— at least at the corporate level. Without adequate current profits, the company would incur the risk of adverse investor reaction and a concomitant unavailability (or at least increased cost) of capital with which to finance future growth. On the other hand, unless certain minimal strategic expenditures were made on an on-going basis, the long-term competitive (and profit) position of the company would deteriorate. Nevertheless, within such limits, management had considerable discretion.

THE COMPANY

Both current and future profitability were of high priority to Sigtronics' corporate management. Said Robert Ferris, President:

> Like many major diversified corporations, we aspire to "Blue Chip" status in the eyes of the investment community. This has meant a steadfast commitment to rewarding our shareholders with a consistently and dependably high return on their investment. As a consequence, we cannot afford to forego either short-range or long-range profitability, even for the cause of trading off one temporariliy for the other. We need to preserve both at all times, at least insofar as it is within our ability to do so.

The company operated, as did many "diversified majors" with a sizable corporate staff and used 6 group vice presidents to oversee the operations of the divisions which were grouped according to like markets and technologies. (See Exhibit D-1 for an organization chart.) Each group vice president had 4–6

EXHIBIT D-1   Sigtronics, Inc.:: Partial Organization Chart

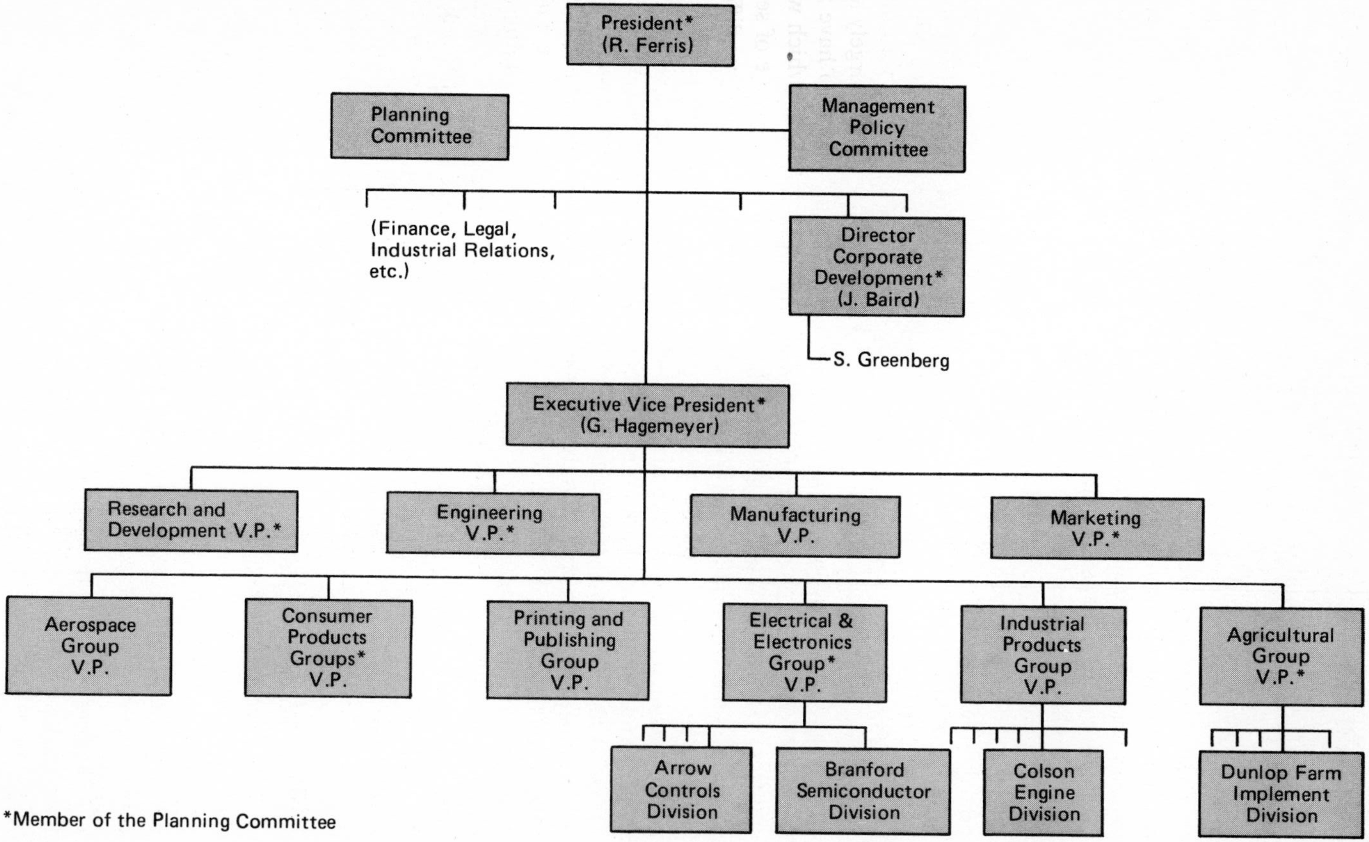

*Member of the Planning Committee

divisions for which he was responsible and this involved participation in their long-range planning and budgeting processes.

With prime interest rates expected to go above the 10% mark by the end of 1978 and profit margins chronically below those of many of its major competitors, there was growing concern that external funds would be limited for the company over the next few years. Still, the corporation had set ambitious growth and profitability targets, and in order to meet its short-term profit objectives, strategic expense funds would be limited to 4% of sales. Therefore, management sought to spend its limited strategic funds to maximum advantage.

PROPOSED SOLUTIONS

In order to do this more effectively, the corporate planning staff was asked to consider ways in which corporate management could take a greater part in managing the affairs of the divisions so that they coincided more readily with group and corporate interests. One area being considered for more attention was that of strategic expenses. In the past, they had been decided upon largely at the discretion of the division managers, but it now seemed desirable to have them more closely reviewed and adjusted to accord with those activities which would contribute the most to group and corporate objectives. In the course of several discussions with others in the company, Greenberg had developed three different approaches:

Project Approach

Under this method, divisions would submit to their group managements various projects which the group vice presidents would then consolidate into a single list, rank-ordered in terms of desirability from a group viewpoint. This ranking would take place at meetings attended by division personnel. Also attending these meetings would be a three-person corporate task force consisting of representatives from the marketing, engineering, and planning departments. This task force would then develop a single, consolidated list of division projects for all the groups ranked according to corporate priorities. This final list would be the basis for allocating corporate resources.

Statistical Approach

This method was designed to apportion the company's resources among the groups based on a number of "external factors" which could be calculated from data gathered by surveying the groups. These factors would be averaged according to a formula such as the one below and the resulting score would be converted to a percentage figure so that the total for all the groups would equal 100%.

$$\text{Overall Group Score} = \frac{\text{Factor 1} + \text{Factor 2} + \text{Factor 3}}{3}$$

Where Factor 1 = 1987 Market + 10-year Growth + Technological
                    Growth Potential[1]

       Factor 2 = 1987 Market + Technological Growth Potential

       Factor 3 = 1977 Sales + 1977 Market + 1987 Market + 10-year
                    Growth + Technological Growth Potential

Analytic Approach

The purpose of this method was to maximize the ratio:

$$\frac{\text{Corporate Profit Before Taxes}}{\text{Corporate Strategic Expenses}}$$

$$\text{Where} \quad \frac{\text{Corp. PBT}}{\text{Corp. SE}} = \frac{\Sigma\ (PBT_1 + PBT_2 + \ldots + PBT_n)}{\Sigma\ (SE_1 + SE_2 + \ldots + SE_n)}$$

and 1, 2, . . ., n refer to divisions 1 to n.

In general, the idea was to allocate the individual amounts of SE on the basis of the estimated improvements of PBT which would result, always attempting to gain the largest increase in PBT for a given amount of SE. More specifically, the divisions were asked to estimate their 1983 PBT based upon their actual SE budgeted for 1978, 0.9 × actual, and 1.5 × actual. It was then possible to computerize a procedure whereby all divisions were cut back to 0.9 × their budgeted amounts and the resulting funds reallocated to those divisions projecting the greatest increase in PBT provided funds could be restored (to 1.0 × actual) or increased (to 1.5 × actual). In this way, the same absolute amount of strategic expenses was expected to yield a PBT for the corporation about 15% higher than if every division proceeded as planned with its budgeted strategic expenses. This approach would be applicable at the group level as well as to individual projects within a division.

A TRIAL APPLICATION

While examining ways to more satisfactorily allocate strategic expense funds, Greenberg had come up with the idea of using the simplified situations of four representative divisions to test both the logic and the practicality of some of the

---

[1]Technological Growth Potential was a ranking assigned to each of the company's six groups. It was arrived at by assigning arbitrary weights to each of four factors for each group's major product lines: breakthrough opportunity (the probability of major technological developments being introduced to the product line by 1982); new product potential (the relative number of new products conceivable for each group); importance of cost reduction (the degree to which cost reduction was important to the product lines success); and styling (the relative importance of styling on the success of the product line). A score for each major product line was thus calculated and these were combined to give a group score which was then used to develop a group ranking.

methods proposed. She thought that by trying to cope with a specific problem involving the distribution of strategic expense funds, the Planning Committee[2] would be able to evaluate the methods described above or perhaps devise new and more effective approaches to the problem. In any event, they would be able to focus on the main issues from a new and more concrete perspective. Greenberg explained this approach to the Planning Committee:

> In many ways, these four divisions are representative of the diversity inherent in a firm like Sigtronics. What is not so clear is how we are to go about making intelligent investments for the future in such dissimilar units. Our task will be that of allocating limited strategic expense funds to these four divisions in a way that best serves the long-term interests of the corporation.
>
> We have past performance data and future projections for each division, along with a short summary of respective product lines and industries. Histories of strategic expenditures and forecasted needs for strategic funds have also been provided. For simplicity, let's assume that in each division depreciation funds are reinvested in new plant and equipment to remain competitive. Let us further assume that net worth is proportional to sales in each case.
>
> If strategic expense funds within the company are going to be constrained to about 4% of sales, one would expect to be able to predict the level of future strategic funds for these divisions. However, whereas past performance data show total strategic expenditures for the four divisions around 4 or 5% of aggregate sales, strategic fund requests for 1978 through 1982 far outstrip that percentage of sales. [At this point, Greenberg displayed Table 1 shown on page 616.]
>
> The real challenge will be to resolve the discrepancies between what is available (presumably an amount approximating 4% of sales) and what has been requested by the divisions. To do this properly, we must not only keep within the limit of funds available, but we must allocate these funds to the four divisions in a manner which would most effectively improve the future position of Sigtronics.

Greenberg then distributed thumbnail sketches of the four sample divisions which were intended to provide some basis for distributing the strategic funds for 1978. These descriptions follow:

ARROW CONTROLS DIVISION

The products of this division included a wide range of circuit breakers, automatic switches, bus ducts, and miscellaneous electrical controls and accessories. Most of the products were for industrial use and were sold nationally to original

---

[2]Consisted of nine of the top officers of the company, including Ferris, President; Hagemayer, Executive Vice President; and Baird, Director of Corporate Planning.

TABLE 1
STRATEGIC EXPENSE FUNDS—AVAILABLE AND REQUESTED
(Dollar amounts in millions)

	Year	Available Strategic Funds for 4 Divisions (Based on 4% of Actual or Projected Sales)	Strategic Funds Invested or Requested by 4 Divisions (Based Upon Their Past and Projected Needs)
	1973	$4.3	$4.5
Actual	1974	4.7	5.0
Operating	1975	5.1	5.6
History	1976	5.4	6.0
	1977	5.8	6.7
	1978	6.3	8.5
	1979	6.9	11.2
Estimated	1980	7.6	15.0
	1981	8.3	20.5
	1982	9.0	29.0

equipment manufacturers or to industrial supply houses. All of the manufacturing operations were concentrated in one location in facilities which had been built largely during World War II.

Past Performance

Sales growth in recent years had been rapid, growing at a 12% compound annual rate, and 1977's net sales were in excess of $42 million. This division enjoyed the largest market share in the industry, with the next two competitors having approximately 15% each and most of the remaining sales divided among a dozen smaller firms. Largely because of this industry leadership, the division had been able to command healthy margins. As a consequence, it had been one of the most profitable divisions in Sigtronics. (Operating results for the past five years are shown in Exhibit D-2.)

Looking Ahead

The outlook for the industry largely influenced the Arrow Controls Division's projections for future operations. After an anticipated market growth of 11% in 1978, it was expected that primary demand for electrical controls would plateau or even decline to a more stable 5% growth per annum. Through heavy investments in aggressive marketing programs, however, the division forecasted sales growth rates up to 15% per annum and an increased market share. (Projections are shown in Exhibit D-2.)

EXHIBIT D-2   Arrow Controls Division
(Dollar amounts in millions)

Past Operating Results

Year Ended Dec. 31	Net Sales	Net Income*	Market Share	Strategic Funds Invested*
1973	$27.1	$2.0 (7.4%)	30.4%	$1.3 (4.8%)
1974	30.3	2.1 (6.9%)	31.2	1.4 (4.6%)
1975	33.7	2.7 (8.0%)	31.7	1.7 (5.0%)
1976	37.6	3.2 (8.5%)	32.0	1.9 (5.0%)
1977	42.6	3.8 (8.9%)	32.8	2.1 (4.9%)

Projected Results

Year Ended Dec. 31	Net Sales	Net Income*	Market Share	Strategic Funds Requested*
1978	$48.5	$4.4 (9.1%)	33.5%	$2.4 (4.9%)
1979	55.8	4.5 (8.1%)	34.7	2.8 (5.0%)
1980	63.2	5.1 (8.1%)	35.5	3.2 (5.1%)
1981	70.8	5.3 (7.5%)	36.0	3.8 (5.4%)
1982	78.0	5.5 (7.1%)	36.1	4.6 (5.9%)

*Figures in parentheses indicate percentage of sales.

BRANFORD SEMICONDUCTOR DIVISION

The division produced and marketed many electronic components including diodes and rectifiers, transistors, and a number of special devices and circuit elements. Most of the division's output went to industrial supply houses where it was further distributed to manufacturers of electronic components. Some of the division's products were sold to other divisions within Sigtronics.

Past Performance

Semiconductor devices had been in great demand since the mid-1950s, largely as a result of the great scientific and technological development effort precipitated by the launching of Sputnik. Growth in the industry had been rapid and sustained; 1977's total market sales had increased by as much as 20% from 1976's volume. In general, 15% per annum in sales had characterized the industry.

The Branford Semiconductor Division had matched industry sales growth, but had never managed to sustain superior growth. This was because many firms competed with the division, and consequently, product innovations within the industry were frequent and often short-lived. Great amounts of research and development funds were necessary just to remain competitive with the more than

200 firms in the industry. No one of these firms seemed capable of achieving more than a 15% share of the market. However, there were signs of the industry entering a consolidation phase, and the companies that emerged would be larger and more profitable than most present firms.

Division profits had been uneven and well below corporate averages due to start-up expenses in the mid-1950s and depressed semiconductor business in the early 1960s and 1970s. Even in 1974 and 1976 losses of $100,000 and $400,000, respectively, had been incurred. (Operating results for the past five years are shown in Exhibit D-3.)

Looking Ahead

Profits were regarded as having excellent possibilities for growth as shown in the division's five-year projections. According to the division manager:

> For the immediate future we see no slowdown in the projected indus-
> try sales growth rate of 15% per year. By investing as we have in product
> development projects, we should be able to maintain our share of market
> at 5% or even increase it slightly.
> For example, we have plans to develop a wide range of new products
> which are either offered by others or are under development. These

EXHIBIT D-3   Branford Semiconductor Division
         (Dollar amounts in millions)

Past Operating Results

Year Ended Dec. 31	Net Sales	Net Income*	Market Share	Strategic Funds Invested*
1973	$16.4	$0.1 (0.6%)	4.8%	$0.7 (4.3%)
1974	19.8	−0.2 (−%)	4.9	0.9 (4.5%)
1975	23.0	0.1 (0.4%)	4.9	1.1 (4.8%)
1976	26.2	−0.4 (−%)	4.9	1.5 (5.7%)
1977	30.7	0.6 (2.0%)	5.0	2.2 (7.2%)

Projected Results

Year Ended Dec. 31	Net Sales	Net Income*	Market Share	Strategic Funds Requested*
1978	$35.2	$0.7 (2.0%)	5.0%	$3.2 (9.1%)
1979	40.8	1.2 (2.9%)	5.0	4.9 (12.0%)
1980	47.8	1.9 (4.0%)	5.1	7.3 (15.3%)
1981	55.0	2.8 (5.1%)	5.1	11.0 (20.0%)
1982	64.0	4.5 (7.0%)	5.1	17.0 (26.6%)

*Figures in parentheses indicate percentage of sales.

products include thermoelectric cooling and generating devices, solar cells, and micro-miniature circuits. Although they are much more complex and costly to develop than previous products, only by keeping up with other firms can we remain competitive.

At the same time, we feel that additional strategic funds will be necessary to provide for improved production methods so that we can increase our yields. Only by making these investments now can we expect to become respectably profitable within the next few years. Our projections reflect these improved operations. Frankly, if we don't become more profitable soon, the company may have to rethink its decision to stay in the electronic component field.

(The projections for the division are shown in Exhibit D-3.)

COLSON ENGINE DIVISION

This division was characterized by a stable, concentrated product line of gasoline engines under 3 horsepower which were used to power a variety of devices such as compressors, power lawn mowers, rototillers, irrigation pumps, etc. All of the division's production output was sold to original equipment manufacturers and industrial supply houses (for replacement use).

There had been very few technological changes in recent years. Consequently, one corporate executive expressed the opinion that development costs (such as a staff of 20 product development engineers) were a needless expense in such a division.

> This is a very mature field, and about all they [the development engineers] do is change the appearance now and then and occasionally rearrange the controls. From a corporate standpoint, we might do much better to invest elsewhere.

Past Performance

As shown in Exhibit D-4, profitability had been well above the corporation average of 4% return on sales, with 1977's net income representing 9% of sales. The cash throw-off in 1977 was slightly more than $8 million, making the division a substantial generator of funds within the company.

Outlook

Although market share had dropped from 57% in 1973 to 55% in 1977, it was expected that the division could match industry sales growth in the future, thus retaining its share of the market. The annual growth rate for the industry was forecast as a steady 3%, down from 5% in 1973. Strategic funds would be needed in moderate amounts to support promotional programs aimed at maintaining market share. (Projections were as shown in Exhibit D-4.)

EXHIBIT D-4   Colson Engine Division
(Dollar amounts in millions)

Past Operating Results

Year Ended Dec. 31	Net Sales	Net Income*	Market Share	Strategic Funds Invested*
1973	$46.0	$3.7 (8.0%)	57.0%	$1.6 (3.5%)
1974	47.4	4.0 (8.4%)	56.0	1.7 (3.6%)
1975	49.0	4.2 (8.6%)	55.3	1.7 (3.5%)
1976	50.3	4.5 (8.9%)	54.8	1.8 (3.6%)
1977	52.0	4.7 (9.0%)	55.0	1.8 (3.5%)

Projected Results

Year Ended Dec. 31	Net Sales	Net Income*	Market Share	Strategic Funds Requested*
1978	$53.6	$4.8 (9.0%)	55.2%	$1.9 (3.5%)
1979	51.1	4.9 (9.6%)	55.0	2.0 (3.9%)
1980	57.0	5.1 (8.9%)	55.0	2.2 (3.9%)
1981	58.8	5.3 (9.0%)	55.1	2.3 (3.9%)
1982	60.6	5.5 (9.1%)	55.2	2.4 (4.0%)

*Figures in parentheses indicate percentage of sales.

DUNLOP FARM IMPLEMENT DIVISION

For many years this division had attempted to gain entry to the huge farm equipment market. It offered a limited line of high quality, multi-purpose implements for use on small farms where it was thought operators could not afford the substantial inventory of specialized equipment typically found on larger farms. Distribution of this division's product line was handled through a small group of independent farm equipment dealers.

Because the farm implement industry was dominated by a few large manufacturers with extensive distribution channels, product acceptance was hampered by lack of a strong nationwide service organization.

Past Performance

Extensive product development costs had depressed the division's profitability in recent years, and the industry as a whole had suffered a sharp decline in the *rate* of sales growth in 1975. That same year, the Dunlop Division had introduced a new product line with disappointing sales results, leading to a loss in excess of $3 million. (Results for the past five years are show in Exhibit D-5.)

EXHIBIT D-5   Dunlop Farm Implement Division
              (Dollar amounts in millions)

Past Operating Results

Year Ended Dec. 31	Net Sales	Net Income*	Market Share	Strategic Funds Invested*
1973	$18.3	$0.8 (4.4%)	2.1%	$0.9 (4.9%)
1974	19.8	1.1 (5.6%)	2.2	1.0 (5.1%)
1975	22.0	−0.5 (−%)	2.3	1.1 (5.0%)
1976	21.6	−3.2 (−%)	2.2	0.8 (3.7%)
1977	20.7	−1.7 (−%)	2.0	0.6 (2.9%)

Projected Results

Year Ended Dec. 31	Net Sales	Net Income*	Market Share	Strategic Funds Requested*
1978	$20.9	−2.0 (−%)	1.9%	1.0 (4.8%)
1979	21.2	−1.0 (−%)	1.9	1.5 (7.1%)
1980	21.5	0.0 (−%)	1.8	2.3 (10.7%)
1981	21.7	1.0 (4.6%)	1.7	3.4 (15.7%)
1982	22.0	1.0 (4.5%)	1.7	5.0 (22.7%)

*Figures in parentheses indicate percentage of sales.

Outlook

With farm equipment sales growth projected at 5% per year, division management anticipated a decline in market share unless substantial increases in strategic funds could be obtained for expanding channels of distribution and service facilities. By aggressively marketing existing product lines, it was thought that stable profitability could be achieved by 1981.

Case E
International Engineering, Inc.

In late 1970s much attention was focused on utility companies and the role they would play in supplying additional amounts of electricity to meet the growing energy demands created by business, industry, and home consumers. While geothermal, wind, solar, fusion, and breeder reactors might be the energy sources of tomorrow, the electric utility companies rely on either fossil fuel or nuclear power plants to generate electricity today and for the next few decades. Whereas nuclear power plants might in the future be the most economical and efficient means of producing electrical power, today they present many drawbacks, both economical and social, which have resulted in utilities placing more reliance on fossil fuel generating systems. Because of the relative scarcity of natural gas and the escalating cost of fuel oil, most of the fossil fuel plants that were in operation in 1980 or would be coming into operation in the next few years were of the coal-fired type.

One company that was heavily involved in serving the utility industry was International Engineering, Inc. (IEI), a Michigan-based firm that designed, manufactured, and sold fossil fuel and nuclear steam supply systems and components for use in generating electricity. Of the approximately 1500 coal-fired power plants in operation in the United States in 1980, about 600 of them were designed, manufactured, and built by IEI. Exhibit E-1 shows where most of these coal-fired plants were located and the areas where the growth of coal-fired plants was expected to occur over the next few years. Coupled with this growing market in coal-fired steam generating systems was a growing market in replacement sales, i.e., sales of those parts of a generating station that eventually wear out or break. The growth rate of this replacement market over the next few years had been estimated at about 5 percent per year. Replacement sales was a sizeable amount of IEI's total sales picture, accounting for about 3 percent of total sales. Exhibits E-2 and E-3 show IEI's financial statements for the year 1979.

Realizing this growth potential of both coal-fired generating stations and the accompanying market for replacement parts, one could expect a steady growth of sales of each over the next few decades. Such was not the case, however, for one particular product of IEI's replacement line, that of coal pulverizer rings and rolls.

EXHIBIT E-1   Present and Potential Areas for Coal-fired Power Generation Plants in the U.S.

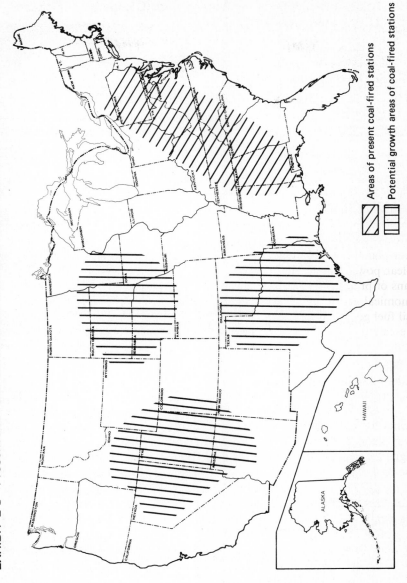

Areas of present coal-fired stations

Potential growth areas of coal-fired stations

Source: Company records.

EXHIBIT E-2   International Engineering, Inc.: Comparative Financial Statistics, 1970–1979

(Dollars in Thousands, Except per Share Amounts)	1979(5)	1978	1977(5)
Summary of Operations			
Net Sales	$2,757,504	$2,331,751	$2,044,764
Costs and Expenses—			
Cost of sales	$2,373,357	$2,006,266	$1,776,518
Selling, general and administrative expenses	213,402	178,041	145,742
	$2,586,759	$2,184,307	$1,922,260
Operating Income	$ 170,745	$ 147,444	$ 122,504
Other Income and (Deductions)—			
Interest expense	(16,663)	(18,400)	(11,563)
Miscellaneous, net	32,499	29,972	22,068
Income Before Income Taxes and Extraordinary Items	$ 186,581	$ 159,016	$ 133,009
Taxes on Income	88,940	78,700	65,820
Income Before Extraordinary Items	$ 97,641	$ 80,316	$ 67,189
Extraordinary Items (3)	—	—	—
Net income	$ 97,641	$ 80,316	$ 67,189
Net Income per Share (2)—			
Income before extraordinary items	$ 5.96	$ 4.97	$ 4.17
Extraordinary items (3)	—	—	—
Net income	$ 5.96	$ 4.97	$ 4.17
Average Shares Outstanding (2)	16,371,638	16,171,116	16,117,125
Cash Dividends Declared—			
Total	$ 35,892	$ 29,105	$ 24,098
Per share—			
Common	2.20	1.80	1.50
Preferred	—	.85	1.70
Other Financial Statistics			
Current Assets	$1,428,639	$1,252,542	$1,086,841
Current Liabilities	1,144,337	978,948	894,123
Working Capital	284,302	273,594	192,718
Property, Plant and Equipment, net	515,983	450,866	437,145
Investments and Other Assets	136,756	132,171	128,948
Deferred Income Taxes and Investment Tax Credit	232,981	222,999	169,960
Long-term Debt	144,386	139,639	147,270
Shareholders' Equity			
Amount	559,674	493,993	441,581
Per share (4)	34.26	30.58	27.30
Capital Expenditures	$ 146,741	$ 74,904	$ 122,055
Depreciation and Amortization	66,138	52,567	39,630
Orders Received	$2,897,763	$2,298,490	$2,111,246
Unfilled Orders	2,986,465	2,879,929	2,968,556
Employees	43,286	45,729	44,770
Shareholders of Record	26,742	26,451	26,596

1. In 1974, the Company changed to the last-in, first-out (LIFO) method of inventory valuation with respect to certain domestic inventories (generally inventories other than those involved in long-term contract work). The LIFO method was adopted because the rapid increase in prices would have resulted in an overstatement of profits if use of the average, or first-in, first-out (FIFO) method were continued, since inventories sold were replaced at substantially higher prices. The effect of this change was to reduce net income for the year 1974 by $5,887,919 equal to $.37 per share.

2. Net income per share was based on the average number of shares outstanding. Average shares outstanding include (a) the average number of common shares outstanding, (b) common shares issuable on the conversion of the Series A Convertible Preferred Stock, prior to redemption in July, 1978, (c) in the years 1970 through 1974, estimated shares to be released from escrow based on earnings of certain companies subsequent to acquisition and (d) in the years 1971, 1972, 1973 and 1979, the assumed exercise of all outstanding stock options. The average number of shares outstanding in each period has been adjusted where necessary to give effect retroactive to a 2-for-1 stock split in 1970, a 3-for-2 stock split in 1977, and shares issued in connection with significant poolings of interest.

1976(5)	1975	1974	1973	1972	1971	1970
$1,830,925	$1,711,151	$1,428,028	$1,168,578	$1,054,532	$ 960,910	$ 879,204
$1,601,773	$1,513,297	$1,253,616	$ 998,987	$ 902,596	$ 819,794	$ 747,439
122,117	109,317	94,336	87,484	77,181	69,857	65,984
$1,723,890	$1,622,614	$1,347,952	$1,086,471	$ 979,777	$ 889,651	$ 813,423
$ 107,035	$ 88,537	$ 80,076	$ 82,107	$ 74,755	$ 71,259	$ 65,781
(9,989)	(10,119)	(11,704)	(9,561)	(8,643)	(6,273)	(5,964)
8,147	5,024	5,472	6,885	6,387	3,845	3,135
$ 105,193	$ 83,442	$ 73,844	$ 79,431	$ 72,499	$ 68,831	$ 62,952
50,990	38,850	33,660	36,340	32,980	32,100	30,630
$ 54,203	$ 44,592	$ 40,184	$ 43,091	$ 39,519	$ 36,731	$ 32,322
		(2,700)		(16,000)		
$ 54,203	$ 44,592	$ 37,484(1)	$ 43,091	$ 23,519	$ 36,731	$ 32,322
$ 3.36	$ 2.77	$ 2.50	$ 2.70	$ 2.48	$ 2.34	$ 2.09
—	—	(.17)	—	(1.00)	—	—
$ 3.36	$ 2.77	$ 2.33(1)	$ 2.70	$ 1.48	$ 2.34	$ 2.09
16,121,660	16,083,514	16,080,781	15,952,219	15,930,967	15,722,697	15,467,769
$ 21,188	$ 20,137	$ 18,617	$ 16,320	$ 15,160	$ 14,195	$ 13,237
1.316	1.25	1.152	.997	.958	.917	.85
1.70	1.70	1.70	1.70	1.70	1.70	1.70
$ 876,259	$ 717,029	$ 662,049	$ 523,588	$ 484,278	$ 458,427	$ 388,275
663,412	529,623	494,088	373,170	329,435	315,977	281,544
212,847	187,406	167,961	150,418	154,843	142,450	106,731
358,741	315,850	297,339	266,536	219,096	203,145	182,731
54,643	35,977	38,111	40,622	39,976	64,820	65,215
99,638	57,802	41,669	14,946	9,557	20,931	19,104
128,176	116,497	121,242	121,490	107,116	103,193	75,348
398,417	364,934	340,500	321,140	297,242	286,291	260,225
24.31	22.12	20.49	19.15	17.64	17.15	15.47
$ 81,446	$ 50,621	$ 61,796	$ 57,330	$ 38,747	$ 42,336	$ 35,370
33,030	29,653	27,744	23,868	19,765	17,972	15,723
$1,738,626	$1,527,288	$2,515,965	$1,999,142	$1,220,497	$ 979,133	$1,130,262
2,980,098	3,132,481	3,347,114	2,288,011	1,477,500	1,350,050	1,337,121
42,843	45,938	40,765	35,316	34,950	33,374	32,645
25,536	25,212	24,758	21,305	21,549	21,390	19,252

3. Represents, in 1972 and 1974, a provision for loss on the disposition of the holding in United Nuclear Equipment Corporation, less in each case the effect of applicable income taxes ($15,000,000 in 1972 and $2,500,000 in 1974).
4. Based on net assets and common shares outstanding at year-end.
5. Includes Thompson Company for periods subsequent to October, 1976, Lumco Inc. for the periods subsequent to November, 1977, and Basic Incorporated for the period subsequent to January, 1979.

EXHIBIT E-3   International Engineering, Inc.: Financial Reporting by Business Segments

The Company's equipment, products and services are classified into the following business segments: (a) design, manufacture, installation and service of steam generating systems and equipment for the electric utility industry including nuclear steam supply systems; (b) design, engineering and construction services (principally through its subsidiary, The Lummus Company), primarily for the chemical, petrochemical and petroleum industries; (or equipment supplied to industrial markets) and (d) products and services supplied to industrial markets. The following tables present financial data by business segment:

(Dollars in Thousands)	1979	1978	1977
Sales (1)—			
Steam generating systems, equipment and services for the electric utility industry	$ 926,220	$ 815,767	$ 747,808
Design, engineering and construction services	351,719	308,438	300,698
Equipment for industrial markets	815,563	688,815	606,338
Products and services for industrial markets	664,002	518,731	389,920
Total	$2,757,504	$2,331,751	$2,044,764
Operating Profit—			
Steam generating systems, equipment and services for the electric utility industry	$ 65,166	$ 56,985	$ 46,451
Design, engineering and construction services	27,979	27,663	24,664
Equipment for industrial markets	81,167	62,823	53,477
Products and services for industrial markets	25,948	20,819	13,147
Total	$ 200,260	$ 168,290	$ 137,739
Equity in Net Earnings of Associated and Other Companies (2)	4,340	1,397	1,775
Interest Expense	(16,663)	(18,400)	(11,563)
Unallocated—			
Corporate expense	(16,356)	(14,443)	(12,141)
Miscellaneous, net	15,000	22,172	17,199
Consolidated income before income taxes	$ 186,581	$ 159,016	$ 133,009

December 31,	1979	1978	1977
Identifiable Assets—			
Steam generating systems, equipment and services for the electric utility industry	$ 432,133	$ 385,962	$ 358,021
Design, engineering and construction services	151,989	135,746	135,230
Equipment for industrial markets	548,756	515,815	550,387
Products and services for industrial markets	451,069	349,927	334,883
Total	$1,583,947	$1,387,450	$1,378,521
Investments in Associated and Other Companies (Equity Basis) (2)	50,713	33,172	20,988
Corporate and Unallocated Assets, net (3)	448,300	416,325	254,765
Consolidated	$2,082,960	$1,836,947	$1,654,274

1. Includes only sales to unaffiliated customers (intersegment sales are not significant) and no single customer accounts for 10% or more of the consolidated sales.
2. Companies accounted for under the equity method of accounting (20% or more owned) are located principally in the United States, Europe and other foreign areas. The principal companies included in this category are not vertically integrated with the operations of the Company and its consolidated subsidiaries. Such companies are engaged in the manufacture and sale of steam generating equipment for utility and industrial use and other equipment, products and services for industrial markets.
3. Includes primarily cash, marketable securities and corporate facilities.
Depreciation and amortization by business segment for the years 1979, 1978 and 1977 were as follows: (a) steam generating systems, equipment and services for the electric utility industry $18.0 million, $12.2 million and $11.8 million; (b) design, engineering and construction services $3.3 million, $3.7 million and $2.9 million; (c) equipment for industrial markets $22.3 million, $20.1 million and $12.2 million and (d) products and services for industrial markets $21.6 million, $16.0 million and $12.2 million. Similar amounts charged to corporate and unallocated assets were $.9 million in the year 1979, $.6 million in the year 1978 and $.5 million in the year 1977.

Prior to burning, coal to be used in the furnaces of generating plants was first fed into a coal pulverizer, where it was finely ground to the consistency of talcum powder. This enabled the coal to be burned much more efficiently. The ring and roll unit is responsible for crushing the coal. There are three ring and roll units per pulverizer and anywhere from five to ten pulverizers per power plant. The roll was capable of crushing anywhere from 250,000 to 500,000 tons of coal before having to be replaced, with the rings generally lasting up to three times as long as the rolls. IEI's replacement market for these rings and rolls was estimated to be in the neighborhood of $5 million to $6 million per year.

However, within the last two years IEI's market share of pulverizer replacement rings and rolls had been decreasing while the overall market for such items had been increasing. The reason for this decline in sales was that IEI had met stiff competition from two other manufacturers of rings and rolls. These manufacturers were Helmick Corp. and Weatherly Company. They had succeeded in capturing a large percentage of the replacement market for rings and rolls by pricing their products lower than IEI's and by giving better delivery dates. Also, the quality of Helmick's rolls was believed to be superior to IEI's rolls since many customers were reporting longer life with Helmick's rolls than with IEI's rolls.

IEI's marketing department was faced with the problem of preventing future sales of rings and rolls from being lost to competitors and regaining the sales of those customers who had formerly purchased rings and rolls from IEI but were now purchasing from competitors.

BACKGROUND

International Engineering was originally formed in 1912 as a manufacturer of locomotive superheaters. Its growth was marked over a period of years by the acquisition of similar types of companies. Along the way it acquired much knowledge and experience in the field of fuel combustion which eventually enabled it to become one of the leading manufacturers of boilers and other steam-generating equipment.

With emphasis on growth and diversification, the company evolved as a diversified international company serving many markets with annual sales of about $1.7 billion. Through its design and manufacturing facilities it provided a variety of energy-related systems and engineering services world-wide to electric utility, petroleum, petrochemical, metallurgical, and other industrial markets. IEI produced nuclear and fossil-fueled steam supply systems and oil and gas production processing equipment and designed and constructed petrochemical, petroleum-refining chemical, and other related process plants. Other products included refractories and minerals, pulp-processing machinery, pollution-control equipment, and building products.

IEI was organized into four main groups to carry out the corporate functions as described above. These groups were the Power Systems Group, the Engineering Group, the Process Equipment Group, and the Industrial Products Group. The largest of these was the Power Systems Group, its principal market being the electric utility industry. This group was mostly concerned with the design and manufacture of fossil and nuclear-fueled steam supply systems and their related components. Within this group was Power Systems Services, the prime responsibility of which was serving the "after" market for energy-related projects. An organizational chart showing Power Systems Services in the overall IEI structure is presented in Exhibit E-4.

One "after" market was that of coal pulverizer replacement rings and rolls. Until 1974 IEI had experienced very little competition in the sale of replacement rings and rolls to electric utility companies. During the 1960s and early 1970s, the Griffin Wheel Company tried unsuccessfully to enter the market. Aggressive marketing programs on the part of IEI and the superiority of its product over that of Griffin Wheel forced the latter to withdraw from the market.

Concurrent with IEI's increasing sales of replacement rings and rolls during the early 1970s were increasing delays in delivery to customers. Being cast metal products, rings and rolls were manufactured at IEI's foundry located in Middletown, Ohio. This foundry manufactured all of the cast metal parts in IEI's product line. Because of the large volume of work that was being done at the foundry in the early 70s and the resulting backlogs, delivery of rings and rolls could be promised for no sooner than 38 weeks. While plans were being made to expand the foundry in the near future, it would be some time before this increased capacity would allow the reduction of delivery time for rings and rolls. In the interim IEI found it necessary to acquire the services of an outside firm, Weatherly Foundry & Manufacturing Co., to help produce these rings and rolls. Even with Weatherly Company manufacturing all of the rings and the larger sized rolls, IEI could only reduce its delivery time to 24 weeks.

ENTER HELMICK CORP.

In the final quarter of 1973, Helmick Corporation, a small company of about 87 employees with sales of approximately $3.5 million, purchased Griffin Wheel Company. Helmick Corporation was involved in the manufacturing of grey iron and alloy castings. Helmick set up its own equipment and immediately entered the ring and roll market. It embarked on a strategic marketing program in an attempt to penetrate this market. This program consisted primarily of:

1) promising new customers delivery within 2–4 weeks
2) pricing their rings and rolls 30–40% less than IEI's

It also appeared that Helmick's rolls were of a better quality than IEI's, with some utility companies claiming that Helmick's rolls lasted longer than IEI's rolls. This was probably due to the differences in construction and manufacturing techniques of the two rolls. The IEI roll had a center of grey cast iron with a 2-inch outer ring of ni-hard, a nickel-based high-strength steel alloy. The Helmick

EXHIBIT E-4 International Engineering, Inc.: Power Systems Services Organizational Chart

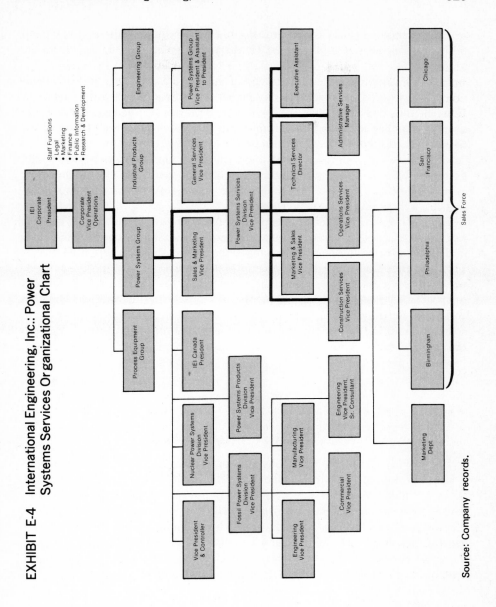

Source: Company records.

roll was composed solely of ni-hard. Because the Helmick rolls were made entirely of ni-hard it was profitable for Helmick to buy back the old rolls from the utilities.

Helmick's initial marketing strategy of cutting delivery time and price evidently had worked, as an increasing number of utility companies were favoring Helmick rolls and rings over IEI. While price played an important part in the utilities' supplier selections, the promise of shorter delivery time and increased life influenced their decisions even more. With a shorter lead time, the utilities did not have to plan so much in advance. But more important, a shortened lead time coupled with a longer life meant that utilities would not have to stockpile as many rings and rolls for future use. This would result in savings on storage costs as well as on taxes for inventory.

From 1974 to 1976, Helmick enjoyed a steady growth in the sales of its rolls and rings. As sales increased, Helmick, as had IEI, began to experience increases in delivery time to the point where it was promising delivery within 24 weeks. This lead time was somewhat flexible in that Helmick was still promising 2–4-week delivery periods to new customers, but giving the 24-week delivery period to established customers. Having successfully penetrated the market, Helmick also raised the price of its rolls and rings to the point where Helmick's prices were comparable to IEI's. The current prices of a typical roll manufactured by both IEI and Helmick are as follows:

IEI Price: $1900   Helmick Price: $2100
                                     $\underline{-300}$ (buy back of used roll)
                                        1800

WEATHERLY FIGHTS BACK

IEI recently completed its expansion program of the Middletown foundry at a cost of $7 million. With the availability of this additional foundry capacity, IEI no longer required the services of Weatherly Foundry & Manufacturing Company, which consequently faced a substantial drop in revenues from the loss of the ring and roll casting business it had been doing for IEI. Total sales of Weatherly Co. for 1979 had been $4.2 million, of which $2.2 million had been from rings and rolls. Unable to face such a large loss of sales, Weatherly made a major marketing effort in selling rings and rolls directly to the utilities. This did not prove to be difficult since when they had been making rings and rolls for IEI they would often ship the finished product directly to the customer, rather than to IEI. Thus Weatherly not only acquired the manufacturing expertise of pulverizer rings and rolls from IEI but became familiar with IEI's customers and dealt with them directly. With the elimination of IEI, Weatherly was now able to approach the utility companies and offer the same product that IEI had been selling but at a savings of about 60 percent over what IEI had been charging, and with a superior delivery period.

IEI'S SALES PICTURE FOR RINGS AND ROLLS

The entrance of both Helmick and Weatherly into the coal pulverizer ring and roll replacement market had an adverse effect upon IEI's market position. Exhibit E-5 shows IEI's market share of rings and rolls over the last 10 years. In the years 1974–1979, IEI went down from holding a high market share for rings of about 43 percent to a low of about 14 percent; and from a high market share for rolls of about 50 percent to a low of about 22 percent. Exhibit E-6 gives a tabular breakdown of the purchase of rings by 55 utility companies for the period 1974 through 1979. Exhibit E-7 shows 12 of IEI's present customers who were either considering purchases of rings or had already purchased rings manufactured by IEI's competitors. It is evident from Exhibit E-7 that the majority of IEI's sales of rings were being lost to Helmick Corp., which in the past had been concentrating mainly on the roll market but was attempting to penetrate the ring market as well.

REFURBISHING OF ROLLS

The refurbishing of rings and rolls, a process whereby metal plates were welded to the surfaces, had been in existence since about the early 1950s when Cleveland Electric Illuminating Company began to hard surface rings and rolls. The process did not catch on and until recently had insignificant effects upon the sales of new rolls. However, with the improvement of welding materials and depositing techniques, the process was starting to appeal to many of IEI's present customers.

In this process the roll was power brush cleaned, mounted on a rotating surface, preheated, and welded. The process took up to eight hours for some of the larger rolls. Major equipment requirements were an automatic welder and positioner and rotating machinery. Initial capital costs were estimated at $75,000. Once a refurbishing facility was set up, it required only one or two workers for its complete operation, thus involving little additional capital outlay. The process was presently being aggressively marketed by two welding material suppliers.

Several companies were already in the business of refurbishing and others were expected to enter the market shortly. Following is a list of the geographic areas that were being served by refurbishing companies:

West Coast—Rebuilders, Inc.
Southeast—Southern Tempering
Mid-Atlantic—Consolidated Metal Services, Inc.
Midwest—Kuhar Co. and A&R Industries

Rebuilders, Inc. had been quite successful in its operations, with the other four companies expected to gain an increasing amount of refurbishing business in the future. In addition, Detroit Edison, Consumers Power, and Dayton Power & Light were presently refurbishing rolls that had been purchased from IEI. The

EXHIBIT E-5   IEI's Market Share of Rings and Rolls, 1970-1979

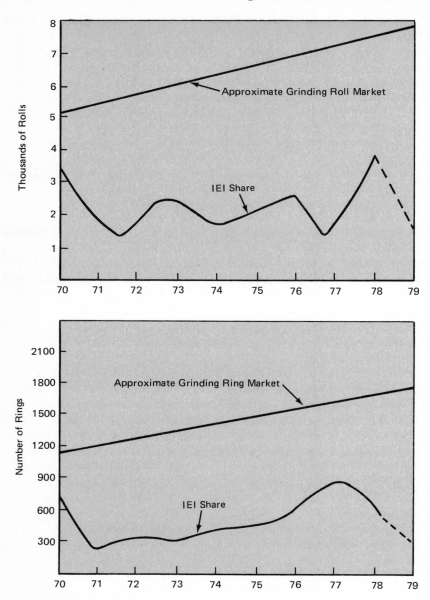

Source: Company records.

EXHIBIT E-6   IEI Ring Sales Analysis by Customer

	1974	**1975**	**1976**	**1977**	**1978**	**1979**
Dairyland Power	0	3	3	6	6	0
Montana Power	2	0	0	4	0	0
Salt River Project	0	0	0	2	0	0
Southwestern Pub. Svc.	0	0	0	0	2	0
Alabama Power	1	11	48	16	7	0
Central Illinois Light	1	1	3	2	0	0
Central Illinois Pub. Svc.	5	2	3	0	5	0
Cincinnati Gas & Electric	23	6	8	14	14	0
Cleveland Electric	19	16	24	62	13	11
Columbus & Southern	12	7	5	9	13	0
Commonwealth Edison	0	20	22	13	11	0
Dayton Power & Light	4	3	5	5	2	0
Detroit Edison	11	15	15	13	12	0
Georgia Power	13	6	18	30	16	10
Gulf Power	10	11	13	9	0	10
Illinois Power	1		10	8	6	7
Indianapolis Power	13	7	5	30	15	1
Interstate Power	4	2	3	6	5	0
Iowa Power & Light	4	5	0	2	3	0
Kansas City Power	0	3	8	11	15	0
Kansas Power & Light	2	0	8	18	0	0
Louisville Gas & Electric	8	8	18	22	8	2
Metropolitan Edison	0	4	6	1	0	0
Minnesota Power & Light	3	3	9	6	8	2
N.Y. State Electric	1	7	15	21	18	1
Niagara Mohawk Power	0	2	11	28	7	6
Northern States Power	0	2	2	0	1	0
Ohio Edison	19	1	29	4	21	0
Pennsylvania Electric	11	35	33	45	0	4
Philadelphia Electric	0	0	7	30	0	0
Carolina Power & Light	7	6	10	22	3	12
Potomac Edison	0	0	1	0	3	2
Public Service of Indiana	0	4	13	8	6	0
Rochester Gas & Elec.	0	2	11	14	5	0
Upper Peninsula Gen.	3	4	5	1	5	0
Utah Power & Light	6	4	13	10	8	1
Virginia Electric Power Co.	0	0	0	0	0	19
Wisconsin Elec.	5	13	4	8	33	0
Pacific Power & Light	0	3	3	3	15	6
Consumers Power	19	15	3	16	32	5
Duke Power	8	35	24	47	14	0
Duquesne Light	0	5	8	6	8	6
Electric Energy	6	10	0	20	6	0
Northern Indiana Pub. Svc.	0	0	6	4	2	7
Otter Tail Power	0	0	0,	0	0	2
Potomac Elec.	0	3	6	10	5	4
Union Electric	0	0	7	16	0	3
Wisconsin Pub. Svc.	3	0	1	4	0	0
Penn. Power & Light	8	12	22	22	12	0
So. Carolina Elec.	0	3	3	8	4	0
Tenn. Valley Authority	32	39	56	46	52	17
Arizona Public Svc.	1	1	2	1	2	0
Kentucky Utilities	3	1	7	3	0	0
New England Power	0	0	0	0	15	0
Florida Power	0	0	0	0	0	10

Source: Company records.

EXHIBIT E-7   Tabulation of Survey, Rings Investigation

Customer	Competitors Present
Cleveland Electric	Helmick
Consumers Power	Helmick
Central Illinois Pub Svc.	Helmick
Duke Power	Helmick, Alabama Iron
Carolina Power & Light	Helmick
Detroit Edison	Helmick
Northern Indiana Pub. Svc.	Helmick
Pennsylvania Electric	Helmick, Weatherly
Penn. Power & Light	Helmick, Weatherly
Virginia Electric Power Co.	Helmick
Georgia Power	*Georgia Iron Works
Duquesne Light	Weatherly

*Emergency delivery required only minor purchase procured.
Source: Company records.

following utility companies were contemplating using the refurbishing process in the future:

Alabama Power	Louisville Gas & Electric
Cincinnati Gas & Electric	Montana Power
Columbus & Southern	Pacific Power & Light
Georgia Power	Salt River Project
Kansas Power & Light	Tennessee Valley Authority

Cost comparisons for new and refurbished rolls are as follows:

Size	Refurbished	Present (1980) Pricing
863	$1500	$1620
943	1925	2310
1003	2500	5270

It was evident that the cost of refurbishing was less than that of purchasing new rolls, especially larger rolls.

Once a roll had been refurbished its life appeared to be substantially improved over the life of a similar new roll. While there was no documented evidence to support this, various unproven reports had been received by IEI indicating that an improvement in life was being experienced by refurbished rolls. In particular, Detroit Edison and Pacific Power & Light reported longer life with refurbished rolls. To determine whether this was true, a test of a set of rolls that had been refurbished by Southern Tempering Company has been undertaken at the Widows Creek Station of the Tennessee Valley Authority. At last report, the refurbished rolls had pulverized about 250,000 tons of coal and still had showed no signs of failure. Based on current wear rates it was estimated that the rolls would probably be capable of crushing an additional 500,000 tons of coal before being replaced or refurbished. In comparison, new rolls supplied by IEI for use at the Widows Creek Station had had an average life of about 250,000 tons.

A $75,000 refurbishing facility was capable of refurbishing 15 rolls a week or 750 rolls per year. Ten of these facilities would therefore yield about 7500 refurbished rolls per year, which represented approximately the total market available for IEI grinding rolls. Total replacement sales for IEI grinding rolls for the 1980 year would total about 2000. In addition, a roll could be refurbished up to 15 times before having to be replaced. The recent trend of the utility companies in refurbishing their old rolls as opposed to buying new ones posed a real threat to IEI's future in the highly profitable replacement coal-grinding roll business.

Being an original equipment manufacturer, IEI had certain advantages over its lesser known competitive suppliers in dealing with its utility customers. In endorsing the refurbishing process which was developed primarily by a welding metal supply company, IEI would jeopardize this advantage and lose the ability to differentiate its product. It would put its sales engineers at a disadvantage when, in the field, they must answer to the utility companies as to whether it was better to refurbish or to replace a grinding roll. IEI's acceptance and use of the process would encourage many utility companies to make the small investment necessary to set up their own refurbishing facilities, as several had already done. Lesser known companies that were already involved in refurbishing would make use of IEI's acceptance of the process to increase their own business and compete on price.

Because refurbishing facilities could be small one- or two-worker operations requiring little capital investment, they would for the most part be regional or local businesses. If IEI were to enter the refurbishing market it would be necessary to establish several shops regionally located in order to compete favorably with local companies.

The refurbishing of old rolls would mean a definite loss of business for the recently completed foundry expansion. Whether or not IEI decided to go into the refurbishing business, this loss of foundry business would continue. Since this loss was not acceptable, IEI must increase its sales of new grinding rolls to offset it.

IEI's ORDERING PROCESS FOR RINGS AND ROLLS

The sales department had the responsibility of attaining new customers for the purchase of coal pulverizer replacement rings and rolls from IEI. While there might be considerable contact on the part of the sales engineers with the utility companies in the initial stages of acquiring them as customers, once the account had been established there was virtually no personal contact between IEI and the client utility companies when purchases of rings and rolls were made. For the most part the sales department was concerned with special or new orders, the ordering of replacement rings and rolls being a fairly routine matter on the part of both the utility companies and IEI.

Throughout the United States, IEI had several district offices to handle orders placed by utility companies for parts. See Exhibit E-8. When a utility company desired to order a replacement ring or roll, it simply sent the order to the appropriate district office. The district office processed the order and sent it to the Parts Operations Department in Plymouth, Michigan.

The Parts Operations Department had the responsibility of filling orders for all replacement and non-replacement parts that IEI marketed for both nuclear and fossil fuel plants. The Parts Operations Department handled orders for more than 50,000 parts. Total yearly sales for Parts Operations, in 1979, amounted to about $40 million for fossil fuel parts and $1 million for nuclear parts, the bulk of their work obviously being concerned with processing orders for fossil fuel parts.

The Parts Operations Department checked each order against the original invoice to make certain that the customer was receiving the correct part. Once the order had been checked, the parts group then placed the order with the Middletown Foundry. The foundry gave the Parts Operations Department a shipping date based upon its current backlog of work. In turn, the Parts Operations Department notified the customer when to expect shipment of the part. Shipment from the foundry was normally by truck, usually the fastest and cheapest means of transporting the part to the customer. Usually shipment by truck could be made to anywhere in the continental United States within two to three days.

To keep track of all orders that were placed with the Parts Operations Department, IEI used a computerized tracking system. This system followed the order from its initial placement at the district office to final delivery to the customer, insuring minimal delay in order processing and filling.

MARKET SURVEY

In order to provide the marketing and sales groups with information on current and future trends in the marketplace and to help the marketing group in determining how resources might be allocated over the next two years, a survey was conducted on a group of IEI customers in major metropolitan areas of the United States. The survey was developed, conducted, and tabulated by Health-width Inc., an independent survey company. In this survey 45 business executives of various IEI customer companies were personally interviewed. While the results of the entire survey cannot be presented herein, two areas of the survey were of prime interest to IEI in regard to its marketing problem with replacement sales of coal pulverizer rings and rolls.

One of these areas was concerned with determining the relative importance of those factors that tended to influence a purchaser to buy from a particular

EXHIBIT E-8 International Engineering, Inc.: Power Systems Services Sales Territories

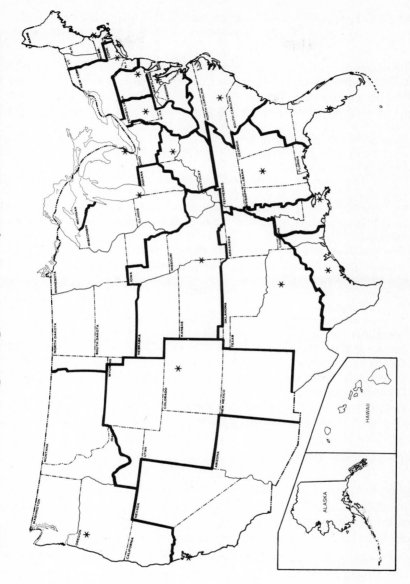

Source: Company records.

EXHIBIT E-9   Coal Pulverizer Rings and Rolls Market Survey
              Percentage of Respondents Rating the Buying Factors as Crucial
              or Very Important

1. Dependability and quality of product or service	100.0%
2. Company reputation in this product or service category	87.8
3. Company's engineering capabilities	85.3
4. Company's reputation for meeting promised delivery date	82.9
5. Company's design capabilities	80.5
6. Responsiveness and flexibility of company to customer needs and requirements	78.1
7. Maintenance service and back-up capabilities offered by company	78.1
8. Promptness of reply to customer inquiries and requests	78.0
9. Length of company experience in this product or service category	75.6
10. Previous favorable experience with this company	73.9
11. Reputation of company for completion of projects on time and within budget	73.2
12. Company's field construction capabilities	63.3
13. Price of product or service	68.3
14. Amount of technical support information provided by company	63.4
15. Projected time of delivery	61.0
16. Quality of company's personnel	61.0
17. Commercial terms and conditions offered by company	51.2
18. Company's field labor relations	43.9
19. Recommendation by consulting engineer	24.4
20. Amount of sales support contact provided by company sales representatives	17.1

Source: Company records.

supplier. Exhibit E-9 presents the results of this study in which 20 factors were evaluated on a 5-point scale ranging from "crucial" to "not at all considered." From the results of this survey those individuals interviewed tended to rate the following as being very important in the buying decision:

1) Quality of the product
2) Ability to supply product within a reasonable time period
3) Warranty or back-up service that accompanies product
4) Responsiveness to customer needs
5) Engineering and design capabilities

In another part of the survey the respondents were asked to evaluate how pricing affected their organization's decision-making process regarding the selection of supplier companies. The following is a list of the questionnaire statements and the percentage of respondents who agreed with them:

31.7%   A) In most cases, the lowest priced quote for the product or service is the major determinant.

22.0%   B) In most cases, our firm will pay a small (up to 5%) price premium for a product or service if the supplier offers a better quality, delivery, or service.

24.4%   C) In most cases, our firm will pay a meaningful premium (10% or more), assuming the quality, delivery, or service justifies such a premium.

14.6%   D) In most cases, the price of the product or service is one of the secondary considerations. Our firm bases its purchasing decision on more primary factors such as performance, reputation of supplier, product quality, delivery, and service.

7.3%   E) No answer.

The information contained in this survey, while not pertaining just to the sales of rings and rolls but of the entire line of IEI's products and services, gave the marketing department some insight concerning what areas to concentrate on in their marketing strategy to regain their market share of coal pulverizer ring and roll sales.

IEI's MARKETING STRATEGY

It was evident that if IEI was to regain its former share of the replacement market for coal pulverizer rings and rolls, it would have to meet or beat the competition in all of the following product areas:

1) delivery time
2) quality
3) price

The area needing immediate improvement, and the most crucial, was that of delivery. Longer delivery times mean higher costs for utilities. IEI's delivery time of 24 weeks was clearly unacceptable. However, with the expansion of the Middletown Foundry, IEI had the extra capacity it needed to manufacture, within a reasonable time period, all of the rings and rolls that it could sell.

The $7 million foundry expansion was regarded as the most modern facility in the country, employing the latest casting techniques. One such technique was that of centrifugal casting. Both Weatherly and Helmick statistically cast their rings and rolls, a more costly process because of the amount of labor and time involved. Centrifugal casting was much more efficient and economical, requiring less labor and enabling parts to be cast at a faster rate. It was unlikely that Helmick or Weatherly would be capable of similar major improvements in their foundries because of the large costs involved. Neither company had the necessary cash for such an investment. IEI's new facility, which would be devoted primarily to the manufacturing of rings and rolls, was capable of producing

21,000 rolls a year, with an estimated market of 8000 rolls a year. Thus, it was evident that IEI had a definite edge on its competitors in manufacturing rings and rolls.

The entire foundry manufactured over 8000 individual parts that were sold by IEI. Because about 50 different types of rings and rolls were manufactured by IEI, it was economically unfeasible to stock these items. Instead, a system had been set up whereby all orders for rings and rolls received by the foundry were to be guaranteed ready for shipment within 4 weeks, which essentially was the same as stocking an item. The district sales offices and the Parts Operations Group in Plymouth had been given explicit instructions to expedite all orders for replacement rings and rolls. Orders that had previously taken about 3 weeks to process would now be processed within 2 weeks or less. Thus, the maximum lead time for rings and rolls had been reduced from 24 weeks to 6 weeks.

The marketing department had the task of informing the utility companies of the improved lead time. Two phases were planned. The first phase, which had already started, would consist of personal contact by the sales department with the utilities, while the second phase would consist of individual mailings to the utility companies. For these mailings a list would be drawn up of all past, present, and potential customers for IEI replacement rings and rolls. A letter would be sent to these firms telling of IEI's six-week delivery period. Enclosed with the letter would be a special four-page color brochure describing IEI's ring and roll line. This brochure would emphasize IEI's current position as a leader in the design, development, and construction of fossil fuel plants, a statement that could not be made by any of IEI's present competitors in the ring and roll replacement business.

The sales department, while not directly under the control of the marketing department (see Exhibit E-4), relied heavily upon marketing and worked closely with this group. Thus, when the marketing people approached sales with the objective of and strategy for regaining IEI's market share of replacement rolls and rings, the sales group responded favorably. Immediately the sales department representatives were calling upon the utilities and informing them of the six-week delivery time for IEI's replacement rings and rolls.

Initial reports received by marketing from sales were not encouraging. Instead of taking advantage of the significantly shortened lead times, many of the utilities found it very difficult to believe that IEI could offer such lead times. The marketing people were now faced with the task of making believers out of these utility companies which had become disenchanted with IEI's service over the last few years. Perhaps the mailings, which would be going out very shortly, would have some impact on the utilities, but the marketing people felt that they would probably have to come up with some other means of enticing the utilities to purchase replacement rings and rolls from IEI. This enticement would probably have to be in the form of a price reduction or some type of allowance if IEI did not meet its promise of delivery within six weeks from the time the order was placed.

Improvement in the quality of IEI's rings and rolls was something that would take at least one to two years to materialize. Extensive support would be required from engineering in designing, analyzing, and testing various types of rings and rolls. To meet this challenge, $50,000 had been set aside for a program to develop a better quality roll. The object of this program was to develop a roll that would last at least as long as that offered by competition and at a price that was comparable to that of the competition. During the implementation of this program, the marketing group suggested that engineering look into the feasibility of developing a longer wearing roll that would be incapable of being refurbished. It was unlikely that IEI's ring and roll competitors would be able to embark on such a development program because they lacked the engineering and technical resources that IEI possessed as an original equipment manufacturer.

Once the new foundry achieved full operation, IEI expected its price for replacement rings and rolls to drop by at least 10 percent. If this price reduction of rings and rolls was not enough to bring IEI's prices in line with its competitor's, IEI was prepared to cut prices more. The marketing department was presently examining the profit margins, currently 36 to 40 percent of total cost, of the various rings and rolls sold by IEI to determine how much of a price cut could be withstood. It was realized that it might be necessary for IEI to take a loss on the sale of some of its rings and rolls in an effort to increase its market share.

CONCLUSION

Whether IEI's marketing tactics will succeed in reversing the trend of declining sales of replacement rings and rolls remains to be seen. IEI has clearly defined the reasons for this decline, i.e., price, quality, and delivery of their product vs. that of the competition. IEI is now taking the appropriate steps in improving their product to regain a larger share of the market. But one must question whether these problems could have been foreseen earlier and corrective action taken then to avoid the sudden decrease in sales of rings and rolls that apparently came about without much warning. The Vice President of Marketing made the following comments on the whole problem and its solution:

> It is obvious that IEI made a serious mistake in having Weatherly Company ship rings and rolls directly to IEI's utility customers. But even more serious may have been the lack of personal contact with the utilities in regard to sales of rings and rolls. Having successfully thwarted one would-be competitor, Griffin Wheel, from entering the ring and roll market, IEI may have felt, with their status as an O.E.M. and being a leader in the field of fossil fuel plant development, that they occupied a position in the ring and roll market that was relatively safe from any outside competitive forces. It was this dominant position that possibly led IEI to believe that there was no need to have contact with the utility companies in supplying them with replacement rings and rolls. Had this contact been maintained through personal sales calls to the utilities, the

utilities today might not have a despondent attitude toward IEI. It is no wonder that when smaller companies such as Helmick and Weatherly, which dealt more directly with the utilities and gave them what they wanted, i.e., better delivery, quality, and price of replacement rings and rolls, entered the scene the utilities favored doing business with them rather than with IEI.

If IEI should regain its market share of rings and roll sales, and hopefully it will, it must continue to remain in contact with the utilities for such routine orders as rings and rolls. IEI must let the utilities know that it cares about their wants and needs. If this contact is not maintained the situation that now exists may arise again in the years to come.

IEI must take a closer look at the refurbishing process as this poses a very serious threat to the ring and roll business in the future. It is obvious that for larger rolls refurbishing has definite cost advantages over buying new ones. And the fact that a refurbished roll will last up to three times as long as a new roll makes refurbishing look even more attractive. One way of overcoming this problem might be to sell new rolls to the utilities on a contractual basis. Under the terms of such a contract an agreement could be made between IEI and its customer utility companies whereby a purchased roll would be refurbished by IEI for a specified number of times at a specified price. The terms of the contract would be such that it would not be profitable for the utilities to refurbish the roll themselves or have some outside firm refurbish the roll. Or a contract may be set up whereby the utilities just purchase the use of the roll, thereby preventing them from having it refurbished by a competitor. While such arrangements probably would not be as profitable to IEI as selling a new roll every time one wears out, such alternatives would still allow IEI to acquire a sizable share of the market. Having the status of an O.E.M. would make it easier for IEI to secure such contracts in comparison to their smaller competitors, providing the pricing of such contracts is competitive.

Index

A

accumulated cost, 465–467

Ackoff, Russell, 10–11

acquisition, 24

adaptivizing planning, 10–11

adjustment, 332

administered vertical marketing system, 356–357

administrative planning, 32

advertising: comparison, 389–390; definition of, 370; objectives, 379; strategies, 378–390

advertising-copy strategy, 384–390

analogy technique for projecting cost, 441

anti-materialism, and impact on marketing strategy, 83–84

Antimerger Act, 110

appeal: emotional, 387–388; humor, 388–389; rational, 387–388

appraisal: corporate, 40–41; internal, 40–60; of marketing, 60–61

arbitration, 361

assignment of salespeople, 401

attitudinal approach to defining advertising objectives, 380–381

average-commitment strategy, 250–251

B

balanced portfolio, 423

bargaining strategy, 359–360

be-first-in-the-market strategy, 245–246

bottom-up planning process, 27

boundary strategy, 360

brands, competing, 265–266

breakdown methods, 366–367

breakthrough product, 158

budget, impact of on promotion mix, 376

buildup method, 367–370

bundling-pricing strategy, 321–322

business: assessment of strengths of, 426–428, 429; future trends in, 82; mission, 20, 168, 180–182; strategic factors in, 56–58; strategy concepts, 228–230; strategy development, 429, 430–432; unit. *See* strategic business unit

businesses, classification of, 417–419

buyer: need of, 501–503, 504; strengths of, 499–504

C

cannibalism, 260–261

cash consequences, 219

cash cow, 418

CEO: office, 523–524; role of, 525–526

channel: competitive, 346–348; complementary, 344–346; conflict, 358; controller, 355; evaluation, 349–353

channel-conflict-management strategy, 358–361

channel-control strategy, 354–358

channel-modification strategy, 348–354

channel-structure strategy, 328–339

chief executive, role of, 525–526

Clayton Act, 109

Colonial Manor Hospital, 573–591

common thread, 181

communication: and control, 353; with salespeople, 402

community, and effect on corporate environment, 69

comparison advertising, 389–390

compensation, sales, 395–398

competition: between brands, 265–266; and marketing decisions, 113–114; as pricing factor, 299–300; review of, 152–156; three categories of, 106–108

competitive: channel, 346–348; distribution, 346; product, 158

competitive-parity approach, 367

competitive position, assessment of, 426–428, 429

competitor profiling, 207

complementary channel, 344–346

compulsory arbitration, 361

concentration of goods, 327

concentric diversification, 291

conciliation, 361

conglomerate diversification, 292–293

consistency: with environment, 224–225; internal, 224

constraint objective, 21

consumer: confidence and plans to buy, 115; expenditure patterns, 132–136; location of, 126–128

consumerism, 118–123; federal laws concerned with, 80

contingency planning, 26

contractual vertical marketing system, 357

control, 335; communication and, 353; of salespeople, 401–402

copy, 384

core strategy, 209–215

corporate: appraisal, 40–41; diversity, 473; objectives, 169–177, 178; publics, 41–47; vertical marketing system, 356

corporate environment: explanation of, 69–70; three parts of, 69

corporate planning, 18–27; flowchart, 19

corporate strategy: and business strategy, 224; and environmental scanning, 85

corporate-wide planning, and marketing planning, 27–28

cost: accumulated, 465–467; of distribution, 349–351; four techniques for projection of, 441; as pricing factor, 297–298

cost-per-thousand-contacts comparison, 381–382

creativity: and impact on marketing strategy, 83; test for, 194

critique, in OST system, 511

cross-impact analysis (CIA), 90–95, 99, 490–494, 495–496, 506

cross-impact matrix, 454

cultural changes, and effect on marketing, 103–106

culture, and effect on corporate environment, 69

customer: impact of on promotion mix, 375–376; service, 353

customized-products strategy, 274–275

D

decision making, marketing. *See* marketing decision making
decline stage in product life cycle, 409
defensive strategy, 501
Delphi panel, 89; important factors in selection of, 455
Delphi technique, 100, 446–455
demand: analysis of, 158, 160, 300; elasticity of, 300; as pricing factor, 300–303; three types of, 158, 160
demarketing strategy, 252–253
development planning, 23–24
dictatorial strategy, 501
direct-distribution strategy, 328
directional policy matrix, 432–433
discounted cash flow rate of return, 460–462
discretionary income, 129
dispersion of goods, 327
disposable income, 128–129
distribution: competitive, 346; cost of, 349–351; exclusive, 339–341; intensive, 341–342; policies, 344; prior, 453; selective, 342–343
distribution-scope strategy, 339–343
diversification strategy, 289–293
diversity, corporate, 473
divestment, 24, 431–432; total-line, 279–282
dog, 419
durable goods: household availability of, 136; household expenditures for, 135

economy, in 1988, 79
education, 136–138
elasticity of demand, 300
elimination price, 305–306
emotional appeal, 387–388
environment: concept of, 69; constituents of, 70; impact of on pricing, 505; product/market, 69–70, 103; types of, 69, 74–84; corporate. *See* corporate environment
environmental scanning: approaches to, 100; and corporate strategy, 85; example of, 88–95; external information obtained by managers in, 72–73; importance of, 68; and marketing strategy, 84–88; organization and problems of, 95–98; state of the art of, 69–74; systematic approach to, 88–89; techniques of, 98–100
ethics, in making marketing decisions, 111–113
evaluation: of media, 383; of salesperson, 398–401
exclusive distribution, 339–341
existing demand, 158, 160
expansion, internal, 24
expenditure: marketing, 473; patterns, 132–136; R & D, 473
experience, definition of, 465
experience curve: concept, 437–445; construction, 465–470
external environment, definition of, 69
extrapolation procedures as scanning technique, 98

E

early-entry stategy, 246–247
economic climate, 114–116
economic development, international, 189
economic environment, 77–79

F

Fayol, Henri, 4
Federal Trade Commission Act, 110
financial: approach to selection of channel, 335–337; performance profile, 148, 151; planning, 31–32

flexible-pricing strategy, 314–315
Food, Drug and Cosmetic Act, 110
forecasting, as distinguished from planning, 7
foreign investment, U.S., 243
framework-for-pricing-strategy model, 499–504, 505
franchise system, 357
FSCAN, 504, 505–507
functional planning, 22–23
Futurscan (FSCAN), 504, 505–507

G

gamesmanship strategy, 501
gap: analysis, 204; filling the, 204–215
General Electric: Futurscan model developed by, 504, 505–507; SBU structure of, 518–523
generic product, 309
goals, 20; definition of, 168; framework for defining, 168–169; market and product (in OST system), 511; process of setting, 189–193, 194; as response to expectations of corporate publics, 45–47; of strategic business unit, 182–184; technical (in OST system), 511; three types of, 20–21
goods: approach to distribution, 332–335; shopping, 342
government intervention in business, 106–108
gross margin, 332
growth, 187–188; limits of, 123–124; potential, 479, 481–482, 483; stage in product life cycle, 408
growth/survival objective, 21

H

habitat, and effect on corporate environment, 69

hierarchy approach to defining advertising objectives, 380
horizontal: competition, 107; diversification, 292
humor appeal, 388–389

I

improved product, 158
incipient demand, 158, 160
income, 128–132
increasing-the-price strategy, 311–313
indirect-distribution strategy, 328
industry: dynamics of, 156–158, 159–160; life cycle of, 216–219; price-sensitive, 297; volume-sensitive, 297
industry attractiveness, assessment of, 426–428
inside-out approach to planning, 25–26
institutional dynamics, 117–118
integration: corporate-level, 224; definition of, 290; top-level, 523–525
intensity, 465–468; investment, 473, 474; multiplier, 468–469
intensive distribution, 341–342
internal: appraisal, 40–60; consistency, 224; deployment, 219; environment, 69; expansion, 24; rate of return, 460–462
international economic development, 189
International Engineering, Inc., 622–642
international-market strategy, 242–244
interpenetration strategy, 360
intertype competition, 107
introduction stage in product life cycle, 408
intuition technique for projecting cost, 441

inventory approach to developing advertising objectives, 379–380

investment: intensity, 473, 474; U.S. overseas, 243

investment proposals: evaluation of, 457, 459–464

invest-to-exit strategy, 431

invest-to-grow strategy, 430, 431

invest-to-maintain strategy, 430, 431

invest-to-regain strategy, 430–431

issue assessment, 206–207

J

Johnston, Inc., 592–609

K

keep-out price, 305–306

key-markets strategy, 254

L

labels, private, 266–267

laggard-market-entry strategy, 247–249

latent demand, 158, 160

leadership, technological, 189

leasing strategy, 318–321

legal implications of consumerism, 122

legal requirements and marketing strategy, 108–111

life cycle: of industry, 216–219; product, 408–413, 414

light-commitment strategy, 251–252

line-simplification strategy, 276–279

local-market strategy, 240

M

maintaining-the-price strategy, 307

management: characteristics of operational, 509, 510; value orientation of top, 47–54

manufacturer, original equipment, 268

marginal approach to promotion budget, 365–366

market: changes in scope of, 239; goal (in OST system), 511; impact of on promotion mix, 374–375; penetration, 351–353; performance profile, 148, 150

market-commitment strategy, 249–252

market-dilution strategy, 252–254

market-entry strategy, 245–249

market-geography strategy, 239–244

market-harvesting strategy, 254

marketing: application of experience curve concept to, 441–442; appraisal of, 60–61; effect of social and cultural changes on, 103–106; effect of strategic planning on, 528–536; expenditures, 473; impact of multibusiness strategic planning on, 227; outline for measuring effectiveness of, 62–66; simulation, 482, 483–487; and social trends, 81–82

marketing decision making: approaches to, 3; and strategic planning process, 4

marketing decisions, paradigm of, 35–37

marketing effectiveness, outline for measuring, 62–65

marketing mix, impact of on promotion mix, 376–377

marketing planning, 30; and corporate-wide planning, 27–28; and planning in other functional areas,

28–32; and strategy formulation, 12–18

marketing strategy: dimensions of, 11, 231–232; environmental scanning and, 84–88; impact of anti-materialism on, 83–84; impact of personal creativity on, 83; impact of social trends on, 81–82; legal requirements and, 110–111; major elements of, 211–212; politics and, 108; resources and, 54–55; study of present, 145–146, 147

marketing system, vertical, 355–358

market-scope strategy, 232–239

market segmentation: analysis, 207; criteria for, 233–235

market share, 185–187, 473, 474; pricing strategy to build, 324–325

market strategy. *See* marketing strategy

matrix: cross-impact, 454, 491–494, 495–496; directional policy, 432–433; multifactor portfolio, 426–433; portfolio, 413, 415–426; pricing tactics, 502–503; product evaluation, 497, 498

maturity stage in product life cycle, 408–409

measurement: objective, 21; vs. profit, 183

media: definition of, 378; evaluation, 383

media-selection strategy, 378–383

mediation, 361

merger, definition of, 290

mission, 20, 168, 180–182

model building, as scanning technique, 100

models, special-purpose, 494, 497–507

momentum: definition of, 202; measurement of, 202–203

motivation of salespeople, 395–401

multifactor portfolio matrix, 426–433

multimarket strategy, 237

multiple-brand positioning, 260–262

multiple-channel strategy, 343–348

multiple-product strategy, 271–272

N

national: income, 128; security, 189

national-market strategy, 241–242

need: of buyer, 501–503, 504; of seller, 502–503, 504

negotiated strategy, 501

new products, pricing strategies for, 303–306

new-product strategy, 282–289

noise, 384

O

objectives, 20; of advertising, 379–381; corporate, 169–177, 178; definition of, 168; framework for defining, 168–169; pricing, 296–297; process of setting, 189–193, 194; product/market, 184–189; as response to expectations of corporate publics, 45–47; as result of value orientation, 51–54; selling, 390–391; of strategic business unit, 182–184; three types of, 20–21

OEM, 268

one-price strategy, 313–314

operating environment, 69

operational management, characteristics of, 509, 510

optimizing planning, 10

organization, changes in, 523–525

original equipment manufacturer, 268

OST system of Texas Instruments Inc., 509, 511, 513–518

outside-in approach to planning, 25–26

P

payback period, 457, 459
penetration: of market, 351–353; pricing, 305–306
percentage-of-sales approach, 366
performance: evaluation of past, 146–151; measure (in OST system), 511
personal income, 128
personal selling, 370; strategies, 390–402
PIMS program, 472–479, 480
planner, role of strategic, 526–528
planning: administrative, 32; approaches to, 25–27; characteristics of strategic, 509, 510; concept of, 4–11; contingency, 26; corporate, 18–27; definition of, 6–7; development, 23–24; as distinguished from forecasting, 7; effect of on marketing organization, 528–536; financial, 31–32; flowchart, 19; functional, 22–23; initiation of, 9–10; philosophies of, 10–11; processes, 27; production, 30–31; requisites for successful, 8–9; schedule, 27; significance of, 7–8; staff and, 26–27; strategic, 18–22. *See also* marketing planning, product/market planning, and product/market strategy
PLC. *See* product life cycle
policy, 168
political: environment, 77; risk, 78
politics, and influence on business, 106–108
population, 124–126; projected growth of, 127

portfolio: balanced, 423; developing a, 412–413, 414; matrix, 413, 415–426; unbalanced, 423–424, 425
portfolio matrix, multifactor, 426–433
positioning: multiple brands, 260–262; a single brand, 258–260
postponement-speculation theory, 330–331
premium price, 304–305
present-value index, 462
present-value method for evaluating investment proposals, 459–460
price: choice of, 505; elimination, 305–306; keep-out, 305–306; premium, 304–305; promotional, 305–306; restrained, 305; sensitivity, 300; umbrella, 304–305
price-flexibility strategy, 313–315
price-leadership strategy, 322–324
price-sensitive industry, 297
pricing: computation of target-return, 298; factors, 295–303; objectives, 296–297; penetration, 305–306; skimming, 303–305; tactics matrix, 502–503
pricing strategy: to build market share, 324–325; effect of costs on, 297–298; for established products, 306–313; four types of, 501; impact of environmental factors on, 505; model for choosing, 499–504, 505; for new products, 303–306; quadrangle, 501–502, 504
prior distribution, 453
private labels, 266–267
probabilistic system dynamics modeling capability (PSD), 506–507
product: and effect on corporate environment, 69; evaluation matrix, 497, 498; generic, 309; goal (in OST system), 511; imitation, 286–288; impact of on promotion mix, 374; improvement/modification,

283–286; innovation, 288–289; intensity, 465–468; location of in life cycle, 410–412; performance profile, 148, 150; portfolio matrix, 413, 415–426; quality, 473; three categories of, 158
product-design strategy, 273–275
product-elimination strategy, 275–282
product intensity multiplier, 468–469
production planning, 30–31
product life cycle (PLC), 408–413, 414; product portfolio and, 422–423
product-line-pricing strategy, 315–317
product-line-strategy model, 497–499
product/market: environment, 69–70, 103; objectives, 184–189; study of present strategy of, 145–146; thrust, 152–161
product/market planning: conceptual scheme for, 200–202; integration of at the SBU level, 215–223
product/market strategy: evaluation of, 224–226; review of, 219, 221. *See also* product/market planning
product-overlap strategy, 265–268
product portfolio, and product life cycle, 422–423
product-positioning strategy, 257–262
product-repositioning strategy, 262–265
product-scope strategy, 269–273
product strategy: dimensions of, 256–257, 258; implications, 419–422
profiling of competitors, 207
profit: economics analysis, 207; impact of market strategy (PIMS), 472–479, 480; impact of strategic planning on, 474; key factors which influence, 473; vs. measurement, 183

profitability, 184–185; index, 462
promotional price, 305–306
promotion-expenditure strategy, 363–370
promotion-mix strategy, 370–378
promotion strategies, 363–378
Protestant ethic, 104–105
pruning-of-marginal-markets strategy, 253
PSD, 506–507

Q

question mark, 418–419

R

R & D expenditures, 473
rate of return, internal (or discounted cash flow), 460–462
rational appeal, 387–388
reducing-the-price strategy, 307–311
regional-market strategy, 240–241
regression technique for projecting cost, 441
regulatory environment, 79–80
replacement rate, 332
repositioning: among existing customers, 263; among new users, 263–264; for new uses, 264–265
resources: considered in finalizing strategy, 225; as factor of appraisal, 54–60; and marketing strategy, 54–55; measurement of, 55–60; scales for measuring, 60
restrained price, 305
return-on-investment approach, 366–367
return on investment (ROI), 459, 473
risk: analysis, 462–464; political, 78; of a strategy, 225
Robinson-Patman Act, 110
ROI, 459, 473

S

sales: compensation, 395–398; promotion, 370
sales-motivation-and-supervision strategy, 395–402
salespeople: assignment of, 401; communication with, 402; control of, 401–402; evaluation of, 398–401; supervision of, 401–402
satisfying planning, 10
SBU. *See* strategic business unit
scanning, environmental. *See* environmental scanning
scenario building, 456–457, 458; as scanning technique, 99
scope, in OST system, 511
searching time, 332
sector organization, 524–525
segmentation: criteria for market, 233–235; of market, 207
selective distribution, 342–343
seller: need of, 502–503, 504; strengths of, 499–504
selling: personal, 370; strategy, 390–395
sensitivity analysis, 463–464
service: customer, 353; quality of, 473
Sherman Antitrust Act, 109
shopping goods, 342
Sigtronics, Inc., 610–621
simulation, 464; marketing, 482, 483–487; technique for projecting cost, 441
single-brand positioning, 258–260
single-market strategy, 235–237
single-product strategy, 270–271
skimming pricing, 303–305
sleeper effect, 386
social: changes and effect on marketing, 103–106; contribution, 189; environment, 80–84; trends, 449; trends having marketing significance, 81–82

special-purpose models, 494, 497–507
spend-as-much-as-can-be-afforded approach, 366
spending, consumer, 134
staff and planning, 26–27
standard-products strategy, 274
standard-product-with-modifications strategy, 275
star, 417–418
strategic business unit (SBU): compendium of strategies for, 220; definition of, 142; financial record of, 222–223; identification of, 215–216, 217; objectives of, 177, 179–184; profitability and cash position of, 221; situation analysis of, 216–219; strategy review of, 219; structure of General Electric, 518–523
strategic planner, role of, 526–528
strategic planning, 18–22; characteristics of, 509, 510; effect of on marketing organization, 528–536; impact on marketing of, 227; and marketing decision making, 4
strategy: advertising, 378–390; bargaining, 359–360; boundary, 360; channel-conflict-management, 358–361; channel-control, 354–358; channel-modification, 348–354; channel-structure, 328–339; concepts, 11–12, 228–230; defensive, 501; definition of, 20; development of business, 429, 430–432; dictatorial, 501; dimensions of market, 231–232; dimensions of product, 256–257, 258; direct-distribution, 328; distribution-scope, 339–343; diversification, 289–293; essence of, 68; formulation and marketing planning, 12–18; gamesmanship, 501; implications of experience curves, 445; indirect-distribution, 328; interpenetration, 360; market-commitment, 249–252; market-dilution, 252–254;

market-entry, 245–249; market-geography, 239–244; market-scope, 232–239; multiple-channel, 343–348; negotiated, 501; new-product, 282–289; options, 430–432; personal selling, 390–402; prerequisites to successful, 228–229; product-design, 273–275; product-elimination, 275–282; product-overlap, 265–268; product-positioning, 257–262; product-repositioning, 262–265; product-scope, 269–273; promotion, 363–378; as result of value orientation, 51–54; selection of, 209–215; selling, 390–395; and structure, 509–523; study of present, 143–146; superorganizational, 360–361. *See also* marketing strategy, pricing strategy, product/market planning, and product/market strategy

strengths: business, 426–428, 429; of buyer and seller, 499–504

strengths and weaknesses: analysis of, 161–164; meaning of, 140; studying, 140–142; systematic approach for measuring, 142–143

strong-commitment strategy, 249–250

structure, strategy and, 509–523

supernumerary income, 130

superorganizational strategy, 360–361

supervision, of salespeople, 401–402

supporting strategy, 209–215

synergy: definition of, 164; measurement of, 165

system-of-products strategy, 272–273

T

target-return pricing, 298

technique, 437

technological: changes, 116–117; environment, 74–77; leadership, 189

Texas Instruments Inc., 509, 511–518

TIA. *See* trend-impact analysis

time of consumption, 332

tool, 437

top-down planning process, 27

top management, value orientation of, 47–54

total-line divestment, 279–282

total-market strategy, 238

trend-impact analysis (TIA), 89–90, 487–490; as used in Futurscan, 506

U

umbrella price, 304–305

unbalanced portfolio, 423–424, 425

U.S. investment abroad, 243

V

value orientation: importance of in corporate environment, 48; measurement of, 48–51; and objectives and strategy, 51–54; of top management, 47–54

variables, identification of for success in industry, 207–209

vertical: competition, 108; marketing systems, 355–358

volume-sensitive industry, 297

voluntary arbitration, 361

W

Wheeler-Lea Act, 110

Wilmington Corporation, 538–572

woman, role of, 104

workability, of a strategy, 225–226